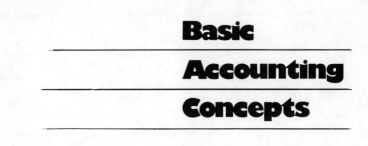

Basic
Accounting
Concepts

Basic

Accounting

Concepts

Hershel M. Anderson

Bernard A. Coda

James W. Giese

North Texas State University

Goodyear Publishing Company, Inc.,

Santa Monica, California

Library of Congress Catalog Card Number: 73-81262
Current Printing (last digit):
10 9 8 7 6 5 4 3 2

Y-1028-3
ISBN: 0-87620-102-8

Project Supervisor: Rhona B. Johnson, Publications Development Corporation

Printed in the United States of America

contents

two • CLASSIFIED FINANCIAL STATEMENTS

three • DOUBLE-ENTRY BOOKKEEPING

four • THE PROBLEMS OF RECOGNITION, CLASSIFICATION, AND MEASUREMENT

preface

This text is the culmination of several years of thought and work. We have in-flicted three previous versions of it, in preliminary editions, on our students over a six-year period. Our persistence can be traced to two firm conclusions we reached before beginning the project. First, we agree with our many colleagues who believe that the traditional content of the introductory course in account-ing does not serve the needs of the vast majority of students who take the course. Most students who take only one or two courses in accounting leave the subject with no real understanding of accounting measurements nor of their uses and limitations. Second, we are convinced that this failure can be attributed to a considerable extent to the traditional introductory chapters that stress the bal-ance sheet equation. This traditional approach obscures a basic relationship that students must grasp if they are to understand accounting. That relationship is the one between the cash flow of an enterprise and its net income. Having reached this second conclusion, we set about to develop content for an introduc-tion to accounting that emphasizes the important relationship between cash flow and net income.

The text begins, after an introductory chapter stressing the historical develop-ment of accounting, by explaining the importance of cash measurements for contemporary accounting in a monetary economy. From this, definitions for revenues and expenses based on cash flows are developed using simple formulae. The balance sheet is then "derived" based on these same formulae, giving the student a more precise understanding of how accountants use words such as assets, liabilities, and equities. We believe the approach is pedagogically sound because the student is confronted first with periodic cash receipts and disburse-ments, amounts that can be defined operationally. In this way, the student learns how and why accountants smooth cash flows in income measurement and how the balance sheet is, in large measure, a by-product of income measurement.

Part Two of the text, following the introduction to basic concepts, discusses the content, uses, and limitations of the three basic financial statements. The student is introduced to basic statement analysis, a theme stressed throughout the remainder of the text. Only after a discussion of the basic concepts and the financial statements is the student confronted in Part Three with the double-entry method, and this is written to give maximum flexibility to the instructor. While the book generally deemphasizes double-entry record-keeping, the Teacher's Manual does provide two outlines and assignment schedules, one for minimal instruction in double-entry and a second with maximum emphasis on record-keeping, given the constraints of the book.

The latter two parts of the book cover the usual gamut of income-measurement problems and the use of financial statements. Throughout these parts, dialectic arguments, which presumably lead to the conclusion that some alternative method is theoretically superior to others, are given short shrift. Instead the student is provided with pragmatic information about when and why corporate management prefers the various alternatives. This approach focuses the student's attention on the effects of using the alternative methods. In these chapters, the statement of changes in financial position is treated as a basic statement and the effects of various transactions on this new statement are an integral part of the text.

The text by design can be used as a one-semester (or term) introduction to financial accounting at every level.

In our effort to produce a text which is a real departure from tradition, numerous accounting educators have provided helpful advice and criticism. (Perhaps no book in accounting has been reviewed as many times as the one between these covers.) In listing the names of these helpers and critics, their endorsement of the new approach of the book or of its content is in no way implied. Indeed, many of our reviewers stoutly oppose this attempt to break with tradition. But even the most severe critic can often help a project. In one way or another we owe a debt to the following colleagues: Jon Booker, University of Southern Illinois; Lou Davidson, University of Texas; Nicholas Dopuch, University of Chicago; Charles Horngren, Stanford University; Thomas Keller, Duke University; John Klingstedt, University of Oklahoma; A. Mosich, University of Southern California; James Winjum, University of Michigan. We wish to thank them all, and others who have critiqued the manuscript in one of its many versions.

The discontent of accounting educators with the introductory course is clearly evidenced by the many new titles published in the last decade. We are convinced that what you have in your hands now is not just *another* one to add to the long list. We have something different, and whether it is for the better or worse, only time can tell. In any event, being different, it deserves your attention.

Denton, Texas   Hershel M. Anderson
September, 1973   James W. Giese
                                                         Bernard A. Coda

BASIC CONCEPTS

OF ACCOUNTING

1

The Nature and Purpose of Accounting

Economic conditions in the United States for the past two decades are expressed by the phrase "the affluent society." We have enjoyed an abundance of economic goods—food, clothing, household appliances, automobiles, to name a few. Our material prosperity, although certainly not enjoyed equally by all members of our society, is without parallel in the history of mankind. This cornucopia of goods and services is possible because of our complex industrial system. This system, which includes not only free enterprise but also many governmental units, is characterized by intense mechanization, automated operations, specialization of both equipment and personnel, and large organizational units. The successful operation of the industrial system depends on specialized training and education of our citizens and a general willingness on the part of most people to cooperate in maintaining and improving the system.

The complexity of the system can be illustrated by considering the production and distribution of a simple item, a food blender. The container on the blender and its top are made of plastic. Most plastics are by-products of the petroleum industry and are made of hydrocarbons extruded from raw petroleum not suitable for gasoline, oil, or other products. The metal in the blender, primarily steel, is the end result of a process involving raw ore, scrap steel, coking coal, numerous other raw materials, a huge transportation network, and a highly organized system of steel furnaces and mills. Once made the steel must be formed into parts to fit the blender design. The blender is powered by an electrical motor that requires the use of other metals, especially copper, and the use of the blender depends on the availability of electricity in the home. Finally, to regulate the speed of the motor the blender is fitted with an elaborate power-control device, which was probably derived as a technological by-product of the aerospace industry.

Even for a relatively simple product, the flow of materials and necessary components is quite complicated. Think also of the number of people involved in making the raw materials, in transportation, in actual fabrication and assembly

3

of the blender, and in planning the activities at each step in the process. All of this must happen before a salesman can show and demonstrate the blender in your local store. In short, the industrial system may be characterized as an intricate flow of materials and products propelled by human effort, intelligence, and ingenuity. The role of accounting in the process is to provide economic information about the production and distribution processes and claims of the different people involved.

A formal definition of *accounting is the process of identifying, measuring, and communicating economic information to permit informed decisions.* This definition emphasizes the fact that accounting accumulates data about the economic activities in society to provide people with the information they need to make decisions affecting the system. Should the business be continued, expanded, or contracted? Should one go to work for Company A or stay with Company B? Is the manager of the store in Des Moines doing a good job? Should we reelect the city council or throw the "rascals" out? These are the kinds of decisions that are based, in part, on accounting information.

In summary, accounting observes, measures, and communicates *useful* information about economic *transactions*. The concept of a transaction is a basic one in accounting. A transaction is an identifiable event that affects the ownership, enjoyment, or condition of economic resources. In the blender example, the flow of goods and the activities of the people involved are transactions.

The remainder of this chapter, and much of the remainder of the entire book, is an expansion of this description of the nature and purpose of accounting. The sections of this chapter which follow cover (1) the nature of business activity, (2) the principal uses of accounting, (3) the historical development of accounting, and (4) the interaction of accounting and the environment.

Business Activity

Most of the entities in our society, individuals, families, business enterprises, and divisions of government, are continually involved in economic transactions. The study of accounting in this text is approached from the viewpoint of a particular type of entity, the business enterprise. Much of what one learns about accounting for a business enterprise is, however, with slight modification, applicable to other types of economic entities. A *business entity* or *business enterprise* is an entity that controls scarce resources and uses them to produce goods and services with the primary objective of earning a profit. The diagram presented in Fig. 1–1 shows a generalized description of the activities of a business enterprise and provides a basis for an elementary understanding of the notion of *business profit* or *business income*.

The boxes in Fig. 1–1 represent either people or objects and the arrows represent activities. The activities represented by the arrows are types of economic transactions—events that affect the ownership, enjoyment, or condition of economic resources.

Figure 1-1: Diagram of the Activities of a Business Entity

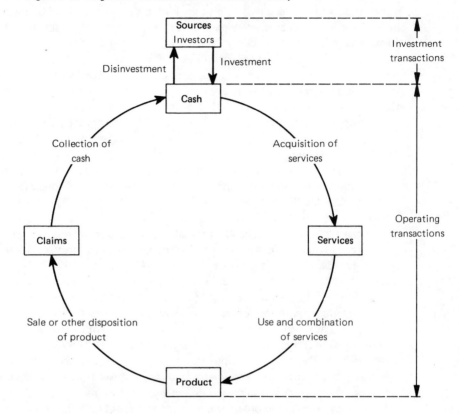

Description of the Diagram

Investors are participants in a business who furnish resources and who, to some degree, choose the business entity's objectives and the means of accomplishing its objectives. The two general types of investments are debt investments and owner investments. *Debt investments* are those made by investors who contribute cash or other resources in exchange for a promise to be repaid the amount originally contributed at a determinable date plus interest, the rental cost of money. *Owner investments* are those made by investors who contribute cash or other resources in exchange for the right to share in profits and the right to share in the proceeds upon liquidation of the business enterprise. If the business has been successful, owners may receive much more cash than they originally contributed. The transactions between a business entity and its owner investors and debt investors are *investment transactions.*

The respective rights of debt investors and owner investors of a business depend partly on the legal forms of the business organization. In a *proprietorship*, one individual is the owner and he holds *legal* title to resources of the business and is personally liable for all debts. A *partnership* is a joint enterprise of two or more legal persons. Title to the business resources is held by the partnership and, in most cases, every partner is jointly and severally liable for all partnership debts. Finally, businesses may be organized as *corporations*, which are recognized as legal entities separate from their owners. Corporations are formed by securing a charter from a governmental unit. The corporation then issues or sells *shares* to owner investors. The shareholders control the corporation through the election of a board of directors. The directors establish policy and also appoint the corporate officers who actually control the operations. The corporation holds title to all resources and it, not the shareholders, is liable for the debts of the business.

Cash assumes considerable importance in modern-day business activity. Not only is cash typically the beginning and end of a business entity's operating cycle, as shown by the circular portion of the diagram in Fig. 1-1, but it also serves as a medium of exchange and as a common denominator. The person who has cash can readily exchange it for all kinds of goods and services, which means freedom of action. The term *cash* is used throughout this text in a very broad way: Cash is more than currency (coins and bills), for it includes not only currency but also deposits with banks, checks, money orders, and any other legal instrument that can be redeemed for cash at a bank. Thus cash in accounting is synonymous with the concept of money in economics.

Money or cash is the most common unit of measurement used in accounting. Transactions are expressed in terms of cash or *cash-equivalent value* to permit comparisons and arithmetic manipulation of transactions. For example, a business may spend money for factory labor and for TV advertising—very dissimilar activities. By assigning a cash or money value to the two transactions, the two activities may be added to obtain the total amount spent in both transactions.

ACQUISITION OF SERVICES. The first step in the *operating cycle* of a business is the acquisition of services. The term *services* includes items ordinarily thought of as material products or goods. In accounting, goods are "bundles of services." Consider two merchants: One rents the building that houses his business operations, and the other merchant owns the building in which the business operates. The merchant who rents his building gets the same bundle of services as the merchant who owns his building, namely, protection from the elements.

Examples of various types of services that businesses typically acquire include labor services, protection services (insurance), advertising services, and bundles of services such as raw materials, supplies, land, buildings, and equipment. Certain legal rights, for example, a patent that gives a business an exclusive right to use certain technical knowledge or processes, are also services. Leases, franchises, trademarks, and copyrights are other examples of legal rights that are valuable services.

PRODUCTS. Products are the goods and services a business furnishes to its customers. A business converts services previously acquired into new products which are useful to its customers. A business may furnish products to its customers by adding one or more of three types of utility: time utility, place utility, and form utility. An example of a business that provides time utility is a meat-locker operation. Customers store meat to have it available at the proper time. Automobile dealers provide place utility by making cars available to customers in appropriate places. An appliance manufacturer changes the form of raw materials and thus furnishes form utility. A business entity may provide all three types of utility.

The combination of services into a new product is a transaction in accounting. This use of the term *transaction* is broader than its use in law and among the public generally. In law, a transaction involves two parties, but, in accounting, combinations of services are *internal* transactions because the combination affects the condition of services acquired.

SALES. In most businesses, the critical step in the operating cycle is the sales transaction. This step in the cycle is an important one for businessmen because it provides a test of how well the preceding transactions have been performed. Has the business acquired useful services and effectively combined them into a product that can be sold at a profit?

COLLECTION OF CASH. In exchange for its products, a business receives a claim to cash. The claim may be settled immediately, as in a cash sale, or after some delay, as in a credit sale. When a customer delays the cash settlement, the business's claim against the customer is called an *account receivable.* The collection of cash is important because it is only when cash has been realized that the business has freedom of choice. The business can return cash to owners, pay off creditors, or acquire different services which can be combined into some new product.

In Fig. 1-1, investments and disinvestments are in the form of cash. Occasionally, investments may be made "in kind"; for example, a shareholder may transfer title to land to a corporation in exchange for the corporation's stock. The corporation thus acquires services, land in this example, by issuing stock instead of expending cash. On rare occasions, a business may trade or barter its own product for new services. For *in-kind* investments and *barter* transactions, the accountant usually treats the transaction as though an intervening cash transaction had occurred. The values assigned to the services acquired are the values that would have resulted if the transaction had been a cash transaction—the cash-equivalent value.

Business Income

Investors in a business entity furnish resources to the business with the hope of getting back more than they initially contributed. Of course, investors risk losing some or all of their investment. Refer again to the cash box in Fig. 1-1. A business spends cash to acquire services that are used in production (*cash outflow*), and a business receives cash from customers in exchange for products (*cash inflow*). If the amount of cash received from customers over the life of the business exceeds the amount of cash spent for services, this excess is *income* or *profit*. In the reverse situation, the excess cash outflow for services over the cash inflow from customers is negative income or loss. In general, business income (profit) is the increase in economic resources arising from operations. Over the life of the business the increase in economic resources is generally represented by an increase in cash or money; a decrease in economic resources is a loss (negative income). The monetary unit is used to measure income.

Of course, there is no guarantee that income will result from the operation of the business. Many things must happen between the acquisition of services and inflow of cash from customers. We generally assume, however, that a firm earning a profit does so because it operates efficiently. Losses, on the other hand, generally arise because of inefficient operations. Thus, profit or income is widely used as an *index of efficiency.*

Calculation of income for a completed business or venture is quite simple. A completed venture is one where all the services acquired have been used up or otherwise disposed of, where all products have been sold to customers, and where all claims have been settled with a cash exchange. Under these conditions, one need only determine the cash on hand after all investors have been repaid their original investments. If, for example, a completed venture has $5,000 on hand after the investors have been repaid, this increase in cash is income. This same amount can be determined by comparing the cash paid out for services with the cash received from customers in the operating cycle.

The calculation of income or loss for a business still in progress is much more complicated. The major objective of this book is to describe the procedures and rules used to calculate income for an on-going business concern.

Principal Uses of Accounting

The main function of the accounting process is to provide information about economic activity to the persons interested in a business. Accounting serves many different individuals who must make decisions about a business entity.

Managers use accounting information to make decisions about product pricing, distribution of profits to owners, adopting new business processes and procedures, introducing new products, expanding or contracting the scope of market coverage, and determination of wages and salaries. Managers also rely on the accounting process for a record of services controlled by the company, debts owed, capital invested, and cash on hand.

Investors use accounting information to select investment opportunities from among those available. Should money be invested in Corporation A? Or in Corporation B? Should amounts previously invested be withdrawn? Investors also use accounting information to evaluate managerial performance.

Agents of the government may use accounting information to decide whether or not a business is serving the public interest. Has the business paid the amount of taxes required by law? Are the business's prices reasonable and in accord with relevant statutes? Is the enterprise violating antitrust legislation? Does the accounting information in any way indicate that new legislation is desirable or that old legislation is no longer necessary?

Customers must decide whether an entity's prices are fair and reasonable. *Suppliers* must determine whether or not to anticipate future sales to the entity. *Employees* must decide what wages and working conditions can be bargained for under the circumstances. Each of these groups needs accounting information to assist them with their decisions.

The accounting process begins with the identification and measurement of the financial or economic effect of transactions. The object of the process, however, is the communication of information to the interested parties just listed to enable them to make decisions. The transactions identified and measured are classified and interpreted in various ways and serve as the basis for accounting *reports.*

Many reports prepared by accountants are intended for the use of the managers of the business. Some common examples of the reports prepared for *internal* use by business management include budgets, various cost reports, statements of cash balances, cash receipts, and cash disbursements. In this textbook, however, we will be concerned mainly with reports prepared for *external* parties, primarily investors, governmental agencies, and the general public. The following three types of reports are communicated to external parties:

1   Report of the calculation of income or profit. This report is variously referred to as *statement of profit and loss, statement of income,* or *statement of operations.*
2   Report that shows the economic resources controlled by the business and the claims of owner investors and debt investors against the resources. This report is variously called a *balance sheet* or *statement of financial position.*
3   Report that shows investment transactions, acquisitions of services, and other changes in financial position during the year. The preferred title is *statement of changes in financial position*. Other titles that are sometimes used are *statement of funds* and *statement of sources and application of funds.*

These three reports together are commonly called the *financial statements.* The reports are provided to external parties at least on an annual basis, and many businesses issue financial statements for external use on a quarterly basis. The annual financial statements of several large corporations are presented in Appendix D.

Of the three reports, the balance sheet has the longest history. Only within the last four decades have publicly held corporations regularly provided statements of income to their shareholders and the public. The inclusion of a statement of changes in financial position as a part of the financial statements is of even more recent origin. The content and use of these three reports will be discussed in the remaining chapters of Part I and in Part II.

Historical Development of Accounting

The antecedents of modern accounting go back at least four or five thousand years. An essential element of the process is the recording of economic events; such record-keeping was commonplace in the Babylonian culture over four thousand years ago. The Babylonians had special schools for training governmental and commercial clerks and held the clerical profession in high esteem. In all the ancient civilized cultures—the Babylonian, the Egyptian, the Greek, the Roman—records were kept of economic transactions.

The most important event in the history of accounting was the development of unitary record-keeping, a method called *double-entry bookkeeping*. Just when and how double-entry bookkeeping came into being is unknown. We do know that the method was developed by the clerks and scholars of northern Italy some time prior to 1400 A.D. A complete explanation of the double-entry system was first reduced to writing in a treatise on mathematics by a Franciscan monk, Luca Pacioli whose book was published in 1494.

During the period when double-entry bookkeeping was developed, the cities of northern Italy were the trading and banking centers for the civilized world, the cross-roads between the older cultures of the Near East and the rapidly developing cultures of western Europe. During this era, an agrarian economy was being replaced with a trading economy, with a corresponding increase in credit transactions. In addition, several traders would often join together in a venture, creating the need for a record of the amount invested by each and the profit due to each investor. Furthermore, trading ventures required records of the goods and other resources on hand as well as records of credit transactions. The double-entry system was ideally suited to serve these needs. The method is a unified, closed system for recording economic resources on hand, credit transactions, and the investments of owners. Of more importance, the system provides a method for computing income and relating the income to the capital invested in the business. The basic elements of accounting have remained unchanged since the days of Pacioli.

Subsequent Developments

Following the development of double-entry bookkeeping in Italy, the method soon spread throughout western Europe. During the two centuries following publication of Pacioli's book, all Europe was undergoing the transition from complete reliance on agriculture to some light manufacturing and trade. The manufacturers and traders had the same needs for economic information as the earlier Italian traders. By this time, Europe and particularly Great Britain were on the threshold of the Industrial Revolution.

Impact of Industrialization

Before the advent of heavy manufacturing, business ventures generally lasted for relatively short periods. Financial statements for such ventures were generally prepared irregularly, often when the venture was terminated or when the owners were faced with a major decision. In most cases the entrepreneur could change the product or service being manufactured because he had little invested in buildings, machines, and other resources with long lives. Thus financial statements were prepared only when the owners felt a need to "sum up" results and take a look at what they should do next.

The Industrial Revolution changed much of this. To take advantage of the new machines, such as the automatic loom and the steam engine, the entrepreneur was faced with a large investment of capital in properties that would last for a number of years. The machines had to be housed in large buildings specifically designed for the purpose, and these factory buildings further increased the long-term investment. From a relatively insignificant beginning in textiles, industrialization proceeded at a rapid pace until now most of our economic activity is characterized by high initial capital investment in plant and equipment which has a long life. Examples from our present economy include railroads, steel mills, and automobile plants.

This industrialization forced accountants to realize that many business units continue to exist indefinitely. Indeed, *continuity of enterprise* is presently an accurate description of most businesses. This continuity of enterprise resulted in the widespread practice of preparing *regular* accounting reports. Owners and other interested parties could not be expected to wait until the venture was terminated years later before receiving some facts about how the enterprise was progressing. Thus *periodicity*, a division of the life of a business into annual segments, is another feature of modern accounting.

The Financial Revolution

A necessary accompaniment of the Industrial Revolution was a change in the legal organization of businesses. During the trading era, most businesses were owned by individuals, or by groups of individuals joined together in partnerships. In those days, one person or a small group of persons could pool their wealth and have enough capital to support the venture. As often as not, accounting records included personal transactions of the owners, such as amounts spent for food, as well as the transactions of the business.

With technological advances and the resulting increase in the investment required, the wealth of a large number of individuals was necessary to finance a venture. Conveniently, joint-stock companies had developed in Great Britain to raise capital from the public to finance large trading ventures such as the Hudson Bay Company. The descendant of joint-stock companies is the modern business corporation which has developed in response to needs of present-day business. Briefly, the corporation has the following important characteristics:

1   It is a legal entity completely separate from its shareholders.
2   Ownership of the corporation can be subdivided without practical limit through the issuance of additional ownership shares.

3   The shareholders' liability for corporate indebtedness is limited to the amount originally contributed. If the corporation fails, the shareholder cannot normally be sued by corporate creditors.

4   Most corporations have an unlimited life and their shares are traded readily among investors.

Widespread use of the corporation makes the continuity of enterprise assumption a realistic one in most situations. Absentee ownership by shareholders who do not manage the business also makes periodic financial statements more important. Absentee owners will not entrust their economic resources to the management of a corporation without some assurances that the resources will be effectively used to produce a profit. The spirit of trust between owners and managers is based, in large measure, on the accounting reports that tell the owners how well their resources are being utilized. Finally, the use of the corporate form has necessitated the exclusion of the owners' personal financial transactions from the records of the business. Whether organized as proprietorships, partnerships, or corporations, accountants now insist that the business be treated as a *separate entity* and that personal transactions of owners be excluded from accounting records and reports for the business.

To summarize, double-entry bookkeeping provided a method for accountants to record systematically the economic events of a business and to prepare financial statements. With industrialization came businesses that had an indefinite economic life because of industrial technology. Continuity of life made periodic financial statements a practical necessity. Corporations became the dominant legal form in response to the need for large amounts of capital and unlimited life. Because of absentee ownership of corporations, businesses are treated as separate entities and the accounting process is concerned only with business transactions.

Interaction of Accounting and the Environment

The historical sketch in the preceding section shows the ideas or concepts of the accounting process as being shaped by the economic environment in which the process is carried on. Although the environment shapes the process, there can be little doubt that the reverse is also true—the accounting process has been influential in shaping our economic environment. Italian traders developed and used the double-entry method to make a profit calculation and to provide other information. As this method spread across Europe, the method itself carried with it the idea that wealth or capital could be employed to produce income. The spread of this idea, which is basic to capitalism, has had a tremendous impact on the economic life of the Western World and has, in turn, helped to shape our social values.

Other examples can also be cited to show that the accounting process has been instrumental in shaping our lives. For example, the federal government, as well as several state governments, depend primarily on the income tax for their revenues. This tax is based on the most important measurement of the accounting process, namely, net income or profit. The tax, therefore, depends on the widespread ability of taxpayers, by use of the accounting process, to calculate income. Another important influence of accounting on our lives has been the growth of capital markets which are made possible by the existence of reliable periodic financial statements.

Stewardship and Capital Markets

As the use of the corporate form expanded rapidly in the nineteenth and twentieth centuries, elaborate markets also grew up to handle the trade in corporate securities. When a corporation is originally formed, or when an existing corporation wishes to expand rapidly, the necessary resources are often acquired by issuing ownership *shares* in exchange for cash or other resources. These shares give the shareholder a claim to a portion of the corporation's income and to a portion of the cash and other resources at liquidation. The corporation may also issue its bonds or notes (debt investments) for cash or other resources that entitle the investor to a periodic interest payment and to a return of the principal amount at maturity.

The remarkable fact about present-day capital markets is that investors are willing to invest cash in corporations through the remote facilities of the market. Widows in Sioux City are willing to invest in a corporation through the market even though they have never seen the physical facilities of the business and do not know (and in most cases do not even know the names of) the corporate management. People are willing to make such investments in part because the accounting process provides them with periodic financial statements indicating how well the management is performing its stewardship function.

The need to have statements that report on the stewardship of property is partly responsible for the existence of the accounting process. From Roman slaves to overseers of feudal estates in England, down to today's corporate managers, records and reports have been prepared to show the master, lord, or shareholder how the affairs progressed in his absence. The reports of corporate managers to their shareholders are the financial statements.

Role of the Independent Accountant

The National Security Acts of the early 1930s and the "blue sky laws" of most states were passed in response to the stock market crash of 1929. The most important provisions of the regulatory laws require the corporations to make *fair disclosure* of all essential facts to the investing public. An important specific provision of most of these laws is that the annual financial statements of publicly held companies must be *audited* by an independent public accountant. In most jurisdictions, audits can only be performed by a licensed Certified Public Accountant (CPA), an individual who meets certain educational and experience requirements, and who has passed a fairly rigorous examination.

Audits of annual statements of public corporations were first required in Great Britain in the nineteenth century. About the turn of the present century, British public accountants came to the United States to audit U.S. branches of British companies. From this small beginning, the public accounting profession has grown until there are now over 100,000 licensed CPA's. The profession is regulated by law in all 50 states, and also enforces a code of ethics comparable to that for lawyers and doctors.

Each year, every publicly held company must contract with a CPA for an audit of its records and financial statements. The independent accountant must examine the records and statements to determine whether, in his opinion, the statements *fairly present* the company's income, financial position, and changes in financial position. Standards or concepts that guide the work of the independent accountant include the following:

1   *Generally accepted accounting principles.* The company's statement must be prepared in accordance with generally accepted accounting principles. These are rules and procedures that must be followed in the computation of income and preparation of the balance sheet.
2   *Consistency.* The principles or rules must be applied consistently from year to year.
3   *Full disclosure.* The financial statements must disclose all significant facts about the year's operations and the financial position.
4   *Materiality.* In determining the facts that must be disclosed, only material events need be considered. Transactions that have an immaterial effect may be ignored.

The first of these standards is by far the most important. The rules and procedures that you will study in the remainder of this text are "generally accepted accounting principles."

Sources of Accounting Principles in the United States

The Security and Exchange Acts of the 1930s created the Securities and Exchange Commission (SEC) and bestowed certain powers upon it. These powers have been extended by subsequent legislation, and the SEC now has sweeping powers to determine the rules, procedures, and methods used to account for and report the economic and financial activities of almost any corporation that sells significant amounts of securities to the general public. The SEC publishes a numbered series of statements called *Accounting Series Releases.* Other governmental agencies that have a considerable amount of power to influence accounting practices for regulated industries include the Federal Power Commission, the Interstate Commerce Commission, the Civil Aeronautics Board, and the Federal Communications Commission.

The extensive power granted to the SEC is, for the most part, latent power because the SEC has chosen to encourage the accounting profession to develop its own rules, procedures, and methods. The generally accepted principles of accounting developed by the accounting profession are influenced by a number of organizations: the American Institute of CPA's (AICPA), the American Accounting Association (AAA), the National Association of Accountants (NAA), and the Financial Executives Institute (FEI).

The AAA is an organization controlled by university professors. It publishes a periodical, *The Accounting Review*, as well as monographs on important accounting topics. The AAA also contributes to the profession through work of its special and standing committees, the regional and national meetings it sponsors, and other activities as well. The NAA is controlled by industrial accountants and publishes a periodical called *Management Accounting*. Membership in the FEI, publisher of a periodical entitled *Financial Executive*, is limited mainly to top-level financial managers of the larger corporations.

The most important accounting organization is the AICPA, whose members are practicing independent accountants. (Only CPA's are admitted to membership.) It publishes monthly *The Journal of Accountancy*, several other periodicals, and numerous books and monographs that disseminate information about accounting.

The term "accepted principles of accounting" was first used in a report of a joint committee of the AICPA and the New York Stock Exchange in 1934.* This committee established the broad standard that the financial reports of all listed companies must conform to generally accepted principles of accounting and that these principles must be used consistently. Following this joint report, the AICPA formed a committee and gave it the power to *establish* generally accepted principles when doubt arose concerning the propriety of a given practice. This committee issued numerous *Accounting Research Bulletins* between 1939 and 1959. In 1959 the committee was reorganized and given a new name, the Accounting Principles Board (APB). From 1959 through 1972, the APB issued numerous *Opinions* establishing generally accepted principles. The APB commissioned practitioners and scholars to do research projects on the important accounting problems. Beginning in 1973, a new body, the Financial Accounting Standards Board, assumed the responsibility for the promulgation of accounting principles. Unlike the APB whose members served part time, the new Standards Board is comprised of seven full-time members who have severed their employment connections with accounting firms, corporations, and other organizations. This new arrangement should give the members an opportunity to study problems and develop principles without the pressure of other work. The new arrangement should also increase public confidence in the decisions reached, because the members of the Standards Board are in a position to examine problems without bias and without pressure from clients and others who might be affected adversely by their decisions.

Audits of Corporate Accounts (New York: American Institute of Certified Public Accountants, 1934).

Taken together, the *Accounting Research Bulletins* and the *Opinions* of the APB and Financial Accounting Standards Board provide a fairly comprehensive source for generally accepted principles. Without them, the accountant would have no place to turn for rules. The power of the AICPA to make rules that are binding for accountants has been recognized by the SEC and by the courts.

The Challenge of Accounting

You should not conclude from the preceding discussion that accounting is nothing more than learning the rules of the AICPA. Generally accepted principles are, for the most part, only broad statements that serve as standards or guidelines. In addition, there are acceptable alternative ways to account for the same facts. The application of the rules to a particular company requires intelligence and imagination as well as a thorough knowledge of the rules.

Finally, the transactions that must be measured and reported are constantly changing because of changes in the capital markets, in the relationship of business to government, in the technology used in production, and in the goods and services produced. Thus the accountant often encounters novel transactions for which no clear rules have been developed. Transactions of this type make the accountant's task both challenging and rewarding.

An example will give you an indication of the difficulties that can and do arise. For several years, business corporations have participated with the federal government to provide training for unskilled workers from city ghettos and underdeveloped rural areas. The training includes both classroom work and on-the-line training. In the on-the-line training, the trainee is not only learning the work; he is also making a product. The accountant is faced with the task of dividing the total costs involved between the two functions. The allocation is essential to determine how the corporation is coming out on the government contract for the training and to determine the costs that must be assigned to the product on which the trainee worked.

Cooperation between business and government is essential to national defense and will become even more important when we finally face the problem of cleaning up our environment. Accountants today are faced with problems such as calculating the costs to society connected with the use of throw-away containers and the costs to various industries to reduce harmful emissions into our air, lakes, and rivers. Entirely new industries will undoubtedly come into existence as a result of this effort, just as the space industry followed from a national decision to explore space. The accountant will not be a spectator. Indeed, in these new endeavors, as in the past, the accountant will be in the thick of it, trying to provide essential information to business managers and to government on which good decisions may be based.

QUESTIONS

1 What is the purpose of accounting?

2 Name three activities that accounting performs in attaining its objective.

3 What is an economic transaction?

4 What is a business enterprise?

5 What are the steps or activities of an enterprise?

6 When is value added to a good or service in the operating cycle?

7 Describe the financing activities in the operating cycle.

8 Describe the operating activities in the operating cycle.

9 At what point in the business cycle is it known that resources have increased because of the business operations?

10 Write a brief essay on the social importance and uses of income in the evaluation of an enterprise's performance. How is an enterprise evaluated as to its success or failure based on income? Should criteria other than income be used to judge the performance of an enterprise?

11 Explain how accounting information might be used by each of the following groups:
   [a] Managers
   [b] Investors
   [c] Agents of government
   [d] Customers
   [e] Suppliers
   [f] Employees

12 Distinguish between internal and external accounting reports.

13 Identify and describe the three financial statements that a business enterprise whose stock is actively traded is required to furnish to external parties.

14 A number of professional accounting organizations determine the generally accepted accounting principles followed by accounting practitioners in their daily work. For some of the more important of these professional organizations, list the organization's name, describe the nature of its membership, and explain how the organization influences the work of accountants.

15 Speculate about why many of the ideas, rules, and procedures (generally accepted accounting principles) determined by professional organizations change more frequently than broad concepts that developed in response to changes in our social, legal, and economic environment.

16 [a] What are the principal characteristics of a corporation?
   [b] Why has the corporate form of organization proven so successful in our highly developed industrial economy?

17 Explain the meaning of [a] time utility, [b] place utility, and [c] form utility. Identify and describe a business that provides all three kinds of utility to its customers.

18 Explain the importance of cash in the business world. How is cash related to the business's objective, to business transactions, and to accounting measurements?

19 What assurances do shareholders in large corporations have that the companies' managements will not falsify information on the financial statements? In this connection, what is meant by consistency? By fair disclosure? By materiality?

20 One often hears that modern computers will soon replace all accountants. In fact, however, the use of computers seems to have increased the demand for accountants. Comment.

PROBLEMS

1   Match the items listed on the left with those listed on the right by placing the appropriate number in each blank.

_____ [a]   Economic activity

_____ [b]   Economic transaction

_____ [c]   Business entity

_____ [d]   Business income

_____ [e]   Cash

_____ [f]   Services

_____ [g]   Balance sheet

_____ [h]   Income statement

_____ [i]   Cost valuation

_____ [j]   Capital

[1]   Economic resources and legal rights that are useful to a business

[2]   Involves the use of scarce resources by people

[3]   Common denominator

[4]   An accepted indicator of business efficiency

[5]   A report showing monetary amounts for revenues, expenses, and income

[6]   Serves customers to earn a profit

[7]   Amount of cash paid for something

[8]   Accumulated wealth used to gain additional wealth

[9]   Events that affect the ownership, enjoyment, or condition of scarce resources

[10]   A report showing monetary amounts for assets, liabilities, and owners' equities.

2   Listed below are a series of transactions. Identify the point in the operating cycle at which they occur.

[a]   Cash of $1,000 is received from a customer.

[b]   Labor services costing $100 and materials costing $200 are consumed in the production of a new product.

[c]   Electrical energy costing $80 is acquired.

[d]   Products with a value of $800 are transferred to a customer in exchange for his promise to pay $800 in 30 days.

[e]   The bank grants a loan of $5,000 to the business.

[f]   The services of a building are used in the process of forming a new product.

[g]   A customer pays cash for services performed last month.

[h]   An owner of the business contributes $6,000 to the business.

3   The T Company has been in operation since January 1, 19X1. The cash inflow of T Company during the period from January 1, 19X1 through December 31, 19X1 was as follows:

Receipts from debt investors	$ 10,000
Receipts from owners	25,000
Receipts from customers	100,000
	$135,000

Cash disbursements during the same period were as follows:

Payment of interest to debt investors	$ 1,200
Payments for employee's salaries	50,000
Payments to suppliers for material used in production of goods	60,000
Payments to owners	5,000
	$116,200
Cash on hand	$ 18,800

[a]   Is T Company a successful company?

[b]   Why? Support your conclusion in part by quantitative evidence.

4   Refer to Problem 3 above. Cash transactions for T Company for the second year of opera-
      tions (19X2) were

Cash receipts from customers	$150,000
Payment of interest to debt investors	$ 1,200
Payment for employee's salaries	65,000
Payments to suppliers for materials used in production of goods	70,000
	$136,200

Evaluate the success of operations for 19X2. Support your conclusions with quantitative
evidence.

5   A major cause of air pollution are the exhaust fumes from automobiles. For many years,
      some automobile manufacturers have been very profitable and the stocks in these profitable
      corporations have been considered good investments. The accounting process, in short,
      judged these businesses as successful ones. It is now apparent that the cost to our entire
      society of reducing air pollution will be quite high. What is there about the nature of our
      present accounting process which permitted this apparent error?

CASE   A group of professors from the College of Arts and Sciences organized the
       Minibuck Investment Club. Each member agreed to contribute $25 a month
       which would be pooled and invested in the stock of a company that was listed
       on either the New York Stock Exchange or the American Stock Exchange. The
       objective of the club was to invest the funds in companies that were successful
       and that were expected to be successful in the future. The members believed
       that if they invested in successful companies their investments would be safe
       and furthermore that the investment's value would increase because of the
       company's success.
          Professors Jenkins and Brabham were appointed to a committee to develop a
       set of criteria by which the relative success of a company could be measured.
       After extended meditation, Professor Jenkins presented the following criteria to
       be used in determining the success of a company:

[a]   Popularity of the company's product. If a company's product is not
       popular or well accepted it cannot be a success.

[b]   The expectation that the demand for the company's product will con-
       tinue. If a company is making a novelty or a "fad" item its success might
       be doubtful.

[c]   The lack of any adverse publicity such as damage suits and antitrust suits.
       If the company's image has been tarnished, the acceptance of the com-
       pany's product may decrease.

Professor Brabham examined the criteria proposed by Professor Jenkins and
concluded that they would be impossible to use because of the difficulty of

measuring popularity and the expected future demand for the company's product. In addition he stated that most corporations produced many different products. How could the popularity and demand of different products be added together? Furthermore, many companies make products for other corporations and governmental agencies; for example, the Boeing Aircraft Company does not have many customers for its 747 jet airliner or any of its other large jet aircraft. The criteria suggested would eliminate this company and many like it from consideration. Professor Jenkins replied that Professor Brabham should develop another set of criteria for evaluation of the companies. Brabham responded that he had tried but every criterion he developed seemed to have some major defect. He suggested that they contact a member of the business faculty for advice.

Required:

Prepare a set of criteria that you would use in selecting companies in which to invest. After each criterion, write a brief paragraph to support its use.

2

Concepts of
Income
Measurements

The traditional financial statements prepared periodically for business enterprises are the balance sheet and the income statement. Conceptually, these two statements are reports of two different, although related, measurements. The balance sheet is traditionally thought of as a report of the *wealth* of the enterprise at a specific time. The income statement, on the other hand, is traditionally conceived of as a report of the *change in wealth* resulting from economic activities for a period of time. In the preceding chapter we learned that double-entry bookkeeping provided mankind with the first systematic means of accumulating economic data. Our ideas (concepts) about wealth and income have developed gradually in the centuries after the widespread use of double-entry bookkeeping.

One purpose of this chapter is to explore the basic concepts of wealth and income. A second purpose is to identify some of the reasons for measuring wealth and income. In the process we will explain and illustrate some basic practical problems in the measurement of income and wealth. The objectives of income determination, and to some extent, practical problems with measurement, have led accountants to abandon the measurement of income based on the *stock concept*, and to depend primarily on the *flow concept* of income.

Wealth and the Stock Concept

Primitive notions of wealth are as old as recorded history. Wealth is, of course, a store of economic resources. The idea of income is also very old; the Roman Empire levied a tax on income. In ancient times, both wealth and income were thought of in terms of tangible physical objects. A man's wealth, for example, was commonly reckoned in terms of the slaves, land, jewels, and precious metals that he owned. His income was expressed in terms of new lambs or calves born, the grain harvested, or the precious metals received from his activities for a year. Only in modern times, and primarily since the use of the double-entry system, have we measured wealth and income in monetary units and sought to connect the two measurements in monetary terms.

Monetary Measurement of Wealth

Today, if we pose the question, "What is Mr. Y worth?," we will not be given an inventory of his physical possessions. Instead, we will be told that his worth or wealth is $X (or pounds, marks, etc., depending on the country). Other terms commonly used for wealth are *net worth, proprietorship, capital,* and *equity.* Over the years, we have become accustomed to translating physical wealth into a common denominator, its presumed monetary value. This permits us to speak of wealth in a brief and seemingly precise manner, namely, in monetary units.

The measurement of wealth is not complete with the assignment of monetary value to the economic resources (assets) of an individual or business. After this task is complete, a subtraction must be made for monetary claims of other parties to the resources, the individual's or business's *liabilities.* Thus wealth is the net of the monetary value of resources (assets) after subtracting the liabilities (also expressed in monetary terms). The common mathematical expression for this equation is assets minus liabilities equals wealth (A – L = W). For example, if a business has assets valued at $50,000 and liabilities of $15,000, its wealth or net worth is $35,000. We may also say that the net *stock* of goods or resources is $35,000 at the time the wealth measurement is made. Frequently, for a business entity, wealth is also referred to as proprietorship.

Stock Concept of Income

Although the ideas just explained are very commonplace in our present culture, the monetary measurement of wealth was a most important step in the development of a concept of income. Given a precise amount for wealth, economists were able to develop a general definition of income in monetary terms. Thus, instead of an enumeration of physical resources gained during a period, income could be defined as a single monetary amount—the change in monetary wealth over a period of time.

BASIC DEFINITION. The classic definition of income from economic literature states: Income is the amount of wealth that a person or other entity can dispose of during a time period and be as well off at the *end* of the period as at the beginning. In other words, income for an individual is the amount of his consumption adjusted for changes in his stock of goods or wealth.

To illustrate this important idea, imagine the following facts concerned with the wealth of an individual. On January 1, 19X1 the wealth of the individual was $45,000. During 19X1, he consumed $16,000. On January 1, 19X2, he takes another inventory of his wealth. At this time he owns assets valued at $72,000, and he owes creditors, commonly called *liabilities*, $18,000. The wealth or net worth of the individual at January 1, 19X2 is $54,000, the excess of assets over liabilities ($72,000 – $18,000). What then, are the results of his year's operations?

Consumption for 19X1		$16,000
Change in wealth:		
Wealth at 12/1/X2	$54,000	
Wealth at 12/1/X1	45,000	
Increase in wealth		9,000
Income for 19X1		$25,000

By comparing the wealth at the end of 19X1 with wealth at the beginning, we find that wealth increased, and, under the stock concept, this increase in wealth plus the individual's consumption is the income for the year, $25,000.

The following is a simple equation for income where Y is income, C is consumption, W_0 is wealth at the beginning of the period and W_1 is wealth at the end of the period:

$$Y = C + (W_1 - W_0)$$

Income is thus the individual's consumption plus the increase in his wealth or less the decrease in his wealth. Substituting the amounts from the preceding example,

$$Y = \$16,000 + (\$54,000 - \$45,000)$$
$$= \$25,000$$

By this means, income and wealth can be expressed as single monetary amounts. Note the monetary amount represents changes in values of various resources and the acquisition of new resources as well as the acquisition of cash. In accounting, cash is defined broadly as currency, bank deposits, and other items that are readily convertible to currency.

APPLICATION OF STOCK CONCEPT TO BUSINESS ENTERPRISES. The example in the preceding section dealt with the wealth and income of an individual. The ideas presented there were originally developed to measure only the income of individuals. However, the stock concept is often used to measure the income of a business concern. Use of the concept for businesses gives rise to additional problems. First, the beginning point for measuring income is not consumption—business ventures do not "consume" but instead provide profits or income that the owners of the business can use for consumption. Thus the income of a business is basically the change in wealth under the stock concept. Second, many businesses are organized as corporations, legal entities that are separate and apart from the corporation's shareholders. Over the years it has become conventional for accountants to treat all businesses, whether corporations, partnerships, or proprietorships, as separate entities. The economic transactions of the individual owners are not mingled with the transactions of the business for the computation of wealth and income of the business. This separation of business activities from the economic activities of owners means that there are transactions between the business entity and its owners. Generally, two types of such transactions do **not** affect the income of the business:

1 Investments. If owners make investments in the business during a period, the wealth of the business increases. However, this increase is not income to the business because the business is organized to earn wealth through productive activity. The owners' investments decrease their wealth and, considering the business and the owners together, no one is better off as a result. Thus, investments by owners must be subtracted from the change in wealth of a business entity to arrive at the income of the business. Our previous equation is expanded (I represents the investment during the period):

$$Y = (W_1 - I) - W_0$$

The subtraction of I adjusts the ending wealth to the amount that it would have been given if no new investments were made. Note that consumption is not a variable in the computation for a business.

2 Distributions (disinvestments). A parallel, but opposite condition exists when a business entity distributes its resources to its owners. Such distributions decrease the wealth but they are not connected with operations. In addition, distributions or disinvestments result in a corresponding increase in owners' wealth. Thus, to measure income by a comparison of wealth at the beginning and end of the period, the distributions must be added to the change. The complete formula for applying the stock concept to the computation of income for a business has both investments and distributions during the period is as follows (with D being the amount of distributions):

$$Y = (W_1 - I + D) - W_0$$

The subtraction of investments (I) and the addition of distributions (D) adjusts wealth at the end of the period (W_1) to the amount it would have been, given no new investments and no distributions. Restated in its usual form the equation is

$$Y = W_1 - W_0 - I + D$$

To illustrate, assume that Company X had wealth at the beginning of a period of $10,000; wealth at the end of the period was $15,000; during the period Company X distributed $2,000 to the owners; and the owners invested $3,000 during the period. By substituting these facts in the above equation, we would get the following result:

$$
\begin{aligned}
Y &= W_1 - W_0 + D - I \\
&= \$15,000 - \$10,000 + \$2,000 - \$3,000 \\
&= \$4,000
\end{aligned}
$$

In this example, income (Y) is a positive amount, indicating that income accounted for a $4,000 increase in the net worth of the business. If the facts had been such that Y was negative, such a negative value would indicate that operations generated a loss or decrease in wealth.

Limitations of the Stock Concept

The measurements just discussed seem to be very precise and neat. However, like many measurements, they are often misunderstood and therefore misused. In addition, the actual measurement of wealth and the computation of income based on changes in wealth are difficult, if not impossible, tasks.

THE PROBLEM OF AGGREGATION. Wealth, or net worth, refers to real things—land, machines, securities, cash, etc. Assignment of monetary values to these real things is an abstraction, and the summation of these values is a further abstraction from reality. Once wealth is computed in monetary terms, people frequently make the mistake of thinking of the wealth as cash or money. Yet, obviously a business cannot exhaust wealth such as its plant and inventory. If it did, it would go out of business.

Similarly, people often confuse income with cash or money. Yet income, as measured with the preceding formulas, is basically a change in wealth and, in real terms, there may be no cash on hand at all. A business often, therefore, cannot spend its income because the increase in wealth may already be invested in inventory or some other noncash asset.

These common misconceptions of wealth and income apply not only to measurements with the stock concept but to all accounting measurements of these amounts. The stock concept does have, however, some inherent limitations that reduce its usefulness.

THE VALUATION PROBLEM. Computation of income using the stock concept requires a periodic evaluation, in monetary terms, of the resources and liabilities of the business enterprise. This means an "inventory" of all resources and liabilities must be made periodically (annually) with monetary values assigned to all items. This creates two problems: How do we determine objective values for assets? And, does the approach furnish enough information about the causes of increases and decreases in wealth?

● Objectivity: The value of an economic resource is, in the final analysis, the amount of future economic benefits that can be derived from it. For an asset used in business, benefit means the amount of income that the resource or group of resources will produce in the future. The value of an asset now is, therefore, the discounted value of net future cash receipts from the property.* Needless to say, expectations about the future vary widely among individuals, depending on a number of factors. A businessman seeking a loan at the bank for a new

*See Appendix A for an example of how the present value of a property can be determined, given an interest rate and expected net cash flows.

venture is likely to be very optimistic. The banker, on the other hand, is likely to be less sanguine. In short, the value of an economic resource is essentially a *subjective* estimate.

Market values can be determined, of course, for a number of properties. There are active markets for corporate securities, for some basic raw materials (steel, aluminum, etc.), and for some industrial equipment. Valuation of most land and buildings is not so objective. In addition, many intangible assets of a business, such as patents, trade names, labor relations, and customer goodwill, can only be valued by subjective means. Moreover, there is the question of whether to assign values to individual assets, groups of assets, or the whole collection of assets as a single unit.

• Information: Income as measured using the stock concept has limited useful-ness. This measure produces a single numerical result. It does not provide any measure or information about the economic activity that caused the change in wealth. For example, Company X's income of $4,000 in the preceding exam-ple does not provide any information about the activities of Company X. Was the income a result of producing a product or service or was it merely caused by a change in asset valuation? The stock concept does not provide an answer.

Because of the inherent subjectivity of the measurement of wealth, the prac-tical problems involved, and limited usefulness, over the years accountants have developed another set of ideas for income measurement, namely, the *flow con-cept*. It is used by most businesses and is fundamentally the same as the con-cepts used to compute income for the federal income tax. Most of the remainder of this book is devoted to the flow concept, which is the basis for generally accepted accounting principles.

The Flow Concept

Before the Industrial Revolution, when most businesses were owned by a single individual or family, the objective of income measurement was the determina-tion of the change in wealth. The individual proprietors were interested primar-ily in their personal economic status. With industrialization and the resulting complexity of operations, owners and managers of businesses needed detailed information about the activities of the business. They needed answers to ques-tions such as: How were sales of product X in relation to the cost of producing the product? What was the labor cost and the cost of materials used? For the reason just explained, the measurement of income based on a stock of goods is not a practical way of obtaining this information in a large business. Questions such as these can only be answered efficiently by an analysis of the activities of the business during the time period. The flow concept of income measurement is based on the *analysis of activities*, or *transactions.*

Importance of Cash

In the beginning of the trading era, the wealth of an individual or of a business could be thought of in terms of the physical objects owned and available for consumption or use. At that time barter was commonplace. Money, which was then made of precious metals, was primarily thought of as a "store of value" and not as a medium of exchange.

Compare the conditions just described with our present economic environment, which can be characterized as a monetary economy. Today we have a well-developed stable banking system, as well as an extensive system of credit. Most of our money (cash) is represented by figures on bank records. To acquire goods or services for consumption, or for use in a business, we must have money. The hard fact of our economic life is cash: How much do we have? How much will we receive in the future? How much must be spent in the future? Recall that cash is defined broadly in accounting to include currency and anything convertible to currency.

Referring to Fig. 1-1, the diagram introduced in Chapter 1, the important block in the diagram is cash. It is important to the business manager because only when he has cash can he change the direction of business operations. Once the choice is made to acquire certain services, the manager is committed to the combination of these services into a product, and to the sale of this product to his customers; the alternative would be to liquidate the acquired services, probably at a loss. For example, consider what the results would be if you set up a plant to produce airplanes and then found that you could not sell a sufficient number of them to make a profit. Conversion of the plant to the manufacture of some other product would almost certainly result in a huge loss. Only after the sale and collection of cash from the originally intended customer, if ever, does the manager have a new option—continue the old operation or shift to some new product or service. The cash block, of course, is also important to the investors and creditors. Shareholders must look to the cash position for dividends; creditors must look to the cash position for interest payments and repayment of loans.

The facts about cash are objective information that cannot be colored by the optimism of management or other subjective evaluations. As explained earlier, valuation of resources in terms of expected future benefits is difficult; however, the accountant can keep a record and report the amount of cash spent for the acquisition of services and measure and report cash received from customers. In keeping records on the operation of a business, therefore, the accountant's attention is focused on cash spent for acquisition of services (cash outflow) and on the cash collected from customers (cash inflow).

Recognition of the importance of cash inflow and outflow from the operation of a business has led accountants to the concept of income known as the flow concept. Using this concept, income is measured by the following equation:

$$\text{Income} = \text{revenue} - \text{expenses}$$
$$Y = R - E$$

The relationship between "flow" income (revenue less expenses) and the cash flow of the business is explained in this and the next two chapters.

Definitions of Revenue and Expense in a Completed Venture

The calculation of income using the above formula (income = revenue − expenses) depends on reliable, useful definitions for revenue and expense. In the remainder of this chapter, definitions for revenue and expenses that are applicable to a completed venture will be developed.

Revenue for a completed venture is defined as follows:

$$\text{Revenue} = \text{Cash receipts} - \text{Investment receipts}$$
$$R = CR - IR$$

In this equation CR refers to total cash receipts and IR to the portion of cash receipts paid in by investors. Thus, revenue for a completed venture is equal to total cash receipts minus cash investments by owners and creditors.

Referring to Fig. 2–1, note that cash receipts of businesses arise from only two sources, receipts from investors and collections from customers. The cash received from investors is *not* revenue and does not increase income because the business is organized to earn income from its productive effort. In short, revenue arises from cash receipts from customers which result from operations.

Figure 2–1

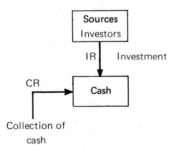

The cash receipts of a business are a measurement of the cash flowing into the entity during a specified time period. Assume, for example, that the total cash receipts of a completed venture were $90,000 of which $15,000 was received from investors. Revenue is obtained by use of the following formula:

$$\text{Revenue} = \text{cash receipts} - \text{investment receipts}$$
$$R = CR - IR$$
$$= \$90,000 - \$15,000$$
$$= \$75,000$$

The expenses of a completed venture are defined as follows:

Expenses = cash disbursements − investment disbursements (disinvestments)
E   =   CD   −   ID

In this equation again CD refers to total cash disbursements and ID to a portion of disbursements, disinvestments by owners. The important transactions are indicated in Fig. 2–2. Note that disbursements to owners are *not* expenses; expenses in a completed venture are the amounts spent to acquire services in business operations.

Figure 2–2

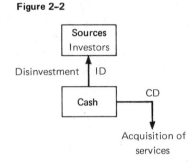

Cash disbursements means the amount of cash paid out by a business during a specified time period—in this case, the completed venture. To extend the previous example, assume that the venture in question had total cash disbursements of $62,000; dividends of $5,000 were paid to investors; cash disbursements for operations were $57,000.

Expenses = Cash disbursements − Investment disbursements
E   =   CD   −   ID
     = $62,000   − $5,000
     = $57,000

If income is a measurement of operational effectiveness, expenses must be defined as the cash paid out as a result of operations, as opposed to financial transactions.

In summary, revenue for a completed venture is cash received from customers in the course of operations, and expenses are cash disbursements made by the business in the course of operations. Income is therefore the difference between cash inflow and outflow from operations:

Income = Revenue − Expense
Y   =   R   −   E
     = $75,000 − $57,000
     = $18,000

This measurement of income tells the interested person how much cash was increased as a result of the venture. By concentrating on cash inflow and outflow, the accountant has some objective, reliable facts on which to base his income computation.

Example

Dan Roberts and Jim Richards are bank executives who occasionally invest in real estate. In January, 19X1, a real estate broker called their attention to a 50-acre tract of land that was zoned for residential property and was already plotted for development. The asking price for the land was $180,000. The plot called for 130 residential lots which Dan and Jim believed could be sold for $3,000 each or a total of $390,000.

With the expectation of a good profit, they formed a partnership, Acres. The partnership agreement specified that both partners would participate in management of the venture (in their spare time) and that profits and losses would be divided equally. The agreement also provided for liquidation of the partnership when all lots were sold. A joint bank account was opened in the partnership name. Each partner contributed $50,000 to the venture on February 1, 19X1.

On February 2, 19X1 the land was purchased for $180,000 and immediately mortgaged to a bank for $175,000. The rate of interest on the loan was 7 percent per annum. The loan agreement provided for repayment as the lots were sold.

The partners made the following expenditures during the spring of 19X1 to complete the development:

Cost of paving and curbing for streets and alleys	$42,000
Cost of sewage and water lines	56,500

The development work was completed in July of 19X1, and the lots were placed on the market. Most lots were sold through real estate agents who were paid a 6 percent commission on the sales price. Dan and Jim also ran several ads in the local newspaper to promote sales. The sale of all lots required a two-year period; the final lot was sold on July 30, 19X3. Total cash realized on the sales was $384,000. The following selling costs were incurred:

Sales commissions	$18,700
Advertising	6,500
Miscellaneous	3,100
Total	$28,300

In accordance with the loan agreement, the loan was repaid as well as $17,250 for interest. At the end of July the partners were ready to make an accounting before liquidation.

Statement of Cash Receipts and Disbursements

Figure 2–3 is a statement of cash receipts and disbursements. This statement shows all cash transactions, both financing and operating, which occurred during the period from February 1, 19X1 to July 31, 19X3. Trace each amount on the statement back to the recitation of facts above. Note the heading on the statement showing the name of the business, the title of the statement, and the period involved.

Figure 2-3

Acres	Statement of Cash Receipts and Disbursements from February 1, 19X1 to July 31, 19X3			
Cash receipts:				
Investments by partners				
Dan Roberts	$50,000			
Jim Richards	50,000	$100,000		
Proceeds from bank loan		$175,000		
Sale of lots		384,000	$659,000	
Cash disbursements:				
Land		$180,000		
Paving and curbing		42,000		
Assessment for water & sewage		56,500		
Sales commissions		18,700		
Advertising		6,500		
Miscellaneous		3,100		
Interest on bank loan		17,250		
Repayment of bank loan		175,000	$499,050	
Cash balance, on hand, July 31, 19X3			$159,950	

The difference between cash receipts and cash disbursements gives the cash balance on hand at the end of the venture because this statement shows all transactions from the inception of the venture. There was no beginning cash balance. The difference between cash receipts and cash disbursements can also be identified as the *change in cash*:

Change in cash = Cash receipts - Cash disbursements
$$\Delta C \quad = \quad CR \quad - \quad CD$$

Measurement of Income

The above statement of cash receipts and disbursements is *almost* a statement of income because the venture was *complete* when the statement was prepared. Revenue and expenses can be determined easily by eliminating the financial transactions:

Income = Revenue – Expense
  Y   =   R   –   E

Revenue = Cash receipts – Investment receipts
  R   =   CR   –   IR
     = $659,000 – ($175,000 + $100,000)
     = $384,000

Expenses = Cash disbursements – Investment disbursements
  E   =   CD   –   ID
     = $499,050   – $175,000
     = $324,050

  Y   = $384,000 – $324,050
     = $59,950

Revenue is $384,000, that is, the total receipts of $659,000 after subtracting $100,000 investment by owners and $175,000 borrowed from bank. Expenses are $324,050, that is, the total cash disbursements after subtracting the repayment of the bank loan. The income is $59,950, that is, the difference between revenue and expense ($384,000 – $324,050).

The income statement for the venture can now be prepared and is shown in Fig. 2–4.

Figure 2–4

Acres	Statement of Income for the period from February 1, 19X1 to July 31, 19X3	
Revenue—sale of lots		$384,000
Expenses:		
Cost of land	$180,000	
Paving & curbing	42,000	
Water and sewage	56,500	
Sales commissions	18,700	
Advertising	6,500	
Miscellaneous	3,100	
Interest on bank loan	17,250	324,050
Net income		$ 59,950

Compare this statement with the one for cash receipts and cash disbursements. Note the changes in the heading, the terms used, and the elimination of the financing transactions. The statement user now has a measurement dealing with the *operations* of the enterprise only; financing transactions have been eliminated. With this statement, including the breakdown of expenses by objects, informed decisions can be made about the success of the venture. If Dan and Jim contemplate other similar ventures, they have information about various costs incurred and revenues produced.

TREATMENT OF INTEREST. The calculation of income just presented brushes lightly over one of many inconsistencies in accounting. Notice that the amount paid for interest is not treated as a disinvestment or investment disbursement; only the amounts paid on the principal are subtracted from total cash disbursements to obtain total expense.

The partners invested $100,000 in the venture and the bank "invested" $175,000 in the form of a loan. If the partners had withdrawn $10,000 each during the life of the venture their withdrawals would be treated as disinvestments or investment disbursements like the loan repayment of $175,000. Similarly, if the venture had been organized as a corporation, any dividends to shareholders would be treated as a disinvestment. All investment transactions between investors and the business are excluded from the income computation with the single exception of interest. Traditionally, interest is treated as an expense, whereas dividends and withdrawals are treated as disinvestments. The distinction is a legal and traditional one, not a logical one.

Upon liquidation of the Acres partnership, each partner will receive cash in the amount of his net worth as shown above. This amount represents a return of his cash investment plus one-half of the profit or income from the venture.

Stock and Flow Methods Compared

Both the stock and flow methods are useful in decision-making. Their relative advantages and disadvantages are compared in the following discussion.

Stock Method for a Completed Venture

Computation of income using the *stock concept* is also relatively easy for a completed venture. Arrange the facts in the Acres illustration as follows:

Wealth at beginning	$W_0 = 0$
Wealth at end	$W_1 = \$159{,}950$
Investment during period	$I = \$100{,}000$
Distribution during period	$D = 0$

Recall that the equation for the computation of income under the stock approach is

$$Y = W_1 - W_0 - I + D$$

Substituting the above amounts in the equation

$$Y = \$159{,}950 - 0 - \$100{,}000 - 0$$
$$= \$59{,}950$$

This amount agrees with the income computed using the flow approach.

Two important factors made the agreement between the stock and flow easy to achieve and easy to understand: First, wealth at the end of the period consisted only of cash, and, second, the venture was completed. The significance of the first factor is readily apparent because measurement of cash presents no problems. The impact of the second factor, completion of the venture, is less obvious but more important.

An Uncompleted Venture

An income figure for a completed venture is calculated in terms of the results of completed transactions. Income for an uncompleted venture may be calculated

1   in terms of anticipated benefits from transactions not yet completed, or
2   by assigning values to noncash assets in terms of disposal prices or other valuations, or
3   by holding judgment in abeyance concerning transactions not yet completed.

The first method works well only when interested parties have thorough first-hand knowledge of the plans and activities entailed in the venture. Even under these circumstances, the method requires a lot of guesswork and usually entails a number of assumptions that are sometimes based on little more than blind faith. For these reasons, one or another of the two remaining methods is typically used at a later time even in those situations where someone calculates an initial estimate of income with the first method.

The second method—assigning values to noncash assets—lends itself to a stock approach to income determination. The third method—holding judgment in abeyance on uncompleted transactions—lends itself to a flow approach to income determination. For ventures of limited size controlled by individuals who have first-hand familiarity with venture activities, either a stock or a flow approach is usually practical. Also, either view may be worthwhile depending on the nature of the assets employed in the venture and the intended use of the information.

CONFUSION ABOUT EQUALITY OF RESULTS. As expressed previously, the direct result of a stock approach to income determination involves taking inventory of assets and assigning values to them; and the direct result of a flow approach involves measuring revenues, inflows of assets, and expenses (consumption of assets to generate revenue). It is important to note that the stock approach indirectly involves flows—the activities and attendant flows of assets that give rise to changes in the stocks of assets that are inventoried and valued at different points in time. Likewise the flow approach indirectly involves stocks. As a result of the flows over time, stocks exist at any point in time. Because stocks and flows are related in the way described, it is easy to commit the error of believing that stock and flow approaches will yield equivalent measures of income (equal monetary amounts) for an uncompleted venture just as they did for a completed venture. Such is not the case.

The stock approach forces an indirect monetary measure of flows, and the flow approach forces an indirect monetary measure of stocks. Only in the case of a highly improbable coincidence would the amounts of the forced measures (flows in the stock approach and stocks in the flow approach) equal the amounts calculated directly (flows in the flow approach and stocks in the stock approach).

For example, assume a businessman purchases a plot of land for $10,000 on which to operate a trailer court. Suppose that, a year later, similar plots are selling for $11,000 and that the businessman is, in fact, offered $11,000 for his plot of land. At any given point in time the plot of land will be part of the businessman's stock of assets. Note, however, that under the flow approach the land would be valued at $10,000. A change in value would be recognized only on the basis of a completed transaction, namely, sale of the land. Judgment is held in abeyance on uncompleted transactions, hence a $10,000 valuation. Under the stock approach, the land would be valued at $11,000. Obviously the amount of income and net assets differs under the two approaches even though a stock approach indirectly entails flows and a flow approach indirectly entails stocks.

THE CASE FOR THE FLOW APPROACH. In a mature economy, ventures are large and complex, and they continue over long, indefinite time spans. Interested parties may have conflicting interests and they rarely have first-hand familiarity with venture activities. Under these circumstances, an approach to income determination that minimizes difficulties in measurement and supplies information about the economic activities that generate income (loss) is definitely advantageous and may be absolutely essential. In such circumstances, practicing accountants have opted for a flow approach. Contemporary practice may not always apply a pure flow approach but it definitely emphasizes the flow approach. Although there is currently some sentiment for mixture of stock and flow approaches or for use of one to supplement the other, these are matters for study in advanced courses. The first order of business is to acquire an understanding of the flow approach together with its strengths and weaknesses.

MODIFIED CASH FLOWS. An important key to minimizing measurement problems and simultaneously provide information about the economic activities that generate income with the flow approach lies in focusing attention on cash flows. The flow approach involves accounting in terms of modified cash flows. This means that even when the income effects of transactions are recognized at points in time other than when cash inflows or outflows occur, the measurements involved are made in terms of cash inflows and outflows. To comprehend this approach fully as it applies to uncompleted ventures, one must understand the terms accruals and deferrals.

Accruals and Deferrals

The calculation of income for the real estate venture exemplified in this chapter was made at the termination of the venture. The purpose of the example was to provide the student with a basic understanding of the flow concept of income. Such short-term ventures are not typical in our modern economy.

In addition to those concepts already defined (revenue, expense, cash receipts, cash disbursements, investment, and disinvestment), calculation of income on a *periodic basis* for a going concern requires an understanding of two additional concepts, accruals and deferrals.

The Accounting Period

Most businesses in our economy continue in existence indefinitely once they are established. We do observe that some mature businesses fail and that others are bought out by larger organizations. However, the normal expectation for an established business is for an indefinite life. The causes of this observed stability are the industrial and financial revolutions discussed in Chapter 1. If the business is to continue indefinitely, a periodic accounting of the progress of the enterprise is essential for all interested parties.

An *annual* accounting for all businesses has become a well-entrenched convention. Many concerns conduct the annual reckoning as of December 31, commonly referred to as the *calendar year* basis. Many businesses have adopted the *natural business year* for the accounting period. In most businesses, there is some point in every year when activity is relatively low. For department stores, the end of January is a time of very low activity, the Christmas buying rush and subsequent exchange period is over, and spring and Easter traffic is light. Inventories are generally at low levels, and the management's time can be devoted to summing up the preceding twelve-months' work. Thus, many department stores end their fiscal years on January 31. For other businesses, the summer months are months of low activity. The year adopted, whether a calendar year or a natural business year, is called the *fiscal year*. The annual reckoning is an ever-present consideration to accountants, managers, investors, tax collectors, labor leaders, and many others. In most businesses, accounting reports are prepared on a monthly basis for internal management. In addition, corporations whose shares are listed on the stock exchanges must release financial statements each quarter. These interim reports are significant but the most important accounting is on an annual basis.

The Matching Concept

The definitions for revenue and expense given earlier in this chapter are inadequate for the measurement of income of a continuing business. A comparison of cash receipts with cash disbursements for a limited time period, even after excluding investment transactions, will usually give a distorted picture of the progress of the enterprise and of the efficiency of operations.

If income is to serve as a periodic index of effectiveness in a going concern, revenue must be something more than cash receipts, and expenses something more than cash disbursements. Refer to the real estate venture described in the preceding pages. On February 1, 19X2 let us assume that lot sales amounted to $100,000 and expenditures were as follows:

Cost of land	$180,000
Paving and curbing expenses	42,000
Water and sewage expense	56,500
Sales commissions	5,000
Advertising	4,000
Miscellaneous expenses	2,000
Interest expense	10,000
Repayment of bank loan	75,000
	$374,500

Measurement of income by excluding only financing transactions would be as follows:

$$R = CR - IR$$
$$= \$375,000 - (\$175,000 + \$100,000)$$
$$= \$100,000$$

$$E = CD - ID$$
$$= \$374,500 - \$75,000$$
$$= \$299,500$$

$$Y = \$100,000 - \$299,500$$
$$= -\$199,500 \text{ (loss)}$$

This is an absurdity; the unsold lots and unpaid bills must be considered if the measurement of income is to be significant. To get a meaningful income measurement, we must define revenue as the *accomplishment* of the business for the *fiscal period*. Expenses must be defined as the *effort* expended by the business to produce the revenue or accomplishment. The difference, then, between the revenue or accomplishment and the effort expended to produce the revenue will be a measure of the net accomplishment of the business. The annual income measurement tells the interested parties whether the management has been effective in moving toward its objectives. Periodic income determination is the process of adjusting cash receipts to measure revenue (accomplishment) and cash expenditures to measure expenses (efforts) and computing the difference, the value added or income for the period.

Accruals

A general definition of the verb *accrue* is "something added by way of ordered growth." One may say, for example, that interest accrued on the principal of a note, meaning that the debtor must repay not only the principal amount, but also an additional sum for interest. The noun accruals generally means either the process of accruing or that which is accrued. In accounting, these terms are used in a way very similar to their general meaning. To accrue is to *add on* to some amount, and an accrual is either the process of adding on or the *amount* which is added on. Specifically, certain accruals or additions must be made to cash receipts of an entity in order to convert the amount of cash receipts into a measure (revenue) which represents the accomplishments for the fiscal period. Also certain additions must be made to cash disbursements to measure expenses representing the effort expended by the business.

Deferrals

A general definition of the verb *defer* is "to put off to a future time." In accounting, a deferral is the process of *putting off*, or is the amount of the cash receipt or cash disbursement which is put off or deferred to a future fiscal period. Specifically, deferrals are amounts subtracted from cash receipts to determine revenue or accomplishment of a business for a fiscal period; or deferrals are amounts subtracted from cash disbursements to determine the efforts expended by a business for a fiscal period.

The need for deferrals is readily seen if one considers the transactions of a business that is just beginning operations. Would all of the cash outlays in the early years of operation for plant, equipment, and other long-lived assets be treated as expenses as the cash is spent? These cash expenditures will contribute to the operations of the business for several years. To subtract them from revenue as the cash is disbursed would understate the income of the early years of operations and result in greatly overstated income in later years.

Thus, the cash spent for plant and equipment must be deferred and included in expenses as the resources are used up or consumed by business operations. A similar need arises for the deferral of cash receipts when customers pay for products in advance, before the business has produced and delivered such products.

The measurement of accruals and deferrals and the resulting definitions of revenue and expense for a continuing business are discussed in the following chapter. The computation of periodic income by adjusting net cash flow for accruals and deferrals is called the *accrual basis* of accounting. Only the accrual basis is generally accepted for reporting to external parties. Occasionally, some businesses will compute their income on the *cash basis*, particularly for income tax purposes. This terminology is misleading, however, because the so-called cash basis is not a strict cash basis. Some adjustments for accruals and deferrals must be made to obtain "cash-basis" income. Thus an understanding of the concepts of accruals and deferrals is essential to an understanding of accounting.

QUESTIONS

1   Compare the stock concept and flow concept of measuring income. List some of the advantages and disadvantages of each method.

2   Define the following words:

[a]   Revenue   [e]   Income

[b]   Expense   [f]   Wealth

[c]   Accrual   [g]   Liabilities

[d]   Deferral

3   Why should an individual or business want to measure income?

4   The flow concept of income is based on the inflow and outflow of cash over the life of the business. Why is cash so important?

5   In measuring income under the stock concept why should additional investment and withdrawal (disinvestments) be considered?

6   Why is it difficult to determine the value of resources?

7   What is the "aggregation problem" in measuring income using the stock approach? Does use of the flow approach eliminate the aggregation problem?

8   Why should accountants be concerned about the objectivity of their measurements?

9   What are some possible substitutes for income as a measure or index of efficiency?

10   For a completed venture, both the stock and flow concepts provide equally objective and practical measures of income. Why?

11   Why does the income of a modern-day corporation need to be measured periodically?

12   What is a balance sheet or statement of financial position?

13   Why is the matching concept so important in the measurement of income using the flow concept?

PROBLEMS

1   The following information was compiled by J. Erwin after he operated his insurance agency for one year:

Cash on deposit	$3,500
Loan from city bank	1,500
Receivable due from Insurance Co.	400

Required:

[a]   Compute Erwin's net worth.

[b]   Assuming Mr. Erwin started the business at the beginning of the year with an investment of $1,000 and has not made any withdrawals, what is his income for the year?

[c]   Assume the same facts as in requirement [b] except that Mr. Erwin withdrew $5,000. What is his income?

2   By applying the formula for measuring income using the stock concept, compute the income for 19X1 in each of the following cases:

[a]   On January 1, 19X1, value of assets was $10,000 and liabilities amounted to $3,000. On December 31, 19X1, assets totaled $12,500 and liabilities were $3,500. There were no distributions (disinvestments) to owners during 19X1 and no new investments.

[b]   Same facts as part [a] above, except that distributions to owners during 19X1 were $2,500.

[c]   Same facts as part [a] above, except that distributions to owners during 19X1 were $2,000 and owners made new investments totaling $5,000 during the year.

3   Compute the answers to the following expressions:

[a] ΔC =

if CR = $180,000
CD = $172,000

[b]   R =

if Y = $18,000
E = $43,000

[c]   E =

if R = $84,000
Y = $16,000

[d]   CR =

if IR = $27,000
R = $61,000

[e]   CD =

if ID = $19,000
E = $56,000

[f]   Compute income using information in parts [d] and [e].

[g] ΔC =

if IR = $139,000
ID = $47,000
R = $116,000
E = $87,000

4   Calculate the income for a completed venture from the following information by using first the equation for the stock concept and then the equation for the flow concept:

ABC Company

Statement of Cash Receipts and Cash Disbursements for Life of Business

Cash receipts:		
Sale of product	$175,000	
Owner's investment	100,000	$275,000
Cash disbursements:		
Cost of product	$ 80,000	
Salaries & wages	30,000	
Supplies	10,000	
Advertising	20,000	
Miscellaneous	10,000	
Disbursement to owners	125,000	$275,000
Cash balance following complete liquidation		$0

5   Listed below are the cash receipts and disbursements for a completed venture:

Cash receipts:		
From customers	$52,000	
From bank loan	10,000	
From owners	18,000	$80,000
Cash disbursements:		
Operating expenses	$54,000	
Interest on loan	600	
Repayment of loan	10,000	
Withdrawals	3,000	67,600
Cash balance		$12,400

[a]   Compute income for the venture using the equations given in the chapter.
[b]   Prepare a balance sheet for the business.

6   The C Real Estate Agency was organized in 19X1 and the venture was terminated in 19X3. The cash receipts and disbursements for the life of the venture were as follows:

Cash receipts:
From Commissions	$214,000	
From bank loan	15,000	
From owners	22,000	$251,000
Cash disbursements:		
Salaries	$167,000	
Rent	5,000	
Utilities	2,000	
Advertising	26,000	
Interest	80	
Repayment of loan	15,000	
Withdrawal by owners	20,000	235,080
Cash balance		$ 15,920

[a]   Compute the income for the C Real Estate Agency by using the revenue and expense equations.
[b]   Prepare a detailed statement of income.
[c]   Prepare a balance sheet for the C Real Estate Agency at the end of the venture. The owner of the agency is John Timothy.

7   Bob and Herbert Brown decided to go into the Christmas tree business for the Yuletide season 19X1. Below are listed chronologically the transactions in which the partners engaged.

19X1

August 10: Each partner contributed $4,000 to the venture and agreed to divide the profit equally. A bank account was opened in the name of the partnership, Brown Brothers.
August 10: Borrowed $5,000 from the bank on a short-term note. The $5,000 plus interest of $200 are to be repaid on February 10, 19X2.
August 20: Leased a vacant corner lot on a busy intersection. Rental for a four-month period amounted to $800. This amount was paid to the lessor on August 20.
August 30: Paid $440 for a sign, for lights, and other items needed to operate the lot.
September 16: Leased a large van and made three trips to Oregon to locate and purchase trees. Cash spent on the trips was as follows:

Cost of trees	$8,400
Travel expense (gas, oil, etc.)	1,300
Truck lease	1,800

November 15 to December 25: Sales of Christmas trees for the holiday season amounted to $14,000. Additional expenses incurred were as follows:

Operating expenses (utilities, etc.)	$ 420
Salaries for helpers	1,230

19X2

February 10: Repaid bank loan with interest of $200.

Required:

[a]   Prepare a statement of cash receipts and cash disbursements for the Christmas tree business from inception to completion.

[b]   Prepare an income statement for this venture.

[c]   Prepare a balance sheet for the business at the end of the venture.

8   Mr. Gee purchased land adjacent to a railroad siding a mile outside of the city of Newburg for $10,000. He constructed buildings, loading docks for both railroad cars and trucks, and fences; and has been operating a lumber yard on the site for the past ten years. In the interim the city of Newburg has grown by leaps and bounds and for all practical purposes Mr. Gee's lumber yard is now located in the heart of the city. As a result Mr. Gee recently received an offer of $125,000 for the land used as a site for his lumber yard.

[a]   With strict application of the flow approach, what value would be placed on the lumber yard site?

[b]   With strict application of the stock approach, what value would be assigned to the lumber yard site?

[c]   Assume the buildings, loading docks, and fences will be completely worn out in one more year and will have to be demolished and replaced at that time. Also assume that on the edge of town a new site that is better suited than the present site to the needs of a lumber yard is available at a price of $15,000. Under these circumstances what value would you assign to the lumber yard site? Present reasons for your answer.

[d]   Assume the buildings, loading docks, and fences will serve the needs of the lumber yard for 20 more years. Also assume that it would cost $200,000 to build compar-able assets that will last 20 years on a new site. The new site will cost $15,000 and Mr. Gee will be lucky to break even if he has buildings, loading docks, and fences demolished (salvage will just about cover wrecking costs). Also assume that Mr. Gee can sell his present site for $125,000 only if all structures are cleared away (i.e., the new owner would have no use for them). Mr. Gee's lumber business is very profit-able and he wants to continue to operate it. An acquaintance of questionable honesty has noted that Mr. Gee could collect $180,000 for his structures from the insurance company if they were completely destroyed by fire. However, Mr. Gee is meticulously honest and plans to take precaution against fire as thoroughly as he has in the past. Under these circumstances what value would you assign to the lumber yard site? Present reasons for your answer.

[e]   Consider the nature of the activities of most, extremely large, modern corporations. With regard to the bulk of their assets, explain why you believe the circumstances more nearly approximate those in parts [c] or [d].

9   The S Corporation was organized on January 1, 19X1. Presented below are the cash receipts and cash disbursements for 19X1.

Cash receipts from customers		$ 84,000
Cash receipts from owner investors		100,000
Total cash receipts		$184,000
Cash paid for labor	$48,000	
Cash paid for material and other services	34,000	
Cash paid for building	80,000	
Total cash payments		162,000
Cash balance, 12/31/X1		$ 22,000

Required:

[a]   Which of these transactions are financial transactions? Which are operating transactions?

[b]   How much better off is the S Corporation on December 31, 19X1 than it was on January 1, 19X1?

[c]   What is the income of the S Corporation in 19X1? Show your computation. If, for some reason, you cannot compute the income, list the additional facts that you would need to measure income for the year.

10   J. D. Rockfall's cash receipts and cash disbursements are presented below:

J. D. Rockfall

Statement of Cash Receipts and Cash Disbursements

Cash receipts:		
Repayment of loan by son		$85,000
Dividends from stock		1,000
Interest received from government bonds		3,000
Total cash receipts		$89,000
Cash disbursements:		
Purchase of government bond	$50,000	
Purchase of certificate of		
deposit from local bank	10,000	
Investment in G Corp.	20,000	
Total cash disbursement		80,000
Increase in cash		$ 9,000

Required:

[a]   Identify the financing activities in J. D. Rockfall's cash transactions.

[b]   Identify the operating activities in the above cash transactions.

[c]   Did Rockfall have a successful year? Why or why not?

[d]   What other information would you like to have to measure Rockfall's economic success?

11   An income statement for the O Company is presented below:

O Company

Statement of Income for the Period March 1, 19X1 to June 30, 19X3

Revenue		$416,000
Expenses:		
Salaries and wages	$160,000	
Materials	180,000	
Other expenses	20,000	
Total expenses		360,000
Net income		$ 56,000

Harold Clarke, the owner of O Company, invested $50,000 in the business on March 1, 19X1. He borrowed $100,000 from his bank on April 1, 19X2, and repaid $75,000 on May 30, 19X3. Mr. Clarke also withdrew $25,000 during this period.

Required:

Prepare a statement of cash receipts and cash disbursements for the period from March 1, 19X1 to June 30, 19X3. (Suggestion: Use the equations for R and E developed in Chapter 2; solve them for cash receipts and cash disbursements.)

12   Presented below are statements of cash receipts and disbursements of Companies A and B covering the three-year life of each company. Examine the information presented and draw conclusions as to which company performed best. Support your conclusion with appropriate quantitative data.

	Co. A	Co. B
Cash receipts:		
From owners	$ 50,000	$100,000
From bank loan	100,000	50,000
From customers	300,000	200,000
Total receipts	$450,000	$350,000
Cash disbursements:		
Salaries	$ 30,000	$ 80,000
Rent	25,000	10,000
Advertising	40,000	6,000
Supplies	110,000	20,000
Interest	8,000	4,000
Repayment of bank loans	100,000	50,000
Withdrawals by owners	100,000	150,000
Total cash disbursements	$413,000	$320,000

CASE   John Cochran purchased the N Laundry from its previous owner on April 30, 19X1 for $50,000. The laundry included land, building, equipment, and supplies. Mr. Cochran invested an additional $10,000 which he deposited in a bank account under the name of N Laundry. In December of 19X1, Mr. Cochran contacted James Strange, a local public accountant, and requested that Mr. Strange help him determine the income of the laundry business for the eight months of 19X1.

Mr. Strange found that Mr. Cochran had followed the practice of depositing all cash receipts in the bank and paying all cash disbursements by check. Mr. Strange proposed that he prepare a statement of cash receipts and disbursements and adjust this statement for items that were not revenues or expenses. Mr. Cochran objected stating that it would take considerable effort to prepare a detailed statement of cash receipts and cash disbursements. Mr. Cochran suggested that they merely determine the net worth of the business as of December 31, 19X1, subtract the beginning net worth of $60,000 from that figure, and the difference would be the income for the period. The net worth at the end of the period could be easily determined by adding the ending cash balance and the value of the land, building, equipment, and supplies.

Required:

[a]   Describe the adjustments that would be necessary to measure revenues and expenses if a record of cash receipts and disbursements were available.

[b]   Identify the main problem that would arise in the determination of ending net worth.

[c]   Draw a conclusion as to whether the stock or flow approach is best under the circumstances. Support your conclusion by itemizing the advantages and disadvantages of measuring income under each approach. Relate your conclusion to the primary purpose of income measurement.

3

Measurement of
Revenues and
Expenses

The objective of this chapter is to describe the measurement of revenues and expenses of a continuing business to enable us to compute income on a periodic basis. The general elements necessary to measure revenue and expense are defined, and the equations for the flow concept of income are developed. In short, this chapter covers the basic concepts of income measurement found in use today.

Measurement of Revenue

Income is defined under the flow concept as revenue minus expenses ($Y = R - E$). To compute income, therefore, we must first measure revenue and expense.
    Revenues are defined as follows:

Revenues are the values of goods and services transferred to external parties in exchange for cash or a promise of a future cash inflow, and are measured by cash inflows either received or expected.

Further explanation of this definition is required in order to develop a method by which revenue can be measured.

Revenue Recognition

In Chapter 2 revenue or accomplishment was equated with the cash received from operations (sale of product or service) at the end of the income cycle or completed venture. If periodic income is to be measured in a continuing business, we must first answer the questions: *How much is the revenue for the accounting period? How much was produced or accomplished during this period?* This problem is commonly referred to as the *recognition* problem. To measure revenue, we must select one point in the operating cycle of the business where activities are sufficiently complete for accomplishments to be measured.

Referring to the diagram of business activities (Fig. 1-1), three steps can be eliminated as clearly inappropriate for revenue recognition. Certainly, there is no earning or accomplishment when the entity secures resources from owners or creditors. Similarly, the final step in the cycle, the return of resources to owners and creditors (disinvestment), should have no bearing on the measurement of income. Finally, accountants have traditionally refused to attribute any revenue as a result of the acquisition of services. Although this first step in the operating cycle is a very important one and the success of the business may depend on its ability to acquire services at favorable prices, the amount of accomplishment cannot be objectively measured until the services acquired are used in production or transferred to customers in the form of a finished product.

Depending on the circumstances, the remaining three steps in the operating cycle are feasible bases for the recognition of revenue:

Combination of services (production)
Sale of product to customers
Collection of cash from customers

In many *service* businesses where the customer pays cash, these three steps may occur simultaneously or virtually so. For example, in a barbershop the service is produced (hair is cut), the sale is complete (customer looks in mirror and nods approval), and the cash is collected within a short interval. In other businesses, the first two steps may occur simultaneously, but there is a time lag before the last step. For example, a repair shop may complete repairs on a TV or on a wristwatch several days or weeks before the customer accepts the work and pays the repair bill. In most businesses, however, there is a considerable time lag between each step. Goods are produced; after a time a customer is found and a sale is consummated on *credit*; and finally, after another wait, cash is collected. Depending on the circumstances, revenue may be recognized at any one of these three points.

EXAMPLE. Assume that a manufacturing concern was organized and operated for its *first* year with the following results:

Units of product completed during year	1,000 units
Units sold during the year	800 units
Units paid for by customers	600 units
Sales price per unit	$90 per unit

These facts present the normal situation where production precedes the sale and the sale is made on credit with the cash collected later. Revenue for this first year can be calculated as follows:

Based on cash collected, or *cash basis*, $54,000
Cash is collected for 600 units at $90 per unit. Use of the cash basis would be appropriate if grave doubts existed about the company's ability to collect cash eventually. For example, if the sales are to firms in a foreign country

and a revolution is expected momentarily, it would be misleading to include in revenue the sales price of the units sold but not yet paid for by customers.

Based on units produced or **production basis**, $90,000

The most optimistic view is that of recognizing revenue as the goods are produced. In this case, 1,000 units were produced with an estimated sales price of $90 per unit. This basis is unacceptable in the usual case because it cannot be determined just how many of the 200 units remaining on hand at the end of the period will eventually be sold, nor what the sales price will be. The production basis is acceptable in gold mining operations because the U.S. government buys the entire output at a set price.

Based on units sold or **sales basis**, $72,000

This amount is obtained by multiplying the 800 units sold by the sales price. This basis is the middle ground between the other bases. It is acceptable in most businesses because most customers pay their debts. The sale, not production, is the critical point in the cycle for most businesses.

GENERAL RULES. Because of the complexity of our economy any one of the above bases may be the most appropriate point for the recognition of revenue, depending on the good or service produced and on the method used to distribute the product. The general rules for determining when revenue should be recognized are as follows:

1   There is an exchange agreement with an outside party.
2   Cash or a legal right to receive cash in the future is received.
3   The business has delivered the product or performed substantially all of the services required by the transaction.

For most businesses in our economy, the three tests are met when the product is sold to a customer. In this initial discussion of the measurement of revenue we will assume that revenue is recognized at the point of sale. Use of the other bases for recognition, cash and production, will be discussed in Chapter 10.

Revenue Flow

A set of typical transactions illustrating the revenue flow would include the following:

1   An agreement is reached between the seller and the buyer specifying the terms of the sale (if in writing, this agreement is usually called a **sales invoice**).
2   The seller delivers the product sold to the buyer or performs the service for the buyer.
3   The obligation of the buyer to pay cash to the seller is recorded by the seller along with other claims to cash which the company has received (this file of claims is usually called **accounts receivable**).
4   Cash is collected from the buyer, thereby increasing cash receipts.

5   The claim against the customer is removed from the file of accounts receivable.
6   Finally, the record of cash on hand is updated to reflect the cash receipt and to increase the cash balance.

Note that after steps 1 and 2 above the criteria for revenue recognition are met: There is an agreement with the customer—the agreement, evidenced by the sales invoice, includes the promise of the customer to pay cash in the future; and the product is completed and delivered to the customer. A time lag usually exists between the sales agreement, delivery of goods or performance of the service, and the collection of cash. If all these events occurred simultaneously, as in the illustration given earlier of the haircut, the time lag would be eliminated. Because of our credit economy, however, the time lag is generally an important consideration. The seller keeps, in some form, three essential records concerned with revenue flow, the file of claims against customers (accounts receivable), the record of cash receipts from customers, and a record of his cash balance (including cash on hand, deposits in banks, and other sources). These records are needed to compute periodic revenue.

ACCRUALS AND DEFERRALS. When a service is performed or a product delivered prior to the receipt of cash, all three criteria for revenue recognition are fulfilled. This recognition of revenue is not, however, reflected in the cash receipts. Recall from Chapter 2 that an accrual is an *addition* made in the measurement of revenue. We must accrue, or add on to cash receipts, an amount equal to the revenue recognized but not yet settled by a receipt of cash. The business maintains a file of uncollected claims (accounts receivables) against customers for products delivered but not yet settled in cash. This file is increased when a credit sale is made and decreased when the customer settles the claim with the payment of cash. Our measurement of revenue in this text will reflect these accruals by the use of the symbol AR (A symbolizing accrual, and R referring to the measurement of revenue, in this case a revenue accrual).

Occasionally customers pay cash before the three criteria for revenue recognition are met. An advanced payment may be required by the seller before the product is made, although this arrangement is rare. In other situations, the buyer may make partial or complete payment for the product prior to its delivery. Lay-away plans in retail stores are examples of this latter situation. When cash is received before the criteria for recognition are met, a *deferral* of the cash receipts is necessary. As explained in Chapter 2, a deferral is a *subtraction* made to measure revenue. The symbol DR is used to represent a revenue deferral (the D symbolizing deferral, and the R again relating to the measurement of revenue).

THE REVENUE EQUATION. The equation for revenue developed in Chapter 2 for a completed venture was as follows:

$$R = CR - IR$$

The formula must be amended, however, for use in a continuing business to consider the effects of accrued revenues and deferred revenues. The change in revenue accruals must be added to cash receipts to determine revenue; the change in revenue deferrals must be subtracted from cash receipts to determine revenue. Investment transactions (cash receipts from debt investors and owner investors) must still be subtracted from cash receipts as illustrated in Chapter 2 to determine revenue.

You will notice in the paragraph above that emphasis is placed on the word *change*—the change in accruals and change in deferrals. Symbol Δ, which was introduced in Chapter 2 with respect to the change in cash (ΔC), will be used to reflect change in the revenue accruals, ΔAR, and change in the revenue deferrals, ΔDR. The change is the difference between the amounts at the end of the accounting compared to the beginning amounts. The change in accruals of revenue (ΔAR) is the difference between the accounts receivable at the end of the period (AR_1) and at the beginning of the period (AR_0),

$$\Delta AR = AR_1 - AR_0$$

The change in revenue deferrals is similarly computed as

$$\Delta DR = DR_1 - DR_0$$

The expanded revenue equation is

$$R = CR + \Delta AR - \Delta DR - IR$$

It defines *periodic* revenue for a continuing business.

Example of Revenue Measurement—Transaction Basis

To simplify the addition of accruals and deferrals to the revenue equation, let us assume that no financing or investment transactions occur during the period. With this assumption the value for IR is zero in all examples unless otherwise specified. Eliminating this variable the revenue equation is

$$R = CR + \Delta AR - \Delta DR$$

We will use the following facts to illustrate the computation of revenue for a single transaction. J Automotive Repairs agrees with Jonathan Black to overhaul his car for $250. Revenue is not recognized when the agreement is reached, because the third criterion for revenue recognition has not been met; namely, Joe has not yet performed the services specified in the agreement.

Assume further that Joe completes the overhaul and delivers the car to Mr. Black. Mr. Black accepts the overhauled car and agrees to pay $250 in 30 days. Revenue is recognized at this point because all three criteria for revenue recognition are met. This transaction would affect revenue for the period as follows:

$$R = CR + \Delta AR - \Delta DR$$
$$= (0) + (\$250) - (0)$$
$$= \$250$$

Revenue accruals increased by $250 but no cash has been received, and there has been no change in deferred revenues. Note that the result is not revenue for the accounting period but the revenue resulting from this single transaction.

At the end of 30 days, Mr. Black mails a $250 check to J Automotive Repairs. The effect of this transaction is

$$R = (\$250) + (-\$250) - (0)$$
$$= 0$$

Cash receipts are increased by $250, but accrued revenue is decreased by $250 when Black pays his bill; the net effect on revenue is zero.

As a second example of the effects of a single transaction, assume that Mr. Tim Markers delivered his foreign car to Joe's shop and requested that Joe install a new motor. Joe did not have the required motor and parts but agreed to order the motor and do the work if Mr. Markers would pay him $300 in advance. Mr. Markers agreed to these terms and paid Joe $300. The effect of this transaction on revenue is

$$R = (\$300) + (0) - (+\$300)$$
$$= 0$$

The services have not been performed, and, therefore there is no increase in revenue. As a result of the transaction, cash is increased, but this increase is offset by an increase in deferred revenue which must be subtracted from cash receipts to obtain the recognized revenue. Several weeks later the motor and necessary parts are received and installed. When Mr. Markers accepts the work on the car, the acceptance has the following effect on revenue:

$$R = (0) + (0) - (-\$300)$$
$$= \$300$$

The performance of the service decreases the deferred revenue which results in the recognition of revenue.

In this example revenue measurement was made on a transaction by transaction basis. Income is a measure of activity for a period of time. Consequently, the variables for income measurement, revenue and expense, will reflect all activities during the accounting period. Just as the speed of an automobile is measured in miles per hour, income is measured for a year, a month, or some other period.

Example of Revenue Measurement—Periodic Basis

As explained previously, the files or records of cash receipts, revenue accruals, revenue deferrals, and investments transactions are essential for the periodic measurement of revenue. The most common method of maintaining these records is double-entry bookkeeping, a method which is explained and illustrated in Chapters 8 and 9. The files or records for revenue accruals and revenue deferrals provide the information necessary to compute the changes in these variables—the amounts of the variables at the beginning and end of the measurement period.

Figure 3-1 is a schematic representation of the measurement of revenue for a period. This diagram shows the additions to and subtractions from the period's cash receipts for revenue accruals and revenue deferrals. The signs (+ and -) can be rationalized by expanding the revenue equation to include beginning and ending balances instead of changes in accruals and deferrals. (Investments are assumed to be zero to simplify the illustration.)

Figure 3-1: Periodic Revenue Measurement

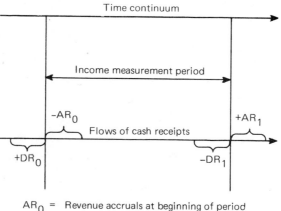

AR_0 = Revenue accruals at beginning of period
AR_1 = Revenue accruals at end of period
DR_0 = Revenue deferrals at beginning of period
DR_1 = Revenue deferrals at end of period

The equation is

$$R = CR + \Delta AR + \Delta DR$$

If the beginning and ending balances are included in place of the changes, the equation is

$$R = CR + (AR_1 - AR_0) - (DR_1 - DR_0)$$

When the parentheses are removed:

$$R = CR + AR_1 - AR_0 - DR_1 + DR_0$$

Note that the signs for the variables are those that appear on Fig. 3-1. The addition or subtraction of the changes in AR and DR is thus a convenient way of showing the effect of two variables, the beginning and ending balances, on the measurement of periodic revenue.

The need for the additions and subtractions of the variables is readily explained if one recalls the definition of revenue and the reason for measuring it. Revenue is a measure of what a business has accomplished during an accounting period—the value of goods and services transferred to external parties. Revenue or accomplishment is measured so that a comparison can be made with the expenses incurred during the same period. This comparison of revenue and expense gives some indication of the efficiency of the operations. To accomplish this purpose:

AR_1 must be added to cash receipts because that was the amount of unpaid claims from customers for products received; the cash will be collected in the following period.

AR_0 must be subtracted from cash receipts because these were claims against customers at the beginning of the period which were paid during the period and are included in cash receipts (or in AR_1); yet this amount was included in revenue in the previous period.

DR_1 must be subtracted from cash receipts because this is the amount of cash received from customers where the revenue is not yet earned; this amount will be added to revenue in future periods.

DR_0 must be added to cash receipts because this amount was excluded from revenue in the prior period; the revenue was either earned in the current period or, if not, the same deferred amount is included in DR_1.

To illustrate the periodic measurement of revenue, assume that the records of P Incorporated disclosed the following information relating to revenue for the year 19X2 [receipts from investments (IR) are assumed to be zero to simplify the example] :

Cash receipts for year	$297,000	
	At 1/1/X2	*At 12/31/X2*
Accrued revenues	$62,000	$71,000
Deferred revenues	8,000	12,000

Revenue for P Incorporated for 19X2 would be

$$R = CR + \Delta AR - \Delta DR$$
$$= \$297,000 + (\$71,000 - \$62,000) - (\$12,000 - \$8,000)$$
$$= \$297,000 + \$9,000 - \$4,000$$
$$= \$302,000$$

In the above example, revenue accruals increased by $9,000 at the end of the year compared to the beginning. Claims against customers for completed work or products, not yet reflected in cash receipts, increased and, therefore, an addition to cash receipts is necessary to show the recognized revenue. The revenue deferrals also increased which means that at the end of the year more cash had been received from customers prior to the recognition of revenue than at the beginning of the year. This increase of $4,000 is included in cash receipts and must be subtracted to determine the recognized revenue.

If the beginning balance is larger than the ending balance the change will be negative and the effect on revenue for accruals and deferrals is the opposite of that shown above. To illustrate a negative change, assume that the records of P Incorporated disclosed the following information for 19X3 (refer to the previous example for the relevant information as of 12/31/X2):

Cash receipts, 19X3	$367,000
Accrued revenue, 19/31/X3	66,000
Deferred revenue, 12/31/X3	9,000

The revenue for 19X3 would be determined as follows:

$$
\begin{aligned}
R &= \$367,000 + (\$66,000 - \$71,000) - (\$9,000 - \$12,000) \\
&= \$367,000 + (-\$5,000) - (-\$3,000) \\
&= \$367,000 - \$5,000 + \$3,000 \\
&= \$365,000
\end{aligned}
$$

Here the accrued revenues decreased, meaning that cash receipts are higher than the revenue that should be recognized for this period. The negative change is therefore subtracted. For revenue deferrals, the negative change arises because cash received in advance was lower at the end of 19X3 than at the beginning, resulting in an increase in recognized revenue for the period.

In summary, the information needed to measure revenue on a periodic basis is cash receipts, the revenue accruals and revenue deferrals at the beginning and end of the period, and the cash receipts from investors. It might be noted that the accruals and deferrals at the beginning of the first year of operation are zero. The changes in accruals and deferrals for the first year are, therefore, the ending balances of accruals and deferrals.

Measurement of Expense

Expense is the second variable in the computation of income. Expenses are defined as follows:

Expenses are the value of services consumed in the process of producing revenues and are measured in terms of the cash disbursements or expected cash disbursements necessary to acquire the services.

In this definition, the term service is used in a broad sense to include not only personal services of individuals but also the services stored in materials, buildings, and all other economic resources. Further explanation of this definition is required in order to develop a method by which expenses can be measured.

Recognition of Acquisition Costs

Expense is usually measured by the acquisition cost of the services consumed in the productive process. The acquisition cost of a service is generally the exchange price (cash paid) at the date of acquisition or purchase. Just as revenue is not recognized until the three criteria discussed previously are met, the acquisition cost of services is not recognized until three similar criteria are satisfied. These criteria are

1   There is an agreement with an outside party.
2   There is a cash payment or an obligation to make a future cash payment. In a few cases, the payment for services is made by a "barter" transaction, where property other than cash is given for services. Barter transactions are discussed in Chapter 11.
3   Generally, the services are received by the business. Contracts for the delivery of future services create special accounting problems which are discussed in Chapters 11, 12, and 13.

The essential steps in the acquisition process are briefly described below:

1   The business enters into an agreement with the party supplying the service. This agreement may be a labor contract with a union or employee, a purchase invoice for materials, or some other contract.
2   The supplier of the service provides the business with the item covered by the agreement in step 1.
3   The business makes a record of the amount owed the supplier for the service. This record is commonly called the *accounts payable* file. In some cases, the cash payment for the service may occur simultaneously with the receipt of the service; however, there is usually a time lag which means a record of accounts payable is essential.
4   Cash is disbursed or paid to the supplier for the service. Payment is normally made with a check, not currency.
5   When the supplier is paid the accounts payable file must be changed or updated to indicate that the liability has been settled or paid.
6   Finally, the record of cash disbursements must be updated to include the cash disbursement for the service.

The crucial records from the acquisition transactions needed to compute expenses are the amount of cash disbursements for services, the amount owed for services (accounts payable), and the cash paid to investors (ID). The record of cash disbursements is also used to compute the balance of cash.

Expense Flow

In a completed venture, expense is the acquisition cost of all services consumed during the venture. When the life of a venture is divided into accounting periods, then periodic income is measured by matching the effort expended (expense) to produce the period's revenue or accomplishment. (Remember: matching of revenue and expense each period provides us with an income computation that can be used to judge the efficiency of operations.)

The first step in measuring periodic expense is to determine the basis used to recognize revenue—cash basis, sales basis, or production basis. In this chapter we will assume that the sales basis is used. With this basis for revenue recognition, the periodic expense is the acquisition cost of the services consumed to produce the goods or services *sold* during the period. Measurements of periodic expenses for the other bases of revenue recognition are discussed in later chapters.

A basic concept of accounting is that the *costs* of services *attach* to the product and that the costs can be allocated, traced, and finally matched against the revenue produced by the sale of the product. For example, if a mechanic in an auto repair shop works on three jobs during one day, we assume that part of his salary for that day attaches to his work on each job. To compute the profit on each job, the salary is allocated (along with all other costs) and matched against the revenue from each job. The allocation of salary between the jobs normally would be based on the time spent on each job.

ACCRUED EXPENSES. The cash payment for services usually lags behind the delivery of the service to the business. The service may be entirely or partially consumed in the productive process before payment is made for the service. Thus the actual cash disbursements during an accounting period may not include the acquisition cost of all services consumed in that period. Labor cost is a good example of a service that is often consumed prior to the cash payment.

To illustrate, assume that an auto repair shop has operated for one year. On Wednesday, December 31, all repair work was completed and the customers had accepted the work and paid cash for it. The owner pays his repairmen every other Friday for the hours worked during the two weeks ending on that day. During the year, $48,500 was paid the repairmen. As of Wednesday night, the last day of the year, the owner owed his repairmen $900 for the hours worked through Wednesday. This obligation will be settled at the normal time, Friday evening when the biweekly pay checks are made out. The total expense for repairmen for the first year is

Cash paid for wages during year	$48,500
Add: Unpaid wages at Dec. 31	900
	$49,400

The amount which is added to cash disbursements is a cost accrual.

Acquisition costs are accrued when the three criteria for recognition discussed on p. 54, 55 are met. Note that the acquisition cost may be accrued prior to the use of the service in production. This possibility and payment for services prior to their use in production create the need for deferred expenses.

DEFERRED EXPENSES. Many services are acquired prior to their use so that they will be available when needed in the productive process. Indeed, some services are typically acquired several years before they are consumed in production. Examples are buildings, automobiles, and capital equipment. To measure expense for the accounting period, these acquisition costs incurred in advance must be allocated between the cost of products sold in the current period (expenses) and the acquisition costs available for future use.

Over the years, accountants have developed numerous rules to guide them in making the allocation of cost between current expense and future (deferred) expenses. The basic rules will be discussed later in this chapter, along with other problems of cost allocation. The basic steps in the allocation of acquisition costs are explained below:

1   The acquisition cost of all services available for use in the business are determined. This amount includes not only the services paid for (CD for the period) and the accrued expenses, but also all acquisition costs of past periods not consumed in production in prior periods.
2   Some services are used and a new product results.
3   Other services are not used in the current period but are deferred to later periods. A record is prepared of the services not consumed in the current period.
4   Some of the new products are sold to customers during the accounting period. The total cost associated with the sales (assuming the sales basis of revenue recognition) becomes expense of the period.
5   Some of the new products may still be on hand at the end of the period. As with the unused cost of the original services, the cost of the unsold products must also be deferred to a future accounting period. A record is made of the cost of products carried forward into the next period.

Expense measurement is thus a process of *allocating* a part of the total acquisition cost of services available to the revenue recognized in the current period. Acquisition costs not assigned to revenue of the current period are deferred expenses (also commonly called *deferred costs*).

EXPENSE EQUATION. Expenses are measured, then, by the cash disbursements (CD) of the period plus the change in accrued expenses (ΔAE) minus the change in deferred expenses (ΔDE). In every case, of course, cash disbursements for investment transactions must be subtracted from the cash disbursements. Including investment transactions (ID), the equation for expense measurement is

$$E = CD + \Delta AE - \Delta DE - ID$$

Example of Expense Measurement—Transaction Basis

Recall the example in the revenue section of this chapter relevant to J Automotive Repairs. The acquisition cost of the parts for the repair of Mr. Black's car was $108. These parts, items regularly required by Joe's customers, were acquired from a wholesale automotive supply house along with other parts and supplies. The total invoice price of all the items acquired, including the parts needed for Black's car, was $500. Joe agreed to pay the supplier this amount, $500, at the end of 30 days. The expense equation would be affected as follows when the parts costing $500 were acquired:

$$E = CD + \Delta AE - \Delta DE$$
$$= 0 + (\$500) - (\$500)$$
$$= 0$$

Accrued expenses were increased by $500 and deferred expenses were increased by $500. The effect on current expense is zero because the goods were not used to produce revenue at the time of the acquisition.

When the $108 of parts were used on Mr. Black's car, the expenses were as follows:

$$E = CD + \Delta AE - \Delta DE$$
$$= 0 + 0 - (-\$108)$$
$$= \$108$$

The parts used on Mr. Black's car decreased the expense deferred to the future and, consequently, resulted in an expense when the parts were used.

Upon payment of the $500 to the supplier, the effect on expense was

$$E = CD + \Delta AE - \Delta DE$$
$$= \$500 + (-\$500) - 0$$
$$= 0$$

Note that payment of the liability (account payable) for the parts did not result in an expense. The expense arose only when the parts were used in the repair work.

Assume that a mechanic who worked on Black's automobile earned $90 in wages. Assume further that the wages were not paid until sometime after the work was performed. With these facts, the expense computation would be

$$E = CD + \Delta AE - \Delta DE$$
$$= 0 + (\$90) - (0)$$
$$= \$90$$

After the mechanic was paid the $90, the effect on expense was

$$E = \$90 + (-\$90) - (0)$$
$$= 0$$

The accumulated expense for the repair of Black's automobile is $198; that is, $108 for parts used and $90 for labor.

Although expenses can be determined after each transaction for those services that can be directly identified as used to produce specific amounts of revenue, the transaction by transaction basis for measuring expenses is neither convenient nor practical for most operations. In addition, some elements of expense cannot be identified with a particular item of revenue, such as the revenue from overhauling Mr. Black's car. For example, how much of the rent of the garage building should be allocated to the repair of Black's car? How much of the acquisition cost of tools required to overhaul the motor should be allocated to the Black job? For most purposes, expenses are measured for an entire accounting period.

Example of Expense Measurement—Periodic Basis

A business needs to accumulate a record of cash disbursements, accrued expenses, deferred expenses, and cash disbursements for investments if it is to measure expense on a periodic basis. The record of accrued expenses and deferred expenses includes sufficient information to permit the measurement of the change in these items from the beginning to the end of the period.

Figure 3-2: Periodic Expense Measurement

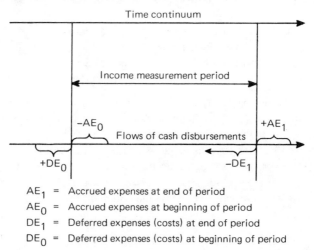

AE_1 = Accrued expenses at end of period
AE_0 = Accrued expenses at beginning of period
DE_1 = Deferred expenses (costs) at end of period
DE_0 = Deferred expenses (costs) at beginning of period

Figure 3-2 is a schematic representation of the measurement of expense for an accounting period. (Disbursements to investors are ignored to simplify the diagram.) The basic expense equation,

$$E = CD + \Delta AE - \Delta DE$$

can be expanded to include the beginning and ending amounts for accruals and deferrals:

$$E = CD + (AE_1 - AE_0) - (DE_1 - DE_0)$$

When the parentheses are removed the equation becomes

$$E = CD + AE_1 - AE_0 - DE_1 + DE_0$$

These signs for the accruals and deferrals appear on Fig. 3–2 and are verbally rationalized as follows:

AE_1 must be added to cash disbursements because it is the cost of services acquired, whether used or not, which have not been paid for at the period's end; the cash payment will come in a later period.

AE_0 must be subtracted from cash disbursements because this amount was added to expenses (or acquisition cost) in the previous period; if the cash payment was made in the current period, cash disbursements include an amount already considered in the expense measurement in a previous period. If some costs accrued at the beginning of the period are still unpaid at the end of the period, the amount will require a future cash payment and is included in accrued expenses at the end of the period (AE_1).

DE_1 must be subtracted from cash disbursements because these costs (future expenses) were not consumed or used up in the current period; they will become expenses in a later period.

DE_0 must be added to disbursements because they are costs deferred in an earlier year; this amount must be considered in the total acquisition cost which could have been consumed in the current period. Costs deferred from previous periods (DE_0) may not be used up (and become expenses) in the current year. That portion of deferred costs at the beginning of the year not consumed are included in the amount of deferred costs at year end (DE_1).

The addition or subtraction of the changes in accruals and deferrals is, as explained earlier, a convenient way of thinking about the combined effect of two variables, the beginning and ending amounts.

To illustrate periodic expense measurement, we will expand the facts for P Incorporated, used earlier in the example of the computation of revenue. Investments are excluded to emphasize the effects of accruals and deferrals.

Records relevant to expense measurement for P Incorporated for 19X2 were as follows:

Cash disbursements		$269,000
Balances as of	*12/31/X1*	*12/31/X2*
For accrued expenses	$33,000	$41,000
For deferred expenses	84,000	78,000

Expense for 19X2 would be as follows:

$$E = CD + \Delta AE - \Delta DF$$
$$= \$269,000 + (\$41,000 - \$33,000) - (\$78,000 - \$84,000)$$
$$= \$269,000 + (\$8,000) - (-\$6,000)$$
$$= \$269,000 + \$8,000 + \$6,000$$
$$= \$283,000$$

The accrued expenses increased by $8,000 and this amount, representing unpaid claims for services, is added. The deferred expenses decreased also resulting in an addition. The unused costs remaining for use in future years was less at the end of the period than at the beginning.

Referring back to the revenue calculation for P Incorporated, for 19X2 on p. 53, the revenue is $302,000. Income for 19X2 would be $19,000:

$$
\begin{aligned}
\text{Income} &= \text{Revenue} - \text{Expense} \\
Y &= R - E \\
&= \$302,000 - \$283,000 \\
&= \$19,000
\end{aligned}
$$

Major Problems in Allocation of Costs

The allocation of cost between the current period and future periods, that is, distinguishing between the amount of current expense and the amount of deferred expense, is one of the most difficult problems in accounting. This section will deal with the basic rules for allocating the cost of merchandise and the cost of long-lived assets, the two most important costs in many businesses.

COST OF MERCHANDISE. The term *merchandise inventory* refers to the property of a business which is held for sale to customers in the ordinary course of business. Residential houses are merchandise to a developer who built them for resale; wheat is merchandise inventory to a wheat farmer; and shoes are merchandise inventory to a shoe store. The purpose for which the property is held, sale to customers, and not the type, grade, or value of property, is the characteristic that distinguishes merchandise inventory from other property. Other properties, such as office supplies and shop supplies, used in operations may also be referred to as inventory. Merchandise inventory, however, means the property held for sale to customers, not for use in the business.

A retail establishment adds value to a product by changing its place utility, by moving the product from the manufacturer's or wholesaler's warehouse to the neighborhood store where it can be inspected, judged, and purchased by the customers. The retailer also adds time utility; the merchandise is held by him until the customer desires it.

DETERMINATION OF DEFERRED EXPENSE. At the end of an accounting period in a retail establishment some merchandise will be on hand, not yet sold. The accounting problem is to divide the acquisition cost of merchandise available during the period between two amounts: (1) cost of the merchandise sold, which must be treated as an expense and matched against the sales revenue; and (2) the acquisition cost of the inventory still on hand, which must be deferred and matched against the revenue of a future period. This allocation of the acquisition cost is normally accomplished in the following manner:

1 A physical count is made of the merchandise at the end of the period.
2 Acquisition cost per unit is calculated for each type of merchandise in the inventory.

3   Unit costs are applied to the quantities on hand to determine the cost of the inventory.

The cost of the inventory on hand is the amount to be deferred. Determination of the acquisition cost per unit (step 2 above) may be quite difficult, depending on the type of business and the method of operation.

Retail inventory is normally purchased in lots from manufacturers or wholesalers. The size of the lots and the frequency of purchase depends on the type of merchandise and the size of the retailer. Produce in a supermarket may be acquired on a daily basis in relatively small lots, whereas a small clothing store may purchase a year's supply of some standard items of apparel at one time. The manufacturer or wholesaler will provide the retailer with a document called an *invoice*, which details the quantities and price for each type of merchandise in the shipment. The invoice also shows the net amount due for the merchandise in the shipment and serves as a basis for payment. The net amount due is the total acquisition cost. Unit acquisition cost is determined by dividing the total cost by the number of units acquired.

An example of an inventory worksheet which might be used to compute the cost of inventory is presented below:

Item	Quantity on hand	Cost per unit	Total
Suits (Style No. 101)	40	$60.00	$2,400.00
Dresses (Style No. 20)	10	16.00	160.00
Handkerchiefs (men's)	110	.25	27.50
. . .	. . .	. . .	. . .
Total inventory cost			$26,220.50

When the work listed in the three steps above is completed, the amount to be deferred for acquisition cost of inventory is known. Then the accountant can compute the *cost of goods sold*, which is the label used to describe the periodic expense for merchandise sold.

• Computation of Cost of Goods Sold: To illustrate the computation of cost of goods sold, imagine a small clothing store which was organized in January of 19X1. Assume the following relevent information at December 31, 19X1:

Cash paid for merchandise during year	$75,000
Cost of merchandise delivered during 19X1 but not paid for during 19X1	6,000
Cost of inventory at December 31, 19X1	9,000

The cost of merchandise not paid for was determined by adding up the unpaid invoices for merchandise received on or before December 31, 19X1. The cost of inventory was determined in the manner described earlier. A schedule for the computation of cost of goods sold would be

Cash paid for merchandise (CD)	$75,000
Add: Merchandise purchased but not paid for in	
19X1 (ΔAE)	6,000
Cost of goods purchased in 19X1	$81,000
Less: Cost of inventory (ΔDE)	9,000
Cost of goods sold (E)	$72,000

Assume for 19X2 the following relevent information:

Cash paid for merchandise	$100,000
Cost of merchandise purchased during 19X2 but	
not paid for	7,500
Cost of inventory at 12/31/X2	11,000

The computation of cost of goods sold for 19X2 would be

Cash paid for merchandise, 19X2 (CD)		$100,000
Add: Change in accruals (ΔAE)		
Accruals on 12/31/X2	$ 7,500	
Accruals on 1/1/X2	6,000	1,500
Cost of goods purchased in 19X2		$101,500
Less: Change in deferrals (ΔDE)		
Deferrals, 12/31/X2	$11,000	
Deferrals, 1/1/X2	9,000	2,000
Cost of goods sold, 19X2 (E)		$ 99,500

Note that this schedule is only a verbalized form of the formula for computing expense:

$$E = CD + \Delta AE - \Delta DE$$
$$= \$100,000 + (\$1,500) - (\$2,000)$$
$$= \$99,500$$

A more comprehensive treatment of the methods and rules used to determine the quantities and the prices that together make up the deferred cost for inventory is discussed in Chapter 12.

LONG-LIVED ASSETS. The term long-lived assets refers to the properties used in a business that benefit two or more accounting periods. Long-lived assets are distinguished from inventory by the fact that they cannot be subdivided into distinct physical units for cost allocation purposes. This category includes properties such as land, buildings, production equipment, delivery equipment, fixtures, and furniture. Most of these "bundles" of service potentials last for several years. The important point to remember is that these properties (with the exception of land) are used up in the production and sale of goods and services just as the inventory is used up as sales are made.

Generally the allocation of the cost of long-lived assets is based on time:

$$\frac{\text{Acquisition cost}}{\text{Useful life}} = \text{Cost per time period}$$

At the end of an accounting period the portion of the cost not yet expired must be deferred to later periods. First, however, acquisition cost for long-lived assets must be defined.

• Acquisition Cost: Essentially, the cost of long-lived assets is the total cash outlay at the time of acquisition necessary to place the assets in use. Imagine this situation in a new retail store: Store fixtures for the display of merchandise are acquired for $10,000 from a manufacturer in a distant city. Under the sales contract, the purchaser must pay the freight which amounts to $500. When the fixtures arrive, a local carpenter is paid $250 to assemble them and put them in place. Finally, toward the end of the first year, $100 annual property tax is paid to the city on the fixtures. Should these incidentals be treated as expenses in the first year or should they be added to acquisition cost and spread over the useful life of the fixtures? The freight and assembly costs are just as necessary to the *use* of the fixtures as the original $10,000 purchase price. These two costs benefit all years during which the fixtures are used to generate sales revenue. The tax, on the other hand, is usually treated as an annual charge that benefits only the current year. The acquisition cost is $10,750.

• Computation of Depreciation: The acquisition cost of a long-lived asset is allocated over its useful life. For tangible properties, such as buildings, equipment, and fixtures, the portion of the total cost allocated to each accounting period is called **depreciation**. For intangible assets (such as patents and copyrights) the allocated part for each year is referred to as expense, with some appropriate descriptive word. The allocated part of a patent cost, for example, is called **patent amortization**. The allocation made at the end of each accounting period for each long-lived asset is

$$\frac{\text{Unexpired cost at first of accounting period less salvage value}}{\text{Remaining useful life from first of accounting period}} = \text{Expense for accounting period (depreciation)}$$

where:

Unexpired cost at first of period is the original acquisition cost less the sum of the amounts allocated to expense in *all* previous years.

Salvage value is the amount that the enterprise expects to realize when a long-lived asset is disposed of. Some long-lived assets (i.e., an insurance policy) may have no value at the end of their useful life, whereas others will have some scrap value (machinery, buildings).

Remaining useful life from first of period is the remaining life from the beginning of the accounting period. A new estimate should be made each accounting period. The time used should be the period the business expects to use the asset.

The computation of depreciation may be illustrated by using the facts on the acquisition of the store fixtures above. The acquisition cost was

Contract price	$10,000
Freight	500
Assembly	250
	$10,750

Assume further that the accounting period is one year and that the fixtures were acquired January 1, 19X1. At December 31, 19X1, the salvage value is estimated at $1,000. The expected life from January 1, 19X1 was ten years. The depreciation would be

$$\frac{\$10,750 - \$1,000}{10 \text{ years}} = \$975.00 \text{ per year}$$

Depreciation expense for 19X1 would be $975.

Note that this computation is different from the one for inventory. To determine inventory the deferred expense was computed first, and the cost of sales (expense) computation was based on the deferral:

Cash paid for merchandise, 19X1	$xxx
Add: Change in accruals (ΔAE)	xx
Cost of goods purchased in 19X1	$xxx
Less: change in deferrals (ΔDE)	xx
Cost of goods sold in 19X1 (E)	$xxx

For long-lived assets, the expense is computed directly. The expense amount is then used to compute the deferred cost:

Acquisition cost of fixtures	$10,750
Less: Depreciation for 19X1	975
Deferred expense at 12/31/X1	$ 9,775

The formula

$$\begin{aligned} \text{Depreciation} &= CD + \Delta AE - \Delta DE \\ &= \$10,750 + (0) - (\$9,775 - 0) \\ &= \$975 \end{aligned}$$

could be used. This is mere exercise because the original computation of depreciation serves as the basis for the $9,775 deferred expense or cost.

Extending the example to 19X2, assume that the salvage value is revised upward to $2,000 because of improvement in the market for used fixtures. The depreciation would be

$$\frac{\$9,775 - \$2,000}{9 \text{ years}} = \$864 \text{ (rounded)}$$

Note that the remaining life is only 9 years from January 1, 19X2. The deferred expense at December 31, 19X2 is

Deferred expense at first of period	$9,775
Depreciation for 19X2	864
Deferred expense at end of period	$8,911

The formula computation would be

$$\text{Depreciation} = CD + \Delta AE - \Delta DE$$
$$= 0 + 0 - (\$8911 - \$9775)$$
$$= \$864$$

The depreciation computation above is commonly referred to as the *straight-line method*. This method of allocation is generally used for intangible items. Several other methods are used, however, for tangible properties, as discussed in Chapter 14.

Example

In this example, entitled C Bookstore, Inc., we discuss:

1   Computation of net income annually for a three-year period, including one *loss* year
2   Reconciliation of net income for the three-year period to the increase in cash.

The essential facts can be summarized as follows: Five businessmen decided to establish a new bookstore near the campus of a local college. To minimize their personal liability, they decided to organize the business as a corporation. A charter for a corporation with an unlimited life was obtained from the state with the name of C Bookstore, Inc. The founders estimated that $25,000 in capital would be needed for the store. A manager with some bookstore experience was located and hired. Operations started in January, 19X1.

First Year

In early January, each of the five organizers contributed $5,000 to the corporation in exchange for 1,000 shares of common stock. A bank account was opened in the corporate name. A suitable store building was leased for $500 per month, payable monthly in advance. Fixtures and shelving were installed for $8,000 in cash.

During 19X1, merchandise was acquired and sold. Sales clerks were employed and paid on a weekly basis. All cash receipts were deposited in the bank and all disbursements were made by check. In January, 19X2, the manager prepared a statement of receipts and disbursements for 19X1 based on records kept for cash receipts and disbursements (Fig. 3-3). The category, "other operating expenses," includes salary expense, casualty insurance, rent, and numerous other items. These items are grouped in this example to reduce detail. In the analysis of cash receipts and disbursements, numerous classifications may be used if such detail improves the informational content of the income statement derived from the statement of receipts and disbursements.

Figure 3-3

C Bookstore, Inc.	Statement of Cash Receipts and Disbursements for the Year Ended December 31, 19X1		
Cash receipts:			
Sale of common stock		$ 25,000	
Cash collected from customers		125,000	$150,000
Cash disbursements:			
Fixtures		$ 8,000	
Merchandise		104,000	
Other operating expenses		30,310	142,310
Cash balance, December 31, 19X1			$ 7,690

After all operations were completed for the first year, the manager assembled the following information:

1 Amount of cash due *from* customers for credit sales was $6,000.
2 The manager estimated that the fixtures would be used for ten years from January 1, 19X1 and that they would have a scrap value of $500 after ten years.
3 The store owed publishers and suppliers $9,500 at December 31, 19X1 for merchandise delivered prior to the year's end. Merchandise inventory at Dec. 31, 19X1 was $20,000.
4 Relative to other operating expenses, salaries unpaid at the end of 19X1 amounted to $400. Also, on March 1, 19X1, $360 was paid for a three-year casualty insurance policy.

Based on this information and the statement of cash receipts and disbursements, the manager was able to compute revenues, expenses, and income for the year 19X1.

REVENUE COMPUTATION. The formula for periodic revenue is

$$R = CR + \Delta AR - \Delta DR - IR$$

The actual amounts for the year 19X1 come from the following sources: The total cash receipts of $150,000 comes from the statement of cash receipts and disbursements (Fig. 3-3). The cash receipts from the owner's investment of $25,000 is also shown on that statement. The accrued revenue at the end of the year (cash due from customers) of $6,000 is one of the amounts determined by the manager from other records. Substituting these amounts:

$$R = \$150,000 + (\$6,000) - (0) - (\$25,000)$$
$$= \$131,000$$

Because 19X1 is the first year of operations, the $6,000 owed by customers at the end of the year is the change in accrued revenues (ΔAR) for 19X1.

EXPENSE COMPUTATION. If total cash disbursements and the totals for accruals and deferrals are used, then one calculation could be made for all expenses. However, it is usually helpful in planning and analysis to classify expenses into several functional classifications and compute the amount for each. In this example, expenses are classified as depreciation of fixtures, cost of merchandise sold, and other operating expenses. A separate calculation is made for each.

• Depreciation of Fixtures: The depreciation expense for the fixtures is calculated directly by using the formula explained earlier in the chapter:

$$\frac{\text{Acquisition cost at first of year less salvage}}{\text{Remaining years of life at first of year}} = \text{depreciation expense for year}$$

Substituting amounts for C Bookstore, Inc.:

$$\frac{\$8,000 - \$500}{10 \text{ years}} = \$750 \text{ depreciation per year}$$

The depreciation expense can then be used to compute the deferred cost at the end of the period, that is, $8,000 original cost less depreciation of $750 leaves $7,250, the cost deferred to later years.

• Cost of Goods Sold: Computation of cost of goods sold involves the use of the cash spent for merchandise, the accounts payable (AE) at the end of 19X1, and the merchandise inventory (DE) at the end of 19X1:

$$
\begin{aligned}
E &= CD + \Delta AE - \Delta DE - ID \\
&= \$104,000 + (\$9,500) - (\$20,000) - 0 \\
&= \$93,500
\end{aligned}
$$

Again note that because 19X1 is the first year of operations, the ending balances for accruals and deferrals are the changes.

• Other Operating Expenses: Expenses such as salaries and casualty insurance are included in this category. For salaries, the accrued expenses amounted to $400 at year end. The insurance premium of $360 applies to three years beginning on March 1, 19X1. Thus 10 months of the total cost expired in 19X1, leaving 26 months as a deferred cost to later periods. The deferred cost is 26/36 X $360 or $260. By expense formula, other operating expenses are

$$
\begin{aligned}
E &= CD + \Delta AE - \Delta DF - ID \\
&= \$30,310 + (\$400) - (\$260) - (0) \\
&= \$30,450
\end{aligned}
$$

INCOME COMPUTATION. Following the computation of revenues and expenses for the various classifications, the manager could prepare the income statement (Fig. 3–4). Note that the words used to describe the revenue and expenses on the income statement differ from the terms on the statement of cash receipts and disbursements. For example, the cash paid for merchandise adjusted for accruals and deferrals becomes cost of goods sold. Terminology for other items is similarly changed to reflect the transformation from cash receipts and disbursements to revenues and expenses.

Figure 3-4

C Bookstore, Inc.	Statement of Income for the year 19X1	
Sales revenue		$131,000
Expenses:		
Cost of goods sold	$93,500	
Other operating expenses	30,450	
Depreciation of fixtures	750	124,700
Net income for year		$ 6,300

Second Year

Operation of C Bookstore, Inc. was continued throughout 19X2. In January, 19X2, in view of the profit earned in 19X1, the directors declared a dividend of $5,000. October 1, 19X2, the company was forced to borrow $10,000 from the bank to pay some bills. This note was due on September 30, 19X3, with interest due at that time. The statement of cash receipts and disbursements for 19X2 is shown in Fig. 3-5.

Figure 3-5

C Bookstore, Inc.	Statement of Cash Receipts and Disbursements for Year 19X2	
Cash receipts:		
Collections from customers	$154,000	
Bank loan	10,000	$164,000
Cash disbursements:		
Merchandise	$131,000	
Other operating expenses	34,200	
Cash dividend	5,000	170,200
Change in cash		$ (6,200)

COMPUTATION OF REVENUE AND EXPENSES. The manager of the bookstore assembled the following information connected with operations for 19X2:

1 Amount due from customers for credit sales as of December 31, 19X2 was $4,000.

2   Unpaid salaries at the end of 19X2 were $750.

3   Unpaid invoices for merchandise at December 31, 19X2 were $12,500. The cost of the inventory at December 31, 19X2 was $18,200.

4   Interest owed to the bank was $150.

By using the information contained on the statement of cash receipts and disbursements and the information about accruals and deferrals, one can calculate revenue and expenses for 19X2.

- Revenue: Substituting the amounts in the revenue formula:

$$R = \$164,000 + (\$4,000 - \$6,000) - (0) - (\$10,000)$$
$$= \$164,000 + (-\$2,000) - (0) - (\$10,000)$$
$$= \$152,000$$

The amounts of the beginning balance for accrued revenue, $6,000, are obtained from the previous income computation.

- Cost of Goods Sold: Substituting amounts for cost of goods sold into the expense formula:

$$E = CD + (AE_1 - AE_0) - (DE_1 - DE_0)$$
$$= \$131,000 + (\$12,500 - \$9,500) - (\$18,200 - \$20,000)$$
$$= \$131,000 + (\$3,000) - (-\$1,800) - (0)$$
$$= \$135,800$$

Again, the beginning balances for accrued expenses, $9,500, and the beginning deferred cost for inventory, $20,000, are obtained from the previous year's income computation.

- Other Operating Expenses: The cash disbursed for operating expenses must be adjusted for the change in the accrual for salary expense and for the change in the deferral for casualty insurance. For the casualty insurance, 10 months expired in 19X1 and another 12 months in 19X2; thus, at the end of 19X2, the deferred cost is for 14 months (36 months less 22 expired). The cost deferred is 14/36 X $360 or $140. By using the beginning balances for accrued expenses and deferred costs for the 19X1 income computation, one can calculate other operating expenses for 19X2:

$$E = CD + (AE_1 - AE_0) - (DE_1 - DE_0)$$
$$= \$34,200 + (\$750 - \$400) - (\$140 - \$260)$$
$$= \$34,200 + (\$350) - (-\$120)$$
$$= \$34,670$$

- Depreciation of Fixtures: The deferred cost for fixtures at the beginning of 19X2 was $7,250, that is, the $8,000 original cost less the $750 expense assigned to 19X1. The depreciation calculated for 19X2, assuming the same salvage value and noting that the remaining life in 19X2 was only 9 years, is

$$\frac{\$7,250 - \$500}{9 \text{ years}} = \$750 \text{ depreciation expense for 19X2}$$

Because the original salvage value and the original estimated life were unchanged, therefore the expense is the same in 19X2 as in 19X1. The cost of fixtures deferred to years after 19X2 is $6,500, that is, $7,250 less the expense for 19X2 of $750.

• Interest Expense: Information collected by the manager indicates that no interest was actually paid during 19X2 and thus no amount for interest appears in the disbursements on the statement of cash receipts and disbursements. Interest accrued (owed but not paid) at the end of 19X2 was $150. By expense formula, interest expense was:

$$E = (0) + (\$150 - 0) - (0)$$
$$= \$150$$

Recall from Chapter 2 that interest, although a payment to debt investors, is treated as an operating expense, unlike all other disinvestments.

INCOME COMPUTATION. Once revenues and expenses are known, income can be computed by preparing an income statement (Fig. 3-6) since that statement is just another way of expressing the formula $Y = R - E$. You should note that, in addition to the adjustment of cash receipts and disbursements for accruals and deferrals, the $10,000 cash receipt from the bank loan is not included in revenue as calculated above. Similarly, the cash disbursed for dividends are not an expense in the income statement.

Figure 3-6

C Bookstore, Inc.	Statement of Income for the Year 19X2	
Sales revenue		$152,000
Expenses:		
Cost of goods sold	$135,800	
Other operating expenses	34,670	
Depreciation of fixtures	750	
Interest expense	150	171,370
Net income (loss) for year		$(19,370)

Third Year

The losses experienced in 19X2, which were attributed to very stiff competition from older established bookstores, were very discouraging for the five shareholders. Business for 19X3 was not much better and, as a result, the business was terminated in December 19X3. On December 31, 19X3, the corporate charter was revoked and the lease on the building was canceled. In December all personnel and suppliers were paid off, the inventory was disposed of by a "going out of business" sale. The bank loan, along with the interest due of $600, were paid on September 30, 19X3. The casualty insurance policy was canceled but no refund was obtained for the remaining two months of its life. The fixtures and furniture were sold for $7,500. All accounts receivable were collected. The remaining cash was *not* returned to the shareholders in 19X3. A statement of cash receipts and disbursements for 19X3 is shown in Fig. 3–7.

Figure 3–7

C Bookstore, Inc.	Statement of Cash Receipts and Disbursements for the Year 19X3	
Cash receipts:		
Collections from customers	$129,000	
Sale of fixtures	7,500	$136,500
Cash disbursements:		
Merchandise purchased	$ 87,400	
Other operating expenses	28,000	
Interest paid	600	
Bank loan	10,000	126,000
Increase in cash		$ 10,500

- Revenue: In the computation of revenue from sales, the cash received from customers is adjusted for the change in accruals:

$$R = \$129,000 + (0 - \$4,000) - (0)$$
$$= \$125,000$$

The beginning balance is the negative change because all receivables were collected before December, 19X3. The revenue from the sale of fixtures is the cash received of $7,500; no adjustments are required for accruals or deferrals because the entire sales price was collected in 19X3.

- Cost of Goods Sold: As with revenue from sales, the changes in accruals and deferrals are both negative, that is, the amounts of the beginning balance for accounts payable and inventory:

$$E = \$87,400 + (0 - \$12,500) - (0 - \$18,200)$$
$$= \$87,400 + (-\$12,500) - (-\$18,200)$$
$$= \$93,100$$

- Other Operating Expenses: The computation of this expense parallels that for cost of goods sold. The beginning balance of salaries payable, $750, reduces the expense, and the remaining deferred cost of the casualty insurance, $140, increases the expense.

E = $28,000 + (0 − $750) − (0 − $140)
  = $28,000 + (−$750) − (−$140)
  = $27,390

• Cost of Fixtures Sold: The expired cost of the fixtures is based on the cost deferred to 19X3 from 19X2, namely $6,500:

E = 0 + (0) − (0 − $6,500)
  = $6,500

In 19X3, the total remaining cost must be recognized as an expense because the fixtures were disposed of. This expense could be divided between depreciation for 19X3 and the remaining cost, but such division would probably serve little use. Note that the depreciation process *did not* result in valuation of the fixtures. After three years of use, they were sold for $7,500, considerably more than the residual based on the estimates of salvage value and useful life used to assign costs to 19X1 and 19X2.

• Interest Expense: Calculation of interest for 19X3 is

E = $600 + (0 − $150) − (0)
  = $600 − $150
  = $450

The interest expense accrued at the end of 19X2 is subtracted from the interest paid to obtain the expense for 19X3.

INCOME COMPUTATION. Preparation of an income statement for 19X3 will give the income for that year (Fig. 3–8). Note that the cash repaid to the bank in 19X3 does not enter into the income computation.

Figure 3–8

C Bookstore, Inc.		Statement of Income for the Year 19X3
Revenues:		
From book sales	$125,000	
From sale of fixtures	7,500	$132,500
Expenses:		
Cost of goods sold	$ 93,100	
Other operating expenses	27,390	
Cost of fixtures sold	6,500	
Interest expense	450	127,440
Net income for year		$ 5,060

VERIFICATION OF INCOME COMPUTATIONS. The income computation for each year of the three-year period can be verified by computing the change in cash over the life of the venture. Income (losses) are reflected in an increase (decrease) in cash when the income cycle has been completed. The sum of the incomes from the three income statements is

19X1	$ 6,300
19X2	(19,370)
19X3	5,060
Total income (loss)	$ (8,010)

This amount must agree with the decrease in cash of the shareholders:

Amount contributed	$25,000
Less: dividend	5,000
Net contributed	$20,000
Cash on hand, 12/31/X3	11,990*
Decrease in cash	$ 8,010

The two amounts agree, indicating that the accruals, deferrals, and investment transactions have been properly treated for the three-year period.

The question should be asked: Of what value to the owners of Campus Bookstore, Inc. was the computation of income? Specifically, could they have seen just how bad their situation was in 19X2 by looking at the cash flow only? The business had a negative cash flow of $6,200 but this amount was much less than the negative income (loss) of $19,370. Without the adjustment of cash flow for changes in accruals and deferrals they may not have realized the extent of their peril. They could have lost their entire investment.

QUESTIONS

1   At what stages in the income cycle may revenue be recognized?
2   At what points in the income cycle would each of the following enterprises recognize revenue and why?
    [a]   A retail clothing store
    [b]   A shoeshine stand
    [c]   A private passenger bus line
    [d]   A gold mining company
    [e]   A highly risky venture with a Vietnamese company to grow rice
3   What are the two primary factors that make the use of accruals necessary?

*Cash on hand at the end of 19X3 is the algebraic sum of the changes in cash for the three years, as shown on the statements of cash receipts and disbursements:

19X1	$ 7,690
19X2	(6,200)
19X3	10,500
Cash balance, 19X3	$11,990

4   Briefly explain why the sales basis is more appropriate than the cash basis for recognizing revenue in most businesses.

5   What effect does the periodic measurement of income have on matching revenues with expenses?

6   What are revenue accruals and why should they be considered in measuring revenue?

7   What are cost accruals and why should they be considered in measuring expenses?

8   What are the general rules for the recognition of revenue?

9   What are the general rules for the recognition of expenses?

10   Describe an accounts receivable file and its relevance to the measurement of revenue.

11   Describe or define the following terms:

     [a]   Sales invoice

     [b]   Remittance advice

     [c]   Deposit slip

     [d]   Receiving report

     [e]   Purchase agreement or order

12   What are the rules for the recognition of acquisition cost?

13   What are revenue deferrals and what is their relevance in the measurement of revenue?

14   What are cost deferrals and what is their relevance in the measurement of expenses?

15   List three types of business in which revenue deferrals would be a significant amount.

16   What is the basic allocation problem in accounting for costs?

17   Describe the process followed to determine the deferred cost for the ending inventory.

18   What is the nature of a long-lived asset? Give five examples of typical long-lived assets.

19   What is the formula or equation for computing depreciation? Which of the variables in this equation are estimates?

20   Would the need for adjusting cash receipts and disbursements for revenue accruals and cost accruals to compute income be unnecessary if we develop the so-called moneyless society?

PROBLEMS

1   Compute the effect of each of the following transactions on the revenue and expense for M Incorporated. Do not be concerned with *total* revenue and expense for the period; calculate the effect of each transaction independently. The company uses the sales basis.

     [a]   Purchases merchandise for $1,000 cash to be sold at a later date.

     [b]   Sold merchandise that cost $350.

     [c]   The sales price in part [b] was $600, and the customer agreed to pay in 30 days.

     [d]   Collected the cash of $600 from the customer in part [c].

     [e]   Paid wages of sales personnel for the week amounting to $800. The entire week fell within the accounting period.

     [f]   Paid $10,000 for a storage shed which will last several years.

2   L Apartments, a proprietorship, operates an apartment building. The building is owned by Realty Corp and L Apartments leases it and then rents apartments to tenants. Following is a statement of cash receipts and disbursements for the *first month* of operations, January, 19X1:

L Apartments

Statement of Cash Receipts and Disbursements for January, 19X1

Cash receipts:

Owner's investment		$ 5,000
Cash collected from tenants		28,000
		$33,000

Cash disbursements:

Lease payment to Realty Corp. for January	$15,000	
Salary expense	1,800	
Maintenance materials	500	
Other expenses	2,800	
Withdrawal by owner	3,000	23,100
Increase in cash		$ 9,900

Other information as of January 31, 19X1:

Amounts owed by tenants for January rent	$2,000
Unpaid salaries	400
Maintenance material purchased but not paid for in January	100
Maintenance materials on hand at end of January	200

Required:

[a] Compute the total revenue for January.

[b] Compute the total expense for January.

[c] Compute January's income

3   Use a letter to indicate whether the following events, which affected the Jones Company (a shoe manufacturer) in 19X1, would result in increasing or decreasing [a] revenue, [b] expense, [c] deferred cost, [d] deferred revenue, [e] investment, [f] accrued revenue, [g] accrued cost, or [h] none of these. (The same event may affect more than one variable.)

[1] Administrative salaries earned by employees but not yet paid

[2] Receipt of cash from bank loan

[3] Leather purchased with a cash payment for manufacture of shoes but not yet used

[4] Partial expiration of the cost of a building owned and used during the operating period

[5] Sale of shoes on account

[6] Sale of shoes for cash

[7] Cost of materials used in the manufacture of shoes sold

[8] Cost of new machine not yet used in production acquired on credit terms

[9] Withdrawal of cash that had been invested by owners

[10] Commissions paid to salesmen

[11] Investment of additional cash by the owners

[12] Sale of shoes in exchange for a note receivable

[13] Doubling of the market value of one of its buildings since acquisition, as a result of an increased demand for commercial property

[14] Sale of government bonds that were purchased to earn interest on cash not needed for operations at the time the bonds were purchased.

[15] Receipt of an order from a mail-order house for 5,000 pairs of shoes (the shoes are not yet manufactured)

4   Complete the following independent expressions (IR and ID are zero):

[a]   Y =

      where E = 46,000
          CR = 85,000
        ΔAR = 7,000
        ΔDR = 2,000

[b]   Y =

      where R = 72,000
         CD = 84,000
       ΔAE = 18,000
       ΔDE = 4,000

[c]   CR =

      where R = 68,000
          E = 63,000
       ΔAR = 6,000
       ΔDR = -2,000

[d]   CD =

      where E = 34,000
          R = 43,000
       ΔAE = 6,000
       ΔDE = -4,000

[e]   ΔAR =

      where CR = 48,000
          R = 50,000
       ΔDR = -3,000

[f]   ΔAE =

      where CD = 16,000
          E = 44,000
       ΔDE = -4,000

[g]   Y =

      where CR = 91,000
         CD = 95,000
       ΔAR = 8,000
       ΔDR = -0-
       ΔAE = 6,000
       ΔDE = -7,000

[h]   ΔDE =

      where ΔC = 4,000
          R = 62,000
         E = 58,000
       ΔAR = 6,000
       ΔAE = 5,000
       ΔDR = -0-

5   As of the end of the period, which of the following is a revenue accrual, an expense accrual, a revenue deferral, or expense deferral? Explain each answer.

[a]   Interest due on a bank loan
[b]   Uncollected interest on a loan you made to another
[c]   Rent collected in advance
[d]   Inventory on hand and unsold
[e]   Unpaid employees' salaries
[f]   Unexpired insurance premiums
[g]   Cost of building less depreciation
[h]   Rent paid in advance for the use of equipment
[i]   Large amounts of postage on hand
[j]   Investment in G.M. stock

6   Given the following information, compute this year's income:

	Beginning balance	Ending balance
Building	$120,000	$110,000
Equipment	50,000	48,000
Inventory	4,000	3,000
Advances from customers	3,000	5,000
Accounts receivable	8,000	11,000
Accounts payable (merchandise)	5,000	3,000
Cash disbursements for the period (no disinvestments)		75,000
Cash receipts for the period (no investments)		130,000

7 Given the following information, compute the cost of goods sold for the month of December:

	12/1/X0	12/31/X0
Inventory on hand	$1,000	$1,500
Accounts payable (inventory)	400	200
Cash payments for inventory during December		4,000

8 You are given the following information concerning the purchase of a new press by a local newspaper. Compute this period's depreciation and deferred cost at the end of the period:

Initial cost	$250,000
Freight and crating	3,000
Specialist salaries in assembly and trial run	4,000
Materials used in trial run	200
Maintenance cost of press for the period	300
Estimated salvage	10,000

It was estimated that the press will have a useful life of 12 years.

9 You are given the following information concerning the S Abstract Co. for 19X1:

	1/1/X1	12/31/X1
Accrued expenses		
Rent	$ 200	$ 250
Salaries	200	200
Miscellaneous	235	220
	$ 635	$ 670
Due from clients:	$1,200	$ 1,000
Cash Receipts for 19X1:		
Services performed		$25,825
Cash disbursements for 19X1:		
Rent		$ 2,700
Salaries		13,400
Miscellaneous		1,955
Dividends		2,000
		$20,055

[a] Compute the income for 19X1.
[b] Prepare an income statement for 19X1.

10 Matt Brown, a highway construction engineer, organized his own construction corporation. Mr. Brown contributed $50,000 to the corporation in exchange for 500 shares of stock. In addition, Mr. Brown was able to sell an additional 400 shares of stock for $40,000. The corporation was awarded a contract for $500,000 to build a section of road for the state, payment was to be received upon completion of the contract. Necessary road equipment was acquired and work progressed in an orderly manner in 19X1. A statement of cash receipts and disbursements for 19X1 is presented as follows:

B Construction Corp.

Statement of Cash Receipts and Disbursements for year 19X1

Cash receipts:

From issuance of corporate stock	$ 90,000	
Loans from bank	150,000	$240,000
Cash disbursements:		
Road equipment	$ 50,000	
Salaries of workers	80,000	
Road materials	60,000	
Salaries of officers and office help	20,000	
Miscellaneous	7,000	$217,000
Change in cash		$ 23,000

The state highway engineers estimated that the contract was 50% complete.

[a]   Can the income of the B Construction Corp. be measured at the end of 19X1? Explain.

[b]   Assuming that some form of income measurement must be made for 19X1, suggest a method of measuring income for 19X1.

[c]   What are the deferrals under your suggested approach, if any?

[d]   What are the accruals under your suggested approach, if any?

11   During 19X2 B Construction Corp. completed the road contract and received payment in full. A statement of cash receipts and disbursements for 19X2 is presented below:

B Construction Corp.

Statement of Cash Receipts and Disbursements for Year 19X2

Cash receipts:

Proceeds from contract		$500,000
Bank loan		100,000
		$600,000
Cash disbursements:		
Salaries (workers)	$ 90,000	
Road materials	100,000	
Salaries (officers)	20,000	
Miscellaneous	3,000	
Bank loan repayment	250,000	
Interest	15,000	478,000
Change in cash		$122,000

Other data:

[1]   Road equipment is expected to have a life of ten years with a salvage value of $5,000.

[2]   As of December 31, 19X2 there were no additional accruals or deferrals.

Required:

[a]   Compute the income for the two-year period for B Construction Co.

[b]   Prepare an income statement for the two-year period.

12   W Apartment House, Inc. had cash receipts and disbursements for 19X2 as follows:

Rent received	$273,000
Bank loan	15,000
Total cash received	$288,000
Mortgage payment	$144,000
Interest	23,000
Repayment of bank loan	10,000
Salaries and wages	30,000
Other operating expenses	37,000
Total cash disbursements	$244,000

Other financial information:

	12/31/X1	12/31/X2
Cash balance	$ 6,000	?
Rent receivable	2,000	$ 3,500
Accrued wages	1,800	2,100
Accrued interest	2,200	1,700
Accrued operating expenses	1,500	1,800
Land	200,000	200,000
Building*	800,000	

Required:

[a]   Compute income for 19X2.

[b]   Prepare an income statement for 19X2.

[c]   What is the cash balance at December 31, 19X2?

*The building has a remaining estimated life of 25 years on January 1, 19X2 with no salvage value.

13   Inventories for the three departments of O Department Store were

	12/31/X4	12/31/X5
Men's clothing	$26,500	$28,900
Women's clothing	37,300	42,700
Other soft goods	64,000	57,400

Accrued costs for merchandise for each department were

Men's clothing	$12,400	$13,700
Women's clothing	5,800	14,300
Other soft goods	21,700	19,600

Cash receipts and disbursements were

	Cash receipts	Cash disbursements
Men's clothing	$126,900	$ 94,200
Women's clothing	187,200	113,700
Other soft goods	226,700	167,600

Revenue accruals were

	12/31/X4	12/31/X5
Men's clothing	$15,800	$13,300
Women's clothing	21,200	23,500
Other soft goods	32,100	27,600

Required:

Compute the revenue and cost of goods sold for each of the departments.

14   B Store, Inc., a local department store, has been in operation for several years. Cash receipts and disbursements for 19X6 are shown below:

Cash receipts:		
From customers	$520,000	
Bank loan	50,000	$570,000
Cash disbursements:		
Merchandise	$375,000	
Salaries	120,000	
Utilities	35,000	
Miscellaneous expense	28,000	
Dividends	25,000	$583,000
Change in cash (decrease)		($13,000)

Information concerning accruals and deferrals for the year was

	1/1/X6	12/31/X6
Accounts receivable	$ 92,000	$125,000
Accounts payable		
(merchandise)	60,000	64,000
Accrued salaries	3,500	1,500
Deferred miscellaneous		
expense	2,000	2,500
Merchandise inventory	106,000	134,000
Deferred cost of furniture		
& fixtures	88,000	76,000

Required:

[a]   Compute the income for 19X6.
[b]   Prepare an income statement for 19X6.

CASE   Sam Irvin, an electronics engineer, hit on an idea to improve the automated answering device that can be attached to a telephone to record messages while the telephone patron is away from the office or home. To capitalize on the idea, he formed a corporation, S Devices, Inc. He contributed $50,000 of his own savings for 1,000 shares of common stock and then sold another 1,000 shares to friends for an additional $50,000. A local bank agreed to furnish additional cash needed on short-term notes.

Sam rented some space and set up a laboratory to make a pilot model of the device. This work continued throughout 19X1, but the pilot model was still not complete at December 31. Sam, who has had some accounting training, prepared the following income statement for 19X1:

S Devices, Inc.
Statement of Income for Year Ended December 31, 19X1

Revenues		$0
Expenses:		
Development costs of pilot model	$125,000	
Rent on laboratory	12,000	
General administrative expense	18,000	$155,000
Net loss for year		($155,000)

These expenses were the cash actually paid adjusted for accrued expenses at the end of the year.

In early 19X2, the device was perfected and patented, and then shown to a national telephone company. Sam could not manufacture and sell the device directly to users because the telephone companies can generally control the types of equipment connected to their lines. Sam thought the wisest course would be to let the telephone company worry about manufacturing and distribution, leaving Sam free to work on new inventions.

Representatives of the telephone company agreed that the new device was superior to those in use. They made the following offer to Sam:

[a]   S Devices, Inc., holder of the patent, would grant the telephone company the exclusive right to make and sell the device for a period of five years beginning on April 1, 19X2.

[b]   The telephone company would pay the corporation $100,000 in cash on April 1, 19X2.

[c]   In addition, for each unit manufactured and installed by the telephone company, the corporation would receive a royalty per unit. The royalty per unit increases according to the following schedule: If 50,000 units or less are used in the five-year period the royalty is $5 per unit. If more than 50,000 units but 100,000 or less are used, the royalty is $10 per unit. If over 100,000 units are used the royalty will be $20 per unit.

[d]   Unit royalties are to be paid monthly as units are put in use, based on the number of units actually put in use. Escalation of royalties will be paid for past units in a lump sum if and when the number used exceeds the amounts specified in provision [c] above. For example, the telephone company will pay S Devices, Inc. only $5 per unit until 50,000 units are placed in use. At that point it will pay in lump sum an additional $5 on the 50,000 units, raising the per unit royalty to $10.

The directors of S Devices Inc. decided to accept the offer and the agreement was signed effective April 1, 19X2. The telephone company paid the initial $100,000 and set up a production line for the device. Working as fast as possible, the first units were ready for demonstration in October, 19X2. The device did not sell well in the remainder of 19X2. It was more expensive than other similar ones available and there were some questions raised about maintenance costs. However, 15,000 units were placed in service in October, November, and December. Under the terms of the agreement, the telephone company paid S Devices Inc. $75,000 (15,000 units at $5 each).

After the agreement was signed in April, 19X2, Sam immediately began work on an apparatus which, when connected to a phone, would automatically dial numbers and deliver a message. Sam thought it could be used by clubs, churches, and other organizations to remind members of meetings, etc. During the remainder of 19X2, Sam spent $86,000 on the new project. Rent expense on the laboratory was $12,000, the same as 19X1; however, general administrative expenses increased to $28,000 in 19X2 (adjusted for accrued expenses).

In preparing the income statement for 19X2, Sam reasoned that actual receipts from royalties of $75,000 was understated. The units actually placed in use in 19X2 averaged 5,000 per month. At that rate 300,000 (5,000 X 60 months) should be in use by the end of the five-year contract. He thus reasoned that revenue from royalties should be $300,000, that is, the 15,000 units times the maximum royalty of $20 per unit. Based on this expectation, he prepared the following income statement for 19X2:

S Devices, Inc.
Statement of Income for Year Ended December 31, 19X2

Revenues:		
Payment for five-year contract	$100,000	
Royalties received and accrued	300,000	$400,000
Expenses:		
Development cost of new project	$ 86,000	
Rent	12,000	
General administrative expenses	28,000	$126,000
Net income		$274,000

Required:

[a]   Write a critique of Sam's income computations for 19X1 and 19X2.
[b]   Prepare revised statements of income for 19X1 and for 19X2 based on your critique in part [a].

4

Measurement of Financial Position

The income of a business is an indication of its operating efficiency. The income statement is historical, it reflects past operations. But people interested in a business usually want to know how successful the business will be in the future. For example, an investor who owns stock in a corporation wants to know how much income the corporation will earn in future years. If the prospects are bleak, he may choose to sell his shares and invest in another corporation or in some other property. If high profits are expected, he will probably choose to continue his investment.

Income measurements for *past* accounting periods are, therefore, used as a basis for estimating the income in future periods. The decision-maker also gets some important information essential to the prediction of future income from the statement of financial position or balance sheet. This statement provides the person who is attempting to predict income of a business with a partial list of economic resources available for future use and a list of the fixed claims (liabilities) which must be settled in the future. The objective of this chapter is to explain the measurement of financial position, that is, how to prepare a balance sheet. We will also examine the relationships between the measurement of income and the measurement of financial position.

Components of a Statement of Financial Position

The measurement of financial position is similar to the measurement of wealth which was explained in Chapter 2. The statement of financial position or balance sheet contains many of the components that would appear in an accurate measurement of wealth. Indeed, the balance sheet prepared by accountants is usually the *only* approximation of the wealth of a business available to decision-makers. Because of the rules that accountants use to measure income, however, the measurement of financial position does not result in a precise statement of the wealth of a business.

Traditional Balance Sheet Equation

The statement of financial position has historically been called a *balance sheet*. The traditional equation for the balance sheet is

Assets = Liabilities + Proprietorship

The symbols used are

$$A = L + P$$

If assets are defined as the present value of the economic resources of the business, and the liabilities are defined as the present value of all claims against the business by creditors, the balance sheet would be a statement of wealth. The equation can be rearranged to give a measurement of wealth:

$$A - L = P$$

In this equation the proprietorship would be the net worth or wealth of the owners.

For example, assume that a corporation has assets or resources with a present value of $750,000. The corporation owes creditors and debt investors $400,000. The net worth or wealth of the corporation is, therefore,

$$
\begin{array}{ccc}
A & - & L & = & P \\
\$750,000 & - & \$400,000 & = & \$350,000
\end{array}
$$

A balance sheet that measures the assets and liabilities at present value and presents the remainder, proprietorship or shareholders' equity, would be a statement of wealth.

Problems of understanding the balance sheet arise because accountants still use the terms assets and liabilities on the statement. The objects and claims and their values that appear under the captions "assets" and "liabilities" do not always include all resources owned and all claims against the resources. And, of more importance, values shown for some assets and liabilities are *not* their present values. Recall from an earlier discussion in Chapter 2 that the present values of resources can be determined only if one knows the amount of income that the resources will produce in the future. Similarly, the precise valuation of claims or liabilities depends on precise knowledge of future events. Usually, we can only make very rough estimates of future income and of payments for many liabilities. Thus the accountant, despite the continued use of the terms assets and liabilities, does not attempt to measure the wealth of a business. Instead, the accountant's balance sheet, or statement of financial position, is primarily a by-product of the measurement of income under the flow concept described in Chapter 3.

Relationship of Balance Sheet to Income Measurement

The balance sheet is a listing of assets, liabilities, and proprietorship at a *point in time*, usually at the end of an accounting period. In recent years, the traditional equation has been simplified to

Assets = Equities

The term *equities* includes all claims against the assets, whether they are the claims of creditors, employees, debt investors, or owner investors.

Unlike the balance sheet, the income statement is a measure of economic activities over a *period of time*, the accounting period. A business begins an accounting period with certain assets and equities, shown on the balance sheet at the beginning of the accounting period. The activities during the period are summarized on the income statement. In addition, the activities *change* the stock of assets and equities which are on hand at the *end* of the accounting period. For example, a business begins the year with $10,000 of cash on hand, one of its resources or assets. During the year, cash receipts (CR) were $115,000 and cash disbursements (CD) were $109,000. These activities during the year, which enter into the measurement of income, also change the asset, cash on hand, at the end of the period. The change in cash (ΔC) is +$6,000 ($115,000 − $109,000) and the asset cash at the end of the year is $16,000 ($10,000 + $6,000).

In a similar way, all other activities during the year, which are considered in the measurement of income, change the assets and equities. To prepare a balance sheet we need a rearrangement of the variables used to measure income into an equation that will permit us to measure the assets and equities at the end of the period.

SOME NEW TERMS FOR CORPORATIONS. To accomplish the objective set out in the preceding paragraph, some new symbols must be introduced. Because of legal requirements in some instances and by long tradition, accountant's make a distinction on the balance sheet between investor's contributions with a fixed or determinable date for repayment (debt investments) and investor's contributions without a fixed repayment date (owners' investments). Most debt investments not only specify a fixed or determinable date for repayment but usually include a provision for fixed, periodic interest payments. The business that cannot make the fixed payments required by the debt contract can be forced into bankruptcy. Owners and stockholders typically have legally binding claims against the business. They risk their resources in return for a share in the profits after other claims are satisfied. To show this distinction on the balance sheet, the investment transactions, I, must be divided into debt or creditor investments, DI, and owner or stockholder investments, OI.

For proprietorships and partnerships, income or profit is added directly to the owners' equity for presentation on the balance sheet (losses are subtracted directly). If the business makes a profit, the owners' claims increase and the total claim is shown as one amount on the balance sheet. On the other hand, when proprietors or partners withdraw cash or other property, the withdrawals reduce their claims and the remainder is shown as a single amount.

For a corporation, laws require a *separate* statement of the owners' investments (OI) and the accumulated profits and losses. As a general rule, dividends can be paid to shareholders only to the extent of past income. For corporations, then, the balance sheet must show owners' investment (OI) and a separate item for the accumulated past income less losses and dividends. This latter amount is called *retained earnings*, and the symbol used is RE. Dividends paid to shareholders during a period, which would be the equivalent of ID for proprietorships and partnerships, will be represented by the symbol S.

To illustrate, assume that the balance sheet of C Corporation shows retained earnings of $150,000 at the beginning of a period. This is a part of the shareholders' equity or claims against the corporation, but it is shown separately because of the legal requirement. During the ensuing year the corporation earned a profit of $75,000 and paid dividends of $50,000. The change in the retained earnings for the period is

$$\Delta RE = Y - S$$
$$= \$75,000 - \$50,000$$
$$= \$25,000$$

The retained earnings at the end of the year is thus $175,000, the beginning balance of $150,000 plus the positive change (excess of income over dividends) of $25,000. The total claims or equity of stockholders has increased as a result of the year's activities.

Retained earnings for a corporation is a measure of the aggregate income or profits from its organization less the aggregate distributions in the form of dividends (S) to owner investors (shareholders) as of the date of the balance sheet. The change in retained earnings (ΔRE) is the difference between income and dividends for a specified period. Retained earnings, then, represents the past profits that have been retained and used in carrying on the economic activities of the corporation. Owner investors have a residual claim to the retained earnings of a corporation.

AN EQUATION FOR BALANCE SHEET CHANGES. As explained earlier, the income of a business for a period can be described as the changes in the assets and equities of the business during the period. A more accurate description of the accounting process is that the accountant measures income and then uses the changes in the variables in his income measurement to obtain the value of assets and equities at the end of the period:

Assets and equities at beginning of period
±Changes in variables used in income measurement
=Assets and equities at the end of period

The appendix to this chapter shows the algebraic manipulations of the income equation necessary to arrange the variables used in income measurement in what we will call the balance sheet change equation, which is

$$\Delta C + \Delta AR + \Delta DE = \Delta AE + \Delta DR + \Delta DI + \Delta OI + \Delta RE$$

Note that the equation includes the change in retained earnings (ΔRE) which assumes that the business is organized as a corporation. Changes that affect assets or resources are placed on the left side of the equality sign and those that affect equities are placed on the right-hand side. The fact that the changes in the assets of a business are exactly equal to the changes in the claims against the assets or equities is hardly mysterious—after solving for income (Y), the identical amounts used in that computation are merely rearranged in the manner shown above. To repeat, the accountant's balance sheet is a by-product of his income measurement.

ACCOUNTING DEFINITIONS OF ASSETS AND EQUITIES. The equation for balance sheet changes shown above also affords a precise basis for the definition of assets and equities. For these general terms, we can now substitute terms that we used for the measurement of income. The equation, Assets = Equities, becomes

$$C + AR + DE = AE + DR + DI + OI + RE$$

A mock-up or pro forma statement of financial position is shown in Fig. 4–1.

Figure 4–1

Any Corporation		Statement of Financial Position Date	
Assets		Equities:	
Cash (C)	$ XXX	Accrued expenses (AE)	$ XXX
Accrued revenues (AR)	XXX	Deferred revenue (DR)	XXX
Deferred expenses (DE)	XXX	Debt investment (DI)	XXX
Total assets	$XXXX	Owner investment (OI)	XXX
		Retained earnings (RE)	XXX
		Total equities	$XXXX

A brief review of meanings assigned to terms in the measurement of income and how they relate to the general concepts of assets and equities and the use of a balance sheet will be helpful at this point.

Cash (C). Cash is an obvious resource or asset. The amount of cash on hand at the end of an accounting period, as shown on the balance sheet, is an important consideration in predicting the success of future operations. The business must have a sufficient amount of cash to meet immediate demands for wages, creditors, and other claims.

Accrued revenues (AR). Amounts that have been earned by the business by the delivery of products prior to the collection of cash are accrued revenues or accounts receivable. They represent claims against others and indicate the amount of cash to be collected in the future for work already completed. Like cash, accrued revenues are an indication of the resources available to settle future claims. For most businesses, the bulk of the accounts receivable will be collected within a month or two. Most accrued receivables are therefore *liquid* assets, which means they will be converted into cash in the near future.

Deferred expenses (DE). Economic resources available for use in the production of future revenues are deferred expenses. A record of the deferred expenses or costs provides the decision-maker with information useful in determining the future of the business. There must be a sufficient supply of services on hand to meet the demands of customers for products and to provide a backlog of services needed to create new products in future periods. Frequently the major part of a business's total resources are invested in deferred expenses.

Deferred expenses may take many forms. Some common examples are supplies, merchandise, plant, equipment, and land. A deferred expense may also be an investment in securities of another business, a deposit for the future delivery of goods or services, or an intangible item such as a patent, copyright, or trademark. The primary characteristic of a deferred expense is an outlay of cash with the expectation that revenue will result sometime in the future. Deferred expenses are measured by an equitable and rational allocation of the original cash outflow between the services used and the services available for future use. The services consumed are expenses of prior periods; the services remaining are deferred expenses representing future utility. In most businesses, merchandise inventory and plant and equipment are the major deferred expenses.

Taken together, cash, accrued revenues, and deferred expenses are the resources available to the business for future operations. To repeat, the definition of assets used by accountants does not purport to measure the current value of all properties and rights of the business. Cash and accrued revenues are stated or measured in current values. The amounts shown for deferred expenses, such as inventories, plant, and equipment, may vary considerably from the current value of the resources.

Accrued expenses (AE). Promises to pay cash in the future for resources already acquired are accrued expenses. These liabilities are claims that must be settled by the use of cash on hand, or the cash realized from the collection of accrued revenues, or from cash generated by future sales, or from cash obtained from additional investments. The decision-maker interested in the future should compare the accrued costs with the resources available to settle the claims. For example, if the accrued expenses exceed the cash on hand and other liquid assets, the company may face a financial crisis which would disrupt future operations and drastically change the estimate of future income or profit.

Deferred revenues (DR). Commitments to deliver goods or perform services at some future time are deferred revenues. Generally cash has been received in exchange for the promise to deliver goods or services in the future. As with accrued expenses, deferred revenues are claims against the available resources of the business (liabilities). Most businesses do not have deferred revenues because their customers either pay when the product is delivered or after the product is delivered. The major exceptions are magazine and other subscriptions, down payments for special products, and premiums paid on various types of insurance.

Debt investments (DI). These investments are also claims against the assets of the business which must be settled usually with a cash payment. In addition, most debt contracts call for payment of interest in addition to the repayment of the original *principal* amount. Recall from Chapter 2 that the payment of interest is the only financing transaction that affects the computation of income—interest is treated as an expense.

The time of repayment of debt contracts is often an important fact in predicting the future of a business. If large amounts must be repaid in the near future, cash and liquid assets must be available for settlement of the claim. If the principal of the debt is due in small installments, or in total at some remote time, the existence of the claim may be less critical.

Owner investments (OI). The residual claim to the resources of the business is the owner investment. These claims are satisfied only after all others have been met. On the other hand, the equity of the owners is increased by profits, and it is the expectation of profit that encourages the owners to risk their capital. Unlike debt investors who risk their capital for a limited return in the form of interest in exchange for some security, the owner investors carry the greatest risk with the hope of large profits.

Retained earnings (RE). As explained previously, laws regulating corporations require a separation of the amounts invested by shareholders from the accumulated profits and losses. Dividend payments are usually restricted to the amount of past profit. This law prohibits the payment of resources to shareholders to the extent which might endanger the prior claims for accrued costs, deferred revenues, and debt investments. The shareholders' original investment can only be returned to him after all other claims are settled.

Equities, therefore, include accrued expenses, deferred revenues, debt investments, owner investments, and retained earnings. The principal use of this information in the prediction of future income is to answer the following question: Are operations of the company producing cash sufficient to meet the claims or liabilities as they become due? Other uses of the information contained on the balance sheet to predict future income will be discussed in Chapters 6 and 17.

Example of Use of Equations

Two different equations were included in the preceding discussion. One of these was an expansion of the basic balance sheet equation, Assets = Equities, to include the variables used to summarize activities in the measurement of income. Thus,

$$C + AR + DE = AE + DR + DI + OI + RE$$

The second equation was the rearrangement of the equation for income computation into a format consistent with the balance sheet equation. This equation shows the *changes* in the amounts on the balance sheet as a result of the period's operations:

$$\Delta C + \Delta AR + \Delta DE = \Delta AE + \Delta DR + \Delta DI + \Delta OI + \Delta RE$$

Note again that the equality of this equation is a truism because the same amounts were originally used to compute income (Y), and income, once determined, is included in this new equation as a variable in the change in retained earnings $(\Delta RE = Y - S)$.

To obtain the balance sheet at the end of an accounting period, the equation for changes in the balance sheet is added to the beginning balance sheet. This operation is shown below with subscript 0 referring to the beginning balance sheet and subscript 1 referring to the balance sheet at the end of the accounting period. The equation for changes is the summary of activities between the two dates.

$$
\begin{aligned}
C_0 + AR_0 + DE_0 &= AE_0 + DR_0 + DI_0 + OI_0 + RE_0 \\
+\ \Delta C + \Delta AR + \Delta DE &= \Delta AE + \Delta DR + \Delta DI + \Delta OI + \Delta RE \\
\hline
= C_1 + AR_1 + DE_1 &= AE_1 + DR_1 + DI_1 + OI_1 + RE_1
\end{aligned}
$$

To illustrate the use of the equations, assume the following facts: Any Corporation was formed on December 31, 19X0, by a group of owner investors. Their total original contribution was $100,000 in cash. For this investment they obtained shares in the corporation. The statement of financial position of Any Corporation on Jan. 1, 19X1 is shown in Fig. 4-2.

Figure 4-2

Any Corporation	Statement of Financial Position as of January 1, 19X1
Assets:	Equities:
Cash $100,000	Capital stock $100,000

The records and files of Any Corporation showed the following activities for the entire year 19X1:

Cash receipts (CR)	$205,000
Cash disbursements (CD)	288,000
Accrued revenues (AR), 12/31/X1	14,000
Deferred expenses (DE), 12/31/X1	115,000
Accrued expenses (AE), 12/31/X1	17,000
Deferred revenues (DR), 12/31/X1	2,000
Debt-investment receipts (DIR)	20,000
Debt-investment disbursements (DID)	10,000
Shareholder dividends (S)	0
Owner-investment receipts (OIR)	0
Owner-investment disbursements (OID)	0

A summary of the year's operations is obtained by the following computations.

Revenue:
$$R = CR + \Delta AR - \Delta DR - DIR - OIR$$
$$= \$205,000 + \$14,000 - \$2,000 - \$20,000 - 0$$
$$= \$197,000$$

Expenses:
$$E = CD + \Delta AE - \Delta DE - DID - OID$$
$$= \$288,000 + \$17,000 - \$115,000 - \$10,000 - 0 - 0$$
$$= \$180,000$$

Income:
$$Y = R - E$$
$$= \$197,000 - \$180,000$$
$$= \$17,000$$

Change in cash:
$$\Delta C = CR - CD$$
$$= \$205,000 - \$288,000$$
$$= (-\$83,000)$$

Change in debt investment:
$$\Delta DI = DIR - DID$$
$$= \$20,000 - \$10,000$$
$$= \$10,000$$

Change in retained earnings:
$$\Delta RE = Y - S$$
$$= \$17,000 - 0$$
$$= \$17,000$$

The change in owner investment is zero because no new investments were made by the shareholders during the year. What about changes in the accruals and deferrals of revenues and expenses? Note that this is the first year of operations and that the amounts for AR, DE, AE, and DR are zero at December 31, 19X0. Because of this fact the change in every case is a positive change equal to the ending balance. For example, the change in accrued revenue would be

$$\Delta AR = (AR_1 - AR_0)$$
$$= (\$14,000 - 0)$$
$$= \$14,000$$

The same holds true for other accruals and deferrals.

The preparation of the balance sheet at the end of the year is accomplished simply by listing the assets and equity items in a balanced format. The balance sheet for Any Corporation is shown in Fig. 4–3. The amounts shown for accruals and deferrals are from the records and files above.

Figure 4–3

Any Corporation		Balance Sheet, December 31, 19X1	
Assets:		Equities:	
Cash	$ 17,000	Accrued expenses	$ 17,000
Accrued revenues	14,000	Deferred revenues	2,000
Deferred expenses	115,000	Debt investments	10,000
		Owner investment	100,000
		Retained earnings	17,000
Total assets	$146,000	Total equities	$146,000

The amounts appearing on the balance sheet are the monetary measures as of the date of the balance sheet. The amount for cash and revenue accruals is the actual cash or the cash expected to be collected. These amounts can be computed. For example, the $17,000 ending cash balance for Any Corporation can be computed as follows:

$$C_1 = C_0 + \Delta C$$
$$= \$100,000 + (-\$83,000)$$
$$= \$100,000 - \$83,000$$
$$= \$17,000$$

Most accountants, however, will not relie entirely on the arithmetical computation but will verify the actual cash on hand and cash on deposit. The amounts for accruals and deferrals are *always* the accruals and deferrals at the end of the period. Even if a continuing record is maintained the accuracy of the ending balance should be verified. Accruals may be confirmed by the customer or supplier and deferred costs should be physically counted whenever possible. Of course, if a continuing record is not maintained the amounts are determined by listing the unpaid sales invoices for the revenue accruals and the unpaid invoices from *all* suppliers of goods and services for expense accruals. Remember that the monetary measures for expense deferrals are the acquisition cost less amounts allocated to expense in the current and prior periods.

The amounts that appear on the balance sheet for the debt investment and owner investment are computed by using the following general equations:

$$I_1 = I_0 + \Delta I$$

The computation for the debt investment balance for Any Corporation is

$$DI_1 = DI_0 + \Delta DI$$
$$= (0) + \$10,000$$
$$= \$10,000$$

In this case the ending balance was equal to the change in debt investment because the beginning balance was zero.

There were no owner-investment receipts or disbursements during the year; consequently the change in owner investment was zero and the ending balance of the owner investment is equal to the beginning balance of the owner investment. If all of the computations are correct including the computation of income, the total assets will equal total equities. The ending balance sheet equation shown on p. 91 will balance.

Example

This section is a continuation of the C Bookstore, Inc. example at the end of Chapter 3. The objectives of this example are to:

1   Prepare a statement of financial position for the end of each of the three years.
2   Show the relationship between the income statements in Chapter 3 and the statements of financial position.

The five organizers contributed a total of $25,000 to the corporation to begin operations. The statement of financial position immediately following the investment of the $25,000 by the organizers is shown in Fig. 4-4.

Figure 4-4

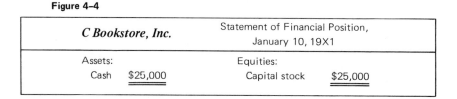

C Bookstore, Inc.	Statement of Financial Position, January 10, 19X1
Assets:	Equities:
Cash $25,000	Capital stock $25,000

First Year

The accruals and deferrals as of December 31, 19X1 were*

Accrued revenues	$ 6,000
Deferred expenses (fixtures)	7,250
Deferred expenses (merchandise)	20,000
Deferred expenses (casualty insurance)	260
Accrued expenses (merchandise)	9,500
Accrued expenses (wages)	400

(Refer to Chapter 3 for an explanation of these individual items.) The statement of financial position as of December 31, 19X1 can be prepared by listing the ending balances for the above accruals and deferrals and the computed amount for ending cash balance of $7,690 (see Fig. 3-3) and the retained earnings of $6,300. Because 19X1 is the first year of operation and no dividends were paid, the retained earnings are equal to the income for the year 19X1.

*Note that for the first year of operation the changes are the same as the ending balances.

Each major classification of the deferred expenses, such as merchandise, pre-paid insurance, and fixtures is shown separately to provide additional informa-tion for the reader. For the same reason, accrued expenses are subdivided into informative categories relating to the various expenses. Frequently, the descrip-tive titles used on the formal balance sheet will be changed to convey more information to the reader. For example, in the formal statement of financial position (Fig. 4–5), accrued revenues are listed as accounts receivable from sales, which is the traditional language used to describe accrued revenue on the balance sheet.

Figure 4–5

C Bookstore, Inc.		Statement of Financial Position, December 31, 19X1	
Assets:		Equities:	
Cash	$ 7,690	Accounts payable	
Accounts receivable		(merchandise)	$ 9,500
from sales	6,000	Wages payable	400
Merchandise inventory	20,000	Capital stock	25,000
Prepaid insurance	260	Retained earnings	6,300
Fixtures	7,250		
	$41,200		$41,200

An examination of this statement shows that assets have increased from $25,000 to $41,200 during the first year, a net increase of $16,200. The sources of this increase in assets were an increase in accrued expenses (accounts payable for merchandise and wages payable) of $9,900 and an increase in re-tained earnings (income) of $6,300. The total increase in equities was, there-fore, $16,200, the same as the increase in assets. The itemization of assets by type, such as cash, accounts receivable, and merchandise inventory, enables the reader to understand something about what is available for future operations. Equities are similarly subdivided to provide the reader with the nature of the claims against the assets.

Second Year

The accruals and deferrals as of December 31, 19X2 for the C Bookstore, Inc. were

	12/31/X2
Accrued revenues	$ 4,000
Deferred expenses (merchandise)	18,200
Deferred expenses (insurance)	120
Deferred expenses (fixtures)	6,500
Accrued expenses (merchandise)	12,500
Accrued expenses (wages)	750
Accrued expenses (interest)	150

Again, the statement of financial position is prepared by listing the above accruals and deferrals, the ending cash balance of $1,490 (the beginning cash balance of $7,690 less the decrease in cash for the year of $6,200—see Fig. 3-5 for details of this decrease), and the deficit (retained earnings) of $18,070. The computation of the ending deficit is as follows:

Balance of retained earnings, 1/1/X2	$ 6,300
Less:	
Dividends	$ 5,000
Loss for 19X2	19,370
Total decrease or change in retained earnings	($24,370)
Balance of retained earnings (deficit), 12/31/X2	($18,070)

The formal statement of financial position is presented in Fig. 4-6.

Figure 4-6

C Bookstore, Inc.		Statement of Financial Position, December 31, 19X2	
Assets:		Equities:	
Cash	$ 1,490	Accounts payable	
Accounts receivable		(merchandise)	$12,500
from sales	4,000	Wages payable	750
Merchandise inventory	18,200	Interest payable	150
Prepaid insurance	140	Loan payable to	
Fixtures	6,500	bank	10,000
		Capital stock	25,000
		Retained earnings	
		(deficit)	(18,070)
Total assets	$30,330	Total equities	$30,330

A comparison of the statement of financial position as of December 31, 19X2 with the same statement for December 31, 19X1 reveals that total assets have decreased from $41,200 to $30,330, a decrease of $10,870. This decrease resulted from the loss of $19,370 and the payment of the $5,000 cash dividend, a total of $24,370 less an increase in loans of $10,000 and an increase in accrued costs of $3,500, a total increase in liabilities of $13,500. The net decrease in total equities is $10,870 ($24,370 – $13,500), which is equal to the decrease in assets.

Third Year

The C Bookstore, Inc. was liquidated at the end of the third year. Because of the liquidation, all accruals and deferrals at December 31, 19X2 were zero. The statement of financial position just prior to distribution of cash to the shareholders is shown in Fig. 4-7. The change in retained earnings is the income for the year, $5,060; no dividends were paid. The reconciliation of the accumulated deficit (retained earnings) is as follows:

Deficit as of 12/31/X2	$18,070
Change in deficit (income, 19X3)	5,060
Deficit as of 12/31/X3	$13,010

Figure 4-7

C Bookstore, Inc.		Statement of Financial Position as of December 31, 19X3	
Assets:		Equities:	
Cash	$11,990	Capital stock	$25,000
		Deficit	(13,010)
Total assets	$11,990	Total equities	$11,990

When the corporation is finally liquidated the original investors will receive only $11,990. This return to the owners can be explained by summarizing the income, losses, and dividends for the three-year period. The net income and losses for the three years shows a net loss of $8,010 (refer to p. 74) which reduces the owners' equity. The owners' equity is further reduced by the $5,000 dividend, a total reduction of $13,010. The original investment of $25,000 less the total reduction for net losses and dividends leaves an equity of $11,990 ($25,000 – $13,010). This equity is equal to the remaining assets, cash of $11,990.

QUESTIONS

1 What information is provided by a balance sheet?
2 While depositing a check at a local bank, the teller showed you a balance sheet of the bank and commented that the net worth of the bank was now $847,000. Would a balance sheet of a bank be a statement of net worth?
3 List the components of a balance sheet.
4 Which assets are generally measured at present value?
5 Which assets are measured at acquisition cost?
6 Which equities are measured at present value? Which equities are measured by acquisition value?
7 Why are some balance sheet components measured at present value and other components measured at acquisition cost?
8 What is the traditional balance sheet equation?
9 Define the following terms:

[a]	Asset	[e]	Capital
[b]	Equity	[f]	Retained earnings
[c]	Liability	[g]	Dividends
[d]	Proprietorship	[h]	Capital stock

10 Define the following terms:

[a]	Cash	[e]	Accrued expenses
[b]	Accrued revenue	[f]	Debt investments
[c]	Deferred expenses	[g]	Owner investments
[d]	Deferred revenue		

11   What is the relationship of the balance sheet to the income statement?
12   Explain how you would use a balance sheet in deciding whether or not to invest in a
      corporation.
13   The income statement measures the activities of a business for a period of time. What does
      the balance sheet measure?
14   Why do corporations show a separate amount for owner investments and for retained
      earnings?
15   Why should a corporation not pay dividends in excess of the amount of retained earnings?

PROBLEMS

1   At 65, Mr. Smith retired from a large U.S. corporation. He still considered himself produc-
     tive, and over the past five years he developed what was once a hobby into a profitable gun
     repair shop. His balance sheet as of December 31, 19X5 is presented below:

Gun Repairs
Balance Sheet, December 31, 19X5

Assets		Equities	
Cash	$ 1,500	Accrued expenses	$ 1,750
Accrued revenue	2,000	Deferred revenue	250
Deferred costs	10,000	Bank loan	5,000
		Smith, equity	6,500
	$13,500		$13,500

Cash information for operations in 19X6 were

Cash receipts:	
From customers	$8,000
Additional investment (Smith)	500
	$8,500

Cash disbursements:	
Operations (including interest)	$2,400
Withdrawals	3,000
Payment on bank loan	2,500
	$7,900

Information for accruals and deferrals at December 31, 19X6 were:

Accrued revenue	$2,500
Deferred costs	9,200
Accrued expenses	1,550
Deferred revenue	400

Required:

[a]   Using the general formulas for revenue and expense, compute income for 19X6.
[b]   Prepare a balance sheet as of December 31, 19X6.

2   On January 1, 19X1, Mr. Townley seized on the opportunity to purchase a small gift shop
     which he had admired for years. It took him all month to complete the purchase, and be-
     cause he wanted to know his "position" before starting February operations, he asked you

to prepare him a balance sheet as of January 31, 19X1. Mr. Townley gives you the following information:

Cash receipts:		
Townley's investment		$10,000
Bank loan (made on 1/1/X1, due		
in 6 months, interest rate 5%		
per year)		2,000
		$12,000
Cash disbursements:		
Purchase of building, furniture,		
& fixtures		$ 9,000
Purchase of inventory (existing)		2,000
		$11,000

Required:

Prepare a balance sheet as of January 31, 19X1.

3   You are given the following information concerning the remainder of Mr. Townley's operations for 19X1 (continuation of Problem 2):

Cash receipts (2/1/X1 to 12/31/X2):	
Townley, additional investment	$ 1,000
Collection from customers	15,000
	$16,000
Cash disbursements (2/1/X1 to 12/31/X2):	
Merchandise inventory	$ 4,000
Salaries	3,000
Insurance for 3 years	720
Purchase of delivery truck (used)	900
Other operating expenses	450
Repayment of bank loan	2,000
Interest on bank loan	50
Withdrawals	4,000
	$15,120

Accruals and deferrals at December 31, 19X1 were

Merchandise inventory	$1,000
Accounts receivable (sales)	2,000
Office supplies on hand	20
Insurance (unexpired)	500
Delivery truck	800
Building, furniture, & fixtures	8,500
Accounts payable (inventory)	1,400
Unpaid salaries	100

Required:

[a]   Prepare an income statement for 19X1.

[b]   Prepare a balance sheet at December 31, 19X1.

4   You are given the following information concerning Mr. Townley's operations in 19X2 (continuation of Problems 2 and 3):

Cash receipts:

Collections from customers	$12,000

Cash disbursements:

Merchandise inventory	$ 3,000
Salaries	3,000
Other operating expenses	475
Withdrawals	4,000
	$10,475

Accruals and deferrals at December 31, 19X2 were

Merchandise inventory	$2,000
Accounts receivable (sales)	1,500
Office supplies on hand	20
Insurance (unexpired)	260
Delivery truck	700
Building, furniture, & fixtures	4,000
Accounts payable (inventory)	1,400
Unpaid salaries	100

Required:

[a]   Prepare an income statement of 19X2.
[b]   Prepare a balance sheet at December 31, 19X2.

5   H Corporation has operated as a management consultant firm for several years. The balance sheet as of December 31, 19X1 was

H Corporation
Balance Sheet, December 31, 19X1

Assets		Equities	
Cash	$ 2,200	Accrued salaries payable	$ 830
Accounts receivable	18,500	Accrued operating expenses	
Office equipment	8,000	payable	1,170
		Capital stock	23,000
		Retained earnings	3,700
	$28,700		$28,700

Cash transactions for the year 19X2 were

Cash receipts:

From customers	$62,000
From bank loan	3,000
	$65,000

Cash disbursements:

Salaries	$26,000
Operating expenses	36,800
Dividend	2,500
	$65,300

[a]   Based on the following information concerning accruals and deferrals at December 31, 19X2, compute the income for 19X2:

Depreciation of equipment, 19X2	$ 800
Accounts receivable	19,200
Accrued salaries payable	910
Accrued operating expense payable	1,000
Accrued interest on bank loan	60

[b]   Prepare a balance sheet for H Corporation as of December 31, 19X2.

6   Ryan, Schultz & Johanson, Attorneys at Law's statement of income for 19X2 is presented below:

Revenues		$128,000
Expenses:		
Salaries	$45,000	
Rent	12,000	
Utilities	5,000	
Taxes	1,600	
Dues & subscriptions	4,000	
Supplies	2,000	69,600
Income		$ 58,400

Ryan, Schultz & Johanson each withdrew $15,000 during the year. Accounts receivable increased $8,000; accrued wages increased $800, accrued taxes decreased $200, and accounts payable for supplies increased $700. Prepare a statement of cash receipts and disbursements for the firm.

7   The balance sheet of Ryan, Schultz & Johanson (see Problem 6) at the beginning of 19X2 was

Ryan, Schultz & Johanson, Attorneys at Law
Balance Sheet, December 31, 19X1

Assets:		
Cash	$ 6,800	
Accounts receivable	10,000	
Total assets		$16,800
Equities:		
Accrued expenses	$2,000	
Accounts payable (supplies)	100	
Capital, Ryan	4,900	
Capital, Schultz	4,900	
Capital, Johanson	4,900	
Total equities		$16,800

Required:
Prepare a balance for the firm as of December 31, 19X2.

8   Duggan Matthews, a recently discharged air force pilot, was anxious to start a crop-dusting business that would enable him to take advantage of his exceptional skill as a pilot. He knew that he could buy a plane and a spray rig at the reasonable price of $15,000.

Although Matthews was willing to invest his life savings of $18,000, he needed additional capital. Pesticides for jobs he contracted would have to be paid for in cash, and some of the farmers would be unable to make immediate payment for his services.

Matthews was not able to secure a loan because the venture was too risky. Finally he approached Mr. Razor Banks, a retired crop duster. Mr. Banks had invested his earnings from crop dusting wisely and had accumulated a substantial amount of personal wealth. His sentimental interest in crop dusting and his admiration for Mr. Matthews's skill as a pilot induced him to furnish the necessary financial backing subject to the two following conditions:

1   He wanted to avoid risking his entire personal fortune in case of an accident with the plane which could involve substantial damage to people or property.
2   He wanted to share in the profits.

The obvious way to satisfy his conditions was to form a corporation. By incorporating, risk would be limited to the amount invested in the business; and, as a shareholder, Mr. Banks would be entitled to receive a pro rata portion of any dividends distributed. The two men agreed that Matthews should receive a commission amounting to 35% of gross billings to customers to compensate him for the high risk involved in flying so near the ground. (Salaries and commissions to officers and shareholders are treated as expenses to a corporation.) The commissions were not to be paid until cash was actually collected from customers. The men also decided to prepare financial statements every three months. Matthews believed he could stay busy most of the year by working in Latin America, the United States, and Canada.

A brief summary of transactions for the first quarter, January 1 through March 31, 19X6 follows.

A-1   Sold 2,000 shares of stock to Matthews for $18,000 and 2,000 shares to Banks for $18,000.
A-2   Purchased the plane for $15,000 cash.
A-3   Billed customers for services rendered $120,000.
A-4   Collected $70,000 from customers.
A-5   Paid $24,500 in commissions to Matthews.
A-6   Paid $45,000 for pesticides.
A-7   Paid $500 for operating expenses—clerical assistance, telephone bills, telephone answering service, accounting fees, insurance, etc.
A-8   Borrowed $5,000 from Mr. Banks.
A-9   At the end of the quarter, P Corporation had the following unpaid bills on hand:

For operating expenses	$ 200
For pesticides	1,000

A-10   Accrued interest on the loan from Mr. Banks amounted to $50.
A-11   The plane and spray rig had an estimated life of five years.
A-12   The inventory of pesticides was $18,000.

Required:

[a]   Prepare a statement of cash receipts and disbursements.

[b]   Prepare an income statement for the first quarter of operations. Show your computations for revenues and expenses.

[c]   Prepare a balance sheet as of March 31, 19X6.

9   A summary of transactions (continuation of Problem 8) for the second quarter, April 1
through June 30, 19X6 was as follows:

B-1   Billed customers $140,000 for services rendered.

B-2   Collected $130,000 from customers.

B-3   Paid $45,500 in commissions to Matthews.

B-4   Paid $40,000 for pesticides.

B-5   Paid $650 for operating expenses.

B-6   At the end of the second quarter P Corporation had the following unpaid bills
on hand:

| For operating expenses | $150 |
| For pesticides | 750 |

B-7   The inventory of pesticides was $2,500.

B-8   Accrued interest on the loan from Mr. Banks amounted to $200.

B-9   The corporation paid $6,000 in dividends.

Required:

[a]   Prepare an income statement for the second quarter. Show your computations for
each revenue and expense item.

[b]   Prepare a balance sheet as of June 30, 19X6.

CASE   Harry Tucker spent ten years selling cars for a local automobile dealer. For the
past three years he has served as the used car sales manager. Mr. Tucker was able
to save $25,000 during this period. In early April, Mr. Carl Essex, the owner of
a well-established used car lot, offered to sell Mr. Tucker his used car lot. After
a period of negotiation Mr. Tucker agreed to purchase Mr. Essex's stock of used
cars for $21,000 and the office furniture and equipment for $500. Mr. Tucker
also agreed to lease from Mr. Essex the used car lot and small sales building for a
five-year period at an annual cost of $3,000. The fifth year's rent was to be paid
in advance. The rent for the first four years was to be paid at a rate of $250 per
month on the first of each month.

A physical inventory was made on April 30, 19X1. The used car inventory
was $21,000. Mr. Tucker paid Mr. Essex $24,500 as agreed. The local bank
loaned Mr. Tucker $15,000 at 9 percent interest for six months. Mr. Tucker
began operations on May 1, 19X1.

During the last eight months of 19X1, Mr. Tucker was active buying and selling used cars. He followed the practice of depositing all cash receipts in his
business account. All cash disbursements were paid by check. A record of all
cash receipts and disbursements appears in Schedule 1.

On December 31, 19X1, Mr. Tucker took an inventory of his used cars. He
listed each car by model, make, and serial number. In a column to the right of
each model, make, and serial number he inserted the cost of each car that he had

purchased. For those units that he had taken in trade for another car, he showed no cost value. His inventory consisted of 30 cars, 20 of which were purchased and 10 of which were received in trade. The total cost of the 20 purchased was $28,000. Other accruals and deferrals are shown in Schedule 2.

SCHEDULE 1

T Auto Sales

Cash Receipts and Disbursements, April 30 to December 31, 19X1

Cash receipts

Investment by Mr. Tucker		$25,000
Loan from bank		15,000
From customers		128,000
		$168,000

Cash disbursements:

Initial payment to Mr. Essex		
Used cars	$21,000	
Rent advance	3,000	
Furniture & equipment	500	$ 24,500
Eight month's rent		2,000
Insurance		1,200
Advertising		4,000
Licenses and taxes		600
Used cars—other		123,000
Utilities bills (power, light, heat)		800
Withdrawal		10,000
Telephone service		380
		$166,480

SCHEDULE 2

Accruals and Deferrals as of December 31, 19X1

Contracts receivable		$2,300
Unpaid utility bills		140
Unpaid taxes		220
Prepaid insurance		400
Prepaid rent		3,000
Furniture & equipment (cost)	$500	
Estimated depreciation (8 months)	50	
deferred to future years		450

Required:

[a] Prepare a balance sheet as of May 1, 19X1.

[b] Prepare an income statement for the eight-month period ended December 31, 19X1.

[c] Should the used cars received in trade be given some value in the inventory?

[d] The ten used cars received as trade-ins had an estimated sales value of $12,500. The amount allowed as trade-in value on the cars purchased by customers was $13,800. The wholesale value of the cars at the time they

were received was $11,000. If the cars should be shown in the inventory at some value, which of the three values listed above should be used? Justify your selection.

[e] Prepare a corrected income statement and balance sheet to put into effect your suggested valuation in part [d] above.

Appendix: Derivation of the Equation for Balance Sheet Changes

The equation for income is

$$Y = R - E$$

This formula can be expanded to include all the variables required to measure income by substituting the revenue and expense equations for these terms in the income equation. The expanded formula is

$$Y = (CR + \Delta AR - \Delta DR - DIR - OIR) - (CD + \Delta AE - \Delta DE - DID - OID - S)$$

Note that the expense equation above also includes the symbol for dividends (S), based on the assumption that we are concerned with a corporation. Also the investment transactions are divided into debt investment (DIR and DID) and owner investment (OIR and OID).

When the parentheses in the above equation are removed, we have

$$Y = CR + \Delta AR - \Delta DR - DIR - OIR - CD - \Delta AE + \Delta DE + DID + OID + S$$

The terms in this expression which deal with related transactions (cash, investments, etc.) can be collected to simplify the expression:

$$Y = (CR - CD) + \Delta AR - \Delta DR - \Delta AE + \Delta DE - (DIR - DID) - (OIR - OID) + S$$

The equation can be shortened by the following definitions:

$$\Delta C = (CR - CD)$$
$$\Delta DI = (DIR - DID)$$
$$\Delta OI = (OIR - OID)$$

When these terms are substituted into the equation, we obtain

$$Y = \Delta C + \Delta AR - \Delta DR - \Delta AE + \Delta DE - \Delta DI - \Delta OI + S$$

The preceding equation is thus a summary of all activities for the accounting period and, taken together, these changes account for the differences between the assets and equities at the beginning of the period and at the end of the period. The balance sheet equation, Assets = Equities, requires a summation of variables under two categories. Similarly, the changes in the above equation must be organized so that all variables will have a positive sign.

The changes that affect assets or resources are placed on the left side of the equality sign and those affecting equities are placed on the right side to conform with the balance sheet equation. (This is accomplished by rearranging the terms and multiplying by -1.)

$$\Delta C + \Delta AR + \Delta DE = \Delta AE + \Delta DR + \Delta DI + \Delta OI + (Y - S)$$

The last term $(Y - S)$ was previously defined (for a corporation) as ΔRE, or the change in retained earnings. By substituting this final term, we obtain the following equation which accounts for changes in assets and equities over an accounting period:

$$\Delta C + \Delta AR + \Delta DE = \Delta AE + \Delta DR + \Delta DI + \Delta OI + \Delta RE$$

With this equation, the accounting measurement of income under the flow concept is related to the statement of position or balance sheet.

two

CLASSIFIED

FINANCIAL

STATEMENTS

5

Classified Financial Statements: The Statement of Income

The purpose of accounting is to supply economic information to decision-makers. Accountants prepare a variety of reports for a variety of users. In the present chapter and the two which follow the reports prepared by accountants primarily for the use of outsiders—investors, creditors, and the general public—will be considered. This chapter covers the income statement and is followed by a discussion of the balance sheet in Chapter 6. Chapter 7 deals with the newest addition to the list of external accounting reports, the statement of changes in financial position. Together these three reports, the statement of income, the balance sheet, and the statement of changes in financial position are referred to as financial statements.

Financial statements are useful to many groups of people who are interested in business:

1   Owners and prospective owners including individual owners, partners, and stockholders
2   Managers who may or may not be the owners
3   Current and prospective creditors, long-term and short-term
4   Governmental units
5   Employees and their representatives
6   Investment dealers and investment counselors
7   Trade associations
8   Customers and the general public

A basic decision of an owner is whether or not to continue his investment in the business. Under some circumstances, owners also decide whether or not the old managers should be replaced with a new team. Sometimes owners must decide if their investment should be expanded or contracted. Prospective owners must reach a decision on the desirability of acquiring an interest in a business.

Owner managers and other managers make most of the decisions concerned with the operations of the business. Some of the more important decisions made by managers are to add to or drop products or product lines; to expand or to contract productive capacity; to increase or to decrease the size of the work force; to borrow additional funds and from where to borrow them; to retire debts prior to maturity or to wait until they mature. The information included in the external financial statements is usually inadequate to answer all these questions. For this reason, accountants prepare many internal reports. A discussion of these internal reports is beyond the scope of this text.

Debt investors are interested in a business's ability to meet payments of interest and principal as they fall due. They also want assurance that the business has adhered to agreements and stipulations made at the time credit was extended. Prospective lenders must determine a business's capacity for debt and the degree of risk involved.

Governmental units, local, state, and federal, require information from businesses in connection with legal regulations of their activities, administration of tax laws, and the collection of economic statistics. Investment brokers and counselors make the same decisions made by owners and creditors either in their own behalf or as representatives of other parties. Employees and their representatives are interested in job security and the potential for improving working conditions and pay scales.

Trade associations accumulate, classify, and distribute industry statistics for the benefit of enterprises within the industry. Customers and the general public want assurances that prices are fair and that the sources of supply are dependable.

Financial statements are usually the most important single source of information available to external parties who are interested in a business's activities. Financial statements are normally prepared and released on an annual basis. Corporations, whose shares are traded on organized security exchanges such as the New York Stock Exchange and the American Stock Exchange, are required to issue interim financial statements quarterly. Recall from the discussion in Chapter 1 that there exists a body of "generally accepted accounting principles" that governs the measurement of income and net worth. These principles are derived primarily from custom, but also from the pronouncements of various professional organizations and governmental bodies (see pp. 13–16). Generally accepted accounting principles must be followed in the preparation of the annual financial statements also. Before turning to a discussion of the principles that relate to the preparation of financial statements, the role of the independent auditor in the preparation of financial statements must be considered.

Financial Statements and the Auditor

Federal security laws provide that the annual financial statements of corporations whose securities are traded in interstate commerce be audited by an independent accountant. The security laws in many states also require an annual audit for some corporations. Annual audits are performed by a firm of independent accountants who, with a few exceptions, are qualified to practice as certified public accountants. At the completion of an audit, the independent accountant issues an *opinion* about the financial statements which he has examined. Figure 5-1 is an actual opinion, issued by the accounting firm, Peat, Marwick, Mitchell & Co., covering the financial statements of Green Giant Company for the accounting period ended March 31, 1971.

Figure 5-1

Accountants' Report

The Board of Directors and Stockholders
Green Giant Company:

We have examined the statement of financial position of Green Giant Company and subsidiaries as of March 31, 1971 and 1970 and the related statements of earnings and retained earnings and source and application of funds for the respective years then ended. Our examination was made in accordance with generally accepted auditing standards, and accordingly included such tests of the accounting records and such other auditing procedures as we considered necessary in the circumstances.

In our opinion, such financial statements present fairly the financial position of Green Giant Company and subsidiaries at March 31, 1971 and 1970 and the results of their operations and source and application of their funds for the respective years then ended, in conformity with generally accepted accounting principles applied on a consistent basis.

Minneapolis, Minnesota
May 7, 1971

Peat, Marwick, Mitchell & Co.

Reprinted from the 1971 financial statements of Green Giant Company and Subsidiaries.

The opinion in Fig. 5-1 is commonly called an *unqualified opinion* because the second paragraph states that the financial statements "present fairly" the financial position and the results of operations. The unqualified opinion indicates that the auditors are satisfied with the accounting system of the company and the financial statements based on their records and measurements. The unqualified opinion is most common and is referred to as the standard auditor's opinion.

In a few cases, a middle paragraph might be inserted in the standard opinion expressing doubt or disagreement over the value assigned to some accruals or deferrals or over the treatment of an investment transaction. In a *qualified opinion*, the final paragraph might then be altered to read: "In our opinion, except for the treatment of [the excepted item] discussed above, the statements present fairly . . ." Occasionally the examination by the auditor will lead to the expression of an *adverse opinion* in which the auditor will express his belief that the financial statements do not fairly present the financial position and the results of operations. On still other occasions, the report will contain a *disclaimer of opinion* when the auditor has been unable to obtain sufficient evidence to justify an unqualified, qualified, or adverse opinion.

Users of published financial statements should always begin with the auditor's report. The auditor's opinion is the best index of the reliability of the statements. The auditor's opinion has value because of the standards observed by independent accountants in the performance of their duties.

Auditing and Reporting Standards

The introduction to accounting principles in the first four chapters has shown that there is no single, comprehensive set of rules governing the accounting measurements and financial statements for all businesses. Alternative practices may be followed, depending on the circumstances. For example, revenue may be recognized on the sales basis, cash basis, or production basis. Other important alternatives exist for the computation of deferred costs of plant and equipment as well as inventories. In addition, accountants will differ over the monetary values assigned to the various accruals and deferrals. Measurement of accruals and deferrals often depends on the estimation of future events, and thus there is room for considerable difference of opinion. For example, What is the estimated life of a building? How much cash will be collected on the accounts receivable?

Because of the many alternatives that exist in accounting and because the value of accruals and deferrals must be based on future events, in the absence of precise rules, the accounting profession has developed some broad guidelines called *standards*. In forming his opinion on the financial statements of a company, the independent auditor does not apply precise rules and tests. He must, however, make certain that his work and the financial statements conform to the standards.

The unqualified opinion in Fig. 5–1 contains four key phrases which refer to auditing and reporting standards:

1   In accordance with *generally accepted auditing standards*
2   *Presents fairly*
3   In conformity with *generally accepted accounting principles*
4   Applied on a *consistent basis*

The statement user must have some appreciation of the standards observed by independent accountants in order to know how much reliance he may place on the audited financial statements.

An independent accountant's opinion containing a qualification may be found on p. 541 of Appendix D, where the auditor's opinion is qualified relative to the consistent application of accounting principles. Note that the final phrase of the second paragraph reads "in conformity with generally accepted auditing principles applied on a consistent basis during the period after restatement of the 1970 consolidated balance sheet as explained in Note 7." If you refer to Note 7, entitled "Long-Term Construction Contracts," you will find an explanation of the change and the effects of the change on the balance sheet items. (Treatment of long-term construction contracts is covered in Chapter 10.) The independent accountant's report must be carefully read to be sure that there are no qualifications relative to the four auditing and reporting standards discussed above.

AUDITING STANDARDS. The first paragraph of the auditor's opinion is commonly referred to as the scope paragraph. It describes the work done by the auditor in very general terms. The paragraph states that the financial statements were "examined" and that the examination was made in accordance with "generally accepted auditing standards." The auditing standards are concerned with the professional competence of the auditor, with independence of attitude, and with the amount of evidence gathered during the examination.

• Competence: To meet the auditing standards, the accountants conducting the examination must have adequate training and experience in accounting and auditing. This standard generally means that one or more of the accountants are CPA's. When assistants are used who are not certified, they must be closely supervised by the licensed (certified) accountant.

• Independence: The accountants conducting the examination must maintain an independent attitude toward the business under examination. The auditor cannot own stock in the company or be an officer or director of the company. Family and close financial relationships between the auditor and a shareholder, officer, or director of a company normally impair the auditor's independence. In addition, the independent accountant must use due care in the conduct of the examination.

• Sufficient Evidential Matter: An audit conducted in accordance with generally accepted auditing standards is one in which the auditor exercised professional care and obtained enough evidence or facts to sustain the opinion rendered on the financial statements. The kind and amount of evidence obtained in an examination varies widely depending on the circumstances. Three types of evidence obtained in virtually every audit are

1 Confirmation of cash balances in banks by direct correspondence between the bank and the auditor
2 Confirmation of the balance of accounts receivable. Confirmation is obtained by corresponding directly with some of the debtors to make sure the claim exists and that the amount of the claim is correct.
3 Physical observation of inventories by the auditor

Note that this evidence is concerned with the crucial asset, cash, and with some important accruals and deferrals.

REPORTING STANDARDS. The second paragraph in the auditor's report is called the opinion paragraph. The key phrases in this paragraph refer to the reporting standards that guide the profession.

• Present fairly: In an unqualified opinion, the auditor must state that the financial statements are a fair presentation of the company's financial position (balance sheet), the results of the operations (income statement), and the changes in financial position (statement of changes in financial position). Fair presentation means that there has been *fair disclosure* of all relevant facts. A fact is considered relevant if there is reason to believe that the people who use the financial statements, and who are reasonably well informed about financial matters, will be influenced by the information. The person using the statements must have some assurance that he is not being misled by the omission of vital information. That the information included is not in error is not enough. Under the convention of fair disclosure, all relevant information must be included.

Information that is not an integral part of the body of an accounting report but that has a bearing on conclusions an informed user would draw from the report should be disclosed in notes to the financial statements. Sometimes it is necessary to include notes about events that take place after the close of the accounting period. For example, a balance sheet of a business dated December 31 might not be prepared until February of the following year. If a fire destroyed half of the business's assets during the month of January, a prominent disclosure of the extent of the fire damage must be included in the balance sheet even if the fire took place after the balance sheet date. A good illustration of an informative note necessary for fair disclosure is Note 9 of the financial statements of the Green Giant Company on p. 517 of Appendix D. The note is entitled "Pending Acquisitions" and it informs the statement user that sometime after the end of Green Giant's accounting period, March 31, 1971, the company is committed to acquire two other corporations. The note goes on to give information about the acquisitions, including the shares and other securities of Green Giant that will be issued to acquire the new companies and the size and profitability of the companies to be acquired. Additional information such as this could influence some investor who is trying to make a decision to buy or sell the stock of the Green Giant Company.

Fair disclosure requires complete reporting of material information and appropriate classification and summarization of this information. Of course, the financial statements cannot disclose every financial event that occurs during the accounting period. The standard of fair disclosure must be qualified by the convention of *materiality*. The accountant is required to disclose only material events; trivial happenings, which would clutter up the statements and make the cost of preparing financial statements prohibitive, may be ignored.

To determine whether a given fact is material, the accountant must consider both its absolute and relative importance. For example, assume that you are examining the financial statements of a corporation that has revenue of $1,000,000 for the year and expenses of $900,000. Included in the expense total is $250 for ball point pens and similar items which are given away to customers. The expense of $250 has been classified as an office supply expense. The cost of the pens is more accurately described as advertising expense. To correct the error, however, would not materially change the results because the amount is insignificant *relative* to total expense. Now suppose that the revenue is $1,000,000,000, that expenses are $900,000,000, and that $250,000 has been incorrectly classified as office supply expense. The relative importance of the error is the same; but the $250,000 is large in absolute terms, and some correction may be required. There are no precise rules that the accountant can rely on to determine whether an item is or is not material. He must exercise his independent judgment in each case.

GENERALLY ACCEPTED ACCOUNTING PRINCIPLES. Financial statements must conform to generally accepted accounting principles. Remember that these principles include many alternative practices and that the judgment of the accountant concerning future events affects the valuation placed on accruals and deferrals. This standard does mean that the accountant is *not* free to use any imaginable practice. He must follow the customary rules and the standard of fair disclosure requires him to disclose the practice followed.

CONSISTENCY. A final reporting standard is consistency. This standard is important because of the many alternative principles which the accountant may use. Once a business adopts a given accounting method or procedure, the business must continue to use it in subsequent accounting periods. The purpose of this standard is to make the accounting reports of a given business for a given accounting period comparable to the accounting reports of that same business for other accounting periods.

Interperiod comparison is one of the basic techniques used to make decisions about a business operation. By comparing the income statements of several years, for example, we can determine if the income is relatively stable or if the general trend is an increase or decrease in income. The financial statements for one accounting period do not afford a sound basis for most decisions. For this reason, generally accepted accounting principles specify that the financial statements include information for the current period and the preceding period as a minimum standard. Without the standard of consistency, the necessary interperiod comparisons would be less reliable as a basis for decisions.

Fair disclosure and consistency together lessen the confusion caused by the existence of alternative methods and procedures. The accountant consistently adheres to a given method or procedure once adopted and he discloses in the financial reports exactly which methods and procedures are being consistently applied. Sometimes there are good and sufficient reasons for failing to follow a practice consistently. If a change in methods or procedures becomes necessary, fair disclosure takes on additional significance. The accountant must disclose the following when there is a change in method or procedure:

1 The original method or procedure
2 The newly adopted method or procedure
3 The reason for the change
4 Effects of the change on the financial reports, especially on the amount of income

Taken together, the existence of these reporting standards—fair disclosure of material facts, adherence to generally accepted accounting principles, and consistency—gives the statement user assurance of the reliability of financial statements.

Conservatism

Accountants prefer to present their findings on the basis of facts; they try to present information that is objective and verifiable. The facts about the operations of business, like all other facts about human actions and natural phenomena, are not easily determined. As in other fields, objectivity and verifiability are relative terms. A fact is objective and verifiable if two independent observers reach essentially the same conclusions. For example, the cash paid for services, evidenced by an invoice, contract or receipt, is a relatively objective fact which can be verified by independent observers.

As previously explained, sometimes the accountant faces situations where more than one alternative permits objectivity and verifiability to an equal degree. When facing a choice between such alternatives, accountants frequently handle the dilemma by choosing an alternative that is pessimistic with respect to asset valuation and income determination. This tendency on the part of accountants to use pessimistic values is referred to as conservatism. This does not mean that accountants intentionally understate and overstate values; it means only that when presented with a range of possible values they traditionally favor the pessimistic. Where uncertainties about values exist, the lower values are assigned to assets and revenue, and the higher values are assigned to liabilities and expenses.

In the past, accountants were often ultraconservative. They intentionally understated assets and revenues, and they overstated liabilities and expenses. Emphasis was placed on the amount of cash that could be realized in the event of liquidation. Accounting reports were prepared primarily for bankers granting short-term credit to the business, and their interest was in the *liquidity* of the company. The bankers wanted to know if the company would have sufficient cash to repay the debt even if the manager's expectations for profits failed to materialize. This viewpoint is essentially a short-term interest in the value of the business's assets.

In recent years, greater emphasis has been placed on the information needed by stockholders and long-term creditors. These parties are less interested in the immediate value of resources owned by the firm than short-term credit grantors. Instead, stockholders and long-term creditors are interested in the long-term profitability of the operations—the expected future income. As a result ultraconservative valuations are not generally accepted as good accounting practice. Nevertheless, when judgment and estimation are required and there is a possibility of error, accountants still prefer to err on the pessimistic side.

Choosing cost as the appropriate index of asset valuation rather than other, more optimistic standards is a good example of a conservative practice. Consider, for example, a corporation that purchases land for $100,000. If the value of the land increases to $150,000, and the corporation continues to hold it, no accounting action is taken. The asset is still shown at $100,000, the deferred cost; no gain or revenue is recognized until the land is sold and the gain realized. The convention of conservatism leads the accountant to anticipate *no* gains but to anticipate losses. The statement user who is not aware of the traditional conservatism of accountants can often draw incorrect conclusions about the operations of a business.

Form and Content of the Statement of Income

Prior to the Great Depression of the 1930s, many corporations released only balance sheet information. Absentee owners of American corporations had very little, if any, information about revenue and expenses of their companies. After the market plunge in 1929, many people were convinced that corporations should publish a statement of income or statement of profit and loss. The belief was widely held at the time that with more information investors in corporate securities would establish a "better" price in the market and the market would not fluctuate as wildly as it did in the 1920s. Because of this sentiment, the federal government and most states passed laws aimed at regulating the information released by corporations to shareholders and the general public. An important effect of these laws was to force corporations to publish information about income.

Smaller businesses that depended primarily on bank credit for capital were reluctant to issue information about income. Bankers and other lending institutions did not wish to offend their customers by asking them how much money they were making. But with the widespread publication of income information by corporations, the taboo was removed, and banks now expect their borrowers to provide both a balance sheet and a statement of income.

The statement of income provides facts the investor or lender may use for judging the economic activities of a business. Analysis of a business based on income will be illustrated at the end of this chapter.

Content of the Statement of Income

The content of the statement of income has been the principal subject of the earlier chapters of this book. The concepts discussed in Chapters 2 and 3 deal primarily with income determination. For example, the unit of accounting is the *business entity*, which is considered distinct and separate from owners and other interested parties. The raw materials of accounting are the *transactions* of the business entity. The basic transactions are investments, acquisitions of services, combinations of services, disposition of services, and cash collections. Income measurement is based on the assumption, a valid one for most businesses, that the enterprise will continue to operate indefinitely. *Continuity* of enterprise is the basis for many accruals and deferrals in the income computation. For example, depreciation of a building over its estimated useful life would be nonsense unless one assumed that the business would continue for at least that long. The idea that most businesses will continue to operate indefinitely is also referred to as the *going concern* concept. Continuity of enterprise is one factor in our economic environment that creates the problem of *periodicity*. If we assume an indefinite life for the business, interim or periodic measures of operations are essential; we cannot wait indefinitely to find out how the venture is going. Periodic measurement of income, in turn, leads to the adjustments of cash flow for accruals and deferrals. Without these adjustments, periodic cash flow would fluctuate widely and have little value as a measure of operating efficiency.

The following discussion of revenue and expense and of the matching concept is a brief review of the basic concepts of income measurement introduced and illustrated in Chapters 2 and 3. Students who do not understand this summary should reread and study those earlier chapters.

REVENUE AND EXPENSES. Revenue is an entity's inflow of cash (or other assets that are easily converted to cash) from customers in return for goods or services furnished by the business. The accountant recognizes only realized revenues in his calculations of an entity's income. Expense is the outflow of assets associated with realized revenue: the cost of services used up or transferred to the customer in order to earn revenue. Broadly speaking, revenue is a monetary measure of an entity's accomplishment, and expense is the monetary measure of an entity's effort.

Accountants do not recognize revenue until it is realized. *Realization* for accounting purposes takes place only after the following three requirements, which were discussed in Chapter 3, are met:

1   The business entity must have a transaction with an outside party.
2   The entity must receive cash or other money resources readily convertible into cash.
3   The goods and/or services transferred to the outside party must have reached a satisfactory degree of completeness. In short, the revenue must be earned.

In the typical case, all three of these requirements are met at the point of sale. At the time of sale the entity usually receives cash or a money resource that is easily converted to cash in a short period of time. A sale is a transaction with an outside party; and the entity usually delivers a completed product or service to the customer at the point of sale.

MATCHING CONCEPT. Matching is the process of comparing an entity's effort or expense (the cost of services used up to supply goods and services to customers) to its accomplishment, that is, realized revenue. Although effort precedes accomplishment chronologically, the two are compared in reverse order. The accountant first applies the three requirements for revenue realization to determine the amount of revenue for the accounting period. Next he determines the cost of services used up to produce that amount of realized revenue. He then compares the two and calculates income.

Certain expenses can be matched with revenue on a transaction basis. The cost-flow assumption permits the accountant to trace costs to the services transferred to customers and this cost outflow or expense can be matched against the revenue realized from the transaction. Costs that are traced and matched against revenue transactions are frequently called **product costs**. It is not always practical or necessary to trace costs to individual transactions. The periodicity concept permits matching on the basis of time. Once the accountant determines the amount of revenue realized in an accounting period, he can then estimate the cost of services used up during that same accounting period and match revenue and expenses on a period basis. Costs that are considered to be expenses because they were used in a period are called **period costs** (see Chapter 11).

Form of the Statement of Income

Two basic formats are used to report revenues, expenses, and income. One form of the income statement is referred to as the single-step statement, and the second format as the multiple-step statement.

SINGLE-STEP STATEMENT. An example of a single-step statement is shown in Fig. 5–2. Note that all revenues are grouped and totaled, all expenses are grouped and totaled, and one subtraction is made to obtain net income. This format is identical to that illustrated in Chapter 3.

Figure 5–2

H Company	Statement of Income for Year Ended December 31, 19X1	
Revenues:		
Revenue from sales	$310,000	
Interest earned	5,000	$315,000
Expenses:		
Cost of goods sold	$ 60,000	
Salaries and wages	110,000	
Depreciation	40,000	
Advertising	20,000	
Insurance	6,000	
Utilities	12,000	
Taxes	20,000	
Interest	10,000	
Miscellaneous	4,000	282,000
Net income		$ 33,000

A good illustration of an actual single-step statement is that of the Green Giant Company on p. 513 of Appendix D. Note the statement is entitled a "Statement of Earnings and Retained Earnings" because it includes the computation of the new balance of retained earnings at the bottom. On the upper portion, revenue from sales is shown as one amount. All expenses are grouped together and their total is subtracted from revenue to arrive at income, referred to as net earnings by this company.

MULTIPLE-STEP STATEMENT. The simple format of the single-step statement is not widely used by practicing accountants. Traditionally, expenses have
been deducted in a series of steps that gives some intermediate remainders. The
procedure followed on the multiple-step statement is to make an addition or
subtraction for a single item and thereby direct the reader's attention to the
expense and to the remainder. Two items commonly singled out for special presentation are cost of goods sold and income taxes. An example of a simple
multiple-step statement is shown in Fig. 5-3.

Figure 5-3

T Corporation	Statement of Income for Year Ended December 31, 19X1	
Revenue from sales		$950,000
Cost of goods sold		522,000
Gross profit on sales		$428,000
Operating expenses:		
Selling expenses	$148,000	
General and administrative expense	94,000	
Depreciation	40,000	
Interest expense	12,000	294,000
Net income before income taxes		$134,000
State and federal income taxes		62,000
Net income		$ 72,000

When the multiple-step format is used, the intermediate remainders (before
net income) can be useful to the statement user. The remainder after subtracting cost of goods sold, a product cost, from sales revenue is called **gross profit**
or **gross margin**. In some industries, the gross profit can be helpful for intercompany comparisons to indicate operating efficiency and market strength.
Income taxes, a period cost, are commonly treated separately to highlight the
portion of the income that must be paid to governmental units. The management of the company cannot control tax rates, to include tax expense with
the other operating expenses fails to call attention to what the income might be
in the absence of the tax. Note that this fact is highlighted by calling the intermediate remainder "net income **before** income taxes."

The treatment of cost of goods sold and income taxes in Fig. 5-3 is only one
example. Under different circumstances, accountants might choose other items
of revenue and expense for separate treatment on the multiple-step statement.
Some accountants will wish to provide more information about expenses. The
caption "selling expenses" might be further detailed as salaries, commissions,
advertising, etc. General and administrative expenses could be similarly displayed. Detailed expense breakdowns are not usually provided, however, on
financial statements issued to the public.

EXTRAORDINARY ITEMS.* There is one group of revenue and expense items that must be treated separately on the statement of income, even where the accountant elects to use the single-step format for all other revenues and expenses. The revenues and expenses that must be treated separately are called *special, extraordinary,* or *nonrecurring* transactions. Opinion No. 9 of the Accounting Principles Board of the American Institute of Certified Public Accountants defines extraordinary items in the following way:

They will be of a character significantly different from the typical or customery business activity of the entity. Accordingly, they will be events and transactions of material effect which would not be expected to recur frequently and which would not be considered as recurring factors in any evaluation of the ordinary operating processes of the business.

Opinion No. 9 goes on to list the following examples of extraordinary transactions:

Examples of extraordinary items . . . include material gains or losses (or provisions for losses) from (a) the sale or abandonment of a plant or a significant segment of the business, (b) the sale of an investment not acquired for resale, (c) the write-off of goodwill due to unusual events or developments within the period, (d) the condemnation or expropriation of properties and (e) a major devaluation of a foreign currency.

It is important to note from this list of examples that extraordinary items must be material in amount, not connected with the normal operations of the business, and events that occur only rarely. Such extraordinary items are segregated from the other revenues and expenses and are shown at the bottom of the statement.

As an example of the presentation of these items, assume that the T Corporation, whose statement of income is shown at Fig. 5-3, sold a plant (land and buildings) during 19X1. The sales price was $100,000, the revenue from the sale. The deferred cost of the plant (original cost not yet included in depreciation expense) at the time of the sale was $65,000. Gain or profit would be

Sales price	$100,000
Deferred cost	65,000
Gain on sale	$ 35,000

The $35,000 gain is clearly a material amount relative to the net income of $72,000 (Fig. 5-3). This transaction is, therefore, an extraordinary item and must be shown separately at the bottom of the statement.

Typical treatment of such unusual sales is to net the revenue from the sale and the deferred cost and show only the gain (or loss if the deferred costs exceed the revenue realized at disposition). In addition, the extraordinary gains and losses are shown net of their effect on the income taxes. If we assume, for example, that T Corporation must pay an income tax of $10,500 on the

*At the time of this writing the Accounting Principles Board is deliberating a change in the definition of extraordinary items. The outcome could substantially alter the discussion of extraordinary items here, especially in Chapters 5, 6, and 7. Check with your instructor for the most up-to-date information.

$35,000 gain, the net economic gain after income taxes would be $24,500 ($35,000 − $10,500).* Extraordinary gains and losses are shown net of income tax because they appear at the bottom of the statement, after the income tax on the recurring operating income has been deducted.

To report the extraordinary item, the following section would be added at the bottom of Fig. 5–3:

Income before extraordinary items	$72,000
Add: gain on the sale of plant and equipment	
(net of income taxes of $10,500)	24,500
Net income including extraordinary items	$96,500

In the preceding example, note that the gain on the disposition, which was the difference between the revenue from the sale and the deferred cost of the plant, was reduced by the income tax that must be paid on the gain. The net amount of $24,500 is the final economic gain, that is, revenue less deferred cost and tax liability. Note that the income tax, where a property disposition results in a loss, has the same effect as disposition at a gain—the income tax reduces the economic effect of the loss. For example, assume that the plant of T Corporation with a deferred cost of $65,000 sold for a price of $20,000. The loss would be $45,000 before the tax effect. If the deduction of the loss on the T Corporation's federal tax return reduced the tax by $21,600, the net economic effect of the loss would be only $23,400 (the $45,000 loss less the reduction in taxes due to the loss of $21,600).** The extraordinary item would then be shown as

Income before extraordinary items	$72,000
Loss on sale of plant and equipment (net of	
income tax reduction of $21,600)	23,400
Net income including extraordinary items	$48,600

The segregation of the unusual, nonrecurring gains and losses is important to the statement user. By definition, these gains and losses cannot be expected in the future. The amount used to predict future income is, therefore, the income before extraordinary items.

Figure 5–4 is an actual reproduction of the income statement for A. O. Smith Corporation for the years ended December 31, 1970 and 1971. Note that the word "consolidated" appears in the heading. Some business operations include several corporations. In such cases a *parent* corporation will hold a controlling interest in its *subsidiary* corporations. Despite the existence of more than one corporation, the entire operations of the business are reported as if they were carried on by a single entity. The statements of the parent and its subsidiaries

---

*The tax of $10,500 would be the federal income tax on the gain, assuming the gain qualified for capital gain treatment.

**The tax effect of $21,600 is based on the assumption that the loss would reduce ordinary income which is taxed at 48% generally. The tax reduction would be 48% of the $45,000 loss, or $21,600.

Figure 5-4: Statement of Income

A. O. SMITH CORPORATION	1970	1971	
CONSOLIDATED STATEMENTS OF EARNINGS AND RETAINED EARNINGS			**EARNINGS**
	$413,097,543	**$456,845,662**	NET SALES
Years ended December 31, 1970 and 1971			OPERATING COSTS AND EXPENSES:
	358,911,167	**392,657,178**	Cost of goods sold
	34,375,607	**36,767,912**	Selling, general and administrative
	393,286,774	**429,425,090**	
	19,810,769	**27,420,572**	PROFIT FROM OPERATIONS
			OTHER INCOME (deductions):
	(4,224,122)	**(5,672,414)**	Interest expense
	2,337,701	**1,867,182**	Miscellaneous—net
	(1,886,421)	**(3,805,232)**	
	17,924,348	**23,615,340**	EARNINGS BEFORE INCOME TAXES
	8,900,000	**11,400,000**	PROVISION FOR INCOME TAXES (1971 after investment tax credits, flow through method, of $475,000)
	9,024,348	**12,215,340**	EARNINGS BEFORE EQUITY IN EARNINGS (LOSSES) OF UNCONSOLIDATED AFFILIATES AND EXTRAORDINARY ITEMS
	(1,737,344)	**592,886**	EQUITY IN EARNINGS (LOSSES) OF UNCONSOLIDATED AFFILIATES—NET
	7,287,004	**12,808,226**	EARNINGS BEFORE EXTRAORDINARY ITEMS
	2,146,000	**(1,760,000)**	EXTRAORDINARY ITEMS, net of applicable income taxes (Note 5)
	$ 9,433,004	**$ 11,048,226**	NET EARNINGS
			PER SHARE OF COMMON STOCK:
	$2.95	**$5.23**	Earnings before extraordinary items
	.87	**(.72)**	Extraordinary items
	$3.82	**$4.51**	Net earnings
			RETAINED EARNINGS
	$101,197,733	**$107,174,231**	BALANCE AT BEGINNING OF YEAR
	9,433,004	**11,048,226**	NET EARNINGS
	110,630,737	**118,222,457**	
	3,456,506	**3,430,865**	CASH DIVIDENDS, $1.40 per share
	$107,174,231	**$114,791,592**	BALANCE AT END OF YEAR (Note 3)

See accompanying notes.

Reprinted from the 1971 financial statement of A. O. Smith Corporation.

are combined or consolidated. Accounting procedures for consolidation will be discussed in Chapter 16.

The statement of income of A. O. Smith Corporation is something of a hybrid—it is not a single-step statement but also not a typical multiple-step statement because the cost of goods sold is not subtracted as a separate item. The income tax expense and net earnings (and losses) from subsidiaries not included in the consolidated statements are subtracted individually. Note that the last item before "net earning" is "extraordinary items, net of applicable income taxes." A description of what these items consist of can be found in Note 5 to the statements reproduced on p. 540 of Appendix D.

Finally, it is important to note, at the bottom of the statement of income, the way in which the information about retained earnings is handled: The beginning balance is added to net income (net earnings) for the year and dividends are deducted to arrive at the ending balance, which appears on the balance sheet.

Use of the Statement of Income in Financial Analysis

The starting point for the computation of both revenue and expense is cash flow or cash receipts and disbursements. Apart from the elimination of investment transactions, the other two adjustments, accruals and deferrals, are timing adjustments. Accruals and deferrals arise because some cash transactions do not occur in the same accounting period as the critical accounting events, the earning of revenue and the utilization of services. This definition of income can be usefully characterized as *adjusted cash flow*. The net income is the cash flow from operations (after excluding investment transactions) that would have resulted if cash had been collected at the point of sale and if cash had been disbursed only when services were consumed.

Viewed in this manner, net income can be used as a fairly reliable predictor of what future cash flows will be. If we *assume* that the conditions that prevailed in the past years will continue into the future, the net income or adjusted cash flow of future periods can be predicted with some degree of accuracy. Admittedly, the assumption just made is a large order. To predict future income based on past results, trends of the past must continue into the future for many variables such as product sales, sales prices, labor efficiency, wages, and taxes. All of these factors *do*, in fact, vary, and the variances will cause the future income to deviate from the predicted amount. Despite this fact, conditions in the *near* future of a business will be reasonably similar to the past in many cases, and income can be used as a predictor of future cash flow. If future changes can be predicted, then past income can be adjusted to provide a more adequate predictor.

Future net cash flow is the single most important fact in assessing a business: cash must be used for the dividends of shareholders; cash must be used to pay off long-term liabilities; cash is the item required for wage increases, for research on new products, for expansion of plant and other facilities, and for payment of taxes. In short, the future growth (success) of the company depends on its ability to collect more cash from operations than it spends on operations. If used with care, the income figure can serve as a basis for predicting future cash flow.

The typical uses of the statement of income in financial analysis are discussed in the following sections. Before proceeding to this discussion, however, one final word of caution is necessary: Financial statements audited by independent accountants are reliable information but subject to the limitations inherent in the accounting process. Many accruals and deferrals are based on estimates of future events. In addition, the tendency toward conservative valuation on the part of accountants often results in understatement of income and asset values. And, finally, the terms used on the balance sheet (assets, liabilities, equities, etc.) have precise definitions in accounting which do not always agree with the common usage of these terms.

Comparative Statements of Income

A common use of the statement of income is a comparison of the business's operating results for the present period with the results of the preceding periods. These *intracompany* comparisons can be made based on the *absolute* amounts that appear on a series of statements of income. Potential investors' or creditors' prediction of future income is usually more reliable if based on several periods rather than a single period. As mentioned earlier, the audited financial statements of a business usually will show statements of income for two years, the current and preceding year. In addition, the annual reports to stockholders of most large corporations show operating statistics for an extended period— seldom less than five years and often for ten or more. Operating information provided usually includes revenues, operating expenses, and net income. Financial reporting services, such as *Moody's* and *Standard and Poor's*, also provide historical data on operations for an extended period.

A line graph is an efficient method of showing trends in intracompany comparisons of operating results. The line graph in Fig. 5–5 shows the history of revenues and operating expenses for a ten-year period, and the area between the two lines is the history of net income. Various statistical methods are available for the projection of these historical data into future operations. Historical comparisons (interperiod) of absolute amounts can only be made for a single company (intracompany). When comparisons are made between companies (intercompany), operating results must be converted to ratios. Preparation of a common-size statement of income facilitates such comparisons.

Figure 5–5: Line Graph Showing Trends in Operating Results

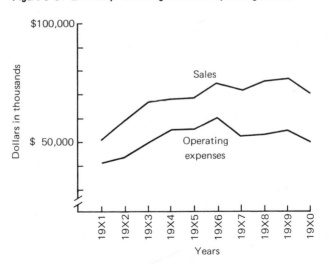

Common-Size Statement of Income

Figure 5–6 is a multiple-step statement of income which includes a common-size statement. The statement also shows a typical breakdown of selling expenses and general and administrative expenses. A cursory glance at the actual statements of income in Appendix D (pp. 483, 496, 506, 513, 527, 535) shows that reports for external parties rarely show as much detail concerning expenses as is included in Fig. 5–6. The column to the right of the absolute amounts shows the ratio of each amount on the statement to revenue from sales. For example, cost of goods sold is shown as 60 percent of the revenue from sales:

$$\frac{\text{Cost of goods sold}}{\text{Revenue from sales}} = \frac{\$180,000}{\$300,000} = \$0.60$$

Figure 5–6: Common-Size Statement of Income

G Company	Statement of Income for Year Ended December 31, 19X1	
	Amount	Percent of sales
Revenue from sales	$300,000	100.0%
Cost of goods sold	180,000	60.0
Gross profit on sales	$120,000	40.0
Operating expenses		
Selling expenses:		
Salaries and commissions	$ 30,000	10.0
Advertising expense	12,000	4.0
Depreciation of fixtures	8,000	2.7
Depreciation of building	3,000	1.0
Delivery expense	7,000	2.3
Store supplies	2,000	0.7
Miscellaneous expenses	1,000	0.3
Total selling expense	$ 63,000	21.0
General and administrative expenses:		
Office salaries	10,000	3.3
Depreciation of building	3,000	1.0
Depreciation of office furniture	4,000	1.3
Taxes	3,000	1.0
Bad debts	2,000	0.7
Insurance	2,000	0.7
Utilities	2,000	0.7
Miscellaneous expense	1,000	0.3
Total general and administrative expenses	$ 27,000	9.0
Total operating expense	$ 90,000	30.0
Net income before income taxes	$ 30,000	10.0
Federal and state income taxes	12,000	4.0
Net income	$ 18,000	6.0

The ratio is converted to a percentage by multiplying by 100. The statement user can also determine at a glance just how much of each sales dollar was required to cover cost of sales, income taxes, and other expense items. A common-size statement is a useful aid in making interperiod comparisons within a single company. By comparing the percentage of an expense item for several years, the analyst can determine how the expense item is affected by changes in sales revenue. Some expenses change roughly in proportion to a change in sales. Cost of goods sold, for example, will normally increase if sales revenue increases— more services must be acquired if sales are to increase. Other expenses remain relatively fixed in amount, for example, depreciation on long-lived assets. Recognition of the characteristics of the various expenses, revealed in part by the common-size statement, is an essential step in the prediction of future income.

The ratios displayed on the common-size statement of income are a necessary part of intercompany (more than one company) comparisons. Most analysts, shareholders, or potential investors are seeking an answer to the general question: Is the company successful? This question can only be answered in a relative way because there are no hard and fast definitions of success. If a useful answer is to be obtained, the question must be rephrased: How do the operations of the company compare with those of other companies? Comparison of the operations of two companies in different industries is a risky and complicated undertaking. However, comparisons between companies in the same industry (intraindustry), as well as the interperiod comparisons for the same company can be based on the ratios that appear on the common-size statement. The ratios normally used for such intraindustry comparisons are the gross profit ratio and return on sales.

GROSS PROFIT RATIO. This ratio is computed as follows:

$$\frac{\text{Gross profit}}{\text{Revenue from sales}} = \text{Gross profit ratio}$$

This ratio is widely used as a standard of performance in retail and wholesale operations. It provides a basis for comparing the efficiency of the merchandising operations. In a chain of dry good stores, for example, a good manager might be expected to "gross" 30%, meaning his gross profit ratio for the year should be 30%. To meet this standard, the manager must buy merchandise that can be sold in a reasonable time at a good markup. If the manager repeatedly makes unwise purchases, and markdowns are necessary to sell the merchandise, his gross profit percentage will be lower.

Within a given trade, the standard for a "good" gross profit ratio is common knowledge. In addition, Robert Morris Associates periodically compiles actual averages of many operating ratios from retail and wholesale trades. A person with only limited knowledge of a given type of retail or wholesale operation can obtain a rough idea of standards from this publication.

Gross profit comparisons are useful only when the businesses compared have very similar operations. Comparisons of gross profit between manufacturing operations is risky because of the diversity of operations. One electronics company may manufacture radios, televisions, and aerospace components, whereas another firm within the same general industry may concentrate on electronic kitchen utensils and military equipment. Indeed, most manufacturing corporations have widely diversified product lines.

RETURN ON SALES. A second important ratio is

$$\frac{\text{Net income}}{\text{Revenue from sales}} = \text{Return on sales}$$

For the G Company statement of income (Fig. 5–6), the return on sales is .06 (or 6%). Because our income tax laws may affect two companies in radically different ways, analysts often use net income before income taxes as the numerator and thereby improve the comparability of the ratio.

Like the gross profit ratio, standards exist for a "good net" within each retail and wholesale line. Return on sales is a more general measure of efficiency than the gross profit ratio because all operating expenses are being compared.

What constitutes a good net varies widely among industries. A well-managed chain of food stores may net only 2 percent whereas a good furniture store may net from 12 to 15 percent. Thus, interindustry comparisons of this ratio do not tell us much about the efficiency of the operation. Like the gross profit ratio, return on sales must be used carefully in the analysis of most manufacturing operations because of the diversified operations of many corporations. For example, the products of LTV, Inc., a so-called *conglomerate* corporation, range from aerospace products to sporting goods, from meat packing to steel production. Comparison of the gross profit percentages of a corporation such as LTV, Inc. with another corporation with a completely different group of products has only limited usefulness.

The Securities Exchange Commission already requires businesses with more than one product line (or line of business) to report separately the results of operation for each product line (or line of business) within the corporation. This requirement applies only to the annual reports which every company under its jurisdiction must file with the SEC. As this book is in preparation, the AICPA is considering divisional or product line reporting of operating results as a requirement for all financial statements prepared for external users. If this change is made, gross profit comparisons by product lines will be possible even for diversified corporations.

Net Income and Corporate Shares

We have previously discussed the importance of the corporate form of organization in our economic system. By using this type of business organization, corporate managers are able to assemble large amounts of capital from the sale of capital stock to absentee owners. Once issued by the corporation, the shares can be traded between shareholders without interrupting corporate operations. If a shareholder no longer wishes to participate in a corporation, he does not withdraw his capital; he merely sells his shares to another absentee owner. The markets for corporate shares are highly organized and are subject to fairly stringent regulations.

After a corporation issues or sells its shares in the market, subsequent trading in the stock has no direct effect on the accounting records of the issuing corporation. For example, a corporation may issue a million new shares of stock and receive $10 per share or $10,000,000. This transaction is an investment by owners (OI). The same shares will normally be traded later among shareholders at other prices. If the corporation is successful over a period of years, the price of its shares will usually increase—the $10 price may increase to $25, $100, or some other amount. With a series of losses, the trading price may be less than the issue price. In any event, subsequent trading prices have no direct effect on the financial statements of the issuing corporation.

Two important measurements that traders in the capital market use to set the price of corporate shares involve the use of the net income figure reported on the statement of income. These two measurements are *earnings per share* and the *price-earnings ratio*. A third ratio which sometimes affects the price of shares is the *dividend yield*. These three measurements serve as a basis for determining the trading price of a share, although just how each trader translates the ratios into prices is not well understood.

EARNINGS PER SHARE.* The annual net income of a corporation divided by the average number of shares of capital stock outstanding gives earnings per share. Assume that a corporation had 100,000 shares of capital stock outstanding throughout 19X1 and that the net income (after taxes) was $550,000. Earnings per share was $5.50:

$$\frac{\text{Net income}}{\text{Average number of shares outstanding}} = \frac{\$550,000}{\$100,000} = \$5.50$$

Earnings per share is thus the prorated amount of income per share. Income is translated into a per share amount because the market establishes the value on a per share basis. Earnings per share can then be related to market price per share by use of the price-earnings ratio.

Because of the importance of earnings per share in establishing stock prices, the independent accountant is now required by generally accepted practice to include a calculation of earnings per share on the statement of income. These amounts appear on the statement of income, typically following the final amount for income (see Fig. 5–4)—the income per share or earnings per share appear below the net earnings. Furthermore, accounting principles specify that the calculation of earnings per share is made *before* extraordinary items, gains or losses per share for extraordinary items, and the final net earnings per share. This

*The difficulties of computing earnings per share because of common stock equivalents and potential dilution is briefly considered in Chapter 15.

breakdown is shown on Fig. 5–4. The calculation is for both the current and preceding years. Separate treatment of the extraordinary items presumably permits the trader to base his future expectations on "normal" operating results.

PRICE–EARNINGS RATIO. The market price of a share of capital stock divided by earnings per share gives the price–earnings ratio. To continue the preceding example, assume that the market price of each of the 100,000 shares outstanding was $110. The price–earnings ratio was

$$\frac{\text{Market price per share}}{\text{Earnings per share}} = \frac{\$110}{\$5.50} = \$20$$

In this case the stock is trading at a price which is 20 times the annual earnings per share. The price–earnings ratio in this case would be quoted as 20 to 1.

The reciprocal of the fraction for the price–earning ratio gives the *rate of return* on market price, another method of expressing the relationship between market price and earnings. Using the same facts, the rate of return on market value would be

$$\frac{\text{Earnings per share}}{\text{Market price per share}} = \frac{\$5.50}{\$110.00} = \$0.05 \text{ (or 5\%)}$$

The corporation earned income at a rate of 5% based on the current market price of its stock.

DIVIDEND YIELD. A final ratio is the rate of dividend yield based on present market value of the share. Assume that the corporation which earned $5.50 per share actually distributed $3.30 on each share during 19X1, a total distribution of $330,000 ($3.30 per share times 100,000 shares outstanding). The dividend yield was

$$\frac{\text{Dividend per share}}{\text{Market price per share}} = \frac{\$3.30}{\$110.00} = \$0.03 \text{ (or 3\%)}$$

The dividend yield can be compared directly with the inherent rates that can be earned on the same dollars invested in savings accounts, bonds, and other interest-bearing investments.

Undue reliance on dividend yield can lead to incorrect conclusions for many corporations. Most corporate directors and managers do not distribute all of the current earnings as dividends. Indeed, some corporations follow the policy of paying no dividends. The income earned that is not distributed as dividends is reinvested in new products and plant expansion or used to acquire other productive resources. The typical pattern is for a corporation to grow by means of retaining earnings. If the operation is successful, the income earned also increases as the earnings are retained and invested in the operation.

The increased earnings, finally, results in an increase in the market price of the shares. A more reliable measure of yield, therefore, includes not only the dividends received but also the change in the value of the share for the year:

$$Yield = \frac{Dividends\ received\ +\ \Delta Market\ price\ per\ share}{Market\ price\ per\ share}$$

To continue the foregoing example, assume that the market price per share was $105 at the first of the year. (Recall that the price at the end of the year was given as $110.) The shareholder not only received cash dividends of $3.30; he also enjoyed an increase of $5 per share in the value of the stock. Thus,

$$Yield = \frac{\$3.30\ +\ \$5.00}{\$110} = \frac{\$8.30}{\$110} = 7.54\%$$

When the change in stock value is included in the calculation, the resulting percentage for yield is a better base for comparison with the rate of return on other investment opportunities.

When deciding to buy or sell a corporate share, the investor usually begins with the following three measurements: earnings per share, price–earnings ratio (or rate of return on market price), and the yield. By using these facts, plus numerous others that might give some indication of the future success of the enterprise, investors decide to buy or sell in some mysterious way. Some of these "additional" facts are found on the balance sheet, the subject of the next chapter.

QUESTIONS

1   List the various groups of people interested in financial statements. Comment on how each group would use financial information.
2   Why are corporations whose stocks are listed on organized stock exchanges required to have their financial statements audited annually?
3   Why should an auditor be independent?
4   How is the competence of an auditor determined?
5   List the various types of opinions that independent auditors may give and describe each opinion very briefly.
6   What are the auditing standards observed by independent public accountants? Should auditors have the power to establish their own standards?
7   Describe the concepts of fair disclosure and materiality. Is there any relationship between these two concepts?
8   What is the concept of consistency? Why is consistency important for the measurement of income?
9   Which of the usual financial statements gives a better indication of future operations?
10 What basic assumption is made when *past actions* are used as a means of *prediction*? What are some of the factors that partially negate this assumption?
11 Both averages and trends are used as analytical tools. Which is a better indication of future operations? Why?
12 What is the underlying assumption for the use of accruals? What major problem does this create?
13 What are the requirements for revenue realization? When are these requirements usually met?
14 What concept enables the accountant to compare efforts with accomplishments?

15   What are extraordinary items? How should extraordinary items be shown on the income
      statement? List four different items that would be classified as extraordinary items.
16   Why are income taxes classified separately on the statement of income?
17   Describe and comment on the uses of
      [a]   The single-step statement of income
      [b]   The multiple-step statement of income
18   What is a common-size income statement? Can common-size statements be used to com-
      pare companies in different industries? Explain your answer.
19   Select the income statement ratios you would use to analyze a particular company and
      explain how you would use each ratio.

PROBLEMS

1   Given the following information, prepare a multiple-step statement of income for the ABC
     Corporation's operations in 19X1.

Sales	$100,000
Capital stock sold during the period	150,000
Interest income	1,500
Advertising expense	5,000
Depreciation expense (building)	8,000
Rental expense (equipment)	2,000
Selling expenses	4,000
Administrative expenses	5,000
Marketable securities that became totally worthless during 19X1	10,000
Cash paid for inventory	17,000
Net increase in inventory during period	1,000
Federal taxes	15,000
State taxes	5,000

2   Prepare a single-step income statement for 19X2 in proper form for the W Corporation
     from the following information:

Revenue from sales	$235,000
General and administrative expenses	41,000
Income taxes	11,700
Selling expenses	53,000
Cost of goods sold	114,000
Gain on sale of assets (net of income tax effect)	3,000
Casualty loss—fire (net of income tax effect)	7,300

3   The following list of transactions was completed by the H Company during 19X1. The
     H Company had revenue from sales during 19X1 of $10,000,000 and net income before

extraordinary items of $800,000; total assets at December 31, 19X1, amounted to $6,000,000. Indicate which of the following transactions should be classified as extra-ordinary or special items and shown at the bottom of the statement of income

[a] Because of a threatened strike in the industry within which the H Company operates, during the month of December sales to customers were unusually large. Company officials estimate that, due to the threat of the strike alone, December sales were increased by $300,000 and that the gross profit on these sales amounted to $120,000.

[b] In March, 19X1, fire destroyed a wing of the plant. The underpreciated cost of the building (deferred cost) was $110,000. Insurance proceeds were $250,000, resulting in a gain of $140,000.

[c] In November, the company sold a delivery truck which had an undepreciated cost of $1,200. Sales price was $1,500.

[d] In November, the H Company also sold a plot of land which had been held for possi-ble expansion. The land had cost $200,000 when acquired and the sales price was $350,000.

[e] Profits were high in 19X1, and the Board of Directors wished to reward top manage-ment. In December 19X1, the president and vice-presidents were paid bonuses total-ing $120,000.

[f] The value assigned to the finished goods inventory (deferred cost) at December 31, 19X0 was $1,250,000. In April, some errors were found in the additions on the inventory sheets. The inventory should have been $1,235,000. This error is to be corrected at the end of 19X1.

4 The multiple-step statement of income of the G Company for 19X1 is as follows:

G Company

Statement of Income for the Period Ended December 31, 19X1

Sales revenue		$5,000,000
Cost of goods sold		3,200,000
Gross profit on sales		$1,800,000
Operating expenses	$400,000	
Administrative expenses	350,000	
Interest and other financial charges	60,000	810,000
Net income before income taxes		$ 990,000
Federal and state taxes on income		420,000
Net income		$ 570,000

[a] Prepare a common-size income statement based on these data. (Carry percentages to nearest one-tenth of 1 percent.)

[b] What uses can be made of the common-size statement?

5 [a] Appendix D contains the financial statements of several large corporations whose stocks are traded on a major exchange. Select one of the corporations and compute the statement of income ratios which you believe would be useful in making a deci-sion regarding investment in the corporation. Justify the use of each ratio.

[b] What additional information would you like to have before reaching a decision?

6 The statements of income of the W Corporation for the last five years in condensed form are as follows:

	19X1	19X2	19X3	19X4	19X5
Sales	$64,800	$81,000	$98,800	$145,800	$141,100
Cost of goods sold	43,200	53,400	65,000	94,200	98,600
Selling expenses	6,760	9,200	12,160	16,300	17,200
General and administrative expenses	6,200	7,000	7,600	12,860	11,020
Income taxes	2,592	3,420	4,212	6,732	4,284
Net income	6,048	7,980	9,828	15,708	9,996
Shares outstanding	10,000	10,000	12,000	12,000	12,000
Market price per share	10	12	11	20	13
Dividends per share	0	0	0	1	1

Required:

[a] Compute the following ratios for each year:
   [i] Return on sales
   [ii] Gross profit ratio
   [iii] Earnings per share
   [iv] Price–earnings ratio
   [v] Dividend yield (excluding appreciation in market value)

[b] Based on the foregoing information, write a short paragraph justifying why you would or would not invest in the W Corporation.

7 Statistics from the statement of income of the M Corporation are

Total revenue	$10,000,000
Cost of goods sold	5,800,000
Total operating expenses	3,000,000
Income taxes	500,000

There were no extraordinary items during the year. The corporation had 500,000 shares of capital stock outstanding during the year, and the market value of the stock was $21.00 per share at the end of the year. The company distributed total dividends of $400,000 during 19X1.

Prepare the following ratios for 19X1:

[a] Gross profit
[b] Return on sales (before income taxes)
[c] Return on sales (after income taxes)
[d] Earnings per share
[e] Price–earnings ratio
[f] Rate of return on market price
[g] Dividend yield

8 *Fortune Magazine* publishes annually a directory of the 500 largest corporations. Secure from your library this directory and prepare a report as follows:
[a] For the five largest companies, compute or list the return on sales.
[b] For these same five corporations compute or list the earnings per share, broken down into ordinary and extraordinary components of income per share.
[c] Comment on the significance of these two ratios in judging the performance of the companies.

9 Go to the library, refer to *Standards and Poor's*, and look up the three largest automobile manufacturing companies, General Motors, Ford Motor Company, and Chrysler Corporation.

  [a] Prepare a table to show the sales, percentage of operating income to sales, and income for each company for the last four years.

  [b] Prepare a similar table to show net income and earnings per share.

  [c] Which company would you recommend to your father as the best investment? Justify your recommendation.

  [d] What additional information would you like to have relative to the statements of income of these three corporations?

10 On p. 494 of Appendix D is a summary of operating results and other information for the ten-year period ended June 30, 19X1 for Gould Inc.

  [a] Take into consideration the operating data only and compute for each year two ratios that you might use in evaluating the company's efficiency.

  [b] Although this summary gives earnings per share, it omits one vital piece of information needed to compare Gould's operations with those of other companies. What is that information? What ratios could you compute with the missing data? Where could you find the missing information?

CASE The S Company operates a number of sand and gravel pits. It has been a very successful company and is currently seeking additional funds for expansion. Schedule 1 shows the past ten-year summary of the company's statements of income and some related ratios.

  In 19X9, the S Company changed its method of depreciation from an accelerated method to a straight-line method. If the accelerated method had been used in 19X9, depreciation expense would have been $10,000 more. Prior year's income was not adjusted to reflect this change in accounting method.

  A friend who knows nothing about accounting has asked you to analyze the S Company's financial statements and advise him whether or not he should invest in this company. Among other things, he has specifically raised the following questions:

  [a] Can he compare the income of the corporation for the different years?

  [b] What effect does the change in depreciation method have on the company's performance? If the average number of shares outstanding was 5,415, what effect did the decrease in depreciation have on earnings per share?

  [c] Which reporting standard assures your friend that changes in accounting methods are disclosed?

SCHEDULE 1

S Company

	19X9	19X8	19X7	19X6	19X5	19X4	19X3	19X2	19X1	19X0
Revenue	$461,000	$406,700	$443,500	$446,500	$412,900	$363,700	$350,100	$333,600	$369,900	$364,300
Cost of production	176,600	143,200	155,900	162,500	140,500	121,100	119,300	102,300	109,100	127,800
Employment costs	205,600	187,200	191,600	186,400	179,500	161,200	160,800	162,300	170,000	157,600
Depreciation and depletion	25,300	35,500	34,400	32,500	33,600	30,800	26,600	21,000	20,800	19,000
Other costs	6,800	5,300	5,700	3,000	3,400	3,500	3,700	2,900	1,800	1,700
Income taxes	21,300	18,200	31,000	34,500	32,300	26,800	23,300	26,100	37,800	32,700
Income	25,400	17,300	24,900	27,600	23,600	20,300	16,400	19,000	30,400	25,500
Income as percent of sales	5.5%	4.2%	5.6%	6.2%	5.7%	5.6%	4.7%	5.7%	8.2%	7.0%
Income per share	$4.69	$3.19	$4.60	$4.62	$3.91	$3.30	$2.56	$3.05	$5.16	$4.25

Classified Financial Statements: The Balance Sheet

A balance sheet shows the net effect of a business's past transactions from inception until the balance sheet date. For example, the cash balance that appears on the balance sheet is the net difference of all cash receipts and cash disbursements as of the balance sheet date. The balance sheet discloses the assets that are available for future operations and the claims against those assets.

Content of the Balance Sheet

Assets are cash, accrued revenues, and deferred costs. Equities (claims against assets) are accrued expenses, deferred revenues, debt investments, owner investments, and retained earnings. The balance sheet equation as developed in Chapter 4 is

$$C + AR + DE = AE + DR + OI + RE$$

Note that assets are on the left side of the equality sign and equities are on the right side. Thus, the balance sheet equation can be written

$$Assets = Equities$$

The following sections discuss the nature of assets and equities and their valuation.

Nature of Assets

The assets of a business are the money resources and means of production or services which it controls. Often the entity owns its assets, but ownership in the strict legal sense is not required. Any beneficial interest acquired as the result of an external transaction is an asset.

The notion that a beneficial interest other than legal ownership may be an asset is a relatively new idea in accounting. For example, a business may buy a truck on a conditional sales contract, whereby title does not pass until all install-ments have been paid. The payments on the truck may not be completed for some time, for instance, let us assume for three years. During that three-year period the business does not have title and does not own the truck in the legal sense. Nevertheless, the entity has control and use of the truck during the three years. Despite the lack of legal ownership, the truck is an asset because the business controls it and has a beneficial interest in it. Another example is a lease agreement which may give the business (the lessee) an interest in the property even though legal title is held by the lessor.

To the general public, the word asset means any useful quality or property. One often hears remarks such as "Neatness is an asset." Without doubt, in the minds of most laymen the word asset has a more general meaning than that actu-ally assigned to it by accountants. Many of the things owned by a business and many of the useful qualities found in a business are not listed under assets on the balance sheet. Special skills and *esprit de corps* of a work force or of the management may make a valuable contribution to the business, yet these assets do not appear on the statement. Finally, the business may own tangible proper-ties that were acquired without an outlay of cash or the original cash cost may have been allocated to expense in prior periods. In these cases the assets, although useful to the business, will not appear on the balance sheet.

Valuation of Assets

Perhaps the most frequent error made in understanding the balance sheet is to assume that the dollar values shown for assets represent the present market value of the assets and that the total asset value is, therefore, the total fair market value of the resources of the business. This interpretation is wrong on two counts. First, as discussed previously, the balance sheet does not show all the assets of most businesses. Second, the dollar values used for many assets has little or nothing to do with their present fair market values.

Cash is valued on the balance sheet by count and the amount which appears for cash represents the dollars on hand, on deposit, or in some other equally liquid form. Revenue accruals (accounts and notes receivable from customers) are valued at the amount of cash the business expects to receive—net realizable value. Thus cash and revenue accruals are generally shown at current or present value.

Expense deferrals, which comprise most of the assets on the usual balance sheet, are shown at *cost*. Cost is the cash paid, or the present value of cash to be paid in the future, for the asset at the time of acquisition. In rare cases, property is acquired by an exchange of property other than cash. In these cases, the cost is the cash-equivalent value. The transaction is handled as though the old asset (traded in) were sold at its present fair market value and the cash used to buy the new asset. For example, assume that land originally costing $10,000 but having a fair market value of $15,000 is traded in for land and a building. The cost of the new property is $15,000, the cash-equivalent value. Under the federal income tax laws, the cost of the new asset would be recorded as $10,000, and some accountants would argue for this valuation. The preferred practice, nevertheless, is to recognize the fair market value at the date of acquisition as the valuation of the new property.

Values that appear on the balance sheet do not represent fair market values in all cases. And certainly the total value of all assets does not represent the total market value of the business. Even if all assets were shown, and all were valued at fair market value, the entire business might be worth more or less than the sum of the value of its recognized assets. There will always be some qualities or properties in a business that cannot be recognized, isolated, and fairly valued. By contrast, because of inefficient operation and for other reasons, the business as a going concern might be worth less than the individual assets used in the business. In this event, the owners may wish to liquidate the business because the sale of the individual assets would yield a higher value than continued operations.

Nature of Equities

Equities are claims against the assets. In addition, the equities indicate the *sources* of the assets. In terms of the balance sheet equation, equities are expense accruals (AE), revenue deferrals (DR), debt investments (DI), owner investments (OI), and retained earnings (RE).

Equities are divided into two groups—liabilities and capital. Thus, another form of the balance sheet equation is

Assets = Liabilities + Capital

A liability arises anytime the entity acquires money resources or services from a creditor with a promise to return cash, services, or goods at a determinable future date. An entity discharges or liquidates a liability by transferring assets, usually cash, to an external party without receiving assets in exchange.

Assets transferred to a business by one acquiring an owner's interest in the entity gives rise to an equity called *capital. Proprietorship* and *owner's equity* are synonyms for capital, and in a corporate enterprise capital is often called *stockholder's equity*. Income, not distributed (RE), either increases assets or decreases other equities. For this reason, capital is usually divided into two major classes: *Contributed capital* arises when owners transfer their personal assets to the entity; the other class of capital, *retained earnings* or *undivided profits*, arises when an entity's net assets increase as a result of its operations.

Valuation of Equities

Most equities are valued at the cash cost required to settle the claim against the business. For expense accruals, the amounts that appear on the balance sheet are the cash payments required in the following periods. Revenue deferrals are valued at the cash amounts received in advance of revenue recognition. Bank loans and other debt investments are shown at the present value of future cash payments required to settle the claim, using the interest rate in effect when the debt originated. Valuation of the owner's equity (proprietorship or stockholder's equity) is measured by the cash-equivalent value of the property contributed, at the time of contribution plus income reinvested in the business.

In the discussion of asset valuation, we noted that the valuation of deferred costs did not represent market value and that, in addition, the concept of assets in accounting does not include all valuable *qualities* present in a business. As a result, the amount that appears on the balance sheet for owner's equity is not always a fair valuation of the ownership or net worth of the business.

To illustrate this point, refer to the skeletal balance sheet in Fig. 6-1. On the equity side, the first item is valued at the amount of cash required for settlement. Revenue deferrals are valued at the amount of cash received in exchange for a promise to deliver a specified quantity of goods or services in the future. In the balance sheet (Fig. 6-1), the dollar value shown for owners' equity would equal the present value of the business only if:

1   All assets were valued at present market value. By all assets we would include valuation of all qualities that contribute to operations such as management skills, secret processes, and labor efficiency.
2   All claims against the business other than the owners' claims are stated at present value. As with assets, many claims may be uncertain and therefore not shown. For example, a pending law suit against the company may not be shown although it may eventually result in a cash payment for settlement.

Thus, the owners' equity does not usually represent the fair value of the owners' interest. The amount shown for owners' equity is nothing more nor less than the difference between the values assigned to assets and liabilities under accepted accounting rules.

Figure 6-1

X Company		Balance Sheet, December 31, 19X1	
Assets:		Equities:	
Cash	$ 1,000	Expense accruals	$ 2,000
Revenue accruals	3,000	Revenue deferrals	500
Deferred costs	6,000	Owners' equity	7,500
	$10,000		$10,000

Form of the Balance Sheet

In all preceding illustrations, the balance sheet has been merely a listing of assets and equities. The totals derived in this manner, as indicated in the preceding section, have only a limited usefulness. Traditionally, various subtotals for assets and equities have been used in financial analysis as will be shown later in this chapter. Subtotals are obtained by dividing the assets and equities into *classes.* Accountants use a combination of three different bases for classification of assets and equities on the balance sheet:

1   Assets and equities may be classified or grouped based on their *nature.* Thus, if a business owns a fleet of delivery trucks, the deferred cost of the trucks may be classed together and designated "trucks" on the balance sheet.
2   Assets and equities may be classified based on their *functions.* For example, if both trucks and cars are used for delivery, the deferred costs of both may be grouped together and designated "delivery equipment" on the balance sheet.
3   Finally assets and equities may be classified based on *time.* For example, some resources will be used in the very near future whereas others will be used over a long period of time. Delivery equipment might be classified as a "long-lived asset."

Very often the different bases for classification are superimposed on each other as shown on Fig. 6–2.

Figure 6-2

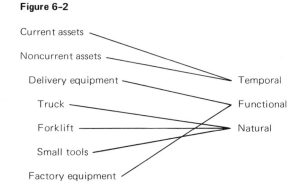

The definitions of the various classes and the arrangement of the classes on the balance sheet are discussed in the following sections.

Current Classifications

The balance sheet was the first external accounting report to be used widely. In the nineteenth century, the growth of business in the United States, particularly in transportation, required a corresponding expansion of credit. Businesses were forced to go beyond their immediate owners for the capital needed for growth and expansion. In a few cases, corporations were formed and stocks and bonds sold to the public. Most businesses sought to obtain the needed capital by borrowing from banks and other financial institutions. Most of this borrowing was short-term (due within one year) or intermediate-term (due in about five years).

The balance sheet was the report normally used by businesses to convince the lender that the loan requested would be repaid. The form of the balance sheet adopted at that time is still generally used today; its prominent feature is the ability of the business to repay short-term (and intermediate-term) debts.

Imagine that you are a banker and that you have been asked to make a short-term loan to a business. The only financial information provided you about the business is a balance sheet. What information on the balance sheet would be most important to you? If the loan is due in one year, you would want to know how much cash the business has now and how much cash the business can expect to receive in the next year. In addition, you would need to know how much the business owes which must be repaid in the next year. With only the balance sheet, you would be limited to considering what accountants refer to as current assets and current liabilities. Because of their importance for credit purposes, these classes of assets and liabilities are given the first position on the balance sheet.

CURRENT ASSETS. Cash and items that will be converted to cash within one year or within an operating cycle, whichever is longer, are current assets. Cash, notes receivable, accounts receivable, marketable securities, and inventories are examples of current assets. Various deferred costs, such as unexpired insurance, deferred advertising expense, and prepaid interest are also classed as current assets. Deferred costs are classed as current assets because the business will not have to spend cash to acquire these items within the next year or operating cycle.

The key term in this definition of current assets is the operating cycle. A modified diagram of the operating cycle is shown in Fig. 6–3. The important aspect of the operating cycle as it relates to the current classification is the time that expires from the point of cash expenditures until conversion back to cash is completed.

Figure 6–3: Modified Operating Cycle

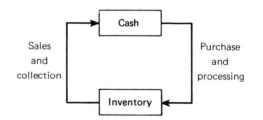

The length of the operating cycle of some businesses may be several years whereas for other businesses the cycle may last only a few days. A grocery supermarket is an example of business that has a very short operating cycle. An extended business cycle usually results from a lengthy processing period or from a delay in collections. Processing whiskey requires several years, and an automobile retailer often takes up to 36 months to complete collections. When the operating cycle is longer than a year, current assets may include assets that will not be converted to cash within one year. The inventory of a distiller of whiskey is a current asset although the inventory may be held for a number of years. The receivables of a business that sells on the installment basis may be current even though they will not be collected within one year.

The current classification of assets ignores the important distinction between revenue accruals and expense deferrals. The classification "current" includes most revenue accruals and some cost deferrals such as inventory and other types of prepaid operating expenses. The bases of valuation of these two types of assets are totally different: Revenue accruals are valued at net realizable value, whereas the cost deferrals are valued at their acquisition costs. Despite this weakness, the total for current assets is the best approximation of the cash available to the enterprise in the near future, provided that the only information to work with is the balance sheet.

CURRENT LIABILITIES. Liabilities that require the expenditure of a current asset within an operating cycle or a year, whichever is longer, are current liabilities. All liabilities that do not fall due within an operating cycle or a year, whichever is longer, are long-term liabilities. Examples of current liabilities are notes payable, accounts payable, advances from customers and other deferred revenues, and various accrued expenses such as accrued wages payable and accrued interest payable. Note that the idea of an operating cycle is used in this definition in the same manner that it was used in the definition of current assets. Usually, liabilities are settled for cash, but deferred revenues may be settled by the delivery of inventory or services. These advances are treated as current liabilities because the asset required to settle the claim, inventory, is a current asset.

The classification of current liabilities ignores the distinction between expense accruals, revenue deferrals, and debt investments. Money borrowed from a bank is an investment transaction, but if the loan is due within one year or a longer operating cycle, the investment is classed as a current liability. The total for current liabilities is the closest approximation that can be made to the cash payments due in the coming year if the only information available is the balance sheet.

A term often used in the analysis of the balance sheet is **working capital**. It is determined as follows:

Total current assets	$xxxx
Less: Total current liabilities	xxx
Working capital	$xxxx

Thus working capital is the portion of current assets that will *not* be required to settle the current liabilities.

Noncurrent Asset Classifications

Assets that do not fit into the current classification are normally subdivided into several classes: investments, plant and equipment, intangible assets, and other assets.

Investments as an asset class on the balance sheet should not be confused with investment transactions in the income calculation. A business may invest capital in another business. Previously we have viewed the investment transaction from one side only, the side of the enterprise *receiving* the capital. On the other side of the transaction, the party who provides the capital has a cash disbursement. The cost of the investment would be deferred, since the cost would not be used up as long as the investment continues. The deferred cost would appear on the investor's balance sheet as an asset.

For example, assume that Corporation A buys a new stock issue of corporation B for $100,000. To B, the cash receipt (CR) is an owner investment (OI) and increases the owner's equity or contributed capital on its balance sheet. To Corporation A, on the other hand, the transaction is an acquisition of services. The acquired services may be expected future dividends, gain on subsequent sale of the shares, some control of the policies of Corporation B by placing someone on B's Board of Directors, or some other service. In any event, the investment in Corporation B is a deferred cost and appears as an asset of Corporation A's balance sheet.

Normally investments are noncurrent, such as the investment of a parent company in the stock of a subsidiary corporation. The investment would be current only if the investing company intended to sell the corporate stock or security in the next year. Investments classified as current assets are described as marketable securities. Such short-term investments are primarily cash substitutes. Assume that a corporation has a temporary excess of cash which will be needed several months later for the acquisition of new services. Should they leave the excess cash in their checking account at the bank where it will earn no interest or dividends? Certainly not. The cash should be invested in bonds, stocks, or other securities which will produce some income until it is needed. Thus marketable securities, current assets, are in reality another form of cash.

The noncurrent deferred costs for investments are shown under a separate classification and appropriately titled "investments." These assets are usually represented by stocks or other corporate securities. In some cases, a business may loan another business money or furnish the other business with services that will not be repaid in the coming year or the next operating cycle. If the loans are evidenced by a note, they would be shown as "long-term notes receivable," and classified as an investment. If there is no note, the deferred costs are usually described as "advances to Company X." Such long-term advances are quite common between parent and subsidiary companies and between affiliated businesses (where one individual owns two corporations, for example). Occasionally, a business will invest in land, speculating on an increase in value.

Plant and equipment, another asset classification, are assets that are (1) noncurrent, (2) used in the operations of the business, and (3) tangible. Tangible assets are those that can be seen and touched. Examples of assets classed as plant and equipment are land, buildings, vehicles, machines, and furniture. Land may be classified as plant and equipment or as an investment, depending on the purpose for which it was acquired: If acquired for use in operations, it would be included under plant and equipment; if acquired for speculation, the land would be classified as an investment.

Intangible assets, a third class of noncurrent assets, are like plant and equipment in that they are noncurrent and are related to the operations of the business. They differ from plant and equipment in that they have no tangible or physical existence. Examples of intangible assets are patents, franchises, copyrights, organization costs, trademarks, and goodwill.

Assets that do not fit into any of the four classes described above are classed as *other assets*. Long-term prepaid expenses and deposits which are to be left with suppliers for an indefinite period are classed as other assets.

The following list is a brief summary of the definitions of the five usual classes of assets:

1   Current assets—cash, items that will be converted to cash within a year or during the operating cycle (whichever is longer) and items that enable an entity to avoid a cash expenditure within a year or during the operating cycle (whichever is longer).
2   Investments—noncurrent assets that are *not* used in the operation of the business
3   Plant and equipment—noncurrent assets (services) that have a tangible physical existence and are used in the operation(s) of the business
4   Intangible assets—noncurrent assets (services) that do not have a tangible physical existence and are used in the operations of the business
5   Other assets—any asset that does not fit into one of the above four categories or any asset from a major asset category that is not used on a particular balance sheet.

Noncurrent Equity Classifications

Liabilities that are not due within a year or the next operating cycle are classed as long-term liabilities. Some examples would be mortgages payable, bonds payable, long-term advances from customers or others, and bank notes that are not due for several years.

For an unincorporated business, the owner's equity will usually be shown as one amount and appropriately described. In a partnership with a limited number of partners, each partner's equity may be shown separately. The class title normally used is *capital*, but owner's equity or *net worth* is used by some accountants. The owner's equity section of a partnership statement might appear as follows:

Partners' capital:
Thomas H. Griffin $205,000
Kieso G. Franklin   112,000
Total capital $317,000

These amounts include not only the partners' original contributions but also their shares of past income and losses, less any distribution to them.

For an incorporated business enterprise, capital is divided into two major classes on the balance sheet. This twofold division is also possible for partnerships and proprietorships; but it is not normally used. The basis for the division of capital is separation of amounts contributed to or invested in the business by parties acquiring an owner's interest from the amounts earned by business operations. Contributed capital includes the amounts received by the corporation in exchange for shares of stock. The name given to that part of capital generated by operations of the business is retained earnings. Although it is now considered a less acceptable term, earned surplus is sometimes used as a synonym for retained earnings. The two main divisions of capital, then, are *contributed capital* and *retained earnings*. The capital section, usually called *stockholders' equity* on a corporate balance sheet would appear as follows:

Stockholders' equity:	
Contributed capital	$1,000,000
Retained earnings	500,000
Total stockholders' equity	$1,500,000

Beginning with the opening balance of retained earnings and adding the income or subtracting the loss for the period recognizes the changes in retained earnings caused by the economic activities for the accounting period. Subtraction of dividends paid recognizes the changes caused by distribution of profits. Sometimes the calculation described is included in the capital section of the balance sheet, as shown in Fig. 6–4. The retained earnings section of the balance sheet is often placed on a separate statement entitled the "statement of retained earnings." When a statement of retained earnings is used, the only balance shown for retained earnings on the balance sheet is the ending balance. Sometimes the calculation of the ending balance of retained earnings is shown on the bottom of the statement of income, as in Fig. 5–4.

Figure 6–4: Stockholders' Equity

Contributed capital		$1,000,000
Retained earnings:		
Balance, 1/1/19X1	$400,000	
Add: Net income for 19X1	150,000	
	$550,000	
Less: Dividends paid, 19X1	$ 50,000	
Balance, 12/31/19X1		$ 500,000
Total stockholders' equity		$1,500,000

The following list is a brief summary of the definitions of the three usual classes of equities:

1   Current liabilities—equities that require the expenditure of current assets or their renewal in the form of another equity that requires the expenditure of a current asset

2   Long-term liabilities—equities that are not due and will not mature within a year.
3   Stockholders' equity or owners' equity—equities arising from the contribution of owners to the business and from the retention of income in the business

Critique of Traditional Classifications

As noted earlier, the traditional classifications used on balance sheets are not consistent with the classifications of transactions used in the measurement of income. Current assets include both accrued revenues and deferred costs. Current liabilities include accrued expenses, deferred revenues, and short-term debt investments. These temporal classifications are no doubt useful for short-term credit purposes. Many accountants believe, however, that the mixing of unlike items within the same balance sheet classes might cause statement users to make mistakes and that these mistakes could be avoided by a change in balance sheet classes.

Paramount among the problems is the nature of the principal items included in current assets. That grouping includes cash and accrued revenues, which are valued at expected cash realizable value, as well as inventory, which is valued at acquisition cost. Thus, heterogeneous values are added together and treated as a single amount. One suggested alternative for balance sheet classification would group cash, accrued revenues, and other items that are expected to be converted to cash *in the amounts shown* on the balance sheet as a separate class. An additional class would be the "current" deferred costs, inventories, and other short-term deferred costs, which are valued at acquisition cost. A similar change might be made in current liabilities by segregating the deferred revenues. This scheme would preserve the valuable temporal classifications and, at the same time, avoid the possibility of misleading users by adding together items that are valued in quite different ways. This problem will be discussed further in this chapter in the section dealing with analysis of the balance sheet.

Example of a Classified Balance Sheet

Figure 6–5 shows the actual balance sheets of Gould, Inc. and its subsidiaries, at June 30, 1971 and 1972; this is an example of a classified balance sheet. The form used by that company is referred to as the *account* form: Assets are presented on the left and the liabilities and equities on the right. Note that current assets, the most liquid (near cash) form of assets, are shown first, with other classes listed generally in order of liquidity. Investments can be converted to cash more readily than plant and equipment, etc. On the equity side, current liabilities are given the first position, with long-term liabilities and owners' equity listed in that order. Long-term liabilities are shown above owners' equity because the liabilities have seniority; in the event of liquidation, the liabilities must be settled before distributing assets among the shareholders.

Figure 6–5

Assets

June 30	1971	1970
Current Assets		
Cash	$ 15,814,248	$ 13,112,347
Marketable securities at cost, which approximates market price	7,948,354	14,482,457
Accounts receivable less allowances: 1971 — $415,591; 1970 — $778,840	51,689,218	49,327,483
Inventories — Note B	66,165,838	70,526,361
Other current assets — Note D	8,185,791	6,769,604
Total Current Assets	149,803,449	154,218,252
Investments and Other Assets		
Unconsolidated subsidiaries at underlying equity — Note A	865,170	269,437
Affiliated companies at cost	5,029,297	4,748,316
Other assets — Note D	7,989,471	4,412,311
Total Investments and Other Assets	13,883,938	9,430,064
Property, Plant and Equipment—on the basis of cost		
Land	3,852,538	3,931,954
Buildings	52,551,384	47,732,348
Machinery and equipment	96,955,789	86,941,540
Construction in progress	8,901,664	4,038,184
	162,261,375	142,644,026
Less allowances for depreciation	(75,910,172)	(71,289,844)
Total Property, Plant and Equipment	86,351,203	71,354,182
Cost of Acquired Businesses in Excess of Net Assets at Acquisition Dates — Note A	52,384,110	51,941,262
Total Assets	$302,422,700	$286,943,760

See notes to financial statements.

Reprinted from the 1971 financial statements of Gould Inc. and Consolidated Subsidiaries.

The last item under assets, "cost of acquired businesses in excess of net assets at acquisition dates," is essentially a deferred cost similar to other deferred costs such as plant and equipment. Generally, this item arises in the accounting process of combining or consolidating the records of the parent company with those of its subsidiaries. This process is discussed in some detail in Chapter 16.

Under liabilities the term "deferred credits" has the same meaning as deferred revenue (DR); "Deferred income taxes," however, is a vague use of the term deferred. The amounts, $13,049,982 in 1972 and $5,459,736 in 1971, are taxes that must be paid in the future, but not within the coming year. These obligations would be more appropriately described as "income taxes payable."

In the stockholders' equity section, note that there are two kinds of capital stock issued and outstanding—preferred stock and common stock. The distinctions between different kinds of capital stock are explained in Chapter 15. Additional paid-in capital is a part of contributed capital, usually amounts paid by stockholders in excess of the par value of the stock. Paid-in capital should not be confused with retained earnings.

Finally, note that the accountants for Gould, Inc. have grouped many accounts and reported them as a single amount on the statements. All accounts payable and accrued expenses are shown as a single amount. Similarly, all

Liabilities and Stockholders' Equity

June 30	1971	1970
Current Liabilities		
Notes payable	$ 15,458,000	$ 18,267,748
Accounts payable and accrued expenses	42,074,715	38,928,586
Income taxes — Note C	2,886,372	3,651,622
Current maturities of long-term debt	9,089,308	2,360,176
Deferred credit — current	37,950	688,251
Total Current Liabilities	69,546,345	63,896,383
Long-Term Debt less current maturities — Note E	65,249,491	66,488,940
Deferred Credits (principally federal income taxes)	4,971,179	2,278,301
Minority Interest in Subsidiary	39,994	80,297
Stockholders' Equity — Notes E and F		
Preferred Stock—par value $1 a share: Authorized—3,000,000 shares Issued—none		
Common Stock — par value $4 a share: Authorized — 20,000,000 shares Issued — 1971 — 5,016,953 shares; 1970 — 4,980,969 shares	20,067,812	19,923,876
Additional paid-in capital	27,387,335	26,676,384
Earnings retained for use in the business	117,305,807	109,880,037
Less cost of Common Stock in treasury: 1971 — 81,853 shares; 1970 — 85,326 shares	(2,145,263)	(2,280,458)
Total Stockholders' Equity	162,615,691	154,199,839
Commitments and Contingencies — Notes G and I		
Total Liabilities and Stockholders' Equity	$302,422,700	$286,943,760

machinery and equipment is shown as a single amount. For long-lived assets, the original cost is shown and the portion of the cost charged to expense in prior years is subtracted to arrive at the deferred costs.

Several arrangements other than the account form are used for the balance sheet. In the *report* form, the assets are listed by classes in the order of liquidity, with the equities listed *below* the assets. Figure 6-6 is a skeletal presentation of the report form. An example of an actual report form is the balance sheet of the Singer Company on p. 528 of Appendix D.

Figure 6-6: Report Form for Balance Sheet

Assets:	
Current assets	$ xxx
Investments	xxx
Plant and equipment	xxx
Total assets	$xxxx
Equities:	
Current liabilities	$ xxx
Long-term liabilities	xxx
Stockholders' equity	xxx
Total equities	$xxxx

Still another form of the balance sheet is one in which current liabilities are subtracted from current assets to show the working capital (Fig. 6–7). An example of an actual working capital form is the balance sheet of the Green Giant Company on p. 514 of Appendix D.

Figure 6-7: Working Capital Format for Balance Sheet

Assets:		
Current assets	$xxxxx	
Less: Current liabilities	xxx	
Working capital		$ xxx
Investments		xxx
Plant and equipment		xxx
Total assets		$xxxx
Equities:		
Long-term liabilities		$ xxx
Stockholders' equity		xxx
Total equities		$xxxx

As a final example of the various balance sheet formats, the stockholders' equity is obtained by subtracting liabilities from total assets (Fig. 6–8).

Figure 6-8: Balance Sheet Format Showing Stockholders' Equity

Current assets		$ xxxx
Investments		xxxx
Plant and equipment		xxxx
Total assets		$xxxxx
Less: Current liabilities	$xxx	
Long-term liabilities	xxx	xxxx
Net assets or stockholders' equity		$ xxxx
Capital stock		$ xxx
Retained earnings		xxx
Stockholders' equity		$ xxxx

The form used will depend primarily on the preferences of the individuals responsible for the financial statements. The accountants for the business and the independent auditors usually choose the desired format. For regulated companies, the state or federal regulatory agency may specify not only the content of the statements but also the form. In some situations, the statements sent to the regulatory agencies differ materially from the financial statements released to the public.

Analysis of the Balance Sheet

The content of the balance sheet is determined by the measurement of income. Assets are cash, revenue accruals, and expense deferrals. Equities are expense accruals, revenue deferrals, and net effects of investment transactions and past income. The dollar amount for *total assets* is *not* the value of the business in any meaningful sense. Neither is the amount of *owners' equity* the value of the owners' economic interest in the business in any meaningful sense. Despite these limitations, the balance sheet conveys useful information to someone who must make decisions about a business. Properly analyzed, the information on the balance sheet can be used by investors, by creditors, and by others as a basis for sound decisions.

The Current Ratio

An important piece of information disclosed on the balance sheet is the business's potential for repaying short-term debts. Current assets, cash, and items that will be converted to cash soon are given a prominent position among the assets. Current liabilities, the existing claims against the current assets, are given a prominent place among the equities. A comparison of current assets and current liabilities is thus a useful indication of a firm's ability to repay *new* short-term loans. The comparison is usually expressed in a ratio known as the current ratio:

$$\text{Current ratio} = \frac{\text{Current assets}}{\text{Current liabilities}}$$

Assume that a company has current assets of $560,000 and current liabilities of $280,000, then the current ratio is

$$\frac{\text{Current assets}}{\text{Current liabilities}} = \frac{\$560,000}{\$280,000} = 2.0$$

For every dollar of current liabilities there are two dollars of current assets. An alternative way of stating the ratio is to say that current assets are 200% of current liabilities.

It requires a good deal of information not included on the balance sheet to decide whether a given current ratio is a "safe" position. Is the company in an industry that has good prospects? Can the inventory be sold? Can the receivables be collected? Perhaps the most important consideration is the nature of the company's operation. For example, a very low ratio may be quite acceptable for a public utility, such as an electric company, because these companies have very little inventory and other deferred costs included in their current assets and the current receivables are usually collected within the following month (customers who do not pay have their service discontinued). At the other extreme, a jewelry store with a large, slow-moving inventory and installment receivables would need a high current ratio to be in a safe position.

The Quick Ratio

Some of the doubts associated with the use of the current ratio can be eliminated by computation of the quick ratio, also called the *acid-test* ratio. As noted earlier, the classification current assets includes not only cash and accrued revenue but also certain deferred costs, primarily inventory, which presumably will be converted to cash soon. Thus, the current ratio is based on the expectation that the inventory can and will be sold and that the resulting receivables will be converted to cash. This weakness of the current ratio is eliminated by computation of the quick ratio:

$$\text{Quick ratio} = \frac{\text{Quick assets}}{\text{Current liabilities}}$$

Quick assets are current assets less inventory and other deferred costs. The deferred costs of short-term investments (marketable securities or cash substitutes) that the business expects to sell in the next year should be included in the quick assets.

Assume that the company with current assets of $560,000 has inventories of $245,000, and there are no other deferred costs included in the current assets. The quick assets are

Current assets	$560,000
Less: Inventory	245,000
Quick assets	$315,000

Then the quick ratio is computed as follows, assuming current liabilities of $280,000:

$$\frac{\text{Quick assets}}{\text{Current liabilities}} = \frac{\$315,000}{\$280,000} = 1.12$$

Here again, just what constitutes a "good" ratio depends on some facts not shown on the balance sheet. Can the receivables be collected? Can the liabilities be extended? The importance of this ratio is that it provides a more certain measure of a company's ability to pay its short-term obligations because the deferred costs are excluded from the current assets.

Other Ratios

The current ratio and the quick ratio both indicate short-term debt-paying capabilities. These are the most widely used ratios based on the balance sheet alone. There are, however, some other ratios that can give an inkling of long-term prospects.

One of these is the ratio of long-term debt to value of plant and equipment. One common method of securing long-term debt is to place a mortgage or a pledge on real estate, the land and buildings of the business. A public utility, for example, will mortgage its plant and transmission lines to provide security to the mortgage bondholders. The usefulness of this ratio is limited because the plant and equipment is valued on the balance sheet at *deferred* cost. Assume that a company has a long-term debt of $720,000 and deferred cost for plant and equipment of $2,605,000. The ratio of long-term debt to plant and equipment is

$$\frac{\text{Long-term debt}}{\text{Plant and equipment}} = \frac{\$720,000}{\$2,605,000} = 27.6\%$$

This ratio indicates that the company's long-term debt is 27.6% of plant and equipment.

Another important ratio is that of long-term debt to owners' equity, indicating the relationship of the long-term equity from the owners to the long-term equity from the lenders (debt investors). Assume that a company has long-term debt of $720,000 and that the total owners' equity is $3,000,000. The ratio of long-term debt to owners' equity is

$$\frac{\text{Long-term debt}}{\text{Owners' equity}} = \frac{\$720,000}{\$3,000,000} = 24\%$$

For this company, a large portion of the long-term capital comes from the owners. Where the ratio is low, the likelihood that the company will be able to repay the long-term liabilities is greater. What is considered a safe ratio, as with all ratios, depends on the type of business and numerous other factors.

Both of these ratios can give creditors a false sense of security. Creditors, in the final analysis, must depend on successful future operations to generate the cash needed for payment of interest and return of principal. When assets are sold in liquidation, cash often is insufficient to pay creditor claims.

Interstatement Analysis

In Chapter 5 and in prior sections of Chapter 6, various ratios used in the analysis of income statements and balance sheets have been presented. This section is concerned with the ratios and techniques used in analyzing relationships existing between these two financial statements, namely, the statement of income and the balance sheet.

Profitability

A statement of income shows the revenue, expenses, and income in absolute amounts, but income is a relative concept. To answer the question, "Was income sufficiently large to continue the operation of the business?," knowledge about the total business investment and its relationship to income is desirable, if not absolutely necessary. For example, assume that Company X has income of $50,000. The owners of the business need to determine if this is sufficient income to justify continued operations. If the total investment (total assets) in the business is $200,000, the owners may decide to continue the business; but if the investment in the business is $2,000,000, the answer to the question might be different. Income is a relative measure; only by relating income to total investment (total assets) or total stockholders' equity can a reasonable answer to the question be obtained.

Return on Total Assets

The ratio, return on total assets, is computed with the following formula:

$$\frac{\text{Net income before interest}}{\text{Total assets}} = \text{Return on total assets}$$

Assume that company Z has an income of $20,000 before interest and total assets of $200,000. Rate of return on total assets is

$$\text{Return on total assets} = \frac{\$20,000}{\$200,000} = 10\%$$

This ratio is also referred to as *return on investment*. The formula adds interest back to income because the objective is to determine how much each dollar invested produced before distributions were made to either debt investors or owner investors. If the operations are not earning a rate of return equal to or greater than the rate that could be earned in other ventures with comparable risk, then, perhaps the investment should be diverted to other activities. If the owners believe that the low return is due to inefficient operations that can be corrected in a short period of time, they may decide to continue the operations. In the long run, each activity must earn a return equal to or greater than that which could be earned in other ventures with comparable risk. Otherwise, the activity should be discontinued.

Risk is the degree of uncertainty about the future of an activity. A manager or investor will generally anticipate a higher rate of return from a volatile business, such as ladies fashions, than from a stable business, such as a public utility. Or, for example, the rate of return on an investment in a toy manufacturing company is usually expected to be higher than the rate of return from a grocery operation. There is greater risk involved in the production and distribution of ladies clothing and of toys than there is in the distribution of food products and in public utilities.

Return on Stockholders' Equity (Owners' Equity)

The ratio, return on stockholders' equity (owners' equity), is computed as follows:

$$\text{Rate of return on stockholders' equity} = \frac{\text{Income}}{\text{Stockholders' equity}}$$

To continue the preceding example, where company Z had total assets of $200,000 and an income of $20,000 before deduction of interest, assume these additional facts: (1) the interest expense for the year was $4,000 leaving a net income of $16,000 after interest; (2) the company's total liabilities were $100,000, including both long-term and current liabilities, leaving a stockholders' equity of $100,000 ($200,000 total assets less $100,000 liabilities). Then the rate of return on stockholders' equity is

$$\text{Rate of return on stockholders' equity} = \frac{\$20,000 - \$4,000}{\$100,000} = 16\%$$

This ratio indicates the return produced for each dollar invested by shareholders, including reinvested income (retained earnings). By evaluating this ratio with his level of confidence in management and other environmental factors, a shareholder may be able to determine whether or not he wishes to continue his investment in the company. He will undoubtedly look at other factors some of which will be discussed later.

It is important to note carefully the differences between the two foregoing ratios. On the one hand, return on total assets indicates how much income (expressed as a percentage) was earned on all assets employed in the business. To obtain a meaningful percentage, the income figure used must be the income produced before payment to investors. Thus, interest expense is not treated as an expense for this purpose. On the other hand, the return on stockholders' equity is an indicator of the rate of return on the amounts invested by the stockholders. For this reason, the income produced, reduced by interest payments to debt investors, is related to the stockholders' investment.

Trading on the Equity

Notice that the rate of return on total assets and the rate of return on stockholders' investment differ by 6% (16% – 10%). This indicates that shareholders are getting a greater return on their investment than the rate earned on the total assets invested in the business. At first glance, this appears impossible, but upon examination it can be explained quite easily. Recall that return on total assets is computed by adding interest expense to income and dividing by total assets; but return on shareholders' investment is computed by dividing income (after deducting interest) by shareholders' equity.

What would the results have been if Company Z had financed operations entirely with owners' capital? In that event, the owners' equity would have been $200,000, the same as the total assets, the net income would have been $20,000, because there would have been no interest, and the return on stockholders' equity would have been 10% ($20,000/$200,000), the same as the return on total assets. Instead, however, Company Z has used the capital of others, current liabilities and long-term debt, and has earned a greater return on this capital (10%) than the rate of interest paid for the use of it. The stockholders' investment was $100,000, yet they earned $16,000 after interest. Thus they have gained $6,000 by using borrowed capital.

To compute the gain from trading on the equity, assume the equities of company Z were as follows:

Current liabilities	$ 50,000
Long-term note (8% per annum)	50,000
Stockholders' equity (including contributed capital and retained earnings)	100,000
Total equities	$200,000

Assume that no interest was paid for the current liabilities; the entire $4,000 interest was paid on the long-term note ($50,000 X 8% = $4,000). Recall that the return on total assets was 10%. The gain from trading on the equity can be computed as follows:

Amount earned on current liabilities (10% return on assets X $50,000)		$5,000
Amount earned on long-term note (10% return on $50,000)	$5,000	
Less: 8% Interest on $50,000	4,000	1,000
Total gain from trading on the equity		$6,000

When this amount is added to the $10,000 earned on the stockholders' equity ($100,000 X 10%) the net income available to shareholders is $16,000, the actual net income.

Liabilities must be paid before the corporation can return any funds contributed by shareholders. This requirement increases the risk of the shareholders and decreases the risk of the holder of a liability. As a result of this assumption of risk, the shareholder receives a larger return if the return on total assets is greater than the rate of interest paid on the liabilities. By borrowing funds at a rate lower than the expected return on total assets, management can enhance the income of stockholders. However, if the interest rate is higher than the rate of return on assets, the rate of return on stockholders' equity is decreased. This financing concept is known as *trading on the equity* or *using leverage*.

Return on total assets and return on stockholders' equity are often used to make comparisons between companies within an industry and between companies in different industries. The ratios afford a much better basis for comparison than absolute amounts of income and assets. One should remember, nevertheless, when using these ratios that many assets are valued at cost and the carrying value of assets between companies may vary widely depending on time of purchase, depreciation computations, etc. Earnings per share is often a better base for intercompany and interindustry comparisons.

Investment in a company with the expectation of a future return is replete with uncertainty. Complete reliance on data supplied by financial statements is not advisable. Environmental data, including changes or expected changes in technology, economics, and politics, must also be considered. For example, investment in a company operating in Cuba a few years before Castro's revolution would have been a mistake no matter how impressive the financial statements looked. This is not to deny the importance and utility of financial data, but only to alert the statement user to the uncertainties of the future; all relevant information should be considered.

The interpretation or analysis of financial statements will be continued in each of the remaining chapters. Funds flow statements, their content and use, are discussed in the next chapter. The final chapter of this text, Chapter 17, includes a comprehensive illustration of the analysis of financial statements, including some additional ratios as well as the interpretation of the basic ratios discussed in Chapters 5 and 6.

QUESTIONS

1 What is the basic nature of assets?

2 List the major subclassifications of assets as they relate to the measurement of income. Give examples for each category.

3 List and define the major classifications of assets as found on the conventional balance sheet. Give examples for each classification.

4 Could both classifications as described in your answer to Questions 2 and 3 be shown on the same balance sheet? Which system of classification provides the most useful information in view of our present economic environment?

5 List the major classifications of equities as found on the conventional balance sheet. Give examples for each classification.

6 List the major classifications of equities as related to the measurement of income. Give examples of each classification.

7 What is the operating cycle? What bearing does the operating cycle have on the traditional classification of assets and equities on the balance sheet?

8 Describe how each classification of assets is valued for the purpose of measuring income. Why are the classifications valued differently?

9 Describe how each classification of equities is valued for the purpose of measuring income. Why are the classifications valued differently?

10 Why are some investments or securities classified as current assets whereas other investments or securities are classified as noncurrent assets?

11 Distinguish between tangible and intangible assets. Give examples of each type.

12 What are the differences between the way a corporation's owner investment is classified and the way the owner investment of a proprietorship or partnership is classified?

13 Describe the different forms of the balance sheet. Do you feel it would be desirable to require all companies to use the same form?

14 If you were to speculate about which of two businesses was the better performer on the basis of a single financial ratio, which ratio would you choose? Explain your choice.

15 E Incorporated has a return on total assets of 8% and a return on shareholders' equity of 12%. What is the probable cause of the difference?

16 W Company has a return on shareholders' equity of 8%, and yet Mr. Champlin, a shareholder, computed the rate of return on the market price of his holdings at only 5%. Explain the difference.

17 Mr. Perplexed operates a retail clothing store and earns a gross profit on sales of 60% which is 20% above the average for others in the industry; yet his return on total assets is only 4%,

barely half the average for others in the same line. Mr. Perplexed asks you to explain why he can do so well on his sales and yet do so poorly on his rate of return. What is the most probable cause? List some other factors that might explain the situation.

18   Mr. Satisfied operates a jewelry store and earns a gross profit of 50%. He believes that he must be doing extremely well because his neighbor who operates the local supermarket has a gross profit of only 12%. Explain why you agree or disagree with Mr. Satisfied.

19   If you heard that the small drug store on the corner had an annual profit of $15,000, you would consider it to be a successful operation; on the other hand, if you learned that General Motors Corporation had a profit for the year of $15,000, you would conclude that the corporation had a bad year. Why?

20   If you were contemplating an investment in a company, list five significant pieces of information you would like to have other than information in the firm's financial statements.

PROBLEMS

1   Indicate the balance sheet classification for each of the following items. Use the traditional balance sheet classifications given in the text. If you cannot determine how an item should be classified, state the additional information you would need.

[a]	FICA (social security) taxes withheld from employees	[i]	Postage stamps on hand
[b]	Cash surrender value of life insurance	[j]	Factory tools
[c]	Prepaid fire insurance premiums	[k]	Cash deposited with a local utility company
[d]	Accrued vacation pay	[l]	Patents
[e]	Loans to officers of the corporation	[m]	Copyrights
[f]	Accrued interest on bonds payable	[n]	Bonds payable in nine months
[g]	Customers' accounts with credit balances	[o]	Bonds payable in two years
[h]	Subscription revenue received in advance		

2   The following information appears on the records of J Store Inc. at August 31, 19X2:

Accounts payable (merchandise)	$ 60,000
Accounts receivable	80,000
Accrued interest revenue	1,500
Accrued salaries and wages	6,500
Advances to suppliers	3,200
Cash surrender value of insurance	2,000
Bonds payable in annual installments of $20,000	140,000
Bank—general checking account	45,000
Bank—payroll checking account	500
FICA taxes payable	1,000
Federal income taxes withheld from employees' wages	2,500
Inventory (merchandise)	120,000
Inventory (supplies)	8,000
Organization costs	2,000
Plant and equipment	90,000
Stockholder's contributed capital	100,000
Retained earnings	42,200

Required:

Prepare a classified balance sheet for J Store Inc. as of August 31, 19X2.

3   Using the following data from the records of the XYZ Company, prepare a statement of income for the year ended December 31, 19X3 and a balance sheet as of December 31, 19X3. The amounts shown are as of December 31, 19X3. The revenues and expense amounts are for the year. The balance of retained earnings at the beginning of 19X3 was $4,480. (Hint: $\Delta RE = Y - S$.)

Cash	$ 7,000
Accounts receivable	17,000
Inventory of merchandise	24,000
Supplies inventory	1,800
Investment in bonds (long-term)	30,000
Furniture and fixtures (net)	16,000
Accounts payable	27,860
Deferred service revenue	2,800
Capital stock	60,000
Sales of merchandise	200,000
Cost of goods sold	130,000
Salaries expense	56,000
Rent expense	12,000
Advertising expense	1,100
Interest revenue	240

4   The stockholders' equity sections for firms A and B are as follows:

	A	B
Contributed capital	$ 900,000	$ 500,000
Retained earnings	100,000	500,000
	$1,000,000	$1,000,000

Required:

[a] Which set of figures, those for A or those for B, makes the more favorable impression?

[b] List at least five reasons for being cautious about reaching a firm conclusion as to whether one of the firms is superior to the other on the basis of this partial information. Consider factors such as (i) the number of years the firm has been in business and (ii) the amount invested in assets.

5   [a] Consider each of the following transactions individually and indicate the transactions that would increase **working capital** and those that would decrease working capital.

[1] A note payable to the bank falls due and the firm renews the note for another six months.

[2] A note payable to the bank falls due and the firm pays the note with cash.

[3] A note payable to the bank falls due and the firm persuades the bank to replace it with a new note due in five years.

[4] A firm borrows $3,000 from the bank on a short-term note.

[5] A firm buys a new machine for $10,000 and pays cash for it.

[6] A firm buys a new building for $100,000 and pays cash of $20,000 giving a mortgage note with annual installments for the balance coming due over the next 20 years.

[7] A corporation issues bonds due in 20 years and receives $250,000 cash in exchange.

[8]   A corporation issues capital stock and receives $250,000 cash in exchange.

[9]   A corporation issues bonds in exchange for a new building. If sold for cash the bonds would have sold for $250,000.

[10] A company declared and paid a dividend of $4,000 to its shareholders.

[11] A company sold a vacant lot that it was holding for speculation.

[12] The company paid an account payable to a supplier in cash.

[13] Inventory with a book value of $5,000 was destroyed by fire.

[b]   Go through the transactions listed in part [a] a second time and indicate the effect of each transaction on (i) the current ratio and (ii) the quick ratio.

6   The rate of return earned on total assets for firm X is 14% and for firm Y is 10%.

Required:

[a]   All other things being equal, would you prefer to invest in firm X or firm Y?

[b]   Suppose that the book value of the assets for each firm is $100,000 but that firm X would have to spend $200,000 to replace its assets whereas firm Y would have to spend $125,000 to replace its assets. How does this information affect your original appraisal?

[c]   Suppose book values and replacement costs are the same for both firms but that one firm is a life insurance company and the other an off-shore drilling company in the oil industry. How does this information affect your original appraisal?

7   Mr. Z owns all of the stock of the F Corporation. The corporation's balance sheet is summarized as follows:

Assets	$1,500,000	Liabilities	$ 400,000
		Shareholder equity	1,100,000
	$1,500,000		$1,500,000

Mr. Z has been offered $1,200,000 for his stock. He believes this is a good offer because it exceeds by $100,000 the valuation of his equity shown on the balance sheet. Just to be sure, he asks your advice before deciding to accept the offer. Briefly summarize what you would tell Mr. Z about the dollar amounts that appear on the balance sheet.

8   Comparative financial statements for the ABC Company are as follows:

ABC Company
Balance Sheet

Assets:	12/31/X2	12/31/X1
Cash	$ 10,000	$ 25,000
Accounts receivable	24,000	31,000
Inventories	84,000	76,200
Plant and equipment	140,000	120,000
Other	5,000	–
Total assets	$263,000	$252,200
Liabilities:		
Accounts payable	$ 40,000	$ 25,000
Other current liabilities	7,000	5,000
Bonds payable, due in 19X9	120,000	130,000
Total liabilities	$167,000	$160,000
Stockholders' equity:		
Contributed capital (10,000 shares)	$ 70,000	$ 70,000
Retained earnings	26,000	22,200
Total stockholders' equities	$ 96,000	$ 92,200
Total equities	$263,000	$252,200

ABC Company

Statement of Income

	19X2	19X1
Sales	$800,000	$720,000
Cost of goods sold	400,000	370,000
Gross profit	$400,000	$350,000
Operating expense	360,000	320,000
	$ 40,000	$ 30,000
Bond interest expense	7,200	7,800
Income before income tax	$ 32,800	$ 22,200
Federal income tax	9,000	5,000
Net income	$ 23,800	$ 17,200

ABC Company

Statement of Retained Income

	19X2	19X1
Retained earnings, beginning balance	$22,200	$20,000
Net income for year	23,800	17,200
	$46,000	$37,200
Dividends	20,000	-15,000
	$26,000	$22,200

As of December 31, 19X2, stock of the ABC Company was selling on the open market for $35 per share.

Required:

[a] For the year 19X2 compute the following ratios for the ABC Company:
    [i] Current ratio
    [ii] Quick ratio
    [iii] Ratio of long-term debt to plant and equipment
    [iv] Return on total assets before income tax
    [v] Return on total assets after income tax
    [vi] Return on shareholders' equity after income tax
    [vii] Gain from the use of financial leverage, trading on the equity
    [viii] Gross profit percentage
    [ix] Return on sales
    [x] Earnings per share
    [xi] Price–earnings ratio
    [xii] Dividend yield

[b] Is the ABC Company more liquid or less liquid in 19X2 as compared with 19X1? Compare working capital and the appropriate ratios for each of the two years to support your conclusion.

[c] Are long-term creditors more secure or less secure in 19X2 as compared with 19X1? Use the ratio of long-term debt to plant and equipment and the ratio of long-term debt to shareholders' equity to support your conclusion.

[d] Assume that the return on total assets in future years will be the same or better than it was in 19X2. Was ABC Company wise or unwise in its decision to reduce the amount of long-term debt? Explain your conclusion.

9   The following is a list of the assets, equities, revenues, and expenses of the G Company for 19X7 and 19X8. (Note: Use one column for the amounts for 19X7 and one column for the amounts for 19X8.)

	19X8	19X7
Cash	$ 21,000	$ 10,000
Marketable securities	7,000	55,000
Accounts receivable	63,000	42,000
Inventory, merchandise	78,000	58,000
Prepaid expenses	7,000	5,000
Land (speculation)	32,000	23,000
Land (plant site)	50,000	50,000
Buildings and equipment	153,000	127,000
Patents	35,000	1,000
Notes payable	7,000	8,000
Accounts payable	41,000	27,000
Accrued expenses payable	20,000	15,000
Taxes payable	18,000	20,000
Miscellaneous current liabilities	4,000	4,000
Long-term debt	142,000	103,000
Contributed capital	47,000	47,000
Retained earnings	147,000	130,000
Dividends	15,000	14,000
Sales	669,000	628,000
Cost of goods sold	420,000	401,000
Depreciation expense	15,000	12,000
Interest expense	7,000	5,000
Selling expenses	90,000	85,000
General and administrative expense	70,000	65,000
Federal income tax	32,000	29,000

Required:

[a] Prepare a comparative statement of income showing the information for both years and a classified statement with expenses segregated into appropriate classes.

[b] Prepare a comparative balance sheet showing the information for both years and a classified statement with assets, liabilities, and shareholders' equity appropriately subclassified.

10 Mr. Barclay operates an appliance store. The current year has been a poor one for appliance dealers generally with most dealers earning only 3% on total assets. Mr. Barclay is, therefore, very pleased with his 5% return on total assets. On the basis of the following partial financial statements, determine whether or not Mr. Barclay has done better than average in the appliance business:

Current assets		$ 50,000
Investments		100,000
Plant and equipment		100,000
Total assets		$250,000
Revenue from sales		$400,000
Dividends and interest on investments		10,000
		$410,000
Cost of goods sold	$200,000	
Operating expense	197,500	
		397,500
Net income		$ 12,500

11   Condensed balance sheets and income statements for M Incorporated are

M Incorporated
Balance Sheet as of December

	19X1	19X2	19X3	19X4	19X5
Cash	$ 50,000	$ 47,930	$ 60,950	$ 72,500	$ 86,500
Accounts Receivable	20,000	32,000	27,500	41,000	33,700
Inventory	18,000	23,000	26,500	16,200	23,300
Plant and equipment	100,000	90,000	80,000	70,000	60,000
Total assets	$188,000	$192,930	$194,950	$199,700	$203,500
Current liabilities	$ 35,000	$ 48,000	$ 30,000	$ 43,500	$ 57,600
Long-term liabilities	50,000	50,000	50,000	30,000	30,000
Contributed capital	100,000	100,000	110,000	110,000	110,000
Retained earnings	3,000	(5,070)	4,950	16,200	5,900
	$188,000	$192,930	$194,950	$199,700	$203,500

M Incorporated
Statement of Income for Year Ended December 31

	19X1	19X2	19X3	19X4	19X5
Sales	$150,000	$175,000	$225,000	$280,000	$340,000
Cost of goods sold	$100,000	$140,000	$160,000	$190,000	$257,000
Selling expense	15,000	20,000	24,000	30,000	50,000
General and administrative expenses	25,000	23,070	23,980	34,750	43,300
Total expenses	$140,000	$183,070	$207,980	$254,750	$350,300
Net income (loss)	$ 10,000	$ (8,070)	$ 17,020	$ 25,250	$ (10,300)
Dividends	7,000	0	7,000	14,000	0
Change in retained earnings	$ 3,000	$ (8,070)	$ 10,020	$ 11,250	$ (10,300)

Required:

Using selected ratios, analyze the foregoing statements and write a paper making recommendations concerning an investment in M Incorporated.

CASE   William Berry organized a livestock auction market in 1965. A livestock auction ring and the necessary corrals were constructed. The ring consisted of an entrance gate, a holding or viewing arena, an exit gate leading to a scale for weighing, and an exit from the scale to the holding pens. The ring was surrounded by seats for buyers and viewers. The corrals were a series of holding pens of varying sizes which were used to hold the cattle from the time they were delivered to the yards until they entered the auction ring. After they were sold the holding pens were used to yard the livestock until they were picked up by their buyers. The land for the auction ring and the corrals cost $2,000. The cost of constructing the auction ring was $11,500 and of the corrals, $6,500. The cost of constructing the ring and yard was low because materials were purchased at a bargain price from an abandoned military installation.

An auction market serves as an agent for the seller. Buyers come and actively bid on the livestock presented for sale. The highest bidder is awarded the cattle. Mr. Berry did buy livestock on each sale day if he felt they were selling below their market value. The cattle purchased by Mr. Berry were held and sold at the next sale date. The revenue of the livestock auction was primarily from commissions charged to the sellers. The livestock which he purchased and held to a later sale might or might not be sold at a profit. In most years, a small loss resulted from the cattle-trading activities.

Mr. Berry operated the sale ring in 1965, 1966, 1967, and 1968. The sales ring was reasonably successful in the first four years. Early in 1969, Mr. Berry had an opportunity to buy an irrigated farm. He was able to borrow $35,000 from a local bank by mortgaging the livestock auction market. Mr. Berry used the $35,000 to make the down payment on the farm and assumed a mortgage of $50,000.

Mr. Berry did not want to operate the sales ring and the farm as a single unit. He, therefore, maintained a separate record for each operation. The mortgage on the sales ring was part of the equities of the livestock market operation. In the fall of 1969 the banker requested a balance sheet and income statement of the livestock auction market. Berry had also borrowed $5,000 from the bank on a 90-day note to use in operation of the auction barn. Mr. Berry's bookkeeper prepared the balance sheet and income statement as presented in Schedules 1 and 2. The auction ring and corrals had an estimated life of 25 years and no salvage value. The accumulated depreciation was the depreciation taken for the five years of operation.

When the bookkeeper presented Mr. Berry with the financial statements, he was visually upset. He made the following comment to the bookkeeper: "This statement shows I am bankrupt and I just borrowed $35,000 from the bank. Either that banker is a blubbering idiot or the statements you prepared are flat wrong."

SCHEDULE 1

Livestock Auction Market

Balance Sheet as of December 31, 1969

Assets			
Current assets:			
Cash		$ 1,250	
Cattle inventory		6,350	
Feed and supplies		3,800	
Total current assets			$11,400
Plant and equipment:			
Land		$ 2,000	
Auction ring and yards	$18,000		
Less: Accumulated depreciation	3,600	14,400	
Equipment:	$ 3,000		
Less: Accumulated depreciation	1,500	1,500	
Total plant and equipment			17,900
Total assets			$29,300

Equities		
Current liabilities:		
Bank loan (90-day note)	$ 5,000	
Accounts payable	1,200	
Wages payable	2,000	
Other current payables	400	
Total current liabilities		$ 8,600
Mortgage payable		35,000
Total liabilities		$43,600
William Berry, net worth (deficit)		(14,300)
Total equities		$29,300

SCHEDULE 2
Livestock Auction Market

Statement of Income for Year Ended December 31, 1969

Revenues:		
Commission from livestock		$62,000
Sales of livestock	$26,840	
Cost of livestock sold	26,980	(140)
Gross revenue		$61,860
Expenses:		
Auctioneer	$ 2,500	
Feed and supplies	14,500	
Wage expense	21,800	
Payroll taxes	1,040	
Property taxes	460	
Licenses	500	
Interest expense	840	
Repairs and maintenance	6,000	
Depreciation	1,120	
Utilities	1,900	
Professional fee	2,000	
Total expenses		$52,660
Net income		$ 9,200
Less: Owners withdrawals		10,000
Net decrease in capital		($ 800)

Required:

[a] The balance sheet was prepared in accordance with generally accepted accounting principles. Explain why the balance sheet shows a net deficit for Mr. Berry.

[b] Compute the following ratios:
    [i] Return on total assets
    [ii] Return on owner equity
    [iii] Return on sales
    [iv] Gain from trading on the equity

[c] Comment on the validity of each of the above ratios. If you were the banker, would you renew Mr. Berry's 90-day note?

7

Statement of Changes in Financial Position

The traditional financial statements, the statement of income and the statement of financial position, do not disclose directly many important financial events which occur in business enterprises. For example, given statements of income and of financial position, the statement reader cannot determine the investment in long-lived assets during the current accounting period. He can compare the deferred costs for long-lived assets shown on the balance sheet at the end of the period with that at the beginning of the period. This comparison, however, will show only the net change and will not reveal the amounts spent for new additions to plant and equipment, retirements or dispositions of plant and equipment, and depreciation for the accounting period.

As with additions to long-lived assets, the statements of financial position and income fail to provide information about other important events. Information that cannot always be obtained directly from balance sheets and income statements includes

1 The actual cash receipts and cash disbursements, either in total, or by object or function, from operations
2 Acquisitions of new plant and equipment
3 Expenditures of assets or issuances of stocks or bonds for new long-term investments, perhaps involving acquisitions of whole business firms
4 Cash realized on disposition of plant and equipment, investments, and other extraordinary activities
5 New capital received from debt investors and debts paid during the year
6 New capital received from owner investors and the resources distributed to owner investors to redeem outstanding stock or for other purposes

In recent years more and more companies have issued a third report which is called the *statement of changes in financial position, statement of cash flow, statement of changes in working capital, or statement of sources and applications of funds.* Opinion No. 19 of the Accounting Principles Board of the American

Institute of Certified Public Accountants, issued in March, 1971, requires that a statement summarizing changes in financial position be presented as a basic financial statement. Opinion 19 recommends that the title of the statement be "statement of changes in financial position."

Changes in financial position have been viewed as an analysis of the sources and application of cash or an analysis of the sources and applications of working capital (current assets minus current liabilities). A statement of changes in financial position that reports only the results of transactions that either change cash or working capital may exclude certain financing and investing transactions. For example, a transaction in which the company exchanges debt-investment securities for property would not affect cash or working capital. Opinion 19 requires that all significant investing and financing transactions be shown. In summary, a statement of changes in financial position should show:

1   Cash or working capital provided by operations
2   Cash or working capital provided by extraordinary transactions. Items shown as extraordinary items on the income statement should also be shown separately on the statement of changes in financial position. This information should immediately follow the section on cash or working capital provided by operations.
3   If working capital format is used, changes in each element of working capital should be disclosed in a separate schedule.
4   Outlays for purchase of long-term assets (identifying separately such items as investments, property, and intangibles)
5   Proceeds from sale of long-lived assets now shown as extraordinary items. Major categories, such as investments, property, and intangibles, should be shown separately. Items affecting cash or working capital should be separated from items not affecting cash or working capital.
6   Conversion of long-term debt or preferred stock to common stock
7   Issuance and repayment of long-term debt
8   Issuance and purchase of a company's own capital stock for cash or for assets other than cash
9   Dividends in cash or in kind or other distributions to shareholders

The objectives of this chapter are to discuss the form and content of the statement of changes in financial position and to present a method for preparing this type of statement that will provide some understanding of its uses and limitations.

Cash Flow Approach to Statement of Changes in Financial Position

The flow of cash and its importance to the entity is emphasized throughout this book. The measurement of income is the process of adjusting cash inflows and cash outflows for accruals, deferrals, and investment transactions. Changes in cash within a given period may be analyzed by preparing a statement of cash receipts and cash disbursements or by analyzing the changes as either sources or applications (uses) of cash. The format that presents sources and applications of cash is required by APB Opinion No. 19.

In Chapter 3 we used the information on beginning balance sheets, the statements of cash receipts and disbursements, and the ending accruals and deferrals to prepare statements of income and ending balance sheets. A simple rearrangement of the formulas used in Chapter 3 enables us to reverse the computations to determine cash inflows and outflows for the accounting period under consideration.

$$R = CR + \Delta AR - \Delta DR - DIR - OIR \qquad (1)$$
$$E = CD + \Delta AE - \Delta DE - DID - OID - S \qquad (2)$$

If we solve equations (1) and (2) for cash receipts and cash disbursements, we have:

$$CR = R - \Delta AR + \Delta DR + DIR + OIR \qquad (3)$$
$$CD = E - \Delta AE + \Delta DE + DID + OID + S \qquad (4)$$

These equations for CR and CD can be solved for the total amounts and can also be used to compute amounts received from various individual sources and amounts disbursed for individual functions or objects, if the comparative balance sheet and the statement of income contain the necessary details.

A Schematic Framework

Equations (3) and (4) summarize all possible sources of cash inflows and outflows. The basic objective of the statement of changes in financial position is to provide information about causes of cash inflows and outflows. Net cash flows from operations are to be shown separately from other cash flows. Therefore, equations (3) and (4) are each divided into two parts to show separately the cash flows from operating transactions and the cash flows from financing transactions (see Fig. 1–1). Equation (3) can be broken down as follows:

Operating transactions: $$CR_o = R - \Delta AR + \Delta DR \qquad (5)$$
Financing transactions: $$CR_f = DIR + OIR \qquad (6)$$

Accounting Principles Board Opinion No. 19 requires that net operational flows be separated from inflows of resources from other sources. Equations (5) and (6) separate operational transactions from financing transactions but do not separate ordinary operational inflows from extraordinary resource inflow. Recall the discussion in Chapter 5 on the disclosure of extraordinary items on the statement of income. Extraordinary gains and losses usually arise because of the disposition of long-lived assets. Sale of an asset, such as goodwill, not previously recognized for accounting purposes, and a settlement of a liability for more or less than the recorded value are other examples. These extraordinary inflows of resources should be shown separately from the ordinary operational activities. Because of these requirements, the net changes in accruals and deferrals should be analyzed to permit separate disclosure on the statement of changes in financial position.

Just as equation (3) provides the input for computing inflows of resources, equation (4) provides the input for computing the outflows or uses of resources. Equation (4) can be broken down as follows:

$$\text{Operating transactions:} \quad CD_O = E - \Delta AE + DE \tag{7}$$
$$\text{Financing transactions:} \quad CD_f = DID + OID + S \tag{8}$$

Disbursements of cash for financing purposes are shown separately from operational activities. Financing transaction outflows are shown as a part of the application section and should be disclosed individually. Cash disbursements for operational activities are to be segregated into those costs that are consumed currently (expenses) and those that are to be consumed over extended periods (deferred costs). For this reason, the amounts spent for long-lived assets acquired during the period are shown as a use of resources. Current depreciation, cost depletion, and amortization of long-lived assets are subtracted from expenses to show the net cash outflow for current operations. The flow chart in Fig. 7-1 presents a schematic diagram for computing cash inflows and outflows from information available in the statement of income and the comparative statement of financial position.

There are three major sources and three major uses of funds. The major cash inflows are from ordinary operations, dispositions of assets (extraordinary items), and financing activities. The three major outflows are expenses, acquisitions of long-lived assets, and disbursements to debt and ownership equity interests. Cash inflows and outflows from current operations are shown together or netted to meet the APB Opinion No. 19 requirement that the net cash inflow from operations should be shown as a net or single item. Changes in current deferred costs, inventories, prepaid items, etc., and changes in accrued expenses, accounts payable, accrued wages, etc., are shown as increases or decreases in computing the cash outflow from operations. Changes in deferred revenue and accrued revenue items are handled similarly.

Example of Preparation of a Statement of Changes in Financial Position—Cash Approach

The R Company is a small retail entity operating in a medium-size metropolitan area. Figure 7-2 is a comparative balance sheet, and Fig. 7-3 is a statement of income and a statement of retained earnings. The numbers in parentheses on the comparative balance sheet and statement of retained earnings will be used to reference changes in accruals and deferrals from the balance sheet and the statement of retained earnings to the statement of changes in financial position (Fig. 7-4), and the supporting schedule of cash inflows and outflows from operations (Fig. 7-5). The list on page 173 explains the numbered items:

Figure 7-1: Flow Chart for Statement of Changes in Financial Position

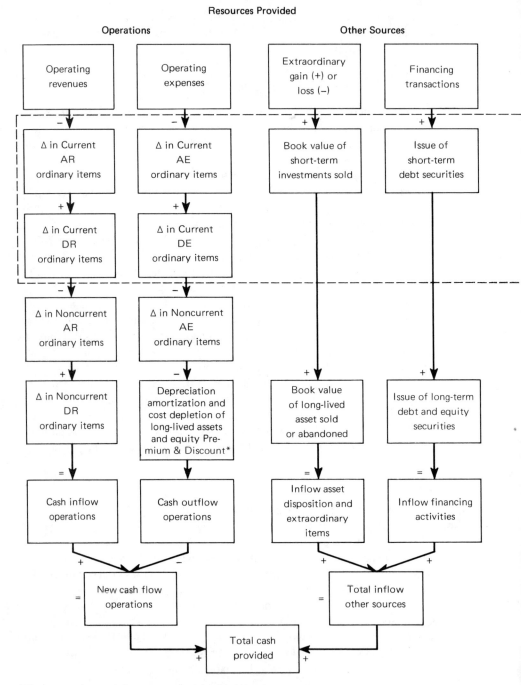

*Equity premium and discount are explained in later chapters.

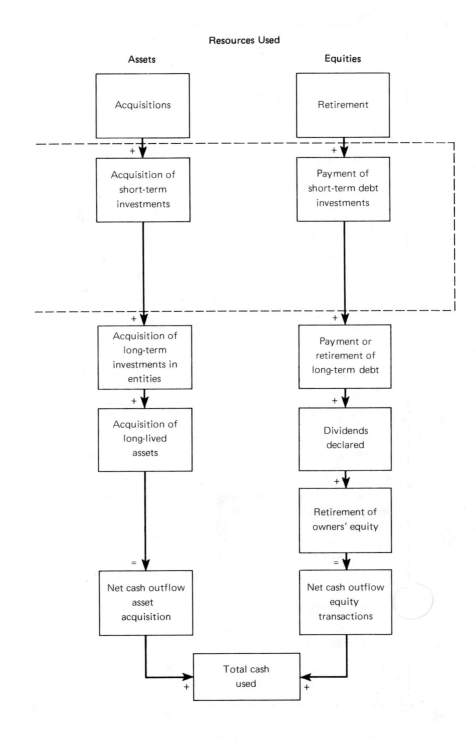

Figure 7-2

R Company			Balance Sheet
	12/31/19X0	12/31/19X1	Change
Assets:			
Cash	$ 5,000	$ 20,000	$15,000
Accounts receivable (1)	10,000	30,000	20,000
Inventory (2)	20,000	17,000	-3,000
Plant and equipment (3)	40,000	43,000	3,000
	$75,000	$110,000	$35,000
Equities:			
Accounts payable (merchandise) (4)	$ 2,000	$ 6,000	$ 4,000
Notes payable—bank, due 7/1/19X2 (5)	0	5,000	5,000
Income taxes (6)	10,000	20,000	10,000
Accrued salaries (7)	1,000	500	-500
Mortgage payable (8)	30,000	28,000	-2,000
Common stock	20,000	20,000	0
Retained earnings (9 & 10)	12,000	30,500	18,500
	$75,000	$110,000	$35,000

Figure 7-3

R Company	Statement of Income for Year Ended December 31, 19X1	
Revenue:		
Sales		$197,000
Expenses:		
Cost of goods sold	$110,000	
Salaries and other operating expenses	25,000	
Depreciation of plant and equipment	5,000	140,000
Net income before income taxes		$ 57,000
Income taxes		20,000
Net income before extraordinary items		$ 37,000
Extraordinary gain [disposal of plant and equipment (11)		3,000
Net income (10)		$ 40,000
Statement of Retained Earnings		
Balance 12/31/X0		$ 12,000
Income for year (10)		40,000
		52,000
Dividends paid (9)		21,500
Balance, 12/31/X1		$ 30,500

Figure 7-4

R Company	Statement of Changes in Financial Position for Year Ended December 31, 19X1		
Cash provided:			
Cash provided by operations (schedule of cash inflows and cash outflows)		$38,500	
Cash provided by extraordinary item:			
Gain on disposal of plant and equipment (11)	$ 3,000		
Book value of item sold (3)	23,000		
Proceeds of disposal		26,000	
Loan from bank (5)		5,000	
Total Cash Provided			$69,500
Cash applied:			
Acquisitions of plant and equipment (3)		$31,000	
Payment on mortgage (8)		2,000	
Payment of dividends (9)		21,500	
Total Cash Applied			54,500
Increase in Cash			$15,000

Figure 7-5

R Company	Schedule of Cash Inflows and Outflows from Operations for Year Ended December 31, 19X2		
Cash inflows from operations:			
Sales from operations		$197,000	
Less: Increase in accounts receivable (1)		20,000	
Total cash inflows from operations			$177,000
Cash outflows from operations:			
Total expenses (including income taxes)	$160,000		
Plus: Decrease in accrued salaries (7)	500	$160,500	
Less: Decrease in inventory (2)	$ 3,000		
Depreciation (3)	5,000		
Increase in accounts payable (4)	4,000		
Increase in income taxes payable (6)	10,000	22,000	
Total cash outflows from operations			138,500
Net cash inflow from operations			$ 38,500

1   Increase in accounts receivable of $20,000. The increase in the revenue accrual, accounts receivable, increased revenue and consequently income increased, but cash did not. Therefore, $20,000 must be deducted from revenue to compute cash inflows as shown on schedule of cash inflows and outflows from operation.

2   Decrease in inventory of $3,000. The decrease in the cost deferral, inventory, did not require the expenditure of cash during the current period. Cash to acquire this inventory was expended in a prior period; therefore, $3,000 has to be subtracted from expenses to arrive at cash outflows for the period.

3   Increase in plant and equipment of $3,000. From an examination of the statement of income we know that $5,000 of depreciation was deducted. This amount should be subtracted from expenses because it did not require an expenditure of cash during the current period. The extraordinary gain shown on the income statement was from disposal of plant and equipment. Inquiry revealed that the book value of the equipment sold was $23,000. The total decrease in plant and equipment was $28,000 (depreciation of $5,000 plus remaining cost of equipment sold of $23,000). However, plant and equipment increased by $3,000 (item 3 of the comparative balance sheet). A reasonable assumption would be that additional equipment costing $31,000 was purchased. The net effect on plant and equipment would be an increase of $3,000 (the $31,000 increase minus the $5,000 depreciation and the $23,000 cost of equipment sold). These items appear on either the supporting schedule of cash inflows and outflows or the statement of changes in financial position.

4   Increase in accounts payable of $4,000. This increase in accounts payable of $4,000 did not require the expenditure of cash in the current period; therefore, $4,000 is subtracted from expenses on the schedule of cash inflows and outflows from operations.

5   Increase in notes payable of $5,000. The increase in notes payable represents a new loan from the bank. This was a debt-investment receipt and is a source of cash. This item is shown on the statement of changes in financial position.

6   Increase in income taxes payable of $10,000. The increase in income taxes payable of $10,000 did not require a current expenditure of cash. Therefore, $10,000 is subtracted from expenses to arrive at the cash outflows from operations.

7   Decrease in accrued salaries of $500. The decrease in accrued salaries indicates that $500 more was spent for salaries this period than was incurred. Therefore, $500 must be added to expenses to arrive at cash outflows.

8   Decrease in mortgage of $2,000. A decrease in the mortgage of $2,000 indicates that $2,000 of cash was applied to reduce the mortgage, an investment item. This item is shown as a use of cash.

9 & 10   Increase in retained earnings of $18,500. An increase of $18,500 should be analyzed in more detail. Retained earnings were increased by the income of $40,000 and decreased by dividends of $21,500, that is, a net change of $18,500. The dividend of $21,500, an investment transaction, is a use of cash.

All items of change between the comparative balance sheets have been explained. Subtracting the cash applied from the cash provided gives the change in cash of $15,000.

The schedule of cash inflows and outflows from operations (Fig. 7–5), may be included as a part of the formal statement of changes in financial position. A separate schedule is easier to follow when there are several adjustments to revenues and expenses. The objective is to present a clear and informative report. Reporting firms have discretion over format but must show in the statement itself or in supporting schedules the nine items listed on p. 167.

Working Capital Approach to Statement of Changes in Financial Position

The working capital approach is a method of showing changes in financial position that many corporations use in their published financial statements. The APB approved this approach in Opinion No. 19 but requires a separate schedule or tabulation of the change in each element of the working capital whenever it is used.

Working Capital Defined

Working capital is the difference between current assets and current liabilities. When funds are defined as working capital, the funds statement explains the change in working capital for the year. At present, this definition of funds is the most widely used in published financial reports.

A Schematic Framework

The possible sources and application of working capital are the same as those for the cash approach. The three major sources of working capital are operations, dispositions of assets (extraordinary items), and financing activities. The three major outflows of working capital are expenses, acquisitions of long-lived assets, and disbursements to debt and ownership equity holders. Figure 7–6 charts the flows of working capital provided and applied. Notice that Fig. 7–1 differs from Fig. 7–6 in that the former includes changes in current accrued revenues, current deferred expenses, current accrued expenses, current deferred revenues, and current debt-investment equities. (The dotted lines on Fig. 7–1 outline the items left out on Fig. 7–6.)

The working capital approach combines the sum of current assets minus current liabilities into a single pool and then identifies various activities of the entity that cause inflows or outflows from the pool.

Figure 7-6: Flow Chart for Statement of Changes in Financial Position

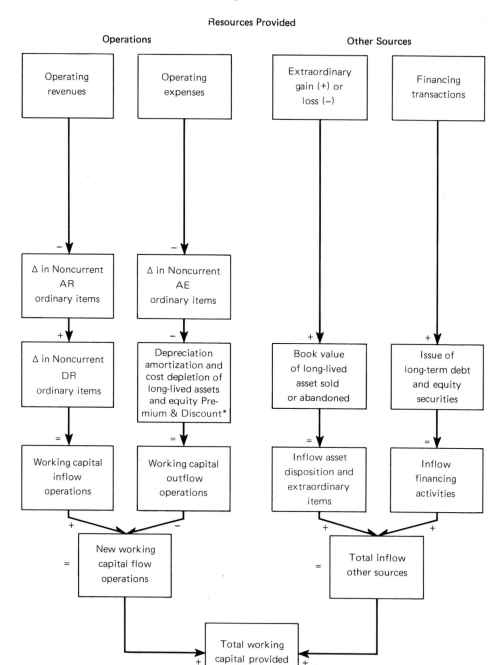

*Equity premium and discount are explained in later chapters.

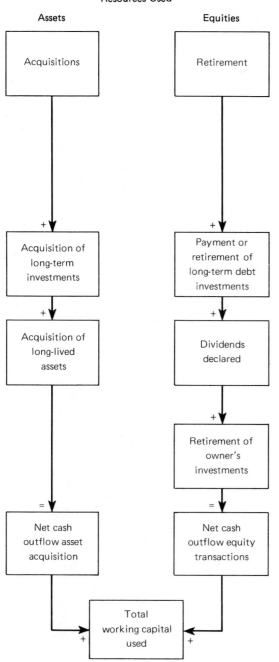

Example of Preparation of Statement of Changes in Financial Position—Working Capital Approach

The first step in preparing a statement of changes in financial position (working capital approach) is to prepare a schedule of changes in working capital (Fig. 7-7).

Figure 7-7

R Company	Schedule of Changes in Working Capital Year Ended December 31, 19X1		
	12/31/19X0	12/31/19X1	Change
Cash	$ 5,000	$20,000	$15,000
Accounts receivable	10,000	30,000	20,000
Inventory	20,000	17,000	-3,000
Total current assets	$35,000	$67,000	$32,000
Less: Current liabilities			
Accounts payable	2,000	6,000	4,000
Notes payable	0	5,000	5,000
Income taxes payable	10,000	20,000	10,000
Accrued salaries	1,000	500	-500
Total current liabilities	$13,000	$31,500	$18,500
Working capital	$22,000	$35,500	$13,500

The items appearing on Fig. 7-7 are limited to those items that are classified as current assets or current liabilities. With the information on this schedule, one can prepare a new comparative balance sheet that summarizes current assets and current liabilities as one item, namely, working capital. Figure 7-8 shows such a balance sheet for the R Company. (Compare this form with the more detailed balance sheet, Fig. 7-2.)

Figure 7-8

R Company	Comparative Balance Sheets for Working Capital Approach		
	12/31/19X0	12/31/19X1	Changes
Assets:			
Working capital (Fig. 7-6)	$22,000	$35,500	$13,500
Plant and equipment	40,000	43,000	3,000
Total assets	$62,000	$78,500	$16,500
Equitles:			
Mortgage payable	$30,000	$28,000	$-2,000
Common stock	20,000	20,000	0
Retained earnings	12,000	30,500	18,500
Total equities	$62,000	$78,500	$16,500

Figure 7–9 presents a statement of changes in financial position using the flow through approach and the working capital definition of funds.

Figure 7–9

R Company	Statement of Changes in Financial Position Working Capital for Year Ended December 31, 19X1. Add Back Approach		
Sources of working capital:			
Working capital provided by operations			
Revenues		$197,000	
Expenses	$160,000		
Less: Expenses not using			
working capital	5,000		
Expenses using working capital		155,000	
Net working capital from operations			$42,000
Extraordinary items providing working			
capital:			
Gain on disposal of plant and			
equipment		$ 3,000	
Book value of items sold		23,000	
Total working capital from			
extraordinary items			26,000
Total working capital provided			$68,000
Application of working capital:			
Acquisition of plant and equipment		$ 31,000	
Payment to reduce mortgage		2,000	
Payment of dividends		21,500	
Total application of working capital			54,500
Increase in working capital			$13,500

The methods and illustrations presented up to this point have used what accountants call the *flow through* approach in analyzing the net resources provided from operations. This approach adjusts revenues and expenses for changes in balance sheet items that did not affect inflows or outflows of cash or working capital during the current period. The flow through method combined with a cash definition of funds provides a more informative report than other commonly used approaches. Despite its superiority, it is seldom used in published financial statements.

Historically, the purpose of a funds flow statement was to explain changes in working capital, not the changes in financial position. The historic objective emphasizing the reasons for changes in funds could be most conveniently satisfied by what accountants call the *add back* method which is discussed and illustrated in the next section. Even with adoption of the broader objective of reporting all changes in financial position, most companies continue to use the add back approach combined with a working capital definition of funds. Perhaps widespread acceptance of the flow through approach and the cash definition of funds will eventually come. In the interim, an understanding of the add back approach and the working capital definition of funds is essential because published statements most frequently employ this format.

The Add Back Method

The add back method starts with income from operations and adds back those expenses that do not require the use of working capital. In like manner, revenues that do not increase working capital are subtracted. Because of contemporary practices with regard to recognition of revenue, significant adjustments of net income for revenues that do not provide funds should be rare.* Typically, the important adjustments are for expenses such as depreciation, amortization, and cost depletion. In recent years changes in the balance of deferred income taxes have also become an important adjustment.

Accounting Principles Board Opinion No. 19 requires that income from ordinary and extraordinary items be disclosed separately. Figure 7-10 presents the statement of changes in financial position for the R Company using the add back method and the working capital definition of funds. The schedule of working capital changes appears at the bottom of Fig. 7-10.

Figure 7-11 is an actual consolidated statement of changes in financial position for A-O Smith Corporation. Note that the statement presents changes for two years.

Appendix D presents the financial statements of several publicly held corporations. Each set of financial statements includes a statement of changes in financial position. All of these statements use the add back method. Green Giant Company and subsidiaries and Indian Head, Inc., and subsidiaries use a working capital definition of funds; Singer Company and its consolidated subsidiaries and Gould, Inc., and its consolidated subsidiaries use a cash definition. Both of the latter companies show changes in short-term accruals and deferrals as sources or uses of resources from activities other than ordinary operations. A precisely correct presentation would show that changes in accounts receivable, inventories, accounts payable, accrued expenses, and other deferred credits do result from ordinary operations. For this reason these companies are likely to mislead some statement users. Their adherence to a traditional format is understandable, but it is outdated.

Continued evolution and refinement of both the content and format of the statement of changes in financial position should result in published reports similar to the ones presented for R Company in Figs. 7-4 and 7-5. To most laymen the term funds probably means cash. If this is true, a report purporting

---

*As explained in previous chapters, accountants usually recognize revenue only when liquid resources are acquired.

Figure 7-10

R Company	Statement of Changes in Financial Position Working Capital for Year Ended December 31, 19X1. Flow Through Approach		
Sources of working capital:			
From operations:			
Income before extraordinary items		$37,000	
Add: Depreciation		5,000	
Total from operations before extraordinary items			$42,000
Extraordinary item:			
Gain		$ 3,000	
Book value of items sold		23,000	
Total from extraordinary items			26,000
Total Provided			$68,000
Application of working capital:			
Acquisition of equipment		$31,000	
Mortgage payable		2,000	
Dividends		21,500	
Total application			54,500
Increase in working capital			$13,500
Increase (decrease) in elements of working capital:			
Cash			$15,000
Accounts receivable			20,000
Inventory			(3,000)
Accrued salaries			500
Accounts payable			(4,000)
Notes payable			(5,000)
Income taxes payable			(10,000)
Total net increase in working capital			$13,500

to show funds provided by operations should use cash as the definition of funds. The concept of working capital, although generally understood by the professionals in the financial community, may not be well understood by laymen.

No matter what definition of funds is employed or what approach (the flow through or add-back) is taken, a clearly presented statement of financial position provides valuable information to a statement user. At the present time it is commonplace for large corporations to acquire collections of assets and even whole businesses by issuing stocks and bonds instead of paying cash. Under such circumstances, a statement that reports these significant financial transactions is essential for a proper evaluation of performance, position, and prospects. In addition, the statement provides valuable clues about the degree of a firm's conservatism, or lack of it, with regard to revenue recognition and its choices concerning capitalization versus expensing. For example, firms in the franchising business have been known to recognize revenue on the basis of contingent

Figure 7-11

A. O. SMITH CORPORATION	1970	1971	
CONSOLIDATED STATEMENT OF CHANGES IN FINANCIAL POSITION			**WORKING CAPITAL**
			SOURCE:
	$ 7,287,004	$12,808,226	Earnings before extraordinary items
	9,850,821	10,792,192	Depreciation
	627,275	2,700,000	Deferred income taxes
Years Ended December 31, 1970 and 1971	1,737,344	(592,886)	Equity in (earnings) losses of unconsolidated affiliates
	677,674	1,414,952	Other items not involving working capital
	20,180,118	27,122,484	Total from operations exclusive of extraordinary items
	2,146,000	(1,760,000)	Extraordinary items
	1,419,672	3,969,870	Amounts applicable thereto not involving working capital
	3,565,672	2,209,870	Total from extraordinary items
	34,291,224	—	Proceeds from sale of debentures, less related costs of $708,776
	—	1,340,293	Long-term borrowings—banks
	451,797	688,253	Proceeds from exercise of stock options
	58,488,811	31,360,900	
			USE:
	3,456,506	3,430,865	Cash dividends paid
	1,641,438	2,033,528	Payments on long-term debt
	23,267,000	17,335,205	Plant and equipment expenditures
	5,450,815	412,665	Investment in subsidiaries and affiliates
	—	2,100,000	Prepaid pension costs
	1,494,850	1,098,612	Purchase of treasury stock
	1,936,001	917,231	Deferred model change-over expenditures
	266,034	1,413,159	Other
	37,512,644	28,741,265	
	$20,976,167	$ 2,619,635	INCREASE
			INCREASE (DECREASE) IN COMPONENTS OF WORKING CAPITAL:
	$ 2,123,520	$(1,387,518)	Cash and marketable securities
	5,707,364	1,858,073	Receivables
	8,809,957	(329,300)	Inventories
	3,031,647	3,943,682	Accounts payable
	2,512,633	3,389,956	Income taxes
	(1,205,045)	(3,676,229)	Accrued payroll
	(3,909)	(1,179,029)	Other
	$20,976,167	$ 2,619,635	

See accompanying notes.

Reprinted from the 1971 financial statements of A. O. Smith Corporation.

long-term receivables. Other firms have capitalized intangibles, such as market research expenditures, when recovery through operations is highly questionable. A well-prepared statement of changes in financial position makes it easier to detect such undesirable practices. Finally, information about funds flow needed for more traditional purposes, such as for determining the availability of liquid resources for dividends and expansion and for detecting an impending liquidity crisis, are provided by a statement of changes in financial position.

QUESTIONS

1   The material in Chapters 5 and 6 dealing with the analysis of financial statements explained the typical uses made of the balance sheet and statements of income. In the decision-making process, what information might an investor look for in a statement of changes in financial position that uses the cash approach? The working capital approach?

2   A company may be highly profitable and yet have no cash currently available for dividends. List some reasons for a shortage of cash in a profitable company.

3   Without referring to the text, write out the equations for revenue and expense. Then, solve the equations for CR and CD.

4   The equations used in the text for the computation of income are ideally suited for the preparation of a statement of funds if "funds" is defined as cash. On the other hand, the equations are not well suited to other definitions of funds. Why is this true?

5   Choose the approach to the statement of changes in financial position that you believe presents the most useful information to the statement user and write a brief defense of your choice.

6   Why is depreciation added to net income to obtain the funds provided by operations when the add back method is used?

7   Is depreciation a source of cash or working capital? Explain.

8   Summarize the information that should be shown in a statement of changes in financial position as specified by APB Opinion No. 19.

9   Why should changes in resources caused by extraordinary items be shown separately from those resulting from ordinary operations?

10   The APB specifies that resources provided and used by operations are to be netted but that acquisition and disposition of long-lived assets are to be shown separately on the statement of changes in financial position. Discuss the pros and cons of this approach.

11   Compare and contrast the flow through and add back methods in the presentation of the statement of changes in financial position. Present the advantages and disadvantages of each approach in a report addressed to nonaccountants.

12   Write a critique of the format used by A. O. Smith Corporation in the statement of changes in financial position in Fig. 7-11.

PROBLEMS

1   Indicate whether the following changes in account balances would be a source or an application of resources using (i) the cash definition and (ii) the working capital definition:
   [a]   Increase in accounts payable
   [b]   Decrease in accounts receivable
   [c]   Increase in investment in the stock of another company
   [d]   Retirement of bonds payable
   [e]   An exchange of the company's stock for merchandise inventory
   [f]   The conversion of bonds payable to common stock of the company
   [g]   The issuance of bonds in exchange for plant and equipment
   [h]   An increase in prepaid insurance
   [i]   The expense arising from the amortization of patent costs
   [j]   A decrease in the inventory of factory supplies.

2   The H Company revenue from sales for 19X2 was $122,000. Accruals and deferrals related to revenue were:

	December 31	
	19X1	19X2
Accounts receivable	$10,000	$13,000
Advances from customers	4,500	6,000

How much cash did the company collect from customers in 19X2?

3   The H Company statement of income for the year 19X1 shows $85,000 for cost of goods sold (expense). Accruals and deferrals related to cost of sales for 19X1 were

	December 31	
	19X0	19X1
Accounts payable (merchandise)	$18,000	$15,000
Merchandise inventory	20,000	24,000

How much cash did the company pay for merchandise during 19X1?

4   The following is a condensed balance sheet of the B Company:

B Company
Balance Sheet as of December 31, 19X4

Assets:	19X3	19X4
Cash	$ 30,000	$ 20,000
Accounts receivable	50,000	60,000
Inventory	60,000	65,000
Prepaid expenses	10,000	15,000
Land, buildings, and equipment		
(net of depreciation)	60,000	90,000
Total assets	$210,000	$250,000
Equities:		
Accrued expenses	$ 5,000	$ 10,000
Accounts payable (merchandise)	40,000	50,000
Bonds payable	50,000	40,000
Contributed capital	110,000	130,000
Retained earnings	5,000	20,000
Total equities	$210,000	$250,000

The following is a condensed statement of income for the B Company for 19X4:

B Company
Statement of Income for Year Ended December 31, 19X4

Revenue		$265,000
Cost of goods sold	$167,000	
Operating expenses	73,000	240,000
Net income		$ 25,000

Depreciation for the year was $12,500. Capital stock valued at $20,000 was issued in exchange for a tract of land. Cash dividends of $10,000 were paid during the year. The accrued and prepaid expenses on the balance sheet relate to operating expenses.

Required:

[a]   Prepare a statement of changes in financial position using the cash approach
[b]   Prepare a statement of changes in financial position using the working capital approach.

5   The following are a statement of financial position and a condensed statement of income for the S Products Company:

S Products Company
Balance Sheet

	December 31	
	19X1	19X2
Assets:		
Working capital	$410,000	$420,000
Investments	75,000	120,000
Land	45,000	45,000
Buildings and equipment	285,000	390,000
Patents	21,000	18,000
Total assets	$836,000	$993,000
Equities:		
Convertible 5% bonds	$220,000	$200,000
Contributed capital	450,000	570,000
Retained earnings	166,000	223,000
Total equities	$836,000	$993,000

S Products Company
Statement of Income for Year Ended December 31, 19X2

Revenues		$1,240,000
Cost of goods sold	$743,000	
Selling expenses	152,000	
General and administrative expenses	134,000	
Depreciation	65,000	
Income taxes	66,000	1,160,000
Net income before extraordinary items		$ 80,000
Extraordinary loss from sale of plant and equipment		23,000
Net income		$ 57,000

Required:

Prepare a statement of changes in financial position for the S Products Company using the net working capital definition of funds. Additional information is as follows:

[a]   Investments are in securities actively traded. No sales were made in 19X2.

[b]   Book value of plant and equipment sold was $32,000. Proceeds of the sale were $9,000.

[c]   Patents had an estimated life of seven years from beginning of the year. Patent amortization is included as part of cost of goods sold.

[d] $20,000 of convertible bonds were converted to common stock.

6   The following information is available for the T Corporation for the year ended December 31, 19X8:

Balance Sheet

	December 31	
	19X7	19X8
Assets:		
Cash	$ 8,000	$ 10,000
Accounts receivable	15,000	20,000
Prepaid advertising expense	1,000	800
Inventory	10,000	15,000
Plant, property, and equipment (net)	50,000	60,000
Total assets	$84,000	$105,800

Equities:

Accounts payable (inventory)	$ 5,000	$ 5,600
Notes payable, due in 19X9	––	10,000
Accrued interest payable	2,000	1,500
Accrued salaries	7,000	7,500
Mortgage payable, due in 19X4	25,000	25,000
Common stock	30,000	30,000
Retained earnings	15,000	26,200
Total equities	$84,000	$105,800

Statement of Income

Revenues:

Sales		$279,700

Expenses:

Cost of goods sold	$100,000	
Salaries	19,000	
Depreciation expense	5,000	
Advertising expense	1,000	
Interest expense	3,500	128,500
Net income before income taxes		$151,200
Income taxes		70,000
Net income		$ 81,200

Statement of Retained Earnings

Balance, 12/31/19X7	$ 15,000
Income for the year	81,200
	96,200
Dividends	70,000
Balance, 12/31/19X8	$ 26,200

There were no sales or other dispositions of plant and equipment during the year.

Required:

[a]   Prepare a statement of changes in financial position using the cash approach.
[b]   Prepare a statement of changes in financial position using the working capital approach.

7   The following are the financial statements for the H Corporation for the year ended December 31, 19X2. There were no dispositions of plant and equipment during this period.

Balance Sheet

	December 31	
	19X1	19X2
Assets:		
Cash	$ 11,000	$ 19,000
Accounts receivable	8,000	9,000
Inventory	15,000	16,000
Prepaid advertising expense	1,000	1,200
Plant, property, and equipment	150,000	149,000
Total assets	$185,000	$194,200

Equities:

Accounts payable (inventory)	$ 15,000	$ 15,500
Notes payable, due in 19X3	4,000	4,000
Advances from customers (services to		
be performed in 19X3)	12,000	12,000
Salaries payable	2,000	3,000
Mortgage payable, 19X8	48,000	48,000
Common stock	91,000	91,000
Retained earnings	13,000	20,700
Total equities	$185,000	$194,200

Statement of Income

Revenues:		
Sales		$200,000
Expenses:		
Cost of goods sold	$100,000	
Salaries	40,000	
Depreciation	10,000	
Advertising	1,900	
Utilities and insurance	5,000	
Interest	3,100	160,000
Net income before taxes		$ 40,000
Income taxes		15,000
Net income		$ 25,000

Statement of Retained Earnings

Balance, 12/31/19X1	$ 13,000
Net income for the period	25,000
	38,000
Dividends	17,300
Balance, 12/31/19X2	$ 20,700

Required:

[a] Prepare a statement of changes in financial position using the cash approach.

[b] Prepare a statement of changes in financial position using the working capital approach and the add back method.

8 The P Company statement of changes in financial position for 19X2 is as follows:

P Company
Statement of Changes in Financial Position (Net Working Capital)
for Year Ended December 31, 19X2

Sources of working capital:	
From operations:	
Income	$190,000
Add: Depreciation	27,000
	$217,000
Bonds issued	100,000
Stock issued	50,000
Total working capital provided	$367,000

Application of working capital:	
Acquisition of plant and equipment	$210,000
Payment of dividends	60,000
Acquisition of stock of the I Corporation	85,000
Increase in working capital	12,000
Total application of working capital	$367,000

The balance sheet of the P Company at December 31, 19X2 is as follows:

Assets:	
Working capital	$124,000
Investments	228,000
Plant and equipment	217,000
Total assets	$569,000
Equities:	
Bonds payable	$180,000
Common stock	250,000
Retained earnings	139,000
Total equities	$569,000

Required:

Prepare a balance sheet at December 31, 19X1, similar to the one for December 31, 19X2.

CASE   As director of public relations for E Products, Inc., you have received the following letter from an irate shareholder. Write a letter to the stockholder answering the questions raised. Your letter should, of course, placate the shareholder.

Mr. John P. Summit, President
E Products, Inc.
110 Glenn Plod
Huntsville, Alabama

Dear Sir:

Eight years ago, I purchased 1,000 shares of your stock for $80. My broker assured me that your operation would be successful. Your stock price has increased, I will admit, to $105 and you have consistently shown a reasonable profit. Two things, however, worry me.

First, during the eight years I have not received a single dividend from your company. And, with inflation the way it is today, the $105 I can get for my stock would buy just about the same goods and services as the $80 I invested eight years ago.

Second, in the annual report I received yesterday you stated in your "President's letter" that, and I quote your very words: "Regretably, due to our expansion program no cash is available for dividend payments." Now I can see that the cash balance of $1,200,000 is low relative to your current liabilities of $14,500,000. But that is not the point. The Statement of Changes in Financial Position shows that working capital increased by $10,000,000 during this year alone. I have checked back and found that working capital has been increasing almost every year. What is more, the Balance Sheet tells me that you have held back the money you have made. In black and white, it says: "Retained earnings—$58,650,000." That's a pretty large sum.

Now, I don't want to accuse you or your bookkeeper of falsifying records or stealing the corporation's money. But I would like to have someone explain to me in plain English why you cannot pay a dividend and what has happened to all the money you say you have been making.

Yours very truly,

A. V. Erage

three

DOUBLE-ENTRY

BOOKKEEPING

8

Introduction
to Data
Processing

The preceding chapters have been devoted to a discussion of the basic concepts of accounting, to the basic measurements of accounting, and to the form and content of external financial statements. Up to now, we have generally ignored the problems of gathering, classifying, and summarizing the economic data that are the raw material for accounting measurements and financial statements. Every business must have a data processing system that will provide the economic data essential to the accounting process.

The data-processing method used will vary depending on the size of the business and numerous other factors. Data may be accumulated in the form of hand-written figures on paper, printed figures from a machine, holes in a punched card or paper tape, magnetic dots on tape, or any combination of the above forms. Regardless of the form used, data gathering systems do have many common facets. This chapter describes the basic ideas of data processing generally and the basic rules of a very old and widely used method for gathering data, namely, double-entry bookkeeping.

Data Processing Systems

Any organized data collection system established to achieve specific results must have the following elements: all data affecting the end results must enter the system (recordation); data must be properly identified and grouped with "like" data (classification); data must be quantified in such a manner as to permit the application of a measurement concept (measurement); data must be available in a suitable form for decision-making on a timely and consistent basis (reporting). The development of a data system depends on the objectives of that system. The reporting requirements of accounting are many and varied; the discussion up to this point has been limited to the external reports of accounting. Although information reports generated by accounting are not and should not be limited to reports described in the preceding chapters, it is assumed for the purpose of this chapter that the information requirements of an accounting system are limited to the statement of income and the balance sheet. This simplifying assumption will facilitate our discussion of data processing systems.

Classification

An objective of any information system is to order "bits" of data in a useful manner. Data gathered at random without any attempt to relate them to other data or observations are useless: They do not tell us what has happened in the past nor do they help us predict the future. To be useful, data must be ordered and reduced to symbolic representations capable of exposing relationships between transactions and events. Classification is the simplest type of ordering; that is, like things are grouped together. A classification system that is effective must define the attributes of the data being classified in terms of the objectives of the system.

Accounting is concerned with supplying economic information about entities (primarily business enterprises) to persons interested in the entity. The object of accounting observations is economic activity. It is not sufficient merely to report that a business is involved in economic activity. The financial statements, instead, are an attempt to depict in a precise way the result of economic activity. Reports detailing every transaction of a business would be unintelligible. Thus, classification is essential to informative reports.

The first characteristic of the classification structure of an information system is the statement of objectives—what information is needed by the user. Previous chapters presented the reasons why the statement of income and related balance sheet are useful. Justification for the various classifications for each statement were given. The end product of accounting, the financial statements, determines the classification system used in accounting. A classification system is a functional process. The basis of the classification system must be *significant* to the objective of the system.

A second major characteristic of a classification system is that the classes must be *mutually exclusive*. There should be no overlapping between classes so that a bit of information could be placed in two or more different classes and yet be correctly classified. A third characteristic is that the system of classes must be *exhaustive*, that is, every bit of information entering the system must fit into some class, but only one.

The preceding description of a system of classification is an ideal description. The financial statements of a business, which are the objectives of accounting classification, are continually changing. Both the operations of the business and the generally accepted rules of accounting change constantly, and, as a result, the system of classification in accounting is also in a fluid state. The accountant must respond by changing his system of classification to provide the information needed to make his measurements and prepare the financial statements.

Observation and Measurement

The economic activity of a business is a series of interrelated events called **transactions**. Accountants observe, measure, and record each transaction in classes that show its effect on the business enterprise. Transactions occur as goods and services, are acquired or distributed by the business, and as services are changed by operations within the enterprise. The data system must provide for the observation and recording of each such transaction.

When a transaction is observed, some unit of measurement must be used to record the transaction's economic effect. In some cases, physical units may be used. For example, if five "parts" are issued from the storeroom to the manufacturing plant, this event may be measured by "number of parts" and recorded in this manner. The measuring unit, however, is usually a monetary unit (the dollar). The rules developed by accounting to measure the economic effect of transactions in monetary terms are quite complex. In fact, these rules comprise the principal subject matter of accounting. In the simplest situation, the exchange or market price is recorded where the business enters into a cash transaction with another party. Special rules have been developed by accountants to assign monetary values to other events. For example, barter transactions are recorded at their cash-equivalent value—an estimate of the cash that would have changed hands if the transaction had been a cash transaction. Other rules apply to the measurement of depreciation, cost of goods sold, revenue recognition, and many other events that are more complicated than a simple cash transaction.

Double-Entry Bookkeeping

The role of double-entry bookkeeping in the development of modern accounting was discussed briefly in Chapter 1. Economic records have been kept, of course, throughout recorded history. Double-entry bookkeeping, which was developed sometime between 1200 and 1500 A.D., provided a system for the **monetary** measurement of profit or loss for a period or from a venture and also integrated the recording of profit and loss with the monetary amount added to net worth. Double-entry bookkeeping was, in short, a major technological breakthrough for Western culture. Even today, double-entry is still the most widely used method of keeping the accounts for a business.

Development of Double-Entry Bookkeeping

The first man to use double-entry bookkeeping, although history does not record his name, was probably not consciously aware of the fact that he was using an information system with the several characteristics just discussed. Like most important technological developments, double entry probably just happened, and the system, once developed, was found useful. As trade and small manufacturing grew in importance across Europe, the double-entry system became important as a valuable system for recording, classifying, and measuring business events. Two major milestones in the development of double-entry bookkeeping were (1) the legal requirement for stewardship records in Ancient Rome, and (2) the use of personal accounts which led to the development of the account form.

LEGAL AND STEWARDSHIP REQUIREMENTS. Early Roman law required the head of every family to keep a cash book or record of cash receipts and disbursements. Later a record of debt transactions also had to be included. For the wealthy Roman, these transactions were numerous and a record for each borrower and each lender was essential. In most cases, educated slaves were made responsible for the record-keeping function. In addition, the slaves engaged in trade on behalf of their masters. It was beneath the dignity of the Roman patrician to engage in trade, and to do so he would run the risk of losing his political rights as a Roman citizen. The slaves, called *stewards*, maintained records of their economic transactions and periodically made an accounting to the master. As a result of these requirements, detailed records of cash and credit transactions had been kept for centuries prior to the advent of the double-entry system.

PERSONAL ACCOUNTS AND DEVELOPMENT OF THE ACCOUNT FORM. The first records of financial transactions were probably memoranda to serve as memory aids. Credit was extended to customers early in history. The merchant needed a reminder of these debts or receivables. The merchant, in turn, received credit from his suppliers, called *payables*, and thus a record of the amount due was also necessary as a memory aid. Records of receivables and payables were known as personal accounts.

Although we do not know exactly when or where, at some point in time a page in a book was dedicated to each debtor (receivable) and to each creditor (payable). Also at some point, this page was divided vertically. Splitting the page in half vertically gave the early bookkeeper two advantages. First, he could easily associate the payments from debtors or payments to creditors with the original transactions. For example, an amount loaned to a debtor could be entered on the left side of the page and subsequent repayment could then be placed opposite the loan on the right side.

Second, the net position of each debtor and creditor could be easily determined. If transactions were listed chronologically on the account page for a debtor, the record would appear as follows:

June 3	Loaned Customer A	$423.75
June 7	Loaned Customer A	627.05
July 2	Customer A repaid	323.06
July 9	Loaned Customer A	814.00
July 10	Customer A repaid	509.40
	etc.	

Imagine 30 or 40 transactions over a year's time. Now think about how much trouble it would be to compute A's net indebtedness at year's end. By rearranging these facts on a split page with loans on the left side and repayments on the right, one obtains

Customer A

June 3	Loaned A	$423.75	July 2	A repaid	$323.06
June 7	Loaned A	627.05	July 10	A repaid	509.40
July 9	Loaned A	814.00		etc.	
	etc.				

Now when the bookkeeper needs to know the net amount that customer A owes the business, he can add up the loans and then the repayments, and finally subtract to obtain A's ***balance***. The advantages of a split account were readily apparent to medieval bookkeepers who had to struggle along without the modern adding machine.

In time, the use of the split page became common for all financial records, not just for records of receivables and payables. In the early days of bookkeeping, an account was a page divided into two sides. For identification purposes, the left side was called the ***debit*** side and the right side was called the ***credit*** side. Figure 8-1 shows a blank account page. The form of the account has changed but the debits are still on the left and the credits are on the right. When punched cards and electronic tapes are used for financial records, the account will not be a page, only a ***storage location***, divided into debit and credit compartments in some manner. An account is, therefore, a location for storing information with two positions in it—the debit position and the credit position.

Figure 8-1

Account Form

ACCOUNT NO.

DATE	EXPLANATION	POST. REF.	DEBIT	DATE	EXPLANATION	POST. REF.	CREDIT

Concept of Duality

Although first used to record receivables and payables, the account form was later used to maintain a record of all assets or properties of the business. Use of the account form somehow led to the recognition that every transaction has a dual effect.

When a business acquires assets, it must either give up some other asset to complete the transaction or recognize an increase in liabilities or equities. The following examples will clarify this point:

1   A business uses $10,000 cash to acquire a building. A bookkeeper would recognize one aspect of this transaction by increasing an account for buildings by $10,000. He would also recognize the $10,000 decrease in cash.

2   A business pays $300 for a three-year fire insurance policy. Cash decreases by $300 and a new service, insurance, increases by $300.

3   An individual invests $5,000 of his personal cash in a business venture. The bookkeeper for the business would recognize an increase in the cash account of $5,000 and the corresponding increase of $5,000 in the owner-investment account, namely, capital.

4   A business borrows $2,000 from a bank. The bookkeeper would recognize a $2,000 increase in the cash account and also a $2,000 increase in a debt-investment account, that is, a bank loan, a liability.

It is also possible to have transactions that decrease both assets and claims against assets:

5   The bank loan in transaction 4 is repaid. Cash would then decrease by $2,000, and the liability account, the bank loan, would also decrease by $2,000.

Both effects of each transaction must be recognized to have a complete record of the status of the business. The dual effect of transactions is also evident in the basic balance sheet equation: Assets = Equities.

Debit–Credit Mechanism

Recognition of the dual effect of each transaction and the use of the two-sided account did create a problem in recording transactions. The basic classifications of information on the balance sheet and statement of income are assets, equities, revenue, and expense. Thus, every transaction must affect one or more of the four major categories just cited. The final step in the development of double-entry bookkeeping was a technique of recording each transaction that would change the left side (debits) of one account and change the right side (credits) of another account by an equal amount. Although just how and when this happened is lost in the Dark Ages, a set of rules was developed that permits every transaction to be analyzed in such a manner that the debits and credits to the accounts are always equal. In addition, these rules for transaction analysis which provide for equal debits and credits are also consistent with the basic definitions of assets, equities, revenues, and expenses.

Just as the axioms in math, these rules for debits and credits are not "truths"; they represent, instead, an orderly, although arbitrary, manner of recording transactions to yield a desired result. As with axioms of math, these rules must be accepted and learned if double-entry bookkeeping is to be mastered. The rules are as follows:

1   An asset account is increased by debiting and decreased by crediting the account.
2   An equity account is increased by crediting and decreased by debiting the account.
3   A revenue account is increased by crediting the account and decreased by debiting the account.
4   An expense account is increased by debiting and decreased by crediting the account.

These rules are presented schematically in Fig. 8-2 by using T accounts. The plus (+) and minus (-) indicate increases and decreases, respectively.

Figure 8-2: Schematic Presentation of Debit-Credit Rules

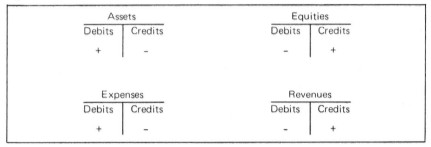

The rules for debits and credits can be directly related to the equation for changes in the balance sheet developed in Chapter 4, that is, for a corporation,

$$\Delta C + \Delta AR + \Delta DE = \Delta AE + \Delta DR + \Delta DI + \Delta OI + \Delta RE$$

In the balance sheet format, where all signs in the equation are "plus," account categories on the left of the equality sign carry debit balances, that is, an increase on the debit side. Account categories on the left of the equality sign carry credit balances, that is, an increase on the credit side. The symbol for the change in retained earnings (RE) can be expanded as follows:

$$RE = (Y - S)$$

Because the income (Y) is revenue minus expenses, therefore

$$RE = (R - E) - S$$

If these symbols are used in the equation for changes in the balance sheet, then

$$\Delta C + \Delta AR + \Delta DE = \Delta AE + \Delta DR + \Delta DI + \Delta OI + R - E - S$$

If we rearrange the equation to provide for only positive signs, we have

$$\Delta C + \Delta AR + \Delta DE + E + S = \Delta AE + \Delta DR + \Delta DI + \Delta OI + R$$

Thus, correspondence of the equation to the rules for debits and credits is re-established. Assets and expenses appear on the *left* side of the equation, and accounts for these items are *increased* with a *debit*—a debit is an entry on the left side of the account. If there is an account for dividends paid, it is also increased by a debit. On the *right* side of the equation are changes in equities and revenues, and these accounts are *increased* by a *credit*—a credit is an entry on the right side of the account.

The following examples illustrate application of these rules.

EXAMPLE A. Stockholders invest $10,000 cash in the business. The asset account, cash, is increased by $10,000; the equity account, capital stock, is increased by $10,000:

Cash			Capital Stock	
Debit	Credit		Debit	Credit
(a) $10,000				(a) $10,000

EXAMPLE B. A service truck, a deferred expense, is purchased for $4,000. The cash account is decreased by $4,000; the account delivery equipment, which is a deferred expense and therefore an asset account, is increased by $4,000:

Cash			Delivery Equipment	
Debit	Credit		Debit	Credit
(a) $10,000	(b) $4,000		(b) $4,000	

EXAMPLE C. Services are sold for $1,000 cash. The cash account is increased by $1,000; revenues are increased by $1,000:

Cash			Revenue	
Debit	Credit		Debit	Credit
(a) $10,000	(b) $4,000			(c) $1,000
(c) 1,000				

EXAMPLE D. Wages of $700 were paid to employees. Cash is decreased by $700; the expense account, wages, is increased by $700:

Cash			Wages Expense	
Debit	Credit		Debit	Credit
(a) $10,000	(b) $4,000		(d) $700	
(c) 1,000	(d) 700			

EXAMPLE E. Merchandise inventory is acquired for $1,500; payment is to be made in 30 days. Merchandise inventory, a deferred expense or asset, is increased by $1,500; accounts payable (merchandise) account is increased by $1,500:

Merchandise Inventory			Accounts Payable (Merchandise)	
Debit	Credit		Debit	Credit
(e) $1,500				(e) $1,500

In a similar fashion, all transactions can be entered into the accounts. The accounts used depend on the transactions of the business. If a different type of transaction occurs, a new account is used to classify and record the economic consequences of the new transaction.

The equality of debits and credits gives a useful arithmetic check on the bookkeeper's work. Not only should total debits equal total credits, but the total of all debit account *balances* should equal the total of all credit account *balances*. The balance of an account is the difference between the total of the debits and the total of the credits in the account. An account has a debit balance if the total debits exceed the total credits. Likewise, the account has a credit balance if the total credits exceed the total debits. In the example above, after transaction (d) the cash account has a debit balance of $6,300:

Cash	
(a) $10,000	(b) $4,000
(c) 1,000	(d) 700
$11,000	$4,700
Balance $6,300	

The Bookkeeping Cycle

The essential elements of the double-entry system were covered in the preceding sections. Mechanical features of systems in use by U.S. businesses vary widely depending on the size of the business and numerous other factors. Hand-written records may be used entirely for small businesses. For larger firms, posting machines, punched card machines, and/or electronic computers may be used to keep the accounts. In all situations, however, accounts with debit and credit entries are basic. In the following pages, a system using hand-written records will be explained and illustrated. This description will also introduce several new terms common to all double-entry systems, from the corner store to General Motors.

TRANSACTION RECORDING. The accounting system of a business must provide means for observing and recording each transaction. For example, a sale to a customer by a department store is observed and recorded by a sales clerk either by preparing a sales receipt slip or by ringing it up on a cash register. The disbursement of cash is recorded by preparing a check stub or by making a duplicate copy of the check. As shipments of goods are received, receiving reports are prepared. In some manner, the system must provide for a record of each transaction by some designated employee. The initial record is not necessarily made by accounting personnel. Virtually every member of a business takes part in the process. The accounting department will normally assist the other departments in the design of forms appropriate for recording their transactions, but the initial record, commonly called a **source document**, is usually prepared by operating personnel, not by accountants.

The accounting department receives copies of source documents, analyzes and classifies transactions recorded on them, and eventually records them in the accounts. Each transaction (sale, purchase, receipt, disbursement, etc.) is analyzed to determine the accounts to be debited and the accounts to be credited. Transactions are analyzed to determine the effect of each transaction on revenues, expenses, accruals, deferrals, and investments. Once the effect of a transaction on the above categories is determined, the event is entered in the appropriate accounts by applying the debit–credit rules discussed in the preceding section. Each business enterprise will have a **chart of accounts**, which is a list of all accounts in current use in the accounting system.

JOURNALS. Analyzed transactions are classified or sorted into accounts by using a device called a **journal** or **book of original entry**. Journals contain the following information:

1   Date of the transaction
2   Name of account or accounts to be debited
3   Name of account or accounts to be credited
4   Monetary amounts for the debits and credits
5   An explanation of the transaction

Journals are of two types: general journals and specialized journals. General journals are, as the name implies, designed so that any transaction may be recorded in them. Specialized journals are designed to record particular types of transactions. The form of a general journal and entries therein are shown in Fig. 8–3.

A transaction is entered in the general journal in the following manner: (1) The name of the account to be debited is written on the extreme left edge in the account title and explanation column; (2) the account to be credited is written on the line below, and is slightly indented; (3) the dollar amounts to be debited and credited are entered into the columns with these designations. Below the account titles for the debit and credit entries, an explanation of the transaction is given.

Specialized journals are columnar forms that facilitate the sorting and summarizing of transactions; as the name implies, each specialized journal contains only the particular type of transaction designated. A cash disbursements journal, Fig. 8–4, accumulates the total credits (decreases) to cash, and classifies the

Figure 8-3

General Journal

DATE		DESCRIPTION OF ENTRY	ACCT NO	DEBIT	CREDIT
19X1					
Jan	2	Cash	1	25000 00	
		(Capital stock	13		25000 00
		Investment of $25.000			
		by shareholders)			
	3	Land	4	2000 00	
		Building	5	20000 00	
		Cash	1		12000 00
		Notes payable	12		10000 00
		(Purchase of lot at corner			
		of Hickory & Oak for $22.000			
		$12.000 cash now; balance			
		in 60 days. Est. life of			
		bldg. 25 years)			
	3	Furniture and fixtures	6	8000 00	
		Notes payable	12		8000 00
		(Purchase of furniture &			
		fixtures for store. Est.			
		life. 10 years)			

debit entries by appropriate account. A sales journal, Fig. 8-5, accumulates the total sales transactions, and shows whether each of the transactions was made for cash or credit.

Specialized journals may be used for the purchase of merchandise, for payrolls, for cash receipts, or any class of transaction encountered frequently in a business. The number of columns used in the journals may be increased or decreased, and the headings changed to fit the needs of each business. The format for specialized journals will vary because it is based on the nature of the transactions of a particular business.

LEDGERS. A general ledger is the collection of all accounts for a business. Traditionally, the accounts are arranged in the general ledger in the order they appear on the balance sheet and statement of income, beginning with the first account on the balance sheet. The first account in the general ledger is cash, the next perhaps accounts receivable, etc., through the asset and equities accounts, then the revenue accounts, and finally the expense accounts. Typically, the ledger is a loose-leaf arrangement.

Figure 8-4

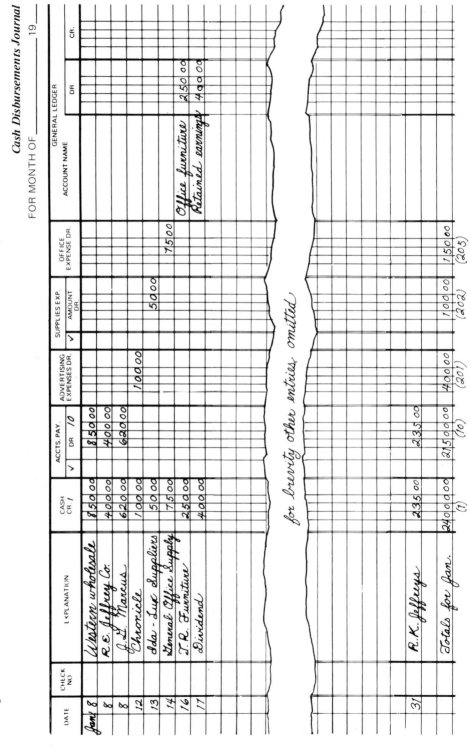

Cash Disbursements Journal

FOR MONTH OF _____ 19___

DATE	CHECK NO	EXPLANATION	CASH CR. 1	ACCTS. PAY. ✓	ACCTS. PAY. DR 10	ADVERTISING EXPENSES DR.	SUPPLIES EXP. ✓	SUPPLIES EXP. AMOUNT DR	OFFICE EXPENSE DR.	GENERAL LEDGER ACCOUNT NAME	GENERAL LEDGER DR	GENERAL LEDGER CR.
Jan. 8		Western wholesale	850 00		850 00							
	8	R.E. Jeffrey Co.	400 00		400 00							
	8	J.L. Marcus	620 00		620 00							
	12	Chronicle	100 00			100 00						
	13	Ida-Lue Suppliers	50 00					50 00				
	14	General Office Supply	75 00						75 00			
	16	T.R. Furniture	250 00							Office furniture	250 00	
	17	Dividend	400 00							Retained earnings	400 00	

for brevity other entries omitted

	31	R.K. Jeffreys	235 00		235 00							
		Totals for Jan.	24000 00		2150 00	400 00		100 00	150 00			
			(1)		(10)	(201)		(202)	(205)			

Figure 8-5

Sales Journal

DATE	CUSTOMER	TERMS	Ref.	DEBITS ACCTS. REC.	CASH SALES	CREDIT SALES REVENUE
1971						
Jan 5	R.J. Duncan & Co.	n/50	R1	800 00		800 00
5	Brown Machine Co.	n/30	R2	400 00		400 00
5	Ross Florist	2/10, n/30	R3	600 00		600 00
5	Cash Sales				1200 00	1200 00
6	Martin & Black	2/10 n/30		700 00		700 00
6	Cameron, Inc.	2/10, n/30	R4	300 00		400 00
6	Cash Sales				1100 00	1100 00
31	Cash Sales				1400 00	1400 00
	Totals for Jan			2100 00 (2)	800 00 (1)	2900 00 (✓)

The entries in the journals are transferred to the appropriate accounts in the ledger. This process is called *posting*. After each journal entry has been posted to the ledger accounts, the balance of the account is computed by summing the debit and credit side of each account and determining the balance—the amount by which the debits exceed the credits or vice versa.

One of the reasons for the use of specialized journals is apparent if one considers the problem of posting journal entries to the ledger. In a specialized journal, similar transactions are grouped and recorded. After a designated period of time, the columns of the specialized journals are totaled and this *total* amount for each column is entered or posted to the general ledger. In Fig. 8-5, for example, the total of the sales column can be posted as a credit to sales revenue, and this will include all sales for June. Similarly, other column totals on specialized journals can be posted as a single amount. Transactions recorded in the general journal must be posted individually.

In addition to the general ledger, most firms will have one or more subsidiary ledgers which give the details of the summary account in the general ledger. The summary account in the general ledger is known as the control account. A commonly used subsidiary ledger is the one for accounts receivable. The *control* or summary accounts receivable in the general ledger will show the balance due from *all* customers. The *subsidiary* accounts receivable ledger will contain the amount due from *each* customer. The sum of the balances in subsidiary accounts for individuals should equal the balance in the control account if all entries have been handled correctly. If the balances do not agree, an error has occurred.

Figure 8-6 is a diagram showing the use and relationships of a subsidiary ledger to the control account and journals. In Fig. 8-6, sales are charge (credit) sales, and the sales journal is posted on a daily basis.

TRIAL BALANCE. When the balance of each account has been computed, a two-column listing of the balances of the accounts in the general ledger is prepared: The left column is for accounts with debit balances, and the right column is for accounts with credit balances. This list is a trial balance, as shown in Fig. 8-7.

If the bookkeeping process has been carried out correctly, with no arithmetical or mechanical mistakes, the sum of the debits should be equal to the sum of the credits. The trial balance is prepared for the purpose of determining the equality of debits and credits. That debits and credits are equal, however, does not automatically imply the correctness of the bookkeeping process. If wrong amounts were entered originally, if the correct amounts are entered in the wrong account, or if a transaction is left out completely, the account balances will not reflect the condition and activity of the enterprise correctly. The trial balance does give proof that the debit–credit mechanism was followed correctly, and it also gives assurance that the balancing of the accounts was correct.

In addition to the trial balance of the general ledger, a schedule is prepared from the subsidiary ledgers listing the balance of each account. The sum of these balances should be equal to the balance of the control account in the

Figure 8-6

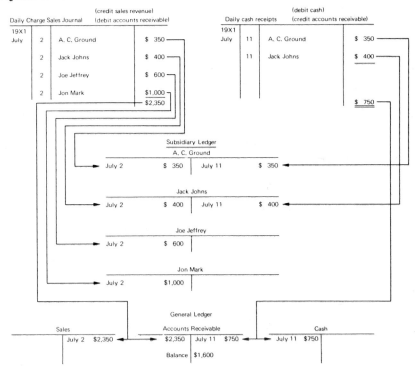

Figure 8-7

Furniture Co. Inc., Trial Balance, January 31, 19X1

Account	Debit	Credit
Cash	1740000	
Accounts receivable	160000	
Merchandise Inventory	2385000	
Land	200000	
Building	2000000	
Furniture and fixtures	825000	
Accounts payable		235000
Other accrued expenses		
Notes payable		1900000
C. Apple capital		2500000
C. Apple, withdrawal	40000	
Sales revenue		2900000
Cost of goods sold		
Advertising expense	40000	
Supplies	10000	
Office expense	15000	
Other operating expense	120000	
	7535000	7535000

general ledger. Agreement with the balance in the general ledger indicates that the individual transactions have been accounted for in total. A schedule of the subsidiary accounts in Fig. 8–6 is given in Fig. 8–8. The sum of the individual account balances in the subsidiary ledger should always equal the balance of the control account.

Figure 8–8: Schedule of Accounts Receivable

Joe Jeffrey	$ 600
Jon Mark	1,000
Balance of control account	$1,600

To summarize, the steps explained up to now in a double-entry bookkeeping cycle consist of (1) journalizing transactions, (2) posting to the ledger, and (3) preparing a trial balance. Other steps will be explained and illustrated later in the text.

Locating Errors

Because people are fallible, errors occur in all data processing systems. One of the principal advantages of the double-entry method is that the existence of many types of errors are exposed by the mechanics of the system. Debits should always equal credits; if not, an error has occurred. Disagreement between the control account and the trial balance of subsidiary accounts also indicates that an error has been made. Unfortunately, however, although the double-entry mechanism does indicate that an error exists, it does not indicate where the error was made.

There are many ways to make an error in recording, posting, and balancing the accounts. The more frequent errors are

1 Arithmetical errors. The process of adding or subtracting is incorrectly performed.
2 Transposition errors. The digits of a number are inverted; that is, 25 is recorded as 52.
3 Slide errors. The number is moved one or more columns to the right or left; that is, $84.00 is written as $840.00 or $8.40.
4 Posting errors. A debit is posted or listed as a credit or vice versa.

The amount of the difference between the debit total and the credit total on the trial balance can provide clues about the nature of the error. A difference of $1, $100, or $1,000, etc., is frequently an error in addition or subtraction. A transposition error is always divisible by 9, for example, if 83 is erroneously recorded as 38, the difference is 45, a number divisible by 9. A slide error is also divisible by 9. Posting a debit as a credit or vice versa causes a difference that is divisible by 2, for example, if the debit total is $10,843 and the credit total is

$10,467, the difference, $376, is divisible by 2, indicating the possibility that a credit of $188 may have been incorrectly posted as a debit. An inspection of the accounts may reveal this amount, and the posting error can be corrected.

Frequently the error may be located quickly by examining the difference between the debits and credits on the trial balance for the above characteristics. If the error is not located in this manner, the steps in the bookkeeping cycle should be retraced until the error is found. A suggested sequence of steps might be as follows:

1   Recalculate the totals for debits and credits in the trial balance.
2   Retrace account balances on trial balance to each account.
3   Recalculate the balance of each account.
4   Trace the postings from the ledger accounts to the journals.
5   Verify the equality of debits and credits in the journals.

Careful completion of these steps should uncover the error.

A reminder: The equality of debits and credits on the trial balance does not mean that the accounts correctly reflect the economic activities and financial condition of the business. The trial balance is a test of *mechanics*. Measurement of income and financial position in accordance with good accounting principles depends on analysis of the transactions as explained in Chapters 2, 3, and 4. The relationship between the bookkeeping process and measurement of income and financial position is discussed in Chapter 9.

Example

On July 1, 19X1, Bill Carter formed a corporation and issued capital stock for $25,000 cash. Carter purchased the stock himself and is to be the president of the newly formed corporation. Carter formed the corporation to purchase J Cleaners from its present owner, George Oakley, so he named the corporation J Cleaners, Incorporated. The corporation paid Oakley $50,000 for the assets of J Cleaners broken down as follows:

Land	$ 5,000
Building	30,000
Cleaning equipment	14,000
Cleaning supplies inventory	1,000
Total purchase price	$50,000

In the past, Oakley ran the cleaners on a cash and carry basis and the business had not been profitable. Carter has secured commitments from three large industrial firms to provide laundry services for worker's uniforms, provided he will extend the service on credit terms. He expects that the additional business from the three big customers will make J Cleaning, Incorporated a profitable operation. All other customers will continue to be on a cash and carry basis.

Formal Accounts

Carter decides to use a double-entry set of accounts and hired a bookkeeping service to set up the accounts. An employee of the bookkeeping service will visit the corporation each week and pick up the records of each transaction for entry in the formal records. After an analysis of the business transactions, the bookkeeping service decided to use the following journals and ledgers:

General journal—to record transactions of particular importance and transactions that do not fit into the specialized journals (Fig. 8–9)

Figure 8–9

J Cleaners, Incorporated   *General Journal*

DATE	DESCRIPTION OF ENTRY	ACCT. NO.	DEBIT	CREDIT
July 1	Cash	100	25000 00	
	Capital stock	400		25000 00
	(To record original invest- ment in business by issuance of stock for cash)			
1	Cash	100	25000 00	
	Mortgage Payable	300		25000 00
	(Mortgage from 1st Fed. Savings on land & bldg. for 20 years payable at $179.11 per mo. including in- terest at 6%)			
1	Cash	100	5000 00	
	Note payable - 1st State Bank	230		5000 00
	(Chattel Mortgage on equip- ment payable at $97.25 per mo. for 5 years, Interest rate 6¼%)			
1	Land	160	5000 00	
	Building	165	30000 00	
	Cleaning equipment	150	14000 00	
	Cleaning supplies inventory		1000 00	
	Cash			50000 00
	To record the purchase of J. Cleaners, Incorporated George Oakley)			

Cash receipts journal—to record cash receipts from cash sales and from collections on accounts. This journal will, therefore, have columns for cash (debit), cleaning revenue (credit; to record the cash sales), and accounts receivable (credit; to record collections on accounts) (Fig. 8–10)

Figure 8–10

J. Cleaners, Incorporated
Cash Receipts Journal

Date	Explanation	Ref.	DR Cash	CR Cleaning Revenue	CR Accounts Receivable
Jul 6	Weekly cash sales		305 00	305 00	
12	S Mfg. Company		105 00		105 00
13	Weekly cash sales		410 00	410 00	
16	A Incorporated		72 00		72 00
17	A Supply Company		164 00		164 00
20	Weekly cash sales		377 00	377 00	
24	S Mfg. Company		134 00		134 00
27	Weekly cash sales		335 00	335 00	
30	A Supply Company		110 00		110 00
31	Cash sales for last day of July		216 00	216 00	
			2228 00	1643 00	585 00
			(100)	(500)	(110)

Charge sales journal—to record charge sales to the three industrial firms to which credit will be extended. This specialized journal will have one column, the total of which will be a debit to accounts receivable and a credit to cleaning revenue (Fig. 8–11).

Figure 8–11

J Cleaners, Incorporated
Charge Sales Journal

Date 1971	Customer	DR-CASH CR-Cleaning Revenue
Jul 3	S Mfg. Company	105 00
6	A. Incorporated	72 00
10	S Mfg. Company	134 00
10	A Supply Company	164 00
16	S Mfg. Company	110 00
21	A. Incorporated	96 00
22	S Mfg. Company	118 00
22	A Supply Company	182 00
		981 00
		(100)(500)

Figure 8-12

X Cleaners, Incorporated
Cash Disbursements Journal

Date	Explanation	Cash CR	Salaries DR	Cleaning Supplies DR	General Ledger Account	Amount DR
Feb 1	Bertha Andrews	2000	2000			
6	Linda Potts	1800	1800			
6	Joan Carrico	2150	2150			
9	S Corporation	4500		4500		
9	C. Insurance	16000			Prepaid Insurance (130)	16000
13	Bertha Andrews	6000	6000			
13	Linda Potts	5500	5500			
13	Joan Carrico	6250	6250			
15	V. Cleaners	6000		6000		
16	Chamber of Commerce	1800			Other Expenses (608)	1800
17	S Corporation	17800		17800		
20	Bertha Andrews	6000	6000			
20	Linda Potts	5500	5500			
20	Joan Carrico	6250	6250			
23	City of Itasca (water & electricity)	4300			Utilities (605)	4300
27	Bertha Andrews	6000	6000			
27	Linda Potts	5500	5500			
27	Joan Carrico	6250	6250			
30	Bill Carter	50000	50000			
		159600	109200	28300		22100
		(100)	(601)	(120)		

Cash disbursements journal—to record all cash disbursements. This journal will have four columns (Fig. 8–12):

1   Cash (credit)—to record the disbursements
2   Cleaning supplies inventory (debit)—to record disbursements for cleaning and laundry supplies
3   Salary expense (debit)—to record disbursements for wages paid to employees
4   General ledger (debit)—to record debits to all general ledger accounts for which no special column is provided

General ledger—the chart of accounts for J Cleaners, Incorporated with the account numbers assigned, is shown in Fig. 8–13.

Subsidiary ledger (accounts receivable)—an account will be opened for each industrial customer to which credit is extended.

Figure 8–13

J Cleaners, Incorporated		Chart of Accounts
Type	Account tital	Account No.
Assets	Cash	100
	Accounts receivable	110
	Cleaning supplies inventory	120
	Prepaid insurance	130
	Equipment	150
	Land	160
	Building	165
Equities	Accounts payable (cleaning supplies)	200
	Accrued wages	210
	Accrued taxes (property)	215
	Other accrued expenses	220
	Notes payable	230
	Mortgages payable	300
	Capital stock	400
	Retained earnings	410
Revenues	Cleaning revenue	500
Expenses	Salaries	601
	Cleaning supplies expense	602
	Insurance	603
	Taxes	604
	Utilities	605
	Depreciation	606
	Interest	607
	Other expense	608

To finance the business, Bill Carter purchased capital stock for $25,000 with personal funds. In addition, the company borrowed $25,000 by mortgaging the land and building. The mortgage plus 6% interest, will be repaid over a 20-year period by monthly payments of $179.11. The company also borrowed $5,000 by mortgaging equipment. This note, plus 6 1/4% interest, will be repaid over a five-year period by monthly payments of $97.25. Of course, a bank account was opened for the new business. These beginning transactions, including a record of the acquisition of the business from Oakley, were recorded in the general journal (Fig. 8-9).

The other transactions of J Cleaners, Incorporated for the month of July were recorded in the appropriate journals (Figs. 8-10 to 8-12). In the cash receipts journal, the cash sales are recorded as a weekly total because to record each cash sale would serve no purpose. With this exception, the journals, including the general journal, include all transactions for July.

Posting to Ledgers and the Trial Balance

The agreement between J Cleaners, Incorporated and the bookkeeping service firm provided for the preparation of financial statements each month. President Carter believed that this would provide him with better control of the operations, particularly in the first months. For this reason, the bookkeeping service totaled the journals and posted the results to the ledgers at the end of July.

The general ledger for J Cleaners, Incorporated is presented in Fig. 8-14. The account form used is the T account to conserve space and present the pertinent information. Any one of several account forms might have been used, depending on the circumstances. The student should trace each posting from the journals to the ledger. To assist in this process, the source of each entry in the ledger has been identified by the following symbols:

GJ—General journal
CR—Cash receipts journal
SJ—Charge sales journal
CD—Cash disbursements journal

For the general journal, each debit and credit is posted individually to the general ledger. Also, each entry in the general ledger column of the cash disbursements journal is posted individually to the general ledger. For all other amounts, the column totals are posted to the ledger account indicated by the column heading; for example, the column total of the charge sales journal is posted as a debit to accounts receivable, and also as a credit to cleaning revenue.

The subsidiary ledger of accounts receivable is shown in Fig. 8-15. The entries in this ledger are the individual transactions of the charge sales journal, which are debited to each customer's account, and the cash receipts from each of the charge customers in the cash receipts journal. The trial balance of the subsidiary ledger is then prepared (Fig. 8-16) to be certain that the total of the balances of customer accounts is the same as the balance of the control account

Figure 8-14

J Cleaners, Incorporated

General Ledger

Cash (100)

GJ	$25,000.00	GJ	$50,000.00
GJ	25,000.00	CD	1,596.00
GJ	5,000.00		
CR	2,228.00		
July balance	$5,632.00		

Accounts Receivable (110)

SJ	$981.00	CR	$585.00
July balance	$396.00		

Cleaning Supplies Inventory (120)

GJ	$1,000.00
CD	283.00
July balance	$1,283.00

Prepaid Insurance (130)

CD	$160.00
July balance	$160.00

Equipment (150)

GJ	$14,000.00
July balance	$14,000.00

Land (160)

GJ	$5,000.00
July balance	$5,000.00

Buildings (165)

GJ	$30,000.00
July balance	$30,000.00

Note Payable (230)

GJ	$5,000.00
July balance	$5,000.00

Mortgage Payable (300)

GJ	$25,000.00
July balance	$25,000.00

Bill Carter, Capital (400)

GJ	$25,000.00
July balance	$25,000.00

Cleaning Revenue (500)

CR	$1,643.00
SJ	981.00
July balance	$2,624.00

Salaries (601)

CD	$1,092.00
July balance	$1,092.00

Utilities (605)

CD	$43.00
July balance	$43.00

Other Expenses (605)

CD	$18.00
July balance	$18.00

in the general ledger. For J Cleaners, Incorporated, the amounts, $396.00, do agree. This control device is very important where the system contains numerous subsidiary accounts.

Figure 8-15

J Cleaners, Incorporated	Subsidiary Ledger—Accounts Receivable

S Mfg. Company

SJ	$105.00	CR	$105.00
SJ	134.00	CR	134.00
SJ	110.00		
SJ	118.00		
July balance			
	$228.00		

A Incorporated

SJ	$72.00	CR	$72.00
SJ	96.00		
July balance			
	$96.00		

A Supply Company

SJ	$164.00	CR	$164.00
SJ	182.00	CR	110.00
July balance			
	$72.00		

Figure 8-16

J Cleaners, Incorporated	Trial Balance of Subsidiary Ledger— Accounts Receivable July 31, 19X1
S Mfg. Company	$228.00
A Incorporated	96.00
Supply Corporation	72.00
Balance—accounts receivable (110)	$396.00

Finally, the balances of the general ledger accounts are determined by summing the debits and credits in each account and subtracting for the difference. The balances thus determined are listed and the trial balance is totaled to determine the equality of debit and credit balances. Figure 8-17 is a trial balance for J Cleaners, Incorporated as of July 31, 19X1.

Adjustments for Accruals and Deferrals

A trial balance such as the one presented in Fig. 8-17 does not contain the information needed to prepare the financial statements. The information on the trial balance is, for the most part, a summary of *cash* transactions. To measure income and prepare the financial statements, the accountant must now look beyond the cash transactions and recognize all accruals and deferrals of revenue and costs at the end of July. The trial balance serves as a check on the mechanics

Figure 8-17

<table>
<thead>
<tr><th colspan="2">J. Cleaners, Incorporated
Trial Balance
July 31, 19X1</th><th></th><th></th></tr>
<tr><th>Account</th><th>a/c #</th><th>Debit</th><th>Credit</th></tr>
</thead>
<tbody>
<tr><td>Cash</td><td>100</td><td>5638 00</td><td></td></tr>
<tr><td>Accounts Receivable</td><td>110</td><td>396 00</td><td></td></tr>
<tr><td>Cleaning supplies inventory</td><td>120</td><td>1283 00</td><td></td></tr>
<tr><td>Prepaid insurance</td><td>130</td><td>160 00</td><td></td></tr>
<tr><td>Equipment</td><td>150</td><td>14000 00</td><td></td></tr>
<tr><td>Land</td><td>160</td><td>5000 00</td><td></td></tr>
<tr><td>Building</td><td>165</td><td>30000 00</td><td></td></tr>
<tr><td>Note payable</td><td>230</td><td></td><td>5000 00</td></tr>
<tr><td>Mortgage payable</td><td>300</td><td></td><td>25000 00</td></tr>
<tr><td>Capital stock</td><td>400</td><td></td><td>25000 00</td></tr>
<tr><td>Retained earnings</td><td>510</td><td></td><td></td></tr>
<tr><td>Cleaning revenue</td><td>510</td><td></td><td>26240 0</td></tr>
<tr><td>Salaries</td><td>601</td><td>1092 00</td><td></td></tr>
<tr><td>Utilities</td><td>605</td><td>43 00</td><td></td></tr>
<tr><td>Other expense</td><td>608</td><td>18 00</td><td></td></tr>
<tr><td></td><td></td><td>57624 00</td><td>57624 00</td></tr>
</tbody>
</table>

of double-entry bookkeeping and provides the accountant with the raw data needed to measure income. In double-entry bookkeeping, the step following the preparation of the trial balance, the *adjustment of the accounts*, is the critical step in the bookkeeping process. Adjustments are discussed in the following chapter.

QUESTIONS

1 What are the elements of an organized information collection system? Briefly comment on why these elements are necessary.

2 What are the basic characteristics of a classification system? Why are these characteristics essential to a classification system?

3 What are the steps in the bookkeeping cycle?

4 Define each of the following words:

[a] Journal   [d] Ledger

[b] General journal   [e] General ledger

[c] Specialized journal   [f] Subsidiary ledger

5 List four specialized journals and explain why they would be useful.

6 What is the relationship between the general ledger and subsidiary ledger?

7 What is a control account?

8 What are the reasons for using a control account and related subsidiary ledgers?

9 Define the words debit and credit.

10 What is a trial balance? How is it prepared?

11   Define the concept of duality. Give three examples using recent purchases that you have made to illustrate the concept of duality.

12   What are the rules for recording debits and credits in accounts representing assets, equities, revenues, and expenses.

13   The balance sheet change equation developed in Chapter 4 is

$$\Delta C + \Delta AR + \Delta DE = \Delta AE + \Delta DR + \Delta DI + \Delta OI + RE$$

The income equation is

$$Y = R - E$$

The equation for ΔRE is

$$\Delta RE = Y - S$$

Relate these equations to the rules for debits and credits.

14   What is the balance of an account?

15   Describe how a typical sales transaction is initially observed and processed in an accounting system.

16   Transactions recorded to capture information which is presented in a balance sheet or a statement of income are recorded in monetary amounts. Why?

17   What kind of an error could have caused each of the following results on a trial balance?
[a]   Debits total $2,000 and credits total $1,800.
[b]   Debits total $2,000 and credits total $1,955.

18   If a difference in the totals of debits and credits on the trial balance is caused by multiple errors, will the techniques of dividing by 2 or by 9 assist in an effort to locate the errors?

PROBLEMS

1   Give the general journal entry to record the following transactions of a real estate development venture:
[a]   Owner invests $5,000 in the business.
[b]   Land is purchased for $3,500.
[c]   Expenses (salaries, etc.) connected with the development amounted to $800.
[d]   All lots in the tract are sold for $6,000.

2   The following accounts are given:

Cash		Merchandise	
$2,000	$ 300	$1,000	$1,500
1,500	1,000	500	

A. Green, Proprietor	
$300	$2,000
	500

Reconstruct the journal entries from which these amounts were posted.

3   Complete the following statements by inserting either a debit or credit in the blank which follows:
[a]   Increases in revenue accruals are recorded by _____.
[b]   Increases in expense accruals are recorded by _____.
[c]   Decreases in revenues are recorded by _____.

[d] Increases in expenses are recorded by _____.

[e] A decrease in equities that results from declaration and payment of a dividend is recorded by _____.

[f] Increases in revenues are recorded by _____.

[g] Decreases in debt investment are recorded by _____.

[h] Decreases in owner's investments are recorded by _____.

[i] Increases in deferred cost are recorded by _____.

[j] Decreases in deferred revenues are recorded by _____.

[k] Increases in merchandise inventory are recorded by _____.

4   The following transactions were incurred by M Incorporated during August of 19X1, the first month of operations. M Incorporated is a painting contractor.

August 1	Capital stock was issued in exchange for $12,000 cash.
August 2	An office was rented for August by paying $300 cash.
August 3	A painting job was completed and cash of $300 was received.
August 4	Wages of $175 were paid to workmen.
August 5	A paint spray gun was purchased for $800. Payment was to be made in 90 days.
August 6	Paint materials and supplies totaling $350 were purchased. Payment was to be made in ten days.
August 10	A paint contract was completed and the bill for $650 was mailed. The customer, J. Baines, agreed to pay the amount before the end of the month.
August 12	Paid $350 for materials purchased on August 6.
August 15	An advertisement was placed in the local newspaper. Payment of $40 was made.
August 20	A truck was purchased for $3,000 of which $1,000 was paid in cash and the balance was to be paid over the next two years.
August 21	A sign painter painted the Company's name, address, and phone number on each side of the truck. The painter's bill for $125 was paid in cash.
August 25	J. Baines (see August 10) paid his bill of $650.
August 30	Wages of $300 were paid.

Required:

[a] Prepare general journal entries in proper form to record the preceding transactions. (Use account titles that describe what has happened.)

[b] Set up T accounts and post the journal entries to the appropriate accounts.

[c] Prepare a trial balance of the accounts.

5   The P Company had the following balances in the accounts as of October 1, 19X2

	Debit	Credit
Cash	$4,000	
Accounts receivable	6,000	
Common stock		$9,800
Retained income		200

The company completed the following transactions during October:

[1] Bought cleaning supplies, on account, $400.

[2] Bought cleaning equipment for cash, $3,000.

[3] Made sales on account for a total of $1,500.

[4] Borrowed $1,000 at the bank by signing a note payable for that amount.

[5]   Sold and issued common stock for cash, $2,000.

[6]   Collected payments on accounts receivable totaling $3,000.

[7]   Purchased a delivery truck for $5,000. Paid cash of $2,000 and signed a note payable for $3,000.

Required:

[a]   Enter the October 1 balances in T accounts.

[b]   Enter October transactions in the accounts, opening new accounts as needed.

[c]   Prepare a trial balance.

6   The balances of the accounts in the ledger of the H Company on December 31, 19X2 are as follows:

Account No.	Account title	Balance
111	Cash	$66,000
113	Accounts receivables	40,000
115	Merchandise inventory	48,000
116	Prepaid rent	—
131	Land (held as an investment)	40,000
152	Delivery truck	—
153	Accumulated depreciation	—
211	Accounts payable	80,000
212	Salaries payable	6,000
215	Advances from customers	—
311	Capital stock	90,000
315	Retained earnings	18,000
319	Dividends	—
411	Sales	—
511	Costs of goods sold	—
512	Salaries expense	—
513	Other expense	—

To reduce the number of journal entries and subsequent postings, the yearly totals for certain kinds of transactions are listed:

Dates 19X3	19X3 Transactions
January 3	Paid the liability for the December, 19X2, salaries amounting to $6,000
January 3	Purchased a delivery truck for cash, $8,000
January 3	Paid $12,000 rent in advance for 19X3
November 1	Received $1,800 cash in advance from a customer who ordered special merchandise to be delivered in the future
December 31	Purchased merchandise on credit, $195,000
December 31	Sales on account, $180,000; cash sales, $30,000
December 31	Cost of goods sold, $128,000
December 31	Collections on accounts receivable, $170,000
December 31	Payments to creditors, $110,000
December 31	Paid other expenses, $24,000
December 31	Paid salaries, $73,400
December 31	Paid dividends, $4,500

Required:

[a]   Enter the December 31, 19X2 (beginning) balances in the ledger T accounts.

[b]   Journalize the 19X3 transactions.

[c]   Post the transactions to the general ledger.

[d]   Prepare the December 31, 19X3, trial balance.

7   R TV & Electronics Company began business in July 19X1. Rogers sells TV's, radios, stereos, tape-recording and other electronic products for home use. The following are the ledger accounts as of the end of December 19X1:

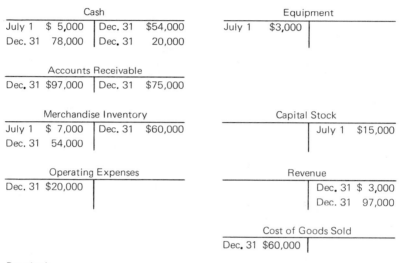

Cash		
July 1 $ 5,000	Dec. 31 $54,000	
Dec. 31 78,000	Dec. 31 20,000	

Equipment	
July 1 $3,000	

Accounts Receivable	
Dec. 31 $97,000	Dec. 31 $75,000

Merchandise Inventory	
July 1 $ 7,000	Dec. 31 $60,000
Dec. 31 54,000	

Capital Stock	
	July 1 $15,000

Operating Expenses	
Dec. 31 $20,000	

Revenue	
	Dec. 31 $ 3,000
	Dec. 31 97,000

Cost of Goods Sold	
Dec. 31 $60,000	

Required:

[a]   Reconstruct the journal entries that were made prior to posting the accounts.

[b]   Determine the balance of each account.

[c]   Prepare a trial balance.

8   Dave Wilcox opened a small specialty shop last year. Dave took bookkeeping in high school but it was not one of his better subjects. Because of a tight budget for his new business, Dave decided to keep the books himself. He bought the journal and ledger forms needed for a complete double-entry system. In applying the rules for debits and credits, he was unable to remember what the textbook had said. He eventually worked out the following rules:

Asset accounts:	Credit to increase
	Debit to decrease
Liability accounts:	Debit to increase
	Credit to decrease
Proprietorship:	Debit to increase
	Credit to decrease

Will this system work? Explain your answer.

9   The R Company entered into the transactions listed in the following table. Show how accountants would record each of the transactions by placing either a plus (+) for an increase or a minus (−) for a decrease and the correct monetary amount in the appropriate columns.

Example: The owners invest cash of $10,000	Asset	Equity	Revenue	Expense
	$+10,000	$+10,000	$0	$0

[a] The company purchases inventory on account for $2,000.

[b] The company pays for the inventory acquired in [a].

[c] Cash sales for $800 are made.

[d] $5,000 is borrowed from the bank.

[e] Wages of $900 are paid.

[f] A machine is purchased for $3,000 cash.

[g] Interest of $50 is paid.

[h] Sales of $12,000 are made on credit.

10   The M Company was established in July of the current year. Its sales and collection for merchandise sold on account during the remainder of the month were as follows:

July 14	Sold merchandise on account to the B Corporation, Invoice No. 1, $460.
July 15	Sold merchandise on account to L Incorporated, Invoice No. 2, $520.
July 17	Sold merchandise on account to M & Company, Invoice No. 3, $750.
July 18	Sold merchandise on account to the J Company, Invoice No. 4, $1,130.
July 19	Received payment for Invoice No. 2 of $520 from L Incorporated for merchandise.
July 22	Sold merchandise on account to M & Company, Invoice No. 5, $480.
July 23	Received payment for Invoice No. 1 of $460 from the B Corporation for merchandise.
July 24	Sold merchandise on account to the D Corporation, Invoice No. 6, $310.
July 25	Sold merchandise on account to E Incorporated, Invoice No. 7, $640.
July 26	Sold merchandise on account to L Incorporated, Invoice No. 8, $190.
July 29	Received payment for Invoice No. 6 of $310 from the D Corporation for merchandise.
July 31	Sold merchandise on account to the J Company, Invoice No. 9, $270.

Required:

[a] Open the following accounts in the general ledger, using the account numbers indicated: accounts receivable, 110, and sales, 500.

[b] Open the following accounts in the accounts receivable subsidiary ledger: B Corporation; E Incorporated; D Corporation; L Incorporated; M & Company; J Company.

[c] Record the transactions for July, posting to the customers' accounts in the accounts receivable ledger immediately after recording each entry. Use a sales journal similar to Fig. 8-5 and a cash receipts journal similar to Fig. 8-10.

[d] Post (i) the cash receipts journal and (ii) the sales journal to the accounts opened in the general ledger, inserting the balances only after the last postings.

[e] What is the sum of the balances of the subsidiary accounts?

[f] What is the balance of the controlling account?

CASE   A group of local citizens organized an athletic club for the purpose of creating a recreational center to encourage fellowship and goodwill among the citizens. The facilities of the Club include a gym, swimming pool, cocktail lounge, and dining room. The Club was financed by charging each member an initiation fee of $250 plus monthly dues of $20. During the first year 500 members joined the club and paid their $250 initiation fees for a total of $125,000. Dues collected during the first year amounted to $54,000. A suitable building was purchased on May 1 for $250,000 including equipment and fixtures. A 6% mortgage for $125,000 with annual payments of $10,000 plus interest each May 1 secured the mortgage note; the balance of $125,000 was paid in cash. The club had difficulty during the early months paying its monthly bills because of a shortage of cash. The later months showed some improvements but the payment of monthly bills was a constant struggle. The Board of Directors agreed to hire a local bookkeeper to assist them in understanding the problem so they could take steps to solve it.

After a period of time, the bookkeeper presented Schedule 1 to the Board of Directors with the statement that its correctness was proved because debits equaled credits. The amounts appearing for wages, food and liquor, taxes and licenses, utilities, and linens, etc., were the actual cash paid for these items. The amount for food and liquor sales is the cash collected from members for these items. After examining the schedule, various members of the Board of Directors raised the following questions:

[a]   What is the amount of our cash balance?
[b]   How much is due from members for dues and charges in the dining room, cocktail lounge, and gym?
[c]   Do we have any unpaid bills?
[d]   What was the income for the period?
[e]   Should the initiation fees be included in revenue?

The manager of the club was able to determine that the members owed the club $7,500 for dues and unpaid food and liquor charges. Unpaid bills for food and liquor were $2,300.

The Board of Directors has asked you to explain why the schedule submitted does not answer the above questions even though debits equal credits. They have asked you to make the measurements you consider necessary to explain the cash shortage.

SCHEDULE 1
Local Athletic Club, Financial Statement

	Debit	Credit
Cash	$282,000	$281,900
Building	250,000	
Wages	35,000	
Food and Liquor	112,000	
Mortgage payable		125,000
Dues		54,000
Initiation Fees		125,000
Food and liquor sales		103,000
Taxes and licenses	5,000	
Utilities	3,000	
Linens, silverware & dishes	1,900	
Total	$688,900	$688,900

9

Completion
of the Bookkeeping
Cycle

The steps in the double-entry cycle discussed in Chapter 8 dealt with recognizing, recording, and classifying the critical transactions of the business *during* the accounting period. The steps in the bookkeeping process explained in Chapter 8 are summarized as follows:

1   Recognition and original recording. Various employees in the business are charged with the responsibility of recognizing and making a record of the critical transactions. The original record may be a sales invoice, a cash remittance (receipt) form, a payroll time card, etc.
2   Double-entry analysis. The transactions are then analyzed to determine the accounts increased and the accounts decreased by the transactions.
3   Journal entry. Once analyzed, a transaction is entered into some journal, either the general journal or some specialized journal.
4   Posting. The journals are posted to the ledger accounts and/or subsidiary ledgers.
5   Account balancing and the trial balance. Periodically, the balance of each account is determined, and the accountant prepares a trial balance of the general ledger to check for mechanical mistakes. Trial balances of subsidiary ledgers are also compared with the control accounts to be certain they agree.

Although the steps just described are all essential to the double-entry system, they do not necessarily occur in order as listed. Several steps may be performed simultaneously. For example, the employee who prepares a sales invoice for a charge sale may enter the transaction in the specialized sales journal at the same time. This is possible because all charge sales have an identical effect on the accounts, and thus analysis of the transaction is no problem. When and how the work is performed depends on the particular system, which should be designed to suit the needs and resources of each business. However, where the double-entry method is used, every step must be performed by someone at sometime.

Many events and transactions that occur *during* the accounting period are not recognized and recorded during the period. In all cases there will be a record of the cash transactions of the business, but the extent to which accruals and deferrals are recognized and recorded varies widely. In every case, the accountant will need to recognize and record some accruals and deferrals after the end of the accounting period. These entries, which are made after the period's end and after the trial balance has been prepared, are called *adjusting entries* or adjustments.

Adjustments

Preparation of the adjusting entries is a crucial step in most accounting systems. The responsibility for recognizing, analyzing, and recording routine and recurring transactions is usually assigned to clerks and other employees who have little or no accounting training. Standard procedures can be developed for most frequently recurring transactions which can be learned and followed by someone who has no knowledge of income measurement and other accounting concepts and rules. At the end of the period, however, a trained accountant must go over the accounts and at that point recognize and record all transactions that affect the net income and financial position of the business.

You may reasonably pose the question: Why wait *until* after the end of the period to adjust the accounts? Why not keep the accounts current so the amounts that appear on the trial balance can be used to prepare financial statements? To answer these questions we must consider the general problem of timing the recognition of transactions in the accounting system.

Timing of Recognition

Adjusting entries are an essential and important step in the bookkeeping cycle because it is impractical and, in some cases, impossible to record all transactions during the period. There are, of course, some transactions that are important enough to warrant immediate recognition. Cash receipts and disbursements usually receive immediate recognition. In the example of J Cleaners, Incorporated in Chapter 8, the accounts receivable were also recognized and recorded immediately. Immediate recognition of these transactions was considered essential for control of the assets involved and for carrying on operations of the business. By contrast, some transactions are not critical to the control and operation of the business. Depreciation of plant and equipment is a good example: No useful purpose would be served by recording depreciation every day. Many transactions are recognized and recorded immediately, whereas others are completely ignored until the end of the period when they are recognized as adjustments.

The timing of recognition in the accounts is related to the nature of accruals of revenue and expense and of deferrals of revenue and expense. In the case of accruals, the recognition problem is due to the time lag between the critical event (sale, use of a service, etc.) and the cash receipt or disbursement. For deferrals of revenues or expense, the cash transaction often occurs before it is possible to determine the effect of the cash transaction on income for the period or the financial position at the end of the period. In addition, some adjustments must be made because of errors in recording transactions during the period.

Adjustments to Correct Errors

Some adjustments may be required because errors were made when transactions were recorded during the period. The double-entry system provides several checks against mechanical errors in posting and balancing accounts. These checks are the trial balance of the general ledger and the trial balances of subsidiary ledgers. Where computers or mechanical equipment is used, other controls will be built into the system to detect posting and arithmetic mistakes.

Another important means of verifying the accuracy of recorded transactions is the bank reconciliation. Most businesses follow the wise policy of depositing all cash receipts in a bank account and making all cash disbursements by checks on bank accounts. Where this policy is followed, the business has two records of cash receipts and disbursements—one kept by the business and one kept by the banks. A reconciliation or comparison of the two records will sometimes disclose an error that must be corrected after the end of the period. Bank reconciliations also assist in locating certain types of transactions that a business may intentionally leave unrecorded until the end of a period. The mechanics of bank reconciliations are discussed in Appendix B.

Adjustments for Accruals

In Chapter 3 it was noted that accruals of revenues and expenses are essential for income measurement because the critical accounting event *precedes* the cash transaction. Stated differently, the cash receipt or disbursement lags behind the important business event. This time lag has several effects on the time when certain accruals are recorded in the accounts. In some cases, the accountant may plan to delay recognition of an accrual in the accounts because of the time lag. In other situations, the delayed recording of the accrual may result from a time lag in the flow of information.

A good example of a planned time lag is the typical method of accounting for wages and salaries. For most businesses wages and salaries earned by each employee are not recorded daily—the clerical expense would be prohibitive. Instead, payrolls are prepared on a weekly, biweekly, or monthly basis. The cost of wages and salaries is recognized only at the end of the payroll period. Most of the time, payroll periods and accounting periods do not terminate at the same time. For this reason an adjustment is typically required for the accrued wages due employees at the end of an accounting period. As in the case of wages, any revenue or expense accrual may be intentionally ignored throughout the period. For example, the interest owed on a bank loan is typically not recorded in the accounts until the end of the period. Interest expense is handled in this way because the efficiency of the business's operations would not be improved by recording the accrual of interest expense on a daily or weekly basis—such frequent accruals would increase the costs of record-keeping. Thus, interest expense is accrued only when income is measured and a statement of position prepared.

Note the difference between salaries and interest and accounts receivable. Most businesses accrue the revenue from sales or services on a transaction basis. When a sale is made to a customer, a credit to revenue is recorded and the asset, accounts receivable, is increased. But the concern here is not to have an up-to-date measurement of revenue. The charge sale is recorded when made to provide a current record of how much each customer owes the business—this information is essential if timely collections are to be made. For a similar reason, purchases of inventory on credit are usually accrued on a transaction basis to give the business a current record of how much it owes its creditors. Keeping up with receivables and payables during the year is essential to efficient operations, but not for the accurate measurement of income.

An example of a time lag resulting from slow communications is the purchase of supplies or inventory from a manufacturer or wholesaler in a distant city. If the goods are shipped "free on board" (f.o.b.) shipping point, title to the goods passes to the buyer when they are delivered by the seller to the common carrier (railroad, motor freight line, or airline). In this case, the cost of the goods should be recognized at that time, and not when the goods are received by the buyer. If the seller mails the invoice to the buyer, several days may pass before he learns of the shipment. In many cases, the goods are received before the invoice arrives. Obviously, the cost of the supplies or inventory cannot be recognized until either the invoice is received or the goods are received. Thus an adjustment may be needed for goods in transit at the end of the accounting period.

Highly sophisticated data systems have been developed to eliminate time lag for some transactions. For example, time clocks in factories may be connected directly to the computer system. As the worker punches in and out, the lapsed time is recorded and each worker's payroll record is updated. With the capability we have for rapid communication and recording, we could eliminate most time lags. In many cases, however, the improvement in the timeliness of the information would not justify the increased costs.

Adjustments for Deferrals

As explained in Chapter 3, deferrals of revenue and expense are necessary because the cash transaction occurs before the critical accounting event. When cash is received or disbursed in such a case, it is often impossible to predict the eventual effect of the cash transaction on income or financial position for the period. In the double-entry system, every transaction affects at least two accounts. In the case of deferrals, the receipt or disbursement of cash changes the balance of the cash account. But what is the other affect?

A typical example is a cash disbursement for inventory during a period. One thing is certain: The cash has decreased and this critical event should be recorded as a credit to the cash account. But what should the accountant debit? If, on the one hand, the inventory is sold before year-end, its cost should be shown as an expense, namely, cost of goods sold. If, on the other hand, the inventory is unsold at year-end, the cost is a deferred cost, or asset, namely, merchandise inventory. The same problem arises if the inventory is acquired on credit terms and the business chooses to recognize the accrued costs (accounts payable) during the period instead of waiting until cash is paid to the supplier.

Accountants normally solve this type of problem by establishing arbitrary or discretionary rules to guide the clerks in recording transactions. To extend the preceding example, the rule may provide that the cost of merchandise will be debited to cost of goods sold or to an account titled purchases in every case. Generally, the costs are left in the discretionary account until year-end when the effect on income is determined. At that point the accounts are adjusted to show up-to-date results of the business operations of the period and an up-to-date representation of financial position at the end of the period.

Discretionary assignment of a debit or credit to an account applies primarily to potential deferred costs and revenues. In making the decisions about which accounts to debit or credit, an accountant is often guided by the probable eventual effects on the financial statements. For example, if a business buys land as a plant site, then the cost of the land will usually be debited to the asset account, land, because this cost will become an expense only when the land is sold, an eventuality with a rather low probability under the circumstances.

For the several reasons just discussed, the amounts on the trial balance are seldom, if ever, the exact amounts for revenues, expenses, assets, and equities. Instead, the information on the trial balance is the raw data with which the accountant begins to measure income and financial position. These measurements were described in Chapters 3 and 4. Once the measurements are made, adjusting entries are prepared to record the measured amounts in the various accounts. Thus, adjustments are the critical step in the bookkeeping cycle. The ability to make the measurements and translate them into adjusting entries is one of the characteristics that distinguishes an accountant from a clerk.

Example of Adjustments

The accounting work at the end of the period usually begins with the preparation of a trial balance. Mechanical errors, if any, are discovered and corrected. At the same time, the company's cash records are reconciled with the bank records, and differences are corrected by appropriate entries. Recall that under the flow concept, the accurate measurement of income and financial position depends on accurate figures for cash receipts and disbursements.

After completion of this work, the accountant begins to gather the data needed to measure income and financial position. The most successful technique is to examine each revenue and expense account shown in the chart of accounts and ask the following question: Is the amount of revenue (or expense) recorded in the account the proper amount in accordance with generally accepted accounting principles? If the recorded amounts are not correct, then an adjusting entry is made to change the revenue or expense balance to the proper amount. All revenue and expense accounts on the *chart* of accounts should be examined. Some accounts may not appear on the trial balance because they have a zero balance. Such accounts must still be examined to ascertain that zero is the right amount.

To illustrate this general technique, assume that you are adjusting the accounts and are currently concentrating on interest expense. The trial balance has two accounts on it related to interest: accrued interest payable, with a credit balance of $450, and interest expense, with a debit balance of $2,800. By checking the records to determine the proper adjustments, the following essential facts are uncovered:

1 No interest was prepaid during the year. This fact eliminates the possibility that part of the $2,800 in the expense account should be deferred to later years.
2 The balance of accrued interest payable ($450) is the amount accrued at the end of the preceding year. No entry was made in the account during the year.
3 By calculation, you determine that interest owed and unpaid at the end of the current year is $600. This amount has not been recorded.
4 The $2,800 debit balance in interest expense is the cash disbursed for interest during the period.

With these facts, the first step is to compute the *correct* interest expense for the year:

$$E = CD + \Delta AE + \Delta DE$$
$$= \$2,800 + (\$600 - \$450) - (0)$$
$$= \$2,800 + \$150$$
$$= \$2,950$$

To adjust the accounts the debit balance of interest expense must be increased from $2,800 to $2,950, which requires a debit entry of $150. The offsetting credit is to the credit balance account, accrued interest payable, which will increase the $450 balance to $600, the amount of interest owed at the end of the current year. The adjusting entry is:

	Debit	Credit
Interest expense	$150	
Accrued interest payable		$150

(To increase interest expense to $2,950 and adjust the liability account)

Note that the above approach will also result in an examination of most of the amounts that appear on the balance sheet. Revenues and expenses can be

measured only after the proper amounts are determined for accruals and deferrals of revenue and expense. The cash balance is verified by the bank reconciliation and the only other amounts on the balance sheet that do not come under
scrutiny as a result of measuring revenue and expense are the investment accounts, particularly the owner-investment accounts. These latter accounts must
be examined directly to determine the correctness of their balances.

To illustrate adjusting entries, assume the existence of a small incorporated
retail establishment, T Incorporated, which is in its second full year of operations. Its accounting system and the timing of recognition of various transactions will be discussed as each adjustment is considered.

THE WORKSHEET. Figure 9–1 is a completed worksheet for T Incorporated
for the year 19X2. Most accountants use some form of worksheet to assemble
the trial balance, the adjusting entries, and the final balances that appear on the
financial statements. The worksheet is normally completed and the financial
statements prepared *before* the adjusting entries are entered in the general journal and posted to the ledger.

The worksheet in Fig. 9–1 is called an *unclassified ten-column worksheet*.
This is only one of many forms found in use. The first two columns (beginning
on the left) contain the trial balance of the general ledger. The trial balance is
usually not prepared separately, as illustrated in Chapter 8, but the balances of
all accounts are entered directly on the worksheet. Given the trial balance (and
a correct figure for cash), the accountant may then turn to the important task
of adjusting the accounts. The third and fourth columns of the worksheet are
used for adjustments. The letters beside each debit and credit are keyed to the
explanation of the entries in the following sections. In the explanation of each
adjustment, note that the timing of the recognition of transactions in the accounts is of paramount importance in preparing the adjusting entry. An accountant must thoroughly understand what has been recorded *during* the period in
order to make the proper adjustments.

Figure 9–1 contains only examples of adjustments for

1   Revenue accruals
2   Expense accruals
3   Revenue deferrals
4   Expense deferrals

The example assumes that all errors made in recording transactions during the
year have already been adjusted. Typically, the accountant will examine revenue and expense accounts in the order they appear on the statements. In the
explanations which follow, adjustments in each of the four categories just mentioned have been grouped together to avoid the confusions that might arise
from taking the accounts in the order on the trial balance.

ACCRUED REVENUE ADJUSTMENTS. A business earns revenue by providing
goods and services for its customers. Some businesses make bookkeeping entries

Figure 9-1

J Incorporated — Worksheet
for Year Ended December 31, 19X2

Account Title	Trial Balance Debit	Trial Balance Credit	Adjustments Debit	Adjustments Credit	Adjusted Trial Bal. Debit	Adjusted Trial Bal. Credit	Statement of Income Debit	Statement of Income Credit	Balance Sheet Debit	Balance Sheet Credit
Cash	2,500.00				2,500.00				2,500.00	
Accounts receivable	3,200.00				3,200.00				3,200.00	
Merchandise inventory	57,900.00			(c) 46,900.00	11,000.00				11,000.00	
Prepaid insurance	180.00			(f) 30.00	150.00				150.00	
Furniture & fixtures	8,000.00				8,000.00				8,000.00	
Accumulated depreciation (furniture & fixtures)		750.00		(g) 750.00		1,500.00				1,500.00
Accounts payable		2,400.00				2,400.00				2,400.00
Accrued salaries payable		300.00		(d) 100.00		400.00				400.00
Note payable due 19X5		3,000.00				3,000.00				3,000.00
Common stock $100 par value		11,000.00				11,000.00				11,000.00
Retained earnings		4,000.00				4,000.00				4,000.00
Sales revenue		76,000.00				76,000.00		76,000.00		
Salary expense	15,800.00		(d) 100.00		15,900.00		15,900.00			
Rent expense	6,000.00				6,000.00		6,000.00			
Advertising & promotion expense	2,200.00			(e) 250.00	1,950.00		1,950.00			
Insurance expense	300.00		(f) 30.00		330.00		330.00			
Utility expense	300.00				300.00		300.00			
Miscellaneous expense	1,070.00				1,070.00		1,070.00			
	97,500.00	97,500.00								
Cost of goods sold			(a) 46,900.00		46,900.00		46,900.00			
Prepaid advertising expense			(e) 250.00		250.00				250.00	
Depreciation expense			(g) 750.00		750.00		750.00			
Interest expense			(b) 180.00		180.00		180.00			
Accrued interest payable				(b) 180.00		180.00				180.00
Income tax expense			(c) 600.00		600.00		600.00			
Accrued income taxes payable				(c) 600.00		600.00				600.00
			48,810.00	48,810.00	99,080.00	99,080.00	73,980.00	76,000.00	25,100.00	23,080.00
Net income for year							2,020.00			2,020.00
							76,000.00	76,000.00	25,100.00	25,100.00

[a] An explanation of letters (a) to (g) is given in the text.

for revenue during an accounting period only when cash is received. Under such circumstances, the business firm's accountant needs to make adjustment for all revenues earned but not yet recorded. This type of situation arises in connection with sales on account if a business elects to record sales during the period only when cash is collected from customers. If a business extends credit to a customer or loans money directly to an outside party, a similar situation can arise. Interest earned during the period may be recorded only if cash is actually collected, thus, making an end-of-the-period adjustment necessary. Adjustments for accrued revenues involve a debit to an asset account and a credit to a revenue account. The firm has earned revenue, and it is entitled to future cash receipts or an asset it is willing to accept in lieu of cash.

In Fig. 9-1, T Incorporated followed the practice of recording charge sales at the time of the sale. This procedure is the same as that used by J Cleaners, Incorporated in Chapter 8. The balance of accounts receivable which appears on the trial balance is the ending balance at December 31, 19X2. No adjustment was required because the proper accruals had been made throughout the year. In this situation, the accountant needed only to check to be sure that all receivables were accrued and that the receivables recorded would probably be collected. The problem of adjusting for bad debts (uncollectible accounts) is discussed in Chapter 10.

• Alternative Treatment: To illustrate the alternative facts that would require an adjustment, assume that T Incorporated made *no* entries in the accounts receivable account during the year. The cash collected, whether for cash sales or charge sales, was credited to sales revenue. Given these facts, the amount on the trial balance for sales revenue, $76,000, is the cash receipts (CR) from customers and the accounts receivables of $3,200 is the beginning balance. Under these conditions, the accountant must determine the amount due from customers at the end of the year. Assume that this amount is $4,000 and that there are no deferred revenues. If the revenue formula is used, then revenue for 19X2 is

$$R = CR + \Delta AR - \Delta DR$$
$$= \$76,000 + (\$4,000 - \$3,200) - (0)$$
$$= \$76,800$$

Now an adjustment is necessary because the revenue account shows $76,000 and not $76,800 which is the correct amount. The balance of accounts receivable must also be increased from $3,200 to $4,000. The adjusting entry in general journal form is

	Debit	Credit
Accounts receivable	$800	
Sales revenue		$800

(To adjust revenue and accounts receivable)

Note carefully that no entry was required on the worksheet because the accruals were recorded throughout the period. The key question in making adjustments is, what transactions were recorded during the period relative to what is needed to measure and report accurately both income and the current financial position.

ACCRUED EXPENSE ADJUSTMENTS. A business firm incurs expense when it consumes services in the process of carrying on its operations. In some cases acquisition and consumption of services may be left unrecorded during the accounting period unless there is a cash disbursement. Thus an end-of-the-period adjustment is required to recognize the expense for services consumed and the liability for the future payment of cash or a substitute satisfactory to the recipient.

• Salary Expense: T Incorporated followed the practice of debiting all cash paid for salaries to the expense account. The liability for accrued salaries was ignored throughout the year. At the end of 19X7, the amount owed to employees was $400, compared to $500 at the end of 19X1. The expense for the year was (there were no deferrals):

$$\text{Salary expense} = CD + \Delta AE - \Delta DE$$
$$= \$16,000 + (\$400 - \$500) - (0)$$
$$= \$15,900$$

The adjustment to show the correct expense and liability, keyed (a) on the worksheet in Fig. 9–1, is

	Debit	Credit
(a) Accrued salaries payable	$100	
Salary expense		$100

(To adjust for decrease in accrued salaries payable)

When this adjustment is extended to the "adjusted" columns, the amount payable becomes $400 and the expense $15,900.

• Interest Expense: Although no accrued interest expense appears on the T Incorporated original trial balance, the accounts do show a long-term note payable of $3,000. Investigation showed that the corporation borrowed $3,000 on March 31, 19X2 to increase working capital. The interest is payable annually on March 31 at the rate of 8 percent per annum. The interest due on December 31, 19X2, is $180 ($3,000 X .08 X 9/12). The expense calculation is

$$\text{Interest expense} = CD + \Delta AE - \Delta DE$$
$$= 0 + (\$180 - 0) - (0)$$
$$= \$180$$

The entry, keyed (b) on the worksheet (Fig. 9–1) is

	Debit	Credit
(b) Interest expense	$180	
Accrued interest payable		$180

(To adjust for unpaid interest on note payable)

Adjustments such as this one for interest can be overlooked unless investigation is extended to all accounts in the chart of accounts, including debt- and owner-investment accounts.

• Income Tax Expense: The federal and state income tax returns of T Incorporated were completed after the adjustments to determine pretax income by the accountant. These returns show a total income tax of $600 for 19X2. At the end of 19X1, the income taxes were accrued and later when payment was made, the amount debited to the liability account. At the end of 19X2, as a result, there were no balances in the accounts for income taxes. The adjustment required at the end of 19X2 is an accrual of the 19X2 tax expense [keyed (c) on the worksheet (Fig. 9–1)]:

	Debit	Credit
(c) Income tax expense	$600	
Accrued income tax payable		$600
(To adjust for the 19X2 income taxes per tax returns)		

Note that this simple accrual is identical with that for interest expense.

• Alternative Treatment: The tax payments for 19X1 could have been debited to an expense account as paid and the accrued liability ignored. For example, assume that income taxes for 19X1 were $950 and that these were recorded at the end of 19X1 in an adjusting entry identical with adjustment (c). The payments, however, during 19X2 were debited to income tax expense. At the end of 19X2, we would then have a cash payment of $950, a beginning accrual of $950, and an ending accrual of $600. The expense calculation would have been

$$\text{Income tax expense} = CD + \Delta AE - \Delta DE$$
$$= \$950 + (\$600 - \$950) - (0)$$
$$= \$600$$

The adjusting entry would then be a debit to the accrued income tax payable account of $350 to reduce the balance to $600 and a credit to income tax expense to reduce the balance to $600.

Accrued income taxes differ from other accrued expenses in that it is difficult to equate the incurrence of the expense with consumption of services. Business firms do get services from governmental units, but there is no direct relationship between the worth of the services and the amount of taxes. In any case a business firm incurs income tax expense on the basis of the current period's income, and a future cash payment will be required. For this reason tax accruals may be grouped with accrued expense adjustments.

• Utility and Miscellaneous Expense: Investigation of these expense accounts revealed no significant unpaid balances for services already consumed nor prepayment for services. No adjustment was required.

DEFERRED COST (EXPENSE) ADJUSTMENTS. Frequently a business will acquire services (assets) and will recognize these acquisitions in the accounts at or near the time of acquisition. As these services (assets) are consumed by the firm's operations they become expenses. Consumption may occur day by day or even second by second. For this reason it is impractical to recognize consumption in the accounts as it occurs. Instead, an end-of-the-period adjustment is made to recognize the increase in expense and the decrease in the asset. This type of adjustment takes its name from the fact that the recording of the expense for services consumed is delayed (deferred) until the end of an accounting period.

Depending on the circumstances, a given type of expense may require an accrued expense adjustment or a deferred cost adjustment or both. If rent is paid in advance, a deferred cost adjustment will be required at the end of the period. Cost of goods sold expense may require both types of adjustment: a deferred cost adjustment for inventory on hand and an accrued expense adjustment for any unrecorded accounts payable.

• Cost of Goods Sold: The trial balance for T Incorporated in Fig. 9–1 does not show an account for cost of goods sold. The following procedures were carried out during the year:

1   The cost of merchandise actually paid during 19X7 was debited to the deferred cost (asset) account, namely, merchandise inventory. This amount was $45,000. The balance of merchandise inventory thus comprised the cash paid of $45,000 and the beginning inventory of $12,500 ($57,500 – $45,000 = $12,500). The ending inventory, determined by a physical count at the end of the year, was $11,000.
2   No accruals were made during the year for merchandise purchased. The balance of accounts payable of $2,000 is therefore the amount due on January 1, 19X2. The accountant determined that $2,400 was owed to suppliers on December 31, 19X2.

With these facts, the cost of goods sold may be calculated as follows:

$$
\begin{aligned}
\text{Cost of goods sold} &= \text{CD} + \Delta\text{AE} - \Delta\text{DE} \\
&= \$45,000 + (\$2,400 - \$2,000) - (\$11,000 - \$12,500) \\
&= \$45,000 + (\$400) - (-\$1,500) \\
&= \$46,900
\end{aligned}
$$

The adjusting entry which appears on the worksheet keyed (d) (Fig. 9–1) is presented in general journal form:

	Debit	Credit
(d) Cost of goods sold	$46,900	
Merchandise inventory		$46,500
Accounts payable		400
(To adjust for cost of goods sold)		

Columns 5 and 6 on the worksheet (Fig. 9-1), entitled the "Adjusted Trial Balance," show the balances of the accounts after adding or subtracting the adjustment (using debit–credit rules). In effect each line on the worksheet is an account. Note the effect of entry (d) on the balances: The credit of $46,500 to merchandise inventory leaves a balance of $11,000 in merchandise inventory account, the correct amount; the credit of $400 to accounts payable increases the balance to $2,400, the amount owed to suppliers on December 31, 19X2. Finally, the debit to cost of goods sold, which is added below the trial balance because it did not appear there, shows the amount calculated by the formula, $46,900.

• Alternative Treatments: T Incorporated could have used several different practices to record merchandise. If, for example, the cost of merchandise purchased on account had been recorded as purchased, the accounts payable would have been $2,400 on the trial balance and merchandise inventory would have been $400 greater, or $57,900. In this situation, accounts payable would not have to be adjusted at the end of the period.

As a second alternative, assume that purchases were not accrued (as on the worksheet, Fig. 9-1) but that all cash payments for merchandise during the year were debited to cost of goods sold. The balance of merchandise inventory would have been $12,500, the beginning inventory, and cost of goods sold would have appeared on the balance sheet with a debit balance of $45,000, the cash paid. The calculation of cost of goods sold would remain unchanged ($46,900). However, the adjusting entry to record the correct balances would be changed to the following:

	Debit	Credit
Cost of goods sold	$1,900	
Merchandise inventory		$1,500
Accounts payable		400
(To adjust for cost of goods sold)		

This entry would increase the debit balance of cost of goods sold from $45,000 to $46,900, decrease the debit balance of merchandise inventory from $12,500 to $11,000, and increase the accounts payable to $2,400.

• Rent Expense: T Incorporated rents its building and pays the rent in advance on the first of each month. Thus the amount paid during the year was the cost consumed and there were no deferred costs or accrued payables to carry forward to the next year and no adjustment was required.

• Advertising and Promotion Expense: Payments for promotion and advertising by T Incorporated were debited to the advertising and promotion expense account. An investigation of the various contracts revealed that there were no unpaid accruals. Analysis of the costs in the account, however, showed that $700 was spent for inexpensive paperweights with the company's name on them. These paperweights were given away to good customers from time to time. At

December 31, 19X2, paperweights costing $250 were still on hand. There was no inventory of advertising supplies at the first of the year. Calculation of the expense is:

$$\text{Advertising and promotion expense} = CD + \Delta AE - \Delta DE$$
$$= \$2,200 + (0) - (\$250 - 0)$$
$$= \$1,950$$

The adjusting entry, keyed (e) on the worksheet (Fig. 9-1) is

	Debit	Credit
(e) Prepaid advertising expense	$250	
Advertising and promotion expense		$250
(To adjust for deferred cost for advertising)		

This entry reduces the expense to the adjusted amount and sets up the new deferred cost.

• Alternative Treatment: The debit of the $700 spent for advertising and promotion expense is a good example of discretionary classification. There was no way to know when the expenditure was made just how much of the cost would be used up in 19X2 and how much, if any, would be available in future years. The accountant could have debited the amount to prepaid advertising expense, a deferred cost account. If this entry had been made, then the adjusting entry would have transferred the consumed cost of $450 from the deferred cost account to the expense account:

	Debit	Credit
Advertising and promotion expense	$450	
Prepaid advertising expense		$450
(To adjust prepaid advertising to show the amount consumed in 19X2)		

This alternative, as with all others, would yield the same end result. Advertising and promotion expense would still be $1,950 and the prepaid advertising expense, $250.

• Insurance Expense: T Incorporated purchases a one-year casualty insurance policy on its inventory and fixtures each year on July 1. In 19X1, the premiums paid were $360, and one-half of this cost was deferred as prepaid insurance at the end of 19X1, giving the balance of $180 in the prepaid insurance account. On July 1, 19X2, the company purchased another one-year policy for $300 and debited this amount to insurance expense. One-half of this premium, or $150, should be deferred and included in expense in 19X3. The calculation of insurance expense for 19X2 is

$$\text{Insurance expense} = CD + \Delta AE - \Delta DE$$
$$= \$300 + (0) - (\$150 - \$180)$$
$$= \$300 - (-\$30)$$
$$= \$330$$

The adjusting entry, keyed (f) on the worksheet (Fig. 9–1) is

	Debit	Credit
(f) Insurance expense	$30	
Prepaid insurance		$30

(To adjust the insurance expense for the cost
consumed during 19X2)

The debit to insurance expense increases the balance of $330, the calculated expense, and the credit to prepaid insurance reduces the deferred cost to $150, one-half of the cost of the new policy.

• Alternative Treatment: The accountant could have debited the cost of the new policy to prepaid insurance. If this procedure had been followed, the balance of prepaid insurance would have been $480 on the trial balance. The adjusting entry would have transferred the $330 of cost consumed to the insurance expense account, leaving a balance of $150 in prepaid insurance.

• Depreciation Expense: The cost of long-lived assets is almost always recognized at the time of acquisition, and the cost is debited to a deferred cost or asset account. At the end of each accounting period, the portion of the cost used up in the current period, depreciation, is set up as an expense.
     Unlike other deferred costs, however, the expense portion is not credited to the deferred cost account. Instead, a *contra* account is used to keep a record of the amount of cost charged (debited) to expense since acquisition. Accounting Principles Board Opinion No. 12* requires that both the original cost of plant and equipment and the depreciation for all past years be disclosed on the balance sheet. A contra account is an account associated with another account but with an opposite balance. The balance of the contra account is normally subtracted from the principle account on the balance sheet. For depreciation, the contra account is titled *accumulated depreciation*, with additional words added to identify the account with the principal account, that is, buildings, furniture and fixtures, etc.
     For T Incorporated, the furniture and fixtures were acquired early in 19X1. The assets have an estimated life of ten years and an estimated salvage value of $500. Annual depreciation is as follows:

$$\text{Depreciation expense} \ = \ \frac{\$8{,}000 - \$500}{10 \text{ years}} \ = \ \$750$$

When costs are incurred for long-lived assets, accountants almost always debit the acquisition costs to the deferred cost or asset accounts because they know the asset will benefit several years. For this reason, the adjusting entry for depreciation is about the only adjustment that has a standard form. The entry to

*American Institute of Certified Public Accountants, *Opinion of the Accounting Principles Board No. 12* (December 1967).

record depreciation of the furniture and fixtures of T Incorporated for 19X2 is keyed (g) on the worksheet (Fig. 9–1).

	Debit	Credit
(g) Depreciation expense	$750	
Accumulated depreciation—furniture & fixtures)		$750
(To adjust for depreciation in 19X2)		

With this adjustment, the balance of the contra account, namely, accumulated depreciation, is increased to $1,500, the total depreciation for 19X1 and 19X2. The original cost, with the balance of the contra account subtracted from it to give a net of $6,500, is shown on the balance sheet.

DEFERRED REVENUE ADJUSTMENTS. A deferred (unearned) revenue occurs when a business firm collects cash from a customer for goods or services to be provided later. Advance collections frequently occur when manufacturers build high cost items according to a customer's specifications. Another example is when a publisher collects subscriptions in advance for periodicals to be delivered monthly over several months or years. Because of the nature of the business of T Incorporated, it had no deferred revenues at the end of 19X2. To illustrate the adjustment for deferred revenues, we will assume some additional facts about a publishing company. (These adjustments are not a part of the T Incorporated example.)

Revenues collected in advance are liabilities. The recipient owes goods or services to the customer who pays in advance. The advance collections are recorded currently because a cash receipt is involved. On the other hand, payment of the liability and the earning of revenue that occurs as goods and services are provided to the customer are frequently ignored until the end of the accounting period, at which time an adjusting entry is made.

As an example, consider a publishing company that collects $150,000 for subscriptions during its first year of operation in 19X1. The summary entry to record these collections is

	Debit	Credit
Cash	$150,000	
Unearned subscriptions		$150,000
(To record advance collections		
of subscriptions in 19X1)		

If at year-end, assuming a calendar year accounting period, $100,000 of the subscriptions collected are still unearned, the revenue formula would show $50,000 of revenue as follows:

$$\text{Revenue from subscriptions} = CR + \Delta AR - \Delta DR$$
$$= \$150,000 + 0 - (\$100,000 - 0)$$
$$= \$150,000 - \$100,000$$
$$= \$50,000$$

Thus, at the end of 19X1, a deferred revenue adjustment would be required. The entry is

	Debit	Credit
Unearned subscriptions	$50,000	
Revenue from subscriptions		$50,000
(To adjust unearned subscriptions and revenue from subscriptions for 19X1)		

To continue the example for another year, assume that collections for new subscriptions in 19X2 are $75,000. The summary entry to record the collections is

	Debit	Credit
Cash	$75,000	
Unearned subscriptions		$75,000
(To record advance collections of subscriptions in 19X2)		

If at the end of 19X2, $90,000 of subscriptions are still unearned, the revenue formula shows that revenue earned is $85,000 as follows:

$$\text{Revenue from subscriptions} = CR + \Delta AR - \Delta DR$$
$$= \$75,000 + 0 - (\$90,000 - \$100,000)$$
$$= \$75,000 + \$10,000$$
$$= \$85,000$$

At the end of 19X2 the deferred revenue adjustment would be recorded by the following entry:

	Debit	Credit
Unearned subscriptions	$85,000	
Revenue from subscriptions		$85,000
(To adjust unearned subscriptions and revenue from subscriptions for 19X2)		

As with many of the entries previously explained, the credit item used to record collections is discretionary. If the collection is credited to a revenue account (revenue from subscriptions) instead of a liability account (unearned subscriptions), the alternative entries for 19X1 and 19X2 are as follows:

	Debit	Credit
Cash	$150,000	
Revenue from subscriptions		$150,000
(To record advance collections of subscriptions in 19X1)		
Revenue from subscriptions	100,000	
Unearned subscriptions		100,000
(To adjust revenue from subscriptions and unearned subscriptions for 19X1)		
Cash	75,000	
Revenue from subscriptions		75,000
(To record advance collections of subscriptions in 19X2)		
Unearned subscriptions	10,000	
Revenue from subscriptions		10,000
(To adjust unearned subscriptions and revenue from subscriptions for 19X2)		

COMPLETION OF THE WORKSHEET. After all accounts are examined and all adjustments prepared and entered on the worksheet, each line on the worksheet is added horizontally, using debit–credit rules, to obtain the adjusted trial balance. As in the original trial balance, accounts with a debit balance after adjustment are shown in the debit column and those with a credit balance in the credit column. The adjustment columns and the columns of the adjusted trial balance are then totaled and each compared for equality of debits and credits to guard against mechanical errors.

If the totals agree, each account balance is then placed in the appropriate debit or credit columns, depending on the account balance as well as on the financial statement on which the account appears. The cash account, for example, has a debit balance and appears on the balance sheet and is thus placed on the worksheet. Sales revenue has a credit balance and appears on the statement of income. In a similar fashion, each account balance is placed in the proper column as either an income statement or balance sheet item.

As a final step the debit and credit columns of the statement of income and balance sheet are summed. On the statement of income columns, an excess of credit balances (revenue) over debit balances (expenses) represents the net income. This net income added to the debit column in the statement of income and the credit (equity) column of the balance sheet makes the totals of each set of columns equal. Where operations result in a loss, the loss is added to the credit column of the statement of income and the debit column (negative equity) of the balance sheet, and the total of both sets of columns are equal.

The worksheet is a convenient tool for assembling the original trial balance, the adjustments, and the balances that appear on the financial statements. When the columns are balanced, the accountant has some assurance that no mechanical mistakes have been made in the calculation of the amounts that appear on the basic financial statements. The same assurances against mechanical errors can, of course, be obtained through careful use of computerized systems.

Preparation of Financial Statements

With the worksheet completed, the accountant has most of the information available to prepare the financial statements. The information for the statement of income and the balance sheet comes directly from the appropriate columns on the worksheet. The statement of sources and application of funds, no matter how defined, is usually prepared by using the techniques described in Chapter 7, requiring the current statement of income and comparative balance sheets.

A multiple-step statement of income taken from the worksheet in Fig. 9–1 is presented in Fig. 9–2, and a classified balance sheet for T Incorporated as of December 31, 19X2, is shown in Fig. 9–3. The format of the balance sheet is the report form. The contra account for accumulated depreciation appears on the balance sheet. Note also that the balance for retained earnings, $6,020, includes the opening balance of $4,000 and the $2,020 net income for 19X2.

Figure 9-2

T Incorporated	Statement of Income for Year Ended December 31, 19X2	
Revenue from sales		$76,000
Cost of goods sold		46,900
Gross profit for year		$29,100
Operating expenses:		
Salary expense	$15,900	
Rent expense	6,000	
Advertising and promotion expense	1,950	
Insurance expense	330	
Utility expense	300	
Depreciation expense	750	
Interest expense	180	
Miscellaneous expense	1,070	
Total operating expenses		26,480
Net income before income taxes		$ 2,620
Taxes on income		600
Net income after taxes		$ 2,020

The principal weakness of the worksheet illustrated in this chapter is the absence of information concerning the classification of amounts that appear on the balance sheet. Other, more complicated forms of the worksheet also provide for the classification of balance sheet items. When the unclassified worksheet is used, additional inquiries may be necessary to determine the proper classification of assets and equities.

Final Steps in the Cycle

An accountant normally prepares financial statements from his worksheets, which are also referred to as working papers. By the time an accountant gathers all information needed to adjust the accounts, the management, shareholders, and others interested in the business are anxious to see the final figures for the year, that is, the financial statements that will be released to the public and sent to regulatory agencies such as the Securities Exchange Commission. In a publicly held corporation, the annual financial statements are mailed to the shareholders before their annual meeting which is usually set approximately $2\frac{1}{2}$ to 3 months after the end of the corporation's fiscal year.

After the worksheet is completed and the statements prepared, the adjusting entries are *formally* entered into the accounts. The adjusting entries on the worksheet are entered in the general journal and then posted to the general ledger. The general journal adjusting entries from T Incorporated are not reproduced; these journal entries [(a) through (g)] appear in the discussion of

Figure 9-3

T Incorporated	**Statement of Financial Position, December 31, 19X2**	
Assets		
Current assets:		
Cash		$ 2,500
Accounts receivable		3,200
Merchandise inventory		11,000
Prepaid advertising expense		250
Prepaid insurance		150
Total current assets		$17,100
Furniture and fixtures (at cost)	$ 8,000	
Less accumulated depreciation	1,500	6,500
Total assets		$23,600
Liabilities and owners' equity		
Current liabilities:		
Accounts payable		$ 2,400
Accrued salaries payable		400
Accrued interest payable		180
Accrued income taxes payable		600
Total current liabilities		$ 3,580
Long-term note payable (8% interest due 3/31/19X5)		3,000
Owners' equity:		
Common stock, $100 par, 200 shares authorized, 110 shares issued and outstanding	$11,000	
Retained earnings	6,020	
Total owners' equity		17,020
Total liabilities and owners' equity		$23,600

adjustments. Figure 9-4 is an abbreviated ledger for T Incorporated in T accounts. The transactions for 19X2 are not shown on the ledger. After the adjustments are posted, the account balances are the amounts that appear on the statements with the exception of retained earnings. After the adjustments are posted, the balance of retained earnings is the opening balance and the net income or loss must be added to this amount to obtain the ending balance. Dividends, if recorded in a separate account, would be subtracted to obtain the ending balance of retained earnings.

Closing Entries

The revenue and expense accounts of a business include information about the operations of the business for an accounting period. These accounts are

Figure 9-4

T Incorporated — Abbreviated General Ledger for 19X2—Showing Adjusting and Closing Entries

Cash

T/B $2,500	

Accounts Receivable

T/B $3,200	

Merchandise Inventory

T/B $57,500	Adj.(a) $46,500

Prepaid Advertising Expense

Adj.(c) $250	

Prepaid Insurance

T/B $180	Adj.(d) $30
Balance $150	

Furniture & Fixtures

T/B $8,000	

Accumulated Depreciation (furniture & fixtures)

	T/B $750
	Adj.(e) 750
	Balance $1,500

Accounts Payable

	T/B $2,000
	Adj.(a) 400
	Balance $2,400

Accrued Salaries Payable

Adj.(b) $100	T/B $500
	Balance $400

Accrued Interest Payable

	Adj.(f) $180

Accrued Income Taxes Payable

	Adj.(g) $600

Note Payable (long-term)

	T/B $3,000

Common Stock

	T/B $11,000

Retained Earnings

	T/B $4,000
	Close 2,020
	Balance $6,020

Sales Revenue

Close $76,000	T/B $76,000

Cost of Goods Sold

Adj.(a) $46,900	Close $46,900

Salary Expense

T/B $16,000	Close 15,900
Adj.(b) $100	

Rent Expense

T/B $6,000	Close $6,000

Advertising and Promotion Expenses

T/B $2,200	Close 1,950
Adj.(c) $250	

Insurance Expense

T/B $300	Close $330
Adj.(d) 30	

Utility Expense

T/B $300	Close $300

Depreciation Expense

Adj.(e) $750	Close $750

Interest Expense

T/B $180	Close $180

Income Tax Expense

Adj.(g) $600	Close $600

Miscellaneous Expense

T/B $1,070	Close $1,070

Key to entries in ledger:

T/B = Balances from unadjusted trial balance.

Adj. = Adjusting entries lettered as shown on Fig. 9-1.

Close = Closing entry referring to journal entry on Fig. 9-5.

frequently referred to as *nominal* accounts, not because they are trifling in importance but because they pertain to a single accounting period. Asset and equity accounts are sometimes referred to as *real* accounts because the balances of these accounts are carried forward year after year.

At the end of each year the balances of the nominal accounts, revenues and expenses, are reset to zero by preparing closing entries. In addition to setting the balances of the revenue and expense accounts at zero (closing them), the closing process records the income or loss for the period in the owners' equity accounts (retained earnings for a corporation). Although closing entries may take many forms, the final effects are to

1   Debit all revenue accounts for their adjusted balances.
2   Credit all expense accounts for their adjusted balances.
3   Credit retained earnings for the income for the year (or debit retained earnings for a loss).

The first two steps close the nominal accounts and the third one transfers the results of operations (the difference between revenues and expenses) to retained earnings. If revenues, which are debited, exceed expenses, which are credited, there will be a credit remainder, the periodic income, to transfer to the retained earnings account thereby increasing its balance. Conversely, if expenses exceed revenue, there will be a debit remainder reflecting a loss, which will reduce retained earnings. Figure 9–5 shows a closing entry for T Incorporated. Note that the amount transferred to retained earnings is $2,020, the income for 19X2. All information needed to prepare the closing entry is contained in the statement of income columns of the worksheet (Fig. 9–1). After closing, the revenue and expense accounts have a zero balance and are ready for the accumulation of the operating results for the coming year.

Figure 9–5

T Incorporated	General Journal	
Closing Entry		
	Debit	Credit
Sales revenue	$76,000	
Cost of goods sold		$46,900
Salary expense		15,900
Rent expense		6,000
Advertising and promotion expenses		1,950
Insurance expense		330
Utility expense		300
Depreciation expense		750
Interest expense		180
Miscellaneous expense		1,070
Income tax expense		600
Retained earnings		2,020
(To close the nominal accounts)		

If distributions to owners, dividends, were made during the year and recorded in a separate account, the debit balance of this account would also be closed to retained earnings as follows:

	Debit	Credit
Retained earnings	$xxxx	
Dividends		$xxxx

(To close the dividend account to retained earnings)

The debit to retained earnings would reduce the balance of that account and show the decreased equity of the owners.

Informal Closing Procedures

The purpose of all closing procedures is the same: to remove the old balances from the nominal accounts and update the balance of retained earnings (or proprietorship) to show the results of the year's operations and distributions to owners. This objective may be accomplished in a number of ways without making formal entries and posting them. Many accountants follow the practice of starting a new ledger every year. The old ledger, whether in the form of handwritten pages, punched cards, or magnetic tape, is simply stored. A new ledger is opened by setting up an account for each item on the balance sheet or for each amount in the balance sheet columns of the worksheet or working papers. Nominal accounts are added to the ledger as the need arises during the year. The old ledger stored away would show the adjusted balances for both the real and nominal accounts.

Closing entries, no doubt, added a sense of mystery to the early use of the double-entry method. That the transfer of the income or loss to the owners' equity accounts brought the real accounts into balance was an astonishing fact to early practitioners. But, as was demonstrated in Chapter 4, the equality of an equation is not effected by moving the terms of the equation across the equality sign, provided the rules of algebra are observed.

After-Closing Trial Balance

After the nominal accounts are closed (or a new ledger started), the accountant should always make certain that the debit and credit balances of the asset and equity (real) accounts are in agreement. This task may be accomplished by a listing of the real accounts in the trial balance format. Another effective method is to compare the after-closing balances with the balance sheet or balance sheet columns on the worksheet. Particular attention should be directed to retained earnings (or proprietorship) because it is the only real account changed by the closing entry.

The Complete Cycle

In summary, the double-entry method involves the following steps:

1 Recognition and original recording of transactions
2 Analysis of transactions using debit and credit rules
3 Entry of transactions in various journals
4 Posting the journals to the general ledger and/or some subsidiary ledger
5 Preparation of a trial balance of the general ledger and of subsidiary ledgers
6 Adjusting the accounts and completion of a worksheet
7 Preparation of financial statements
8 Entry of adjusting entries in the general journal and posting these entries to the ledger
9 Closing the nominal accounts and updating the appropriate owners' equity account
10 Preparation of the after-closing trial balance

This method has served man in his commercial endeavors for about 600 years. After all this time the method remains an important part of every professional accountant's stock-in-trade.

REVERSING ENTRIES. In the explanations and illustrations of the bookkeeping cycle in Chapters 8 and 9, the authors intentionally avoid reversing entries. Familiarity with reversing entries is unnecessary for understanding the accounting process and its uses. In fact, reversing entries complicate accounting mechanics without adding anything conceptually; hence, they make the process more difficult to understand. However, anyone who becomes a practicing accountant is certain to encounter reversing entries and, therefore, needs to understand what they are and how they are used. For this reason, Appendix C contains explanations and examples of reversing entries.

QUESTIONS

1 Describe adjusting entries and explain the purpose of adjusting entries.
2 What are the three general problems that make adjusting entries necessary?
3 For each of the three general problems requiring adjusting entries describe how and why they arise.
4 What are the steps in the accounting cycle?
5 What is the purpose of a worksheet?
6 You overhear a friend state that he can make all necessary adjusting entries without referring to the general ledger accounts or a trial balance. Do you agree with his statement?
7 If an expense accrual has not been recorded prior to preparing the trial balance or the worksheet, indicate the accounts that would be affected and whether they would be increased or decreased.
8 What is the function of closing entries?

9 Why should an after-closing trial balance be prepared?

10 Why are the columns for the adjusted trial balance on a worksheet desirable? Are they absolutely necessary?

11 A friend who operates a drug store purchased a new delivery truck. Indicate whether you would advise him to charge the cost of the truck to an asset or an expense account, and explain why.

12 Explain the difference between measurement of revenue and expense and the adjusting entry process.

13 What are nominal accounts? What are real accounts?

14 Explain how the preparation of a worksheet facilitates the preparation of financial statements.

15 A businessman incurs a deferred cost on June 1, 19X1. When his fiscal year ends on December 31, 19X1 some of the deferred cost is used up and some will be of benefit to future periods.

 [a] Present the debit and credit classification for the adjusting entry on December 31 assuming the deferral was originally recorded in a real account.

 [b] Present the debit and credit classifications for the adjusting entry on December 31 assuming the deferral was originally recorded in a nominal account.

16 Which of the following will give rise to a discretionary classification at the time of initial recording:

 [a] An employer owes accrued wages of $100 to his employees at the end of an accounting period.

 [b] In the middle of an accounting period, a businessman prepays rent for one year on his store building.

 [c] During an accounting period, merchandise is purchased on account.

 [d] During an accounting period, merchandise is purchased for cash.

 [e] A delivery truck is purchased on an installment contract.

 [f] A delivery truck is purchased for cash.

17 [a] Assuming there are no errors on the worksheet, is it possible to determine whether a business experienced a profit or a loss by totaling the balance sheet columns without totaling the statement of income columns?

 [b] Explain the reason for your answer to part [a] in terms of the formulas for revenue, expense, and income presented in Chapter 3.

PROBLEMS

1 S Incorporated records cash transactions and adjusts for accruals and deferrals only at the end of the annual accounting period. During its first year of operation the following cash transactions were recorded:

 [1] Prepaid one year's rent for $3,600 on April 1, 19X1

 [2] Paid $540 for fire insurance for three years on June 1, 19X1

 [3] Purchased office supplies for $450 on September 1, 19X1

 [4] Paid $5,000 for merchandise purchased during 19X1

 The cost of merchandise on hand at December 31, 19X1, the end of the first year of operations, was $500. All of the office supplies were used up at December 31, 19X1.

Required:

 [a] Assume nominal accounts were used for the initial recording and present the necessary adjusting entries as of December 31, 19X1.

[b] Assume real accounts were used for the initial recording and present the necessary adjusting entries as of December 31, 19X1.

[c] Present the initial entries as you would have recorded them and in each case explain why you used the nominal or real account involved.

2 [a] The balance in the prepaid insurance account before adjustment at the end of the year is $1,800. Journalize the necessary adjusting entry required under each of the following *alternatives*:

[1] The amount of the insurance expired during the year is $600.

[2] The amount of unexpired insurance applicable to future periods is $1,000.

[b] A business enterprise pays weekly salaries of $5,000 on Friday, for a five-day week ending on Friday. Journalize the necessary adjusting entry at the end of the fiscal period under each of the following assumptions:

[1] Assume the fiscal period ends on Tuesday.

[2] Assume the fiscal period ends on Thursday.

[c] A delivery truck costs $5,000 and was purchased on January 1, 19X9. Estimated useful life of the truck is five years with no value at the end of five years. Using the straight-line method, make the necessary adjusting entry to record the depreciation on December 31, 19X9, the end of the first year.

3 A number of errors in journalizing and posting transactions are described below. Present the journal entries to correct the errors.

[a] A $40 cash payment for supplies was recorded as a debit to utilities expense and a credit to cash.

[b] Cash of $240 received from a customer on account was recorded as a $420 debit to cash and a credit of $420 to accounts receivable.

[c] Equipment costing $1,000 was purchased for cash and was recorded as a debit to buildings and a credit to accounts payable.

[d] Payment of $400 cash for personal use of John Doe, owner, was recorded as a debit to salary expense and a credit to cash.

4 The S Print Shop, operated by John Smith, has the following statement of income for the month ended October 31, 19X9 (Smith *withdrew* $600 during the month of October for his personal use):

S Print Shop, Statement of Income for Month Ended October 31, 19X9

Sales		$5,000.00
Operating Expenses:		
Salary expense	$1,000.00	
Supplies expense	1,200.00	
Rent expense	300.00	
Depreciation expense	100.00	
Miscellaneous expense	400.00	3,000.00
Net Income from operations		$2,000.00

Instructions:

Using the information found in the preceding statement of income, journalize the necessary closing entry for S Print Shop as of October 31, 19X9.

5 The following trial balance of O Incorporated is presented as of December 31, 19X3:

O Incorporated, Trial Balance for Year Ended December 31, 19X3

	Debit	Credit
Cash	$ 3,900.00	
Accounts receivable	12,000.00	
Merchandise Inventory	135,000.00	
Store supplies	600.00	
Prepaid Insurance	2,200.00	
Store Equipment	19,000.00	
Allowance for depreciation of store equipment		$ 1,800.00
Accounts Payable		5,700.00
Salaries Payable		300.00
Common stock		30,000.00
Retained Earnings		6,800.00
Sales		160,000.00
Salaries	18,000.00	
Rent expense	7,500.00	
Store Supplies expense	800.00	
Other Expenses	5,600.00	
	$204,600.00	$204,600.00

The data needed for adjusting the accounts and preparing a statement of income for the year ended December 31, 19X3 and the balance sheet as of December 31, 19X3 are as follows:

Merchandise inventory, 12/31/19X3	$34,500
Store supplies inventory, 12/31/19X3	400
Prepaid insurance, 12/31/19X3	1,500
Depreciation for current year	1,700
Accrued salaries, 12/31/19X3	500

Required:

[a]   Copy the trial balance in the first two columns of a ten-column worksheet.
[b]   Present adjusting entries in appropriate columnar form for the preceding items.
[c]   Complete the worksheet. Be sure to show income or loss for the year.

6   The following is the trial balance of the M Corporation as of December 31, 19X9:

M Corporation, Trial Balances, December 31, 19X9

	Debit	Credit
Cash	$ 500	
Accounts Receivable	6,000	
Merchandise Inventory	32,500	
Office Furniture and Fixtures	8,000	
Allowance for Depr—Furn. & Fixt.		$ 800
Accounts Payable		2,000
Notes Payable Bank		6,000
Capital Stock		10,000
Retained Earnings		2,200
Sales		40,000
Selling Expenses	6,000	
General and Administrative Expense	8,000	
	$61,000	$61,000

Required:

[a]   By using the preceding trial balance and the following additional information, prepare a ten-column worksheet for the year ended December 31, 19X9.

    [1]   Merchandise inventory as of December 31, 19X9 was $12,500.

    [2]   Accrued office wages as of December 31, 19X9 were $500.

    [3]   Office supplies inventory was $600.

    [4]   Office furniture and fixtures were acquired January 1, 19X8, and estimated life at the date of acquisition was ten years.

    [5]   On December 15, J. T. Marks, a customer, sent a $1,000 check in full payment for an order to be shipped in January. The bookkeeper for the M Corporation recorded the cash receipt by debiting cash and crediting sales.

[b]   Prepare a closing entry in general journal form.

7   H Incorporated was organized on December 10, 19X1, and opened its doors for business on January 2, 19X2. The company issued 1,000 shares of stock for $50,000 cash. A retail store building was leased for two years. The lease required the payment of the first and last month's rent on January 2, 19X2. Monthly rent was $800. The trial balance as of December 31, 19X2 is as follows:

H Incorporated, Trial Balance, December 31, 19X2

	Debit	Credit
Cash	$ 27,200	
Accounts receivable	32,000	
Inventory	0	
Prepaid insurance	1,800	
Supplies	0	
Prepaid rent	1,600	
Furniture & fixtures	35,000	
Accumulated depreciation (furniture & fixtures)		$ 0
Accounts payable		15,600
Notes payable		30,000
Common stock		50,000
Retained earnings		0
Sales		276,700
Cost of goods sold	221,500	
Salaries and wages	39,200	
Rent expense	8,800	
Depreciation	0	
Supplies expense	2,200	
Advertising expense	3,000	
	$372,300	$372,300

Additional data:

[1]   Inventory of merchandise on December 31, 19X2 was $29,700.

[2]   A three-year insurance policy for fire, theft, and other hazards was purchased on March 1, 19X2. The premium was $1,800.

[3]   Supplies inventory was $700 on December 31, 19X2.

[4]   Furniture and fixtures had an estimated life of ten years, with no salvage value. H Incorporated elects to use the straight-line method of depreciation.

[5] Inventory and personal property taxes of $1,500 were assessed for 19X2, payable by January 20, 19X3.

[6] Unpaid wages on December 31 were $1,700.

[7] A sum of $30,000 was borrowed from the bank on October 1, 19X2 for four months. Interest rate, 8 percent.

Required:

[a] Prepare a ten-column worksheet for H Incorporated, 19X2.

[b] Prepare an annual statement of income for H Incorporated in good form.

[c] Prepare a balance sheet for H Incorporated as of December 31, 19X2 in good form.

8   The proprietor of X Retail Store has followed the practice of recording sales revenue only when cash is collected from customers and of recording purchases and expenses only when cash is paid. He has prepared the following statement of income for 19X8 on this cash basis:

X Retail Store, Statement of Income for Year Ended December 31, 19X8

Cash received from customers		$46,100
Cash paid for merchandise	$31,800	
Cash paid for expenses	10,600	42,400
Net Income		$ 3,700

You have been asked to examine the store's operating results and have obtained the following additional information:

Merchandise inventories:

12/31/19X7	$6,800
12/31/19X8	4,700

Accounts payable (merchandise):

12/31/19X7	3,600
12/31/19X8	4,100

Accrued liabilities for expenses:

12/31/19X7	1,600
12/31/19X8	1,900

Accounts receivable (all collectible):

12/31/19X7	5,200
12/31/19X8	4,800

Estimated depreciation for 19X8 on store fixtures purchased in 19X6:   2,000

Required:

[a] Compute the sales, cost of goods sold, and expenses on the accrual basis and prepare a statement of income. (It can only show revenues, cost of goods sold, other expenses, and net income.)

[b] Prepare adjusting entries in general journal form to adjust the accounts for the foregoing items. Assume that the records were correctly adjusted on December 31, 19X7. Cash receipts and cash disbursements were recorded in revenue and expense accounts.

9   [a] Using the following trial balance and data for adjustments, prepare a worksheet for year ended December 31, 19X8.

Trial Balance, December 31, 19X8

	Debit	Credit
Cash	$ 6,000	
Accounts Receivable	18,000	
Inventory, 1/1/19X8	19,000	
Land	60,000	
Building	70,000	
Accumulated depreciation (building)		$ 12,000
Accounts payable		80,000
Liability for sales taxes		650
Capital stock		74,690
Retained earnings		9,640
Sales		410,000
Sales returns and allowances	8,400	
Cost of goods sold	307,000	
Salaries and commissions	89,000	
Advertising expense	7,420	
Miscellaneous expense	2,160	
	$586,980	$586,980

Data for adjustments:		
Inventory, 12/31/19X8	$7,000	
Depreciation for year	1,000	
Salaries owed at year-end	400	

[b]   Prepare a closing entry based on the data in part [a].

10   A trial balance for R–S Corporation as of December 31, 19X7 as well as additional information concerning adjustments are as follows:

R–S Corporation, Trial Balance, December 31, 19X7

	Debit	Credit
Cash	$ 7,409	
Accounts receivable	2,605	
Notes receivable	1,200	
Inventory of merchandise	7,916	
Inventory of store supplies	1,152	
Furniture & fixtures	6,200	
Allowance for depreciation on furniture & fixtures		$ 930
Accounts payable		2,000
Notes payable		2,000
Capital stock		10,000
Retained earnings		2,100
Sales		61,686
Cost of goods sold	40,672	
Store salaries	9,560	
Rent expense	2,160	
Insurance expense	270	
Interest expense	72	
Revenue from interest		30
Revenue from rent		470
	$79,216	$79,216

Additional information provided at December 31, 19X7:

[1]   Inventory of store supplies is $282.
[2]   Inventory of merchandise is $9,000.
[3]   Prepaid insurance is $150.
[4]   Accrued interest revenue is $15.
[5]   Deferred rent revenue is $180.
[6]   Accrued store salaries are $260.
[7]   Deferred interest expense is $10.
[8]   Accounts payable for merchandise is $2,500.
[9]   Depreciation on furniture and fixtures is $620.

Required:

[a]   For each revenue and expense account compute the correct revenue or expense using the equations from Chapter 3.
[b]   Prepare adjusting entries to adjust the accounts as of December 31, 19X7.

11   Based on data for S Company listed in the following:

[a]   Use the revenue and expense formulas to compute the correct revenue and expense balances as of December 31, 19X8.
[b]   Prepare adjusting entries as of December 31, 19X8.

S Company, Trial Balance, December 31, 19X8

	Debit	Credit
Cash	$ 16,000	
Accounts receivable	48,000	
Inventory	295,000	
Unexpired insurance	468	
Notes receivable	4,000	
Land	8,000	
Building	50,000	
Accumulated depreciation (building)		$ 6,000
Accounts payable		22,000
Rent collected in advance		2,400
Liability for sales taxes		600
Capital stock		106,928
Retained earnings (deficit)	3,060	
Sales		360,000
Sales returns and allowances	4,000	
Cost of goods sold	0	
Salaries and commissions	61,000	
Advertising expense	3,600	
Miscellaneous expense	4,800	
	$497,928	$497,928

Additional data:

[1]   The physical inventory was taken on December 31, 19X8, and the total value of goods on hand for resale was $27,000.
[2]   The unexpired insurance consists of the January 1, 19X8 balance of premium on a three-year insurance policy purchased on March 1, 19X7.

[3]   The building has an estimated useful life of 40 years and will be completely worthless at the end of 40 years.

[4]   The land will probably be used by the company for 40 years and then be sold for its fair market value.

[5]   A portion of the building is rented to the former owner of S Company for storage of miscellaneous items. Rent was collected for a four-year lease beginning May 1, 19X8.

[6]   Salaries have been earned by employees since the last payday of December 27, 19X8 and through December 31, 19X8 in the amount of $660. These salaries are unpaid as of December 31, 19X8.

[7]   On October 1, 19X8, the company embarked on a sales campaign and entered into a contract with an advertising company to provide services during the campaign which began November 1, 19X8 and ends January 31, 19X9. The total cost of the services under the contract is $2,400, and they will be provided equally in each of the months. The contract price was paid on the date of the contract, and the $2,400 was charged to advertising expense.

[8]   Interest accrued on the notes receivable as of December 31, 19X8 totaled $24.

[9]   A sales commission of 1 percent *will be paid* to salesmen based on the sales for the year. Payment will not be made until May 1, 19X9, but contracts with salesmen call for commission without regard to profits.

12   The following accruals and deferrals were taken from the balance sheets of Z Store:

	12/31/19X1	12/31/19X2
Unexpired insurance	$ 1,400	$ 2,100
Merchandise inventory	16,500	12,800
Accounts payable (merchandise)	2,300	1,700
Interest payable	340	480
Accounts receivable	27,000	22,000
Deferred rental avenue	2,100	1,800

The statement of income shows the following items:

Revenue from sales	$114,000
Rental revenue	2,700
Cost of goods sold	86,000
Insurance expense	3,200
Interest expense	1,500

Required:

[a]   By using the appropriate equation, compute the cash received and cash disbursed for each of the foregoing items.

[b]   Prepare a statement showing the Z Store cash receipts and disbursements for 19X2.

CASE   Carl Ewing purchased a trucking company on January 5, 19X1 for $100,000. The assets of the trucking company consist of five tractors for $50,000 and five light wheel trailers for $50,000. The life of each tractor is estimated to be five years, and the life of each trailer is estimated to be ten years. The trucking business is very competitive, consequently Mr. Ewing found it necessary to reduce his rates several times during the first three years of operation.

Mr. Ewing engaged the services of a local bookkeeping service which used the double-entry system and prepared financial statements annually. All necessary adjustments were made to measure income and prepare the balance sheet using generally accepted accounting principles. In addition the bookkeeping service prepared comparative statements of income and financial position for each of the three years of operation.

Mr. Ewing received the financial statements and comparative financial statements at the end of the third year. After examining these statements, he drops in to your home and asks you to examine his financial statements. Your father has told Mr. Ewing that you are studying accounting in college. Mr. Ewing leaves the comparative statement with you to study. He comments that he does not understand how his cash balance can continue to increase when the statements of income show that he either operates at a loss or just barely breaks even. He is therefore skeptical of the results produced by using the double-entry system. Furthermore, he cannot understand why the books must be adjusted before the financial statements are prepared. He asks why he cannot just examine the general ledger from time to time and not have to pay the bookkeeping service for adjusting the books and preparing financial statements. Comparative financial statements for E Truck Lines are presented in Schedules 1 and 2.

Required:

Write a report that answers the questions raised by Mr. Ewing.

SCHEDULE 1
E Truck Lines, Comparative Statements of Income as of December 31

	19X1	19X2	19X3
Revenues from trucking	$55,000	$60,000	$48,000
Expenses:			
Salaries	$12,000	$15,000	$13,000
Gasoline and oil	17,000	19,000	14,000
Repairs and maintenance	2,000	3,000	1,800
Taxes, licenses, and road levies	8,400	9,200	7,500
Depreciation	15,000	15,000	15,000
	$54,400	$61,200	$51,300
Net income (loss)	$ 600	($1,200)	($3,300)

SCHEDULE 2
E Truck Lines, Comparative Statements of Financial Position as of December 31

	19X1	19X2	19X3
Assets:			
Cash	16,900	31,700	42,600
Accounts receivable	800	1,200	1,800
Truck (net of depreciation)	40,000	30,000	20,000
Trailer (net of depreciation)	45,000	40,000	35,000
Total assets	$102,700	$102,900	$99,400
Equities:			
Accounts payable (gas and oil)	$ 400	$ 1,300	$ 2,000
Accrued wages	300	500	100
Accrued taxes	1,200	1,500	900
Capital	100,800	99,600	96,400
Total equities	$102,700	$102,900	$99,400

four

THE PROBLEMS
OF RECOGNITION,
CLASSIFICATION,
AND MEASUREMENT

Revenue
Recognition

This chapter and the five that follow deal with some of the more complex problems of recognition, classification, and measurement in accounting. In effect the material in Part Four is a more detailed examination of the accounting problems connected with each step in the income cycle—investments, acquisition of services, combination of services, disposition of services, and the collection of cash.

The present chapter is concerned with sales of goods and services to customers. The allocation of the cost of services between expenses and deferred costs depends on the method used to recognize revenue. The cost of services recognized as expense in a given period depends on whether the business recognizes revenue on the cash, sales, or production basis. The problem of revenue measurement must therefore precede the problem of expense measurement under the matching concept.

Types of Disposition of Services

Disposition of services may be classified in a number of ways. Typically, the business disposes of its services voluntarily. Indeed, the entire sales effort of most businesses may be characterized as enthusiastically voluntary. On occasion, the disposition is involuntary. Services may be lost through a casualty—fire, flood, theft, or other uncontrollable event. Property may also be condemned by a governmental unit and later used for public services—another example of involuntary disposition.

Disposition of services can be classified another way: sale or exchange versus abandonment. In a sale or exchange, the business receives cash or other services for the product or service relinquished in the transaction. In an abandonment, the business receives no new resources as a result of the disposition. Needless to say, dispositions that result in the receipt of some new resources, usually cash or a promise to pay cash in the future, are much more numerous than abandonments. This chapter deals only with sales of goods and services to customers. Other types of dispositions are explained in later chapters.

Sale of Products

The most important accounting decision, which must be made relative to the sale of products and services, is the choice of a basis for revenue recognition. This choice determines the revenue reported each year and, therefore, the income reported. As we will see in the following discussion, numerous factors influence the choice of the basis for recognition. In addition, the amount of revenue recognized is often grounds for serious disputes between the managers of a business and the independent accountants auditing the financial statements of the business.

Bases for Revenue Recognition

Under present generally accepted practice, revenue is usually recognized when the following three criteria are met:

1 The business has a transaction with an outside party.
2 Cash or a legal right to collect cash in the future has been received.
3 The business has performed substantially all services required by the transaction (the earning process is complete).

In Chapter 3, we explained that, for most businesses, the criteria for recognition of revenue are met when the product or services are sold to customers.

Remember that the subject being considered is the recognition of revenue for the measurement of income for a given accounting period. This problem is not directly related to the timing of the bookkeeping record of revenue. The two decisions are usually related, but there is no necessary connection. A business that uses the sales basis *may* accrue revenue as each sale is made, and usually does. Nevertheless, the business could elect to record only cash collections during the period and to adjust the accounts to show revenue on the sales basis at the end of each period. The timing of the *recording* of revenue depends on the accounting system in use; but the timing of the recognition of revenue for the measurement of income depends on when the criteria listed above are met.

SALES BASIS. Most manufacturers, wholesalers, and retailers recognize revenue on the sales basis. Once a sales agreement is reached with a customer and the goods are delivered, the criteria are met. There is a transaction with an outside party, a collection of cash or the receipt of a promise of future cash, and the delivery of the product or service. This constitutes an objective indication that the business has earned the revenue.

A basis for recognition very similar to the sales basis is the *shipments basis.* Many manufacturing operations make products according to the design and specifications of a known customer. A large retail chain, for example, may contract with a television manufacturer for a certain number of sets, built according to the retail company's specifications and finally bearing the company's trade name. The manufacture of the sets may extend over several years with payments made periodically, typically as the sets are received and inspected by the retail company. For these contracts, revenue is usually recognized when the manufactured item is shipped to the purchaser, and, hence, the term shipments basis.

Although application of the three criteria to the sales basis is normally quite simple, problems often do arise. Interpretation of each key word in the criteria may be a problem that can be resolved only by the judgment of the accountant guided by his intelligence and experience.

• Transaction: To recognize revenue, most accountants insist on a completed transaction. At what point in the negotiations is the transaction complete? When there is reasonable certainty that the customer will take the goods? When there is an oral agreement? Or when there is a complete written agreement signed by the customer? The question, of course, is not so important where numerous sales are made for small amounts. However, where the product is sold in large quantities with large amounts involved, the question can become very important. The answer, of course, depends on the circumstances.

• Outside Party: To recognize revenue the business must have an agreement with an outside party. Businesses in financial trouble have been known to "create" customers by forming a bogus or even a legal corporation that buys large amounts of obsolete or slow moving products at high prices. A businessman that needs a good income figure to impress his banker may be able to find a close relative who will agree to purchase a big order. Another term for expressing the requirement of an "outside party" is to say that the transaction must be at "arm's length." This problem becomes particularly critical where a group of corporations are owned by the same group of individuals. For example, a wealthy family group may control several corporations, each treated as a separate entity for accounting purposes. Transactions between corporations with common ownerships are particularly suspect. In a similar status are transactions between a corporation and its shareholders. When the parties are not dealing at "arm's length," operating results and financial position may be manipulated to give an artificial result.

• Liquid Asset: The second criterion states that the cash or a future right to cash must be received in the transaction. As stated, this criterion is perhaps more stringent than the test applied by many accountants. In some cases, revenue is recognized when some very "liquid" asset other than a future promise of cash is received. For example, a customer could pay for merchandise with the stocks or bonds of some corporation. If these corporate securities are traded regularly and the accountant can determine an objective value for them, the revenue is usually recognized. On the other hand, if the valuation of the securities cannot be determined objectively, the revenue recognized is usually limited to the cost of the merchandise. Additional revenue or gain would then be recognized when the securities are sold, provided the sales price is greater than the cost of the merchandise. If the sales price is less, a loss would result. As explained in Chapter 14, revenue (or gain) is frequently recognized when equipment is traded-in for new equipment. Recognition is based on the fair market value of new equipment, certainly not a liquid asset.

• Substantially All Services: Only earned revenue can be recognized. Usually, on the sales basis, delivery to the customer is the point at which the business has performed substantially all services required by the transaction. Where delivery is made by a common carrier, such as a railroad, truckline, or airline, the freight terms establish the time of delivery. If the terms are f.o.b. shipping point, then the buyer pays the freight costs and the merchandise belongs to the buyer during transit. Thus the seller makes the delivery when the merchandise is placed in the hands of the common carrier. If the terms are f.o.b. destination, the freight cost is born by the seller and the goods belong to him during transit. Delivery and recognition of revenue occurs only when the merchandise reaches the buyer.

Problems that are difficult to handle arise when a business on the sales basis performs substantial services following the sale. Warranties and service contracts are examples of agreements that result in "after-costs," that is, costs incurred after the sale. These problems will be discussed in a later section.

CASH AND INSTALLMENT BASIS. The cash basis should be used for the recognition of revenue if there is any doubt about the collectibility of an account. Sales on installment contracts permit the customer to pay for the product over an extended period of time. Most automobiles, appliances, and homes are sold on the installment plan.

Installment sales were not in widespread use until the late 1930s or early 1940s. Since World War II the number of installment sales has become larger each year. At the time installment sales were introduced, most accountants and businessmen believed it was unwise to recognize revenue from this type of sale until the cash was collected. However, the record of the past 30 years shows that losses from installment sales are relatively low; the risk of collection on an installment sale is not much greater than the risk assumed on any credit sale.

The early fear that many people would not pay their contracts made it seem prudent to defer recognition of revenue from installment sales until cash was received. As a result, the federal income tax laws have long permitted the use of the installment basis for the computation of taxable income. The installment method as provided by the Internal Revenue Code allows taxpayers to defer payment of income taxes until cash has been collected from the sale. The tax advantage led many businesses to the use of the installment basis for financial reporting as well as for taxation even in cases where there was little doubt about the collectibility of the receivable. Of course, the sales basis could be used for financial reporting and the installment basis for taxation, but this would mean two accountings with increased costs. The Accounting Principles Board showed its cognizance of this undesirable situation and now requires the sales basis for recognition of revenue on installment sales in the absence of exceptional circumstances with regard to collectibility.*

Most installment sales are sales of goods rather than services. If there is genuine doubt about collectibility and recognition of revenue is to be deferred until cash is collected, the cost of the product sold must also be deferred until cash is collected. The simple method for deferring both revenue and cost is to defer the gross profit, the difference between the sales price and cost of the product.

For example, assume the sale of merchandise for $540 with no downpayment and terms of $15 per month for 36 months. (Financial charges are ignored in this example.) The merchandise cost $360. The gross profit of $180 ($540 − $360) is $33\frac{1}{3}$ percent of the selling price ($180/$540). The method calls for deferral of gross profit recognition until collection occurs. The entries to record the sale are as follows, assuming the record is made at the date of sale:

	Debit	Credit
(Date of sale)		
Installment accounts receivable	$540	
Installment sales		$540

	Debit	Credit
(Date of sale)		
Cost of installment sales	$360	
Merchandise inventory		$360

Installment sales and cost of installment sales are netted against each other and the difference is credited to deferred gross profit on installment sales. The entry is as follows:

	Debit	Credit
Installment sales	$540	
Cost of installment sales		$360
Deferred gross profit on installment sales		180

At the end of the accounting period the unpaid balance is determined, and the balance of the deferred gross profit account is adjusted to the proper balance by using the ratio of profit to selling price: $33\frac{1}{3}$ percent of the unpaid balance in the foregoing example. Assuming the sale was made in January, 19X1, and payments were received for the remaining 11 months, the balance in the installment receivable account would be $375. The deferred gross profit should be $125 (33 1/3 percent of $375). The entry to make the adjustment would be

	Debit	Credit
Deferred gross profit on installment sales, 19X1	$55	
Realized gross profits, 19X1		$55
(To transfer realized profit to revenue account ($180 − $125 = $55)		

---

*American Institute of Certified Public Accountants, *Opinion of the Accounting Principles Board No. 10* (December 1966), p. 149.

Realized gross profit on installment sales is reported on the statement of income as an addition to gross profit from ordinary sales. Installment accounts receivables are shown as current assets on the balance sheet. Deferred gross profit on installment sales is reported on the balance sheet in a variety of ways, although the treatment of the balance as a liability seems to be the most widely accepted practice.

To illustrate the impact that the use of the installment basis can have on reported gross profit, assume that C Company has sales and costs of goods as shown on Fig. 10-1. Using the sales basis, the gross profit for C Company is $200,000, $400,000, and $500,000 for 19X1, 19X2, and 19X3, respectively. Under the installment sales basis, the realized gross profit is $60,000, $220,000, and $390,000 for 19X1, 19X2, and 19X3, respectively. As long as the company's sales increase, the realized gross profit on the installment basis would be less than it would be on the sales basis. Assuming a constant sales pattern and the passage of three years from the time the installment basis is initially used, the realized gross profit would level out and be approximately equal to gross profit on the sales basis. If sales later declined, the installment basis would report a larger profit.

Figure 10-1: Installment Sales Basis and Sales Basis Compared

Sales Basis	19X1	19X2	19X3
Sales	1,000,000	2,000,000	2,500,000
Cost of goods sold	800,000	1,600,000	2,000,000
Gross profit	$ 200,000	$ 400,000	$ 500,000
Collections:			
19X1 sales	$ 300,000	$ 400,000	$ 400,000
19X2 sales		600,000	800,000
19X3 sales			750,000
Totals	$ 300,000	$1,000,000	$1,950,000
Installment Sales Basis			
Realized gross profit:			
19X1	$60,000	$ 80,000	$ 80,000
19X2		120,000	160,000
19X3			150,000
Totals	$60,000	$200,000	$390,000

Assumptions:
1 Gross profit ratio is a constant 20% for the three-year period.
2 Collection pattern is 30% the first year, 40% in each of the last two years.

PRODUCTION BASIS. The production basis is used under two conditions. Industries whose products have a definite market with fixed or predictable prices may recognize revenue as production progresses and prior to an actual sales transaction. A perfect example is gold mining. By law, all gold mined in the

United States must be sold to the U.S. government at a set price. Businesses producing other precious metals and some farm commodities may also qualify for revenue recognition as the product is completed.

A more popular use of the production basis is in industries with long-term contracts. The construction of ships, highways, dams, and buildings are ventures that may require several years from inception to completion. In these situations, use of the sales basis can often seriously distort the net income reported. For example, assume that a small construction company has one contract for $5,000,000 for a building. The construction requires three years and the total cost incurred on the building is $4,500,000. If the company waits until the project is complete to recognize revenue (and income), there is no income in the first two years and then income of $500,000 in the third year. Thus use of the sales basis (completed transaction) can distort income in industries with long-term contracts that cannot use the shipments basis because the product is indivisible.

The construction company in the preceding example could present better statements of income by using the percentage-of-completion method—just another term for the production basis. According to this method the percentage of the total contract performed or produced during the year is recognized. The revenue recognized is the percentage of the contract completed, and this amount is matched against the costs incurred to compute income. The percentage of the contract price earned in a single year is usually computed on the basis of cost incurred using the following fraction:

$$\frac{\text{Cost incurred during year}}{\text{Total estimated cost for project}} = \text{Percentage completed}$$

The total estimated cost is usually determined by engineers or architects. Sometimes engineering estimates are used to estimate the percentage of the project completed on some basis other than the percentage of total cost incurred.

For instance, suppose a contractor undertakes the construction of a ship for which he is to receive $8,000,000, and he agrees to complete the construction within three years. Engineers estimate that 25 percent of the work is completed during the first year, and the contractor incurs costs totaling $1,400,000. Using the percentage of completion method, the following entries would be recorded:

	Debit	Credit
Construction in progress	$1,400,000	
Cash		$1,400,000
Construction contracts receivable	2,000,000	
Construction in progress		1,400,000
Gross profit on contracts		600,000

By the end of the second year the ship is 80 percent complete, and additional costs of $3,400,000 are incurred during the year. Revenue recognized in the second year is 55 percent of the total, or $4,400,000. The 55 percent is the

80 percent completed less the 25 percent recognized in the first year. Entries recorded for the second year are as follows:

	Debit	Credit
Construction in progress	$3,400,000	
Cash		$3,400,000
Construction contracts receivable	4,400,000	
Construction in progress		3,400,000
Gross profit on contracts		1,000,000

In the third year, construction is completed, and additional costs of $1,200,000 are incurred. Entries for the third year are as follows:

	Debit	Credit
Construction in progress	$1,200,000	
Cash		$1,200,000
Construction contracts receivable	1,600,000	
Construction in progress		1,200,000
Gross profit on contracts		400,000

The revenue recognized of $1,600,000 is the remaining 20 percent not earned in the first two years.

On long-term contracts, the buyer usually makes progress payments as the work is being done. When cash is received it is credited to the construction contract receivable account.

Other Problems of Revenue Recognition and Measurement

The major accounting problem associated with operating revenue is the timing of recognition. Classification of revenue does not present a difficult problem. At the present time there are only two major classes of revenue: operating revenue and revenue from all other sources.* The accountant does, however, face several difficult problems of recognition and measurement of revenue connected with events that occur after the sale. Most businesses use the sales basis and a lot can happen after a sale is made. These postsale events result either in a reduction of revenue or in the incurrence of additional costs after the sale.

BAD DEBTS. When revenue is recognized prior to the collection of cash on the sales basis or production basis, the possibility always exists that some customers will not meet their obligations to pay in the future. Some of the receivables will in all likelihood turn into bad debts. For any period, the revenue reported should be the cash already received from sales of that period plus the expected

---

*Supplementary schedules that support the statement of income are sometimes used to break down revenue in other ways such as by product line, by type of customers, and by geographic areas. Under some circumstances such breakdowns are very helpful to the statement user.

future cash receipts. To measure revenue under this rule, most businesses must take into account the probability that a few customers will not pay.

Experience shows that only a small percentage of credit sales prove to be uncollectible. Although the amount is usually small, an accurate valuation of revenue and accounts receivable requires that the total revenue and accounts receivable be decreased by the amount of the expected loss. The accountant or the credit manager can predict, within reasonable limits, the amount of the expected loss. What they cannot predict are the specific accounts that will become uncollectible. For this reason a contra or valuation account is used. A typical year-end journal entry to record the expected loss is

	Debit	Credit
Losses from bad debts	$xx	
Allowance for uncollectible accounts		$xx

The loss from bad debts is related to assets coming into the business, not to services (assets) consumed, thus it is actually a contra revenue account and the statement of income should show gross revenues less losses from bad debts as follows:

Revenues	$xxx
Less: Loss from bad debts	xx
Net revenue	$xxx

In most cases, however, accountants treat losses from bad debts as an expense on the statement of income. Treatment of bad debts as an expense is especially common when a business sells on account to numerous customers, usually final consumers. The usual justification for this approach is that credit policy is an administrative function and any bad debts should, therefore, be included with administrative expenses. In a utilitarian process such as accounting, practical considerations sometimes take precedence over logical niceties.

Accounts receivable are sometimes shown on the balance sheet as follows:

Accounts receivable	$xxx	
Less: Allowance for uncollectible accounts	xx	$xxx

Frequently, disclosure on published balance sheets will be as follows:

Accounts receivable (net allowance for uncollectible accounts)	xxx

The expected loss from bad debts is estimated by either the past experience of the company or by the experience of the industry at large, whichever is the better predictor. Two commonly used methods are percentage of sales and percentage of accounts receivable.

- Percentage of Charge Sales: To estimate uncollectibles based on the percentage of credit sales, a firm determines the percentage of expected losses based on past experience. Assume that historical records of a company disclose the following information:

Total credit sales, 19X1–19X5	$500,000
Actual losses from uncollectibles	$2,500
Expected percentage = $2,500/$500,000 =	0.5%

If sales for 19X6 were $120,000, the following adjusting entry would be made:

	Debit	Credit
Losses from bad debts	$600	
Allowance for uncollectibles		$600

(To record expected losses, estimated to be .5% of sales)

The adjusting entry would be required without regard to the timing of the record of receivables. If the revenue is accrued as each sale is made, the accrued revenue (accounts receivable) is already recorded at year-end and the adjustment is to the revenue and the contra asset account. If the revenue accrual is made at year-end, the allowance account is still needed because the precise accounts that will prove to be uncollectible cannot be determined.

In Chapter 9, all adjusting entries were classified into four categories: revenue accruals, accrued expenses, deferred revenues, and deferred costs. If the adjustment for bad debts is thought of as an adjustment of revenue, the above entry is logically a correction of a previous accrued revenue adjustment. However, if bad debt expense is considered an administrative expense, the adjustment for bad debts is akin to an accrued expense except that the credit account, allowance for uncollectibles, is not shown as a liability on the balance sheet; instead it is subtracted from the accounts receivable.

- Percentage of Accounts Receivable: The estimation of bad debts can also be based on the amount of accounts receivable at the end of the year. The percentage would be determined as follows:

$$\frac{\text{Average actual losses for several years}}{\text{Average amount of receivables}} = \text{Loss percentage}$$

The estimation of losses based on the balance of receivables is usually combined with an *aging* of receivable balances.

Estimation of uncollectible accounts based on an aging of the accounts recognizes that the likelihood of collecting an account decreases as the account gets older. If a firm sells on 30-day terms, the probability that accounts which are over six months old will prove to be uncollectible is relatively high. Thus, a different percentage is used to estimate the bad debts in each age group. The percentage used for each age group is based on past experience. To use this method, all unpaid accounts must be aged. A columnar worksheet, such as that shown in Fig. 10-2, can be used to age accounts. The percentages used might range from $\frac{1}{4}$ of 1 percent for accounts less than 30 days old to 75 percent for accounts over 180 days old.

Figure 10-2: Schedule for Aging Accounts Receivable

Account name	Under 30 days	30–60 days	60–90 days	Over 180 days
J. Andrews			$6,000	$1,500
R. Arnson	$4,000			
(Numerous entries omitted to conserve space.)				
T. Zembrowski	3,000	200		
Totals	$250,000	$120,000	$20,000	$5,000
Estimated loss (percent)	1/4%	2%	10%	75%

An important mechanical difference between the estimate based on aging and that based on a percentage of credit sales is that the aging method yields an estimate of the uncollectible balance, whereas the percentage of credit sales method yields an estimate of the change required in the uncollectible balance. In other words, if an aging estimate shows that the balance in the allowance for doubtful accounts should be $5,000 and the account already shows a credit balance of $1,000, then the adjustment should show a debit to bad debts and a credit to the allowance for uncollectible accounts for $4,000. This differs from the estimate based on the percentage of credit sales which is an estimate of the change required and permits preparation of the adjusting entry without reference to the current balance in the allowance for uncollectible accounts. The fact that the aging method estimates the balance required in the allowance account precludes the possibility of building up an unrealistically high balance in the allowance account as sometimes occurs when the estimate is based on a percentage of credit sales.

• Write-offs and Recoveries: As specific accounts are deemed uncollectible, they are written off against the allowance for uncollectible accounts. The entry takes the following form:

	Debit	Credit
Allowance for uncollectible accounts	$xx	
Accounts receivable		$xx

Sometimes an account written off is subsequently collected. This may occur when a bankrupt, although legally excused from his debts, decides to pay as a matter of conscience or in order to reestablish his reputation. Record-keeping for such a collection is handled with two entries: one to restore the account receivable previously written off and another to record the collection. The purpose of the first entry is to reverse the original write-off and thus provide a record of the collection in the customer's individual subsidiary account. This information would be useful if the customer asks for credit in the future.

• Direct Write-offs: Some businesses follow the practice of recognizing bad debt expense only when an account is deemed uncollectible. No allowance account is used; instead bad accounts are charged to expense at the time they are written off. This practice is not recommended because it does not recognize the lost revenue or expense in the year of the sale but defers the loss to some later year. In some businesses, however, the distortion of income from direct write-offs is not material enough to justify the cost of estimating bad debts and the use of the allowance method.

PRODUCT WARRANTIES. Businesses frequently make sales that require future services. One example is the familiar product warranty or service contract whereby the seller obligates himself to replace parts and/or furnish services for some specified period of time. Recognition and valuation of these future obligations must occur at the time of the sale to achieve a proper matching of revenue and expense.

A controversy exists concerning whether the seller's future obligations should be construed as (1) a basis for accruing future expenditures as expenses or (2) a basis for deferring the recognition of revenue for some part of the selling price. These alternatives may be demonstrated in terms of the revenue and expense formulas as follows:

$$\text{Expense} = CD + \Delta AE - \Delta DE \tag{1}$$
$$\text{Revenue} = CR + \Delta AR - \Delta DR \tag{2}$$

The third criterion for revenue recognition clearly supports the second equation. According to this criterion, revenue cannot be recognized until substantially all services are performed.

Assume that a business sells a machine for $1,000, and the sales agreement provides that the seller will provide free of charge all ordinary repairs for a three-year period. Has the business *earned* the entire $1,000? If we have the additional fact that the same machine can be purchased for $800 without the service contract, then a negative answer is clearly indicated—the $200 charge for the service contract will be earned over the next three years.

Despite the logical support for the deferral of revenue in the foregoing situation, accountants usually handle the problem by recognizing the entire sales price as revenue and then accruing expense for the expected after-costs, that is, the estimated expenses of performing the services under the three-year service contract. If careful estimates are made of future costs, both procedures produce realistic income figures.

An example of recognition and valuation of the accrual of after-costs is as follows. An appliance firm goes into business on January 1, 19X4, and sells $500,000 worth of appliances during the year. Conditions of the sales obligate the firm to warrant major parts for ten years and to supply free servicing for one year. The experience of others in the industry shows that costs of such warranties run about 5 percent of sales price. In 19X5, the firm spends $15,000 for parts and labor services to fulfill warranty obligations. The adjusting entry to accrue estimated after-costs at the end of 19X4 is

December 31, 19X4

	Debit	Credit
Product warranty expense	$25,000	
Estimated accrued expense for product warranties		$25,000

When service expenses are paid during 19X5, they are debited to the estimated warranty expense account:

Various Dates in 19X5
(Summary Entry)

	Debit	Credit
Estimated accrued expense for product warranties	$15,000	
Cash (and other assets)		$15,000

Product warranty expense appears as an operating expense on the statement of income, and estimated accrued expense for product warranties appears as a liability, usually a current liability, on the balance sheet.

SALES RETURNS AND ALLOWANCES. Customers occasionally become dissatisfied with the purchases they have made. Many businesses permit the customer to return a purchased article, even where there is a completed sale and the customer has no legal right to do so. In other cases, the purchase price is reduced to make "allowance" for the actual or claimed defect in the product. Many businesses, particularly retailers, have liberal return and allowance policies based on their belief that the improvement in their customer image is worth the added cost.

Returns and allowances directly reduce the revenue which should be recognized. If the revenue is recorded at the time of the sale, the usual situation, the return or allowance may be recorded by a debit to revenue and a credit to cash or accounts receivable. To maintain a record of the volume of returns and allowances, however, a separate account (a contra revenue account) may be used. If so, the entry to record a return would be

	Debit	Credit
Sales returns and allowances	$xx	
Accounts receivables		$xx

The debit balance of the returns and allowances account is then subtracted from sales revenue on the statement of income to arrive at net sales revenue. Many companies do not report the amount of returns and allowances but merely report the net sales revenue on the statement of income.

On rare occasions, a company may experience wide fluctuations in the sales returns and allowances from year to year. If the amounts are material, the company may use an allowance or valuation account comparable to the procedures used for bad debts to assign the proper valuation to the net revenue for the period.

CASH DISCOUNTS. Business firms frequently offer discounts to encourage customers to pay promptly. Cash has a time value in that a firm is either paying interest to use someone else's cash or foregoing the earnings it could generate with cash. For this reason, it is important for a business to collect from its customers promptly and to handle the collection so as to have the cash available for use as quickly as possible.

The terms of a cash discount are usually stated on the sales invoice in shorthand form, such as 2/10, n/30. The shorthand expression means that a 2 percent reduction in price is allowed if payment is received within ten days of the invoice date; if payment is not made within ten days, the full invoice price is due within 30 days. A customer purchasing $500 worth of merchandise on terms 2/10, n/30 could settle his debt for $490 if he pays within ten days of the invoice date:

Invoice price	$500.00
Cash discount rate	X 0.02%
Cash discount	$ 10.00
Invoice price	$500.00
Less: Cash discount	10.00
Settlement price	$490.00

Accountants record purchases and sales at exchange price net of cash discounts. Passing or missing discounts results in financial earnings for the seller and a financial cost for the buyer, and does not alter the cost of services acquired by the buyer or the sales revenue of the seller. For example, assume that the above sale of the $500 item is recorded at the point of sale. Only $490, revenue net of the expected discount, is recognized:

	Debit	Credit
Accounts receivable	$490	
Sales revenue		$490

If the buyer pays within the discount period, cash is debited and accounts receivable credited for $490. If the buyer passes the discount and eventually pays $500, the $10 discount is similar to interest revenue and is recorded in some account with an appropriate title such as "financial earnings":

	Debit	Credit
Cash	$500	
Accounts receivable		$490
Financial earnings		10

Some accountants prefer to recognize the gross sales price. If the customer pays within the discount period the difference between the receivable balance of $500 and the cash received ($490) is debited to an account entitled "sales discounts." Where this practice is followed, the debit balance of sales discounts is subtracted from revenue, and only net sales revenue is typically reported on the statement of income.

As with sales returns and allowances, cash discounts may be accounted for by using the allowance procedure comparable to that used for bad debts. The amounts involved, however, are usually immaterial.

Care must be exercised in interpreting the percentage figure in the terms of a cash discount. When terms of 2/10, n/30 are quoted, the buyer must pay 2 percent for the privilege of obtaining credit for 20 days (30 – 10). There are 18 periods of 20 days in a year so loss of a cash discount where terms are 2/10, n/30 is equivalent to an annual interest rate of 36 percent (360/20 X 2 percent).

QUESTIONS

1   Unscrupulous businessmen have devised many schemes to increase the profits reported. Study the three criteria for revenue recognition and devise some schemes that would artificially increase the revenue recognized. You may assume that your auditor is a trusting soul.

2   Distinguish between the shipments basis and the production basis for revenue recognition.

3   Three bases are used commonly to recognize revenue. Describe each basis and the business conditions that make the use of each method appropriate.

4   Imagine that you are president of a corporation that is primarily engaged in the manufacture of military equipment for the Defense Department under long-term contracts. In past years, revenue has been recognized on the shipments basis. For the current year, because of cuts in defense spending, anticipated income is low. Suggest a change in methods which might increase income. What effect would the suggested change have on your auditor's report?

5   Why might a company use the sales basis for their financial reports and elect the installment basis for the measurement of income for tax purposes?

6   What basis would a contractor engaged in long-term contracts use for income tax purposes?

7   Percentage of completion of long-term contracts may be based on cost incurred or engineering estimates. For each method, describe circumstances under which it would be appropriate.

8   The allowance method for bad debts is preferable to the direct write-off method in most businesses. Is this statement true? Why?

9   For product warranties and other arrangements that result in after-costs, accountants usually recognize the entire sales price as revenue and accrue the estimated after-cost expenses. Describe an alternative method of handling after-costs. Which is the better method?

10   When the estimate of bad debt expense is based on charge sales, the balance of the allowance account sometimes becomes unreasonably large. This problem is avoided when the expense is based on the balance of accounts receivable. Why?

11   When a customer fails to take a cash discount, the amount of the discount is treated as interest or financial income, and not product revenue. Why?

PROBLEMS

1   The J Hosiery Company is a wholesale house which records revenue as the goods are shipped f.o.b. shipping point. Payment terms are 2/10, n/30. Prepare journal entries for the following events:

[a] Shipped $1,000 order to the T Dress Shop on July 10, 19X3.

[b] Received cash for the invoice in transaction [a] on July 19, 19X3.

[c] Assume cash is received for the above invoice on August 15, 19X3.

2 Imagine that you are an independent accountant auditing the financial statements of Jack Watson, the proprietor of a furniture store. As auditor, you know that the financial statements will be used by Watson in an effort to obtain a sizeable loan from a local bank. Watson uses the sales basis for revenue recognition. How much revenue would you agree to recognize for the year 19X1 in each of the following cases:

[a] On December 28, Watson sold and delivered $3,000 of furniture to his brother. The brother owns a local tavern. No cash was received before December 31, 19X1.

[b] On December 15, Watson sold $2,000 of furniture to Mrs. Wysnitski, with the understanding that the merchandise could be returned if it did not fit in with her new decor. On February 1, the date of the audit, no cash had been collected.

[c] On December 1, Watson shipped $10,000 of furniture to C Furniture Store in a nearby city. The agreement provided that Watson would receive 90 percent of the sales price when and if sold. Cash receipts prior to December 31 were $720.

[d] On December 15, Watson traded furniture with a sales price of $5,000 for a new delivery van. The furniture cost Watson $2,800. The list price of the van was $4,300. The cost price to the auto dealer was $3,600.

[e] On December 31, Watson sold $15,000 of furniture to another brother and received a check in payment. The brother has the furniture stored in Watson's warehouse but avows that he intends to use it to furnish his new home just as soon as he completes a big deal which he is working on. He lives in a two-room walk-up flat now.

3 The G Furniture Mart sells fine furniture on the installment basis. The following data was prepared for 19X1, the first year of operations:

Installment sales	$800,000
Cost of merchandise sold	560,000
Collections on installment contracts for 19X1	600,000

The G Furniture Mart records for 19X2 show the following:

Installment sales	$840,000
Cost of merchandise sold	560,000
Collections on installment sales:	
19X1	150,000
19X2	500,000

Required:

[a] Prepare journal entries to record the revenue, cost of merchandise sold, deferred gross profits, and realized gross profit for 19X1.

[b] Prepare journal entries to record the revenue, cost of merchandise sold, deferred gross profit, and realized gross profit for 19X2.

4 The XYZ Company records all charge sales at *gross* invoice prices and regularly offers a discount of 3 percent for all payments made within ten days of the invoice date. At January 1, 19X8, certain account balances stand as follows:

	Debit	Credit
Accounts receivable (control)	$10,000	
Accounts receivable (allowance for outstanding discounts)		$ 200
Accounts receivable (allowance for sales returns)		200
Accounts receivable (allowance for bad debts)		1,000

During 19X8 the following transactions, among others, occurred:

[a]   In January the $10,000 balance of accounts receivable is cleared through the following events: (i) collections, $8,400, gross less discounts of $200; (ii) uncollectible accounts written off, $1,000; (iii) sales returns, $600.

[b]   Sales on account during 19X8 total $100,000 at gross invoice prices, terms 3/10, n/30, and are recorded at gross.

[c]   Cash *collected* from customers within the discount period totals $87,300.

[d]   Cash collected after lapse of discount period totals $2,000.

Required:

Present journal entries to record the foregoing data.

5   The J Construction Company uses the percentage-of-completion method for recognizing revenue and the related costs. The following is information related to Highway Construction Contract #814 for 19X1, 19X2, and 19X3:

	19X1	19X2	19X3
Construction costs incurred	$800,000	$1,600,000	$ 600,000
Payments received	700,000	1,800,000	1,000,000
Percent completed (certified by state engineers)	30%	80%	100%

[a]   Compute the gross profit from this contract for each of the years involved and prepare appropriate journal entries.

[b]   What income would be reported in each year if J Construction Company used the completed contract method?

[c]   Which system would provide better information to interested parties? Explain your answer.

6   The G Paper Company extends 30-day credit to selected customers. An examination of their accounts for the past five years reveals the following information:

	Credit sales	Actual losses from uncollectible accounts
19X1	$120,000	$1,000
19X2	160,000	1,800
19X3	180,000	2,200
19X4	190,000	2,000
19X5	200,000	1,500

The following is a summary of accounts receivable of G Paper Company for each of the five years with the accounts "aged":

Summary of Aging Schedule, 19X1–19X5

	Balance	Under 30 days	30–60 days	Over 60 days
19X1	$ 25,000	$ 20,000	$ 3,000	$ 2,000
19X2	40,000	32,000	5,000	3,000
19X3	45,000	33,000	8,000	4,000
19X4	50,000	37,000	9,000	4,000
19X5	48,000	36,000	9,000	3,000
	$208,000	$158,000	$34,000	$16,000

Based on actual losses, the probability of loss for each age group is as follows:

Under 30 days	0.25%
30–60 days	3.0%
Over 60 days	50.0%

In the past, the company has used the direct write-off method for bad debts. H. Larson, the owner of G Paper Company, asks you to study this problem and recommend the *best* way to account for bad debts. If a change is needed, he wants to make the change at the end of 19X5.

Required:

Prepare a report for Larson which explains the two alternative ways of treating bad debts. Include in your report, the entries that you would make under the two alternatives at the end of 19X5. Explain the effect of the change in methods on the net income for 19X5.

7 Accounts receivable for M Corporation were reported on the balance sheet at the end of 19X3 as follows:

Accounts receivable		$93,200
Less: Allowance for uncollectibles	$3,850	
Allowance for sales discounts	950	4,800
		$88,400

The firm sells goods on terms of 2/10 E.O.M., n/30; that is, discounts will be allowed if payment is received within ten days of the end of the month (E.O.M.). The M Corporation prepares an aging schedule monthly. At the end of the year the following percentages are applied in arriving at an estimate for uncollectible accounts:

	Estimated uncollectibles
Accounts under 30 days	1/4%
Accounts over 30 days–under 60 days	1%
Accounts over 60 days–under 90 days	5%
Accounts over 90 days–under 180 days	10%
Accounts over 180 days	50%

The following information is pertinent for 19X4:

Sales on accounts	$850,000
Cash collected on account	829,500
Cash discounts allowed	14,500
Sales returns and allowances	3,000
Bad debts written off	4,000
Bad debts previously written off but recovered	400

The aging schedule is summarized as follows:

Accounts under 30 days	$76,400
Accounts over 30 days–under 60 days	8,000
Accounts over 60 days–under 90 days	3,600
Accounts over 90 days–under 180 days	3,000
Accounts over 180 days	1,200

At the end of the year the corporation anticipates sales discounts. Past records indicate that 85 percent of the customers take discounts.

Required:

[a]   Prepare journal entries to record the above information. The M Corporation records credit sales when made.

[b]   Prepare entries to adjust the accounts for uncollectibles and anticipated sales discounts.

[c]   Show how the balances for accounts receivable and related accounts should be disclosed on the balance sheet.

8   The C Company produces and sells small household appliances. The company grants a one-year warranty on all of its products. Warranty expenses for the past five years have averaged 5 percent of sales.

[a]   Discuss the two methods of treating warranties and their relationship to revenue recognition.

[b]   Which method would you recommend? Explain why.

[c]   C Company sales for 19X6 were $925,000. Prepare a journal entry to record the warranty expense accrual for 19X6.

[d]   The warranty costs incurred in 19X7 were $41,000. Prepare the journal entry to record these expenditures.

9   The N Corporation produces and sells a high quality tape recorder for home use. Each recorder carries a one-year warranty. In 19X1, 100,000 units were sold at an average price of $60. It is estimated that 6 percent of the recorders sold will be returned for adjustment or repair. The average cost of adjusting or repairing a set is $8; the average estimated retail sales price for adjusting or repairing a set is $10.

The comptroller has suggested that revenue for the portion of the sales price applicable to the warranty be deferred to the following year. The treasurer of the company wants to accrue the estimated future costs of the warranty in the year of the sale. The president of the company believes that the annual cost of fulfilling the warranty agreement would not materially affect the income of any year. He asks you to prepare a report showing the effect on income under the deferred revenue method, accrued expense method, and recording the warranty cost as an expense in the year incurred. You are to include in your report pro forma journal entries showing how accruals, deferrals, and payments would be recorded under each method. The report is to cover the next three years. Estimated sales for the next three years are

19X2	120,000 units
19X3	122,000 units
19X4	130,000 units

Sales prices and costs are expected to be constant during the next three years.

CASE   Bob Grisly is an all-pro defensive lineman for the local professional football team and a regional folk hero. In early 19X0, he was introduced to Kip Saunders, the owner of a successful local restaurant noted for its excellent barbecued beef. The two men got on well together and decided that they might turn a good profit by combining Kip's secret for good barbecue with Bob's notoriety in the region. The plan they finally developed was a franchise operation under the name "G Barbecue Palaces." Details of the arrangement were as follows:

Bob and Kip would form a new corporation, G Barbecue Palaces, Inc. Each man would contribute $50,000 and each would receive 100,000 shares of the corporation's common stock. Additional funds required would be obtained from bank loans until the business was established and profitable. Then, the two men planned to sell most, if not all, of their common stock to the public and walk away with a sizeable profit with only a few years of effort. (Incidentally, income from the sale of their stock would be taxed by the federal government at much lower rates than their income from playing football and operating a restaurant.)

The corporation would not operate the Barbecue Palaces directly. Instead, franchises would be sold to operators. The initial sales price of each franchise would be $75,000. For this amount the franchisee (operator) would get standardized signs and a barbecue oven patented by Kip. The signs and ovens would be the property of the operator. The franchisee would be required to provide a building, suitable fixtures (except for the patented oven), and all operating capital. The corporation as franchisor would receive 10% of the gross sales from each franchisee. However, the corporation would conduct at its own expense a regional advertising campaign, using television and radio primarily, to tout the quality of the barbecue. The corporation also retained rights to inspect the location and ingredients used by each franchisee to assure cleanliness, good appearance, and quality of the food.

Before actually committing their funds, Bob and Kip retained (and paid out of their own funds) a marketing consultant to give them some idea of the number of outlets they could expect to open. This consultant estimated that from 20 to 30 outlets could be sold in the immediate metropolitan area and that an additional 30 to 40 might eventually be spread over the entire region where Bob's name was well known. Depending on the location of each outlet, annual sales for each could vary between $125,000 and $175,000.

Based on these estimates G Barbecue Palaces, Inc. was formed in May, 19X0. The initial transactions of Bob and Kip are summarized as follows:

[1]   They contracted with a local sign company to design an eyecatching sign for the chain.
[2]   They placed ads in local business publications to attract prospective buyers for the franchises. They also called on banks and others who might know of interested parties.
[3]   They contracted with a local manufacturer to build the barbecue ovens as needed.
[4]   They retained a local advertising agency to begin work on the format for the advertising campaign.

The immediate response was very enthusiastic and they had numerous prospects to purchase the franchises. But there was one problem: Almost without exception the prospects did not have enough capital to pay the $75,000 in cash and also obtain building, fixtures, and operating capital. As a result, Bob and Kip decided to settle for a down payment of $15,000 with the remaining $60,000 due in five annual installments of $12,000 plus interest at 7 percent.

Of course, title to the ovens and signs would not pass to the franchisees until all installments were paid.

They also encountered difficulty with the manufacturer who contracted to build the ovens. He contended that he could provide the ovens at $12,000 each only if they agreed to purchase 40 units over the next three years. For 30 units the price would be $18,000 each, and for only 20 units the price would be $25,000 each. The sign company insisted on a similar arrangement. The signs needed for each outlet would cost $10,000 if 40 outlets were guaranteed; $15,000 each for a guarantee of 30 units; and $20,000 for each outlet with a guarantee of 20 units. Finally the advertising agency insisted on a three-year contract with declining payments of $350,000 for the first year, $125,000 for the second year, and $125,000 for the third year. The agency argued that the bulk of their costs would come in the first year when the campaign was very heavy, to assure a good beginning.

Despite these problems, Bob and Kip decided to go ahead. In the summer and fall of 19X0 they entered into contracts for 12 franchises to become effective in January 19X1. At this time, the down payment of $15,000 would be paid by each franchisee with subsequent installments due on January 2 of the following years. The Grand Opening for these first 12 outlets was planned for February 1, 19X1, with the advertising to begin in mid-January to get the market ready. During the remainder of 19X0, signs and ovens were built and installed. The corporation's additional cash requirements were met by bank loans. For 19X0, G Barbecue Palaces, Inc. reported a net loss of $55,000 consisting of expenses incurred for office help and other miscellaneous expenditures. The major costs incurred for signs, ovens, etc., were deferred into 19X1, as was all revenue.

The Grand Opening was quite successful; with Bob moving from outlet to outlet attracting admirers and customers. From February through the end of 19X1, 8 more outlets were sold. The initial 12 outlets had an average gross of $135,000 each for February through December, 19X1. The remaining 8 averaged only $50,000 each because some were open for only a few months. G Barbecue Palaces, Inc. percentage was

Gross sales:		
12 outlets at $135,000	$1,620,000	
8 outlets at $50,000	400,000	$2,020,000
G's 10% of gross		$ 202,000

In early 19X2, Bob and Kip had their accountant prepare a statement of income. They also told him that they wanted an optimistic approach to the problem. They felt that the 20 outlets were "safe" and that the entire price of $75,000 each would be collected. Also in establishing costs for signs and ovens, they thought that they would eventually have over 40 franchises, citing the marketing consultant's report, and that the lowest costs should be used. Finally, they felt that the advertising, although paid on a declining scale, would benefit all three years equally. Based on these expectations, the following income state-ment was prepared:

G Barbecue Palaces, Inc., Statement of Income for the Year 19X2

Revenue:		
Sale of franchises	$1,500,000	
Royalty on gross sales	202,000	
Total revenue		$1,702,000
Expenses:		
Cost of ovens	$ 240,000	
Cost of signs	200,000	
Advertising	200,000	
Other operating expenses*	120,000	760,000
Net income for the year		$942,000

*These include salaries of office help and other similar items.

Contrary to their professed optimism, Bob and Kip were not so pleased with their enterprise. First, volume in the older outlets opened in February showed a tendency to decrease in later months. This decline was due to several factors: Bob spent his time drawing customers to new openings; the operators, to in-crease profits, tended to reduce the quality of ingredients and cut back on ser-vice; and novelty appeal of football muscle combined with barbecue—especially tough barbecue—seemed to have a short life. The two organizers decided that now might be a good time to sell a good portion of their stock.

To this end, they contacted a group of interested investors. After investigat-ing the situations, the investors come to you for advice concerning the accuracy of the income measurement.

Required:

[a] Write a critique of the statement of income prepared for G Barbecue Pal-aces, Inc., for 19X1. Consider the treatment of each item of revenue and expense.

[b] Prepare a revised statement, taking a more conservative approach to the measurement of income for the year 19X1.

11

Acquisition and Use of Operating Assets: General Considerations

Assets of most business firms may be classified into three major categories: (1) cash, (2) claims to cash, (3) operating assets—deferred costs or services.

The preceding chapter contains a discussion of the basic accounting problems connected with revenue recognition, cash, and claims to cash. The purpose of the present chapter is the presentation of an overview of the basic problems connected with the acquisition and use of services. Referring once again to the diagram of the operating cycle, we will be concerned only with the transactions in Fig. 11–1. A business can earn revenue only as a result of the acquisition and use of services. Here, as elsewhere, emphasis will be placed on the measurement of income, which is an indication of how efficiently a business acquires and uses services or operating assets.

Figure 11–1

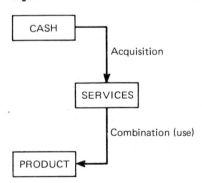

Recognition, Classification, and Valuation

In accounting for the acquisition and use of services, the accountant faces three problems:

1   Recognition. The costs of the services acquired in each accounting period must be recognized in that period; that is, the acquisition cost of services must be included in the computation of income and the effect of the acquisition shown on the periodic financial statements. In addition, the acquisition cost of services must be recognized for what it is, namely, an expense that must be matched against revenue of the current period or a deferred expense or cost that will benefit some future period.

2   Classification. The initial problem in classification of the cost of services is that of assigning the cost to the proper account or category under the broader categories of deferred expenses or current expenses. An expense of the current period may be classified as cost of goods sold, selling expense, or some other category. Deferred expenses may be classified as inventory, equipment, or some asset account. The classification of costs is closely related to the problem of recognition. Costs are classified in a manner that facilitates the recognition of the expense for the period and a proper matching of costs and revenues. The classification of costs as either product or period costs (terms explained in the following) is a good example of a classification that is inseparable from the recognition problem.

3   Valuation. The third problem is the monetary value that should be used as the acquisition cost of services. Valuation is also closely related to recognition and classification because monetary values must be assigned to both the expense of the current period and to the deferred expenses or assets. In addition, the total costs in these two categories, current expenses and deferred expenses, must be classified into the proper categories or accounts for presentation on the financial statements.

You should not get the impression that these three problems can be resolved independently. The purpose of accounting is the measurement of income and other related amounts, and the problems of recognition, classification, and valuation are often so interrelated that all three aspects of the economic events must be considered simultaneously. Recognition and classification are very closely related and are therefore considered together in the following section.

Recognition and Classification

Ignoring for now the problem of allocating the cost of services between the expense for the period and deferred expenses, we must begin with some general rules concerning the *total* acquisition cost to be recognized in a given period. In addition, once recognized, there must be some tentative classification of the acquisition costs.

ACQUISITION OF SERVICES. To begin with a note of caution, the following rules are not concerned with the *timing* of the record of events in the formal accounts. When a transaction or event is recorded and where it is recorded in the formal accounts depends on the design of the bookkeeping system in use. As explained in Chapter 8, the systems in use vary widely depending on the nature and size of the business, the recording equipment used, and numerous other factors.

• Period of Recognition: Acquisitions of services result from transactions between a business and another party who may be either an outsider, or a participant within the company, such as an employee. A transaction to acquire services begins when some agent of the acquiring business plans or recommends the acquisition. The transaction is not fully consumated until the acquiring company takes control of the services and discharges all the obligations incurred. The lapse of time between the beginning and the consummation of a transaction may be a matter of a few minutes or a span of several years.

In general, an acquisition transaction is recognized when a business (1) obtains control of new services or (2) gives up control of either cash or other assets. If the business gives up cash at the same time the services are acquired, it recognizes the newly acquired services and a decrease in cash, as shown in Fig. 11–2:

Figure 11–2: Purchase of Merchandise for Cash

	Debit	Credit
Newly acquired services	$500	
Cash		$500

If control of the newly acquired services precedes payment, the business recognizes these services as well as a liability for the payment to be made later. Subsequently, the payment of cash is recognized, as shown in Fig. 11–3:

Figure 11–3: Purchase of Merchandise on Credit and Payment of Cash Later

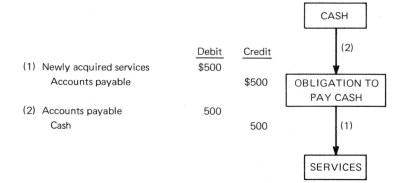

	Debit	Credit
(1) Newly acquired services	$500	
Accounts payable		$500
(2) Accounts payable	500	
Cash		500

If the business pays for services before taking control of them, it recognizes a decrease in cash along with either a claim to services or a claim to return of the cash. Subsequently, the services are recognized by the business when it takes control of them. This method of acquisition is shown in Fig. 11-4:

Figure 11-4: Deposit of Cash with Supplier and Receipt of Services Later

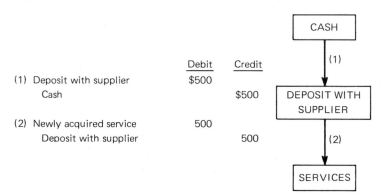

	Debit	Credit
(1) Deposit with supplier	$500	
Cash		$500
(2) Newly acquired service	500	
Deposit with supplier		500

The general rule is to recognize a transaction to acquire services when the entity takes control of the services or when it pays for the services, whichever occurs first.

Most firms prepare a *receiving report* that records the quantity and description of the physical goods received. Personnel services are recorded by punching a *time card* or the preparation of a *time report* by the employee or his supervisor. Although the receiving reports or time cards are not normally recorded in the journals and/or ledgers immediately, documentation of the event is made as soon as feasible after it occurs; procrastination usually means inaccurate data.

• Initial Classification: The initial classification of acquisition costs is not a significant accounting question. Most businesses follow the practice of recording formally the acquisition costs of services soon after the transaction is complete. In most bookkeeping systems for larger businesses, there is an accounting manual that specifies the account to be debited for each cost.

A typical rule followed in the preparation of these manuals is for services that benefit only one year to be debited to an expense account. If the benefits from a service acquired normally extend over a period longer than a year, an asset account is debited. According to this rule, office supplies would probably be recorded as an expense initially, whereas a building would be recorded as an asset. The point to remember is that the initial classification has no effect on the financial statements. It is the allocation of the total costs recognized between current expense and deferred expenses at the end of the period that is important.

USE OF SERVICES. A business acquires services based on its expectation that the services can be used to produce revenues that exceed the costs consumed.

Recognition involves not only the original acquisition cost but also recognition of the critical events indicating that a service has been used up in the production of revenue.

There are many forms and reports prepared to record the use of services. These records are normally made by someone who is in a position to observe directly the production process. For example, in a manufacturing plant a material requisition is normally used to signal the issue of raw materials from the storeroom to the factory. In a wholesale house, shipping or delivery reports are prepared to signal the transfer of goods to customers. Throughout the business operation, various employees make observations about the use of services and prepare reports that serve as the basis for the allocation of costs between current expenses and deferred expenses.

Accountants also use a general classification of costs between **product** costs and **period** costs as an aid in measuring periodic expense. Before turning to the nature and use of these classifications, a general understanding of the behavior of costs relative to the volume of business will be helpful.

• Cost Behavior: Services used relate to productive output in various ways. Some of the possibilities are graphically represented in Fig. 11–5 (a–d).

Figure 11–5: General Pattern of Cost Behavior

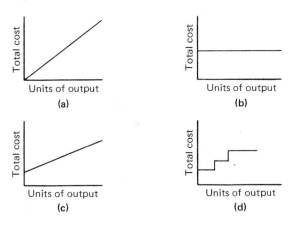

A service or cost that behaves in the manner indicated by graph (a) in Fig. 11–5 is called a *variable cost* because it varies as output varies. The cost of merchandise in a retail store behaves in this manner. Each time a unit is sold the total cost of goods sold increases. If a certain amount of steel is required to make a unit of product, the cost of steel consumed in production will vary directly with the number of units produced.

Graph (b) of Fig. 11–5 shows a cost that is *fixed* in amount relative to production. The cost stays the same no matter how many units are produced. An example of such a cost would be a factory building that will be serviceable for no more or no less than 30 years irrespective of the intensity of the productive activity carried on within the building.

Graph (c) of Fig. 11–5 shows a cost that may be called either **semifixed** or **semivariable**. A certain amount of such a cost must be incurred even if there is no production, but beyond this initial amount the cost varies with production. In some situations, the cost of a factory's power plant behaves in this way. Some minimum cost is incurred to provide the heat and light required even when the plant is not operating. The additional cost required to operate machinery and equipment during productive periods often varies directly with productive output.

Graph (d) of Fig. 11–5 shows a **step pattern**. Factory supervision may behave in this way. Some supervision may be necessary when a plant is idle. As productive activity increases, the amount of supervision required remains level for a range of activity and then jumps to a new level at some point as production increases. The addition of a second shift requires a second shift supervisor, for example.

Because costs behave differently in relation to the volume of activity, it is not always possible to match the cost of a service directly with the revenue it has produced. For example, we cannot identify what portion of our telephone service was used to produce or sell a unit of product. On the other hand, a variable cost clearly related to a product or service can be matched against revenue because these costs vary directly with sales. The problems of matching costs, **other than** variable costs, has been solved by establishing a more-or-less arbitrary classification of costs between those that are associated with the product and those that are associated with an accounting period.

PERIOD AND PRODUCT COSTS. Period costs are costs that are so indirectly related to the productive process that they must be treated as expenses in the accounting period when they are incurred. Some examples of period costs are rent on a store building paid by a retailer, salaries of sales personnel in wholesale, retail, and manufacturing operations, the corporate president's salary in a manufacturing company, and advertising expenses in all types of business. Note that these costs are incurred as time passes or on the occurrence of some event that is only indirectly related, if at all, to the production of goods or services.

Product costs are costs that can be related to the productive process. In manufacturing, product costs include all costs incurred **in the factory**, as opposed to the sales organization or general administration. In retail and wholesale businesses, product costs include the direct cost of merchandise, freight paid to obtain the merchandise, and some other handling charges. Product costs are assigned to each unit of product and they become expenses **only** when the product is sold. Depreciation of the factory building, a fixed cost, is a product cost and is included in the cost of production. The portion of the depreciation assigned to the product not sold at year-end is deferred as inventory costs. However, the portion of factory depreciation assigned to the goods sold is an expense of the period included in cost of goods sold.

Figure 11-6: (a) Period costs and product costs. (b) Office worker services in department store. (c) Factory worker services in a factory.

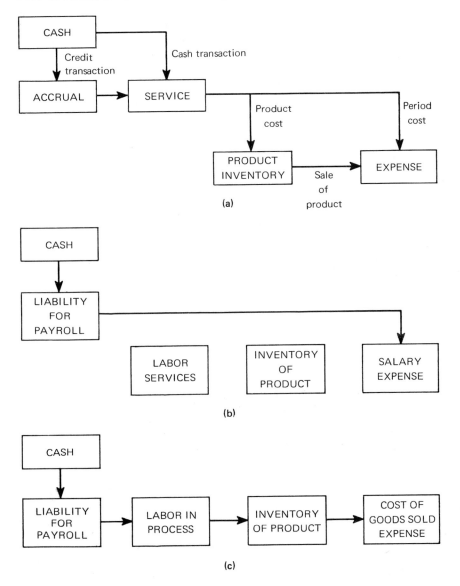

(a)

(b)

(c)

Flow diagram (a) of Fig. 11-6 shows the treatment of period costs and product costs. Note that period costs are assigned directly to expense for an accounting period. Product costs are included in the cost of the product and become expenses when the product is sold.

Diagrams (b) and (c) of Fig. 11-6 contrast the accounting treatment of the costs of office employees with that of factory workers. Office employee services are considered period costs because they cannot be directly identified with a product; they are recognized as expenses of the period. Factory labor, on the other hand, is a product cost because it can be identified with a product and is therefore added to the cost of work in process. When the product is completed the labor costs and other cost associated with the product are transferred to the product (finished goods) inventory; finally when the product is sold, all costs associated with the product are transferred to the expense account, namely, cost of goods sold.

Figure 11-7: (a) Building services in a department store. (b) Building services in a factory.

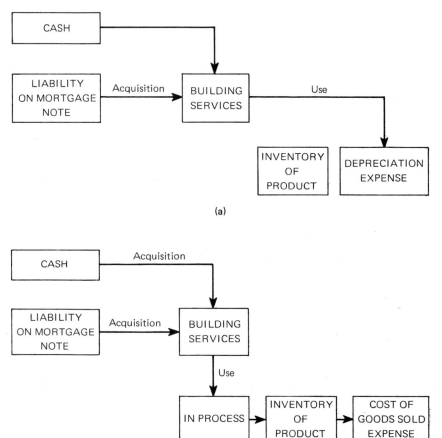

(a)

(b)

Diagrams (a) and (b) of Fig. 11-7 contrast the treatment of depreciation expense in a mercantile concern with that in a manufacturing concern. The flows are similar to the flow of labor services. In a mercantile concern, the depreciation expense is a period cost and is assigned directly to an accounting period. In the manufacturing business, depreciation of factory building is a product cost and becomes a part of factory expense. Costs of operating the factory are assigned to products and become expenses only when the product is sold.

The following transactions can be used to exemplify the distinction between product and period costs:

1   A businessman withdraws $500 from his personal savings account to devote to a venture, namely, a contract to supply souvenir programs for a local play which is to have a three-day run.
2   He contracts for the printing of programs at a price of 32 cents each with an out-of-town printer.
3   He pays $50 for pick up and delivery on a rush order basis.
4   He pays two teenagers $30 each to sell programs for the three evenings the play is to run.
5   He pays the city $10 for a temporary vendor's permit.
6   The teenagers sell the 1,000 programs.

Figure 11-8: Flow and T-Account Diagrams of Souvenir Program Venture

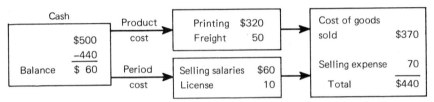

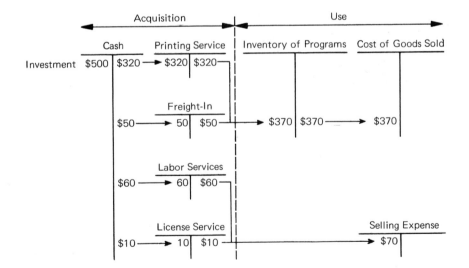

Treatment of these costs is shown in Fig. 11-8. Because of the short period of time involved, in this example the distinction between product and period costs is not significant. However, if a sufficient number of programs were ordered for sale at a Broadway play that is expected to run for more than a year, it would be necessary to allocate the cost of the programs among the years. The selling costs and the license would be period costs and would be expensed in the period when incurred.

Valuation

Accountants value newly acquired services at the cash amount or cash-equivalent value given up by a business in the acquisition. When cash is paid at or about the same time the business takes control of the newly acquired services, the valuation is easy—the amount of cash paid. Complications arise when a business gives consideration other than cash to acquire new services and when the timing of the cash payment (or payments) differs from the time when the business takes control of the new services.

NONCASH EXCHANGES. In noncash exchanges, the accountant's first preference is usually to value the newly acquired services in terms of the fair value (cash equivalent) of the consideration given up in the exchange. If a building is acquired in exchange for 500 shares of the acquiring corporation's capital stock, for example, and the stock could be sold for cash at $100 per share, the exchange would be recorded as follows:

	Debit	Credit
Building	$50,000	
Capital stock		$50,000

Note the effect is the same as though the stock were sold for cash (500 shares at $100 each) and the building were purchased for cash.

As another example, consider the exchange of a tract of land in a rural area for a downtown building site. Assume that the land could be sold for a cash price of $95,000 and that its original cost to the business was $100,000. The exchange would be recorded as follows:

	Debit	Credit
Building site	$95,000	
Loss on exchange of land tract	5,000	
Land tract		$100,000

If the facts are changed so that the book value of the rural land tract is $95,000 and its fair value is $100,000, the exchange would be recorded as follows:

	Debit	Credit
Building site	$100,000	
Land tract		$95,000
Gain on exchange of land tract		5,000

Accountants generally prefer to value noncash acquisitions in terms of fair value of consideration given up, but they will use the fair value of the asset acquired in cases where the amount so determined is either more dependable or where it is easier to calculate.

In the preceding examples, gain or loss was recognized on the exchanges. These gains and losses would affect the measurement of income for the period. Recognition is typical in these cases even though disposition of the old service did not give rise to a cash claim—one test for revenue recognition explained in Chapter 10. The accountant in these "barter" transactions actually considers the single trade as two transactions: First the asset traded is assumed to be sold at its fair value or the fair value of the asset received, and, second, there is an acquisition of the new asset for the value established. The gain or loss is recognized, despite the absence of a cash claim on disposition, to assure that the new asset is recorded at its cash-equivalent value.

DONATED SERVICES. Acquisition of services through donation is a special case of a noncash acquisition where valuation is based on the fair market value of the newly acquired services. Suppose a city donated land with a fair value of $75,000 to a business firm to entice it to open a plant in the city. An acceptable recording of the acquisition would be as follows:

	Debit	Credit
Land	$75,000	
Donated capital (a subclass of contributed capital)		$75,000

Even though the firm acquired the land without a cash payment or other cost, the accountability of the firm's management should be established by recording the acquisition in terms of the fair value of the services acquired. In the event of subsequent disposition of the land, gain or loss would be determined by comparing the amount realized with the carrying value of $75,000.

INTEREST AND FINANCIAL CHARGES. Acquisitions for cash may be as troublesome for accountants as noncash acquisitions when there is a significant lapse of time between the date the business takes control of the services and the date or dates when cash is paid. Money has a time value. The valuation of services at cost means the cash-equivalent amount required for immediate settlement of the obligation. When payment is delayed and both the time span and the monetary amount involved are significant, the cost of the new services must be separated from the financial charges. A financial charge is a cost of deferring the cash payment, and this cost should not be assigned to the new services.

Financial costs are usually called interest. Interest in an agreement may be either explicit or implicit: *Explicit interest* is separately identified in the purchase contract and is paid as such; *implicit interest* is an amount paid that is not separately identified in the contract. The following examples will clarify the meaning of these terms.

Suppose a business borrows $1,000 on a 60–day promissory note bearing interest at 6 percent. When it pays $1,010 to cover its obligation on the note at the end of 60 days, the payment covers $1,000 for the return of principal and $10 for interest. The interest is separately identified and it is actually paid. This is explicit interest.

Suppose a businessman purchases equipment and signs a contract agreeing to pay $525 at the end of six months and another $525 at the end of one year. The contract says nothing about interest. If the same equipment can be purchased for $1,000 cash, there is an implicit interest charge of $50 ($525 + $525 − $1,000) in the contract.

Both explicit and implicit interest should be recognized as a cost of services. In most cases, the interest is treated as a period cost in the year incurred and classified as interest expense or financial charges on the statement of income. In a few situations, the explicit or implicit interest paid during the construction of a plant will be included in the acquisition cost of the plant and recognized as expense as the plant is depreciated.

CASH DISCOUNTS. A cash discount is a reduction in price offered as a concession for prompt payment. The terms of a cash discount are usually quoted in the form of a shorthand expression such as 2/10, n/30, meaning that a 2 percent discount is allowed on any payment made within ten days after receipt of the invoice and that the remainder of the list price is due within 30 days of the invoice receipt. The cash price is the invoice price less the cash discount. If the discount is not taken, the lost discount is an interest cost. Cash discounts given by the seller were discussed in Chapter 10.

For example, assume that a firm buys a machine with a list price of $1,000 from a seller who quote terms of 2/10, n/30. The entry to record the acquisition of the machine would be

	Debit	Credit
Machine	$980	
Accounts payable		$980

If the payment is subsequently made within the discount period, the entry to record the payment of the obligation would be

	Debit	Credit
Accounts payable	$980	
Cash		$980

However, if the obligation is paid after the discount period expires, the entry to record payment would be

	Debit	Credit
Accounts payable	$980	
Discounts lost (a financial charge equivalent to interest)	20	
Cash		$1,000

SUMMARY. The accounting rules for the valuation of new services may be summarized as follows:

1   Services acquired for cash with the cash payment occurring at or near the time the business takes control of the services are equated in value to the amount of cash paid.
2   Services acquired for cash with payment delayed are valued at the cash equivalent required to settle the obligation with an immediate payment. Any explicit or implicit interest paid as a result of the delay is separated and treated as interest, and has no bearing on the valuation assigned to the new services.
3   Services acquired in exchange for considerations other than cash are usually valued in terms of the fair value of the consideration given up in the exchange. Valuation may be in terms of the fair value of the services acquired if the amount is more dependable and/or easier to estimate.
4   Services acquired where no consideration is given, that is, donated services, are valued at the cash-equivalent value of the services.

Example of Interrelations Among Recognition, Classification, and Valuation

In many complicated business arrangements, the accountant cannot isolate and solve independently the problems of recognition, classification, and valuation. To accomplish his basic goals, the measurement of income, wealth, and fund flows, the accountant often must make decisions about recognition, classification, and valuation simultaneously because the problems are inseparable.

A prime example of a set of complicated events where the three problems must be considered together is the accounting for *interperiod tax allocations*. The largest tax paid by most corporations is the federal income tax. That tax is levied at the rate of 22% on the first $25,000 of the corporation's taxable income plus 48% of all taxable income in excess of $25,000.* Accountants have always treated the income tax as an expense, just like other costs of conducting the business. The income tax is unique, however, because, unlike most expenses, it is based on income, which is what the accountant is trying to measure.

Accounting problems arise because the *taxable income* for a corporation is often quite different from the income shown in the financial statements, the *book income*. In the majority of cases, the taxable income is less than the book income because, as a taxpayer, the corporation tries to minimize its tax and chooses tax practices that either defer the recognition of revenue to a later period for taxation or increase the expenses deducted for taxation. These timing

*To avoid two multiplications where the taxable income exceeds $25,000, tax can be computed by multiplying the taxable income by 48 percent and then subtracting the $6,500.

differences in practices are completely legitimate and, in fact, are occasionally encouraged by the federal government. (We should note that there are also some permanent differences, that is, some items included in book income are not subject to the income tax.)

An example is a retailer who sells merchandise on the installment basis. If there is a reasonable expectation that receivables will be collected, the revenue must be recognized on the sales basis for financial purposes. For tax purposes, however, the corporation can elect to use the installment basis and defer recognition of income to a later year and decrease the taxes due in the current year. The current deduction of research and development expenditures and the acceleration of depreciation are other common tax practices that cause taxable income to be less than financial income.

For many years, generally accepted practice has held that the income tax expense reported on the financial statements should be the tax which *would* be paid on the reported income. If the income of the financial statements before taxes is $200,000, then the tax expense reported on the statement of income should be $89,500 [($200,000 X .48) – $6,500]. This amount should be reported even if the taxable income is only $120,000 and actual tax due is, therefore, only $51,100 [($120,000 X .48) – $6,500].

The logic used to support this practice is based on the fact that the lower taxable income results from deferral of income or acceleration of deductions for tax purpose and these are only timing differences. It would, therefore, stand to reason that at some point in time the taxable income should be more than the financial income and the taxes actually paid should exceed the taxes reported on the book income. Thus the difference between the tax expense and current tax liability is a long-term liability. An entry based on the facts above would be

	Debit	Credit
Income tax expense	$89,500	
Income taxes payable (a current liability)		$51,100
Estimated future taxes payable		38,400

When accountants settled on the above practice they forgot to consider several possibilities that have to do with the recognition of the expense, the value assigned to it, and the classification of liabilities:

1 Under normal conditions, will taxable income ever be more than financial income?
2 What happens if the tax rate is lowered (as was the case in the 1960s when the corporate tax was lowered from 52 to 48 percent)?
3 What happens if the law is changed and timing differences become permanent differences?

In any event, additional tax expense has been accrued on many corporate books for many years now and the amounts are becoming very large in some cases. Indeed, many accountants have concluded that there is such a low probability for the long-term liability ever to be paid that it should not be accrued. The growing doubt about the nature of the noncurrent portion of expense is reflected by the words used to describe it on most balance sheets, "deferred credit for income taxes." This title would seem to suggest that the amount is no liability at all, but an amount that will eventually be used to increase income or retained earnings.

To summarize, a clear-cut recognition rule that tax expense should be based on book income leads to serious problems of valuing the future liability, if any, and to a problem of classifying the credit that results from the expense recognition. Unless the rules are changed, the mysterious "deferred credit" could conceivably become the largest amount in the equity section for some corporations. On the balance sheet for Great Northern Nekoosa Corporation (p. 508 of Appendix D), "Deferred Taxes on Income" at December 31, 1971 were almost $43 million, which is only $2.5 million less than the total of all current liabilities. This questionable liability amounts to more than 10 percent of the corporation's total equities.

Application of Accounting Doctrines

The accounting profession has tried to develop rules for the recognition, classification, and valuation of business transactions. These rules, however, are general in nature and do not apply to all transactions; judgment is required in the application of the rules to specific circumstances. To aid in the application of the rules, accountants also have certain doctrines or conventions. The most important doctrines, discussed briefly in Chapter 5, are conservatism, consistency, materiality, and fair disclosure.

Conservatism

This doctrine had its origins in an era when financial statements were used primarily by bankers and other parties who granted short-term credit to businessmen. During that era, conservatism meant an intentional understatement of asset values. The idea was to allow the creditor a margin for safety in the extension of credit to businessmen. A flow approach to income in which assets are valued at cost rather than at liquidation values is a move away from the ultraconservative valuations.

Intentional understatement of asset values is no longer an accepted practice, but conservatism is still practiced by accountants in the form of using a pessimistic bias when there is a choice among several reasonable alternatives. Constant use of liquidation value is not a reasonable choice for valuation of the assets of a going concern—this would be an intentional understatement.

Consistency

The historical developments that led to the deemphasis of conservatism simultaneously led to the development of consistency as a doctrine for making professional judgments. In the 1930s accountants began to notice that most businesses were engaged in continuing activities. The assets controlled by these firms derived their value from earning power, that is, the stream of income generated by using the assets.

Dependence on income measurement as the index of a business's worth makes it imperative that changes in income should result from the economic activities of the business and not from changes in the accounting procedures used to measure income. The circumstances make consistency imperative, including the handling of the problems of recognition, classification, and valuation that relate to accounting for services. The doctrine of consistency means that, in the absence of compelling reasons for a change, the acquisition, use, and disposition of services should be accounted for in the same way period after period.

Materiality

This doctrine is an expression of the utilitarian nature of accounting. As it is related to accounting for services, materiality means that precision in recognition, classification, and valuation are not to be carried beyond the point where the information that results cost more than it is worth.

For instance, consider the purchase of a trash can for $5. The can has an expected useful life of ten years. Strict adherence to accounting rules would require recognition of a deferred cost which would be charged to expense over the ten-year useful life. The doctrine of materiality permits the accountant to treat the cost as an expense in the period incurred because the amount involved is so trivial that precision is not worth the effort required to get it.

Fair Disclosure

Under this doctrine, the accountant must be certain that all relevant information is disclosed by the financial statements. For example, contracts to acquire services in the future are not generally recognized as costs until the transaction is completed. The existence, however, of these contracts must be disclosed in the financial statements. Long-term lease contracts, agreements to provide retirement benefits to employees, and many other executory contracts are also disclosed in footnotes to the financial statements. In some cases contingent future events are disclosed in a middle paragraph of the auditors' opinion. Needless to say, a person using the financial statement should study carefully the auditor's opinion and all footnotes accompanying the statements.

Cost Flows

One major function of accounting is to trace the cost of services from the point of acquisition until they are used in the production of revenue. Services come in a variety of forms such as buildings, equipment, patents, copyrights, and personnel. Some services can be stored and requisitioned as needed in the productive process. Materials, equipment, and buildings are examples of services that can be stored. Other services, often called **energies**, cannot be stored. Examples are electrical energy and human energy. Accountants assume that the nonstoreable services or energies used to produce a physical product become a part of the product and that the cost of the energies should become a part of the cost of the product.

Figure 11–9 shows the general flow of costs through a business. A business exchanges assets or an equity contract for various services needed. Line 1 indicates an exchange of cash or other assets for a service. Line 2 indicates an exchange of an equity contract, an accrued expense, a debt investment, or an owner investment for a service. An exchange could be a mixture of these two. The acquisition of services, of course, is the first step in the process.

Figure 11–9: Flow of Costs (See text for explanation of numbers 1–7.)

Range of Possibilities

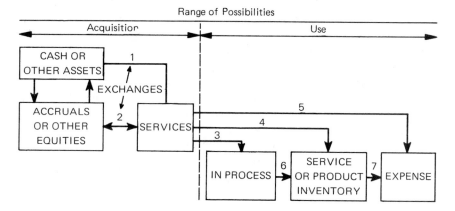

Following the acquisition, the service is used in some way with the expectation of producing revenue. Line 3 indicates that the service is transferred to a production process to be combined with other services to form a new product. When the product is complete, it is transferred to product inventory (line 6), and, after the product is sold, it is transferred to expense (line 7).

Some services are stored temporarily (line 4) as an inventory of product held for resale or an inventory of a service that will be used to produce revenue. When the product is sold or the service is used in the revenue-producing process, it becomes an expense (line 7). Other services are acquired and used immediately in the revenue process, that is, they become expenses when acquired (line 5).

The nature of the activity of a business determines how costs flow through the business. The three principal types of businesses are (1) service enterprises, (2) mercantile firms, and (3) manufacturing industries.

Service Industries

Firms that deal in services, such as barber shops, financial institutions, (banks, savings and loan associations, etc.), and accounting firms, typically treat all services consumed as period expenses. Services treated as period expenses are shown on line 5 in Fig. 11-9. In a barber shop, the cost of labor services (salaries and commissions paid to barbers) and laundry services would be period expenses; the cost of supplies (hair dressings, shaving cream, etc.), buildings, and equipment services would be treated as shown by lines 4 and 7 in Fig. 11-9.

Mercantile Firms

Wholesale and retail businesses treat the cost of some services as product costs and others as period expenses. Traditionally, the invoice price of merchandise net of discounts and allowances has been treated as a product cost by mercantile firms. These costs are inventory costs, as shown by lines 4 and 7 in Fig. 11-9. Most of the other costs in a mercantile business are treated as period expenses. The salaries of management, sales force, and service personnel and the house-keeping costs such as rent, utilities, taxes, and other incidentals are period expenses as shown by line 5. The cost of depreciation for buildings, fixtures, and furnishings along with the costs of insurance and supplies are usually treated as shown by lines 4 and 7.

Freight-in is the cost a mercantile firm incurs to have merchandise transported from the premises of a supplier to the location from which sales are made. Payments for freight-in are usually made to a supplier or a common carrier. If the amounts involved are material, and there is a reasonable basis for associating these costs with units of merchandise, the cost of freight-in should be treated as an inventory cost, as shown by lines 4 and 7 on Fig. 11-9. Freight is a cost necessary to acquire the service and, therefore, the cost of freight should be included in the cost of the service.

Manufacturing and Extractive Industries

The traditional practice in manufacturing and extractive operations has been to treat services used in production as product costs. Services used to carry on general administration, marketing, and financial activities are usually treated as period expenses. It is readily apparent that manufacturing is the prototype for the separation of product cost and period expense.

In a manufacturing operation, product costs are usually divided into three categories: (1) direct materials, (2) direct labor, and (3) manufacturing overhead. Direct materials are the physical items used in production that can be traced to units of product without requiring more effort than the information is worth. Steel is a direct material in the manufacture of automobiles. Direct labor includes the labor services of all employees that can be practically traced to units of product. Manufacturing overhead includes all production costs other than direct materials and direct labor. Examples of manufacturing overhead are indirect labor, indirect materials, factory supervision, maintenance, insurance, utilities, and depreciation of machinery and buildings, that is, the cost of services related to production as opposed to other activities such as general administration, financing, or marketing. Manufacturing overhead is frequently referred to as burden or as manufacturing expense.

Manufacturing expenses are usually grouped together and then allocated to units of product on some practical basis for association. For example, if the direct labor associated with each unit of product is $1.00 and if manufacturing overhead in total is $3,000 as compared with total direct labor of $1,500, then $2.00 of overhead is assigned to each unit of product on the basis of the relationship between total overhead and total direct labor.

As represented in T accounts, a summarization of service flows for a manufacturer is shown in Fig. 11–10.

Figure 11–10: T Account Cost Flow in a Manufacturing Industry

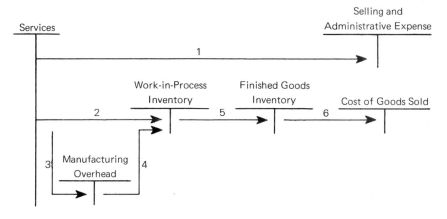

Key to numbers:

Period expenses

1   Flow of services consumed to carry on administrative and selling activities

Product costs

2   Flow of direct materials and direct labor
3   Flow of indirect materials, indirect labor, services of machines, buildings, etc.
4   Allocation of manufacturing overhead to production in process
5   Transfer to finished goods inventory
6   Transfer of finished goods to customer

In the three chapters that follow we consider in detail the accounting problems associated with the acquisition and use of services. Chapters 12 and 13 deal with short-lived services such as inventories and human services. In Chapter 14 we will discuss long-lived assets.

QUESTIONS

1   Briefly describe, in accounting terms, how a business produces a good or service which results in the generation of revenue.

2   What are the three problems an accountant must solve in accounting for the acquisition and use of services?

3   Identify and discuss the generalizations that exist with regard to the accounting rules for recognition, classification, and valuation of the acquisition and use of services.

4   What are the similarities between recognition and classification?

5   Explain the difference between the timing of the recording and the timing of the recognition of the acquisition and use of services.

6   When should a business recognize the acquisition of a service?

7   Explain why the initial classification of the acquisition of a service is not as important as the allocation of the cost between deferred expenses and expenses at the end of the period.

8   List and define the four patterns of cost behavior.

9   Define period costs and product costs. Distinguish these two types of cost by giving contrasting examples of each.

10   Indicate which of the following costs are period costs and which are product costs:
    [a]   Letterhead stationery
    [b]   Janitorial services for a retail store
    [c]   Janitorial services for a factory
    [d]   The rent of a computer used for accounting
    [e]   The rent of a computer used to prepare production schedules in a factory

11   What is the general rule for valuing the acquisition cost of a service?

12   How should noncash exchanges be valued?

13   List and define the two different types of interest.

14   Why is interest usually treated as a period cost rather than a product cost?

15   [a]   Why is it advisable for a business to take a cash discount when offered?
    [b]   Should the cost of a service be increased if the cash discount is not taken? Why?

16   What accounting problems arise when taxable income differs from book income?

17   How do each of the following doctrines affect accounting for the acquisition and use of services?
    [a]   Conservatism
    [b]   Consistency
    [c]   Materiality
    [d]   Fair disclosure

18   What are the general flows of costs in a business?

19   Describe each of the following types of businesses and list some examples of each:
    [a]   Service industries
    [b]   Mercantile firms
    [c]   Manufacturing industries

PROBLEMS

1   An airline purchased a small jet airplane. Present entries to record the acquisition for each of the following transactions. For [b] and [c], give at least two alternatives and indicate the preferable valuation. Explain your preference.
    [a]   The firm paid $100,000 cash for the plane.

[b]   The firm issued 10,000 shares of its own $5 par value stock in exchange for the plane. The current market price of a share of the company's stock is $12.

[c]   The firm exchanged a 50-acre tract of land for the plane. The company turned down a firm offer of $110,000 for the land a week ago. An adjacent tract of land sold for $1,950 per acre a few days ago.

2   A firm purchased land and a building on the land paying cash of $5,000 and signing a 6 per-cent mortgage note for $145,000. An adjoining piece of land of similar size was offered to the firm for $20,000, but the firm decided against buying it.

Required:

[a]   Present a journal entry to record the acquisition of the land and building.

[b]   Explain why the cost of the land should or should not be classified separately.

3   The following independent events were selected from various businesses. For each event, indicate the acquisition cost which should be recognized during the current accounting period.

[a]   100 tons of steel was ordered from a supplier for a total cost of $50,000.

[b]   An attorney was paid $150 as a retainer fee.

[c]   A notice was received from the local tax assessor that the assessed valuation of your property had been increased by $10,000.

[d]   A contract was signed with an automotive repair shop to service all of your vehicles at a monthly cost of $300.

[e]   A bill for $800 was received from the local power company for power used.

[f]   An insurance policy for one period was purchased. The premium was $600.

[g]   A contract to purchase land was signed. The contract requires a down payment of $5,000 and ten annual payments of $10,000.

4   J and Company entered into the following transactions during the current year. Classify the acquisition cost in each transaction as either a product or a period cost.

[a]   Advertising costs of $500 were incurred.

[b]   Factory labor of $1,800 was accrued.

[c]   Depreciation on office equipment was $600.

[d]   The president was paid $15,000 for salary.

[e]   Production materials costing $7,000 were acquired during the year.

[f]   A telephone bill for $400 was received.

[g]   Materials held for use in production were destroyed by fire.

[h]   The company paid freight of $500 on materials purchased for use in production.

[i]   Taxes on the factory building and equipment were $900.

[j]   Taxes on the warehouse used to store finished goods were $540.

[k]   Electrical energy used to operate the office air conditioners and equipment cost $110.00.

[l]   Natural gas consumed in operating the electrical power generator for the factory cost $250.

5   The R Construction Company is negotiating with a heavy equipment manufacturer to pur-chase two large backhoes. The equipment company has offered to make the two backhoes available to R Construction under any of the following arrangements:

[1]   Cash price of $25,000

[2]   Lease the backhoes to R Construction for $6,000 per year for five years and grant an option to buy the backhoes for $1 at the end of the five-year lease

[3]   Sell the backhoes to R Construction for $4,000 plus the payment of $7,000 per year for three years plus annual interest of 8 percent on the unpaid balance

Required:

[a] What is the acquisition cost of the backhoes under each of the arrangements?

[b] Assuming a backhoe has an estimated life of ten years, is the lease proposal a true lease?

[c] What type of interest, if any, is involved in each of the above arrangements?

6   The W Corporation received a bill from the service station for expenditures on its delivery truck. The bill was itemized as follows:

New transmission	$250
Installation of transmission	25
Tune-up	25
Oil change and lubrication	10
Gas	5
Tires	45
	$360

Because monthly financial statements are prepared, the bookkeeper of W Corporation was instructed to record the bill although it would not be paid until the beginning of the next month.

[a] How should each of the items listed be classified—as an expense or as a deferred cost?

[b] Prepare a journal entry to record this accrual.

7   The taxable income and book income for B Incorporated for the past three years are as follows:

	Taxable income	Book income
19X1	$60,000	$70,000
19X2	40,000	40,000
19X3	25,000	15,000

[a] Compute the income tax expense, the income taxes payable, and the estimated future taxes payable for each of the three years for B Incorporated. (Assume that the tax rates are 22 percent on the first $25,000 of income and 48 percent on all income in excess of $25,000.)

[b] Prepare journal entries to record the tax expenses and related accruals.

[c] Should there be a balance in the account "estimated future taxes payable" after 19X3?

[d] Do the accruals of estimated future taxes usually work out as they did for B Incorporated? Why?

CASE   John Lasher has operated a successful advertising agency for many years. Although his agency was successful, Mr. Lasher has always wanted to own and operate a newspaper. Late in 1970, the local newspaper publisher offered to sell Mr. Lasher his newspaper and printing shop for the very favorable price of $100,000.

Mr. Lasher has always kept the books of the advertising agency and has stated many times that accounting is a very simple process. Revenues were just the cash receipts from customers plus the increase or minus the decrease in accounts receivable. Expenses were merely cash disbursements plus or minus, respectively, the increase or decrease in unpaid bills. Of course, additional adjustments were necessary for the investment transactions during the period. Mr. Lasher has always rented offices and equipment for his agency.

Lasher acquired the newspaper in January 19X1 and operated the business for one year. At the end of 19X1, Mr. Lasher prepared the statement of income, Schedule 1, for his newspaper and print shop using the techniques just described.

Mr. Lasher was extremely disappointed with the results of operating the newspaper and print shop. He asks you to examine the statement of income and his operations and to advise him on how he may improve the profitability of the business.

After several days of investigation you discovered the following facts:

[1] Paper stock of approximately $10,000 was on hand as of December 31, 19X1.
[2] Printer's ink, lead stock, and other supplies amount to $3,000 at December 31, 19X1.
[3] Materials and labor on printing jobs in process amounted to $5,000 at December 31, 19X1.
[4] Depreciation on equipment and building for 19X1 was estimated to be $2,500.

Required:

[a] What errors did Mr. Lasher make in preparing the income statement? Were these errors a result of changing from one type of business to another?
[b] Can a corrected statement of income be prepared using the additional facts presented?
[c] If you do not believe that a corrected statement of income can be prepared with the available information, what additional information would you need? Be as specific as possible.

SCHEDULE 1
L News, Statement of Income for Year Ended December 31, 19X1

Revenue:		
Newspaper advertising	$ 85,000	
Paper sales	110,000	
Printing jobs	55,000	$250,000
Expenses:		
Labor (print shop)	$76,000	
News reporters' salaries	25,000	
Editors' salaries	24,000	
Paper stock purchased	58,000	
Printer's ink	12,000	
Type (lead)	16,000	
Taxes and insurance on print shop	7,000	
Utilities	14,000	
President's salary	20,000	252,000
Net loss		($2,000)

12

Inventories

Services are acquired by a business with the expectation that their use or consumption will produce revenue. The principal objective, of course, is to produce something that can be sold at a price exceeding the costs of the services consumed in the process. The general problems of recognition, classification, and valuation were examined in Chapter 11. This chapter and the two that follow consider specific problems in the acquisition and use of various types of resources.

The problems considered will be the recognition and valuation of services when they are acquired and as they are used. Some of the difficulties encountered are exemplified by the following questions: In a department store, what portion of the cost of counters, rugs, and other furnishings are used up during an accounting period? In the manufacture of a new jet airliner, how much of the total cost of research and development should be assigned to the aircraft sold during a given year? In a retail store, where the cost of inventory items has fluctuated significantly during the year, what are the costs of the items sold during the year? And what are the costs of the items still on hand? In order to compute income on a periodic basis, accountants have developed rules and procedures that provide answers for these questions, as well as a large number of similar questions which could be raised.

In this chapter we consider inventories. In Chapter 13, personnel costs and prepaid expenses are considered. In Chapter 14 the problems of accounting for long-lived services will be discussed.

Short-lived services are those services that are acquired in units, batches, or bundles and are expected to be used or consumed in a short period of time, usually within the next operating cycle or year. One type of short-lived service is characterized by a physical existence and comes in measurable units. Merchandise inventory, stationery, and janitorial supplies are typical examples. The unit of measure may be any of a number of units of weight or quantity. For example, an inventory of groceries may be measured by the ounce, the pound, the bushel, can size, the dozen, or some other basis. This type of short-lived asset can be measured in a finite way. For convenience, services of this type will be called *inventories*.

In terms of the equations developed in Chapter 3, the relevant variables in this chapter are all from the equation, $E = CD + \Delta AE - \Delta DE - ID$. The variables related to the acquisition and use of services are expenses (E), cash disbursements (CD), deferred costs (DE) and accrued costs (AE).

Accounting for Inventories

One of the most troublesome problems an accountant must face in most manufacturing and mercantile operations is accounting for inventories. In these businesses, large amounts of capital are invested in inventories. In addition, the volume of inventory transactions is usually very high relative to other types of transactions. As a result, an accurate accounting for inventories is essential to an accurate measurement of income.

In accounting for inventories, the important variables in the expense equation are expense (E) and deferred costs (DE). Accounting for accrued cost (AE) and for cash disbursements (CD) are no different for inventories than for other acquisitions of services. If the cost is recognized prior to the cash disbursement, an accrual of the cost is necessary. The major problem arises in the allocation of the total acquisition cost of inventories between the expense for the accounting period and the deferred costs applicable to future periods. The accounts used to show the results of this allocation of inventory would be cost of goods sold (E) and merchandise inventory (DE).

Acquisitions

Recognition of the acquisition cost of inventories usually takes place with the receipt of the services or when legal title is obtained. As explained in Chapter 10, the shipment terms frequently determine the period in which the cost of goods should be recognized. "Free on board" (f.o.b.) shipping point means that title passes from the seller to the purchaser at the seller's loading dock; f.o.b. destination means that the title does not pass until the goods reach the destination, the purchaser's receiving point. Goods in transit belong to the seller if title has not passed; they belong to the buyer if title has passed.

Some businesses (consignor) will ship goods to another business (consignee) who has agreed to sell the goods or perform some other service for the consignor. Although the consignee has control of the goods, the consignor still has legal title to them and therefore must account for the cost of the goods. In other cases a business may acquire merchandise inventory using money borrowed from a bank or other financial institution, giving legal title to the merchandise as security to the lender. The business (borrower) has control of the merchandise, however, and must recognize the acquisition cost of the inventory and the new liability (note payable). When money is borrowed under this agreement, the lender usually requires the buyer to apply proceeds from the sale of goods to repayment of the loan.

Valuation

The value assigned to inventory is its *cash* acquisition cost. Cash acquisition cost is defined as the amount of cash paid at the time of acquisition to place the inventory in the position where it can be sold or used. Acquisition costs, under this rule, include the net invoice price (invoice price less discounts available) plus freight costs and other handling costs.

The Recording Process

The acquisition and use of inventories may be recorded in the formal records in two different ways. If the *periodic method* is used, the acquisition cost is recorded either in the deferred cost (an asset account) or in an expense account at the time of acquisition. The account originally debited is adjusted *periodically* to show proper cost allocation between expense and deferred cost. Generally the deferred cost account will be used to record the acquisition, but for some types of inventories an expense account is used. This decision is arbitrary and has no effect on the measurement of income.

If the *perpetual method* is used, the acquisition is recorded in an asset account. The use of the inventory is recognized on a transaction-by-transaction basis rather than periodically, thus causing the expense account to increase and the inventory account to decrease each time a unit is used or sold. The perpetual method usually provides better control over inventory costs, but it also requires more effort and increases accounting costs.

The two methods are compared in Fig. 12-1, where the acquisition cost is recorded in a deferred cost account, namely, merchandise inventory, for both methods. With the perpetual method, expense is recorded as each sale is made, whereas, with the periodic method, expense is recorded at the period's end by an adjusting entry that transfers the cost of sales of $7,640 to expense, leaving a deferred cost of $1,530 in the inventory account. The accountant could have recorded the new costs in the expense account using the periodic method. If this is done, the adjusting entry at the end of the period changes the inventory balance to agree with the amount actually on hand. Under these conditions, the adjusting entry is

	Debit	Credit
Cost of goods sold	$440	
Merchandise inventory		$440

This entry reduces the beginning inventory of $2,000, which had remained unchanged throughout the year, to $1,560, the correct amount of deferred cost. This adjustment is consistent with the procedures used in Chapter 3 where the adjustment to CD for the ΔDE is used to compute the expense:

$$E = CD + \Delta AE - \Delta DE$$
$$= \$7,200 + 0 - (\$1,560 - \$2,000)$$
$$= \$7,200 - (-\$440)$$
$$= \$7,640$$

Figure 12–1: Comparison of Periodic and Perpetual Method for Inventory

PERPETUAL

Merchandise Inventory

Balance 400 units @ $5.00	$2,000	1/5 200 @ $5	$1,000	
1/10 800 units @ 5.10	4,080	1/11 200 @ 5	1,000	
1/20 600 units @ 5.20	3,120	3/18 500 @ 5.10	2,550	
		1/22 300 @ 5.10	1,530	
		1/22 300 @ 5.20	1,560	
		Balance	$1,560	
	$9,200		$9,200	

1/31 Balance 300 units @ $5.20 $1,560

Cost of Goods Sold

1/5 200 @ $5.00	$1,000
1/11 200 @ 5.00	1,000
1/18 500 @ 5.10	2,550
1/22 300 @ 5.10	1,530
1/22 300 @ 5.20	1,560
	7,640

PERIODIC

Merchandise Inventory

Balance 400 units @ $5.00	$2,000	1/31 1500 units	$7,640	
1/10 800 units @ 5.10	4,080			
1/20 600 units @ 5.20	3,120			
		Balance 300 @ $5.20	1,560	
	$9,200		$9,200	

1/21 Balance 300 units @ $5.20 $1,560

Cost of Goods Sold

1/31 1500 units	$7,640

Many businesses maintain a subsidiary ledger for inventory. A control account in the general ledger is supported by the subsidiary ledger which includes an account for each inventory item. In some cases the subsidiary records for inventory show the physical count by unit only and do not include a unit cost or any other monetary information. The dollar amounts for inventory in such cases are shown in the general ledger inventory control account only. This method, in effect, uses the perpetual system for control of quantity and the periodic system for cost allocation.

Costing Methods

Figure 12-2 shows graphically how inventory moves through a business. The inventory brought forward from the previous accounting period (DE_0) and the purchases for the current period ($CD + \Delta AE$) are available for use or sale in the current period. Of the goods available only a part is used or sold during the period (E); the balance is available for use or sale in following periods. As mentioned earlier, the accounting problem is to allocate the acquisition cost between the inventory available for future use and the expense of the current period.

Figure 12-2: Inventory Flow

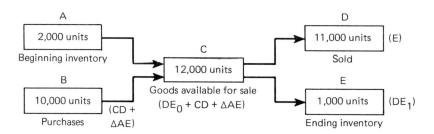

The measurement or allocation problem is aggravated by the fact that the prices paid for inventory fluctuate constantly. Each of the batches acquired in Fig. 12-1 was acquired at a different price. To allocate the cost between the expense account and the inventory account, the accountant must decide which unit cost should be applied to the quantity on hand and which unit cost to the quantity sold. Any one of several commonly used techniques may be employed to solve the problem. Of these techniques, known as inventory costing methods, the more commonly used ones are

1   Weighted average
2   First-in, first-out (FIFO)
3   Last-in, first-out (LIFO)
4   Specific identification

These methods are examined and illustrated in the following sections.

WEIGHTED–AVERAGE METHOD. By this method, the cost price used to value each unit in the ending inventory is the weighted average of all goods available for sale or use. For example, assume that the owner of a sporting goods store is trying to arrive at the inventory value of 28 golf bags (style #14) which he has on hand at year-end. At the first of the year he had 20 style #14 bags on hand, and he had valued them at $18 each in the ending inventory last year. During the year he made three purchases of style #14:

Date	No. of bags	Unit cost
February 10	25	$19
June 15	40	21
August 2	15	22
	80	

At the end of the present year, a physical count shows 28 bags on hand, which means that of the 100 bags available for sale (20 in the beginning inventory plus 80 purchased), 72 were sold. The weighted-average calculation is as follows:

Item	No. of units	Unit cost	Total cost
Beginning inventory	20	$18	$ 360
February purchase	25	19	475
June purchase	40	21	840
August purchase	15	22	330
	100		$2,005

Weighted-average price per unit: $\dfrac{\$2,005}{100 \text{ units}} = \$20.05$

Using this unit value, the allocation of cost between inventory, a cost deferral, and the expense, cost of the goods sold, is

Cost of goods sold (E)	72 @ $20.05	$1,443.60
Inventory (DE)	28 @ 20.05	561.40
Total cost of available units		$2,005.00

FIRST-IN, FIRST-OUT (FIFO). The arithmetic required for a weighted-average calculation is time consuming. Think of the clerical time required if the business handles several thousand different commodities. In addition, use of averages runs counter to good merchandise management. In mercantile concerns, the older items are sold first to minimize the loss through natural deterioration and handling by customers. The FIFO method, therefore, assumes that the oldest goods are sold first and that the inventory contains the most recent purchases and should be valued at the most recent prices. Using the same facts as in the foregoing example, the total costs would be allocated as follows under the FIFO method:

Item	Cost of Goods Sold (E)			Inventory (DE)		
	No. of Units	Unit cost	Total	No. of Units	Unit cost	Total
Beginning inventory	20	$18	$ 360			
February purchase	25	19	475			
June purchase	27	21	567	13	$21	$273
August purchase				15	22	330
	72		$1,402	28		$603

Total cost of goods available: $1,402 + $603 = $2,005

Consistent with the FIFO assumption the first goods acquired are considered sold first and their costs are therefore included in the cost of sales. Inventory is valued at the most recent costs.

LAST-IN, FIRST-OUT (LIFO). An assumption of cost flow exactly contrary to the FIFO assumption has been widely used during the inflationary period since World War II. According to this method, LIFO, the most recent costs are assigned to expense and the oldest costs (including those in the beginning inventory) are used for inventory valuation. Using the same facts again, the allocation between cost of sales and inventory under the LIFO method is

Item	Cost of Goods Sold (E)			Inventory (DE)		
	No. of Units	Unit cost	Total	No. of Units	Unit cost	Total
Beginning inventory				20	$18	$360
February purchase	17	$19	$ 323	8	19	152
June purchase	40	21	840			
August purchase	15	22	330			
	72		$1,493	28		$512

Total cost of goods available: $1,493 + $512 = $2,005

SPECIFIC IDENTIFICATION. This method cannot be used unless the actual cost of each inventory item can be specifically identified. When items are acquired in lots one must determine the cost of each lot and must also identify each inventory item with the lot to which it belonged at the time of acquisition. Assume in this example that the items in the inventory can be identified as follows:

February purchase	10 @ $19	$ 190
June purchase	12 @ $21	252
August purchase	6 @ $22	132
Total cost of inventory (DE_i)		$ 574
Cost of goods sold (E)		1,431
Cost of goods available		$2,005

This method is used only in cases where the inventory items can be easily identified. Each item usually has either a serial number or a high value, or both.

Automobile dealers find it convenient to use specific identification. A jewelry store might also use specific identification for high priced items. Grocery, hardware, or department stores, on the other hand, could not use specific identification as record-keeping costs would be prohibitive. Because of its limited use, in the next subsection, specific identification will not be compared with the three more common methods.

COMPARISON OF METHODS. To compare the effects of the various methods on income, assume that the owner got $30 each for all bags sold in the preceding example and that he did not change his sales price despite the increased costs. Considering this product alone, his revenue was $2,160. His gross profit on this item, under each of the three methods would be as follows:

	Weighted average	FIFO	LIFO
Sales revenue (R)	$2,160.00	$2,160.00	$2,160.00
Cost of goods sold (E)	1,443.60	1,402.00	1,493.00
Gross profit	$ 716.40	$ 758.00	$ 667.00
Inventory value on balance sheet (DE$_1$)	$ 561.40	$ 603.00	$ 512.00

The differences are substantial. Consider the total effect when all the items in the inventory, not just a single item, are taken together. The difference between FIFO and LIFO might be enough to turn net income into a net loss.

Of the three methods, LIFO gives the lowest inventory values, the highest cost of goods sold, and therefore the lowest net income during a period of rising prices. Prices have been rising steadily since the late 1940s when LIFO was first permitted as an acceptable costing method for most taxpayers. Following the acceptance of the method for tax purposes, many businesses began using it for both tax purposes and financial statements. The Internal Revenue Service permits use of LIFO for tax purposes only if the method is also used for financial reporting. Even if an alternate method was permitted by the IRS, the costs of valuing inventory under two methods would be prohibitive for many businesses.

In support of LIFO one can argue that in matching costs with revenue, the costs used should be the most recent costs. Net income is used to predict future operations; thus the most recent costs are the best indicators of future costs. Although this argument may have merit, the fact that LIFO was first adopted into our tax laws and resulted in lower taxes as prices increased is the primary reason for the widespread use of the method.

The most regrettable effect of the use of the LIFO method is the significant understatement of inventory values on balance sheets of many large corporations. If a company has used LIFO since the early 1950s, some of the inventory values that appear on its balance sheet will be 1950 prices. Thus, inventory amounts on the balance sheet may have little relationship to the present fair value of products.

Finally, when a LIFO cost-flow assumption is combined with the perpetual method, a significantly different inventory valuation may result. Refer to the original information concerning golf bags on p. 307. Under the perpetual method for sales made before February 10, the first purchase, the most recent costs for the LIFO valuation are the costs in the beginning inventory, $18 per unit. For sales made between February 10 and June 15 the most recent cost is $19. Thus the perpetual method partially destroys the main advantage claimed for LIFO because some of the older costs are included in cost of goods sold. For this reason most businesses that adopt LIFO use the periodic method for recording the use or sale of inventories. Of course, as previously explained, it is possible to use perpetual records for physical units and allocate costs to expenses and inventory on a periodic basis.

Estimated Cost Methods

Maintaining perpetual inventory records is a costly process for businesses that handle many different products. It is also costly to take a physical inventory and to accumulate unit cost information for a large number of products. For this reason many companies use various methods to estimate inventory costs. Two methods commonly used for estimation are the gross profit method and the retail inventory method.

GROSS PROFIT METHOD. The gross profit method assumes that the rate of gross profit on an item of inventory or class of merchandise remains relatively constant throughout two accounting periods. If this is not a realistic assumption, the gross profit method should not be used. Information necessary for use of the gross profit method includes the sales revenue for the current period, the cost of goods available for sale (the beginning inventory plus the goods acquired during the current period), and the gross profit rate (percentage of gross profit to sales revenue). Cost of goods sold is determined by multiplying the gross profit rate times the revenue from sales to obtain the gross profit. This amount is then subtracted from revenue to obtain cost of sales. The difference between the goods available and the cost of sales is the estimated ending inventory. The method takes advantage of the fact that sales and cost of goods sold relate to the same set of physical items, namely, those sold to customers during the period. By converting the selling prices for these goods to the cost prices and then subtracting the latter from goods available, it is possible to estimate the inventory balance.

For example, assume the following information is available from the records of T Swimfair:

Inventory, January 1	$ 60,000
Purchases, January 1–31	140,000
Goods available for sale in January	$200,000
Sales for January	$225,000
Gross profit rate	40%

Gross profit is $90,000 (40% X $225,000)
Cost of goods sold is $135,000 ($225,000 – $90,000)
Estimated inventory is $65,000 ($200,000 – $135,000)

Figure 12–3 shows the statement of income for January for T Swimfair. If only the statement of income is prepared the estimated ending inventory does not need to be computed.

Figure 12–3

T Swimfair	Statement of Income for Month Ended January 31, 19X2	
Sales	$225,000	(100%)
Cost of goods sold	135,000	(60%)
Gross profit	$ 90,000	(40%)
General and selling expenses	67,500	(30%)
Net income	$ 22,500	(10%)

Accuracy of an estimated inventory based on the gross profit method depends on the validity of the assumption that the rate of gross profit is constant. For this reason, one should be cautious in using the method. Nonetheless, the method is very useful when the ending inventory cannot be counted because of destruction by fire, flood, or other disasters. In some situations, the method is used when it is inconvenient to make a physical count of the inventory such as when financial statements are prepared for interim periods, for example, monthly statements.

RETAIL METHOD. Large retail businesses such as department stores and discount houses have special problems relating to inventories. They may deal in several thousand commodities and the investment in inventory is often very high relative to the total capital employed in the business. Control of inventory in these businesses is the key to their success. They must have a sufficient supply of commodities on hand which customers want, yet they must avoid an oversupply of unwanted or slow-moving commodities. To maintain control, an annual inventory accounting is usually insufficient; monthly, or at least quarterly, inventory valuation is needed for good control. Yet to count the goods on hand physically each month would be very costly. To solve this problem, accountants have developed a method of estimating the inventory values, known as the retail method.

As merchandise is received in a department of a store, a record is maintained of acquisition cost (net invoice price and freight). When the merchandise is received it is *marked up*; that is, the retail price is recorded on the merchandise, usually on a tag or sticker. A record is also maintained showing the retail price of all merchandise entering the department. Finally, a record is kept of the sales made in the department at retail price—the sum of all cash and credit sales. Given this information the retail price of the inventory can be determined by subtracting the sales (at retail price) from the retail price of the goods available. This inventory at retail price can then be converted to an approximation of cost by multiplying the inventory at retail price by the ratio of the cost of goods available over the retail price of the goods available.

As an example, the records for Department A in a department store show the following for June, 19X1:

Inventory June 1 at cost	$15,000
Inventory June 1 at retail price	22,000
Purchases in June at cost	21,000
Purchases in June at retail price	32,000
Sales during June at retail price	36,000

The information is usually arranged in the following manner to facilitate computation of the cost of the ending inventory:

	Cost	Retail price
Inventory June 1	$15,000	$22,000
Purchases in June	21,000	32,000
Goods available for sale in June	$36,000	$54,000
Less: Sales at retail during June		36,000
Inventory June 30 at retail		$18,000
Estimated cost at June 30	$\dfrac{\$36,000}{\$54,000} \times \$18,000 =$	$12,000

This estimation of the cost of ending inventory can now be used in the normal manner to compute the cost of goods sold and the income of Department A for June.

Estimates of cost determined by the retail method are usually checked at least once each year by a physical count of goods on hand. Inventory teams may move from department to department throughout the year making physical counts which can be used to verify the accuracy of the estimates made with the retail method. The physical inventory is valued at retail and reduced to cost by the foregoing procedure.

Frequently firms will reduce their prices for special sales or just to encourage the movement of merchandise. These reductions are called *markdowns*. When markdowns occur a record of all markdowns is accumulated. The total markdowns are subtracted from total retail sales. However, the rate is still computed by dividing the cost of goods available by the total retail sales value before subtracting the markdowns. Cost is thus a smaller percentage of retail value than it would be if markdowns were subtracted in calculating retail. The procedure results in a conservative valuation of the inventory which approximates the lower of cost or market value for the ending inventory because the reduction in the cost percentage is directly related to the decrease in selling prices, the markdowns. In the previous example, had a $3,000 markdown occurred in Department A in June the ending inventory would have been computed as follows:

	Cost	Retail
Goods available, June	$36,000	$54,000
Less: Markdowns		3,000
		$51,000
Sales at retail		36,000
		$15,000
Inventory June 30	$\dfrac{\$36,000}{\$54,000}$ X $15,000 =	$10,000

Cost or Market Valuation

The valuation of inventory is generally based on acquisition cost determined by one of the costing methods discussed in the foregoing. A departure from cost is required whenever the expected proceeds from the disposal of the goods is less than their acquisition cost. The decline in the expected sales value below acquisition may be a result of damage in handling or storage, deterioration, obsolescence, or a general decline in demand resulting in a falling sales price. Usually, a decline in sales value will cause a decline in the replacement cost of the item. This type of departure from cost is known as the *lower of cost or market* (LCM) rule. The application of the rule requires an understanding of what is meant by "market."

A business entity deals with at least two markets: The market in which it sells its products, the *sales* market or *exit market*; and the market in which it buys its goods and services, the *replacement* market or *entry market*. The normal expectation is that the prices in the sales or exit market will be higher than the prices in the replacement or entry market. The customers of the business entity usually do not have access to the entity replacement or entry market. For example, a new car dealer purchases new cars from the manufacturer for less than his expected sales price. The dealer's customers cannot buy directly from the manufacturer.

The term market as used in the LCM rule may be either the acquisition price necessary to replace the good or service in the normal course of operation or expected net proceeds from a sale of the good or service in sales or exit market. The *expected net proceeds* are defined as sales price less all costs necessary to sell the item. The value determined from the sales or exit market is called *net realizable value*. Both replacement cost and net realizable value can be the market value of the LCM rule.

Generally, market value is replacement cost. However, there are two restrictions on the use of replacement cost. Market value should not be more than the expected disposal value less the direct costs of disposals. The direct costs of disposal include all direct costs necessary to complete and sell the item. This restriction is reasonable. The value of an inventory item deferred to a future period should not be more than you expect to realize from its sale. This limit is called the *ceiling* of market value.

For example, assume that a ladies' ready-to-wear store has a dress in stock that cost $35 and normally sells for $50. The current replacement cost of the dress is $30; the store manager believes he can sell the dress for $25. The direct cost of selling is a 10 percent sales commission. The realizable value is $22.50 ($25 – $2.50). Because the realizable value ($22.50) is less than replacement cost ($30), the inventory value of the dress is $22.50.

The second restriction on the use of replacement cost, called *floor* is that the inventory value should not be below disposal value less direct costs of completion and sales and less the normal profit of the entity. Again, this is a reasonable restriction. If the replacement cost is used as market value and it is less than realizable value minus normal profit, it would increase expenses for the current period but reduce expenses in the next period resulting in a transfer of profit from the current period to the future period.

For example, assume that an electronics dealer has a cassette player in inventory that cost $52. The current replacement cost of this item is $35, and the expected sales price is $50. Assuming no additional cost of disposal and a normal profit of 20 percent or $10, the market value using the LCM rule is $40 ($50 – $10). If replacement cost of $35 is used, the income of the current period would be reduced by an amount larger than the expected loss on disposal. The actual expected loss is $2 ($52 – $50). If replacement cost is used, then the recorded loss for the current year would be $17 ($52 – $35). The $10 normal profit is transferred to the future period to avoid recognizing any profit until realized. In effect replacement cost is used only when it is between realizable value (disposal proceeds minus cost to complete and sale), the ceiling, and realizable value minus normal profit, the floor.

To value an inventory, (DE) cost, replacement market, and net realizable value should be determined. The market is computed by applying the foregoing rules. After computing market value, cost and market are compared. If market is less than cost, the inventory is valued at market. If cost is less than market, the inventory is valued at cost. The cost or market comparison may be made item by item, inventory class by inventory class, or applied to the inventory as a whole. Usually the LCM rule is applied to a class of inventory rather than item by item or to the total inventory.

To illustrate the application of these rules, assume that a company has four different commodities in its inventory and that costs are determined on a FIFO basis:

Item	FIFO cost	Market	LCM
1	$12,000	$ 10,000	$10,000
2	8,000	13,000	8,000
3	26,000	25,500	25,500
4	44,000	60,000	44,000
	$90,000	$108,500	$87,500

If totals are compared, cost is substantially lower than market. On an item by item comparison, the LCM valuation is $87,500, that is, $2,500 less than cost.

When the inventory cost is reduced to market, a valuation account may be used which is similar to the contra or valuation account for accumulated depreciation. The entry to record the lower market figure in the preceding example is

	Debit	Credit
Cost of goods sold	$2,500	
Reduction of inventory to market		$2,500

(To reduce inventory to net realizable value)

The credit balance in the valuation account is subtracted from inventory on the balance sheet or shown parenthetically as an adjustment of the deferred cost for inventory.

Financial Statement Presentation

The deferred cost for inventory affects cost of goods sold but does not normally appear on the statement of income. Cost of goods sold is typically shown as a single amount. Other account titles may be used such as cost of products sold, cost of sales, or cost and other operating expenses. The reproduced financial statements in Appendix A are typical of published financial statements.

Inventory costs are shown on the balance sheet as current assets. The following are inventory disclosure requirements recommended by the AICPA:

1   The basis of the valuation must be stated either on the balance sheet or notes to financial statements.
2   If inventories are pledged to secure outstanding obligations, full disclosure of conditions is to be made. (See Note 2, financial statements of Green Giant Company and Subsidiaries, Appendix D, p. 516.)
3   Value of major categories of inventories, such as finished goods, work in process, and raw materials should be disclosed. (See the consolidated balance sheet for Indian Head, Inc., and Subsidiaries, Appendix D, p. 484.)
4   If inventory methods, such as LIFO, that provide values materially different from replacement value are used, then replacement value should be disclosed. (See Note B, notes to financial statements of Gould, Inc., and Consolidated Subsidiaries, Appendix D, p. 500.)
5   The effect of changes in the method of valuing inventory from the method used in preceding years should be disclosed as required by APB Opinion No. 20.*

Inventory transactions are disclosed in the statement of changes in financial position if the cash approach is used. The increase in inventories is a use of cash; a decrease in inventory is a source of cash. The Statement of Changes in Financial Position for Gould, Inc., and Singer illustrate how two companies show these changes. It is permissible and probably preferable to show changes in inventories as part of funds provided or used by operations.

*American Institute of Certified Public Accounts, *Opinion of the Accounting Principles Board No. 20* (July 1971).

If the working capital approach is used, changes in deferred expenses classified as inventory do not appear on the statement of changes in financial position
because inventory is a part of working capital. Changes in inventory do appear
on the schedule of changes in working capital. The Statement of Changes in
Financial Position and Supporting Notes to Financial Statements of Indian Head,
Inc., Great Northern Nekoosa Corporation, and A. O. Smith Corporation in
Appendix D are examples of this approach.

Financial Statement Analysis

Because of the large investment which many manufacturing and mercantile firms
have in inventory, security analysts and other statement users give it a close
scrutiny. As with most ratios, those concerned with inventory must be used
with care. The following are general precautions for using inventory ratios:

1   Standards for comparison are essential.
2   Trends are more important than an absolute amount or a single ratio.
3   The inventory relationships should not be viewed in isolation but should be
    considered along with the whole family of financial ratios.

The following types of relationships are useful relative to inventories:

1   Composition relationships
2   Gross profit relationships
3   Turnover relationships

These relationships are used primarily to judge the adequacy of control over the
amount invested in inventory and to give some indication of profit stability.
Overinvestment can result in losses due to obsolescence and to excessive costs
for interest, insurance, storage, and handling. Underinvestment can mean lost
sales, excessive freight charges, and possibly unfavorable purchase prices.

COMPOSITION RELATIONSHIPS. The ratio of inventory to working capital
or inventory to current assets should be considered along with other ratios to
make judgments about a firm's liquidity. If there is a substantial difference between the current ratio and the acid test ratio, the relationship of inventory to
working capital or inventory to current assets will indicate to what extent the
investment in inventory is the cause of the difference. Given appropriate standards for comparison, a ratio of inventory to total assets may indicate whether
the business has an appropriate amount invested in inventory.

GROSS PROFIT RELATIONSHIPS. The gross profit or margin a firm earns on
its inventory may be determined by either of two relationships: cost of goods
sold to sales or gross profit to sales. One ratio is the reciprocal of the other.
Gross profit, the margin on inventory sold, is an extremely important indicator
of profitability for most wholesale and retail firms and interested parties closely
observe trends in gross profit.

TURNOVER. The ratio of cost of goods sold to the average merchandise inventory cost is referred to as the inventory turnover ratio. If sales are four times the average inventory, the business has sold its inventory, or turned it over, four times during the year.

Turnover is the most frequently used inventory relationship. With appropriate standards for comparison, it is considered the best single index of the amount invested in merchandise inventory. If the ratio is too high, the firm has probably an underinvestment in inventory; if it is too low, the firm has overinvested in inventory. The appropriate range for inventory turnover varies by industry and by firm size so standards for comparison must be carefully chosen.

The ratio of sales to average inventory is sometimes used as a substitute for the turnover ratio. This ratio is affected by changes in markup as well as changes in turnover velocity. If margin is reasonably stable and appropriate standards for comparison are used, sales to average inventory is an acceptable way to measure turnover.

A CAVEAT. A comparison of financial statements of two or more companies in the same industry may be distorted if the companies use different inventory costing methods. The composition relationship, gross profit relationship, and turnover relationship are all affected by the costing method used if prices are fluctuating, as is normally the case. Before making a financial analysis it is advisable to convert inventory value to a value using a common costing method. As pointed out previously, companies should disclose replacement cost if the costing method used is materially different from replacement value.

QUESTIONS

1   One of the basic problems of accounting is the allocation of costs between services consumed and services available for use in future periods. What factors make the allocation of the cost of merchandise different?
2   What is the difference between the periodic inventory method and the perpetual inventory methods?
3   Distinguish short-lived services from long-lived services.
4   Define the following terms:
    [a]   f.o.b.
    [b]   f.o.b. shipping point
    [c]   f.o.b. destination
    [d]   Consignment
5   How are inventories valued?
6   Describe each of the following methods of inventory costing:
    [a]   Weighted average
    [b]   First-in, first-out (FIFO)
    [c]   Specific identification
    [d]   Last-in, first-out (LIFO)
7   Which inventory costing method would show the lowest income in a period of declining prices?

8   Describe two methods of estimating the allocation of costs between deferred costs (inventories) and cost of goods sold.

9   Why do accountants use the lower of cost or market value?

10   Describe the following ratios and indicate how they are used in the analysis of financial statements:

[a]   Gross profit ratios   [c]   Inventories to current assets

[b]   Inventory turnover   [d]   Inventories to total assets

11   Why do firms that use the LIFO method of costing inventories generally use the periodic inventory method?

PROBLEMS

1   The D Company uses the periodic inventory method. During 19X1, transactions in one commodity in the inventory of D Company were as follows:

Item	No. of Units	Unit cost
Beginning inventory	30	$12.00
March purchase	15	14.00
July purchase	45	15.00
October purchase	20	17.00

During 19X1, D Company sold 68 units of this commodity. Based on this information,

[a]   Compute the cost of goods sold and the ending inventory values using the weighted-average method.

[b]   Compute the cost of goods sold and the ending inventory values using the FIFO method.

[c]   Compute the cost of goods sold and the ending inventory values using the LIFO method.

[d]   Prepare the adjusting entry required for each of the three methods, assuming that all acquisition costs are recorded in the costs of goods sold account. The inventory account, which shows the beginning inventory, has not been changed during the period.

2   L Tradefair uses a calendar month as an accounting period. During the month of July, L Tradefair had the following transactions:

July 1   Beginning inventory was $5,000.

July 3   Received an invoice from T & Son for $5,000 merchandise purchased on terms 2/10, n/30.

July 5   Returned $500 worth of goods purchased on the invoice received July 3.

July 7   Paid the invoice of July 3 after deducting $500 for the merchandise returned on July 5.

July 20   Received an invoice from T & Son for $4,000. Merchandise purchased on terms 2/10, n/30.

July 25   Took an allowance of $100, per agreement over the telephone, for damaged goods received in the shipment relating to the invoice received on July 20 and paid the remainder of the amount due in cash.

July 30   Paid $600 freight charges for the month of July.

July 31   Took a physical inventory and determined that inventory on hand cost $2,000.

Required:

Assuming that L Tradefair uses two accounts, merchandise inventory and freight-in, to record inventory acquisitions, prepare the entry to adjust the inventory balance and record cost of goods sold during the month of July.

3   The X Company uses the LCM rule to value inventories. The comparison between cost (determined under the FIFO method) and market value is made on an item-by-item basis. The company uses the perpetual method of accounting for inventories. At the end of 19X1, the following information is available concerning the three commodities sold by the company:

Item	FIFO cost	Realizable value	Replacement cost
1	$402,000	$660,000	$420,000
2	55,500	75,500	55,500
3	210,000	203,500	220,000
	$667,500	$939,000	$695,500

[a]   Prepare an entry to record the LCM valuation.

[b]   Ignoring all other transactions, calculate the gross profit that would be realized in 19X2 if all inventory items are sold in 19X2, assuming that sales are made at the realizable value:

    [i]   Using FIFO cost

    [ii]   Using LCM

[c]   Speculate about why a mercantile concern might choose to adopt LCM rule of valuation on an item-by-item comparison.

4   The cost of the merchandise inventory at the close of the first fiscal year of operations, according to three different methods is as follows:

FIFO, $38,000

LIFO, $33,000

Average, $36,000

If the average-cost method is used, the net income is $18,000.

Required:

[a]   What is the amount of net income if the FIFO method is used?

[b]   What is the amount of net income if LIFO is adopted?

[c]   Of the three methods, which is best for tax purposes?

5   The inventory of the G Nursery was destroyed by fire in October of 19X3. Fortunately, the records of the company were saved. These records revealed the following facts:

	19X1	19X2	To date of fire in 19X3
Sales	$160,000	$200,000	$180,000
Cost of goods sold	128,000	152,800	
Gross profit	$ 32,000	$ 47,200	
Goods available for sale in 19X3 at cost			$163,000

The insurance adjustor has agreed to use the average gross profit percentage of 19X1 and 19X2 to determine the amount of loss from fire.

Required:

[a]   Prepare a schedule to show the estimated inventory value at the date of the fire.

[b]   Explain how the gross profit method might be used for purposes other than to estimate the cost of inventory destroyed by fire.

6 The R Brothers Department Store uses the retail inventory method. The relevant records of the company for 19X2 are as follows:

	Cost	Retail value
Inventory 12/31/19X2	$ 29,000	$ 43,000
Merchandise purchases in 19X2	96,200	144,800
	$125,200	$187,800
Markdowns in 19X2		$ 3,756
Sales in 19X2		130,044

Required:

[a] Compute the inventory using the retail inventory method.

[b] Does the use of the retail inventory method facilitate the costing of the ending inventory when a physical inventory is taken? Why?

7 The G Company had the following transactions dealing with the acquisition and use of merchandise:

July 1 Beginning inventory was 50 units @ $30.
July 10 Sold 30 units @ $40.
July 19 Purchased 40 units @ $31.
July 27 Sold 35 units @ $40.

Required:

[a] Assuming that the G Company uses a perpetual inventory, compute the inventory according to (i) the FIFO method and (ii) the LIFO method.

[b] Assuming that the G Company uses a periodic inventory, compute the inventory according to (i) the FIFO method and (ii) the LIFO method.

[c] Compare the inventory and cost of goods sold values for parts [a] and [b].

8 Sam Wilson prepared the following statement of income for the accounts of the M Hardware Company. Income for the prior year, 19X1, was $273,000. The corporation is not subject to income taxes because of an operating loss carried forward from earlier years.

M Hardware Company, Statement of Income for the Year Ended December 31, 19X2

Sales	$2,800,000
Cost of goods sold	2,100,000
Gross profit on sale	$ 700,000
Selling and general expenses	406,000
Net income	$ 394,000

For the first time, an auditor was engaged late in 19X2 to perform an audit of the company's records. The auditor discovered the following facts:

[1] Merchandise costing $16,000, purchased in 19X2 f.o.b. shipping point, was in transit on December 31, and was received January 5, 19X3. Mr. Wilson did not consider the purchase in any way in 19X2.

[2] Merchandise purchased f.o.b. shipping point and costing $14,000 was in transit on December 31, 19X1. This purchase was recognized in 19X2.

[3] Merchandise on consignment from R Incorporated, valued at $6,000, was inadvertently included in inventory for 19X2. Mr. Wilson had accounted for this inventory correctly otherwise.

[4]   Merchandise costing $7,500 was sold to the J Construction Company in 19X2 but it was stored for J Construction in the M Hardware warehouse. This merchandise was included in inventory on December 31, 19X2.

Required:

[a]   Compute the corrected net income for 19X1 and 19X2.
[b]   What effect will the corrections in part [a] have on the balance sheet at December 31, 19X2.
[c]   Prepare journal entries necessary to correct the accounts at December 31, 19X2.

CASE   The D Company is a small machine shop that makes tools and dies and performs other contract work for large manufacturing companies located nearby. All of the output of the D Company is specialty work made to customer's specifications. Customers usually come to the D Company in emergency situations. They need quick, high-quality service and they are willing to pay for it. Usually, the prices that customers pay to the D Company are minor relative to their operations taken as a whole, and most customers know that the D Company must maintain both a skilled workforce and a substantial inventory of parts and top grade metals in various forms to provide the kind of service expected. Thus, the D Company covers the costs of a heavy investment in inventory by earning a high gross margin on its output.

Late in 19X2, some of D Company's suppliers went on strike, and the D Company was forced to deplete its inventories way below normal levels in order to continue serving its customers. The items used out of the inventory were carried at a value of $75,000, but the D Company paid $175,000 to replace these items when they became available early in 19X3. The large difference exists because the inventory items were valued on a LIFO basis using prices that were paid ten years ago.

The D Company uses LIFO for tax purposes and therefore has to use it for financial reporting. The company uses the calendar year for preparing both tax returns and published financial statements. The president of the D Company is not an accounting expert, but he knows enough about accounting to be worried about the use of the old LIFO layer of inventory during 19X2. He is concerned about the effect on the amount of income tax the D Company will have to pay for 19X2 and about his banker's reaction to the statement of income the president has agreed to send him.

The president of the D Company asks you to examine the facts and consult with him on the matter.

Required:

[a]   What effect, if any, will temporary depletion of the inventory have on the D Company income for 19X2?
[b]   Will there be any effect on the D Company income for 19X3?

[c]   Would there be any difference in the situation if the D Company used FIFO instead of LIFO? Explain.

[d]   Will temporary depletion of the inventory in 19X2 affect the amount of income tax that the D Company has to pay for 19X2? Is this fair?

[e]   You have learned to use a valuation account to reduce inventory to market when market is less than cost. See if you can develop an analogous procedure to normalize the effect of the temporary depletion of inventory levels on the D Company income for 19X2 and 19X3.

[f]   In the absence of special procedures such as the one you developed in part [e], draft appropriate footnotes for the D Company statements of income for 19X2 and 19X3.

13

Personnel Costs
and Prepaid
Expenses

Short-lived services can be divided into three principal types. One type, characterized by physical existence and measurable units, was considered in the previous chapter. A second type of short-lived services are those performed by people. The cost of acquiring and using human services must be recognized and matched with revenue in each accounting period. In many cases accountants find it difficult to relate human services consumed directly to a product. For this reason they are often treated as period expenses. Even though much of the effort of presidents and other executive officers in corporations is devoted to planning for future activities, executive compensation is typically recognized as an expense of the period when the cost was incurred. Personnel costs that can be related directly to productive processes are treated as product costs in the manner described in Chapter 11. Much of the record-keeping for personnel costs is handled through use of a group of procedures commonly called *payroll accounting*. Certain aspects of accounting for personnel costs are handled separately from standardized payroll procedures. Special incentive compensation for executives and pension costs are two important types of such costs.

A third type of short-lived service is one that is consumed by the passage of time or one where consumption depends on some future event. Acquisitions of insurance policies that typically provide protection for periods of from one to five years exemplify short-lived services that expire with the passage of time. A repair and maintenance contract is an example of a service whose use is contingent on a future event. Another example of a service that is consumed as time passes is a retainer fee paid to an attorney for legal services. Services of this third type are commonly called *prepaid expenses.*

Human Services

Acquisitions of the services of humans are the most important of all acquisitions for most businesses. The innovative ability of people and their willingness to work toward a common goal usually have more to do with the success of a business than any other factor.

The accounting problems associated with the acquisition of human services are concerned with the measurement of expenses (E) and accrued costs (AE). Deferred costs are not usually a problem because prepayments for human services are rare. Human services may be either product costs or period costs. Salaries and wages that can be directly traced to the production of a resalable item must be considered as deferred costs until they can be included in expenses upon sale of the product. Salaries and wages that cannot be specifically identified with a given product are period costs and are assigned to expense in the period in which they are incurred. The cost of human services includes not only cash payments to employees but also the many payroll deductions from the employees' compensation. In addition, there are many fringe benefits provided for employees; these must also be included in acquisition costs for human services. Disbursements for payroll deductions and for fringe benefits may lag behind the direct cash payment of wages to employees from 30 days to several years. Examples of fringe benefits are pensions, holiday and vacation pay, medical and life insurance, and bonuses. The more important of these will be discussed in the following sections.

The expense for human services is generally recorded in several accounts. Usually there is an account for wages, and one for each of the fringe benefits. The subdivisions of the expense for human services provides control and planning information for management but they have no effect on the measurement of income.

Payroll Taxes

The Social Security Act was passed by the federal government in 1935. Under the provisions of this act the government makes payments to retired employees, their dependents, or survivors. The wherewithal to make these payments comes from taxes collected from workers and their employers. The taxes are called by a variety of names and initials including Federal Old Age Benefits (FOAB), Federal Insurance Contributions Act (FICA), Old Age Benefits (OAB) and Social Security (SS). All the names and initials refer to a single tax. The initials FICA are used in this text.

The base for the FICA tax is some specified portion of each employee's earnings. At present (1973), everything an employee earns up to $10,800 is taxed. The rate for FICA tax is some specified percentage of the base (e.g., 5.85 percent in 1973). Current law provides for a series of changes in both the base and the rate. Moreover, the law has been changed frequently in the past and further changes are not improbable. Specific rates and bases have no import on the purposes of our discussion so, for convenience, in the examples we will assume a base of everything an employee earns up to $12,000 and a rate of 6 percent. Thus, a worker who earned $15,000 in a year would pay FICA tax of $720 (6 percent of $12,000) and his employer would also pay $720.

The Social Security Act of 1935 also created a Federal Unemployment Compensation Tax (FUT). The FUT is assessed only against employers, not workers. In its present form, the Federal Act is written so as to tax an employer at the rate of 3.2 percent* on the first $4,200 earned by each of his employees. To encourage states to enact their own unemployment legislation, the Federal Act provides for decreasing FUT to a minimum of 0.5 percent if the difference is covered by State Unemployment Compensation Tax (SUT). In other words, if a state assesses unemployment taxes of at least 2.7 percent of the first $4,200 earned by each worker, FUT is reduced to 0.5 percent. All states now have SUT rates of at least 2.7 percent. When SUT exceeds 2.7 percent, the federal rate stays at .5 percent. The law also makes it possible for employers to pay SUT rates below 2.7 percent on the basis of "experience ratings"[†] and still get a FUT rate of .5 percent.

The FICA taxes assessed against workers are not paid to the taxing authority by the worker. Instead, the employer withholds the FICA tax from a worker's earnings and pays the amount withheld to the taxing authority along with the matching amount he pays as an employer. Federal Income Tax Withheld (FIT W/H) is also deducted from an employee's earnings and paid to the taxing authority by the employer.

Other Payroll Deductions

Employers sometimes make agreements with labor unions, under what is known as a check-off system, to withhold the union dues owed to the union by employees. The employer pays amounts withheld directly to the labor union. Employers may also act as collecting agents for charities, insurance companies, and other agencies and organizations. Functioning as a collecting agent complicates payroll accounting because the employer must know how much he has collected and make an accounting to all parties concerned.

Journal Entries for Payrolls and Payroll Deductions

Business firms establish regular pay periods, for example, weekly, biweekly, or monthly. Entries to record the payroll and payroll taxes are prepared at the end of each pay period. Recognition on this basis permits the firm to capture information needed for the financial statements. If only a fraction of a pay period has passed at the time an accounting period ends, adjusting entries must be prepared to record the payroll and payroll taxes for the fractional period.

---

*A special rate of 3.28% applies to 1973. The rate returns to 3.2% after 1973.

[†]An employer who provides stable employment does not cause the state to incur costs in the form of unemployment payments to workers who are unemployed. With a favorable experience rating, SUT may fall well below 2.7 percent without causing the employer to pay more than 0.5 percent in FUT because he still gets credit for SUT of 2.7 percent for the purpose of computing FUT.

For example, assume the following facts about Z Company:

1   The company pays monthly and the total amount earned by the Z Company employees during the current month is $10,000.
2   The FICA taxes are 6 percent on the first $12,000 earned by each employee; FUT is .5 percent, and SUT is 2.7 percent on the first $4,200 earned by each employee.
3   None of the Z Company employees have earnings for the year to date in excess of $4,200 as of the end of the current month.
4   Under an agreement to a check-off system for union dues, the company is to withhold $5 for each of 20 workers and pay this $100 directly to the labor union.
5   The FIT W/H for the current month is $1,400.

Given the above facts, the following entry would be prepared to record the payroll for the current month:

	Debit	Credit
Salary and wage expense (E)	$10,000	
Accrued payroll (AE)		$7,900
FICA tax payable (AE)		600
FIT W/H payable (AE)		1,400
Union dues payable (AE)		100

The entry to accrued payroll taxes assessed against Z Company as an employer is as follows:

	Debit	Credit
FICA tax expense	$600	
FUT expense	50	
SUT expense	270	
FICA tax payable		$600
FUT payable		50
SUT payable		270

The credit balances in the liability accounts for payroll and payroll taxes are removed when the liabilities are paid. For example, payment of cash to employees eliminates the payroll accrual:

	Debit	Credit
Accrued payroll	$7,900	
Cash		$7,900

The accrual of expense is normally recorded each pay period because the liability arises prior to the actual cash payment. Of course, an accrual must also be made at the end of each accounting period to recognize the wages earned but not paid or previously accrued during the year.

Entries such as exemplified in this subsection provide information needed for the financial statements. For other purposes, more detailed subsidiary records must be maintained. Reports to governmental agencies containing a considerable amount of detail must accompany the periodic payments of the liabilities accrued. Also federal law requires employers to maintain individual earnings records for each employee showing hours worked, gross pay, deductions by category, and net pay.

Holidays, Vacations, and Interim Financial Statements

If a firm prepares annual financial statements only, paid holidays and vacation pay may be recorded as incurred. If, on the other hand, a firm wishes to prepare monthly financial statements, recording holiday and vacation pay as incurred will distort some of the measurement figures, particularly income. For example, more employees take their vacations in July than in January, yet offering paid vacations has as much to do with labor services acquired in January as in July. Firms that want to prepare monthly financial statements usually accrue one-twelfth of the annual cost of paid holidays and vacations each month. For example, if a firm expected to pay $3,000 in vacation pay for the year and wanted to prepare monthly financial statements, it would prepare the following entry for $250 (1/12 of $3,000) each month:

	Debit	Credit
Vacation pay expense	$250	
Accrued vacation pay		$250

When employees take vacations and collect cash for their vacation pay, the liability account is debited and cash is credited. The monthly accrual spreads the expense evenly over the year.

Accounting for Pension Costs

Many employers have pension plans for their employees. The plans are designed to provide the retired employees with a supplement to the income received from social security. Pension plans are usually adopted to decrease employee turnover and thus provide a better work force. There are several difficult recognition and valuation problems associated with pension plans.

The employee *earns* his pension payments during his working years, that is, many years before he receives the actual payments. The employer must recognize the cost of the plan as an expense, therefore, during the accounting periods when employees earn the future pension payments. The general form of the entry to accrue the pension expense for a period is as follows:

	Debit	Credit
Pension expense	$xx	
Accrued pension liability		$xx

The expense may be either a period or a product cost, depending on the nature of the services performed by the employee. The difficult problem is determination of the amount of expense which should be recognized each year.

The accounting rule for valuation is to equate the value of services acquired to the cash or cash-equivalent value given as consideration. In the case of pensions, the delay between the acquisition and payment for the service is unusually long. Because of this time lag, the time value of money must be considered. Unfortunately this is only the beginning of the complications. When the desired point of recognition occurs, the accountant does not know how much cash will eventually be spent or when it will be spent. Some employees may sever their relationship with the company before they earn the right to pension benefits. Employees who earn pensions may collect them for varying periods of time, depending on the time of their death and the provisions of the pension plan. Estimates of the amounts and the timing of the payments must be based on actuarial estimates, and different actuaries use different approaches and come up with different answers.

Another complication arises from funding arrangements used to accumulate the money to make pension payments. *Funding* is the practice of creating a separate fund for pensions or placing the funds in the hands of a trustee. Pensions may be fully funded (money to cover all of the estimated costs incurred is set aside), partially funded, or not funded at all. Funds set aside are invested and there is no way to know exactly how much these investments will earn or lose between the time of the investment and the time pension benefits are paid.

The problem is further complicated by what are called *past service costs* and *prior service costs*. Past service costs relate to the pension benefits earned by employees for labor services supplied before a pension plan is adopted. A company might assume that past labor services actually cost more than the amount recognized before the plan is adopted. With this assumption, an adjustment must be made to retained earnings to record the understatements of labor expense in the past. On the other hand, the entity may reason that past service costs were incurred to get present and future labor services. With this assumption, the expense for past services is recognized over the remaining working lives of the workers involved. Prior service costs occur when the original pension agreement is altered so that benefits and the requirements for earning the benefits are changed. The differential between new benefits and original benefits, prior service costs, presents an array of problems identical to those presented by past service costs.

Accountants have generally concluded that past service costs and prior service costs are costs to secure present and future services. These costs are therefore recognized in the current and future periods.

The position taken by APB Opinion No. 8* is that pension or retirement programs will be continued in the future and current costs of future payments should be recognized annually regardless of whether the plan is funded or not. Opinion No. 8 specifies the accounting for pension costs and requires the use of actuarial methods to calculate the current expenses of pensions.

*American Institute of Certified Public Accountants, *Opinion of the Accounting Principles Board No. 8* (November 1966).

Use of Corporate Stocks for Executive Compensation

The federal income tax rates on compensation can be as high as 50 percent. An unmarried corporate executive who is currently earning $100,000 per year gets very little benefit from a pay raise. If his compensation is increased to $150,000, as much as 50 percent of the increase may be paid to the federal government as income tax.* Because of these high rates on compensation, various schemes have been devised to pay executives of large corporations in some way that reduces the tax bite. Most schemes have failed because of careful scrutiny by the IRS. The income tax law does provide for one method, the qualified stock option, which is used widely to compensate executives.

The plan works as follows: The executive is granted an option to acquire stock of the employer corporation. To "qualify" for special tax treatment, the option price, which is the amount the executive must pay the corporation for its stock, must be substantially equal to the fair market value at the date of the grant. Under the tax rules, the executive has five years in which to exercise his option and buy the stock. If the stock's price increases, and the executive has an incentive to see that it does, he may pay much less than the market value for the stock when he exercises his option. For example, an executive may be granted an option to acquire 1,000 shares at a price of $50. Assume that he exercises the option four years later when the stock is worth $80 per share. The executive has an immediate gain or income of $30 per share ($80 value less the $50 cash price), amounting to a total income of $30,000 for the 1,000 shares. The income is not subject to income tax. Generally, if he holds the stock for three years and then sells it for $95, his gain of $45 per share ($95 sales price less $50 cost) must be recognized and included in his income. This gain, however, is a capital gain and receives preferential treatment for income tax purposes; the maximum tax rate on the gain is 35%, not the 50% which applies to compensation or 70% that applies to income from other sources.

From the corporation's point of view, the executive has been compensated. The option presumably motivated him to work hard and he does have an increase in his wealth. The questions to be answered are "What amount should be recognized as an expense?" and "In what period or periods, should the expense be recognized?" In October, 1972, the APB issued Opinion No. 25[†] specifying the techniques for measurement of expense to the corporation and the timing of recognition of the measured amount.

Opinion No. 25 distinguishes between compensatory and noncompensatory stock options and stock purchase plans. A plan is noncompensatory if (1) it is available to substantially all employees, (2) stock is offered based on uniform percentage of salaries and wages, (3) the exercise period is reasonably limited

*The maximum tax rate on earned income is 50 percent but if an executive has income from other sources, a part of his income may be taxed at a 70 percent rate.
†American Institute of Certified Public Accountants, *Opinion of the Accounting Principles Board No. 25* (October 1972).

(usually five years or less), and (4) the discount from market is no greater than normal in regular sales to stockholders. If a plan fails to meet the above rules, it will be considered a **compensatory plan**. The recognition of measurable compensation as an expense by the corporation is required for a compensatory plan. The expense will be recognized in the periods in which the services were received. Compensation is measured by the difference between the market price on the measurement date and the amount the employee is required to pay. If market price is unavailable, the best estimate of market value should be used.

The measurement date is the date when the option price and the number of shares of stock to be issued are known. In many plans the measurement date will be the date of grant. In those cases where the price of the stock to the employee is the market value at the date of the grant, the amount of compensation measured by the stock option will be zero. For executive stock options that qualify for special income advantages, equality of the option price and fair market value is essential. Thus in these situations, the corporation will record no compensation.

In plans where the measurement date is not determinable for a number of years, the amount of compensation is estimated and accrued for the interim period. The amount of the interim accrual will be based on the situation at the time of the accrual. Because of the many uncertainties, adjustments of these interim accruals may be necessary.

If there is a timing difference for the recognition of compensation expense for tax purposes, appropriate income tax allocation is to be made. Tax allocation provisions were discussed in Chapter 11.

The measurement techniques and procedures specified in APB Opinion No. 25 are complex and beyond the scope of this text. The student should be aware of this difficult measurement problem and that a solution is possible. Currently, (1973) an accounting research study is in process that may suggest improvements in current measurement and recognition rules.

Personnel Costs and Limitations of Accounting

The foregoing discussion of qualified stock option plans is only one of a number of factors that leave many accountants dissatisfied with their present capabilities in accounting for human services. A few years ago a family-owned company that manufactured pleasure boats was purchased by a larger firm. The tangible assets of the family-owned company were appraised at 19 million dollars, that is, current fair value not the adjusted cost figures in the accounting records. Yet the larger company paid 40 million dollars for the family-owned company. The larger company indicated that they were paying 21 million dollars in excess of the fair value of the tangible assets to get the trained work force of the other company. Demand for boats was high at the time and the larger company did not have enough skilled labor to produce all the boats they could sell and at the same time maintain the quality of their products. In cases like the one described, the excess payment is usually assigned to **goodwill**. Yet, a significant limitation of accounting becomes very obvious when one considers the value of assets that did not appear in the financial statements of the family-owned company prior to the time the family sold it.

Undoubtedly there are many business firms with valuable human assets that are ignored in financial statements. However, before judging accountants harshly, one should consider some of the problems accountants must face in any attempt to account for these assets. First of all, unless employees are under contract, and very few are, they are free to leave a business whenever they choose to do so. Moreover, for good reasons, accountants adhere to valuation at cost until products are sold to customers and the three criteria for revenue recognition are satisfied as discussed in Chapter 10. In many cases a significant part of the value of human assets comes to a business cost free in the form of inherent abilities or educational training paid for by society. To recognize an increment in value at the time of acquisition would violate general rules that are important for other facets of the accounting process.

Even when a company does attempt to enhance the value of its human resources by spending cash for training, familiarization, organization, and morale building, it would be difficult to decide which of these costs were successful in achieving the intended purpose and which were unsuccessful. If one could decide which of these costs achieved their intended purpose, there remains the problem of deciding which accounting periods benefit from the costs and to what extent. Morale can disappear completely on the basis of a single incident, and employees can terminate their employment on short notice. In view of all these factors, it is not surprising that most personnel costs are treated as period expenses during the period in which they are incurred.

A number of researchers are busy trying to develop accounting techniques and measuring methods to overcome the barriers to better accounting for human services. The authors do not believe that many improvements will be forthcoming in the near future. In the interim, accountants and people who use information generated by the accounting process must tolerate the limitations, and those limitations are severe. Accounting measurements do not include the value of the talent of management nor of the work force.

Other Short-Lived Services

The problems encountered in accounting for other short-lived assets, a number of which are commonly called *prepaid expenses*, are very similar to those for inventories and human services. The costs of supplies and insurance premiums are recognized and valued under the general rules applying to deferred costs. Electrical power and professional services are usually accounted for under the general rules for accruals. Similarly, other short-lived services present either the deferral or accrual problem.

On occasion, utility companies and professional firms, such as attorneys or accountants, require deposits or retainers. Deposits or retainers paid out are deferred until they are applied against the cost of services received or until they are refunded.

The basic concepts and rules in Chapter 11 and this chapter are valid for all types of short-lived services if applied with judgment. For that matter, they apply equally well to long-lived services discussed in Chapter 14. The only difference between prepaid expenses such as prepaid insurance and plant and equipment items is temporal, length of useful life. Buildings and machines are prepaid expenses also even though they are rarely called such.

Financial Analysis for Human and Other Short-lived Services

As short-term services are used up they become expenses classified according to the informational needs of the business that uses the services. Insurance premiums become insurance expense; labor services become wage and salary expense; office supplies become office supplies expense; etc. The ratio of each of these expense categories to sales is often computed so that trends may be studied and comparisons made with industry norms.

Pension and retirement plans and stock options and other incentive plans are complex. Details of these plans are not normally shown in the body of the financial statement but are described in notes to financial statements. To appreciate the varying nature of retirement plans and stock option plans, examine the relevant notes to the six sets of financial statements presented in Appendix D. The note headings vary from company to company but can be easily identified.

Short-lived services on hand, such as prepaid insurance, prepaid rent, materials, and supplies on hand are usually classified as current assets. Given this classification, acquisitions of short-lived services usually have no effect on working capital. Ordinarily the increase in working capital brought about by the acquisition is offset by either a decrease in cash or an increase in a current liability. Acquisition of short-lived services by giving up a noncurrent asset or incurring a noncurrent liability would increase working capital, but such transactions are extremely rare. When short-lived services are transformed into expenses, the effect on working capital is the same as the effect on income, so that, if the income figure is used as a starting point in calculating the change in working capital, then no adjustment is necessary.

When funds are defined as cash, increases in the deferrals for short-lived services result in an application of funds. When the amount of such deferred costs decrease, the decrease is a source of funds.

Classification of the deferred costs of short-lived services as current assets is a tradition of long standing in accounting. Support for this practice is based on the fact that possession of short-lived services enables a business to avoid an expenditure of working capital in the current year. Arguments opposed to the practice include the following:

1   Short-lived services are usually intended for use rather than resale.
2   If short-lived services are exchanged for monetary assets, the proceeds of the exchange will probably be substantially less than the costs of the services.
3   Most businesses replace short-lived services almost as rapidly as they are used.

The authors believe that most users of financial statements would be better served if the deferred costs for inventories and other short-term services were separated from monetary assets. Most business firms maintain a fairly constant investment in these deferred costs. The implication that the amounts invested are available for discretionary use or expenditure may leave a statement user with a mistaken impression of high liquidity.

QUESTIONS

1   What are the problems associated with accounting for human resources?
2   Describe the following payroll taxes:
     [a]   Federal Insurance Contribution Act (FICA)
     [b]   Federal Unemployment Tax (FUT)
     [c]   State Unemployment Tax (SUT)
3   Why should the costs of holidays and vacations be accrued?
4   What are past service costs and prior service costs?
5   Why is the accrual of pension costs a difficult accounting problem?
6   Why do many executives prefer to receive part of their compensation in form of qualified stock options?
7   List the main reasons accountants treat most personnel costs as expenses during the period they are incurred even though future benefits are likely to result.
8   Short-lived assets are traditionally classified as current assets. Does this practice enhance the informational content of the balance sheet? Why?
9   A corporate president receives options to purchase 1,000 shares of his company's stock. The option price and market price of the shares are equal on the date of the grant. A share-holder with a large block of stock in the company commented that this was a great way for him to eat his cake and have it too. He points out that the president will be motivated to increase the value of his shares and that this motivation is cost free to him because of the equivalence of the option price and the market price. Explain why you agree or disagree with the shareholder.

PROBLEMS

1   The R Company pays its employees monthly. The total payroll for the month of March is $11,500. Assume payroll tax rates as follows: FICA, 6 percent on the first $10,800 earned by each employee; SUT, 2.7 percent; and FUT, .5 percent on the first $4,200 earned by each employee. The employees have all pledged to give ½ of 1 percent of their pay to the community fund, and the R Company withholds this percentage each pay period. The FIT W/H for the month is $1,170.

     Required:
     Present entries to record the payroll and payroll taxes for the month of March.
2   The C Corporation adopted a pension plan on January 1, 19X1. The plan provides a pension to all employees at the retirement age of 65. The amount of the pension is determined by years of service and by the average compensations. The company has contracted with S Insurance Company to fund the plan. The past service cost of $225,000 was paid to

S Insurance Company in 19X1. The C Corporation estimated that this past service cost will benefit the company for the next ten years. Consequently, the $225,000 is to be deferred and allocated to expense over the ten-year period.

Current pension costs are to be measured at the end of each year and remitted to S Insurance Company by February 15, of the following year. The current pension costs for 19X1 were $27,000; for 19X2 the costs were $29,000.

Required:

[a]   Compute the pension expense for 19X1 and 19X2.

[b]   Prepare journal entries to record the pension expense for 19X1 and 19X2.

3   The following accounts relating to payments to employees for services appeared on the books of M Company for the year ended December 31, 19X2. All accounts are correctly stated.

	Debit	Credit
Salaries and wages	$156,000	
FICA expense	9,000	
FUT expense	500	
SUT expense	1,500	
Accrued wages payable		$3,000
FICA payable		1,000
FUT payable		500
SUT payable		0

The FICA taxes are payable monthly, FUT taxes are payable annually, and SUT taxes are payable quarterly.

[a]   What is the amount of wages in 19X2 subject to FICA taxes? Assume a 6 percent tax on employer and 6 percent on employees.

[b]   What is the amount of wages not subject to FICA taxes in 19X2?

[c]   What is the amount of wages subject to federal unemployment taxes, assuming a tax rate of .5 percent?

[d]   What is the amount of wages subject to SUT taxes assuming a tax rate of 1.5 percent?

[e]   If accrued wages were $2,500 on January 1, 19X2, what is the amount of wages paid to employees in 19X2?

4   The F Company granted its executives options to acquire 5,000 shares of stock under its qualified stock option plan. The option price was $35 per share, the market price of the stock at the date of the option grant, January 1, 19X1. The option permitted executives to purchase stock at the option price at any time in a four-year period beginning January 1, 19X2. The market price as of December 31, 19X2 was $50 per share. Options for 2,500 shares were exercised in 19X2.

Required:

Prepare pro forma journal entries to record the foregoing stock options and to record the exercise of options in 19X2.

CASE   F Professional Football, Inc., has agreed to issue a contract to P. J. Snapgood containing the following clauses:

[1]   The contract is nonrevocable and is for a term of three years.

[2] Annual cash payments will be as follows:

19X4	$15,000
19X5	20,000
19X6	25,000

[3] If P. J. Snapgood is named rookie of the year in 19X4 or named to the all-pro team or all-star teams in 19X4 or 19X5, then the cash payment shall be increased by $5,000 for each year remaining in the contract.

[4] P. J. Snapgood shall receive an option to buy 1,000 shares of stock of F Professional Football, Inc., in each of the next three years for $25 per share, current market price of the stock.

[5] F Professional Football, Inc., agrees to loan P. J. Snapgood $50,000 in each of the next five years at an interest rate of 3 percent per annum provided that Snapgood is still a member of F football team. Repayment of any loan made pursuant to this agreement shall be made at the rate of 5 percent per annum of the principal of the initial loan plus 5 percent of the principal of any additional loans made. Interest on any loans is also to be paid annually.

P. J. Snapgood was very successful in professional football and was named to the all-pro team in 19X4 and 19X5. He exercised his stock option at the end of each of the three years. He also requested and received a loan of $50,000 in each year.

Required:

[a] How should F Professional Football, Inc., record the cost of the contract with P. J. Snapgood in 19X4?

[b] Should the increased cash payment in 19X5 and 19X6 be considered an expense in 19X5 and 19X6 or should the increase be accrued as an expense in 19X4 and 19X5, the years when he was named all-pro?

[c] If the current market rate of interest is 8 percent, what expenses result from the clause permitting Snapgood to borrow $50,000 annually at 3 percent interest?

[d] What costs should be recorded because of the stock option clause? The market price of the stock at the end of 19X4 and 19X5 is $30 and $35, respectively.

[e] Should costs resulting from the stock option granted and the annual loans of $50,000 be allocated over the three-year contract period or the estimated remaining active playing life of Snapgood? Discuss.

14

Acquisition, Use, and Disposal of Long-Lived Assets: Land, Plant and Equipment, Intangibles, and Natural Resources

Long-lived services are acquired for use rather than for resale and are of benefit to a business for more than one accounting period. Long-lived services that have physical existence are known as *tangible* assets. The major classifications found on financial statements are land, buildings, equipment, and furniture and fixtures. Land acquired for the extraction of natural resources is usually subclassified under the general category land. Rights to the natural resources, such as oil rights or timber rights, however, are usually classified as *intangible* assets because the business does not own the surface rights to the land. Other intangible assets are leaseholds, leasehold improvements, patents, copyrights, trademarks, franchises, organization costs, and research and development costs. Intangible assets are assets that have no physical existence and include the right to control and use physical assets for a limited time or purpose, for example, a leasehold interest.

Problems of accounting for tangible and intangible assets are similar. The general concepts explained in Chapter 11 can be applied; but techniques of recording and classifying differ slightly. The variables of the expense equation connected with accounting for long-lived assets are deferred costs (DE) and expenses (E). Occasionally a problem arises concerning accruals (AE) and investments (DI and OI). Generally, if the deferred cost at the time of acquisition can be measured, the related accrual (A) or investment (DI or OI) can be easily determined. Accruals and investment variables are usually not affected by the allocation of the acquisition cost between expenses (E) and deferred costs (DE).

Acquisition of Long-Lived Services

Many long-lived services are acquired in exchange for cash. Recognition occurs when the service is received or when the cash is paid, whichever occurs first. The classification of long-lived assets is usually by object, that is, buildings, equipment, furniture and fixtures, etc. In larger businesses, the classification may also be a functional classification. In some cases the classification is based on the responsibility for the asset. In general the problems of the initial recognition of acquisition cost and classification of long-lived assets are minimal; the general rules apply with very few exceptions.

Valuation of Long-Lived Assets

Valuation is the most difficult problem in accounting for the acquisition of long-lived services. The general rule is that the cash or cash-equivalent cost necessary to place the asset in use is the value at acquisition. The following examples show applications of this rule:

EXAMPLE 1. The ABC Company purchases a new industrial lathe for $5,000, f.o.b. shipping point, from P Machinery Company. Credit terms are 2/10, n/30. The ABC Company pays freight of $225 to have the lathe delivered to its factory. The costs of installing the lathe are not material. The acquisition cost of the lathe would be computed as follows:

Invoice price	$5,000
Less: Cash discount	100
Net cash price	$4,900
Freight costs	225
Acquisition cost	$5,125

The acquisition cost should be $5,125 even if the cash discount is not taken. If the cash discount is not taken, the additional $100 is charged to interest or financial expenses.

EXAMPLE 2. The D-G Company purchased a new automatic steel-cutting machine from A–D Machine Tool Company for $10,000 f.o.b. destination (D–G's factory) with credit terms n/30 (net in 30 days). Because of the weight and use of this automatic machine, the D-G Company built a special foundation at a cost of $625. Direct labor costs incurred in installation were $200. The costs incurred to adjust the machine to produce parts within the necessary tolerance limits were $340. This included both labor and material used in trial runs. The acquisition cost of the automatic steel-cutting machine would be

Invoice price	$10,000
Installation ($625 + $200)	825
Precision adjustments	340
Acquisition cost	$11,165

Note that implicit interest cost for the 30-day credit terms was not considered. Technically, the present value of the invoice price at date of acquisition should have been used instead of the $10,000 invoice price. Practically, discounts for 30-day periods are usually ignored on the basis that they are not material. All costs incurred to acquire a long-lived service and to make it ready and available for use should be included in its acquisition cost. Costs incurred that are not related to the acquisition should be charged to expense for the period. For example, if the unloading crew for the D-G Company accidentally dropped the automatic steel-cutting machine causing damage of $480, then this amount should not be added to the acquisition cost because it did not improve the efficiency or the effectiveness of the machine. The damages of $480 would be a loss for the period due to negligence.

BARTER TRANSACTIONS. Frequently the acquisition of long-lived assets involves the trade-in of a used item of machinery for a new item. The general rule is that the fair value of the item given up (plus cash or assumed liabilities) are the applicable cost of the item received. The fair value of the item received may be used if it is more easily determined. (See Chapter 11 for a more detailed discussion.)

In some cases the company may issue debt contracts or common stock in exchange for long-lived assets. Both the acquisition of the long-lived asset and the investment obligation should be valued at their current market value. Face value, par value, or stated value is an arbitrary amount designated by the issuing company. Face value generally applies to bonds; par or stated value applies to capital stock issues.

The proper valuation of long-lived assets acquired by a company in exchange for its own investment securities is difficult because:

1 The fair market value of the asset received or the security issued is not readily available.
2 Frequently the parties involved are closely related and the values agreed on are not bargained prices.

For instance, assume that H. L. Williams and A. P. Williams organize a corporation. They issue all the common stock of the corporation in exchange for a tract of land in Florida. Land is a unique item, and the value of one tract may not be comparable to any other tract of land. The stock of the corporation has never been traded; therefore its value is unknown. Finally, the Williamses and the corporation are not independent parties. The valuation of the land and stock could be determined by asking an independent appraiser to value the land. It should be apparent that this valuation would be an approximate value, not a precise measurement. In this situation, the accountant normally adopts a conservative position and values the land and the stock at the original cost of the land to the Williamses.

Some Exceptions to the General Rules

In accounting, as in most other disciplines, one frequently encounters exceptions that prove the general rules. Some exceptions to the general rules for the
recognition, classification, and valuation of the acquisition of services are the
accounting treatments of some leases, research and development costs, goodwill,
and certain other intangibles.

LEASES. In our present-day economy, leases are used for two major purposes.
First, they are used to control assets for a limited period of time. This arrangement is a traditional agreement in which one party agrees to let another party
use specific property for a limited time period in exchange for a specified amount
of cash or other assets or for future cash payments. Daily car rental agreements
and apartment leases are common examples of leases.

The second use of leases is an agreement which has the economic effect of an
installment purchase of the property. Used in this way, a lease is a means of
financing an acquisition of services. This second type of lease agreement has
been very popular since World War II, particularly when firms find it difficult to
raise capital by borrowing or through the issuance of stock.

• The Controversy over Leases: A few accountants are of the opinion that all
lease agreements should be *capitalized* with the lease shown on the balance sheet
as an asset and with offsetting future payments shown as a liability. The verb
"to capitalize" is often used among accountants. It means simply that the acquisition cost of a service is recognized and recorded as an asset or deferred cost.
Costs that are *not* capitalized are expenses of the period in which they are incurred. The Accounting Principles Board concluded in APB Opinion No. 5* that
leases covering only the right to use property in exchange for future rental payments do not create an equity in the property and thus are executory contracts.
An *executory contract* is an exchange of promises where the conditions of the
contract are to be executed in the future. Accountants have traditionally waited
until at least one promise is executed before recognizing an asset or equity. Many accountants are uncomforable about waiting because the economic import of an executory contract is immediate even though the legal import is not firmly established.

The existence of executory contracts, such as leases, is relevant information
and should be disclosed through footnotes to the financial statements. The disclosure of lease agreements is required by APB Opinion Nos. 5 and 31†.

• Criteria for Recognition of Leases as Assets: The problem of accounting for
leases is to determine whether a given agreement is an operating lease or a

---

*American Institute of Certified Public Accountants, *Opinion of the Accounting Principles
Board No. 5* (September 1964).
†American Institute of Certified Public Accountants, *Opinions of the Accounting Principles
Board No. 5* (September 1964) and *No. 31* (June 1973).

disguised purchase in lease form. If the lease creates a material interest in the property for the lessee, the lease should be treated as a disguised purchase. The Accounting Principles Board concluded in APB Opinion No. 5 that if a lease is noncancellable and that if *either* of the two following conditions exists, then the lease should be considered as an installment purchase of the property.

1   The initial term of the lease is less than the useful life and the lessee has the right to renew the lease for the remaining useful life of the property at substantially less than fair rental value.

2   The lessee has the right to acquire the property at a price substantially less than the fair market value of the property during or at the termination of the lease.

If a lease is unilaterally cancellable, it is doubtful that the agreement is in fact a means of financing an asset acquisition. A careful evaluation of the terms concerning the execution of a lease is essential to obtain the facts necessary to determine whether the agreement is a lease in fact or a purchase.

● Accounting for Leases: In those cases where the lease is a lease in fact, lease payments are expenses of the period during which the rent is incurred. Assume the following facts:

1   On January 1, 19X1, the E–J Company leased a building for 20 years from C Realty.

2   The lease does not contain a renewal clause.

3   Annual rental is $3,600 payable in 12 installments at the first of every month.

4   The first and last months' payments were made at the time the lease was signed.

On January 1, 19X1, the payment for the first and last months' rent of $600 was recorded as follows:

	Debit	Credit
Rent expense	$300	
Prepaid rent	300	
Cash		$600

The payment at the beginning of each of the following months was recorded as follows:

	Debit	Credit
Rent expense	$300	
Cash		$300

At the end of the 20–year period, the rental deposit of prepaid rent would be transferred to rent expense.

In cases where a lease agreement is a means of financing the purchase of an asset, the present value of future lease payments would be computed and capitalized. An equal amount would be shown as a liability. Assume the following facts:

1 On January 1, 19X1, the E–J Company leases a new truck for a 30–month period from Big D Truck Sales.
2 The E–J Company has the option to buy the truck at the end of the 30 months for $100.
3 The monthly rental is $300 payable on the first of every month beginning February 1, 19X1.
4 The lease is noncancellable.
5 The truck has an estimated useful life to E–J Company of five years.

This agreement fits both of the criteria established by the Accounting Principles Board and should therefore be treated as an installment purchase. The acquisition cost would be computed as follows, using an interest rate of 12 percent per annum:

From Table A.4 in Appendix A, the present value of an annuity of $1 at 1% for 30 periods is 25.8077	
$25.8077 X $300 =	$7,742.31
From Table A.2, the present value of $1 at 1% discounted for 30 periods is $0.7419	
$0.7419 X $100 =	74.19
Present value of contract	$7,816.50

On January 1, 19X1 the following entry would be made when the lease is signed:

	Debit	Credit
Autos and trucks	$7,816.50	
Contract liability		$7,816.50

The monthly payment would be allocated between interest and the principal amount. The payment made on February 1 would be allocated as follows:

Interest (1% X $7,816.50)	$ 78.16
Principal ($300.00 – $78.16)	221.84
Total payment	$300.00

The March 1, 19X1 payment would be allocated as follows:

Interest [1% X $7,594.66 ($7,816.50 – $221.84)]	$ 75.95
Principal ($300.00 – $75.95)	224.05
Total payment	$300.00

The journal entry to record the March payment would be

	Debit	Credit
Interest expense	$ 75.95	
Contract liability	224.05	
Cash		$300.00

In this manner, the liability will be reduced to zero after 30 payments. The account set up as acquisition cost ($7,816.50) will be allocated to expense over the five-year useful life of the truck.

Businesses using lease agreements to acquire assets usually object to the capitalization of the cost because a large liability results. Often these same companies are not in sound financial condition and the additional liability makes their condition look even worse. Regrettably, many lease agreements that are in fact installment purchases are written so that they do not meet the criteria set out in Opinion No. 5. When this is done, the statement user must depend on the footnotes to disclose the existence of the liability.

Many accountants are dissatisfied with the current treatment of services acquired and obligations incurred by leasing agreements. The issue is unsettled and changes in the recommendations presented in Opinion Nos. 5 and 31 may be forthcoming.

RESEARCH AND DEVELOPMENT. Activities directed toward the creation and/or improvement of products and production processes are referred to as research and development. Most large corporations and many medium and small corporations have research and development programs. With our rapidly changing technology, a business must improve its products and production processes, as well as develop new products continuously just to maintain its relative position. The amount of resources allocated to research and development has increased steadily in recent years. Consequently, the problems of accounting for research and development (R & D costs) have become increasingly important. The principal problem is determining whether an R & D cost should be recognized as an expense or deferred to some future period.

• Types of Research and Development: The typical large company incurs three types of research and development costs:

1   Cost incurred for the administration and management of the R & D department.
2   Cost incurred for projects that are primarily directed toward obtaining new knowledge. These are called *pure* research projects.
3   Cost incurred on projects that are believed capable of either producing new products and/or processes or of improving existing products and/or processes. These are called *applied* research projects.

Costs of administration of the R & D department are similar to the general and administrative costs of the corporation. Most businesses will treat these costs as period costs in the year incurred. Some accountants recommend allocating these costs among the various applied and pure research projects being carried on in the same way that manufacturing overhead is allocated to goods produced, as explained in Chapter 11.

The costs of pure research projects are not expected to produce any direct benefits to the company. The company does expect the investment in pure research to benefit society in general. Only a few companies devote material sums to pure research. Because these projects are not expected to produce benefits directly, their costs are usually treated as period expenses in the year incurred.

The costs of applied research projects are expected to produce economic benefits directly. These costs should therefore be accumulated by projects and periodically each project should be evaluated. If the project has merit the costs should be deferred until the knowledge gained is put to use. The accumulated R & D costs should then be allocated to expense over the expected economic life of the product or process which was the subject of the project. If the evaluation shows that some projects will not produce future benefits, their costs should be treated as an expense of the period.

• Accounting for Research and Development: The procedures outlined fail to make it clear that it is very difficult, and often impossible, to evaluate the future benefits that will be derived from a given project. In addition, the income tax laws and the doctrine of conservatism encourage the immediate write-off of all R & D costs. Most businesses that have R & D departments, as a result, treat these costs as expenses in the period incurred even though this approach is inconsistent with the matching concept.

Companies that capitalize R & D costs usually transfer the project costs to patents or copyrights if a patent or copyright has been granted. Legal costs and other costs are included along with R & D costs in calculating the total acquisition cost assigned to the patent or copyright. If a patent or copyright is not granted the cost of R & D projects is usually shown as deferred R & D costs and then allocated over the periods benefited.

GOODWILL. Some businesses are more profitable than others. Very often the reasons for the higher profits cannot be specifically identified. It may be a combination of customer rapport, employee morale, managerial talent, or some other characteristic that cannot be measured or identified separately. Goodwill is the additional value that is attached to a business because it is a "going concern" earning a good profit.

• Recognition of Goodwill: Accountants will only recognize goodwill when it is "purchased." Goodwill is acquired only when a business or an autonomous department of a business is acquired by another business. Goodwill appearing in the accounts of a company is the acquisition cost of that extra "something" possessed by a going concern which has been acquired by the purchasing company.

• Valuation of Goodwill: The amount allocated to goodwill is the difference between the sum of the market value of the identifiable assets and the total purchase price of the business acquired. In negotiating the purchase price of a business, various methods have been used to value goodwill. These methods are related to the ability of the business to generate above average earnings. The amount calculated as the value of goodwill is a starting point in the negotiations. The final price is the result of bargaining between the buyer and seller.

The two most common methods for measuring goodwill are (1) capitalization of earnings and (2) capitalization of excess earnings. Before either can be applied to an actual situation, certain conditions should exist:

1   Valuation of the identifiable assets should be at *market* value.
2   Earnings should be adjusted to show only normal, recurring amounts. Extraordinary items must be excluded.
3   Earnings should be average earnings for a reasonable number of periods (generally a minimum of five years).
4   Average earnings should be adjusted to show expected trends in the future.

• Capitalization of Earnings: The expected earnings of a business are capitalized at a normal rate of return for that particular industry. For example, assume that the normal rate of return in a wholesale trade is 15 percent. The average annual expected income of T–X Company is $30,000; the fair market value of the identifiable assets is $150,000. Goodwill for T–X Company would be computed as follows:

Total asset value implied ($30,000 ÷ 15%)	$200,000
Fair market value of identifiable assets	150,000
Value of goodwill	$ 50,000

• Capitalization of Excess Earnings: The capitalization of earnings method assumes that the higher earnings will continue and that the normal rate of return is a valid measure of the risk inherent in the industry. In reality, a higher rate should be applied to the *excess* earnings because there is less assurance that the excess earnings will continue to be earned in the future. Competition and changes in demand could have a serious effect on the excess earnings. Because of this higher risk, a higher rate of return is applied to excess earnings than to normal earnings.

As an example, assume that I–X Company's average annual expected income is $30,000, a normal rate of return is 15 percent and the rate for excess earnings is 20 percent. The fair market value of the identifiable assets is $150,000. Goodwill would be computed as follows:

Average expected earnings	$30,000
Normal expected earnings (15% X $150,000)	22,500
Excess earnings	$ 7,500
Goodwill ($7,500 ÷ 20%)	$37,500

Other methods of computing goodwill are also used. Remember, however, that the final price of the company acquired is the price arrived at by bargaining.

• Amortization of Goodwill: With the issuance of APB Opinion No. 17,* the AICPA changed a long-standing view that, in the absence of evidence to indicate

---

*American Institute of Certified Public Accountants, *Opinion of the Accounting Principles Board No. 17* (August 1970).

dissipation of purchased goodwill, the acquisition cost should be permanently capitalized. Opinion No. 17 takes the position that goodwill like most other long-lived assets dissipates as time passes. Continued existence of goodwill would indicate that new unpurchased goodwill had come into existence, and not that purchased goodwill continued to exist. Opinion No. 17 recommends amortization of goodwill through use of the straight-line method over an estimated useful life that is not to exceed 40 years. Methods of amortization and problems encountered in estimating useful lives of long-lived assets are discussed later in this chapter.

OTHER INTANGIBLES. Other common intangibles include patents, copyrights, franchises, trademarks, trade names, brand names, and organization costs. Organization costs include legal and accounting fees, promotional costs, and any other costs incurred to establish an organization. Costs incurred in the acquisition of the preceding intangibles should be accumulated and classified as such. Again, accountants will only recognize the costs actually incurred. The market value of the trade name "Coke" is substantial because of its acceptance by the public. The Coca Cola Company does not show this market value on its statements, however. Usually companies that have developed a trademark, trade name, or brand name do not show any deferred cost for this intangible. When another company acquires the intangible from the originator or predecessor company, an acquisition cost may be recognized.

The failure of financial statements to show the value of trademarks and similar assets is mainly due to the doctrine of conservatism. These assets are not acquired "free of charge." They are developed over time by advertising, careful product control, and in many other ways. But who can tell what part of expenditures made for advertising in the current year will benefit future periods? Which periods will benefit and to what extent? The problem here is identical with that encountered for R & D: How can the future benefits be measured to serve as a basis for cost deferral? When this question cannot be answered, accountants usually treat acquisition cost as a period expense in the year incurred.

Use of Long-Lived Assets

As long-lived assets are used up, the cost of the services consumed is allocated to either the cost of the product or to the expense of a period. Although the basic process is similar, the terminology varies with the different classes of long-lived services. The following terminology is used for the various classes of services.

Depreciation—the measure of the services consumed for tangible assets, such as buildings, machines, vehicles, and tools, in a given period.

Depletion—the measure of natural resources, such as minerals, oil deposits, and timber extracted from land, consumed in a given period.

Amortization—the measure of the services of intangible assets, such as patents and copyrights, used up in a given period.

Long-lived services used up in the production of revenue are difficult to measure. Estimates are made of expected useful life, of the pattern of use, and of the salvage value. The amount of cash a firm expects to realize from disposition of the asset at the end of its useful life is the salvage value. This section treats the various methods of cost allocation, the application of these methods, and special problems arising from the use of long-lived assets.

Cost Allocation Methods

Services of a building, a machine, patent, and similar properties cannot be precisely measured as they are consumed. It cannot be known with certainty how long such services will be economically useful. A physical measure such as a pound or gallon is useful only rarely. Because of these difficulties, the allocation of the cost of long-lived assets is made by using the various allocating methods discussed below.

ASSETS WITH INDETERMINABLE LIVES. The services of some long-lived assets do not diminish with use. Land used as the site of a building does not become less useful with age, for example. Similarly, organization cost does not diminish in value with the passage of time. Under normal circumstances, the cost of the land, organization cost, and other long-lived assets with indeterminable lives are not transferred to expense until they are disposed of by sale or abandoment.

STRAIGHT-LINE OR LEVEL-CIIARGE METHOD. The straight-line or level-charge method assumes the services of an asset are used up in equal amounts during each period of the asset's estimated life. This method is graphically shown in Fig. 14–1.

Figure 14–1: Level-Charge Pattern

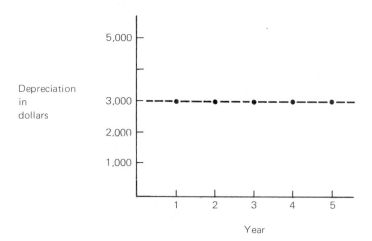

Year

The usual formula for computing depreciation using the straight-line method is

$$\text{Depreciation} = \frac{\text{Depreciable cost}}{\text{Estimated life}}$$

where

Depreciable cost = Acquisition cost - Salvage value

This formula has some limitations because it implies that the periodic depreciation will not change over the useful life of the asset. With the passage of time,
better information relative to the salvage value and estimated life may become
available. Also, the depreciable cost may change because of additions or improvements to the property which benefit several periods and must, therefore,
be deferred. The additional information frequently requires the business to
change the depreciable cost, the estimated useful life, or the salvage value. Depreciation for each time period should be based on the best information available. A more useful formula is

$$\text{Depreciation} = \frac{\text{Remaining depreciable cost}}{\text{Remaining useful life}}$$

where

Remaining depreciation cost = Acquisition cost - Current estimated salvage value -
Accumulated depreciation

Critics of this formula contend that it permits management to vary depreciation from year to year. Of course, there should be some factual support for
changes in salvage value and estimated remaining life to avoid arbitrary changes
in depreciation expense to fit the wishes of management. The estimated variables of the straight-line depreciation formula should be examined each period
and adjusted if necessary to allocate properly the cost of the service to the
periods benefited.

• Example of the Straight-Line Method: Assume that T–X Company buys a
new truck for $16,000 on January 1, 19X1. The estimated useful life is five
years and the estimated salvage value is $1,000. The depreciation for the first
year would be computed as follows:

Remaining depreciable cost = $16,000 - $1,000 = $15,000

$$\text{Depreciation, 19X1} = \frac{\$15,000}{5} = \$3,000$$

At the end of 19X2, T–X Company estimates that the remaining life is three
years from the beginning of year 19X2 and that the estimated salvage value is
$1,000. Depreciation for 19X2 would be computed as follows*:

Remaining depreciable cost = $16,000 - $1,000 -- $3,000 = $12,000

$$\text{Depreciation, 19X2} = \frac{\$12,000}{3} = \$4,000$$

*The reason for treating the change as prospective rather than retroactive is explained later
in the chapter.

DECLINING BALANCE METHOD. The declining balance method results in a decrease in the periodic depreciation as the asset is used. The decreasing-charge pattern of allocation is shown in Fig. 14–2, although this graph does not depict precisely the declining balance method.

Figure 14–2: Decreasing-Charge Pattern

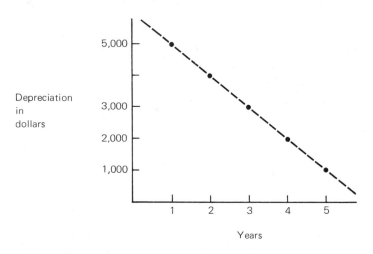

Years

The declining balance method allocates most of the cost of the asset to expense in the early years of the asset's life. A precise but cumbersome formula to compute the depreciation percentage rate is

Depreciation percentage rate $= 1 - n\sqrt{s/c}$

where n = number of periods of useful life, s = salvage value, and c = cost. This constant rate is applied to the undepreciated cost, which is cost less accumulated depreciation, or book value of each asset. Federal income tax rules do not allow the use of the above method in measuring *taxable income*. They do permit 200 percent declining balance or double-declining balance (DDB) for many new assets, and 150 percent declining balance rate for some used assets.* The constant rate is double or 200 percent of the straight-line rate or 150 percent of the straight-line rate. The rate is applied each period to the undepreciated cost of the asset. The formulas for computing double-declining and 150 percent-declining balance are

Straight-line rate $= \dfrac{1}{\text{Estimated life}}$

DDB rate = 2 (Straight-line rate)

150% declining balance rate = 1.5 (Straight-line rate)

Depreciation = DDB rate X Undepreciated cost

= 150% declining balance rate X Undepreciated cost

*A 125 percent rate is permitted for some assets under the Revenue Reform Act of 1969.

Declining balance formulas do not require use of estimated salvage value. When these methods are used, depreciation for the final year of useful life is the difference between carrying value at the beginning of the period and estimated salvage value.

• Example of Double-Declining Balance Method: Assume that T–X Company purchases an asset for $15,000 and it has an estimated life of five years.

Straight-line rate $= \dfrac{1}{5} = 20\%$

DDB rate $= 2 \times (20\%) = 40\%$

Depreciation for each year of the estimated life is given in Fig. 14–3.

Figure 14–3: Depreciation Using Double-Declining Balance

Year	Rate (%)	Undepreciated cost or book value	Annual depreciation	Accumulated depreciation	Ending book value
1	40	$15,000	$6,000	$ 6,000	$9,000
2	40	9,000	3,600	9,600	5,400
3	40	5,400	2,160	11,760	3,240
4	40	3,240	1,296	13,056	1,944
5	40	1,944	778[a]	13,834	1,166

[a] Rounded value.

The cost of an asset is never fully allocated to expense using double-declining balance or variations of this method. For this reason, the federal income tax law, which is the impetus for the use of this method in financial accounting, permits the taxpayer to change from the declining balance method to the straight-line method at any time. If the switch is delayed until the final period of useful life, the undepreciated cost is then reduced to the estimated salvage value. If, for example, the salvage value of the above property is $1,000, the straight-line method could be used in the fifth year to calculate depreciation of $944 and an undepreciated cost equal to salvage value of $1,000.

SUM-OF-YEARS DIGITS METHOD. The sum-of-years digits method (SYD) is also a decreasing-charge method. The formula for sum-of-years digits method is

$$\text{Depreciation}_i = \frac{n + 1 - i}{n(n + 1)/2} \times (c - s)$$

where n = estimated useful life,* i = year of useful life for which depreciation is calculated (first, second, etc.), c = acquisition cost, and s = salvage value. A verbal equivalent formula is

$$\text{Depreciation} = \frac{\text{Remaining years of useful life}}{\text{Sum-of-years digits}} \times (\text{Cost} - \text{Salvage})$$

*The term $n(n+1)/2 = \text{SYD}$; for example, for four-year life, $\text{SYD} = n(n+1)/2 = 4+3+2+1 = 10$.

• Example of Sum-of-Years Digits Method: Assume that T–X Company acquires an asset on January 1, 19X1, for $23,000. The estimated life of the asset is six years, and its estimated salvage value is $2,000. The annual depreciation for each of the six years is shown in Fig. 14–4.

Figure 14–4: Depreciation Using the Sum-of-Years Digits Method

Year	Rate	Annual depreciation	Accumulated depreciation	Ending book value
1	6/21	$6,000	$ 6,000	$17,000
2	5/21	5,000	11,000	12,000
3	4/21	4,000	15,000	8,000
4	3/21	3,000	18,000	5,000
5	2/21	2,000	20,000	3,000
6	1/21	1,000	21,000	2,000[a]

[a]The assumed salvage value is $2,000. Calculations of the amount shown in the table for year 3 using the SYD formula are as follows:

$$\text{Depreciation}_i = \frac{n + 1 - i}{n\,(n + 1)/2} \times (c - s)$$

$$\text{Depreciation}_3 = \frac{6 + 1 - 3}{6\,(6 + 1)/2} \times (\$23,000 - \$2,000)$$

$$= 4/21 \times \$21,000$$

$$= \$4,000$$

PRODUCTION METHOD. Straight-line, double-declining balance, and sum-of-years digits methods are depreciation methods using time as the basis for allocation. The production methods of depreciation are based on the *use* of the asset without regard to the span of time involved. For example, depreciation of a truck may be based on the number of miles driven rather than the time which has elapsed.

The formula for a production method of cost allocation is

$$\text{Depreciation} = \frac{\text{Service units used in current period}}{\substack{\text{Estimated remaining units of service} \\ \text{from beginning of period}}} \times (\text{Undepreciated cost} - \text{Salvage})$$

For example, assume T–X Company acquires a truck for $6,500. The estimated useful service units are 100,000 miles and the estimated salvage value is $500. During the first year the truck was driven 18,000 miles. Depreciation would be computed as follows:

$$\text{Depreciation} = \frac{18,000}{100,000} \times (\$6,500 - \$500) = \$1,080$$

If the truck was driven 22,000 miles the second year and the estimated service units and salvage were unchanged, depreciation for the second year would be

$$\text{Depreciation} = \frac{22,000}{82,000} \times (\$5,420 - \$500) = \$1,320$$

A shortcut in using the method would be to compute a rate per service unit (a rate per mile in this illustration) and multiply this computed rate times the service units used. In the foregoing example, the rate per mile would be 6 cents, that is, ($6,500 – $500)/100,000 = $0.06. Depreciation for 19X1 would be $1080 ($0.06 X 18,000), and for 19X2, $1320 ($0.06 X 22,000). The rate per service unit is satisfactory as long as the variables do not change (estimated service units and estimated salvage value). If these variables change, of course, the rate per service unit will change. The first method is preferable because the estimated variables are explicitly considered each period.

Although the above methods were generally referred to as methods of depreciation, some of the methods are also used to allocate costs of natural resources and intangibles. Most depletion for financial income measurement is based on a production method. The straight-line method is used almost exclusively for amortization of intangibles.

• Selection of Appropriate Method for Allocation: The factors relevant to the selection of an appropriate method of cost allocation for long-lived assets are

1   The base or total amount to be allocated must be determined.
2   The useful life of the services, that is, the span during which the allocation is to occur, must be determined.
3   The pattern for spreading the total allocation, that is, the fraction of the total allocation to be assigned to each accounting period within the useful life, must be determined.

The various methods considered in the preceding section are selected on the basis of conclusions about the three factors just listed.

SALVAGE VALUE. The depreciable base is the acquisition cost less the salvage value under most methods. The amount assigned to salvage value is an estimate based on experience and the current market for similar used items or the asset's anticipated value as scrap. Whether the item will eventually be sold as a productive asset or as scrap depends on the policy of the company and the nature of the asset. The policy of the company should be determined by evaluating the continued use of the long-lived asset and all other feasible alternatives. This type of analysis is called *capital budgeting* and is beyond the scope of this book. The estimated useful life is directly related to the estimated salvage value.

DETERMINATION OF USEFUL LIFE. The useful life of a bundle of services is that period, stated in terms of time or service unit, during which the services make a positive contribution to the enterprise. The useful life of tangible services may expire because of (1) physical exhaustion or deterioration or (2) obsolescence. The useful life of intangible services may expire because of (1) expiration of legal life or (2) obsolescence. Legal life is based on rights granted by governmental authority or rights acquired through contracts with other parties.

Physical exhaustion or deterioration of tangible services, for example, plant and equipment, will prevent these assets from performing a useful function. Physical life is more difficult to predict than legal life. Accountants look to the past experience of other firms, with identical or similar assets for guidelines to use in making estimates of physical life. Often the advice of managers and engineers is considered.

Obsolescence is caused by changes in productive processes, shifts in the demand for products, or the invention of another machine or process that performs the same function more economically and efficiently. The useful life of an obsolete asset ends not because of physical exhaustion, but because the function is no longer beneficial or the function can be performed better by another machine or process. The advent of the jet airliner made prop-driven aircraft obsolete for the major airlines. Thus, the useful life of a long-lived asset must be determined by physical exhaustion or obsolescence, whichever occurs first.

Technological developments, consumer preferences, and other factors that determine an asset's useful life are often outside the control of corporate management. Past experience offers little, if any, assistance and many of the factors involved may be unforeseen or even unforeseeable. These uncertainties have caused managers and accountants to select allocation methods based on expiration of time and methods that allocate larger amounts to the early years of the assets' life. The acceptance and use of decreasing-charge methods for measuring *taxable income* by the IRS has caused a dramatic increase in the frequency of their use for making the measurements presented in published financial statements.

To summarize, the selection of an allocation method is based on judgment. Ideally the method that best measures the use of the services should be used. Unfortunately, criteria for choosing the best method are difficult to identify and many companies base the decision on the tax advantages that can be obtained from the decreasing-charge methods. But then, given the rapid rate of change in technology which results in early obsolescence for many assets, allocation of most of the cost of services to operations over a few short years may be an appropriate decision.

Application of Cost Allocation Methods

Originally the straight-line method was used almost exclusively for all types of long-lived assets. The straight-line method is still used almost exclusively for the amortization of intangibles. Decreasing-charge methods are used mainly for items of plant and equipment; their application to intangibles is not permitted for tax purposes and this tax rule has undoubtedly influenced accounting practice.

The production method is used for the cost depletion of natural resources. Percentage depletion is permitted for measurement of taxable income; it is not acceptable for the measurement of financial income. Percentage depletion is calculated by taking a percentage of gross income from an operation and using this amount as depletion expense for federal income tax purposes. The rates and limitations for percentage depletion are established by Congress. Percentage depletion is not related to the acquisition cost of the natural resources. For this reason, it is not a generally accepted practice for measuring financial income.

A contra account is conventionally used to record depreciation in the double-entry system. The pro forma entry is

	Debit	Credit
Depreciation	$xx	
Accumulated depreciation		$xx

Contra accounts are not ordinarily used in the amortization of intangibles nor in the depletion of natural resources. The pro forma entry for recording the amortization of intangibles is

	Debit	Credit
Amortization of intangibles	$xx	
Deferred cost of intangible		$xx

The pro forma entry for recording depletion is

	Debit	Credit
Depletion	$xx	
Deferred cost of natural resources		$xx

Contra accounts could be used for both intangibles and natural resources, but the conventional practice is to credit the deferred cost directly.

Depreciation expense is material for most businesses. This means that choices of depreciation methods and estimates of useful lives usually have a significant impact on periodic income. For this reason the AICPA requires separate disclosure of depreciation expense, accumulated depreciation, and of methods used to calculate depreciation in published financial statements.* The disclosures may appear in the financial statements or in notes to the financial statements. Opinion No. 12 only implies a need for similar disclosures with regard to amortization and depletion but such a requirement is directly stated in Opinion No. 22.

ALLOCATION FOR FRACTIONAL PERIODS. Long-lived services are rarely acquired or disposed of at the beginning or the end of an accounting period. For this reason it is often necessary to calculate depreciation, depletion, and amortization for fractional periods.

Conventions that are followed in handling amortization for the period of acquisition and the period of disposition include the following:

1   Allocate for a full year in the year of acquisition and do not allocate in the year of disposition irrespective of the date within the period on which the transactions occur.

*American Institute of Certified Public Accountants, *Opinion of the Accounting Principles Board No. 12* (December 1967) and *No. 22* (April, 1972).

2   Reverse the procedure for the year of acquisition and the year of disposition in the preceding convention (1).
3   Allocate for a half-year in both the period of acquisition and the period of disposition.
4   Prorate allocation in the year of acquisition and the year of disposition according to the fractional part of the year the asset is in service, usually to the nearest month.

For example, consider a firm that uses a calendar year accounting period and acquires a truck on April 1, 19X1. The truck is acquired for $5,200, it has an estimated salvage value of $400, it has an estimated useful life of four years, and it is to be depreciated under the straight-line method. Depreciation under each of the four alternative methods is shown in Fig. 14–5. A pro rata portion of the depreciation for each year of an assets' life would be allocated to each accounting year for the double-declining balance and sum-of-the-years digits method in a similar manner.

Figure 14–5: Allocation for Fractional Periods Using Straight-Line Method (Four Alternative Approaches)

Accounting period	1	2	3	4
19X1	$1,200	–	$ 600	$ 900
19X2	1,200	$1,200	1,200	1,200
19X3	1,200	1,200	1,200	1,200
19X4	1,200	1,200	1,200	1,200
19X5	–	1,200	600	300
	$4,800	$4,800	$4,800	$4,800

Method of Presentation on the Financial Statements

The depreciation expense for each period appears on the statement of income along with the other expired costs.

Balance sheet treatment varies widely depending on the size of the business and the accountant's preferences. For small concerns, major assets may be listed separately and the accumulated depreciation shown for each asset:

Plant and equipment:		
Land		$100,000
Building	$250,000	
Less: Accumulated depreciation	110,000	140,000
Equipment	$340,000	
Less: Accumulated depreciation	205,000	$135,000
Total		$375,000

A more common practice, particularly for larger corporations, is to show all plant and equipment combined, net of accumulated depreciation, with the past depreciation disclosed parenthetically (using the foregoing amounts):

Land, buildings, and equipment (net of accumulated depreciation, $315,000)	$375,000

The limited space on the balance sheet is the major cause for condensing the information to a single line item.

Examine the financial statements presented in Appendix D for examples of various methods of disclosing the cost of long-lived assets and the related depreciation, depletion, and amortization. Particular attention should be given the financial statements and notes to financial statements of A. O. Smith Corporation, Singer Corporation, Gould, Inc., and Great Northern Nekoosa Corporation.

As indicated earlier, APB Opinion Nos. 12 and 22 require that the amount of annual depreciation be disclosed on the statement of income or in notes to the financial statements and that the cost of plant and equipment and accumulated depreciation be disclosed in the balance sheet or in footnotes.

FUND-FLOW PRESENTATION. Cost allocation of long-lived assets (depreciation, depletion, and amortization) does not cause a decrease in funds. The expense arises because a *noncurrent* deferred cost expires during the period. Thus, depreciation, depletion, or amortization expense does not reduce funds (working capital or cash). For this reason, depreciation, depletion, or amortization expense is added to net income to obtain the funds provided by operations; that is, these expenses must be removed from the income calculation to show funds provided by operations. A typical statement of funds would appear as follows:

Source of funds		
From operations:		
Net income for year	$250,000	
Plus: Depreciation expense	35,000	
Total funds from operations		$285,000

Because of this addition of depreciation, people often mistakenly say that depreciation expense is a *source* of funds. To the contrary, the source of funds is the revenue, the inflow of current assets, and the depreciation expense is one expense that does not reduce this inflow currently.

Disposal of Long-Lived Assets

Although acquired for use rather than resale, long-lived assets eventually cease to be useful and must be retired, scrapped, sold, or traded. Also assets are sometimes involuntarily disposed of as a result of such things as thefts, fires, and floods. These transactions must be recorded in the accounting records and reported in the financial statements. If material in amount, gains and losses recognized should not affect income from operations but should be classified separately. The reader should also note that the three criteria for the recognition of product revenue discussed in Chapter 10 are also generally applicable to the disposition of long-lived assets by sale.

Sale of Long-Lived Assets

When a firm disposes of an asset, all account balances that pertain to the asset must be removed from the records. The difference between the proceeds from disposal and the carrying value of the asset is recorded as a gain or loss. For depreciable assets, depreciation expense for the fraction of the accounting period prior to the sale is recorded before preparing the entry for disposal.

ENTRIES FOR DISPOSALS. Recording disposals of long-lived assets through sale differs slightly from recording product revenues. The difference is that revenue and expense are netted against each other instead of recording the gross amounts of revenue and expense in separate entries.

As an example, assume that a machine purchased for $6,000 on January 1, 19X3 has been depreciated on a straight-line basis and that the firm uses a calendar year accounting period. If the machine is sold on July 1, 19X6 for $1,600, the following entries are necessary to update depreciation expense and record the disposal:

	Debit	Credit
Depreciation expense	$ 600	
Accumulated depreciation		$ 600
(To record depreciation for a half year)		
Cash	1,600	
Accumulated depreciation	4,200	
Loss on disposal	200	
Machine		6,000
(To record the sale of machinery)		

REPORTING DISPOSITIONS ON FINANCIAL STATEMENTS. The disposal of equipment in the preceding example affects the balance sheet in two ways. The cash proceeds reported increase the cash balance, and the machine and the related accumulated depreciation are no longer reported. On the statement of income, the gain or loss, if material, is reported separately.

On the statement of changes in financial position, these gains or losses should be shown separately although they are included in funds provided from operations. Figure 14-6 shows the presentation of the loss of $200 from the foregoing examples. Other amounts are omitted to highlight the disclosure of the unusual item.

Note that the amount shown on the statement of changes in financial position is the proceeds of the disposal.

Figure 14-6

B Company		Statement of Changes in Financial Position
Funds provided:		
Funds provided by recurring operations		$xx,xxx
Loss on disposal of machine	$ (200)	
Plus: Machine cost	$6,000	
Accumulated depreciation	4,200	1,800
Net proceeds from disposal		$ 1,600
Total funds provided by operations		$xx,xxx
Other sources		$xx,xxx
Total funds provided		$xx,xxx

The statement of sources and application of funds of the Green Giant Company and Subsidiaries (on p. 515 of Appendix D) shows a single item, "Proceeds on Disposal of Property and Equipment." Opinion No. 30 has changed the definition of an extraordinary item subsequent to the time of the publication of the statement in Appendix D*.

Trade of Long-Lived Assets

When an operating asset is traded for another operating asset as opposed to selling it for cash, the new asset must be recorded, the old asset and the related accumulated depreciation account must be removed from the records, and any gain or loss on the transaction must be recognized. In a trade-in, the value assigned to the new asset received is its fair market value, provided this value can be determined with reasonable objectivity. For example, assume that a machine which originally cost $4,000 and which has accumulated depreciation of $3,000 is traded for a new machine. The new machine has a fair market value of $3,900 and the company also pays $2,500 in cash for the new machine. With these amounts, the indicated market value of the old machine is $1,400 ($3,900 value for the new machine less the cash payment of $2,500). There is a gain of $400. The gain is the excess of the value of the old machine of $1,400 over its deferred cost of $1,000 ($4,000 original cost less accumulated depreciation of $3,000). The entry to record the trade is

	Debit	Credit
Machine (new)	$3,900	
Accumulated depreciation (old)	3,000	
Machine (old)		$4,000
Cash		2,500
Gain on trade		400

*American Institute of Certified Public Accountants, *Opinion of the Accounting Principles Board No. 30* (June, 1973).

Recognition of the gain in the preceding example, a generally accepted practice, is clearly inconsistent with one of the three criteria for revenue recognition. Although the transaction is completed and the gain is earned, the company has not received a new liquid asset (cash or a near-cash asset). Instead it has received another operating asset which will be used in the business, a continuing investment in the same kind of property. In addition, difficulties and disagreements often arise over the fair market value to be assigned to the new asset or over the trade-in value of the old asset.

For the reasons just mentioned, a business is not allowed to recognize gains or losses on trade-ins in the measurement of taxable income. The foregoing transaction would be recorded as follows using the income tax method:

	Debit	Credit
Machine (new)	$3,500	
Accumulated depreciation (old)	3,000	
Machine (old)		$4,000
Cash		2,500

The value assigned to the new machine is the deferred cost of the old machine, $1,000, plus the cash paid of $2,500, a total of $3,500. Many accountants prefer to use the method prescribed for income taxes for financial reporting as well. The income tax method avoids disputes over fair market value and violation of the recognition criterion. Use of the tax method has the additional advantages of avoiding duplicate records for taxes and financial reporting. It is probably for these reasons that Opinion No. 29 requires use of the income tax method for all transactions consummated after September, 1973*.

Involuntary Dispostions

Procedures for recording involuntary dispositions covered by insurance are similar to those to record an ordinary sale of a long-lived asset. Proceeds of the insurance recovery simply replace the proceeds of the sale. If a building with a cost of $80,000 and accumulated depreciation of $45,000 were totally destroyed by fire, with a recovery from the insurance company of $30,000, the transaction would be recorded as follows:

	Debit	Credit
Accumulated depreciation	$45,000	
Cash	30,000	
Fire loss	5,000	
Building		$80,000

Given the same facts except that with no insurance, the entry would be as follows:

	Debit	Credit
Accumulated depreciation	$45,000	
Fire loss	35,000	
Building		$80,000

*American Institute of Certified Public Accountants, *Opinion of the Accounting Principles Board No. 29* (May, 1973).

The income tax rules for involuntary conversions are somewhat different from the rules for financial accounting. In some cases, the accountant may choose to record the event using the tax rules.

Gains and losses on trades and involuntary conversions are reported on the financial statements in the same manner as gains and losses on sales. Where material, the gain or loss is shown as a separate item on the statement of income.

Additions and Improvements

Sometimes a firm acquires new long-lived services by adding to or improving assets. Additions are usually easy to identify: They include constructions such as a wing added to a building or the extension of a loading dock. Additions may be classified separately or the cost of the addition may be added to the deferred cost of the existing asset.

Improvements that should be capitalized are sometimes difficult to distinguish from maintenance and repairs that should be expensed as incurred. The general rule is that expenditures that improve performance or extend useful life are capitalized and those that do not improve performance or extend the useful life are expensed as incurred. Ordinary maintenance, such as cleaning, oiling, adjusting, and replacement of minor parts, obviously falls into the expense category. A major overhaul should be capitalized. Between these extremes are expenditures that may be very difficult to classify. In such cases, accountants can only call on their experience and use their best judgment.

QUESTIONS

1   When should the acquisition cost of a long-lived asset be recognized?
2   How are the acquisition costs of long-lived assets normally classified when originally incurred.
3   What is the general rule used to value long-lived assets? Give several examples to illustrate this general rule.
4   How should services received in a barter transaction be valued?
5   Why does the valuation of leases present a special problem?
6   What are the criteria for recognizing leased property as an asset?
7   What are the three different types of research and development expenditures?
8   How are research and development costs usually treated for income measurement? Do you agree with this position? Why?
9   Describe two ways that the value of goodwill may be estimated.
10   How is the amount of goodwill finally determined?
11   Define each of the following:

    [a]   Patents   [d]   Organizational costs
    [b]   Copyrights   [e]   Brand names
    [c]   Trademarks

12   Define the following terms:

    [a]   Depreciation   [c]   Amortization
    [b]   Depletion

13   How are the costs of assets with indeterminate lives allocated to expenses?
14   Describe the straight-line or level-charge method of depreciation and the formula for computing depreciation under this method.

15   Describe the various declining balance methods of depreciation. Give the formula for computing depreciation using the double-declining balance method.

16   Describe the sum-of-years digits method of depreciation and give the formula for its computation.

17   Describe the production method of depreciation.

18   What criteria should be used to select the appropriate method for depreciation?

19   Why does the AICPA require businesses to disclose the depreciation expense, accumulated depreciation, and the method of depreciation used on the financial statements or in notes to the statements?

20   What are the various methods of allocating the costs of long-lived assets for fractional periods?

21   Accountants often have difficulty in distinguishing between an addition or betterment and an ordinary repair. What criteria are used to make this distinction? When doubt arises, what will most accountants do? Why?

22   M Corporation's inventory was completely destroyed by fire. The merchandise cost $500,000 but the insurance proceeds were only $440,000. How should this disposition of inventory be reported on the financial statements?

23   When one asset used in the business is traded for another asset that will be used in the business, the income tax law does not usually permit the recognition of gain or loss. Some accountants do recognize gains in these situations. Explain the difference in practice in terms of the criteria for recognition of revenue.

24   When long-lived assets are sold, the sales price is not treated as revenue. Instead, the deferred cost of the property is offset against the sales price and only the net gain or loss is reported. Why do accountants differentiate between the disposition of assets used in the business from the disposition of products?

PROBLEMS

1   A firm purchased a machine that had an invoice price of $1,000, terms 1/10, n/60. Thirty days after purchase, the firm paid the full $1,000. The firm also paid $750 for installation costs and $75 for trial runs. The installation costs were high because it cost $350 to repair damage to the machine that occurred when it dropped off the hoist while it was being installed.

Required:

[a]   Calculate the acquisition cost of the machine.

[b]   Prepare an entry or entries to record the acquisition cost.

2   H Incorporated purchased three machines for $100,000. The purchase price was reduced by the supplier as a concession to H Incorporated for buying three machines at the same time. If the machines had been purchased separately their prices would have been as follows:

Machine No. 1, $50,000
Machine No. 2, $40,000
Machine No. 3, $30,000

Required:

Present the journal entry to record the acquisition of the three machines. The machines must be classified separately because they have different useful lives.

3   On January 1, 19X1 BKB Company signed a noncancellable ten-year lease on a building. The lease calls for annual payments of $2,000 on December 31 of each of the ten years. The BKB Company uses the calendar year as an accounting period. The company wants to capitalize the lease and recognize it as an asset. The present value of the annual payments of $2,000 each discounted at 6 percent is $14,720.

Required:

[a]   Present all the journal entries the company should make with regard to the lease during the year 19X1.

[b]   Explain why you would or would not approve the treatment of this lease as the acquisition of an asset.

4   During the month of December, 19X8, the F Company purchased and installed a machine to be used in manufacturing operations.

December 1. Machine was delivered to the F Company and an invoice for $10,000 was received. Credit terms are 2 percent cash discount if paid within ten days. Full price of $10,000 is due in 30 days, after which 6 percent will be charged on any unpaid balance.

December 2. Paid $200 to the supplier for a one-year service contract for which the supplier agrees to pay for all maintenance and repairs.

December 4. Paid $500 transportation charge on the machine.

December 8. Paid $1,500 for materials and labor to install the machine.

December 11. The last day of the discount period. No payment on the $10,000 owed the supplier was made.

December 15–20. Testing period for the new machine and for training employees in its operation, during which time all output was scrapped. Labor and materials consumed were $500, as expected and this amount was not considered excessive.

January 31, 19X9. Paid the invoice in cash, $10,050, including $50 interest.

Required:

[a]   For each transaction indicate the amount that should be recognized as a deferred cost and the amount as an expense. Justify your decision.

[b]   Prepare journal entries to record each of the above transactions.

[c]   What amount should be allocated to expense in 19X8 provided the machine was not put into productive use in 19X8?

5   The R Oil Company bought a producing oil lease for a total cost of $1,000,000. The estimated production from the well was 2,000,000 barrels. Production during the first year of ownership was 200,000 barrels which was sold for $500,000. Total costs of production exclusive of depletion was $200,000. The estimated life of the well is five years.

[a]   What method of cost allocation would you recommend to R Oil Company?

[b]   In general journal form record cost depletion for the first year using your suggested method.

6   On July 10, 19X3, S Corporation traded its old delivery truck for a new delivery truck. The acquisition cost of the old truck was $5,000, accumulated depreciation was $3,000. The old truck was acquired on January 5, 19X0. The estimated life of the old truck was five years with no salvage value. The sales price of the new truck was $6,000. S Corporation was allowed $1,200 trade-in value for the old truck. The balance of the purchase price of the new truck, $4,800, was paid in cash.

[a]   Prepare a journal entry to record this trade recognizing gain or loss.

[b]   Prepare a journal entry to record this trade without recognizing gain or loss.

7   S Corporation acquired an asset on January 1, 19X1, at a cost of $21,000. The asset has an
     estimated useful life of four years and an estimated salvage value of $1,000.
     [a]   Compute depreciation for 19X1 and 19X2 using the following depreciation methods:
            [i]   Straight line
            [ii]   Double-declining balance (DDB)
            [iii] Sum-of-years digits (SYD)
     [b]   On June 30, 19X3, S Corporation sold the asset acquired in 19X1 for $8,000.
            Assume that straight-line depreciation was used. Record the sale of the asset and
            prepare any other entries you believe are necessary.
8   In early January, 19X1, the N Company acquired a new milling machine. The total cost,
     including freight, installation, etc., was $20,000. The estimated life of the machine was six
     years. Salvage value is estimated at less than 10 percent and is therefore ignored.
     [a]   Prepare a schedule of depreciation expense for the six-year life under each of the
            following methods:
            [i]   Straight-line
            [ii]   SYD
            [iii] DDB
     [b]   Compute the depreciation expense for 19X1 for all three methods if the machine is
            acquired on May 1, 19X1. (The N Company allocates depreciation to the nearest
            full month.)
     [c]   Prepare journal entries to record the depreciation expenses computed in part [b] for all
            three methods, assuming that the acquisition cost was originally recorded as an asset.
     [d]   A capital addition was made to the machine in January 19X2 (assuming acquisition
            date is May 1, 19X1). The capital improvement to the machine cost $4,000. In
            addition, the remaining life of the machine from January 1, 19X2, is estimated at
            eight years. Compute the depreciation for 19X2 using the straight-line method.
9   The J Corporation purchased a patent from K Corporation for $80,000. The remaining
     legal life of the patent is 16 years. The management of the J Corporation estimates that
     the beneficial life of the patent will be ten years.

Required:

     [a]   Why would the beneficial life be shorter than the legal life?
     [b]   What factors should be considered in selecting a method of cost allocation?
     [c]   Prepare a journal entry to record the acquisition of the patent.
     [d]   Prepare a journal entry to allocate the cost of the patent to expense for the first year.
10   L Incorporated is contemplating the cash purchase of a small manufacturing company
     which produces baseball equipment. The physical assets have been appraised at $500,000,
     but the owners are unwilling to sell for that amount. They claim that the goodwill of the
     company, based primarily on good customer relations, is worth $250,000. The normal rate
     of return for sporting goods manufacturers is approximately 12 percent. The past annual
     earnings of the company have been fairly stable at $72,000 per year.

Required:

     [a]   Calculate the goodwill of the manufacturing company using the capitalization-of-
            earnings method.
     [b]   Calculate the goodwill using the capitalization-of-excess earnings method. Use a
            20 percent capitalization rate.
     [c]   How much would you pay for the operation? If you would need additional facts,
            what would they be?

11   The W Oil Corporation drilled five oil wells in 19X0. Four of the wells were "dry holes."
      The other well proved to be an excellent producer. The cost of drilling each oil well was
      $150,000.

      Required:

      [a]   How should the cost of drilling the four oil wells that are nonproductive be
             accounted for? Explain.
      [b]   Prepare journal entries to record the costs, based on your decision in part [a].
      [c]   Assuming that the estimated production from the active well will be 500,000 barrels
             and that 80,000 barrels were produced in 19X0, record the depletion for the year
             19X0.

12   The C Automobile Company has spent $1,000,000 to develop a more efficient motor and
      drive mechanism. The new model incorporating the new feature is scheduled for produc-
      tion next year. A patent has been granted to C Automobile Company giving it the exclu-
      sive rights to use these new technological improvements. The legal life of the patent is 17
      years, but the normal life for this type of automobile production model is only 3 years. A
      competitive company has just announced the successful and economic development of a
      battery-operated car.
          The president of C Automobile Company asks you to develop a report that will present
      the accounting problems and alternative ways of allocating the $1,000,000 development
      costs to expense. The president also asks you to support your recommendations.

13   James and Shaw, attorneys, purchased all of the law books of another local attorney who
      was retiring from practice. The cost of this law library was $5,000. Mr. James wants to
      charge this cost to expense during the current year, but Mr. Shaw wants to allocate the cost
      of these books to the next three years. They ask you for advice on how the cost of the
      library should be allocated.

      Required:

      [a]   Outline the issues involved in this discussion.
      [b]   Use your knowledge of reference volumes in the local library and any other suitable
             sources to determine the estimated life of the law library.
      [c]   Show how you would record the acquisition of the law library on the books of the law
             firm and how you would record the cost allocation to expense, if any, for the first year.

14   F Mart, a chain of discount houses, has a policy of leasing the store buildings for its opera-
      tions. This policy reduces the capital required for long-lived assets and increases the capital
      available for expansion. In January, 19X0, the firm leased a store in Asheville under the
      following terms:
      [1]   The lease term is 20 years and the lease is noncancellable.
      [2]   Rentals of $30,000 per year will be paid in advance on January 1, beginning with
             January 1, 19X0. F Mart has the right to renew the lease for an additional 20 years
             at an annual rental of $2,000 per year.
      The estimated useful life of the store building is 30 years with no salvage value.

      Required:

      [a]   Is this agreement an operating lease or a disguised purchase? Explain your answer.
      [b]   Assuming that it is a purchase, prepare an entry to record the lease. (Use 10 percent
             for the discount rate.) Prepare entries to record the lease payments on January 1,
             19X0 and January 1, 19X1. Finally, prepare an entry to amortize the cost of the
             building for 19X0, assuming that F Mart's fiscal year ends on December 31, 19X0.

15   The J-M Company traded its 19X4 Chevrolet truck for new 19X8 Ford truck. Details of
        the transaction are as follows:

Date	6/28/19X8
Invoice price	$4,547.18
Discount	547.18
Net price	4,000.00
Trade-in (old truck)	1,000.00
Cash difference	$3,000.00

The 19X4 Chevrolet truck was acquired on January 2, 19X4 for $3,600 cash. Estimated
life was five years. Straight-line depreciation was properly deducted in 19X4, 19X5, 19X6,
and 19X7.

Required.

Make all entries necessary to record the trade if
[a]   Gain or loss is recognized.
[b]   No gain or loss is recognized.

16   On July 5, 19X7, J Furniture Company's delivery truck was involved in an accident while
        returning from making a delivery. The truck was a total loss. J Furniture Company carried
        $100 deductible collision insurance. The insurance company and J Furniture Company
        agreed that the fair market value of the truck just prior to the accident was $800.

        The following information relative to the old truck was taken from the property, plant,
        and equipment account:

Cost of 19X2 truck	$4,200
Accumulated depreciation, 12/31/19X6	$3,150
Estimated life	5 years

Required.

[a]   Prepare journal entries to record the loss of the truck and the receipt of the insurance
        company check.
[b]   Assume that J Furniture Company did *not* carry collision insurance and the other
        party was not at fault. Prepare journal entries to record the loss.
[c]   What effect did the above events have on the flow of funds?

17   The H-A Company sold an industrial lathe on June 1, 19X4 for $300. The lathe originally
        cost $1,200 on January 3, 19X1. It had an estimated life of four years at acquisition and a
        salvage value of $200. Straight-line depreciation was used by H-A Company.
[a]   Prepare journal entries to record the sale of the lathe and its removal from the
        records.
[b]   What effect did the sale of the lathe have on funds flow? If the sales price had been
        $25, what would be the funds flow?

18   B Motor Transport is licensed as a common carrier in the Rocky Mountain states. It oper-
        ates ten trucks on the average. The following transactions occurred in 19X5:
[1]   A new tractor was purchased on June 1, 19X5; an old tractor originally costing
        $10,000 on January 1, 19X0 was traded in. The tractor traded in had an estimated
        life of six years with a salvage value of $1,000. B Motor Transport uses the straight-
        line method to depreciate its tractors. The new tractor's sales price was $12,000;
        the trade-in allowance on the old tractor was $2,000.
[2]   A trailer originally costing $8,000 on July 1, 19X1, was destroyed by fire on

August 30, 19X5. The estimated life of trailers was 20 years with no salvage value. Straight-line depreciation had been properly recorded through 19X4. An insurance check for $4,700 was received.

[3] A 5,000–gallon tank of diesel fuel was lost when a flat bed truck loaded with angle iron backed into the tank, rupturing it. The diesel fuel was uninsured and cost 15 cents a gallon.

Required:

[a] Prepare journal entries to record the preceding transactions.

[b] What effect did each of the transactions have on flow of funds?

CASE   The MMC Corporation, a drug manufacturing company, has a research and development division which has the objective of developing new drugs that will be more effective in combating various human ailments. The research staff proposes projects and includes an estimated project budget that is either approved or rejected by the Board of Directors. Costs incurred on approved projects are accumulated in appropriately identified accounts. Periodically the approved projects in progress are examined to determine whether or not they should be continued. Those that appear profitable are continued; those that do not appear profitable are discontinued. Costs of the discontinued projects are charged to expense in the year of termination. If a project is successful in producing a useful and marketable product, the costs of developing that product are allocated over the estimated life of the product. The administrative and clerical costs of the research and development division that cannot be charged directly to a research project amount to $100,000 per year. These costs are charged to expense in the year incurred.

The president of the MMC Corporation has proposed that all costs incurred by the research and development division be charged to expense in the year incurred on the basis that the expenditures of the division are relatively constant and this procedure would not distort income.

Required:

[a] Comment on the current procedure, considering problems of recognition, classification, and valuation. Be sure to comment on the expensing of administrative costs.

[b] Comment on the president's proposal and write a memorandum either supporting or rejecting the president's proposal.

[c] What is the effect of the current and proposed method on funds flow?

15

Accounting
for Equity
Investments

Transactions between a business and its owners are called investment transactions. This category includes both transfers of capital to the business from the investors and distributions from the business for retirement or repayments, for withdrawals, for interest, and for dividends. This chapter is primarily devoted to investment transactions of corporations. Corporations are the dominant form of organization in our economy, and the investment transactions of corporations are generally more complex than investment transactions in proprietorships and partnerships.

Investments in a corporation are of two types, debt investments (D) and stockholder investments (OI). The distinction between these two types of investments is based on the different legal rights of the two classes of investors and, consequently, the different legal obligations of the corporation. For both types, the corporation enters into a legal contract with the investor, and these legal contracts specify the rights and obligations of each party.

For a debt investment, the contract specifies a *repayment* of capital to the investor of a fixed or determinable amount (or amounts) at some fixed or determinable time (or times). For example, a 90–day note with a bank is a debt contract, which provides for repayment of the amount borrowed in one payment in 90 days. A long-term mortgage, another type of debt contract, normally provides for repayment of principal in a series of periodic payments. Debt contracts usually provide for a payment of interest over the life of the contract in fixed or determinable amounts. Interest is the equivalent of rent for use of capital.

Under a debt contract, the corporation is obligated to make the specified repayments of capital and payments of interest. These legal promises of the corporation provide the debt holder with some security against the loss of his capital and interest. If a corporation does not meet its obligations for payments of interest and principal, legal action can be initiated by the debt holder to secure payment. In some cases, this may result in the liquidation of the corporation.

Generally the claims of debt holders in a corporation have legal priorities over the claims of stockholders.

Legal contracts with stockholders usually do not contain specific provisions for repayment of capital or for payment of specific amounts in dividends. As payment for this additional risk the stockholders share in all profits of the corporation without limit. They also share in losses. However, their maximum loss is limited to the amount of capital contributed. Normally, stockholders cannot sue a corporation to secure repayment of their capital contributions. Furthermore, the stockholders cannot force the board of directors to pay a dividend except under very unusual circumstances. If a stockholder does not like the way a corporation is run, he can only vote for different directors or he can sell his stock.

Two parties are involved in the initial investment transaction, the business entity and the investor. In addition to the initial transaction, investors may buy and sell investments from and to each other. To the business, the investee, the investment is a source of new capital or a repayment of capital or payment for the use of capital. To the investor, the transaction is an acquisition of services, generally a claim against the business for future cash payments. In this chapter, we will discuss the effect of the various transactions on both parties.

Debt Investments

The essential legal characteristic of a debt contract is the enforceable obligation of the corporation to pay a fixed or determinable sum at some fixed or determinable future time. Three common types of debt contracts are single-payment notes, installment notes, and bonds. Other fairly common debt contracts are subordinate debentures, income bonds, and serial bonds. The various debt contracts can be classified based on time of repayment. The various classifications are short-term, which are due in about one year, intermediate-term, which are due in from one to about five years, and long-term, which mature after about five years.

Debt contracts can also be classified based on their security agreements. Investors who lend money to corporations often expect to receive some assurances of eventual repayment beyond the legal promises included in the basic debt contract. For example, the lender may insist that the title to some property be *pledged* to secure eventual payment. A pledge that involves real property, such as land and buildings, is called a *mortgage*; a pledge that involves personal property, such as inventory, furniture, and equipment, is called a *chattel mortgage*. Where there is a pledge agreement in conjunction with a note, the lender has first claim, after the payment of all wages and taxes, on the property pledged if the corporation fails to meet its obligations. Upon default, the lender can force sale of the pledged property and application of the proceeds against his loan.

Corporations may pledge accounts receivable, inventory, or stocks and bonds of other companies held as investments to secure payment of the debt contracts.

Many corporations have long-term security agreements with lending agencies to secure a line of credit for their short-term capital needs. These agreements usually limit the corporate property that can be pledged to other lenders, the amount which may be borrowed from other sources, and the amount which the corporation can pay out as dividends.

Short-Term and Intermediate-Term Notes

The amount of capital necessary to operate a business successfully often fluctuates widely within a year or over a period of a few years. For example, a corporation engaged in a seasonal business, such as toy manufacturing, will need larger amounts of capital as inventories increase in anticipation of the Christmas season. As receivables from sales are collected during the winter, the necessary capital decreases significantly. A business that is expanding its operations by building new plants may need a gradually increasing amount of investment until the expansion is completed and permanent capital needs for the expanded operations can be determined.

In these situations, the corporation normally secures the additional investment for a limited period by borrowing from banks, insurance companies, and other financial institutions. The debt contract in these cases is called a *note*. For seasonal fluctuations in capital requirements, short-term notes are used. Intermediate-term notes are used when the requirements extend for more than one year.

For example, assume that M Corporation needed additional capital to carry its Christmas inventory and therefore borrowed $100,000 on October 1, 19X1 from C Investment Company. The note matures on January 31, 19X2 with interest at 8 percent per annum due at maturity. Both M Corporation and C Investment Company use the calendar year as their accounting period. Journal entries for both parties are shown in Fig. 15-1.

The entries are generally self-explanatory. Upon repayment of the loan on January 31, 19X2, the total interest is allocated between the accrued payables and the $667 interest expense for one month in 19X2 on the books of M Corporation. A comparable entry is made on the C Investment Company books. If either company has numerous transactions of this variety, the accountant might record the entire interest payment (or receipt) in the nominal account and make a single adjustment for the change in the accrual at year-end.

Installment Notes

A popular method of obtaining the capital necessary for the acquisition of operating assets is to borrow money on an installment note which provides for repayment of principal in a series of payments. Often the property acquired is pledged to secure payment of the installments. The method is particularly popular for the acquisition of real estate and equipment.

Figure 15-1: Journal Entries for Short-Term Note

Date and description	M Corporation		C Investment Company	
	Debit	Credit	Debit	Credit
10/1/19X1: Loan agreement is signed and cash transferred	Cash $100,000 Note payable	$100,000	Note receivable $100,000 Cash	$100,000
12/31/19X1: Interest expense and revenue is accrued by the respective parties. Amount is $2,000 ($100,000 X 0.08 X 3/12)	Interest expense $ 2,000 Accrued interest payable	$ 2,000	Accrued interest receivable $ 2,000 Interest revenue	$ 2,000
1/31/19X2: Loan is repaid with interest. Total interest due is $2,667 ($100,000 X 0.08 X 4/12)	Note payable $100,000 Interest expense 667 Accrued interest payable 2,000 Cash	$102,667	Cash $102,667 Note receivable Interest revenue Accrued interest receivable	$100,000 667 2,000

There are two systematic methods for repayment of installment notes: (1) a series of equal principal payments with decreasing payments for interest; (2) a series of equal payments covering both interest and principal. In order to illustrate these two repayment schedules, assume that M Corporation borrows $100,000 on January 1, 19X1 and agrees to repay the loan and 8 percent interest over a period of five years. Real estate is mortgaged to secure the installment note. If repayment provides for a series of equal principal payments, M Corporation would repay the principal in five amounts of $20,000 each. At the end of the first year, interest would be $8,000 ($100,000 X 8 percent); at the end of the second year, interest would be only $6,400 ($80,000 X 8 percent).

Figure 15-2 shows a repayment schedule providing for five equal payments for both interest and principal. The amount of the constant payment, $25,046 in this case, can be determined by using Table A-4 in Appendix A. The installment note can be viewed as an annuity where the present value is known and the interest periods are equal to the number of payments. The unknown amount is the annual payment under the annuity. If we let R equal the annual payment and look up the factor for P5 at 8% on Table A-4, we have the following solution for the annual payment:

$$\$100,000 = R \times 3.9927$$
$$R = \frac{\$100,000}{3.9927}$$
$$= \$25,046 \text{ (rounded)}$$

With this amount determined, the repayment schedule can be readily prepared.

Figure 15-2: Repayment Schedule for Installment Note

Year	Principal balance during year (a)	Interest, 8% of col. a (b)	Principal payment, col. d – col. b (c)	Total payment (d)
19X1	$100,000	$8,000	$17,046	$25,046
19X2	82,954	6,636	18,410	25,046
19X3	64,544	5,164	19,882 .	25,046
19X4	44,662	3,753	21,473	25,046
19X5	23,189	1,857[a]	23,189	25,046

[a] Rounding error included.

Journal entries for installment notes are very similar to those for short-term notes (Fig. 15-1). Where the interest payment dates do not coincide with the accounting period of the business securing the loan or of the investor, the normal adjusting entries are necessary for interest expense (on the borrower's books) and interest revenue (on the lender's books).

Bonds

The methods of obtaining capital discussed in the preceding sections are used normally where the amount of capital required can be obtained from a single lender. Often large corporations require immense amounts of new capital that cannot be supplied by a single lender. In such cases, a corporation may issue bonds and sell them to a number of investors.

A bond is essentially a negotiable note that obligates the corporation, in exchange for the capital provided, to pay interest at a fixed rate at fixed times, and to repay the principal amount at a fixed time. The denomination or principal amount of bonds issued varies widely, typically from $100 to $1,000. There is some evidence to indicate that smaller investors are more likely to buy bonds of lower denominations. On the other hand, the lower the denomination, the more bonds that must be issued to raise the needed amount of capital. Clerical and administrative costs increase, of course, as the number of bonds issued increases.

Bond issues are often secured by mortgages on the plant and equipment of the issuing corporations. Where a mortgage is used, the bonds are usually described as *mortgage bonds*. The security agreements between corporations and their bond holders usually provide for restrictions on dividend payments and further borrowing by the corporations. For most bond issues, a trustee is appointed to protect the interests of the bondholders.

BOND PRICES. Corporate bonds are bought and sold in the capital market in the same manner as other securities. Market prices for bonds are quoted as a percentage of the principal amount. One may read in a financial paper, for example, that the mortgage bonds of a certain corporation are selling for 102. If the bonds have a principal amount of $1,000 each, the price per bond is $1020 ($1,000 X 102 percent).

On first thought, one would expect the price of a note that will eventually return $1,000 at maturity to be $1,000, no more, no less. Trading prices vary from the principal value, however, because of two factors. First, the issuing corporation may be in a different risk class and its bonds may sell considerably below the maturity value because of the risk that the principal will never be repaid. Second, the price may vary from the principal amount because the rate of interest specified on the bonds is more or less than the current market rate of interest. For corporations with sound financial structures, this difference in interest rates is the usual cause for variations between the market price and the maturity value.

Suppose, for example, that you are an investor considering the purchase of a $1,000 corporate bond that will mature in exactly five years and will bring interest at the end of each year at 6 percent. If the bonds are purchased, the corporation will pay you interest of $60 at the end of each year and $1,000 repayment of principal. The total cash return would be $1,300, the $1,000 principal plus $300 interest ($60 for five years). Assume further that the market rate of interest on similar investments is 8 percent. Given these conditions, you will be unwilling to pay $1,000 for the bond—you will be willing only to pay a price that will yield at least an 8 percent interest rate, that is, a price less than $1,000.

The price can be approximated by using the discount and annuity procedures in Appendix A. What is the present value of all future cash payments based on a market rate of interest of 8 percent?

Present value of $1,000 at end of five years at 8% is	
$1,000 X 0.6806 (using Table A–2)	$680.60
Present value of a series of five $60 payments over 5	
years at 8% is $60 X 3.9927 (using Table A–4)	239.56
Total present value of all future payments	$920.16

The market price of the bond would be approximately 92 under these conditions. Note that a 6 percent market interest rate, using the foregoing calculation, would give a price of $1,000, the maturity value.

Thus, if the market rate of interest is more than the interest paid on a bond, then the bond price will normally be less than its maturity value. On the other hand, if the interest paid on the bond is more than the market rate of interest, the bond price will normally be more than the maturity value.

TREATMENT OF BOND DISCOUNTS AND PREMIUMS BY ISSUING CORPORATIONS. For the reasons explained above, the price of a bond will not be the same as its principal or maturity value. There will be some difference even when a corporation with the highest credit rating issues bonds because of market interest rate fluctuations between the time when the decision is made to issue bonds and the time of issuance.

If bonds are sold for more than their maturity value, a bond premium results. For example, if 1,000 bonds with a maturity value of $1,000 are sold for 103, the premium is

Sales price (1,000 X $1,000 X 103%)	$1,030,000
Maturity value (1,000 X $1,000)	1,000,000
Premium	$ 30,000

The premium arises when the bond rate is higher than the market rate. The $30,000 received in cash now will be offset by higher cash payments for interest over the life of the bonds. For this reason the premium is amortized over the life of the bonds and reduces the interest expense to an amount which approximates the lower market rate at the time of issue.

When the bond rate is less than the market rate a discount results. Assume for example that the sales price is only 96. The discount is

Maturity value (1,000 X $1,000)	$1,000,000
Sales price (1,000 X $1,000 X 96%)	960,000
Discount	$ 40,000

The lower sales price is offset by lower cash payments for interest over the life of the bonds. In this situation, the discount is amortized over the life of the bonds and increases the interest expense to an amount that approximates the higher market rate at the issue date.

Figure 15-3 shows the entries for a two-year period and at the maturity date of bonds issued at a premium. The basic data are as follows: M Corporation, which uses the calendar year for its accounting period, issued 1,000 bonds with a maturity value of $1,000 each on March 1, 19X0. Interest at 8 percent per annum is due annually on March 1. The bonds mature in ten years on March 1, 19X10. The issue price was 104 which resulted in a premium of $40,000.

Figure 15-3: Entries for Bonds Issued at a Premium

Date and description	Entries on books of M Corporation		
		Debit	Credit
3/1/19X0: Issue of bonds with maturity value of $1,000,000 at 104	Cash	$1,040,000	
	Bonds payable		$1,000,000
	Bond premium		40,000
12/31/19X0: To accrue interest payable for ten months ($1,000,000 X 0.08 X 10/12)	Interest expense	66,667	
	Accrued interest payable		66,667
12/31/19X0: To amortize premium over the life of bonds ($40,000 ÷ 120 months less 10 months in 19X0)	Bond premium	3,333	
	Interest expense		3,333
3/1/19X1: To pay interest for first year ($1,000,000 X 0.08)	Interest expense	13,333	
	Accrued interest payable	66,667	
	Cash		80,000
3/31/19X1: To accrue interest on bonds (1,000,000 X 0.08 X 10/12)	Interest expense	66,667	
	Accrued interest payable		66,667
3/31/19X1: To amortize premium for 19X1 $\frac{\$40,000}{120 \text{ months}}$ X 12 months	Bond premium	4,000	
	Interest expense		4,000
3/1/19X10: To pay interest for last year of bond's life	Interest expense	13,333	
	Accrued interest payable	66,667	
	Cash		80,000
3/1/19X10: To amortize premium for last two months $\frac{\$40,000}{120 \text{ months}}$ X 2 months	Bond premium	667	
	Interest expense		667
3/1/19X10: To record retirement of bonds at maturity	Bonds payable	1,000,000	
	Cash		1,000,000

Note that the premium is recorded in a separate account with a credit balance. Subsequent amortization of this credit balance over the life of the bonds decreases the interest expense. At March 1, 19X10, the entire premium has been offset against interest expense and the repayment of the bonds is made at maturity value.

When bonds are issued at a discount, the accounting procedures are virtually identical. The discount is recorded in an account with a debit balance and the amortization of the discount results in an increase in the interest expense. For example, assume that M Corporation had issued the bonds at 96, giving a $40,000 discount. All entries would be the same except that amortization of the discount at December 31, 19X0 would be

	Debit	Credit
Interest expense	$3,333	
Bond discount		$3,333

Similar entries over the life of the bonds would reduce the discount to zero and the entry to record the retirement would be the same as that shown on Fig. 15–3.

TREATMENT OF BOND PREMIUMS AND DISCOUNTS BY INVESTORS. The investor in corporate bonds treats the cost of the bonds as a deferred cost. The asset should be classified as a current asset, marketable security, if conversion into cash will occur within the coming year. The deferred expense for bonds that will not be converted into cash within one year should be classified as an investment.

Premiums and discounts are not normally set up in separate accounts by investors. The entire purchase price is recorded in the asset account, whether more or less than maturity value. For instance, assume that an individual buys ten of the 8 percent bonds of M Corporation at 97. The most direct method of recording the purchase is to debit the acquisition cost directly to an asset account, investment in M Corporation bonds. The interest revenue recorded each accounting period is $800 plus a portion of the discount. The entry on the individual's book on December 31, 19X0 who purchases the bonds of M Corporation would be

	Debit	Credit
Interest receivable [10/12 ($10,000 X 0.08)]	$667	
Investment in M Corporation bonds (300/120 X 10)	25	
Interest revenue		$692

If the bonds are held to maturity the amount in the investment account will be equal to the maturity value of the bonds, which is $10,000 in this case. The discount on the bonds at acquisition when amortized to revenue would be added to the investment account. If bonds were purchased at a premium, the periodic amortization of the premium would decrease the investment account to maturity value at maturity. Opinion No. 21 of the APB* requires the amortization of discounts and premiums.

Other Debt Investments

Corporations issue many types of debt instruments in addition to notes, installment notes, and mortgage bonds. *Income bonds*, for example, make the annual payments of interest contingent on corporate profits. *Debentures* are debt instruments with no specific assets pledged as security. *Convertible bonds* are debt instruments that may be exchanged for stock of the issuing corporation at the election of the investor. All types of debts, however, receive accounting treatment comparable to that described for notes and bonds.

Debt-Investment Transactions on Financial Statements

Most debt-investment transactions do not create serious reporting problems. For most of the transactions discussed, their affects on the financial statements are implicit in the accounting treatment described. There are some reporting problems, however, which deserve special attention.

Corporate Statements

When a company raises capital through the use of a debt contract, the debt is a claim against the assets, an equity. The amount of the claim is usually the face amount, and this amount is shown as a liability on the balance sheet. Occasionally, a debt may not provide for interest payments. In this event, the liability should be shown at its present value as opposed to its face amount. Interest paid or accrued on debt contracts is treated as an expense in the income computation. It is good practice to disclose the amount of interest expense on the statement of income to permit the determination of the gain from trading on the equity.

On the balance sheet, liabilities are classified as either current or long-term, depending on their due dates. For installment notes, the portion due within one year is shown as a current liability with the remainder classified as long-term liability. A typical account under current liabilities is "current portion of long-term indebtedness." The unamortized portion of bond premiums and discounts is best reported as an adjustment to the maturity value of the bonds payable. Unamortized premiums would be added to, and unamortized discounts subtracted from, the face amount of the bonds. Using the facts in Fig. 15–3, for example, the balance sheet of M Corporation would show the following at December 31, 19X0:

Long-term liabilities:
Mortgage bonds payable (8%, due on 3/1/19X10)	$1,000,000	
Plus: Unamortized premium	36,667	$1,036,667

*American Institute of Certified Public Accounts, *Opinion of the Accounting Principles Board No. 21* (September 1971).

The current classification of the new debt or the repayment of *current* debt does not change the amount of net working capital, but does cause an outflow of cash. Capital received from new long-term debt contracts, however, represent a source of funds. The funds statement of M Corporation for 19X0 would show the following as a result of the bond issue:

Funds provided:		
Net income (assumed)	$60,000	
Less: Amortization of bond premium	3,333	$ 56,667
Bond issue		$1,040,000

The total sales price of the bonds is the measure of the funds provided. In addition, the premium amortization must be subtracted from the funds provided by operations. The amortization reduced the interest expense (and increased the net income), but it did not decrease the cash (funds) required to pay the actual interest. Amortization of discounts are added to net income to determine the funds provided, and for the opposite reason.

When long-term debt is retired, the amount paid is reported as an application of funds. The cash payment at retirement will reduce the net working capital.

Published balance sheets do not generally contain details of debt investment. Instead the details along with any restrictive covenants are disclosed in notes to financial statements. For example, refer to pp. 499 and 501 of Appendix D, the liabilities and shareholder section of the balance sheet and Note E on long-term debt of Gould, Inc. Note E reports the various types of long-term debt investments, interest rates, maturity dates, and the amounts outstanding. In addition the amount due within one year is presented and a schedule of aggregate maturities appears of each of the following five years.

A review of the debt-equity section and the relevant notes to the financial statement of the other financial reports in Appendix D shows that similar information is provided in each case; however, different formats are used.

Investors' Statements

Interest received or accrued is reported as interest revenue on the investor's statement of income. Gains and losses on sale or other dispositions of debt investments are treated as extraordinary items if material in amount.

The deferred costs of investments are shown as assets until the securities are sold or repaid by the issuer. If the investor expects to sell or otherwise dispose of the asset in the coming period, the asset should be classified as a marketable security and included under current assets. If not, the deferred expenses should be reported under investments, a noncurrent classification.

On the statement of changes in financial position, the acquisition of a noncurrent debt contract is an application of funds. The disposition of the noncurrent debt contract has the same effect on the funds statement as the disposition of long-lived assets.

Stockholder Investments

The stockholders in a corporation do not have as much security as debt investors. Stockholders are not assured a specific, periodic return on their capital and the corporation is not obligated to repay the amount invested at a fixed time. On the other hand, stockholders of a corporation have many rights that debt investors do not have. The stockholders elect the board of directors. The board, in turn, appoints the corporate officers and determines the general operating policies of the corporation. A stockholder also has the right to share pro rata in all distributions of assets to stockholders. These distributions (dividends) are usually paid out of current earnings but stockholders also receive their pro rata share of the corporate assets in the event of liquidation. Finally, stockholders have the right (preemptive right) to acquire their proportional share of any new stock issued by the corporation. For example, a stockholder who owns 10 percent of the common stock of a corporation has the right to acquire 10 percent of any additional common stock issued.

Corporate statutes in all states require that corporations distinguish between paid-in or contributed capital and retained income. The contributed capital, which is recorded in stock accounts and in accounts called *additional paid-in capital*, is the amount paid into the corporation by shareholders in exchange for stock. Contributed capital may also arise from additional assessments on stock, from donations of cash or property by stockholders, and from other transactions between the corporation and its owners.

Retained income or earnings is the portion of the corporation's total capital derived from previous profitable operations. Generally, the amount of retained earnings serves as a legal limit on the dividends a corporation may distribute. This limitation on dividends provides security to debt investors; the contributed capital is a financial "cushion" which can absorb losses and still leave the corporation with enough assets to pay creditors.

Common Stock

When a corporation is formed, its initial capital is obtained by issuing shares of stock to investors in exchange for capital. The shares of stock (capital stock) are legal contracts between the corporation and the investors which specify the rights of the investors and the corporation.

A corporation may have one or more classes of stock. Each class has different rights concerning control of the corporation and participation in dividends and other distributions. One class may have preferences over other classes for dividends or assets in liquidation. Capital stock with such preferences is called *preferred stock*. Every corporation, however, must have one class of stock which has the residual rights and obligations not reserved for or assigned to other classes of stock or debt instruments. This residual class of stock is called *common stock*.

The charter for a corporation, issued usually by a state government, specifies the classes of stock and the number of shares of each class that can be issued. The classes of stock and number of shares specified in the charter is called the *authorized* capital stock. The corporation may not issue all of its authorized shares; some may be held for later expansion or the corporation may find that it is unable to sell all authorized shares. The shares actually sold are called *issued* stock. The corporation often purchases its own shares, called *treasury* stock. The issued stock of a corporation held by the public (not treasury stock) is called the *outstanding* stock.

PAR AND NO PAR COMMON STOCK. Years ago, most stock certificates of corporations showed a face amount or par value. For example, a stock certificate might prominently show $100 as the "par" value per share. Although the practice of showing a par value has declined in recent years, many shares will still show a par value. If par value is used, the par amount is shown in the stock account, and any amounts received in excess of par are shown in an additional paid-in capital account.

For example, assume that the B Company was organized with 10,000 shares of $50 par value common stock authorized. Immediately following organization, the company sold 5,000 shares through an investment banker for $65 per share. The journal entry to record the investment transaction on the corporation's books is

	Debit	Credit
Cash	$325,000	
Common stock		$250,000
Additional paid-in capital (excess over par)		75,000
(To record the issue of 5,000 shares at $65)		

The entire amount received is recorded as contributed capital (owners' investment), but only the par value is shown in the common stock account. For a par value stock, the additional paid-in capital may be called *premium on common stock*.

Occasionally in the past, the investor who bought a par value stock for less than its par value was liable for assessment of the difference if the corporation became insolvent. In addition, the use of par values led to fraudulent practices because brokers selling the stock would represent the par value as the "fair" or market value. For these reasons, many corporations began issuing no-par stock in the 1920s.

No-par stock, as the term indicates, has no face amount. When no-par stock is issued, either state laws or the issuing corporation's directors may establish a *stated value* which is used to allocate the issue price between the stock account and additional paid-in capital account. An alternative solution is to set the par value at a nominal amount, say $1. To illustrate the issuance of no par stock, assume that B Corporation had 10,000 shares of no-par stock authorized and that it issued 5,000 at $65 each. If the board of directors established a stated value of $40 per share, the entry to record the stock issue is

	Debit	Credit
Cash	$325,000	
Common stock, no par ($40 stated value)		$200,000
Additional paid-in capital (excess over stated value)		125,000

(To record issue of 5,000 shares at $65)

The distinction between par value and no par stock has little significance. In both cases, the contributed capital is reported separately from the retained income.

DISTRIBUTIONS TO COMMON STOCKHOLDERS. Rights of common stockholders include the rights to receive distributions out of earnings and distributions of assets when the corporation is liquidated. Distributions of assets earned in the operation of the business are called *dividends*. Dividends are paid on outstanding stock only. At termination of the corporation's existence, the remaining corporate assets, after settlement of all equities having preference in liquidation, are distributed to the common stockholders. This type of distribution is generally called a *liquidating dividend*.

CASH DIVIDENDS. Many corporations declare and pay a cash dividend on a quarterly, semiannual, or annual basis. The dividend declaration usually specifies a dollar amount per share. The following are three important dates connected with a dividend:

Declaration date—the date when the directors meet and make the decision to pay the dividend. In virtually all cases, the corporation is legally obligated to make the payment once declared. Only under rare conditions can the directors change their minds.

Record date—the date when the corporation examines its record of stockholders to determine who owns stock and will receive the dividend declared. A stockholder who sells his stock before the record date or buys stock after the record date will not receive the dividend.

Payment date—the date when the dividend is actually distributed to the shareholders. For cash dividends, payment date is the day when the checks are placed in the mail.

Cash dividends are a liability of the corporation on the declaration date. Failure to recognize the liability at declaration can result in an understatement of current liabilities. Distribution of cash on the payment date settles the liability.

To illustrate the accounting entries, assume that B Corporation uses the calendar year as its accounting period. The corporation has 5,000 shares of common outstanding and declared an annual cash dividend of $1.25 per share on December 1, 19X1. Payment date is January 15, 19X2. The entry at declaration is

	Debit	Credit
Retained earnings	$6,250	
Cash dividend payable		$6,250

(To record declaration of $1.25 per share dividend)

The debit in this entry could be made to an account titled "dividends paid," the balance of which would be transferred to retained earnings at the end of the year.

On the company's balance sheet at December 31, 19X1, the cash dividend payable of $6,250 would be shown as a current liability. When the dividend is paid on January 15, 19X2, the entry is

	Debit	Credit
Cash dividend payable	$6,250	
Cash		$6,250

(To record the payment of dividend declared 12/1/19X1)

The net effect of the two entries is a decrease in cash and a decrease in retained earnings.

STOCK DIVIDENDS. Often a corporation that is short on liquid capital will wish to make some distribution to its stockholders, but a distribution that does not reduce funds needed for new projects and ventures. A popular way of accomplishing these ends is the stock dividend. A stock dividend is the distribution of the stock of the distributing corporation.

A stock dividend is unique in that it does not decrease the corporate assets. The stock dividend affects only the owners' equity section of the balance sheet, that is, the number of shares outstanding is increased. Thus a portion of the balance of retained earnings must be transferred to the capital stock account because that account must at all times show the par or stated value of the stock outstanding. The question that arises is, "How much should be transferred from retained earnings to contributed capital? The par value (or stated value) of the stock issued or its fair market value?" The generally accepted practice is to transfer the fair market value (FMV) of the distributed stock from retained earnings to contributed capital.

For example, B Corporation, which had 5,000 shares of $50 par value common stock outstanding, declared a 10 percent stock dividend. The corporation distributed 500 shares of its own stock which had a market value of $70 at the date of distribution. The entry is

	Debit	Credit
Retained earnings	$3,500	
Common stock ($50 par)		$2,500
Additional paid-in capital (excess over par)		1,000

(To record 10% stock dividend with FMV of $70 per share)

The retained earnings account is reduced by the FMV of the shares. If the FMV had been less than par or stated value, an unlikely occurrence, the amount transferred to contributed capital would have been the par or stated value. The important point to remember concerning a stock dividend is that it does not reduce the corporation's assets and each shareholder still owns the same percentage of the shares outstanding after the distribution.

Preferred Stock

Capital stock of a corporation that has some preferential rights is known as preferred stock. A dividend preference is stated as a percent of par value or a fixed amount per share. Thus a preferred stock issued with a par value of $100 per share may specify that each share is entitled to a 6 percent dividend, or $6 per share; a no par preferred stock may specify an annual $3 dividend per share.

Such a provision should not be confused with the contractual obligation to pay interest on a debt contract. Corporations have no legal obligations to pay periodic dividends on stock, whether common or preferred. A preference as to dividends in a preferred stock contract means that, if the board declares a dividend, the preferred shareholders are entitled to receive their preference percentage or amount before any distribution is made to the common shareholders.

The preference as to dividends may be either *noncumulative* or *cumulative*. If the preference is noncumulative and the board of directors does not declare a dividend in a given year, then the preference has no value to the shareholder. That is, the preference in noncumulative preferred shares applies to the dividends for a single year. The dividend preference in cumulative stock, on the other hand, is carried forward until a dividend is declared. For instance, assume that in 19X1 a corporation issued $100 par preferred stock with a 6 percent cumulative dividend. No dividends were paid in 19X1. If a dividend is declared in 19X2, each preferred share must be paid $12 ($6 for 19X1 and $6 for 19X2) before a dividend can be paid on common. If the preference had been noncumulative, only $6 would be paid to the preferred.

Occasionally, preferred stock has both a dividend preference and the right to participate with common stock on a pro rata basis in any dividends declared in excess of the preference percentage on common and preferred. Stock carrying this right is called *participating preferred stock*. Some preferred stocks also have a *call* provision which means that the corporation can retire any or all of the shares outstanding by payment of a specified sum. Finally, some preferred stocks have preferences over common stock when assets are distributed in liquidation. The contract might provide, for example, that on the liquidation of the corporation, each preferred share will be given assets equal in value to the par value of the preferred before any assets are distributed to the common shareholders.

A preferred stock contract with a cumulative dividend preference, a call feature, and preference to assets on liquidation is difficult to distinguish from some debt contracts. An income bondholder, for example, may have virtually the same rights as a preferred stockholder. Preferred stockholders, however, usually must give up some rights in exchange for these preferences. Preferred stock often has limited voting rights and the dividend return is usually limited.

Convertible Securities

Preferred stock is a "hybrid" investment contract, having some features of residual stock and some features of a debt. Another hybrid contract, and one which has created some serious problems for accountants in recent years, is the convertible contract or security. Although any investment contract may have the convertible feature, long-term debentures that may be converted into common stock at the election of the debenture holder have been used frequently in recent years.

The accounting procedures for convertible securities are, on their face, relatively simple. For example, assume that a corporation sells a subordinate debenture (one which has no collateral agreement) for $1,000, as its face amount. The debenture provides for interest at 7 percent and also provides that the holder may, at his option, convert the debenture into ten shares of common stock of the issuing corporation. Assume further that the stock is no par stock which has a stated value of $75. If the debenture holder elects to make the conversion, which he might choose to do provided the market value of ten shares of stock exceeds the value of his debenture, the following entry would be made to record the retirement of the debenture and the issuance of ten shares of stock:

	Debit	Credit
Debentures payable	$1,000	
Common stock		$750
Additional paid-in capital		250

The general practice is to transfer the carrying value of the debenture to the stock accounts.

For many years, the convertible feature was included in debentures and preferred stocks to enhance their marketability. Recently, however, some shrewd corporate managers have discovered another use for them. Recall from Chapter 6 that earnings per share is perhaps the most important ratio used in the evaluation of securities. That ratio is computed as follows:

$$\frac{\text{Net income (after interest and after extraordinary items)}}{\text{No. of shares outstanding}}$$

What happens if the corporation acquires the stock of another corporation and "pays" for the new corporation's stock by issuing convertible debentures? Assume that both corporations were equally profitable. If the two operations are merged (or consolidated statements are prepared as explained in Chapter 16), the earnings per share are automatically increased (see Fig. 15-4). The total income of the two corporations, we have assumed, is the same before and after the transaction. Because of the convertible debentures used to acquire some of the stock purchased, however, the shares outstanding decreases *relative* to the income. This operation, which has been used often by the so-called conglomerates, leaves the appearance of increased profits and thereby increases the market value of the stock of the acquiring company. These inflated values can be used to acquire yet another company, using some convertible securities, and thus obtain a higher amount for the earnings per share.

Figure 15-4: Convertibles and Earnings per Share

		Corp. A.	Corp. B
[1] Balance sheet of Corp. A and Corp. B prior to the acquisition of Corp. B by Corp. A	Net assets	$2,000,000	$1,000,000
	Stockholders equity	$2,000,000	$1,000,000
Annual average income		$ 200,000	$ 100,000
Shares issued and outstanding	Net income	200,000	100,000
Earnings per share	Shares outstanding	$ 1.00	$ 1.00

			Corp. A and B Combined
[2] Corp. A agrees to acquire Corp. B by issuing 10% convertible debentures for $1,000,000 in exchange for all of Corp. B's outstanding stock	Net assets		$3,000,000
	10% convertible debentures		$1,000,000
	Stockholders' equity		2,000,000
			$3,000,000
Assume the same income before interest of $100,000 on convertible debentures			$ 300,000
Interest expenses less decrease in tax expense	(assume rate of 50%)	$ 100,000 50,000	50,000
Income after interest			$ 250,000
Per share income	$250,000 / $200,000		$ 1.25
Per share income if debentures are converted	$300,000[a] / $300,000		$ 1.00

[a] Upon conversion, interest expense would be eliminated thereby increasing income to $300,000.

Opinion No. 15 of the APB* is intended to curb this possible misrepresentation. That opinion requires that the earnings per share be reported on two bases:

1 Assuming no dilution. The assumption is made that conversion rights will *not* be exercised and, in general, the shares outstanding are used as the denominator.

*American Institute of Certified Public Accountants, *Opinion of the Accounting Principles Board No. 15* (May 1969).

2   Assuming full dilution. The assumption is made that all conversion rights will be exercised and the denominator for earnings per share includes not only the shares outstanding but all shares that may be issued under conversion and certain other rights.

The board evidently believed that this dual presentation would put investors on notice that increases in earnings per share assuming no dilution may not reflect actual increases in profitability.

   For an illustration of the two computations of earnings per share, refer to the financial statements of Great Northern Nekoosa Corporation and subsidiaries, Appendix D, p. 506. The earnings per share are shown as primary and fully diluted for 1970 and 1971.

Reacquisition of Stock

A corporation will from time to time purchase its own outstanding stock. The shares purchased may be cancelled, which means they are no longer legally issued (although still authorized). Reissuance of cancelled shares is subject to the preemptive rights of shareholders, which is the right to acquire a pro rata amount of new shares issued. If not cancelled, the shares purchased are held "in treasury," which means they are issued in the corporate name, but not considered outstanding. Treasury shares can be resold without regard to the preemptive right of the shareholders.

RETIREMENT OF STOCK. Shares purchased and cancelled are said to be retired. Upon retirement, the amounts credited to the contributed capital when the stock was originally issued are removed from the accounts. If the amount paid for retired stock is more than the original issue price, the excess is treated as a dividend and is debited to retained earnings. For example, assume that B Corporation buys 100 shares of its $50 par stock for $82 per share. The stock was originally issued for $65. The entry to record the retirement appears below:

	Debit	Credit
Common stock ($50 par)	$5,000	
Additional paid-in capital (excess over par)	1,500	
Retained earnings	1,700	
Cash		$8,200

(To record retirement of stock)

The debit to retained earnings of $1,700 is based on the rationale that the retiring shareholders are being paid their share of past earnings.

   The purchase price of the retired stock may be less than the original issue price. If so, the credit difference is set up in a new paid-in capital account and appropriately identified. Assume, for example, that B Corporation paid only $57 per share for the 100 shares retired in the preceding example:

	Debit	Credit
Common stock ($50 par)	$5,000	
Additional paid-in capital (excess over par)	1,500	
Cash		$5,700
Additional paid-in capital for retirement of stock		800

The $800 difference becomes a permanent part of contributed capital. An important point to note is that *no gains* or *losses* are recognized as a result of these transactions with stockholders; the differences between retirement costs and issue prices are recorded in equity accounts, not gain or loss accounts.

TREASURY STOCK. The cost of stock reacquired but not cancelled is usually recorded as a debit balance account called *treasury stock*. If B Corporation acquired 100 shares of its $50 par common at $82 and holds the stock in treasury, the entry to record the purchase is

	Debit	Credit
Treasury stock	$8,200	
Cash		$8,200

(To record acquisition of B Corporation common at $82)

Although it has a debit balance, the account balance is not shown as an asset on the balance sheet. Instead, the debit balance is normally shown as a subtraction from the total stockholders' equity.

The rule that no gains and losses are recognized on transactions with shareholders also applies to a resale of treasury shares. Differences between the purchase price and sales price are recorded in stockholder equity accounts. If the resale price is more than cost, the excess is treated as additional paid-in capital. If the B Corporation stock reacquired for $82 is later sold for $90, then the entry is

	Debit	Credit
Cash	$9,000	
Treasury stock		$8,200
Additional paid-in capital (treasury stock)		800

(To record resale of treasury stock at $90)

If the stock is sold for less than cost, the difference is debited to retained earnings. To change the above facts, assume the resale price is only $75:

	Debit	Credit
Cash	$7,500	
Retained earnings	700	
Treasury stock		$8,200

(To record resale of treasury stock at $75)

To repeat, no gains or losses are recognized.

A corporation may have a variety of reasons for the reacquisition of stock. A common reason at present is to provide stock for use in stock option plans. In rare cases, treasury stock may be shown as an asset when the corporation has a contractual obligation to purchase the stock and use it to pay for the services of employees.

Donated Capital

Stockholders and other parties sometimes transfer property to a corporation and receive no stocks, bonds, or other ownership interests in the corporation. A fairly common example is a gift of a plant site from a state or city government to a corporation to encourage location of operations in that area. Donated assets are recorded as services at their FMV and the value is shown in the stockholders' equity section as donated capital.

Retained Earnings

The retained earnings of a corporation is the portion of the stockholders' equity other than contributed capital. Essentially the retained earnings is the sum of all past profits and losses, reduced by the dividend distributions to shareholders $[RE = \Sigma (y - s)]$.* In some cases, particularly in the early years of operations, losses may exceed income. The negative amount is called a *deficit*. The existence of a deficit means that a portion of the contributed capital has been lost as a result of unprofitable operations.

The retained earnings sets the limit for dividend payments. In many states, the amount available for dividends is reduced by the cost of shares held in the treasury. Recognition is shown in the accounts by transferring a portion of the balance of the retained earnings account to another equity account called *appropriated* (or *restricted*) *retained earnings*. For example, when B Corporation purchased 100 shares of treasury stock at $90, the restriction on retained earnings (if required by law) would be recorded as follows:

	Debit	Credit
Retained earnings	$9,000	
Appropriated retained earnings (cost of treasury shares)		$0,000

When the treasury stock is resold, the $9,000 amount is returned to the "unrestricted" retained earnings account. Appropriated retained earnings are shown in the stockholders' equity section with the retained earnings.

Appropriations may also be made at the discretion of the board of directors for plant expansion, expected future losses, and other purposes. These discretionary appropriations can mislead shareholders. By reducing the unrestricted

*This equation is from Chapter 4, where y is the annual or periodic income and s is the annual or periodic dividends.

retained earnings they can lead to the conclusion that the director cannot declare a dividend. In truth, however, the directors can cancel the discretionary appropriations at any time and thereby increase the unrestricted retained earnings. Regardless of the amount of retained earnings, the practical limit on the dividends that most corporations can pay is the cash or other liquid assets not needed in operations.

A common mistake made by persons who do not understand accounting is to confuse the stockholder equity accounts, and particularly retained earnings, with accounts showing the "real" assets of the business. When a corporation is profitable, and only a portion, if any of the income is distributed as dividends, the balance of retained earnings increases. The total assets also increase, but not necessarily the cash or other liquid assets. The cash generated by operations is usually reinvested in operating assets, such as plant and inventories. The use of the term "appropriation" to describe a restriction of retained earnings no doubt contributes to the confusion. In laymen's language, an appropriation is a fund set aside for a purpose. As used by accountants, the meaning is quite different: An appropriation of retained earnings has no effect on, and implies nothing about, the composition of the corporation assets.

Statement Presentation—Corporate Accounts

Transactions with stockholders do not give rise to gains and losses. Thus these transactions are not reported on the statement of income. Stock issues and sales of treasury stock result in an inflow of new funds and will appear under sources on the statement of changes in financial position. Retirement of stock, purchase of treasury shares, and dividends paid with cash or other current assets, reduce the funds available and therefore appear as "applications" on the statement of changes in financial position. Stock dividends do not affect the amount of funds.

Most of the available information about past transactions with stockholders is found on the balance sheet. An example of a stockholders' equity section of a balance sheet, showing the essential facts which should be disclosed is presented in Fig. 15–5, which is taken from the consolidated balance sheets of Great Northern Nekoosa Corporation and Subsidiaries. The complete balance sheets are reproduced on pp. 507 and 508 in Appendix D. The numbers in parenthesis following the words "Stockholders' Equity" refer to notes to the financial statements.

Note that the preferred stock is cumulative and without par value, but is convertible. Note 3 to the financial statements gives the details for the convertible feature of the preferred stock. Note 2 presents the details about debt investments including the convertible features.

The retained earnings are substantially larger than the total capital contributed by both common and preferred shareholders. Retained earnings are in excess of $138 million and contributed capital is slightly over $72 million. This condition is very common for established corporations. The primary source of new capital or growth for most corporations is the reinvestment of earnings.

Figure 15-5: Stockholders' Equity Section of Great Northern Nekoosa Corporation and Subsidiaries

Stockholders' Equity (2, 3, and 4):	December 31 1971	December 31 1970
Capital stock–		
Preferred stock, cumulative, issuable in series, without par value–		
Authorized–3,000,000 shares		
Outstanding–1,882,114 convertible shares at December 31, 1971 (liquidation preference aggregates $26,734,000).............................	$ 25,097,000	$ 26,167,000
Common stock, $10 par value–		
Authorized–9,000,000 shares		
Issued–4,713,056 shares at December 31, 1971	47,131,000	46,509,000
	$ 72,228,000	$ 72,676,000
Additional paid-in capital.......................................	33,941,000	32,348,000
Retained earnings...	138,293,000	132,957,000
Common stock in treasury, 25,000 shares, at cost..	(1,057,000)	–
Total stockholders' equity	$243,405,000	$237,981,000
	$441,144,000	$435,174,000

Reprinted from the 1971 financial statements of Great Northern Nekoosa Corporation and Subsidiaries.

Statement Presentation—Investors' Accounts

An investor may acquire corporate stock directly from the issuing corporation or from another investor in the capital market. In both cases, the cash paid by the investor is to acquire a bundle of services. The cash outlay is debited to an asset account. Assume that an investor acquires 100 shares of B Corporation stock at $90 per share. The entry to record the purchase and set up the deferred expense is

	Debit	Credit
Investment in B Corporation common	$9,000	
Cash		$9,000

(To record purchase of 100 shares at $90)

The deferred cost would be classified as a current asset (marketable security) or an investment, depending on the intention of the management relative to resale. The purchase is an application of funds on the statement of changes in financial position.

Cash dividends received by the investor are revenue and are reported in the statement of income. Traditionally, revenue from dividends is described as *dividend income*, presumably because there are no direct costs to be matched against the revenue to obtain net income from that source. When the investors' income is measured between declaration and payment dates, the declared dividend should be accrued as revenue.

Stock dividends received by investors do not constitute revenue according to generally accepted practices. The stock dividend only increases the *number* of shares that each stockholder owns; the dividend does not change the percentages of ownership among the shareholders, nor does it change the total stockholders' equity in the corporation.

The original cost of a stock investment is deferred until the stock is sold or otherwise disposed of. If the stock becomes worthless, then the deferred cost expires and is shown as an expense (loss) on the income statement. When an investment is sold, the deferred cost is matched against the revenue from the sale. The common bookkeeping practice is to match the cost directly against revenue at the time of sale and record the gain or loss in a new account. Assume the investment in B Corporation stock is subsequently sold for $105 per share. The profit, commonly referred to as a gain, is $1,500, that is, revenue of $10,500 less cost of $9,000:

	Debit	Credit
Cash	10,500	
Investment in B Corporation common		9,000
Gain on sale of investment		1,500
(To record the sale of 100 shares at $105)		

If the stock is sold for $85 per share, the loss is $500, that is, revenue of $8,500 less cost of $9,000:

	Debit	Credit
Cash	$8,500	
Loss on sale of investment	500	
Investment in B Corporation common		$9,000
(To record sale of 100 shares at $85)		

Gains and losses on sales of investments, if material in amount, should be reported as extraordinary items on the statement of income. Sale of noncurrent investments increases the funds of the investor, and the revenue from the sale would appear under sources on the statement of changes in financial position.

QUESTIONS

1 What are the characteristics of a debt investment?
2 Define each of the following terms:
   [a] Short-term debt   [c] Long-term debt
   [b] Intermediate-term debt   [d] Installment debt
3 Describe a process to determine the market value of a bond.
4 What are the advantages and disadvantages of a secured investment as opposed to an unsecured investment to an investor. To the issuing corporation?
5 What factors cause a bond or other debt investment to be sold at a discount or a premium?

6   How should a bond discount or bond premium be disclosed on the balance sheet of the issuing corporation?

7   Define the following terms:

[a]   Mortgage bond   [c]   Debenture
[b]   Income bond   [d]   Convertible bond

8   How are debt investments disclosed on the balance sheet of the investor?

9   Why is the accounting for premiums and discounts different on the books of the investor than it is on the books of the issuing company?

10   Why is the amortization of bond premiums or bond discounts a deduction or an addition to income in determining funds provided by operations on a statement of funds?

11   What are the characteristics of an owner investment?

12   What are the rights of a common stockholder of a corporation?

13   Define the following terms:

[a]   Par value   [c]   No par value
[b]   Stated value   [d]   Market value

14   List and describe some of the typical preferences given to preferred stock.

15   List and comment on the significance of the three important dates connected with a dividend.

16   What is a stock dividend?

17   Define each of the following terms:

[a]   Cumulative preferred stock   [d]   Nonparticipating preferred stock
[b]   Noncumulative preferred stock   [e]   Callable preferred stock
[c]   Participating preferred stock

18   Why would a corporation reacquire some of its shares of stock and hold them as treasury shares rather than retiring the stock?

19   Why do corporations have a separate account called "retained earnings"?

20   Why are gains and losses from the sale of securities by investors usually shown as extraordinary items? Under what conditions would gains and losses from the sale of securities be shown as operating income?

PROBLEMS

1   [a]   Prepare journal entries to record the following note transactions on the books of the R Company:

[1]   The R Company borrowed $1,000 from the J Company on September 1, 19X1. The note is due in six months plus interest at 8 percent per annum.

[2]   The R Company closes its accounts on December 31, 19X1. Give the necessary adjusting entry for interest.

[3]   The note and interest are paid on March 1, 19X2.

[b]   Prepare journal entries to record the effects of the above transactions on the books of the J Company, which also closes its accounts on December 31.

2   [a]   The R Company issued and sold 100 bonds with a face amount of $1,000 each on May 1, 19X1. Bonds are due in five years. Interest is paid annually on May 1, 19X1 at the rate of 7 percent per annum. Give journal entries to record the following on the books of the R Company:

[1]   Sales price of the bonds was 105.

[2]   R Company closes its accounts on December 31. Prepare an entry for the accrual of interest and premium amortization.

[3]   Interest is paid on May 1, 19X2

[4]   Adjusting entries at the end of 19X2

[5]   Entry to record final interest payment and amortization on May 1, 19X6

[6]   Entry to record retirement of bonds at maturity on May 1, 19X6

[b]   Assume the same facts as in part [a] except that the R Company sold the bonds for 96. Prepare journal entries as in part [a].

3   The R Company sold the bonds to the T Investment Corporation. Record the transactions in Problem 2 on the books of the T Investment Corporation:

[a]   Assuming the bonds were purchased at 105.

[b]   Assuming the bonds were purchased at 96.

4   The L Corporation received a charter in early January, 19X1. The corporation was authorized to issue 100,000 shares of no par common stock and 10,000 shares of preferred ($100 par). The stated value of the common stock was set at $10. The preferred shares have a 6 percent dividend preference with a cumulative feature.

[a]   During 19X1, the L Corporation entered into the following transactions with investors. For each transaction, prepare a general journal entry to record properly the transaction in the L Company accounts.

January 20, 19X1: Sold 80,000 shares of common stock for $14 per share.

January 25, 19X1: Sold 5,000 shares of preferred stock for $105 per share.

July 20, 19X1: Reacquired 500 shares of the common stock for $12 per share. Stock will be held in treasury.

October 10, 19X1: Sold 200 shares of the common stock held in treasury. The sales price was $15.

December 31, 19X1: Profits for 19X1 amount to $75,000 (after accounts are closed, this is the balance of the retained earnings). Under state law, an appropriation of retained earnings was made equal to the cost of shares in treasury. (Make only the entry for appropriations; assume the accounts are closed.)

[b]   Prepare the stockholders' equity section of the balance sheet for the L Corporation as of December 31, 19X1. (The student may find it helpful to use T accounts, particularly for part [d].)

[c]   Prepare journal entries to record the following transactions for 19X2:

March 20, 19X2: The remaining shares held in treasury were sold for $16. The appropriation of retained earnings was cancelled.

May 29, 19X2: A stockholder who owned 1,000 shares of common stock became dissatisfied. The corporation purchased his stock for $16 per share and retired (cancelled) it.

September 30, 19X2: To preserve liquid capital, the directors declared and distributed a 10 percent stock dividend on the shares outstanding at September 30. Fair market value of the shares on that date was $17 per share.

December 15, 19X2: The directors declared a $60,000 cash dividend on the preferred shares to pay the preference dividend for 19X1 and 19X2. Payment date was January 15, 19X3.

[d]   Income closed to retained earnings for 19X2 was $150,000. Prepare the stockholders' equity section as of December 31, 19X2.

[e]   Give the entry to record payment of the preference dividend on January 15, 19X3.

[f]   Give the entry that would have been made if the treasury stock sold on March 20, 19X2 had brought only $11 per share.

[g] Give the entry to record the retirement of 1,000 shares of common on May 29, 19X2, assuming the corporation paid only $11 per share for the stock.

[h] What are the effects of the following transactions on the L Corporation statement of funds (working capital)? Explain each answer thoroughly.

    [i] Sale of common and preferred stock in Jan. 19X1

    [ii] Acquisition of treasury stock in July, 19X1

    [iii] Distribution of stock dividend in September, 19X2

5   The following is the equity section of the E Corporation as of December 31, 19X9. Virtually all of the corporation's stock is owned by Bob Lee, who is president and chairman of the board.

E Corporation
Stockholders' Equity Section, December 31, 19X1

Common stock ($100 par)	$ 10,000
Additional paid-in capital	3,000
Retained earnings	150,000
	$163,000

The following lettered items are statements concerned with the equity section of the E Corporation. For each statement, indicate whether it is true or false. If the statement is false, explain the source of the error.

[a] The corporation has 100 shares of stock outstanding.

[b] Bob Lee originally purchased 100 shares.

[c] Lee paid $13 per share for the stock.

[d] The corporation has been unusually profitable based on the assets employed by the business.

[e] Profits (income) since incorporation totalled $150,000.

[f] The E Corporation has one class of stock outstanding.

[g] Based on this balance sheet, the current value of Bob Lee's stock in the company is $163,000.

6   The C Corporation issued 100, 8 percent bonds with a face value of $1,000. The issue price was 102. Interest is payable semiannually on January 1 and on July 1. Bonds mature on July 1, 19X1.

[a] Record the issuance of the bonds on July 1, 19X1.

[b] The C Corporation fiscal year ends on September 30. Record the interest expense accrual and the amortization of premium for the fiscal year ended on September 30, 19X1.

[c] Record the interest payments in 19X2.

[d] Make all necessary adjusting entries to correct the accounts relevant to the bonds for the fiscal year ended September 30, 19X2.

[e] What effect would the above transactions have on the funds flows (use net working capital definition) for fiscal years 19X1 and 19X2).

7   The N Company earned $100,000 the first year of its existence and declared dividends of $40,000 on December 20, 19X4, payable on February 15, 19X5 to stockholders of record as of January 30, 19X5.

[a] Prepare entries to record the foregoing information.

[b] Prepare the stockholders' equity section of the N Company as of December 31, 19X4. On January 10, 19X4, 10,000 shares of no par stock, with stated value of $25 per share, were issued for $30 per share.

[c]   How should the dividends payable be shown on the balance sheet?

[d]   What effect does the declaration and payment of dividends have on the funds statement prepared on December 31, 19X4 if funds are defined as net working capital?

8   Jack Hofman has agreed to sell his 500-acre farm including the buildings to Jeffrey Herman
for $250,000. Mr. Herman has agreed to pay $50,000 down and the balance plus 8 percent
interest in ten equal annual payments. Mr. Hofman and Mr. Herman request that you
determine the amount of the annual payment and prepare a repayment schedule for the
ten-year period showing unpaid principal balance, annual interest, principal payment, and
total annual payment.

9   The J Company was organized with capital stock authorizations as follows:

Common stock, 10,000, par value $10
Preferred stock, 1,000, par value $100

[1]   Plant and equipment owned by N. Bill with a fair market value of $120,000 were
received in exchange for 5,000 shares of common stock and 600 shares of preferred
stock.

[2]   The remaining shares of common stock were sold for $12 per share.

[3]   Of the preferred stock, 200 shares were sold at par.

Required:

[a]   Prepare journal entries to record the preceding transactions.

[b]   Prepare a balance sheet for the J Company following the completion of the preceding
transactions.

10   Robert Hillot inherited $250,000 cash from his uncle on December 1, 19X0. As soon as
this news was known in Hillot's home town, a small community, both bankers actively tried
to convince Bob that he should permit their trust department to manage this money for
him. Bob decided that he would allow a bank to manage his funds, but he was undecided
as to which bank he should select. To help him make the final decision he gave each bank
$100,000 to invest for him on January 1, 19X1. At the end of the year the banks submitted
the following statements:

National Bank

Investment for the Account of Robert Hillot

	Face value	Cost	Market value 12/31/19X1	Interest received or accrued 19X1
USS, 5% debentures due 19X6	$ 70,000	$ 45,000	$44,500	$3,500
P,M,&L, 8% mortgage bonds, due 19X8	20,000	20,500	21,000	1,600
U.P. railroad equipment bonds, 6% due in 19X4	45,000	34,000	33,000	2,700
Uninvested cash	500	500	500	
	$135,500	$100,000	$99,000	$7,800

Bank & Trust Company
Investment for the Account of Robert Hillot

	Face value	Cost	Market value 12/31/19X1	Interest received or accrued 19X1
C Company bonds, 7% due 19X7	$ 48,000	$ 40,000	$ 42,000	$3,360
P & A, 9% debentures due 19X20	29,000	30,000	33,000	2,610
G.S. Corporation, 3% note due 19X4	67,000	29,000	25,000	2,010
Uninvested cash	1,000	1,000	1,000	
	$145,000	$100,000	$101,000	$7,980

Required:

Recommend to Mr. Hillot which bank has performed best. Support your conclusion by schedules showing which bank performed best.

CASE The G City Rockets, a professional hockey team, has rented the city civic arena for the past ten years. The city civic arena had a seating capacity of 10,000. The arena was in poor repair and the management of the Rockets was unable to reach a satisfactory renewal agreement with the city officials. In addition, they believed that an arena with a larger seating capacity could be justified. After a slow start, the G City Rockets had become the "darlings" of G City. The Rockets performed to a full house most of the time. Ticket scalpers were able to sell tickets at double the normal admission price of $4.

The directors of the G City Rocket Corporation approved a plan to build a new multipurpose arena on the north edge of G City. They sought and received approval from the State Commissioner of Finance to issue $3,000,000 of bonds in denominations of $250, a total of 12,000 bonds. Each bond gave the purchaser the right to order a season ticket at the normal market price, currently $100 per season. This right was renewable annually at the option of the season ticketholder for the next 20 years.

The bonds did not pay interest annually but would be redeemed as follows:

[1]   The excess of rental value of the arena over the cost of operating and maintaining the stadium would go into a pool. This pool would accumulate for the first five years. At the end of five years and each year thereafter the balance in the pool would be used to redeem the bonds at the rate of $300 per bond. The bonds redeemed would be determined by lot. The bond

numbers from 1 to 12,000 would be placed in a bowl, stirred, and numbers would be drawn until the required number of bond redemptions were reached. Each year the numbers of the outstanding bonds would be used as the population of the lottery. The bonds redeemed in the fifth year would not exceed $600,000 and no more than $500,000 would be redeemed in any succeeding year.

[2]   At the end of 40 years any bonds still outstanding would be redeemed by the payment of $300 cash to the bondholder.

The seating capacity of the new arena was 15,000 seats. The bond issue was successful in that all 12,000 bonds were sold. The financial plan was very favorable because the current interest rate for bonds with similar risk was 8 percent.

The directors estimated that the rent revenue from the stadium would be $500,000 annually and that the estimated cost would be $200,000, leaving $300,000 as the expected annual contribution to the bond redemption pool. Based on this forecast, all of the bonds should be redeemed at the end of 12 years.

The arena would be owned by a new corporation, R Arena Incorporated whose stock would be 100% owned by the current directors of G City Rocket Corporation. The revenue of the arena would come primarily from the G City Rockets but would be supplemented by other sporting events and concessions.

Robert Buchanan, a local attorney and owner of ten shares of the G City Rocket Corporation has complained that the G City Rocket Corporation is giving to R Arena Incorporated a valuable right, that is, the option of the bondholders to purchase season tickets for the next 20 years. In addition the rental fee paid by the Rockets is equal to or more than the fair market value for the arena facilities. Because of this gift of the option rights to R Arena Incorporated, the income of G City Rocket Corporation will be reduced in the future, and the income of R Arena Incorporated will be increased. R Arena Incorporated would not have been able to issue the bonds for such a low interest rate if the ticket option right had not been attached to the bonds.

Mr. Buchanan asks you to compute the fair market value of the ticket option rights. Prepare a table showing the present value of the bonds assuming an 8 percent interest rate and that the bonds will be redeemed at the rate of $600,000 at the end of the fifth year and $500,000 per year thereafter until they are fully redeemed.

Additional requirements:

[a]   Is Mr. Buchanan correct?

[b]   How should R Arena Incorporated account for these bonds? Should the sale of the bonds be divided between the bond proceeds and deferred revenue? Why or why not?

five

ANALYSIS OF
FINANCIAL
STATEMENTS

16

Consolidated Financial Statements

In Part Five, we will review and illustrate the uses and limitations of financial statements. The ratios and other analytical methods introduced in earlier chapters are used in this part to analyze the financial statements of Kellogg Company. Before attempting this analysis, we must consider two other important accounting problems that affect the way the financial statements are used.

The first of these problems is the construction of consolidated financial statements for a group of companies (subsidiaries) controlled through stock ownership by another corporation (the parent). The basic concepts for preparation of consolidated statements are discussed in this chapter. The second problem is the effect of changing prices on accounting measurements. How price changes relate to the measurement of income and financial position is the subject in the first section of Chapter 17.

Concepts Governing Consolidated Financial Statements

Accountants recognize a business as an entity separate from its owners and from all other participating groups. This separate entity concept, in turn, determines the transactions included in the financial statements of the business. For example, in the case of a proprietorship, only transactions that affect the operations of the business are included in the statements. No personal transactions of the owners can be included.

The separate entity concept is also important in determining the point of realization of revenue. One of the three basic tests for realization is that of a transaction with an outside party. If a person purchases merchandise from a business in an arms-length transaction, he is an outside party, a customer. This holds true even if he has a residual equity interest in the business. For example, consider an individual who owns shares in a corporation, who works for the same corporation, and who also buys merchandise from the corporation. Relative to the corporation, a separate entity, he is an owner, an employee, and a customer.

The accountant's concept of the entity may or may not coincide with what constitutes a "person" under the law. In the case of corporations, the two concepts frequently do coincide. For proprietorships and partnerships, however, accounting is concerned with business operations, whereas the law does not make this distinction. On the other hand, the accountant's entity often includes more than one legal person. A common example is where one corporation owns a controlling interest in several other corporations. Even though these are separate legal persons, there may be only one accounting entity, because the proper accounting entity is the economic entity, not the legal entity. When managerial control, profitability, risk, and potential for growth are similar for a group of related legal entities, accountants usually treat the group as a single unit and prepare one set of statements for the entire group.

Parent and Subsidiary Companies

When one corporation owns a controlling interest in another, the controlling corporation is the parent company, and the controlled corporation is the subsidiary company. To have a controlling interest the parent must own more than 50 percent of the voting capital stock of the subsidiary. The capital stock of the subsidiary held by the parent is called the *majority interest*, and the remainder of the subsidiary's outstanding capital stock is called the *minority interest*.

Sometimes a parent is strictly a *holding* company, that is, the parent does not engage in any operating activities but exists for the sole purpose of controlling the activities of subsidiaries. The relationships between related companies can be very complex. A parent may control one or more subsidiaries and, in turn, can be a subsidiary of another company.

Nature and Purpose of Consolidated Statements

Consolidated financial statements are balance sheets, statements of income, and statements of changes in financial position prepared as though several companies with parent–subsidiary relationships were a single business entity. Both ownership (meaning possession of more than 50 percent of the subsidiary's voting stock) and control are prerequisites for the preparation of consolidated financial statements. In addition, several other prerequisites for preparation of consolidated financial statements include:

1   Ownership and control should be permanent rather than temporary. Either ownership or control could be temporary in nature for a variety of reasons: A foreign government may intend to confiscate a subsidiary company, or a subsidiary may be bankrupt, or bankruptcy may be iminent if not actual, or a parent may plan to dispose of its holdings in a subsidiary.
2   The parent should have a dominant financial interest in the subsidiary as well as control. If large blocks of nonvoting stock are controlled by parties other than the parent, consolidated statements may not be appropriate.

3   Ownership and control should be free from severe restrictions. For example, if a foreign country limits or forbids transfer of a subsidiary's funds to a parent, preparation of consolidated statements may not be appropriate.

Investments in subsidiaries that are not consolidated with other members of a controlled group should appear as assets on the consolidated balance sheet and the majority interest's share of earnings should be included in the consolidated statement of income. Also, unconsolidated subsidiaries should be identified and reasons given for not including them in the consolidated financial statements. If the investment in an unconsolidated subsidiary is material relative to the total assets of the affiliated group, separate financial statements of this subsidiary should accompany the consolidated financial statements.

Consolidated financial statements are prepared to present the financial position and operating results of the controlled group from the viewpoint of the parent corporation. The needs of minority interests and of creditors are best served by the separate statements for each subsidiary. For the majority interest, transactions between the members of the consolidated group are eliminated and like items are combined so that the financial position and operating results may be presented as if the group were a single business. Economically and financially, the controlled group is one business.

Although the concept of consolidated statements is a simple one, the mechanics can be rather complicated. For example, complications arise when the relationships among the companies in the group are complex, when the ownership percentages change, or when the members of the group do not use the same fiscal periods. Such complications are beyond our scope. We will consider a parent with a single subsidiary and identical fiscal periods. Also, we will always assume that the ownership percentage remains unchanged. Consolidation procedures are explained for the balance sheet on the date of acquisition assuming either purchase of a subsidiary for cash or the acquisition of a subsidiary in exchange for capital stock of the parent company. The discussion also covers consolidating procedures after acquisition and will include the preparation of a consolidated statement of income.

Consolidated Balance Sheet at Acquisition

The first examples in the following sections are based on the assumption that the parent acquires its controlling interest in the subsidiary by paying cash for the subsidiary's stock. Situations where the parent issues its own securities for the subsidiary's stock are discussed later.

PURCHASE PRICE EQUAL TO BOOK VALUE. Consolidating procedures are least complicated when the parent acquires a 100 percent interest in a subsidiary for cash and when the amount of cash paid is equal to the book value of the subsidiary's net worth. If P Company buys a 100 percent interest in S Company for

$150,000, the following entry would be used to record the transaction on the P Company books:

	Debit	Credit
Investment in S Co.	$150,000	
Cash		$150,000

The S Company would simply make a record of the fact that the ownership of its shares has been transferred from the original owners to P Company, and it would make no entry that affected the accounts in its general ledger.

When P Company and S Company are consolidated at the end of the accounting period, the account, investment in S Company, on the books of P Company and the shareholders' equity accounts on the books of S Company are eliminated. For the consolidated entity, an investment in S Company becomes the equivalent of an investment in itself, and the outstanding stock of S Company becomes the equivalent of treasury stock. After making the elimination, the remaining assets, liabilities, and shareholders' equity accounts are combined. The process is shown on the worksheet, Fig. 16-1. The worksheet is not a part of the permanent records of either company, and the elimination entries are not recorded on the books of either company. The worksheet is used only for preparation of consolidated financial statements. Figure 16-1 presumes the conditions specified in the preceding paragraph.

Figure 16-1: Worksheet for Preparation of Consolidated Balance Sheet

			Eliminations		
	P Company	S Company	Debit	Credit	Consolidated
Current assets	$200,000	$ 50,000			$250,000
Investment in S Co.	150,000			$150,000	
Noncurrent assets	400,000	150,000			550,000
	$750,000	$200,000			$800,000
Liabilities	$100,000	50,000			$150,000
Capital stock	400,000	100,000	$100,000		400,000
Retained earnings	250,000	50,000	50,000		250,000
	$750,000	$200,000			$800,000

PURCHASE PRICE EXCEEDS BOOK VALUE. Typically a parent pays more than book value for an interest in a subsidiary for reasons such as the following:

1 The general market value of the subsidiary's assets may have increased since they were originally purchased. This increase could be caused by inflation or by appreciation in real economic value or some combination of the two.

2 The assets of the subsidiary may be understated because the subsidiary has employed highly conservative accounting practices.

3 The subsidiary may have assets that are not recognized in accounting as currently practiced, such as a skilled work force. Assets that have no

accounting recognition or cannot be separately identified are lumped together as goodwill after the acquisition.

4   The subsidiary as a whole or some of its individual assets may have unique value for the parent. For example, the distribution channels of the subsidiary may be more valuable to the parent than to the general market.

If specific assets of the subsidiary have a value in excess of their book value, the additional value would be assigned to these assets in the process of consolidation. Any excess that cannot be assigned to individual assets should appear on the consolidated balance sheet as goodwill or more accurately, as "excess of cost over book value of investment in subsidiary." The excess should be amortized as an expense in future years. The amortization period may not exceed 40 years to comply with APB Opinion No. 17.*

Figure 16-2

S Company	Balance Sheet as of January 1, 19X1
Current assets	$ 50,000
Noncurrent assets	150,000
	$200,000
Liabilities	$ 50,000
Capital stock	100,000
Retained earnings	50,000
	$200,000

In order to give an example of an acquisition where the purchase price exceeds the book value, consider a subsidiary with account balances immediately prior to acquisition as shown in Fig. 16-2. Assume that the parent acquires a 100 percent interest in S Company for $170,000, an excess of cost over book value of the subsidiary by $20,000. Assume also that $4,000 of the excess of cost over book value of the subsidiary can be assigned to land held by the subsidiary and that the remaining $16,000 cannot be assigned to any individual asset. The parent would record the acquisition as follows:

	Debit	Credit
Investment in S Co.	$170,000	
Cash		$170,000

The consolidation of the balance sheets of P Company and S Company on the date of acquisition is shown in Fig. 16-3.

*Amercian Institute of Certified Public Accountants, *Opinion of the Accounting Principles Board No. 17* (August 1970).

Figure 16–3: Worksheet for Preparation of Consolidated Balance Sheet

	P Company	S Company	Eliminations Debit	Eliminations Credit	Consolidated
Current assets	$180,000	$ 50,000			$230,000
Investment in S Co.	170,000			$154,000	16,000[a]
Noncurrent assets	400,000	150,000	$ 4,000		554,000
	$750,000	$200,000			$800,000
Liabilities	$100,000	50,000			$150,000
Capital stock	400,000	100,000	100,000		400,000
Retained earnings	250,000	50,000	50,000		250,000
	$750,000	$200,000			$800,000

[a]This is "excess of cost over book value of investment in subsidiary" sometimes labeled "goodwill from consolidation."

To illustrate an acquisition that involves minority interest, assume the same facts as in the preceding example except that P Company acquires only 75 percent of the capital stock of S Company for $127,500. The parent would record the acquisition as follows:

	Debit	Credit
Investment in S Co.	$127,500	
Cash		$127,500

The consolidation of the balance sheets is shown in Fig. 16-4.

Figure 16–4: Worksheet for Preparation of Consolidated Balance Sheet

	P Company	S Company	Eliminations Debit	Eliminations Credit	Consolidated
Current assets	$221,500	$ 50,000			$271,500
Investment in S Co.	127,500			$115,500	12,000[a]
Noncurrent assets	400,000	150,000	$ 3,000		554,000
	$750,000	$200,000			$837,500
Liabilities	$100,000	$ 50,000			$150,000
Capital stock of P Co.	400,000				400,000
Retained earnings of P Co.	250,000				250,000
Capital stock of S Co.		100,000⎫	112,500		37,500[b]
Retained earnings of S Co.		50,000⎭			
	$750,000	$200,000			$837,500

[a]Excess of cost over book value. [b]Minority interest.

Amounts that relate to the capital stock and retained earnings of S Company are combined because the residual of $37,500 is carried into the consolidated balance sheet as a single figure labeled "minority interest." Note that $3,000 instead of $4,000 is added for the increment in the value of the land. Minority shareholders have a 25 percent interest in all of the assets including the land. The $1,000 increment in their interest is unrealized appreciation, not a cost incurred. Some accountants might prefer to add $4,000 to the carrying value of the land and increase the minority interest from $37,500 to $38,500, but this alternative would be inconsistent with generally accepted rules for realization. A consolidated balance sheet based on the foregoing is shown in Fig. 16–5.

Figure 16–5

P Company and Subsidiary	January 1, 19X1
Assets:	
Current assets	$271,500
Noncurrent assets	554,000
Excess of cost over book value of investment in subsidiary	12,000
	$837,500
Equities:	
Liabilities	$150,000
Minority interest	37,500
Capital stock	400,000
Retained earnings	250,000
	$837,500

The presentation of minority interest on consolidated balance sheets is a controversial matter. Some accountants believe that the minority interest should be grouped with liabilities. The basis for this belief is that consolidated statements are intended to represent the equity of the shareholders of the parent company. According to this view, the minority shareholders are outsiders.

Other accountants hold that minority shareholders have a residual equity interest in the consolidated entity and prefer to list minority interest with shareholders' equity. Still other accountants prefer a compromise and list minority interest in an undefined classification between liabilities and the shareholders' equity.

ACQUISITIONS USING PARENT'S SECURITIES. In recent years, the financial community has seen many corporations grow into giant financial enterprises by acquiring other corporations not with cash but by issuing their own securities. In Chapter 15 we explained how, previous to the issuance of Opinion No. 15 of the Accounting Principles Board, the earnings per share of these companies could be increased by using convertible securities. The use of securities to acquire a subsidiary also creates a unique valuation problem affecting the procedures used to prepare consolidated financial statements. When securities are used, the acquisition may be accounted for as a purchase or as a "pooling of interest."

• Purchase Method: Under the purchase method, the procedures are substantially the same as when the subsidiary's stock is acquired for cash. The investment in the subsidiary is valued at the fair market value of the securities issued. Determination of the fair value of the acquiring company's stock is sometimes difficult. The value assigned affects the amounts that will appear in the parent's financial statements and the consolidated statements.

To give an example of a purchase effected by issuing stock, assume the same facts as in Fig. 16-2 except that the parent issues 2,000 shares of its own common stock (stated value $50) for the subsidiary's stock. Assume further that the parent's stock has a fair market value of $85 per share. The entry to record the acquisition in the parent's accounts is

	Debit	Credit
Investment in S Co.	$170,000	
Common stock		$100,000
Additional paid-in capital		70,000

The cost of subsidiary purchased is $170,000 (2,000 shares X $85). Its book value, however, is only $150,000. The excess of cost over book value is accounted for in the consolidated financial statements just as though the stock had been acquired for cash.

• Pooling of Interest Method: In some cases, two corporations merge or combine their operations. One corporation does not buy out the shareholders of another; instead, the two corporations are joined together in a new and larger combined enterprise. Although mergers may be accomplished under many different legal arrangements, the simplest way is for one corporation to issue its own securities to the shareholders of the other corporation. The result is a parent–subsidiary relationship,* with the following qualification: The acquiring corporation (parent) does not record its investment in the acquired company (subsidiary) at the fair market value of the securities issued. The value assigned to the investment is the pro-rated amount of *contributed capital* of the acquired company. The book values of all assets and liabilities, as well as the retained earnings (or deficit) of the acquired company, are included in the consolidated statements. In other words, when the acquisition is recorded as a pooling of interest, there is never an excess of cost over book value. The valuation of the securities issued is based on the rationale that there has been no transaction with outside parties, but only a combination of operations in which the interest of the owners and managers of both companies is continued in the combined enterprise.

For example, suppose a parent company issues 2,000 shares of its own capital stock with a par value of $100,000 and a market value of $170,000 for a 100 percent interest in a subsidiary. The transaction would be recorded as follows in the parent's books:

*In a pooling, the relationship is often more correctly that of brother corporations rather than parent and subsidiary, but the previous terminology is used for convenience.

	Debit	Credit
Investment in S Co.	$100,000	
Capital stock		$100,000

Consolidation of a parent and its subsidiary under the pooling of interest concept is shown in Fig. 16-6. The capital accounts of the subsidiary and the investment account of the parent are completely eliminated, and the credit to balance the entry is made to the retained earnings of the parent. This is permitted because the consolidated entity may show retained earnings of the pooled companies.

Figure 16-6: Worksheet for Consolidation as a Pooling of Interests

	P Company	S Company	Elimination Debit	Elimination Credit	Consolidated
Current assets	$200,000	$ 50,000			$250,000
Investment in S Co.	100,000			$100,000	
Noncurrent assets	400,000	150,000			550,000
	$700,000	$200,000			$800,000
Liabilities	$100,000	$ 50,000			$150,000
Capital stock of P Co.	400,000				400,000
Retained earnings of P Co.	200,000			50,000	250,000
Capital stock of S Co.		100,000	$100,000		
Retained earnings of S Co.		50,000	50,000		
	$700,000	$200,000			$800,000

In the preceding example, we assumed that the par or stated value of the stock issued was the same amount as the contributed capital of the acquired corporation. In some cases, the par or stated value of the issued shares is less than the total contributed capital of the acquired company. Assume the same facts as for Fig. 16-6 except that the 2,000 shares issued by P Company have a par value of $50,000 instead of $100,000. The entry to record the transaction on the P Company books is

	Debit	Credit
Investment in S Co.	$50,000	
Capital stock		$50,000

The elimination entry in the workpapers for consolidation would be

	Debit	Credit
Capital stock of S Co.	$100,000	
Investment in S Co.		$50,000
Additional paid-in capital		50,000

If the par or stated value of the 2,000 shares issued by P Company had been $110,000 instead of $100,000, the entries to record the investment would be as follows:

	Debit	Credit
Investment in S Co.	$110,000	
Capital stock		$110,000

The elimination entry in consolidating workpapers would be

	Debit	Credit
Capital stock of S Co.	$100,000	
Retained earnings	10,000	
Investment in S Co.		$110,000

Consolidated retained earnings are reduced as in the preceding entry only as a last resort. If P Company had any contributed capital, the $10,000 debit would ordinarily be charged against it. The opportunity to preserve the balances of retained earnings in tact is usually one of the reasons why firms choose the pooling method instead of the purchase method.

COMPARISON OF THE METHODS. For a corporation that is growing by acquiring other corporations in exchange for securities, the pooling-of-interest method has two significant advantages over the purchase method. First, the combined financial statements usually show a larger balance for retained earnings because the earnings of the acquired corporation prior to the acquisition are added to retained earnings of the acquiring company.

Second, if the pooling method is used the difference between the equity of the subsidiary acquired and the fair market value of the securities issued by the acquiring company is ignored. In most cases, the cost (fair market value of the securities issued) is greater than the book value of the equities acquired. The low book values may be due to conservative accounting practices, to inflation, or to assets of the acquired company that are either unrecorded or undervalued. Under the purchase method, the additional cost is recorded, and these costs will eventually be expenses or losses and will reduce future net income.

To illustrate the impact that the pooling method has on future income of the affiliated companies, consider a situation where S Company has developed a patent for a nominal cost of $5,000. Suppose the merging companies agree that the patent is worth $200,000 and that the exchange of shares between P Company and S Company is in accord with this agreement: The market value of the P Company shares issued to shareholders of the S Company is equal to the fair value of their interest in S Company and the patent is valued at $200,000. Remember that the purchase method would result in recognition of the fair market value of the stock issued, which is $200,000 in this situation. Under the pooling method, the patent might be valued at its cost of $5,000. The remaining $195,000 would then be assigned to excess of cost over book value, and this amount amortized over 40 years, the maximum period permitted by accounting principles for goodwill amortization. Assuming the patent has a ten-year life, under the purchasing method the annual amortization expense would be $20,000 ($200,000 cost over ten years). Under the pooling method, amortization expense would be

Patent ($5,000 ÷ 10 years)	$ 500
Goodwill ($195,000 ÷ 40 years)	4,875
Total amortization	$5,375

Given these facts the amortization expense is $14,625 ($20,000 - $5,375) less by using the pooling method as compared to the purchase method. For the first years following the acquisition the income of the combined companies would be increased by this amount.

Sometimes the fair value of a firm's assets exceeds book value by millions of dollars. Thus, there is a temptation to use the pooling method even in circumstances where the purchase method is obviously more appropriate.

In an attempt to restrict the use of the pooling method, the APB, in Opinion No. 16,* listed some specific criteria that must be met before a business combination can be accounted for under the pooling method. These criteria relate to conditions that exist prior to the combination, the nature of the combination itself, and to transactions that occur after the combination. The intent of the criteria is to make use of the pooling approach contingent on a continuation of essentially the same business activities and the same shareholder interests.

Consolidated Financial Statements after Acquisition

The procedures for consolidations explained in the preceding section were concerned with elimination or cancellation of intercompany accounts at the date of acquisition. Additional problems arise following the date of acquisition. One additional problem is preparing statements other than the consolidated balance sheet. A second problem is eliminating the effects of transactions between affiliated companies.

INTERCOMPANY TRANSACTIONS. Companies in an affiliated group frequently have transactions with one another. They usually record these transactions in the same way they record transactions with parties outside the affiliated group because they retain their separate legal status. Consolidation ignores legal separation and treats an affiliated group as a single entity. Thus, in consolidation the effects of transactions between consolidated companies must be eliminated.

To give an example of the effect of intercompany transactions, suppose that a parent company buys merchandise from its 100 percent owned subsidiary for $3,000. Of the merchandise purchased from S Company, $1,000 of the merchandise is in P Company's inventory and the remaining $2,000 of merchandise has been resold to the parent company's customers for $2,500. The merchandise originally cost the subsidiary $2,400, and S Company's cost of the merchandise still in P Company's inventory is $800. Figure 16-7 shows the entries in T accounts recorded by the P Company and by the S Company followed by the

*American Institute of Certified Public Accountants, *Opinion of the Accounting Principles Board No. 16* (August 1970).

Figure 16-7: Entries treated as separated transactions on records of parent and subsidiary companies.

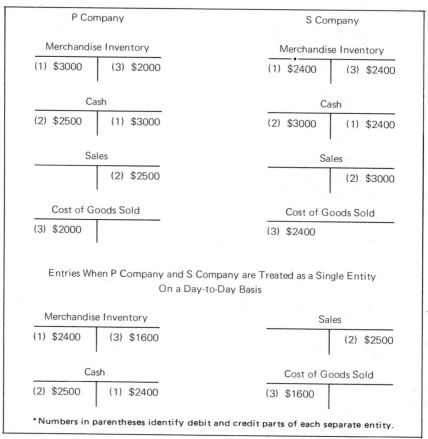

*Numbers in parentheses identify debit and credit parts of each separate entity.

entries that would have been recorded if the records of the affiliated companies were those of a single entity. The differences that arise in recording the transactions are tabulated as follows:

Account	Effects combined (1)	As a single entity (2)	Difference
Cash	$ 100.00	$ 100.00	$ 0
Merchandise inventory	1,000.00	800.00	200.00
Sales	(5,500.00)	(2,500.00)	(3,000.00)
Cost of goods sold	4,400.00	1,600.00	2,800.00

The first column shows the combined effect of the entries actually recorded by companies P and S. The second column shows the effect of the entries as they would be recorded by a single entity, and the third column shows the difference by subtracting column 2 from column 1. (The amounts in parentheses are credit balances.) The differences must be eliminated in the consolidated statements to show the amounts as if companies P and S were one business. The following entry would appear on the worksheet for consolidation:

	Debit	Credit
Sales	$3,000.00	
Cost of goods sold		$2,800.00
Merchandise inventory		200.00

This entry reduces revenue to the amounts received from parties outside the affiliated group. It also reduces cost of goods sold to the cost originally incurred by the S Company for goods transferred by sale to parties outside the affiliated group ($2,000/$3,000 X $2,400 = $1600). In addition, goods that remain in P Company's inventory are reduced to the cost originally incurred by the S Company ($1000/$3000 X $2400 = $800).

Affiliated companies may enter into a number of transactions with one another in addition to the purchase and sale of merchandise. The following are transactions that occur frequently between affiliates and the resulting reciprocal account balances:

1   Intercompany sale of merchandise may require adjustment of balances in sales, cost of goods sold, and merchandise inventory accounts. Also there may be reciprocal balances in accounts receivable and accounts payable.
2   Intercompany loans may require the elimination of notes receivable and notes payable, interest receivable and interest payable, and interest income and interest expense.
3   Intercompany dividends may require elimination of dividends receivable and dividends payable.
4   Intercompany sales of long-lived assets may require the elimination of gains or losses on the sale. If the long-lived assets are subject to depreciation or amortization, these expenses will also require adjustments.

PARENT'S ACCOUNTING AFTER ACQUISITION. Under what is called the *equity method*, a parent company would account for its investment in a subsidiary as shown in Fig. 16–8. (It is assumed that P Company owns 100 percent of S Company.) The parent's initial investment is adjusted to record the subsidiary's income (loss) and dividend distributions. Under this method, the parent's net income before consolidation is always equal to the net income for both parent and subsidiary after consolidation. When a subsidiary that is accounted for by the equity method is consolidated, its net assets (all assets minus all liabilities) are substituted for the parent's investment account and it's equity accounts are eliminated to avoid double counting. In other words, under the equity method, a parent's statements alone differ from consolidated statements in that the algebraic sum of the subsidiary's assets and liabilities are shown as a single number labeled "investment in subsidiary." Probably for this reason, the

Figure 16–8: Equity Basis for Investments in Subsidiaries

Transaction	Entry in Records of P Company	Debit	Credit
1 Subsidiary has income from operations of $25,000	Investment in subsidiary Income from subsidiary	$25,000	$25,000
2 Subsidiary declares and pays a dividend of $10,000	Cash Investment in subsidiary	10,000	10,000
3 Subsidiary has a loss from operations of $5,000	Loss from subsidiary Investment in subsidiary	5,000	5,000

APB, in its Opinion No. 18,* requires use of the equity method to account for subsidiaries that are not included in a consolidation.

Under an alternative to the equity method, called the *cost method*, a parent recognizes income from a subsidiary only when it receives a dividend. The differences between the cost and equity method are shown in Fig. 16-9.

Figure 16–9: Cost and Equity Methods

Transactions	Equity Method Entries	Debit	Credit	Cost Method Entries	Debit	Credit
1 Subsidiary has income from operations of $25,000	Investment in subsidiary Income from subsidiary	$25,000	$25,000			
2 The subsidiary declares and pays a dividend of $10,000	Cash Investment in subsidiary	10,000	10,000	Cash Dividend income	$10,000	$10,000
3 The subsidiary has a loss from operations of $5,000	Loss from subsidiary Investment in subsidiary	5,000	5,000			

The cost method has some application for investments in companies other than subsidiaries. As for controlled subsidiary companies, the cost method can be nothing more than a clerical procedure because, as already explained, accounts are automatically adjusted to the equity basis in consolidated statements. In addition, Opinion No. 18 requires the use of the equity basis for all subsidiaries if the parent issues separate, unconsolidated statements.

*American Institute of Certified Public Accountants, *Opinion of the Accounting Principles Board No. 18* (March 1971).

QUESTIONS

1 Every corporation is a separate legal entity. Accountants, however, prepare financial statements for several corporations as a single accounting entity. Why?

2 What conditions must exist before it is appropriate to prepare consolidated financial statements for two corporations?

3 Corporation Y is a large manufacturing company who owns stock in several other corporations. Would you include the following corporations in the consolidated statements of Corporation Y?

[a] Corporation Y owns 100 percent of the common stock of a bank.

[b] Corporation Y owns 45 percent of another large manufacturing company. The remaining 55 percent of that company's stock is owned by 500,000 small investors and, as a result, Corporation Y effectively controls the company.

[c] Corporation Y owns 100 percent of the capital stock of an Algerian oil company.

[d] Corporation Y owns 55 percent of the common stock of Corporation X. The common stock, however, accounts for only 5 percent of the Corporation X total capital. Nonvoting preferred stock and debentures convertible to common stock account for 60 percent of the capital of Corporation X.

4 Normally, when a parent corporation acquires the stock of a new subsidiary, the cost to the parent exceeds the book value of the subsidiary. Explain why this statement is true.

5 What is the most desirable treatment of the excess of cost over book value in consolidated statements?

6 Distinguish the cost and equity method of accounting for a subsidiary's transaction on a parent's books. Does the use of different methods have any effect on consolidated financial statements? On the parent's separate financial statements?

7 Corporations frequently acquire the stock of a new subsidiary by issuing their own securities to the shareholders of the acquired company. What are the two methods that accountants may use to record such acquisitions? Explain each method.

8 Why do corporate managers frequently prefer to account for a business combination as a pooling even when the combination is in substance a purchase?

9 In general terms, under what conditions is it appropriate to account for a business combination as a pooling of interests?

PROBLEMS

1 The following are the balance sheets of the F and B corporations. The B Corporation is the parent company and F Corporation is the subsidiary company

	B Corp.	F Corp.
Assets:		
Current assets	$ 400,000	$150,000
Investment in F Corp.	250,000	
Other Assets	350,000	100,000
	$1,000,000	$250,000
Equities:		
Current liabilities	$ 200,000	$ 75,000
Contributed capital	500,000	125,000
Retained earnings	300,000	50,000
	$1,000,000	$250,000

Required:

For each of the following independent situations, prepare a consolidated balance sheet for the B Corporation.

[a] The B Corporation acquired 100 percent of the stock of the F Corporation just prior to the date of the foregoing statements. The excess of cost over book value is to be allocated to other assets.

[b] The B Corporation uses the equity method of recording the income of its subsidiary. The F Corporation was formed one year ago. All of F Corporation's stock was issued to the B Corporation.

[c] The B Corporation acquired 80 percent of the F Corporation just prior to the date of the foregoing statements. The assets of the F Corporation are stated at fair market value.

2   The condensed balance sheets of D Corporation and K Corporation are as follows:

	D Corp.	K Corp.
Assets:		
Current assets	$ 800,000	$200,000
Other assets	1,000,000	300,000
	$1,800,000	$500,000
Equities:		
Liabilities	$ 500,000	$100,000
Contributed Capital	1,000,000	350,000
Retained earnings	300,000	50,000
	$1,800,000	$500,000

[a] The D Corporation acquired all of the stock of K Corporation by exchanging 40,000 shares of its own unissued stock. Each share has a par value of $10, and the fair market value of the stock of the K Corporation is $600,000. The D Corporation uses the purchase method to record the acquisition of K Corporation. The excess of cost over book value is attributed to a patent with a remaining life of five years. Prepare a consolidated balance sheet at the date of acquisition.

[b] The D Corporation acquired all of the stock of the K Corporation in exchange for $400,000 of par value of its unissued stock. The market value of the D Corporation stock is $600,000. The D Corporation elects to record the acquisition of the K Corporation by the pooling method. Prepare a consolidated balance sheet at the date of acquisition.

[c] Assume that the expected income of the D Corporation for each of the next five years is expected to be $100,000 before considering any income from the K Corporation. Assume also that K Corporation's income for each of the next five years is expected to be $40,000 without considering the amortization of the patent referred to in part [a]. Compute the difference in the consolidated income of D and K corporations for the five-year period under the pooling method as compared with the purchase method.

[d] Assume that immediately before the combination with the K Corporation, the earnings per share on D Corporation's stock was $1 and that the price–earnings ratio was 15. If this P/E ratio is expected to continue after the combination, compute the expected impact of the purchase versus the pooling approach on the market value of the holdings of an investor who owns 1,000 shares of D Corporation.

3 Data from the accounts of the C Corporation and the I Corporation are as follows:

	C Corp.	I Corp.
Debit accounts:		
Current assets, C Corp.	$ 300,000	
Current assets, I Corp.		$100,000
Investment in I Corp.	200,000	
Noncurrent assets	400,000	60,000
Cost of goods sold, C Corp.	300,000	
Cost of goods sold, I Corp.		150,000
Other expenses	100,000	50,000
	$1,300,000	$360,000
Credit accounts:		
Current liabilities, C Corp.	$ 125,000	
Current liabilities, I Corp.		$ 40,000
Noncurrent liabilities	200,000	50,000
Contributed capital, C Corp.	275,000	
Contributed capital, I Corp.		30,000
Retained earnings, C Corp.	200,000	
Retained earnings, I Corp.		20,000
Sales of C	500,000	
Sales of I		220,000
	$1,300,000	$360,000

Additional information:
[1] The C Corporation owns 100 percent of I Corporation.
[2] Sales from I Corporation to C Corporation were $60,000.
[3] The C Corporation owes the I Corporation $8,000 at the end of the year.
[4] The C Corporation's ending inventory contained $5,000 of intercompany profits on merchandise acquired from I Corporation.

Required:

[a] Prepare consolidated working papers.
[b] Prepare a consolidated statement of income.
[c] Prepare a consolidated balance sheet.

4 **A Company and B Company**
Ledger Balance, Dec. 31, 19X9

	A Co.	B Co.
Current assets (net)	$147,000	$ 57,000
Investment in B Co. stock (100%)	100,000	
Other assets	90,000	39,000
	$337,000	$ 96,000
Current liabilities	$ 52,000	$ 23,000
Capital contributed	160,000	60,000
Retained earnings	125,000	13,000
	$337,000	$ 96,000
Sales	$500,000	$130,000
Merchandise cost of sales	$300,000	$100,000
	100,000	25,000
	$400,000	$125,000
	$100,000	$ 5,000

The A Company acquired 100 percent of the B Company on January 1, 19X9, at which time the B Company had retained earnings of $8,000. During 19X9, one-half of B Company's sales were made to the A Company, and, at the end of the year, the A Company still had on hand 20 percent of the goods bought from the B Company. Also, on December 31, 19X9, the A Company owes the B Company $4,000 for goods purchased, and the B Company owes the A Company $6,000 from a loan made at the end of the year. B Company recorded a 25 percent gross profit on sales of merchandise to A Company.

Required:

[a] Prepare a consolidated position statement.
[b] Prepare a consolidated statement of income (journal entries would be helpful, but are not required).

17

The Problem of
Changing Prices and
a Summary of Financial
Statement Analysis

Financial statements are quantified summaries of the activities and resources of
a business, measured in terms of money. They are general statements, but when
properly used, they can reveal many specific events occurring during the life of a
business. The main objective of the preceding chapters of this text is to explain
the basic concepts underlying the preparation of financial statements. In this
final chapter, attention is focused on the use of these statements when an investment decision has to be made. Before taking up the problem of statement analysis for decision making, we must consider in some detail how the problem of
price changes affects the accountant's measurements of income and financial
position. No one can intelligently use financial statements unless they understand how price changes affect them.

The Problem of Changing Prices

In accounting the measurement unit is money. Unlike money, most measurement units are stable units: Pounds, yards, meters, and miles are constant and,
if properly used, denote the same quantities regardless of when or where they
are used. On the other hand, the monetary values of most economic goods and
services fluctuate constantly. The price of beef may be declining whereas the
price of steel is increasing rapidly. Although the prices of individual commodities change constantly, it is now common practice to prepare averages or indices
of the price changes of a selected group of commodities and, based on changes
in these averages or indices, to refer to the decline or increase in the value of
money.

Despite the knowledge that prices of individual commodities are constantly
changing and that these changes, when averaged, indicate a general change in the
value of money relative to commodities, accountants in the United States persist

in the assumption that the dollar is a stable unit of measurement. Critics of present accounting measurements, both within and outside the accounting profession, have long questioned the wisdom of ignoring price changes. Two basic remedies have been proposed. One group of critics would adjust accounting values by using some general index of price changes. Implementation of this remedy would result in *common dollar* accounting. Others would use *specific* price changes, combined with some general index, and prepare *current value* financial statements. Before turning to a discussion of the proposals and how they would affect our present measurements, a thorough understanding of the differences between specific price changes and general price changes is necessary.

Specific Versus General Price Changes

As noted above the prices of individual commodities are generally increasing or decreasing constantly, although some may remain relatively stable for a year or more. In recent years, prices of most commodities have been increasing. To give a simple example of the accounting problem caused by changing prices, assume that a retail clothing store buys a ready-to-wear men's suit on January 3 for $100. This same suit is sold on May 15 for $150. Assume further that on May 15 the clothing store would have to pay $110 to replace the suit, that is, the wholesalers' or manufacturers' price increased from $100 to $110 between January 1 and May 15. What is the profit on the sale? One could conclude that the store made a profit of $50 (the sales price of $150 less original cost of $100.) A closer analysis of the facts, however, may provide more useful results.

CONCEPT OF HOLDING GAINS. The retailer earned the $50 profit by adding both time and place utility to the suit. He held it for over four months (time utility) in a place convenient for his customer (place utility). By using the replacement cost of $110, a specific price change, it is possible to divide the retailer's gain into two portions:

Selling price	$150
Less: Cost of specific item sold at time of sale (replacement cost)	110
Operating profit	$ 40

Presumably, the operating profit is attributable to the primary goal of the retailer, providing place utility or convenience in location to its customers.

The remainder of the profit, $10 ($50 total less the $40 operating profit), may be attributed to the fact that the suit was bought in January when the cost was lower:

Replacement cost at date of sale	$110
Original cost in January	100
Holding gain	$ 10

In this calculation, the holding gain arises because the retailer purchased the suit when the price of that *specific* commodity was lower. Thus the $10 is due to *holding* (time) a commodity during a period of price changes, increases in this case.

The use of specific prices in this manner is susceptible to attack on three bases. First, accounting for specific price changes would cost too much in most businesses. Second, many accountants argue that the division between operating profits and holding gains is an arbitrary one. The two elements, they maintain, are interdependent—you cannot have one without the other. A third, and perhaps the most damaging criticism of the separation of the profits into two elements is the fact that the calculation ignores changes in prices generally. The calculation involved the price change for only one commodity, namely, a specific price change.

General Price Changes and Price Indices

When prices change, the quantity of goods and services one can buy with a given sum of money also changes. To demonstrate the relationship between changing prices and the purchasing power of money, assume a simple economy that has only three commodities, A, B, and C. Then assume the additional facts presented in the following table. The computations in the table also assume that prices changed gradually during the year and that Prorata amounts were spent at each price.

Commodity	(1) Price 1/1/19X1	(2) Price 1/1/19X2	(3) Increase/ decrease in price (2) – (1)	(4) % Increase/ decrease in price, (3)/(1)	(5) % of all money spent in 19X1	(6) % Weighted increase/ decrease (4) X (5)
A	$100	$120	$20	20	15	3
B	50	40	(10)	(20)	25	(4)
C	200	230	30	15	60	9
					100	8

In this simplified economy, one may conclude that, on the average, prices increased by 8 percent during the year.

The example shows what a general price index (GPI) attempts to measure. Ideally, a GPI is an average of the price changes of all the goods and services in an economy weighted by the money spent for each as a percentage of total expenditures in the economy. Typically, a base point is set equal to 100 and prices at other points are stated in terms of this base. If prices at January 1, 19X1 are used as a base in the foregoing example, then the index at January 1, 19X1 would be 100 and the index at January 1, 19X2 would be 108. Usually average prices for an annual period instead of prices on a specific day are used as a base.

Although an ideal GPI would be based on a weighted average of the prices of all goods and services in an economy, the construction of such an index is not feasible. Instead, indexes are based on selected groups of commodities. There are three major indices used in the United States that purport to show changes in general price levels: The Consumers' Price Index (CPI) shows the average change in the prices of a "basket" of typical consumer goods; the Wholesale Price Index is based on the wholesale price of selected commodities; and the Gross National Product Implicit Price Deflator (GNP Deflator), issued quarterly by the Commerce Department, is the most comprehensive index. Converting dollar amounts at one point in time to dollars with the same general purchasing power is essentially a mechanical process once a GPI has been selected. The conversion involves multiplying the original amount by a fraction. The numerator of the fraction is the index for the year you are "converting to" and the denominator is the index for the year you are "converting from."

As a basis for illustration assume the following index:

Year	19X1	19X2	19X3	19X4	19X5	19X6	19X7
Index	100	105	106	111	115	119	125

If a tract of land purchased for $10,000 in 19X1 is still on hand in 19X7, its purchase price could be converted to current dollars (19X7 dollars in this case) as follows:

$10,000 × 125/100 = $12,500.

If the land had been purchased in 19X2 and reports were being prepared in 19X5, the conversion would be

$10,000 × 115/105 = $10,953.

The amounts obtained, $12,500 and $10,953, are the dollars required in 19X7 and 19X5, respectively, to purchase what $10,000 would have bought when the land was acquired. But note carefully that amounts derived would only purchase the same quantities of the commodities whose prices are included in the index.

REAL AND FICTITIOUS HOLDING GAINS. Given an understanding of how general price changes are measured by indices, the questions can be raised, "Was the $10 holding gain realized by the clothier in our earlier example a real gain? Or can some of the gain be attributed to the fact that prices increased generally?" If the general price level has increased, a portion of the gain may be illusory or fictitious.

In the example of the clothing store, we calculated a holding gain of $10 because the cost price of the suit rose from $100 in January to $110 in May when the suit was sold. If a GPI showed an index of 125 on January 1 and an index of 130 on May 15, it is possible to divide the holding gain into two parts as follows:

Replacement price at May 15	$110.00
Purchase price in current dollars ($100 × 130/125)	104.00
Real holding gain	$ 6.00
Purchase price in current dollars ($100 × 130/125)	$104.00
Purchase price without adjustment	100.00
Fictitious holding gain	$ 4.00
Total holding gain	$ 10.00

Of the $10.00 gain, the retailer obtained $4.00 because the purchasing power of money changed by 4 percent [(130 – 125)/125], and he obtained $6.00 because the price of the article of clothing increased by a larger percentage than the weighted average of all prices (GPI). Because the purchasing power of $104.00 on May 15 is equivalent to that of $100.00 on January 1, the $4.00 gain is fictitious. The remaining $6.00 is a real gain because the retailer obtained $6.00 of general purchasing power ($110.00 – $104.00) that he did not have originally because the price of the suit increased more rapidly than prices generally.

Some Inherent Weaknesses of Price Indices

The division of the holding gain in the preceding example into its real and fictitious components appears neat and precise. However, the amounts involved do not have any real meaning to the person using them, unless he fully understands how the price index employed in the calculation was constructed. There are some inherent weaknesses in all price indices.

First of all, one should remember that an index is an average. The prices of individual items change at different rates and even in different directions. A GPI is typically thought of as reflecting changes in an entire economy even though prices are usually different in various locations. For example, milk in Boston may be priced above or below milk in Dallas. A skid-row alcoholic purchases a basket of goods that differs significantly from that purchased by a Baptist minister. In like manner, oil refiners and clothing manufacturers use a radically different bundle of goods in their operations. The old adage, about the man who, with one foot in an ice bucket and the other one in an oven, is *on the average* comfortable, is an extreme example concerning variations around an average. Variations around average price changes within an economy may not be so extreme but they are often extreme enough to destroy the utility of the index for many purposes.

Quality changes and new products are other problems that result in an inherent weakness in any GPI. The make and model of a car manufactured in 19X5 may be the same as for one manufactured in 19X1 but this does not mean the cars are identical. Deciding what part of a price change is caused by a change in the purchasing power of money and what part is caused by differences in the product itself is difficult, if not impossible.

In summary, we know that prices change. We can directly observe the changes in prices of individual commodities. The change in price may be due, in part, to a change in quality. Of more importance, the change may be due to a general drift in prices for all commodities. However, measurement of a general price change is difficult and the resulting index, for the reasons enumerated, may have only limited usefulness. Keeping all these factors in mind, we now turn our attention to the possible ways of taking price changes into account in the measurement of income and financial position.

Some Proposed Solutions

For simplicity, the various proposals to take account of price changes in accounting measurements will be grouped under two headings, namely common dollar accounting and current value accounting. A discussion of each proposal is clearly beyond our scope here. In general, advocates of common dollar accounting would use a general price index to determine the values used in accounting. Advocates of current value accounting would begin with the specific prices of commodities. The basic difference between these two approaches has to do with how much capital the accounting process should attempt to maintain within the entity. This question is inextricably related to income measurement because income by definition is the amount that can be consumed without reducing the equity or capital of the business.

PRICE CHANGES AND CAPITAL MAINTENANCE. Many accountants believe that the failure of accounting rules to take price changes into account can result in the distribution of a corporation's original capital to the shareholders as dividends. Certainly one purpose of the income computation is to indicate the maximum amount that a business can distribute to its owners without impairing the capital originally invested by the owners. A question that accountants have not been able to agree on is how much capital should be maintained. At least three possibilities are usually considered:

1   The nominal capital originally contributed by the owners; that is, the same number of dollars without respect to any price changes
2   An amount of capital equivalent to the general purchasing power, as measured by some GPI, originally contributed by the owners. For example, if the Consumers' Price Index is used, then, upon liquidation of the business, the owners would receive capital that would enable them to consume the same basket of goods as when the capital was contributed.
3   Enough capital to enable the business to maintain the same scale of operations; that is, an amount that enables the business to replace the specific assets needed to continue operations

To compare these three possibilities using a simple situation, assume that a large group of investors formed a corporation for the purpose of building a sports stadium. They agreed in advance that *all income* from operations would be distributed to the stockholders as dividends annually. The stadium originally cost $30,000,000 and, for simplicity, we will assume that no borrowed funds were used but that the entire cost was contributed by the shareholders. First, let us assume that the owners wish to maintain the nominal capital only; after 25 years they expect to have returned their original $30,000,000 only. In this event, accountants can base their depreciation on the historical cost. By deducting $1,200,000 of depreciation each year for 25 years, revenues not used to cover operating costs will be maintained in the corporation (remember that all net income is paid out as dividends). The capital maintained would equal $30,000,000 after 25 years.*

As an alternative, the owner might wish to maintain capital equivalent to the general purchasing power of their original investment based on the CPI. Assume that the CPI was 120 when the stadium was built and had risen to 180 at the end of 25 years. The purchasing power equivalent of $30,000,000 originally invested would be $45,000,000 ($30,000,000 X 180/120). To maintain this amount of capital, the depreciation policy must be such that revenues of $45,000,000 are diverted from net income and maintained in the business. At the end of the stadium's life the owners have enough capital to buy the same basket of commodities that their $30,000,000 bought when the stadium was built.

Maintenance of the capital based on a general price index does not mean that the owners will be in a position to replace their stadium with a new one at the end of 25 years. Assume that an index of construction costs for materials and labor needed to rebuild the stadium stood at 120 when the first stadium was built but increased to 216 over the 25–year period. The capital needed to re-place the stadium would not be $45,000,000 but $54,000,000 ($30,000,000 X 216/120). Thus to maintain capital sufficient to continue operations, specific prices (or a very specific price index) must be used to calculate how much reve-nue must be retained in the business through depreciation deductions in the income calculation.

Even assuming that $54,000,000 had been maintained in the corporation based on the construction cost index, would the group be in a position to put up a new stadium? Probably not. Tastes and preferences change rapidly. What was considered a good stadium 25 years ago is now outmoded. The investors would probably need to make a considerably larger investment. Thus even when we attempt to maintain capital sufficient to continue operations we must in some way take into account changes in technology, tastes, preferences, and customs.

It should be noted that the decision on the capital to be maintained has a direct impact on the income measurement. In the foregoing example, the de-preciation expense increases as the amount of capital to be maintained increases. Revenues and all other expenses being equal, the reported income would decrease as depreciation increases.

COMMON DOLLAR ACCOUNTING. Advocates of common dollar accounting generally believe that the accountant's income measurement should assure the maintenance of owners' capital which is equivalent to the general purchasing power contributed by them to the business. Accounting values would be ad-justed each year using a GPI so that all values on the statements are expressed in terms of current purchasing power. Assets, for example, although purchased in

---

*Of course, the owners would not want the capital to lay idle but would want it invested in some manner. The investments would increase the income distributed as dividends.

various years, would be shown on the balance sheet for the current year at a value equal to the current purchasing power of their acquisition costs (less, of course, amounts already assigned to expenses). In common dollar accounting, it is necessary to make a distinction between monetary and nonmonetary items because the accounting for the two is quite different.

When general prices change, a business holding monetary assets has an immediate gain or loss. The most obvious monetary asset is cash. Other assets and liabilities are monetary items if a fixed sum of money is to be received or paid regardless of any changes in specific prices or the general price level. To demonstrate how gains and losses occur on monetary items, assume that a firm places $1,000 in a savings account when the GPI is 120 and leaves it in tact until a time when the index has moved to 150. When the price level moves from 120 to 150, it takes $1,250 ($1000 X 150/120) to purchase as much as $1,000 would have purchased when the price index was 120. The amount of the deposit is still $1,000 despite the change in the GPI so the firm loses $250 in general purchasing power ($1,250 – $1,000 = $250).

As illustrated, during periods of inflation, business firms lose on monetary assets, such as notes receivable, because the money eventually received is worth less than the money originally loaned. A firm gains from inflation on monetary liabilities, such as notes payable, because the money repaid is worth less than the money originally borrowed. The effects are the opposite during periods of deflation when the purchasing power of money is increasing. Proponents of common dollar accounting generally agree that gains and losses on monetary assets, being both immediate and "real" in terms of purchase power, should be recognized currently as they arise.

Nonmonetary items are mainly the deferred costs and deferred revenues which do not specify a fixed future receipt or disbursement of cash. Under common dollar accounting, these items are valued in terms of current purchasing power. For example, assume that a firm buys a parcel of land for $10,000 when the GPI is 120 and still holds this land at the end of the current year when the GPI has increased to 150. The business would show the cost of the land in current dollars. The amount would be $12,500 ($10,000 X 150/120 = $12,500). In a similar manner, other nonmonetary items would be shown at values equal to the current purchasing power of the original cash exchange.

Unlike monetary items, proponents of current dollar accounting generally do not feel that gains or losses should be recognized currently on nonmonetary items. This does not mean that adjustments of values to current dollars would not affect the measurement of income. To the contrary, the portions of deferred costs and revenues allocated to the current period would be in terms of current dollars. By referring back to the section on capital maintenance, it can be seen that depreciation expense on the stadium used to compute income would increase as the general price level rises. The portion of the change in value of nonmonetary items which has not yet been allocated to revenue or expense would be shown on the balance sheet as an "unrealized" gain or loss for price level changes.

CURRENT VALUE ACCOUNTING. Reformers who propose to use current values in accounting measurements vary significantly on many questions: What does "current value" mean? Replacement costs? Liquidating value? They also differ on how to treat the problem of specific price changes relative to general price level changes. Should holding gains or losses be separated for operating profits? If so, should holding gains or losses be divided into real and fictitious components? Finally, there is no agreement on when or how gains and losses from specific price changes should be recognized.

Current value accounting, if adopted, would mean essentially a return to stock concept for income determination (see Chapter 2). Emphasis would be placed on the statement of financial position with assets and liabilities shown at their current value. Income would be derived by comparing beginning values for net worth with those at the end of the year. To repeat, no consensus exists as to which gains and losses on specific assets or liabilities should be recognized in the current year and included in the current income computation.

Adoption of current value accounting seems highly unlikely within the foreseeable future. As we will note below, however, the use of current values for some assets, as opposed to historical cost, is probably just over the horizon.

Current Accepted Practice

The problem of price changes, although much discussed, remains an unresolved problem in accounting. Generally accepted practice still requires the accountant to use original dollar exchange amounts (or their equivalent) in all measurements. The American Institute of Certified Public Accountants has made one concession to accountants and others who wish to use common dollar accounting. The APB Statement No. 3, entitled "Financial Statements Restated for Price-Level Changes," recommends that supplementary statements showing the effect of price-level changes be presented along with the basic statements. Before its demise, the Board came very close to making a concession to the advocates of current value accounting. An opinion requiring companies to show their investments in marketable securities, equities of other corporations classified as current assets, at their market values on the balance sheet date was almost issued. Gains and losses because of changes in value during the accounting period would have been recognized and included in income. This possible change is still under study and may yet be promulgated by the new Financial Accounting Standards Board.

These are only minor concessions. To date, only a few companies have issued supplementary statements showing general price level adjustments. And no independent accountant can render an opinion on statements showing current values because of the possible legal liabilities. One should note, however, that if a banker asks for a balance sheet from a prospective borrower, the borrower would be foolish, indeed, if he used historical costs for assets that have appreciated in value.

Until some changes are made to take price changes in account, the intelligent user of financial statements can only remember that the statements show original costs and that these amounts may be more or less than current values. Because of the general conservative valuation of major deferred costs (LIFO for inventory, accelerated depreciation for plant and equipment, immediate writeoff of research and development, to name a few), the amounts on the balance sheets are generally less than current values.

Foreign Exchange Transactions

Although common dollar accounting is not widely used, the ability to convert different kinds of money to a common unit is, nevertheless, an essential skill for anyone using financial statements. Many American corporations now conduct their operations on an international scale. They deal not only in dollars but also in yen, marks, pounds, francs, and other currencies. Since it is meaningless to add unlike units such as marks, francs, and dollars, international companies must translate foreign currencies into dollars in order to make reports that cover all of their operations. For example, a U.S. firm with a German subsidiary would translate marks to dollars in order to prepare reports for the entire operation. The objective of foreign money conversion to dollars is similar to that of price-level adjustments. If one considers a 19X1 dollar a different unit from a 19X2 dollar, then the translation of one to the other is an attempt to measure with a common unit. Likewise, translation of a mark to a dollar is an attempt to measure with a common unit.

Exchange rates among national currencies change quite often. This means that a firm must sometimes choose between a current exchange rate and a past exchange rate as the basis for a translation. Suppose a foreign subsidiary buys a machine in 19X1. Later the exchange rate between the foreign and domestic currencies changes from that existing at the time the machine was purchased. After the change, the firm must decide whether to use the current rate or the past rate to translate the cost of the machine from the foreign currency to dollars. The choices are based on the nature of the item: Is it a monetary or a nonmonetary item?

In present practice, nonmonetary items are translated at a past rate, the one existing at the time the item was originally recognized. No gains or losses are recognized on the translation of nonmonetary items. Monetary items are translated at current rates, and any gain or loss that results from the change in rates is recognized.

Financial Statement Analysis

In this section, the objectives are to identify some of the objectives of statement analysis, to describe the various tools used in analysis, and to give an example of the process by analyzing the financial statement of an actual company. Frequently, statement analysis is confused with the mechanical process of computing certain ratios and trends. These mechanical procedures, we will see, are only the starting point for use of the statements in making an investment decision.

Sources of Information

The financial statements of a particular company include the balance sheet, the statement of income, and the statement of changes in financial position (funds statement). These statements provide the basic facts available to outside parties. Annual financial statements are available for all corporations whose stock is traded on the stock exchanges or in the "counter" markets which are made by stockbrokers. These corporations are called **public corporations**. Most public corporations issue quarterly reports in addition to the annual statements. The published annual report will usually contain comments by the management on the past year's operation and their future expectations.

AUDITOR'S OPINION. The opinion of the Certified Public Accountant is another source of information that should be examined. The usual short-form opinion shown in Chapter 5 is an unqualified opinion. Additional grades of opinion include the qualified opinion, the disclaimer of an opinion, and the adverse opinion.

The unqualified opinion is a statement by the auditor that the financial statements **present fairly** the result of operation and financial position of the company. A **qualified** opinion is a statement by the auditor that the financial statements are fairly presented **except for** or **subject to** a specified condition. Generally an "except for" qualification refers to an inadequate disclosure of some event or lack of consistency in accounting methods used. A middle paragraph in the auditor's certificate may provide the supplementary information. The "subject to" qualification refers to unusual uncertainty about the effect of some future event, for example, the value placed on some account receivable.

A disclaimer of an opinion is a statement by the auditor that he has not obtained sufficient evidence to form an opinion concerning the fairness of the financial statements. This disclosure may arise because of a limitation in the scope of the audit work or from the existence of uncertainties concerning some events that would materially affect the financial statements. An adverse opinion is an opinion that the financial statements **do not** present fairly the results of operations or the financial position of the company.

In addition to the auditor's opinions, the notes to the financial statements are facts that are useful in the analysis of financial statements. They should be read and studied carefully because they contain relevant information about past and expected future events.

SECURITIES AND EXCHANGE COMMISSION (SEC). All public corporations are required to file annual statements with the SEC. Copies of these statements may be obtained by anyone. The standardized 10–K form filed with the SEC provides additional information not usually available in the published reports. The 10–K contains, for example, a detailed schedule of the long-lived assets of the business and related depreciation. It also contains information about officers' salaries and stock ownership of the corporation.

ADVISORY SERVICES. Many organizations compile financial and other statistical information about the major corporations in the United States. Moody's Investor Service and Standard & Poor's compile financial data in annual volumes and in periodic reports. These services are usually available in any major library. Major brokerage firms and other advisory services will provide information about public corporations if you carry an account with the broker or subscribe to their advisory service.

Most industrial, wholesale, and retail trade associations collect and publish average ratios and trends for their industry. Dun and Bradstreet, Inc., Robert Morris Associates, and other credit organizations also provide a wide variety of data on small and medium-sized businesses as well as information about the major corporations.

Objectives of Statement Analysis

An analysis of the financial statements of a company usually has a specific objective. The objective of the analysis is usually phrased as a question. For example, a banker may ask, "Should my bank loan money to Corporation A?" The analysis of the financial statement is then made in an attempt to answer the question and the analysis must be designed to answer that question. The questions and tools used will vary depending on the objective of the analysis. Financial statements are usually analyzed by individuals or companies that are considering the purchase of common stock, preferred stock, or bonds of a corporation, or by someone who is considering the possibility of making a loan or extending credit to the business. Labor leaders, government officials, and others also make frequent use of the statements. Although it is impossible to specify all the questions that can be used by investors and others, the more important ones for debt investors and owner investors are considered in the following sections.

GENERAL INVESTMENT ANALYSIS. A set of general questions is examined in any investment decision. These questions should be answered regardless of the nature of the investment.

1   Is the business, and the industry within which the business operates, performing a necessary and legitimate function in our society?

If the answer to the question is negative, further analysis is probably useless. Facts bearing on this question are general environmental and industrial data not usually found in financial statements. *Fortune* publishes annually a tabulation of the 500 largest corporations in the United States and their ranking as to size. Dun and Bradstreet's services and other advisory services are also useful in answering this question.

2   What is the general reputation of the firm's management?

The management's ability and integrity are one of the most important attributes of a company. The success or failure of most companies depends primarily on the competence of its executive personnel. This is also one of the most difficult factors for an investor to evaluate. The statement of income when compared with statements of income of other companies in the same industry, gives some insight about the relative efficiency and effectiveness of management's ability to produce in that industry. Most financial statement ratios and analyzes also have some bearing on this question. In most investments, however, qualitative factors not revealed by the financial statements should be examined. Such factors should include changes in the management and the reputation of the individuals in their community. The published annual reports generally include a list of directors and officers. A comparison of current officers with officers shown in prior reports may show some changes in management. *The Wall Street Journal* and other financial news media also report important changes in the managements of major corporations. The reputation of individual members of the company's management may be obtained from various sources including credit reporting services and personal references.

3   Are there any legal or political developments that are expected to affect the company's future operation?

Knowledge of the general political environment certainly should be considered. For example, changes in military expenditures and appropriations for aerospace research have had a critical impact on corporations operating in these areas in recent years. Pending antitrust litigation can also have a material impact on a company's future operation. The payment of damage claims can reduce the available resources and, of more importance, public knowledge of the damage claim may decrease acceptance of the company's product by its customers. Investigation by the champions of consumers, such as "Nader's Raiders," may also affect future operations. National issues, such as pollution, are also relevant issues.

Notes to the company's financial statements and the auditor's opinion should disclose impending action of a specific nature. General conditions are not disclosed in financial statements: The investor must depend on his general knowledge or he must research the question in the financial press.

4   What is the trend of the company's economic activities?

Financial statements for a single year do not provide sufficient information about the company's economic progress. Comparative financial statements for periods of five to ten years are desirable if not essential for a financial analysis. Most companies provide some type of summary for the past five to ten years, but the summary is rarely a comprehensive comparison. Refer to Appendix D, p. 494 and examine the Financial Summary: Ten Year Comparison of Gould, Inc. In this summary, selected data are compared for a ten-year period. The information presented in this report is generally informative but does not include comparisons of all items included in the financial statements. The analyst should not hesitate to develop other comparative statistics.

All financial analysis is relative; and, therefore, summary data for a single company should be compared with similar data for other companies in the same industry and with industrial averages. Published summary data for individual companies and for industries generally include some of the more common financial ratios. For example, the summary for Gould, Inc., shows the percentage increase in sales for each year over the preceding year.

The published balance sheet, statement of income, and statement of changes in financial position invariably are presented for the past two years. Significant changes in the components of any of these statements should be analyzed in more detail. Additional analysis may include the examination of the particular component for the preceding five to ten years. An increase or decrease in income over the prior year may or may not be significant. If the general economy has been expanding, an increase in earnings may be expected. On the other hand, if the economy has been weak, a decline in income may be expected. For example, most companies showed a decrease in earnings for their fiscal years ending in late 1970 or early 1971. A change in income, or any other item, must be compared to other companies or to prior periods, if it is to be meaningful.

ANALYSIS FOR DEBT INVESTMENT. Debt investments in a company are of three types: short-term, intermediate-term, and long-term. Short-term debts are those that mature in one year or less; intermediate debts mature from one to five years; and long-term debts are those that mature after five years. These arbitrary time periods are generally accepted in the financial community. The analyses used to determine whether a short-term, intermediate, or long-term debt investment should be made are similar and are considered together.

1   What assurances are there that the principal and interest will be paid?

The financial statements are directly relevant to this question. The debt investor wants to know what assets are available that can be used to pay back the funds invested and the interest. Second, the debt investor is interested in projecting future cash inflows and outflows to determine if they are adequate to meet the interest and principal payments. Equities with a higher priority than the investor's claim should be deducted from assets before arriving at the assets available to satisfy the investor's claim. Mortgages, preferred liabilities in the event of bankruptcy, and partially secured liabilities are examples of preferred claims that may reduce the resources available to unsecured creditors. The following ratios typically are used to answer this question (see Chapters 5 and 6 for an explanation of the ratios):

a   Debt-to-owner's equity
b   Current ratio
c   Quick ratio
d   Rate of return on total assets
e   Rate of return on stockholders' equity

All of these ratios should be compared with industry averages. An investor contemplating a long-term commitment would be particularly interested in the rate of return on total assets over an extended period of time. The safety of long-term debt investment depends on the ability of the company to continue to earn a satisfactory income in the long run. The rate of return should, of course, exceed the interest rate of the loan. Otherwise there is a loss from trading on the equity —a most unhealthy situation.

2 Is the interest rate adequate considering the opportunity cost and the relative risk?

Opportunity cost is the earnings foregone to make the investment under consideration. For example, in lieu of the proposed investment, the funds could be deposited with a savings and loan association with a guaranteed return or interest rate. In addition, the deposit with a savings and loan association is almost devoid of risk, provided it is insured by the federal government. The potential investment should be compared with rates of return on similar investments. Moody's and Standard & Poor's rate long-term corporate bonds as to their potential risk. *Business Week* publishes weekly averages for returns on treasury bills, government bonds, and long-term medium grade corporate bonds. The relevant statistics should be used in any investment analysis.

The question of risk is at least partially resolved in the analysis seeking an answer to Question 1. Another aspect of risk related to debt investment is the potential gain or loss of purchasing power resulting from holding securities with fixed maturity values in periods of changing price levels. If inflation or a decline in purchasing power is expected, a loss in purchasing power will occur. If deflation or an increase in purchasing power is expected, a gain in purchasing power will occur. Explicit consideration should be given to this problem when investing in securities that have fixed maturity values and constant interest rates.

ANALYSIS FOR OWNER INVESTMENTS. An owner investor is generally seeking either current income or investment growth, or a combination of the two. Current income to the investor is measured by the expected dividends. Investment growth is measured by increased earnings and is generally reflected by an increase in the market price of the stock. In recent years, some investors have been selecting owner investments to decrease the loss from the decline of purchase power because of the rate of inflation.

1 What are the future expectations for the industry within which the company operates?

An industry that is declining is probably a poor investment either for dividend income or for growth. Industrial trends and statistics are the best guideline for the future of the industry. If the industry is stable or is expected to become more prosperous, then further investigation about an individual company would prove fruitful.

The future expectation of a particular company or industry are based on its past record or activities. The activities of a corporation are shown by its periodic statements of income. Relevant factors to consider are

a   Changes in revenue for several periods (five to ten years)
b   Changes in major expense for the same period
c   Changes in income before extraordinary items in total dollar and in earnings per share for the periods
d   Changes in the rate of return in total assets for the periods
e   Changes in rate of return in stockholders' equity for the periods
f   Changes in investments in plant and equipment and other long-lived assets over the period

2   What is the corporation's dividend policy? (For investors seeking current earnings primarily.)

Factors that relate to this question include:

a   Past dividends record
b   The proportion of income that is distributed as dividends.

Of course, the general questions and the question relative to future expectations should be answered satisfactorily before seeking the foregoing information.

3   What is the expectation that the market price of the stock will increase? (For investors primarily interested in growth.)

Usually, the market price of stock will not increase without an increase in income. The following facts bear on the growth potential of the company:

a   The historical price–earning ratio in the industry and for the specific company
b   The record of expenditures for research and development
c   The company's ability to introduce new products and processes in the industry

A high historical price–earning ratio (above 20:1) may mean that future growth has already been discounted. However, if the price–earnings ratio has been stable over an extended period, a high price–earnings ratio would indicate that an increase in earnings would be capitalized at a relative low rate resulting in a relative greater increase in the market price.

For example, Gould, Inc., earnings increased from $1.85 per share in 1970 to $2.32 per share in 1971 or 47 cents per share. Assuming an average historical price-earnings ratio of 12, the increase in the market value of the stock should be approximately $5.50 per share. An examination of the range of market price of the stock would indicate whether or not the market had anticipated the increase in earnings or whether the change in market price does not reflect the increase in earnings. If not, an examination should be made to determine why the market has not reacted to the change in earnings. The market reaction may be caused by the quality of earnings, a general reevaluation of the price–earnings ratio of the particular industry, and other more general economic factors.

The quality of earnings is a value judgment based on whether the income will remain stable or continue to increase in the future. This judgment is based on overall knowledge of the industry and the economic strength of the particular company. An increase in income resulting from a change in accounting policies, such as changing from accelerated depreciation to straight-line depreciation, does not indicate general improvement. Only income that is expected to recur should be considered. In every case, extraordinary items should be excluded.

SOME LIMITATIONS OF FINANCIAL ANALYSIS. In evaluating and interpreting the financial position of a company or a group of companies, it is important to be aware of the limitation of ratios and other comparative measures. Measures of liquidity, such as the current ratio and quick asset ratio, are broad measures; they are not precise. A relatively high current ratio does not measure precisely the company's ability to meet maturing obligations. It does imply that generally a company with a reasonable current ratio will be able to pay its debts. All financial ratios and other comparative measures are broad measures that may indicate favorable or unfavorable conditions. Generally additional investigation is necessary to determine the validity of the indicator and the cause of the condition if the indicator or ratio is valid.

Similarly, a ratio is an indicator of a specific condition not of overall performance. The current ratio indicates something about liquidity; it does not provide information about the overall financial management of the company. A company with a low current ratio and the ability to meet all maturing obligations and take all cash discounts is probably better managed financially than a similar company with a higher current ratio.

Ratios and other tools of financial analysis cannot be used effectively alone. Financial analysis requires the selection of a set of ratios or measures that will provide information relevant to a stated decision objective. Final judgment is based in part on the information provided by the set of measures, but the set of measures does not provide the judgment. A debt-to-ownership equity ratio of 90 percent may be either good or bad depending on the company and its industry.

Accounting methods may influence a financial analysis. A firm using the LIFO inventory costing methods may appear to have a higher inventory turnover than another firm using FIFO. For instance, assume there are two companies with a cost of goods sold of $100,000 last year. One company uses LIFO and shows an average inventory value of $20,000; the other company with approximately the same quantity of inventory uses FIFO and has an average inventory value of $40,000. The inventory turnover ratio would be 5:1 and 2.5:1, respectively. The actual rate of inventory turnover may be the same.

An analyst should ascertain that the companies are using similar accounting policies before making comparisons. If companies being compared are using different accounting methods, adjustment should be made. Accounting policies that may affect comparisons would include depreciation, research and development, revenue recognition, pension costs, leasing arrangements, and, of course, inventory pricing.

If a company has made a number of business acquisitions, careful attention should be given to whether the acquisition was treated as a pooling or a purchase.

If a pooling has occurred, there may be an understatement of assets and an over-statement of income. If the purchase method has been used, there may be an unusually large amount charged to goodwill. If so, the amortization policy for goodwill should be examined closely.

Finally, consideration should be given to the complex and difficult process of measuring income and reporting financial activities as described in the first 16 chapters of this text. Recognizing that accounting measures are not precise but only the best measures available given the complexity of the task, an analyst should use extreme care in evaluating ratios based on accounting data. In addition the measuring unit, money, is not stable, as explained in the first section of this chapter. A 1963 dollar is not the same as a 1973 dollar. The measurement of income is a value measurement; the measurement unit for value in accounting is money. Value is based on taste and preference; therefore, change is inevitable. Accountants do a good job of measuring economic activity, given the constraints. However, accountants are trying to measure activities that by their nature are dynamic, and, as a result, their measurements and the analytical ratios based on them must be used with care.

Example of Financial Statement Analysis

The 1972 Annual Report of Kellogg Company and Subsidiary Companies was selected to use as an example in the analysis of financial statements. The basic information provided by Kellogg for 1972 is reproduced in Figures 17–1 to 17–10, as follows:

Figure 17–1.   Financial Review.
Figure 17–2.   Consolidated Statement of Earnings.
Figure 17–3.   Opinion of Independent Accountants.
Figure 17–4.   Consolidated Balance Sheet.
Figure 17–5.   Consolidated Statements of Changes in Financial Position.
Figure 17–6.   Analysis of Changes in Working Capital.
Figure 17–7.   Summary of Accounting Policies.
Figure 17–8.   Notes to Financial Statements.
Figure 17–9.   Consolidated Statements of Capital and Retained Earnings.
Figure 17–10. Ten-Year Financial Review.

These figures are reprinted with kind permission from the 1972 Financial Statements of Kellogg Company.

The assumed objective is the selection of a company whose common stock shows promise for good income and growth in value. We will also assume that the general questions concerning the industry, legal and political developments, and the company's management have been answered satisfactorily.

Figure 17-1

FINANCIAL REVIEW

NET SALES

Consolidated world-wide net sales for 1972 reached $699,221,122. This represents an increase of $22,169,711 over 1971, a growth of 3.3%. Sales growth is somewhat understated due to the lines of business which were sold and discontinued late in 1971. The combined sales of these discontinued operations totaled approximately $18,000,000 in 1971. If 1971 sales were restated to reflect this difference, the sales of the Company would show a 6.1% increase for the current year.

NET EARNINGS

Profits, after taxes, reached $60,512,908 during 1972, an increase of $5,460,739, or 9.9% over 1971. In reporting the Company's "after tax" earnings, it should be pointed out that, although income tax obligations for 1972 totaled $57,400,000 an additional $12,600,000 was expensed for taxes not based on income. Moreover, there were many hidden taxes absorbed which cannot be readily quantified.

Persistent emphasis on cost efficiency resulted in a number of programs which produced savings during the past year. These savings, combined with the profitable sales growth in a number of product lines and countries, were instrumental in producing substantial earnings growth in 1972.

PER SHARE EARNINGS AND DIVIDENDS

Per share earnings increased by 15 cents in 1972. Total earnings per share amounted to $1.66 for the year versus $1.51 in 1971.

Total dividends paid during 1972 amounted to $37,947,235. This represents $1,521,047 more than the total paid in 1971, an increase of 4.2%. Quarterly dividends were increased 2 cents per share during the year which increased the total annual dividend to $1.04 per share for 1972 versus $1.00 for the previous year. Total dividends paid during 1972 represented 62.7% of Company profits for the year.

CAPITAL EXPENDITURES

1972 capital additions were somewhat less than 1971 when an all-time high was recorded. The 1972 amount is, however, significantly higher than expenditures in recent years. We are convinced that this high level of investment in our business is both necessary and justified based on current and predicted growth trends. It is anticipated that capital needs will accelerate even further in the months and years ahead. Current plans are to continue to underwrite this expansion with retained earnings. As our business expands into new ventures, product lines and markets, the possibilities for profitable capital investment are uncovered at an ever-increasing pace. The maintenance and improvement of our physical assets are vital to continuing productive efficiency of our operations.

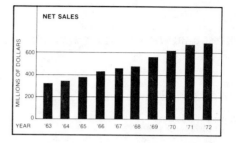

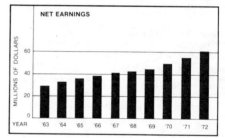

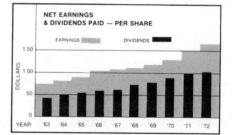

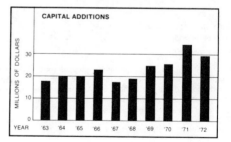

Figure 17–2

KELLOGG COMPANY
and Subsidiary Companies

CONSOLIDATED STATEMENTS OF EARNINGS

	1972	1971
Net Sales	$699,221,122	$677,051,411
Interest and Other Income	5,238,121	3,752,309
	$704,459,243	$680,803,720
Costs and Expenses:		
Cost of goods sold	$436,481,783	$419,962,631
Selling, general and administrative expenses	148,565,956	147,629,752
Interest expense	1,498,596	1,459,168
	$586,546,335	$569,051,551
Earnings before Income Taxes	$117,912,908	$111,752,169
Estimated Income Taxes, including deferred of $2,800,000 in 1972 and		
$900,000 in 1971	57,400,000	56,700,000
Net Earnings for the year	$ 60,512,908	$ 55,052,169
Earnings Per Common Share	$1.66	$1.51

See accompanying Summary of Accounting Policies and Notes to Financial Statements.

Figure 17–3

OPINION OF INDEPENDENT ACCOUNTANTS

To the Stockholders and
Board of Directors of
Kellogg Company

In our opinion, the accompanying consolidated balance sheets and the related consolidated statements of earnings, capital and retained earnings and of changes in financial position present fairly the financial position of Kellogg Company and its subsidiaries at December 31, 1972 and 1971, the results of their operations and the changes in financial position for the years then ended, in conformity with generally accepted accounting principles consistently applied. Our examinations of these statements were made in accordance with generally accepted auditing standards and accordingly included such tests of the accounting records and such other auditing procedures as we considered necessary in the circumstances.

Battle Creek, Michigan
February 12, 1973

Price Waterhouse

Figure 17-4

KELLOGG COMPANY
and Subsidiary Companies

CONSOLIDATED BALANCE SHEETS

	December 31	
	1972	**1971**
CURRENT ASSETS:		
Cash, including certificates of deposit of $51,300,000 in 1972 and $41,600,000 in 1971	$ 56,037,214	$ 47,471,053
United States Government Securities and Other Short-Term Investments, at cost (approximate market)	2,648,562	7,520,537
Accounts Receivable, less allowances of $532,000 in 1972 and $520,000 in 1971	42,116,922	37,901,394
Inventories:		
Raw Materials and Supplies	42,648,552	41,739,463
Finished Goods and Materials in Process	33,478,825	29,928,930
Prepaid Taxes and Other Expenses	12,565,902	11,935,680
Total Current Assets	$189,495,977	$176,497,057
PROPERTY, PLANT AND EQUIPMENT, at cost less accumulated depreciation	191,801,678	180,571,999
OTHER ASSETS:		
Excess of Cost Over Net Assets of Companies Acquired	19,023,385	19,021,299
Other Investments	1,641,280	2,191,590
Patents, Trade-Marks and Goodwill	1	1
	$401,962,321	$378,281,946
CURRENT LIABILITIES:		
Accounts Payable	$ 31,521,090	$ 25,200,042
Foreign Loans	9,755,478	15,465,210
Other Current Liabilities	28,716,668	28,081,854
Estimated Income Taxes	15,211,098	21,318,551
Total Current Liabilities	$ 85,204,334	$ 90,065,657
LONG-TERM FOREIGN LOANS	$ 9,186,220	$ 6,767,913
DEFERRED INCOME TAXES	$ 16,032,969	$ 13,583,696
CAPITAL AND RETAINED EARNINGS:		
3½ % Cumulative Preferred Stock, $100 Par Value — Authorized and issued 89,263 shares, less 64,946 shares in treasury (93,013 less 68,364 in 1971)	$ 2,431,700	$ 2,464,900
Common Stock, $.50 Par Value — Authorized 40,000,000 shares; issued 36,432,807 shares in 1972 and 36,374,232 shares in 1971	18,216,404	18,187,116
Capital in Excess of Par Value	12,614,338	11,501,981
Retained Earnings	258,276,356	235,710,683
	$291,538,798	$267,864,680
	$401,962,321	$378,281,946

See accompanying Summary of Accounting Policies and Notes to Financial Statements.

Figure 17–5

CONSOLIDATED STATEMENTS
OF CHANGES IN FINANCIAL POSITION

KELLOGG COMPANY
and Subsidiary Companies

FINANCIAL RESOURCES WERE PROVIDED BY:	1972	1971
Net Earnings for the Year	$ 60,512,908	$ 55,052,169
Depreciation	14,190,806	15,236,102
Non-Current Deferred Income Taxes	2,449,273	2,040,216
Working Capital Provided by Operations	$ 77,152,987	$ 72,328,487
Sale of Properties and Change in Other Assets	4,238,627	4,638,085
Increase in Long-Term Foreign Loans	2,418,307	
Issue of Common Stock	1,130,072	1,420,485
	$ 84,939,993	$ 78,387,057

FINANCIAL RESOURCES WERE USED FOR:		
Additions to Properties	$ 29,110,888	$ 33,737,534
Cash Dividends	37,947,235	36,426,188
Reduction in Long-Term Foreign Loans		1,620,978
Purchase of Preferred Stock for Treasury	21,627	9,919
	$ 67,079,750	$ 71,794,619
INCREASE IN WORKING CAPITAL	$ 17,860,243	$ 6,592,438

Figure 17–6

ANALYSIS OF CHANGES IN WORKING CAPITAL

INCREASE (DECREASE) IN CURRENT ASSETS:		
Cash	$ 8,566,161	$ 5,440,505
United States Government Securities and Other Short-Term Investments	(4,871,975)	4,253,344
Accounts Receivable	4,215,528	1,703,343
Inventories	4,458,984	5,397,044
Prepaid Taxes and Other Expenses	630,222	857,126
	$ 12,998,920	$ 17,651,362

(INCREASE) DECREASE IN CURRENT LIABILITIES:		
Accounts Payable	$ (6,321,048)	$ (2,914,532)
Foreign Loans	5,709,732	(6,565,678)
Other Current Liabilities	(634,814)	(2,154,929)
Estimated Income Taxes	6,107,453	576,215
	$ 4,861,323	$ (11,058,924)
INCREASE IN WORKING CAPITAL	$ 17,860,243	$ 6,592,438

See accompanying Summary of Accounting Policies and Notes to Financial Statements.

Figure 17-7

SUMMARY OF ACCOUNTING POLICIES

CONSOLIDATION

The consolidated financial statements include the accounts of Kellogg Company and its subsidiaries. Significant intercompany transactions have been eliminated in consolidation.

Assets and liabilities of foreign operations are translated into United States dollars at year-end rates of exchange, except property, plant and equipment (and related depreciation) translated at historical rates. Income and expense accounts, except depreciation, are translated at the monthly average rates prevailing during the year.

Net gains or losses from translations are included in current income. Gains and losses for the years are not material.

INVENTORIES

Inventories are valued at the lower of cost (average) or market.

PROPERTY, PLANT AND EQUIPMENT

Fixed assets are stated at cost. The cost of depreciable property, plant and equipment is depreciated over estimated useful lives using the straight-line method ranging from 2% to 10% for buildings and 5% to 33% for machinery and equipment. Ordinary maintenance and repairs are expensed; replacements and betterments are capitalized. On disposal of assets the costs and related accumulated depreciation are removed from the accounts and any gain or loss reflected in income.

INTANGIBLE ASSETS

The "excess of cost over net assets of companies acquired" is not being amortized because, in the opinion of the Company, there has been no decrease in value.

INCOME TAXES

Income taxes have been provided for differences between depreciation and other expenses as recorded for financial statement and for tax reporting purposes. Investment tax credits are used to reduce current income tax provisions.

No provision has been made for United States income taxes relating to potential future distributions of accumulated earnings of foreign subsidiaries since it is the Company's present intention to utilize these earnings in its foreign operations. As of December 31, 1972 the cumulative amounts of undistributed earnings aggregated approximately $66,000,000.

RESEARCH AND DEVELOPMENT

Research and development costs are charged to expense as incurred.

RETIREMENT PLANS

The Company and its subsidiaries have established various profit-sharing, savings, and pension plans to provide retirement benefits for officers and employees. Expense to the Company and its subsidiaries (and amount funded) under these plans was approximately $12,100,000 in 1972 and $11,700,000 in 1971. The policy is to fund pension costs accrued. Unfunded vested benefits were not material.

EARNINGS PER COMMON SHARE

Earnings per common share is computed by dividing net earnings by the weighted average number of shares outstanding after deducting dividends applicable to preferred stock.

NOTES TO FINANCIAL STATEMENTS

NOTE 1 — FOREIGN OPERATIONS:

The consolidated financial statements include the following amounts applicable to operations outside North America:

	1972	1971
Assets	$ 92,996,000	$ 87,848,000
Liabilities	40,284,000	40,390,000
Net sales	165,731,000	156,345,000
Net earnings	7,239,000	7,444,000

NOTE 2 — PROPERTY, PLANT AND EQUIPMENT:

	1972	1971
Land	$ 9,591,125	$ 9,138,659
Buildings	90,851,566	85,300,341
Machinery and equipment	205,865,722	193,024,125
Construction in progress	13,548,012	15,793,752
	$319,856,425	$303,256,877
Less-Accumulated depreciation	128,054,747	122,684,878
	$191,801,678	$180,571,999

Figure 17–8

NOTES TO FINANCIAL STATEMENTS

NOTE 3 — FOREIGN LOANS:

Foreign loans at December 31, 1972 are payable in instalments from 1973 to 1981 at interest rates from 3.5% to 10%. Maturities during the five years ending December 31, 1977 are listed below.

1973	$ 9,755,478
1974	925,327
1975	1,128,329
1976	652,451
1977	5,517,587

NOTE 4 — PREFERRED STOCK:

Preferred shares may be redeemed at prices from $101.50 in 1973 to $100 after 1985. Each year the Company must offer to purchase 3,750 shares of preferred stock at current maximum prices of $100.50 ($100 after 1975), or apply previously acquired shares (64,946 shares in treasury at December 31, 1972) against this requirement.

NOTE 5 — STOCK OPTIONS:

At December 31, 1972, 135,900 shares of common stock were available for granting of options under stock option plans; 536,859 shares were under option at prices from $19.88 to $29.88 a share, of which 378,059 were exercisable. Shares under the various options are exercisable over four years, beginning one year from date of grant. Options granted are at market value of common stock at date of grant.

The following table sets forth certain other information:

	1972	1971
Options granted (shares)	145,500	3,500
Price per share	$29.88	$27.38
Options exercised (shares)	58,575	74,012
Average exercise price	$19.12	$18.95
Options cancelled (shares)	12,200	11,000

NOTE 6 — FEDERAL TRADE COMMISSION PROCEEDING:

The Federal Trade Commission has commenced a proceeding against Kellogg Company and three other cereal manufacturers, charging that these companies have maintained a "highly concentrated, noncompetitive market structure" in violation of the Federal Trade Commission Act. It is the position of Kellogg Company that it has not violated the Act, and the Company, therefore, intends to contest the charges.

Figure 17–9

CONSOLIDATED STATEMENTS OF CAPITAL AND RETAINED EARNINGS

	Preferred Stock	Common Stock	Capital in Excess of Par Value	Retained Earnings
Balance, January 1, 1971	$2,480,800	$18,150,110	$10,112,521	$217,084,702
Net earnings for the year 1971				55,052,169
Dividends declared:				
Preferred Stock — $3.50 a share				(86,466)
Common Stock — $1.00 a share				(36,339,722)
Stock options exercised		37,006	1,383,479	
Preferred stock purchased for treasury	(15,900)		5,981	
Balance, December 31, 1971	$2,464,900	$18,187,116	$11,501,981	$235,710,683
Net earnings for the year 1972				60,512,908
Dividends declared:				
Preferred Stock — $3.50 a share				(85,726)
Common Stock — $1.04 a share				(37,861,509)
Stock options exercised		29,288	1,100,784	
Preferred stock purchased for treasury	(33,200)		11,573	
Balance, December 31, 1972	$2,431,700	$18,216,404	$12,614,338	$258,276,356

See accompanying Summary of Accounting Policies and Notes to Financial Statements.

Figure 17-10

TEN YEAR FINANCIAL REVIEW

Dollars in Thousands (Except per share figures)

	1972	1971	1970	1969	1968	1967	1966	1965	1964	1963
NET SALES	$699,221	$677,051	$614,412	$566,339	$486,807	$461,689	$442,560	$392,857	$355,995	$328,006
% Increase over previous year	3%	10%	8%	16%	5%	4%	13%	10%	9%	11%
EARNINGS BEFORE INCOME TAXES	117,913	111,752	101,490	95,770	92,635	81,271	75,084	66,132	67,444	58,173
INCOME TAXES	57,400	56,700	51,900	50,600	49,600	39,800	36,000	30,300	34,300	29,500
NET EARNINGS	60,513	55,052	49,590	45,170	43,035	41,471	39,084	35,832	33,144	28,673
% Increase over previous year	10%	11%	10%	5%	4%	6%	9%	8%	16%	15%
CASH DIVIDENDS:										
On 3½% Preferred Stock	86	86	89	92	94	98	100	103	157	306
On Common Stock	37,862	36,340	32,526	29,058	27,236	23,588	21,784	19,954	18,172	15,398
INCREASE IN RETAINED EARNINGS	22,566	18,626	7,903	16,020	15,705	17,785	17,200	15,775	14,815	12,969
DEPRECIATION	14,191	15,236	13,600	12,904	11,579	11,027	11,114	9,467	8,166	8,978
NET EARNINGS per Share on Common Stock*	1.66	1.51	1.36	1.24	1.18	1.14	1.08	.99	.91	.78
CASH DIVIDENDS per Share on Common Stock*	1.04	1.00	.90	.80	.75	.65	.60	.55	.50	.43
CURRENT ASSETS	189,496	176,497	158,846	150,469	162,348	139,427	126,394	111,005	105,674	90,865
CURRENT LIABILITIES	85,204	90,066	79,007	78,218	69,874	60,732	60,880	56,540	56,123	44,547
WORKING CAPITAL	104,292	86,431	79,839	72,251	92,474	78,695	65,514	54,465	49,551	46,318
PROPERTY, PLANT AND EQUIPMENT (Net)	191,802	180,572	168,673	158,739	132,842	127,499	116,354	107,820	92,097	82,083
TOTAL ASSETS	401,962	378,282	347,135	331,085	297,308	268,050	243,358	218,866	202,468	178,159
ADDITIONS TO PROPERTIES	29,111	33,738	26,356	24,624	18,797	17,277	22,962	19,823	20,227	17,641
COMMON STOCKHOLDERS' EQUITY	289,107	265,400	245,347	228,079	211,842	194,450	175,507	159,328	142,050	126,674
NUMBER OF COMMON STOCKHOLDERS	16,398	17,343	15,523	14,604	13,858	12,880	12,257	11,192	10,512	9,993

*Adjusted to give effect to 100% stock distributions in August 1970 and September 1963.

Note that the accountant's opinion, Fig. 17–3, is unqualified. The accountant believes that the statements present fairly the financial position, the results of operations, and the changes in financial position for the years then ended, in conformity with generally accepted accounting principles consistently applied. Remember that there are a number of alternative accounting principles. Figure 17–7, Summary of Accounting Policies, specifies the more important accounting policies that have been adopted.

Additional information about the content of the financial statements and contingencies are given in Fig. 17–8. In Note 6—Federal Trade Commission Proceeding, it is stated that the Federal Trade Commission has commenced a legal proceeding against Kellogg Company and three other cereal manufacturers, charging that these companies have maintained a "highly concentrated, noncompetitive market structure" in violation of the Federal Trade Commission Act. The Kellogg Company does not believe that a violation has occurred and will contest the charges. The independent accountant does not believe that the charge will have any material effect on the company. If the accountant believed that the charged would have a material effect, a "subject to" opinion would have been issued rather than the unqualified opinion that was given. If the reader has any doubts about this matter he should investigate it further.

The first question in the analysis for owner investment is

1 What are the future expectations for Kellogg Company?

How a company is going to perform in the future is based on how well it has performed in the past. Figure 17–10 provides a ten-year financial review. This review shows that sales and earnings have increased in each of the ten years. The increases in sales have fluctuated more than the increase in earnings during the last three years. The small increase in sales for 1972 is partially explained in Fig. 17–1, Financial Review. The discontinuance of an operation would have a negative effect on sales. Standard & Poor's *Standard N.Y.S.E. Stock Reports* for Kellogg Company is shown in Fig. 17–11. The chart relates the price of Kellogg Company stock to seven other packaged food Companies and to 425 industrial companies. The comparisons are made by using specially developed scales. Kellogg has done better than the 425 industrial companies for the last three years and better than the average of the seven packaged foods companies for the past two years. This report also summarizes the activities and recent developments relevant to the company. Sales, common share earnings, dividend data, income statistics, and pertinent balance sheet information are given in the report.

The income statistics for the ten-year period shows earnings per share, dividends paid, price ranges, and price–earnings ratios. Note that the price–earnings ratio has shown a decline from earlier years. The current price–earnings ratio is approximately 17.5 (the current price of $29\frac{1}{4}$ divided by $1.66 the 1972 earnings per share) is still within the range the stock has maintained for the past three years. The market price has been increasing as the earnings have increased. Although the market price has fluctuated during the ten-year period the trend

Figure 17–11[a]

Kellogg Co.

Stock—	Price Apr. 5'73	Dividend	Yield
COMMON (NEW)....................	15⁵⁄₈	[2]$0.54	[2]3.5%

RECOMMENDATION: Accounting for more than 40% of total domestic output of ready-to-eat cereals and firmly entrenched in markets overseas, the company occupies a strong position in this field. While FTC charges alleging a "shared monopoly" in the cereal business may be a restraining factor, the shares (split 2-for-1) have appeal as a conservative investment, as prospects suggest a continuation of the more than two-decade-old earnings uptrend.

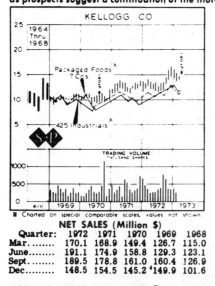

■ Charted on special comparable scales, values not shown.

NET SALES (Million $)

Quarter:	1972	1971	1970	1969	1968
Mar.......	170.1	168.9	149.4	126.7	115.0
June.......	191.1	174.9	158.8	129.3	123.1
Sept.......	189.5	178.8	161.0	160.4	!26.9
Dec.........	148.5	154.5	145.2	[4]149.9	101.6

Sales for 1972 increased 3.3% from the year-earlier level, despite the elimination of some $18 million in sales from discontinued operations. The year-to-year gain would have been 6.1% if these operations were eliminated for 1971. The higher volume was attributed to a strong resumption of domestic demand for ready-to-eat cereals, aggressive marketing efforts, and the introduction of several new products. Margins came under some pressure from mounting grain, labor and shipping costs, although the elimination of certain marginal operations was partially offsetting. Operating income advanced 2.9%. Aided by a sharp rise in other income and a moderate reduction in non-operating charges, pretax income gained 5.5%. After taxes at 48.7%, against 50.7%, net income increased 9.9%.

[3]COMMON SHARE EARNINGS ($)

Quarter:	1972	1971	1970	1969	1968
Mar.......	0.17	0.16	0.14	0.13	0.13
June.......	0.20	0.18	0.17	0.16	0.15
Sept.......	0.27	0.24	0.22	0.20	0.18
Dec.	0.19	0.18	0.15	[4]0.13	0.13

PROSPECTS

Near Term—Sales for 1973 are expected to post a moderate gain from the peak $699.2 million of 1972. The increase should reflect continued growth in demand for the company's established ready-to-eat cereals, benefits from several new cereal products, and an expanded geographic market for "Eggo" frozen waffles. Implementation of a 5.76% price increase on domestic cereals in April should be significant, if competition and possible Government restrictions do not force a rollback.

Although margins are likely to be hampered by rising grain, labor and shipping costs, the price increase should be somewhat offsetting. Greater production efficiencies should be derived from consolidation in Germany and Britain. Assuming no labor disruptions, which were limiting in 1972, earnings for 1973 should be moderately above the record $0.83 a share of 1972, as adjusted for the 2-for-1 stock split of April, 1973. Dividends were raised to $0.13½ quarterly, from $0.12½ (both adjusted), with the September, 1972 payment.

Long Term—Successful new product introductions and diversification of the product line should contribute to sales and earnings potentials.

RECENT DEVELOPMENTS

Several new products introduced during 1972 are now in varying stages of market development. A skillet-prepared stuffing called "Stuf" is entering national distribution, while "Cocoa Hoots" and "Frostins 'N Raisins" cereals, "Rise 'N Shine" breakfast drink, and "Neocitran" for relief of colds are in test market development.

DIVIDEND DATA

Dividends in the past 12 months:

Amt. of Divd. $	Date Decl.	Ex-divd. Date	Stock of Record	Payment Date
0.25...	May 15	May 25	Jun. 1	Jun. 15'72
0.27...	Aug. 21	Aug. 28	Sep. 1	Sep. 15'72
0.27...	Nov. 17	Nov. 24	Nov. 30	Dec. 15'72
0.27...	Feb. 20	Feb. 26	Mar. 2	Mar. 15'73
*.......	....	Apr. 30	Apr. 6	Apr. 27'73

*2-for-1 split.

[1] Listed N.Y.S.E.; also traded Detroit & PBW S.Es.　　[2] Indicated rate (adj.).　　[3] Adj. for 2-for-1 splits in Apr. 1973 & Aug. 1970.
[4] Incl. Fearn International for 12 mos.

[a]Reprinted with permission from Standard & Poor's Corp. Standard N.Y. Stock Exchange Reports, Vol. 40, No. 29, Friday, February 9, 1973. This report was up to date at the time of publication, but subsequent events have been reflected in later reports published by Standard & Poor's Corp.

Figure 17-11 (cont.)

KELLOGG COMPANY

[1]INCOME STATISTICS (Million $) AND PER SHARE ($) DATA

Year Ended Dec. 31	Net Sales	% Oper Inc. of Sales	Oper. Inc.	Deprec.	Net Bef. Taxes	Net Inc.	[2]Common Share ($) Data: Earns.	*Cash Gener-ated	Divs. Paid	Price Range	Price-Earns. Ratios HI LO
1973--	-----	---	-----	----	-----	----	---	---	0.13½	16⅜-13⅞	-----
1972--	699.22	18.4	128.36	14.19	117.91	60.51	0.83	1.06	0.52	16⅞-11½	20-14
1971--	677.05	18.4	124.70	15.24	111.75	55.05	0.76	0.99	0.50	14 -11¼	19-15
1970--	614.41	18.4	113.15	13.60	101.49	49.59	0.68	0.89	0.45	11¼ - 8¾	17-13
1969--	566.34	18.5	104.97	12.90	95.77	45.17	0.62	0.81	0.40	11⅜ - 9¾	18-16
1968--	466.61	20.7	96.46	11.21	91.13	42.33	0.59	0.77	0.37½	11¾ - 9⅜	20-16
1967--	447.10	19.4	86.86	10.64	80.03	40.83	0.57	0.72	0.32½	11½ - 8⅞	20-16
1966--	426.74	19.1	81.69	10.70	73.98	38.48	0.54	0.69	0.30	10⅞ - 7¾	20-14
1965--	385.47	18.6	71.65	9.31	65.05	35.25	0.49	0.62	0.27½	14⅜ -10	29-20
1964--	349.08	20.7	72.24	8.01	66.42	32.61	0.46	0.57	0.25	13½ -10	30-22
1963--	321.58	20.2	64.84	8.83	57.23	28.23	0.39	0.51	0.21¼	11¼ - 6⅞	29-18

[1]PERTINENT BALANCE SHEET STATISTICS (Million $)

Dec. 31	Gross Prop.	Capital Expend.	Cash Items	Inven-tories	Receiv-ables	Current: Assets	Current: Liabs.	Net Workg. Cap.	Cur. Ratio Assets to Liabs.	Long Term Debt	[2]($) Book Val. Com. Sh.
1972--	319.86	29.11	58.69	76.13	42.12	189.50	85.20	104.29	2.2-1	9.19	3.71
1971--	303.26	33.74	54.99	71.67	37.90	176.50	90.07	86.43	2.0-1	6.77	3.39
1970--	284.93	26.36	45.30	66.27	36.20	158.85	79.01	79.84	2.0-1	8.44	3.13
1969--	268.23	24.62	45.28	61.99	35.92	150.47	78.22	72.25	1.9-1	11.70	2.87
1968--	211.86	18.06	79.28	45.99	26.23	157.54	67.57	89.97	2.3-1	1.45	2.86
1967--	199.56	17.07	64.55	42.82	24.38	136.29	59.12	77.17	2.3-1	Nil	2.65
1966--	188.14	18.87	54.41	42.38	22.72	122.84	59.23	63.61	2.1-1	2.46	2.41
1965--	174.29	19.44	48.99	38.22	17.60	108.18	52.63	55.55	2.1-1	2.77	2.17
1964--	150.36	20.07	55.31	31.10	13.25	103.01	54.93	48.08	1.9-1	Nil	1.96
1963--	135.43	17.44	43.25	30.15	11.69	88.53	43.46	45.07	2.0-1	Nil	1.74

[1]Fully consol. aft. 1964; incl. all wholly owned domestic & foreign subs. in prior yrs.; incl. Fearn International aft. 1968. [2]Adj for 2-for-1 splits in 1973 & 1970 & 100% stk. divd. in 1963.

*As computed by Standard & Poor's

Fundamental Position

Kellogg is the leading producer of ready-to-eat cereals, accounting for an estimated 45% of total retail store sales of such products in the United States. Cereals, marketed under the Kellogg name, are sold principally to supermarkets, grocery stores, Government agencies, and other institutions through an extensive organization of grocery jobbers and institutional food products salesmen. Cereal sales accounted for an estimated 85% of total sales in 1972, while snack foods and other products accounted for the rest.

The bulk of sales and earnings is derived from markets in the U.S., Canada and Mexico, but sales in other world markets contributed 24% of the 1972 total, while foreign earnings accounted for 12% of total profits.

Although Kellogg has a well-established position in its market, successful new product introductions are still very important to market expansion.

The company's ready-to-eat cereals include Corn Flakes, Rice Krispies, Special K, Sugar Frosted Flakes, All-Bran, Sugar Pops, Raisin Bran, 40% Bran Flakes, Sugar Smacks, Shredded Wheat, Pep Wheat Flakes, Krumbles, Corn Flake Crumbs, Cocoa Krispies, Concentrate, Stars, Apple Jacks, Product 19, and Frosted Mini-Wheats. The principal raw ingredients used in cereals include corn grits, rice, wheat, oats, sugar, and raisins. Non-cereal products include Pop-Tarts,. Frosted Pop-Tarts, Danish Go-Rounds, and Corn Flake Crumbs Bag and Bake.

The company's main plant is located in Battle Creek, Mich. Other U.S. cereal production facilities are in Omaha, Memphis, and San Leandro, Cal.

Salada Foods, acquired in 1969, produces and markets tea, potato products, preserves and spreads, gelatin desserts, drink mixes, pie fillings, and coffee.

Fearn International, acquired in 1970, makes soup bases, condensed soups, gelatin desserts, pudding and pie fillings, canned gravies and sauces, and Eggo frozen waffles.

In January, 1972 the Federal Trade Commission charged that Kellogg and three other makers of ready-to-eat cereals shared an illegal monopoly. These charges have been denied by the four companies involved, and further action by the FTC is expected.

Common dividends, paid in every year since 1923, averaged 65% of available earnings in the five years through 1972.

Employees: 15,978. Shareholders: 16,398.

Finances

Capital expenditures amounted to $29.1 million in 1972, and should exceed $40 million in 1973.

At December 31, 1972 the cumulative undistributed earnings of foreign operations aggregated approximately $66,000,000.

CAPITALIZATION

LONG TERM DEBT: $9,186,220.

$3.50 CUM. PREFERRED STOCK: 24,317 shs. ($100 par); red. at $101.50 through 1975, and at lower prices thereafter.

COMMON STOCK: 72,865,614 shs. ($0.50 par); 50% controlled by the W. K. Kellogg Foundation.

has been upward. Cash generated per share is the amount obtained by adding the earnings and the depreciation for each year and dividing by the average shares outstanding. This figure can be misleading and should be ignored.

The balance sheet statistics shows the more important components of the balance sheet including working capital. The current ratio for each of the ten years is also shown. Book value per share is the equity of each share of common stock in assets after subtracting all liabilities and the liquidating value of preferred stock. Book value is computed by the following formula:

$$\text{Book value per share} = \frac{(\text{Stockholders' equity} - \text{Liquidation value of preferred})}{\text{Average no. of common shares outstanding}}$$

The computation of book value per share for 1972 for Kellogg is

$$\text{Book value per share} = \frac{\$29,538,798 - \$24,681,755}{\$36,403,519} = \$7.32$$

The per share figures were adjusted for a 2 for 1 stock split in 1970 and 100 percent stock dividend in 1963. Note that Standard & Poor's reports that the company has proposed a 2 for 1 stock split in 1973.

Figures 17–10 and 17–11 provide data covering the last ten years. In addition, Fig. 17–1 displays a review of some of the more important data. Observation of these three illustrations reveals no negative factors.

The rate of return on total assets and common shareholders' equity is given in Fig. 17–12. The rate of return on total assets for years prior to 1971 is not presented because the amount of interest expense was not available for those earlier years. The rate of return to common share equities has been relatively stable and very respectable ranging from 19.8 to 23.2 percent. Based on past activities, Kellogg Company should be profitable in the future. The only cloud is the Federal Trade Commission Proceeding.

Figure 17–12

Kellogg Company	Return on Total Assets and Common Stock Equity	
Year	Return on total assets[a]	Return on common stock equity[b]
1972	15.4	20.9
1971	14.9	20.7
1970		20.2
1969		19.8
1968		20.2
1967		21.3
1966		22.2
1965		22.4
1964		23.2
1963		22.4

[a]Profit is after taxes but before interest. Return on total assets is not computed for 1970 and earlier years because interest expense figures were not available.
[b]Profit is after taxes, interest, and preferred dividends.

The second question in the analysis for owner investment is based on the assumption that the investor also desires a current income. The question is

2   What is the corporation's dividend policy?

The relevant factor, a record of past dividends, is shown in the Ten Year Financial Review, Fig. 17-10. Cash dividends per share of common stock have increased from 43 cents in 1963 to $1.04 in 1972. The expected dividend for 1973 is $1.08. The percentage of income disbursed as dividends has ranged from 55 to 62.5 percent. A shareholder could reasonably expect a continuation of the current dividend policy.

The third question is based on the assumption that the investor is also seeking growth. The question is

3   What is the expectation that the market price of the stock will increase?

This question is perhaps the most difficult one to answer. The market price of a stock is subject to the vagaries of the capital market. Factors such as the current interest rate, the rate of inflation, the current economic outlook and others influence the market. There are, however, some facts that can be of help. The record of past earnings is without doubt the most important. The price–earnings ratio links earnings and the price of the stock. As shown earlier, an increase in earnings will probably result in an increase in the price of the stock. The price increase will approximate the increase in earnings times the average price earnings ratio if the price–earnings ratio remains stable. Although the price–earnings ratio of the Kellogg Company, as shown in Fig. 17-11, has fluctuated from a high of 29 to a low of 13, the range for the last few years has been between 15 and 20.

The record for research and development is not presented in the published financial data of the company. The Summary of Accounting Policies (Fig. 17-7) states that research and development expenditures are charged to expense as incurred. Figure 17-11 in the section on fundamental position reveals that the company has been successful in introduction of new products and that expenditures for research and development in 1971 were $4.5 million.

A compilation of financial information for manufacturers of flour and other grain mill products is presented in Fig. 17-13. The compilation was prepared by Robert Morris Associates and provides the analyst with a basis of comparison. The top portion of the report shows the average composition of assets, liabilities, and equities by company size. The middle section shows income data in percentages. The last section presents various financial ratios. For each ratio, the high, the mean, and the low are given within each size group. For receivables, the average daily collection period is shown and, for inventories, the average days sales are given.

In Fig. 17-14, balance sheet and income data for Kellogg and manufacturers of flour and other grain mill products are compared. Balance sheet and income data are stated in percentages to facilitate comparison. In the last section of Fig. 17-14 the more common financial ratios are compared.

Note that Kellogg's relative liquidity is stronger than the average of the other companies. Kellogg's lower investment in receivables is reflected in a higher sales–receivables turnover ratio. In effect, fewer days sales are tied up in receivables. Kellogg does have a higher relative investment in net fixed assets. Naturally a lower percentage investment in current assets will cause a higher percentage investment in other assets, mainly fixed assets. Kellogg's debt is very low comparatively.

Kellogg's income data show a relatively lower cost of sales and a higher percentage profit on sales. Kellogg's percentage of profit before taxes to net worth and total assets is much higher than the average return of the other companies.

Summary

Our analysis has not answered the question whether an investor should buy or hold the stock of Kellogg Company. Kellogg has shown a steady increase in sales, income, and dividend distributions. The financial structure of the company is excellent. Although the information examined provides positive criteria for investment, the answer to the question posed must be given by each individual investor.

One important aspect of our analysis of Kellogg is the emphasis given to trends rather than short-term fluctuations. Generally the analysis of statements for a single year provides very little, if any, significant information. Analysis of many years does provide information about the growth and development of the company in the past.

In short, the analysis of financial statements does not result in pat answers—there is an element of risk in every investment as there is in most actions. Finally, each individual must make a subjective judgment about what the future holds in store. The information in financial statements is, after all, historical information. As such, the statements cannot tell us what will happen to a company in the future. They can only furnish us with facts that make our predictions of the future something more than a mere guess.

QUESTIONS

1   Distinguish between current values and price-level adjustments.
2   Distinguish between price changes and price-level changes.
3   Relate general price-level adjustments to the problem of capital maintenance.
4   Discuss similarities and differences between price-level adjustments and foreign money translations.
5   Explain the difference between an operating profit and a holding gain.
6   List and discuss some of the difficulties encountered in constructing a general price index.
7   In analysis of financial statements, there must be a basis for comparison. Make a list of the sources of information in your library which provide standards for comparison.

Figure 17–13*

MANUFACTURERS OF—DAIRY PRODUCTS

35 STATEMENTS ENDED ON OR ABOUT JUNE 30, 1971
40 STATEMENTS ENDED ON OR ABOUT DECEMBER 31, 1971

MANUFACTURERS OF—FLOUR & OTHER GRAIN MILL PRODUCTS

27 STATEMENTS ENDED ON OR ABOUT JUNE 30, 1971
15 STATEMENTS ENDED ON OR ABOUT DECEMBER 31, 1971

	DAIRY UNDER $250M	DAIRY $250M & LESS THAN $1MM	DAIRY $1MM & LESS THAN $10MM	DAIRY $10MM & LESS THAN $25MM	DAIRY ALL SIZES	FLOUR UNDER $250M	FLOUR $250M & LESS THAN $1MM	FLOUR $1MM & LESS THAN $10MM	FLOUR $10MM & LESS THAN $25MM	FLOUR ALL SIZES
NUMBER OF STATEMENTS		27	39		75		11	22		42
ASSET SIZE	%	%	%	%	%	%	%	%	%	%
ASSETS										
Cash	8.1	6.0		6.3		5.0	8.3		5.9	
Marketable Securities	1.2	.9		1.0		.0	2.6		7.0	
Receivables Net	19.9	25.9		24.5		33.1	25.3		22.6	
Inventory Net	15.9	25.1		25.6		23.2	21.1		19.9	
All Other Current	1.7	1.1		1.0		2.0	3.9		2.8	
Total Current	46.8	58.9		58.4		63.3	61.2		58.2	
Fixed Assets Net	45.3	33.6		34.2		29.0	33.8		33.2	
All Other Non-Current	7.9	7.5		7.4		7.8	5.0		8.6	
Total	100.0	100.0		100.0		100.0	100.0		100.0	
LIABILITIES										
Due To Banks—Short Term	9.8	12.9		13.9		9.7	15.9		11.5	
Due To Trade	16.9	19.5		17.9		18.1	14.3		9.7	
Income Taxes	1.9	2.1		1.9		4.2	1.5		1.9	
Current Maturities LT Debt	4.5	2.6		3.8		2.2	2.1		1.7	
All Other Current	8.3	5.0		6.3		6.2	6.4		5.5	
Total Current Debt	41.4	42.1		43.8		38.5	40.3		30.4	
Non-Current Debt. Unsub	11.6	12.6		11.9		9.9	14.4		11.7	
Total Unsubordinated Debt	53.0	54.6		55.7		48.4	54.7		42.0	
Subordinated Debt	1.0	1.5		1.7		.5	1.4		.6	
Tangible Net Worth	45.9	43.8		42.6		51.0	43.9		57.4	
Total	100.0	100.0		100.0		100.0	100.0		100.0	
INCOME DATA										
Net Sales	100.0*	100.0*		100.0*		100.0	100.0		100.0*	
Cost Of Sales	71.3	79.1		80.2		83.5	88.6		87.3	
Gross Profit	28.7	20.9		19.8		16.5	11.4		12.7	
All Other Expense Net	26.1	18.6		17.7		13.7	9.8		10.4	
Profit Before Taxes	2.6	2.3		2.1		2.9	1.6		2.3	
RATIOS										
Quick	1.0	1.2		1.2		1.6	1.4		1.6	
	.8	.9		.9		1.0	.9		1.0	
	.5	.6		.5		.7	.6		.7	
Current	1.5	1.9		1.9		2.2	2.3		2.5	
	1.1	1.3		1.2		1.9	1.5		1.7	
	.9	1.1		1.0		1.1	1.2		1.2	

448

Ratio	Col 1	Col 2	Col 3	Col 4	Col 5	Col 6
Fixed/Worth	6 / 8 / 15	4 / 8 / 12	5 / 8 / 12	4 / 5 / 9	4 / 9 / 13	4 / 7 / 11
Debt/Worth	5 / 12 / 21	7 / 11 / 21	7 / 11 / 22	4 / 7 / 19	6 / 15 / 24	4 / 12 / 22
Unsub Debt/Capital Funds	.5 / 11 / 21	7 / 11 / 18	6 / 11 / 21	4 / 7 / 19	5 / 15 / 22	4 / 9 / 22
Sales/Receivables	20 17.9 / 28 13.1 / 38 9.4	17 21.3 / 28 12.8 / 37 9.8	19 18.6 / 28 13.1 / 38 9.6	19 18.8 / 33 10.9 / 144 2.5	22 16.2 / 29 12.4 / 42 8.6	20 17.8 / 29 12.5 / 43 8.4
Cost Sales/Inventory	11 33.0 / 30 12.2 / 80 4.5	10 37.4 / 19 18.6 / 58 6.2	10 34.9 / 22 16.5 / 58 6.2	18 20.6 / 33 10.9 / 0 0	17 21.0 / 25 14.3 / 41 8.8	19 19.4 / 30 12.2 / 52 6.9
Sales/Working Capital	19.3 / 6.8 / -27.5	35.4 / 17.0 / 6.0	31.5 / 15.2 / 4.3	17.3 / 11.2 / 1.0	16.9 / 13.0 / 5.9	18.0 / 13.0 / 5.9
Sales/Worth	10.9 / 5.1 / 3.2	14.9 / 7.8 / 4.6	11.8 / 7.4 / 4.6	3.6 / 4.8 / .6	10.1 / 7.0 / 5.1	9.6 / 6.4 / 4.0
% Profit Bef Taxes/Worth	28.9 / 7.2 / .0	26.3 / 17.7 / 6.9	27.1 / 14.4 / 5.1	28.6 / 14.0 / 3.4	18.0 / 7.3 / 3.8	18.0 / 7.0 / 1.6
% Profit Bef Taxes/Tot Assets	11.3 / 4.0 / .0	11.6 / 6.2 / 2.6	11.1 / 5.7 / 2.1	16.7 / 7.5 / -10.4	7.1 / 3.6 / -.9	11.6 / 4.4 / .6
Net Sales	$40625M	$434153M	$651140M	$26125M	$226308M	$456166M
Total Assets	15440M	125147M	183216M	7511M	64284M	161543M

Robert Morris Associates cannot emphasize too strongly that their composite figures for each industry may *not* be representative of that entire industry (except by coincidence), for the following reasons:

1. The only companies with a chance of being included in their study in the first place are those for whom their submitting banks have recent figures.
2. Even from this restricted group of potentially includable companies, those which are chosen, and the total number chosen, are not determined in any random or otherwise statistically reliable manner.
3. Many companies in their study have *varied* product lines; they are "mini-conglomerates," if you will. All they can do in these cases is categorize them by their *primary* product line, and be willing to tolerate any "impurity" thereby introduced.

In a word, don't automatically consider their figures as representative norms and don't attach any more or less significance to them than is indicated by the unique aspects of the data collection.

* See Footnote Page 1

449

Figure 17-14: Ratios for Kellogg Company, 1971 Compared to Those of Other Manufacturers of Flour and Grain Mill Products

Balance sheet data	Kellogg's (%)	11 other companies,[a] with 250M but less than 1 MM (%)
Assets:		
Cash	12.5	5.0
Marketable Securities	2.0	0.0
Receivables (net)	10.1	33.1
Inventory (net)	18.9	23.2
All other current assets	3.2	2.0
Total current assets	46.7	63.3
Fixed assets (net)	47.7	29.0
All other noncurrent assets	5.6	7.8
Total	100.0	100.0
Liabilities:		
Due to bank (short-term)		9.7
Due to trade	6.7	18.1
Income taxes	5.6	4.2
Current maturities (long-term obligations)	4.1	.2
All other current liabilities	7.4	6.2
Total current liabilities	23.8	38.5
Long-term debt	1.8	49.0
Deferred income taxes	3.6	.0
Net worth	70.8	51.0
Total	100.0	100.0
Income data		
Sales	100.0	100.0
Cost of Sales	61.7	83.5
Gross profit	38.3	16.5
All other expenses (net)	21.9	13.7
Profit before taxes	16.4	2.9
Ratios		
Quick	1.03	1.0
Current	1.96	1.9
Fixed/worth	.67	.5
Debt/worth	.025	.7
Unsubordinated debt/capital funds	—	.7
Sales/receivables	18.0	10.9
Cost of sales/inventory	5.6	10.9
Sales/working capital	7.87	11.2
% Profit before taxes/worth	41.7	14.0
% Profit before taxes/total assets	29.5	7.5
Net sales	680M	26125M
Total assets	378M	7511M

[a]Taken from Fig. 17-13; data compiled by Robert Morris Associates.

8   Make a list of some essential facts often found in the notes to financial statements that cannot be found in the statements themselves.

9   What essential information can be obtained from the auditor's opinion or report?

10   Distinguish between the following opinions:
     [a]   Unqualified
     [b]   An "except for" opinion
     [c]   A "subject to" opinion
     [d]   A disclaimer
     [e]   An adverse opinion

11   Contrast the analysis you would make of a corporation as a debt investor with the one you would make as an owner investor.

12   How can the historical accounting information on financial statements be used to predict future events?

PROBLEMS

1   A firm has sales of $500,000 in 19X6. The average GPI at the time these goods were sold was 120. The goods sold were acquired for $280,000, when the average GPI was 105. Assume the replacement price of the goods was $340,000 at the time of the sale.

Required:

Compute operating gain and holding gain. Then identify any fictitious component in the latter.

2   The C Realty Corporation is a real estate holding company. It operates in the metropolitan area and has acquired building lots during the last 20 years. The following table shows the amount spent for lots in each of several years and the GPI for each year during which the C Realty Corporation purchased lots:

Year	Cost of lots	GPI
1953	$ 10,000	90
1956	12,000	98
1959	25,000	105
1962	40,000	108
1965	35,000	120
1969	60,000	135
1972	20,000	160
1973 (end)		175
	$202,000	

Required:

[a]   On January 1, 1974, Mr. McDonald, the president of C Realty Corporation asks you to determine if the company has lost any purchasing power by investing in land. Prepare a table that shows the cost of the land in current dollars.

[b]   Assume that the C Realty Corporation believes it can sell the land within a short time for $450,000 by selling individual lots. In large blocks, similar property could be purchased for $300,000. On the basis of these estimates compute operating gain, holding gain, and fictitious gain.

3   Below is a comparative balance sheet for N Finance Company.

	December 31	
	19X3	19X4
Cash	$ 20,000	$ 25,000
Notes receivable	300,000	400,000
Marketable securities (stock)	50,000	50,000
Total assets	$370,000	$475,000
Notes payable to banks	$300,000	$380,000
Capital stock	50,000	50,000
Retained earnings	20,000	45,000
	$370,000	$475,000

Assume that the GPI was 132 on December 31, 19X3 and 140 on December 31, 19X4.

Required:

Compute gain or loss in general purchasing power from holding monetary assets and from owing monetary liabilities.

4   On January 1, 19X5, X Company purchased a machine for $10,000. The GPI on January 1, 19X5 was 120. The machine has a ten-year useful life with no expected salvage value. Compute depreciation for 19X8 under the straight-line method in current dollars. Assume that the average GPI for 19X8 was 135.

5   Assume an economy with four commodities that are priced on two different dates:

Commodity	1/1/19X2	1/1/19X3
A	$ 25	$ 26
B	40	42
C	50	53
D	15	24
	$130	$145

Of all the money spent in the economy 10 percent is spent on A, 25 percent on B, 50 percent on C, and 15 percent on D.

Required:

Use January 1, 19X2 as a base and set the index equal to 100 on that date and then compute the index for January 1, 19X3.

6   The financial statements of Green Giant Company and Subsidiaries for 1971 are reproduced on p. 513 through 519 of Appendix D. Prepare a detailed report of the analysis of these financial statements. Use the material in your library to obtain standards for performance. Also look up articles in the financial press to use in answering questions that cannot be answered based on the financial statements. Make one analysis from the viewpoint of a debt investor and another from the viewpoint of an owner investor. Write an essay that includes all the pertinent information, ratios, etc., for each analysis.

7   The financial statements of Gould, Inc. for 1971 appear on pp. 493 through 504 of Appendix D. Refer to the instructions in Problem 6 and prepare two essays to report your analysis.

8   The financial statements of the A. O. Smith Corporation for 1971 appear on pp. 532 through 543 of Appendix D. Refer to the instructions in Problem 6 and prepare two essays to report your analyses.

9   The financial statements of Singer Company for 1971 appear in pp. 521 through 530 of Appendix D. Refer to the instructions in Problem 6 and prepare two essays to report your analyses.

APPENDIX A

Present Value and
Future Value

Most people, given the alternative, would prefer to receive $1,000 today instead of $1,000 a year from today. Money changes in value with the passage of time. The purchasing power of money may change because of inflation which erodes its purchasing power. But of more importance in measuring the value of cash flows is the cost of money in use. Just as a building has a use value or rental value, money has a use value which is referred to as interest. The process of measuring the present value of the right to receive cash in the future is called *discounting*. The process of measuring the future value of an amount of cash invested today is called *compounding*.

When several time periods are involved, interest is earned on interest. For example, if you deposit $1,000 in the local savings and loan association which pays 5 percent interest, at the end of the first year your account will be $1,050 ($1,000 plus interest of $50). If you do not withdraw the interest, at the end of the second year your account will be $1,102.50 ($1,050 plus interest of $52.50). The fifty dollars of interest earned the first year will earn $2.50 interest the second year. This process of calculating the interest earned on interest to determine a future value is an example of compounding.

Discounting is the process of computing the present value of future cash flows, either inflows or outflows. For example, assume that a tract of land is purchased for $1,000 down and the promise to pay $1,000 per year for the next nine years. What is the cost of the tract of land? The sum of the current and future payments is $10,000 but this is not the present value of the future payments. How much would have to be deposited now to assure that $1,000 would be available at the end of each of the next nine years? If $952.38 is deposited now with an institution that is paying 5 percent interest, it will amount to $1,000 at the end of the first year ($952.38 + interest of $47.62). As opposed to discounting, compounding is the process of computing the *future value* of a present amount.

Two factors necessary to the process of discounting or compounding are the time period involved and the discount or interest rate. Usually the time period is stated in number of years, number of months, or number of days. The interest or discount rate is usually stated as a percentage for a stated time period.

Compounding

Let us assume that we wish to know how much a person will have after a number of years if he invests $1,000 at the present time. The assumed interest rate is 8 percent per annum. One method of compounding would be to prepare an accumulation table as shown in Fig. A-1.

Figure A-1: Accumulation Table for $1,000 Interest in Five Years at 8 Percent

End of year	Accumulated investment	Interest
0	$1,000.00	None
1	1,080.00	($1,000 X 8%) = $80.00
2	1,166.40	(1,080 X 8%) = 86.40
3	1,259.71	(1,166.40 X 8%) = 93.31
4	1,360.49	(1,259.71 X 8%) = 100.78
5	1,469.33	(1,360.49 X 8%) = 108.84

The preparation of an accumulation table is a tedious process. Mathematical formulas have been developed to simplify this process. The general formula for computing the future value of a sum invested for n periods at r rate of interest is developed in the following.

The symbols used are

p = Principal or present value of sum invested

$f_{\overline{n}|r}$ = Future value of principal (n periods at r rate of interest)

r = Rate of interest

n = No. of periods

After one period the formula would be

$$f_{\overline{1}|r} = p(1 + r)$$

after two periods,

$$f_{\overline{2}|r} = p + rp + r(p + rp) = p(1 + r)^2$$

after three periods,

$$f_{\overline{3}|r} = p(1 + r)^2 + r[p(1 + r)^2] = p(1 + r)^3$$

and after n periods,

$$f_{\overline{n}|r} = p(1 + r)^n$$

The future value of $1,000 invested at 8 percent interest for five years would be computed as follows:

$$f_{\overline{5}|8\%} = \$1,000(1 + 0.08)^5 = \$1,000(1.46933)$$
$$= \$1,469.33$$

For convenience, mathematical tables have been prepared for computing future values. Table A-1 of this appendix was completed for the principal of one or unity. The future value of any principal can be computed by following the steps presented here and using Table A-1:

Step 1   Locate the appropriate row for the time period n in Table A-1.
Step 2   Locate the appropriate column for the rate of interest, r.
Step 3   Select the compounding factor located at the intersection of the row and column found in steps 1 and 2.
Step 4   Multiply the principal amount or present value times the compounding factor found in step 3 to calculate future value of known principal.

• Example: You have the opportunity to invest $5,000 at an annual interest rate of 8 percent compounded quarterly for ten years. An annual interest rate of 8 percent compounded quarterly for ten years is equivalent to 2 percent rate for 40 periods. The compounding factor located at the intersection of n = 40

Table A-1: $f_{\overline{n}|r\%} = (1 + r)^n$ (f = future value of a single sum)

N ↓ r →	$\frac{1}{3}$	$\frac{1}{2}$	1	2
1	1.0033	1.0050	1.0100	1.0200
2	1.0067	1.0100	1.0201	1.0404
3	1.0100	1.0151	1.0303	1.0612
4	1.0134	1.0202	1.0406	1.0824
5	1.0168	1.0253	1.0510	1.1041
6	1.0201	1.0304	1.0615	1.1262
7	1.0235	1.0355	1.0721	1.1487
8	1.0270	1.0407	1.0829	1.1717
9	1.0304	1.0459	1.0937	1.1951
10	1.0338	1.0511	1.1046	1.2190
11	1.0372	1.0564	1.1157	1.2434
12	1.0407	1.0617	1.1268	1.2682
13	1.0442	1.0670	1.1381	1.2936
14	1.0476	1.0723	1.1495	1.3195
15	1.0511	1.0777	1.1610	1.3459
16	1.0546	1.0831	1.1726	1.3728
17	1.0581	1.0885	1.1843	1.4002
18	1.0617	1.0939	1.1961	1.4282
19	1.0652	1.0994	1.2081	1.4568
20	1.0687	1.1049	1.2202	1.4859
30	1.1049	1.1614	1.3478	1.8114
40	1.1422	1.2208	1.4889	2.2080
50	1.1808	1.2832	1.6446	2.6916

and r = 2 percent is 2.2080. The future value of $5,000 invested at 8 percent per annum compounded quarterly is $5,000 X 2.2080 = $11,040.

Discounting

The present value of the right to receive an amount at some future time is determined by the process known as discounting. The discounting process is the reverse of the compounding process.

If the future value [Eq. (1)] is

$$f_{\overline{n}|r} = p(1 + r)^n \tag{1}$$

then the present value equation should be

$$p_{\overline{n}|r} = \frac{f}{(1 + r)^n} \tag{2}$$

This equation answers the question, How much should be invested now for n periods at r rate of interest to grow to f? The same question may be stated, What is the present value of the right to receive f, in n periods from now, assuming a rate of interest r?

3	4	5	6	8	10
1.0300	1.0400	1.0500	1.0600	1.0800	1.1000
1.0609	1.0816	1.1025	1.1236	1.1664	1.2100
1.0927	1.1249	1.1576	1.1910	1.2597	1.3310
1.1255	1.1699	1.2155	1.2625	1.3605	1.4641
1.1593	1.2167	1.2763	1.3382	1.4693	1.6105
1.1941	1.2653	1.3401	1.4185	1.5869	1.7716
1.2299	1.3159	1.4071	1.5036	1.7138	1.9487
1.2668	1.3686	1.4775	1.5938	1.8509	2.1436
1.3048	1.4233	1.5513	1.6895	1.9990	2.3579
1.3439	1.4802	1.6289	1.7908	2.1589	2.5937
1.3842	1.5395	1.7103	1.8983	2.3316	2.8531
1.4258	1.6010	1.7959	2.0122	2.5182	3.1384
1.4685	1.6651	1.8856	2.1329	2.7196	3.4523
1.5126	1.7317	1.9799	2.2609	2.9372	3.7975
1.5580	1.8009	2.0789	2.3966	3.1722	4.1772
1.6047	1.8730	2.1829	2.5404	3.4259	4.5950
1.6528	1.9479	2.2920	2.6928	3.7000	5.0545
1.7024	2.0258	2.4066	2.8543	3.9960	5.5599
1.7535	2.1068	2.5270	3.0256	4.3157	6.1159
1.8061	2.1911	2.6533	3.2071	4.6610	6.7275
2.4273	3.2434	4.3219	5.7435	10.0627	17.4494
3.2620	4.8010	7.0400	10.2857	21.7245	45.2592
4.3839	7.1067	11.4674	18.4201	46.9016	117.3908

Table A–2: $p_{\overline{n}|r\%} = \dfrac{1}{(1+r)^n} = (1+r)^{-n}$ (p = present value of a single sum)

$N \downarrow$ $r \rightarrow$	$\frac{1}{3}$	$\frac{1}{2}$	1	2
1	0.9967	0.9950	0.9901	0.9804
2	0.9934	0.9901	0.9803	0.9612
3	0.9901	0.9851	0.9706	0.9423
4	0.9868	0.9802	0.9610	0.9238
5	0.9835	0.9754	0.9515	0.9057
6	0.9803	0.9705	0.9420	0.8880
7	0.9770	0.9657	0.9327	0.8706
8	0.9738	0.9609	0.9235	0.8535
9	0.9705	0.9561	0.9143	0.8368
10	0.9673	0.9513	0.9053	0.8203
11	0.9641	0.9466	0.8963	0.8043
12	0.9609	0.9419	0.8874	0.7885
13	0.9577	0.9372	0.8787	0.7730
14	0.9545	0.9326	0.8700	0.7579
15	0.9514	0.9279	0.8613	0.7430
16	0.9482	0.9233	0.8528	0.7284
17	0.9451	0.9187	0.8444	0.7142
18	0.9419	0.9141	0.8360	0.7002
19	0.9388	0.9096	0.8277	0.6864
20	0.9357	0.9051	0.8195	0.6730
30	0.9051	0.8610	0.7419	0.5521
40	0.8755	0.8191	0.6717	0.4529
50	0.8469	0.7793	0.6080	0.3715

$N \downarrow$ $r \rightarrow$	12	14	15	16
1	0.8929	0.8772	0.8696	0.8621
2	0.7972	0.7695	0.7561	0.7432
3	0.7118	0.6750	0.6575	0.6407
4	0.6355	0.5921	0.5718	0.5523
5	0.5674	0.5194	0.4972	0.4761
6	0.5066	0.4556	0.4323	0.4104
7	0.4523	0.3996	0.3759	0.3538
8	0.4039	0.3506	0.3269	0.3050
9	0.3606	0.3075	0.2843	0.2630
10	0.3220	0.2697	0.2472	0.2267
11	0.2875	0.2366	0.2149	0.1954
12	0.2567	0.2076	0.1869	0.1685
13	0.2292	0.1821	0.1625	0.1452
14	0.2046	0.1597	0.1413	0.1252
15	0.1827	0.1401	0.1229	0.1079
16	0.1631	0.1229	0.1069	0.0930
17	0.1456	0.1078	0.0929	0.0802
18	0.1300	0.0946	0.0808	0.0691
19	0.1161	0.0829	0.0703	0.0596
20	0.1037	0.0728	0.0611	0.0514
30	0.0334	0.0196	0.0151	0.0116
40	0.0107	0.0053	0.0037	0.0026
50	0.0035	0.0014	0.0009	0.0006

3	4	5	6	8	10
0.9709	0.9615	0.9524	0.9434	0.9259	0.9091
0.9426	0.9246	0.9070	0.8900	0.8573	0.8264
0.9151	0.8890	0.8638	0.8396	0.7938	0.7513
0.8885	0.8548	0.8227	0.7921	0.7350	0.6830
0.8626	0.8219	0.7835	0.7473	0.6806	0.6209
0.8375	0.7903	0.7462	0.7050	0.6302	0.5645
0.8131	0.7599	0.7107	0.6651	0.5835	0.5132
0.7894	0.7307	0.6768	0.6274	0.5403	0.4665
0.7664	0.7026	0.6446	0.5919	0.5002	0.4241
0.7441	0.6756	0.6139	0.5584	0.4632	0.3855
0.7224	0.6496	0.5847	0.5268	0.4289	0.3505
0.7014	0.6246	0.5568	0.4970	0.3971	0.3186
0.6810	0.6006	0.5303	0.4688	0.3677	0.2897
0.6611	0.5775	0.5051	0.4423	0.3405	0.2633
0.6419	0.5553	0.4810	0.4173	0.3152	0.2394
0.6232	0.5339	0.4581	0.3936	0.2919	0.2176
0.6050	0.5134	0.4363	0.3714	0.2703	0.1978
0.5874	0.4936	0.4155	0.3503	0.2502	0.1799
0.5703	0.4746	0.3957	0.3305	0.2317	0.1635
0.5537	0.4564	0.3769	0.3118	0.2145	0.1486
0.4120	0.3083	0.2314	0.1741	0.0994	0.0573
0.3066	0.2083	0.1420	0.0972	0.0460	0.0221
0.2281	0.1407	0.0872	0.0543	0.0213	0.0085

20	25	30	40	50	
0.8333	0.8000	0.7692	0.7143	0.6667	
0.6944	0.6400	0.5917	0.5102	0.4444	
0.5787	0.5120	0.4552	0.3644	0.2963	
0.4823	0.4096	0.3501	0.2603	0.1975	
0.4019	0.3277	0.2693	0.1859	0.1317	
0.3349	0.2621	0.2072	0.1328	0.0878	
0.2791	0.2097	0.1594	0.0949	0.0585	
0.2326	0.1678	0.1226	0.0678	0.0390	
0.1938	0.1342	0.0943	0.0484	0.0260	
0.1615	0.1074	0.0725	0.0346	0.0173	
0.1346	0.0859	0.0558	0.0247	0.0116	
0.1122	0.0687	0.0429	0.0176	0.0077	
0.0935	0.0550	0.0330	0.0126	0.0051	
0.0779	0.0440	0.0254	0.0090	0.0034	
0.0649	0.0352	0.0195	0.0064	0.0023	
0.0541	0.0281	0.0150	0.0046	0.0015	
0.0451	0.0225	0.0116	0.0033	0.0010	
0.0376	0.0180	0.0089	0.0023	0.0007	
0.0313	0.0144	0.0068	0.0017	0.0005	
0.0261	0.0115	0.0053	0.0012	0.0003	
0.0042	0.0012	0.0004	0.0000	0.0000	
0.0007	0.0001	0.0000	0.0000	0.0000	
0.0001	0.0000	0.0000	0.0000	0.0000	

The present value of the right to receive $1,000 assuming a discount or interest rate of 5 percent per annum is computed as follows:

$$P\overline{1}|5\% = \frac{\$1,000}{(1.05)^1} = \$952.38$$

The present value of the right to receive $1,000 two years from now, assuming a 5 percent interest rate, is computed as follows:

$$P\overline{2}|5\% = \frac{\$1,000}{(1.05)^2} = \frac{\$1,000}{1.1025} = \$907.00$$

Finding the nth value and dividing this value into the future value is an arduous process. Mathematical tables have also been prepared to compute the present value of a single sum. Table A-2 is such a table computed for future value of one or unity. The present value of any sum discounted n periods at r rate of interest can be computed using Table A-2. The following steps are taken in the process of discounting a known future sum:

Step 1 Locate the appropriate row for the number of time periods n.
Step 2 Locate the appropriate column for the rate of interest r.
Step 3 Select the discounting factor located at the intersection of the row and column found in steps 1 and 2.
Step 4 Multiply the future value times the discounting factor found in step 3 to calculate the present value.

• Example: Mr. Z offers to pay you $11,040 in ten years in exchange for a tract of land. What is the present value of this offer? Assume that the annual interest rate is 8 percent compounded quarterly. This is equivalent to 2 percent for 40 periods. The discounting factor located at the intersection of n = 40 and r = 2 percent is 0.4529. The present value of $11,040 discounted for 40 periods at 2 percent is $11,040 X 0.4529 = $5000.01.

The difference of 1 cent between this example and the previous example is caused by rounding.

Annuities

The right to receive a series of equal payments or the obligation to pay a series of equal amounts is known as an annuity. Measurement of the present value and future value of an annuity is briefly explained in this section.

Future Value of an Annuity*

An annuity in arrears is defined as a series of equal payments beginning at the end of the first period and continuing for n periods. The value at the end of

---

*Small letters f and p stand for future value and present value of a single sum; capital letters F and P stand for future and present value of an annuity.

n periods is referred to as the future value of an annuity in arrears. A time continuum to represent this series is

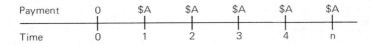

Payment	0	$A	$A	$A	$A	$A
Time	0	1	2	3	4	n

The amount A is equal to the deposit at the end of successive equal time periods. The future value of the annuity is the sum of the future values of each deposit A. It was determined that the future value of a sum was n periods at r interest or $p(1+r)^n$. The future value of a series of such payments would be a sum of a geometric series:

$$p(1+r)^{n-1} + p(1+r)^{n-2} + p(1+r)^{n-3} + \ldots + p(1+r)^0 \tag{3}$$

The first payment would accumulate interest for n – 1 periods; because the deposit is made at the end of the period, the last payment would not accumulate interest. An accumulation table is presented in Fig. A–2 to assist in understanding this process.

Figure A–2: Accumulation Table for Future Value of an Annuity of $1,000 for Four Periods at 5 Percent Interest

Time period	0	1	2	3	4
1		$1,000	$1,050	$1,102.50	$1,157.60
2			1,000	1,050.	1,102.50
3				1,000	1,050.
4					1,000
		$1,000	$2,050	$3,152.50	$4,310.10

Equation (3) is a geometric series. The sum of a geometric series of one or unit is

$$F_{\overline{n}|r} = \frac{(1+r)^n - 1}{r} \tag{4}$$

where n is the number of periods, r is the rate of interest, and F is the future value of the annuity. The future value of a series of equal deposits for n periods is

$$AF_{\overline{n}|r} = \frac{A(1+r)^n - 1}{r} \tag{5}$$

where A is the amount of the annuity.

Again mathematical tables have been prepared to ease the computational process. Table A–3 is a table for computing the future value of an annuity [n payments and (–1) interest periods]. The procedure for using Table A–3 follows the same pattern of steps described for the use of Table A–1 or A–2.

Table A-3: $F_{\overline{n}|\,r\%} = \dfrac{(1+r)^n - 1}{r}$ (F = future value of an annuity)

$N \downarrow$	$r \rightarrow$ $\frac{1}{3}$	$\frac{1}{2}$	1	2
1	1.0000	1.0000	1.0000	1.0000
2	2.0033	2.0050	2.0100	2.0200
3	3.0100	3.0150	3.0301	3.0604
4	4.0200	4.0301	4.0604	4.1216
5	5.0334	5.0503	5.1010	5.2040
6	6.0502	6.0755	6.1520	6.3081
7	7.0703	7.1059	7.2135	7.4343
8	8.0939	8.1414	8.2857	8.5830
9	9.1208	9.1821	9.3685	9.7546
10	10.1512	10.2280	10.4622	10.9497
11	11.1850	11.2792	11.5. 68	12.1687
12	12.2222	12.3356	12.6825	13.4121
13	13.2629	13.3972	13.8093	14.6803
14	14.3071	14.4642	14.9474	15.9739
15	15.3547	15.5365	16.0969	17.2934
16	16.4059	16.6142	17.2579	18.6393
17	17.4605	17.6973	18.4304	20.0121
18	18.5187	18.7858	19.6147	21.4123
19	19.5803	19.8797	20.8109	22.8406
20	20.6455	20.9791	22.0190	24.2974
30	31.4946	32.2800	34.7849	40.5681
40	42.7104	44.1588	48.8864	60.4020
50	54.3053	56.6451	64.4632	84.5794

- Example 1: The future value of an annuity of $1,000 to be paid at the end of four periods with interest at 5 percent is

$$AF_{\overline{4}|5\%} = \$1{,}000(4.3101) = \$4{,}310.10$$

- Example 2: The future value of an annuity of $6,000 for 20 periods with interest at 8 percent is

$$AF_{\overline{20}|8\%} = \$6{,}000(45.7620) = \$27{,}457.20$$

Present Value of an Annuity

The present value of an annuity of n payments of a stated amount at interest rate r with the first payment n periods from now is the value of an annuity at the beginning of the time frame instead of at the end of the time frame, as was the case for the future value of an annuity. The present value of an annuity is the sum of the present values of a series of single sums. Recall Eq. (2),

$$P_{\overline{n}|r} = \frac{f}{(1+r)^n}$$

Thus, the present value of a series of equal payments would be

$$P = \frac{f}{(1+r)^1} + \frac{f}{(1+r)^2} + \frac{f}{(1+r)^3} + \cdots + \frac{f}{(1+r)^n}$$

3	4	5	6	8	10
1.0000	1.0000	1.0000	1.0000	1.0000	1.0000
2.0300	2.0400	2.0500	2.0600	2.0800	2.1000
3.0909	3.1216	3.1525	3.1836	3.2464	3.3100
4.1836	4.2465	4.3101	4.3746	4.5061	4.6410
5.3091	5.4163	5.5256	5.6371	5.8666	6.1051
6.4684	6.6330	6.8019	6.9753	7.3359	7.7156
7.6625	7.8983	8.1420	8.3938	8.9228	9.4872
8.8923	9.2142	9.5491	9.8975	10.6366	11.4359
10.1591	10.5828	11.0266	11.4913	12.4876	13.5795
11.4639	12.0061	12.5779	13.1808	14.4866	15.9374
12.8078	13.4864	14.2068	14.9716	16.6455	18.5312
14.1920	15.0258	15.9171	16.8699	18.9771	21.3843
15.6178	16.6268	17.7130	18.8821	21.4953	24.5227
17.0863	18.2919	19.5986	21.0151	24.2149	27.9750
18.5989	20.0236	21.5786	23.2760	27.1521	31.7725
20.1569	21.8245	23.6575	25.6725	30.3243	35.9497
21.7616	23.6975	25.8404	28.2129	33.7502	40.5447
23.4144	25.6454	28.1324	30.9056	37.4502	45.5992
25.1169	27.6712	30.5390	33.7600	41.4463	51.1591
26.8704	29.7781	33.0660	36.7856	45.7620	57.2750
47.5754	56.0849	66.4388	79.0582	113.2832	164.4940
75.4012	95.0255	120.7998	154.7619	259.0565	442.5925
112.7968	152.6670	209.3480	290.3358	573.7701	1163.9082

or

$$P = f \sum_{x-1}^{n} \left(\frac{1}{1+r} \right)^{x} \tag{6}$$

The sum of the geometric series with f equal to unity may also be expressed as

$$P_{\overline{n}|r} = \frac{1 - (1 + r)^{-n}}{r} \tag{7}$$

Equation (7) can be solved quite easily by using Table A-2 to determine the value of $(1 + r)^{-n}$. Table A-4 was prepared using Eq. (7).

• Example: If a man owed $5,000 at the end of each of the next four years and the interest rate was 8 percent, then the present value would be calculated as follows:

$$P = \$5,000_{\overline{4}|8\%} = (\$5,000)(3.3121) = \$16,560.50$$

A better understanding of this process might be gained by examining the reduction table in Fig. A-3.

Table A–4: $P_{\overline{n}|r\%} = \sum\limits_{i=1}^{n} p_{\overline{i}|r\%} = \sum\limits_{i=1}^{n} (1+r)^{-i}$ (P = present value of an annuity)

N ↓ %→	⅓	½	1	2
1	0.9967	0.9950	0.9901	0.9804
2	1.9901	1.9851	1.9704	1.9416
3	2.9801	2.9702	2.9410	2.8839
4	3.9669	3.9505	3.9020	3.8077
5	4.9504	4.9259	4.8534	4.7135
6	5.9307	5.8964	5.7955	5.6014
7	6.9077	6.8621	6.7282	6.4720
8	7.8814	7.8230	7.6517	7.3255
9	8.8520	8.7791	8.5660	8.1622
10	9.8193	9.7304	9.4713	8.9826
11	10.7834	10.6770	10.3676	9.7868
12	11.7442	11.6189	11.2551	10.5753
13	12.7019	12.5562	12.1337	11.3484
14	13.6565	13.4887	13.0037	12.1062
15	14.6078	14.4166	13.8651	12.8493
16	15.5560	15.3399	14.7179	13.5777
17	16.5011	16.2586	15.5623	14.2919
18	17.4430	17.1728	16.3983	14.9920
19	18.3818	18.0824	17.2260	15.6785
20	19.3175	18.9874	18.0456	16.3514
30	28.5051	27.7941	25.8077	22.3965
40	37.3923	36.1722	32.8347	27.3555
50	45.9889	44.1428	39.1961	31.4236

N ↓ %→	12	14	15	16
1	0.8929	0.8772	0.8696	0.8621
2	1.6901	1.6467	1.6257	1.6052
3	2.4018	2.3216	2.2832	2.2459
4	3.0373	2.9137	2.8550	2.7982
5	3.6048	3.4331	3.3522	3.2743
6	4.1114	3.8887	3.7845	3.6847
7	4.5638	4.2883	4.1604	4.0386
8	4.9676	4.6389	4.4873	4.3436
9	5.3282	4.9464	4.7716	4.6065
10	5.6502	5.2161	5.0188	4.8332
11	5.9377	5.4527	5.2337	5.0286
12	6.1944	5.6603	5.4206	5.1971
13	6.4235	5.8424	5.5831	5.3423
14	6.6282	6.0021	5.7245	5.4675
15	6.8109	6.1422	5.8474	5.5755
16	6.9740	6.2651	5.9542	5.6685
17	7.1196	6.3729	6.0472	5.7487
18	7.2497	6.4674	6.1280	5.8178
19	7.3658	6.5504	6.1982	5.8775
20	7.4694	6.6231	6.2593	5.9288
30	8.0552	7.0027	6.5660	6.1772
40	8.2438	7.1050	6.6418	6.2335
50	8.3045	7.1327	6.6605	6.2463

3	4	5	6	8	10
0.9709	0.9615	0.9524	0.9434	0.9259	0.9091
1.9135	1.8861	1.8594	1.8334	1.7833	1.7355
2.8286	2.7751	2.7232	2.6730	2.5771	2.4869
3.7171	3.6299	3.5460	3.4651	3.3121	3.1699
4.5797	4.4518	4.3295	4.2124	3.9927	3.7908
5.4172	5.2421	5.0757	4.9173	4.6229	4.3553
6.2303	6.0021	5.7864	5.5824	5.2064	4.8684
7.0197	6.7327	6.4632	6.2098	5.7466	5.3349
7.7861	7.4353	7.1078	6.8017	6.2469	5.7590
8.5302	8.1109	7.7217	7.3601	6.7101	6.1446
9.2526	8.7605	8.3064	7.8869	7.1390	6.4951
9.9540	9.3851	8.8633	8.3838	7.5361	6.8137
10.6350	9.9856	9.3936	8.8527	7.9038	7.1034
11.2961	10.5631	9.8986	9.2950	8.2442	7.3667
11.9379	11.1184	10.3797	9.7122	8.5595	7.6061
12.5611	11.6523	10.8378	10.1059	8.8514	7.8237
13.1661	12.1657	11.2741	10.4773	9.1216	8.0216
13.7535	12.6593	11.6896	10.8276	9.3719	8.2014
14.3238	13.1339	12.0853	11.1581	9.6036	8.3649
14.8775	13.5903	12.4622	11.4699	9.8181	8.5136
19.6004	17.2920	15.3724	13.7648	11.2578	9.4269
23.1148	19.7928	17.1591	15.0463	11.9246	9.7790
25.7298	21.4822	18.2559	15.7619	12.2335	9.9148

20	25	30	40	50	
0.8333	0.8000	0.7692	0.7143	0.6667	
1.5278	1.4400	1.3609	1.2245	1.1111	
2.1065	1.9520	1.8161	1.5889	1.4074	
2.5887	2.3616	2.1662	1.8492	1.6049	
2.9906	2.6893	2.4356	2.0352	1.7366	
3.3255	2.9514	2.6427	2.1680	1.8244	
3.6046	3.1611	2.8021	2.2628	1.8829	
3.8372	3.3289	2.9247	2.3306	1.9220	
4.0310	3.4631	3.0190	2.3790	1.9480	
4.1925	3.5705	3.0915	2.4136	1.9653	
4.3271	3.6564	3.1473	2.4383	1.9769	
4.4392	3.7251	3.1903	2.4559	1.9846	
4.5327	3.7801	3.2233	2.4685	1.9897	
4.6106	3.8241	3.2487	2.4775	1.9931	
4.6755	3.8593	3.2682	2.4839	1.9954	
4.7296	3.8874	3.2832	2.4885	1.9970	
4.7746	3.9099	3.2948	2.4918	1.9980	
4.8122	3.9279	3.3037	2.4941	1.9986	
4.8435	3.9424	3.3105	2.4958	1.9991	
4.8696	3.9539	3.3158	2.4970	1.9994	
4.9789	3.9950	3.3321	2.4999	2.0000	
4.9966	3.9995	3.3332	2.5000	2.0000	
4.9994	3.9999	3.3333	2.5000	2.0000	

Figure A-3: Reduction Table for Annuity of $5,000 for four Periods at 8 Percent

Year	Value at beginning of year	Payment	Interest		Principal reduction
1	$16,560.50	$5,000	8% ($16,560.50) =	$1324.84	$3,675.16
2	12,885.34	5,000	8% (12,885.34) =	1030.83	3,969.17
3	8,916.17	5,000	8% (8,916.17) =	713.29	4,286.71
4	4,629.46[a]	5,000	8% (4,629.46) =	370.36	4,629.64[a]

[a]Difference of 24 cents caused by using four-place tables instead of six or eight places.

The following rules should be applied before attempting to solve a problem using annuity tables:

1   Count the number of payments and the number of interest periods. (An annuity in arrears has one less interest period than payment.)

2   If the number of payments equals the number of interest periods, then look up

    a $P_{\overline{n}|r\%}$ if present value is desired

    b $F_{\overline{n+1}|r\%}$ if future value is desired

3   If the number of payments is n and the number of interest payments is (n − 1), then look up

    a $P_{\overline{n-1}|r\%}$ if present value is desired

    b $F_{\overline{n}|r\%}$ if future value is desired

APPENDIX B

Bank
Reconciliations

If a firm deposits all cash receipts intact and makes disbursements only by check, records kept by the firm's bank should duplicate the business's record of cash transactions. Any differences will come only from (1) variations in the timing of recording transactions and (2) errors made by either the bank or the business. It is highly improbable that both the firm and the bank will make the same errors so that the duplicate records can be used to good advantage to assure correct records of cash transactions, which are essential to the flow concept of income.

Periodic reconciliation, usually on a monthly basis, of the cash balance on the firm's books with the cash balance according to the bank is necessary to take advantage of the duplicate records. To reconcile the two sets of records, the balances are brought to agreement by adjusting for errors and for differences in timing. The following is a summary of the potential types of reconciling items:

Book Balance to Adjusted Balance

Balance of the firm's cash account				$xxx
Add:	1	Any proper increases in cash recorded by the bank but not yet recorded by the firm. (An example would be the collection of an item such as a note receivable by the bank acting as the firm's collecting agent.)	$xxx	
	2	Any error on the firm's records that caused the cash balance to be understated. (An example would be writing a check for $59 and recording it as a check for $95.)	xxx	xxx
				$xxx
Deduct:	1	Any proper decreases in cash already recorded by the bank and not yet recorded by the firm. (An example would be the bank's monthly charge for servicing the bank account.)	$xxx	

2 Any error on the firm's books that caused the
book balance to be overstated. (An example
would be recording a $45 receipt from a cus-
tomer as a $54 receipt.)   xxx   xxx

Adjusted balance (same as balance in bank) $xxx

Bank Balance to Adjusted Balance

Cash balance shown on bank's records $xxx

Add: 1   Any proper increases in the cash balance recorded
by the firm but not yet recorded by the bank.
(An example would be a deposit in transit.) $xxx

       2   Any error by the bank that understated the cash
balance. (An example would be crediting the
firm's deposits to someone else's account.)   xxx   xxx

                                                       $xxx

Deduct: 1   Any proper decreases in the cash balance recorded
by the firm but not yet recorded by the bank.
(An example would be checks written that have
not cleared the bank, commonly called *outstanding checks*.) $xxx

       2   Any error by the bank that caused the cash balance
to be overstated. (An example would be crediting
someone else's deposit to the firm's account.)   xxx   xxx

Adjusted balance (same balance as in preceding adjusted book balance) $xxx

Reconciliation of book and bank balances assures the discovery of both intentional and unintentional errors on either set of records if the procedures are
carried out correctly. Reconciliations are usually performed and approved by
individuals who do not have access to cash. Otherwise mishandling of the cash
can be concealed by juggling the figures on the reconciliation.

Procedures for Reconciliations

Banks customarily mail monthly statements to depositors who have checking
accounts with the bank. These statements show the cash balance for the beginning of the month, all the deposits and payments recorded during the month,
daily balances, and the ending balance. Canceled checks and other documents
that support the deposits and payments shown on the bank statement are for-
warded to the depositor along with the statement.

When a firm receives its monthly bank statement, the following procedures
are carried out to make the reconciliation:

1 Daily cash receipts on the firm's records are traced to the deposits listed on
the bank statement. Deposits in transit are readily located by this procedure
and any other differences are identified for further investigation.

2   Canceled checks returned with the bank statement are compared with the firm's record of checks written. This procedure readily locates outstanding checks and any other differences for further investigation.

3   Documents other than canceled checks that accompany the bank statement are examined to discover items recorded by the bank but not yet recorded on the books. Examples would include the bank's monthly charge for services and any collections made on the firm's behalf and not previously reported to the firm.

4   Any remaining differences are probably caused by errors, and the investigation of the records is continued until the source and nature of these differences are located.

Example

N Incorporated had a balance of $3,416 in its general ledger cash account on May 1, 19X6. During the month of May, the company had cash receipts totalling $5,248 and disbursements totalling $6,429.

In comparing receipts per books with receipts per the bank statement, the following facts were revealed:

1   A deposit in the amount of $240 recorded on May 31, 19X6 did not appear on the May bank statement.

2   The deposit for May 6, 19X6 was recorded on the books for $218 and the bank statement showed $236 for the same deposit. Further investigation revealed that a check received from a customer for payment on his account was recorded at $68 on the company's records but was actually made out for $86.

In comparing the canceled checks returned with the bank statement to the firm's record of checks written, the following facts were revealed:

1   Checks No. 273 for $26, No. 276 for $82, and No. 277 for $14 did not clear the bank.

2   A check for $56 returned with the bank statement was a M Incorporated, not N Incorporated, check.

3   Check No. 274 paid on account to T Corporation was written for $726 but recorded for $720 on the company's records.

A collection notice returned with the bank statement showed that the bank had collected a note from one of the firm's customers. The $400 collected for the note, which included $10 interest, appeared on the bank statement but was not yet recorded on the books. Another document returned with the bank statement indicated that the bank had charged $3 to the account of N Incorporated for bank services rendered. The ending balance on the bank statement was $2,470.

The following reconciliation is based on the preceding information:

Book Balance to Adjusted Balance

Balance per books			$2,235
Add:	Error in receipts of May 6	$ 18	
	Note collected by bank	400	418
			$2,653
Deduct:	Error in recording check No. 274	$ 6	
	Bank charge for May	3	9
Adjusted book balance			$2,644

Bank Balance to Adjusted Balance

Balance per bank statement			$2,470
Add:	Deposit in transit	$240	
	Erroneous charge for M Incorporated check	56	296
			$2,766
Deduct	outstanding checks as follows:		
	No. 273	$ 26	
	No. 276	82	
	No. 277	14	122
Bank balance to adjusted book balance			$2,644

The reconciling items used to work from the book balance to the adjusted balance are items not yet recorded on the books or for items recorded errone-ously. To correct the books and to bring them up to date, entries for these items would be recorded as follows:

	Debit	Credit
Cash	$ 18	
Accounts receivable		$ 18
(To correct an error in recording a customer's payment for $68 instead of $86)		
Cash	$400	
Notes receivable		$390
Interest earned		10
(To record the collection of a customer's note together with interest)		
Accounts payable	$ 6	
Cash		$ 6
(To correct an error in recording a payment to a creditor for $720 instead of $726)		
Miscellaneous expense	$ 3	
Cash		$ 3
(To record bank service charge for May)		

Note that no entries are required for the items used to reconcile the bank bal-ance to the adjusted balance. These items are timing differences and will be re-corded in due time or they are errors that must be corrected on the bank's records.

PROBLEMS

1   The R Company receives its bank statement for the month ended June 30 on July 5, 19X5. The bank statement shows a balance of $462. The cash account as of the close of business on June 30, 19X5 shows a balance of $246. The following facts were gathered to prepare the bank reconciliation:

[a]   Receipt for June 30 of $1680 was not deposited until July 1.
[b]   Checks outstanding on June 30 amounted to $1,881.
[c]   Bank service charges of $5 were not recorded by the R Company.
[d]   A deposit of $2,184 was recorded by the R Company as $2,148.
[e]   A customer's check for $36 was returned by the bank because of insufficient funds.

Required:

Prepare a bank reconciliation statement in good form. Prepare any necessary adjusting entries.

2   Use the following information to prepare a reconciliation of the B Company book balance for cash with the bank balance as of May 30, 19X4. Also prepare any journal entries that are necessary according to information revealed by preparing the reconciliation.

Cash balance per books on April 30, 19X4 was $6,276. During May, 19X4, receipts of $12,621 and disbursements of $11,431 were recorded on the books. A comparison of receipts per books with receipts per bank revealed that the deposit of April 29, 19X4 for $450 was not recorded by the bank until May 2, 19X4 and that the deposit of May 31, 19X4 for $520 did not appear on the bank statement. The comparison also revealed the following:

[a]   The bank statement showed a deposit of $256 on May 8 that was not recorded on the books. A collection slip that accompanied the bank statement showed that the bank had collected a note for $250 and $6 of interest accrued on the note for the company.

[b]   The bank statement showed a debit for $80. Investigation revealed that a customer's check for $80 was returned by the bank and marked "NSF" because the customer did not have a balance in his account large enough to cover the check.

A comparison of disbursements per books with disbursements per bank revealed that the following checks written by B Company did not clear the bank:

No. 1184	$ 60
No. 1185	20
No. 1188	125
No. 1189	45

Reversing
Entries

Accountants frequently use reversing entries in the bookkeeping cycle. If used they are made after the closing entries and before preparation of the postclosing trial balance. These entries take their name from the fact that they are reversals of adjusting entries. For example, assume the following adjusting entry for accrued interest was prepared:

	Debit	Credit
Accrued interest receivable	$25	
Interest earned		$25
(To record interest accrued but not received		
as of the end of the period)		

The reversing entry would be

	Debit	Credit
Interest earned	$25	
Accrued interest receivable		$25
(To reverse the adjusting entry for accrued interest receivable)		

When reversing entries are used, they are usually prepared for all adjusting entries involving accrued revenues and accrued expenses. They are also typically prepared for deferred items whenever the initial entry has been recorded in a nominal, as distinguished from a real, account. As explained in Chapter 9 the use of a nominal or real account to record the initial transaction is a matter of discretion.

Account balances at the time financial statements are prepared come out the same with or without reversing entries. The easiest way to demonstrate this is by using examples. In the following, examples of an accrued expense and of a prepaid expense, each covering two accounting periods, are presented. The procedures for using reversing entries in connection with accrued revenues and for revenues collected in advance are accomplished in the same way.

Examples

Assume the following transactions to illustrate the use of reversing entries in connection with an accrued expense:

1   The business firm's first year of operations is 19X1.
2   Only transactions that involve cash disbursements are recorded during the accounting period.
3   During 19X1 the firm paid out $200 cash for interest and had $45 of interest accrued but unpaid at the end of the period.
4   During 19X2 the firm paid out $250 cash for interest and had $65 of interest accrued but unpaid at the end of the period.

In the T accounts on the left (Fig. C-1), the preceding information is recorded making use of reversing entries. In the T accounts on the right (Fig. C-1), the preceding information is recorded without using reversing entries. Information recorded during the period is entered in one summary entry and labeled "period trans.," adjustments are labeled "adj.," closing entries are labeled "to close," and reversing entries are labeled "to reverse." Amounts that will appear on the statements of income as interest expense are $245 in 19X1 and $270 in 19X2. Amounts that will appear as accrued interest expense liabilities on the balance sheets are $45 in 19X1 and $65 in 19X2. Use of reversing entries has no effect on the financial statements.

Assume the following transactions to illustrate the use of reversing entries in connection with a prepaid expense:

1   The business firm's first year of operation is 19X1.
2   Only transactions that involve cash disbursements are recorded during the accounting period.
3   On April 1 of each year the firm pays an annual rental for the coming year. The annual rent for the period April 1, 19X1, through March 31, 19X2, was $1,200. The annual rent for the period April 1, 19X2, through March 31, 19X3, was $1,320.
4   The initial entries are recorded as debits to an expense account as a matter of discretion.

In the T accounts on the left (Fig. C-2), the preceding information is recorded making use of reversing entries. In the T accounts on the right (Fig. C-2) the preceding information is recorded without using reversing entries. Information recorded during the period is labeled "period trans.," adjustments are labeled "adj.," closing entries are labeled "to close," and reversing entries are labeled "to reverse." Amounts that will appear on statements of income as rent expenses are $900 in 19X1 and $1,290 in 19X2. Amounts that will appear as prepaid rent expense on balance sheets are $300 in 19X1 and $330 in 19X2. Use of reversing entries has no effect on the financial statements.

Figure C-1: Comparison of Recording Accrued Expenses with and without Reversing Entries

With Reversing

Interest Expense

Period trans. 19X1 (1)	$200	To close (3a)	$245
Adj. 19X1 (2)	45		
	$245		$245
Period trans. 19X2 (4)	$250	To reverse (6a)	$ 45
Adj. 19X2 (5)	65	To close (6a)	270
	$315		$315
		To reverse 11/1/19X3	$ 65

Accrued Interest Expense

To reverse 1/1, 19X2 (aa)	$ 45	Adj. 19X1 (2)	$ 45
To reverse 1/1/19X3 (bb)	65	Adj. 19X2 (5)	65

Cash

	Period trans. 19X1 (1)	$200
	Period trans. 19X2 (4)	250

Revenue and Expense Summary[a]

Close expense 19X1 (3a)	$245	Close R&E (3b)	$245
Close expense 19X2 (6a)	270	Close R&E (bb)	270

Without Reversing

Interest Expense

Period trans. 19X1 (1)	$200	To close (3a)	$245
Adj. 19X1 (2)	45		
	$245		$245
Period trans. 19X2 (4)	$250	To close (6a)	$270
Adj. 19X2 (5)	20		
	$270		$270

Accrued Interest Expense

	Adj. 19X1 (2)	$ 45
	Adj. 19X2 (5)	20

Cash

	Period trans. 19X1 (1)	$200
	Period trans. 19X2 (4)	250

Revenue and Expense Summary[a]

Close expense 19X1 (3a)	$245	Close R&E (3b)	$245
Close expense 19X2 (6a)	270	Close R&E (6b)	270

[a] Amounts in revenue and expense summary would be combined with other expenses in an actual closing. Also the debit entry for the closing of revenue and expense summary is not shown.

Figure C-2: Comparison of Recording Prepaid Expenses with and without Reversing Entries

With Reversing

Rent Expense

Period trans. 19X1 (1)	$1,200	Adj. 19X1 (2)	$ 300
		To close (3a)	900
	$1,200		$1,200
To reverse 1/1/19X2 (aa)	$ 300	Adj. 19X2 (5)	$ 330
Period trans. 19X2 (4)	1,320	To close (6a)	1,290
	$1,620		$1,620
To reverse 1/1/19X3 (bb)	$ 330		

Prepaid Rent Expense

Adj. 19X1 (2)	$ 300	To reverse 1/1/19X2 (aa)	$ 300
Adj. 19X2 (5)	330	To reverse 1/1/19X3 (bb)	330

Cash

	Period trans. 19X1 (1)	$1,200
	Period trans. 19X2 (4)	$1,320

Revenue and Expense Summary[a]

Close expense (3a)	$ 900	Close R&E 19X1 (3b)	$ 900
Close expense (6a)	1,290	Close R&E 19X2 (6b)	1,290

Without Reversing

Rent Expense

Period trans. 19X1 (1)	$1,200	Adj. 19X1 (2)	$ 300
		To close (3a)	900
	$1,200		$1,200
Period trans. 19X2	$1,320	Adj. 19X2 (5)	$ 30
		To close (6a)	1,290
	$1,320		$1,320

Prepaid Rent Expense

Adj. 19X1 (2)	$ 300	
Adj. 19X2 (5)	30	

Cash

	Period trans. 19X1 (1)	$1,200
	Period trans. 19X2 (4)	$1,320

Revenue and Expense Summary[a]

Close expense (3a)	$ 900	Close R&E (3b)	$ 900
Close expense (6a)	1,290	Close R&E (6b)	1,290

[a] Amounts in revenue and expense summary would be combined with other expenses in an actual closing. Also, the debit entry for the closing of revenue and expense summary is now shown.

Purpose of Reversing Entries

At this point in time reversing entries are often used as a matter of habit and in effect serve no useful purpose at all. Even though reversing entries may have been generally useful in times past, the purposes they served probably could have been achieved more efficiently in other ways.

An effort to make judgments about how and why reversing entries came to be used is a speculative undertaking. Yet it seems reasonable to believe that in times past a major part of the clerical burden involved in keeping accounts of a business was assumed by clerks who did not understand the accounting process. Each clerk probably was trained to record certain types of transactions in a mechanical way. At the end of the period, a trained individual could then prepare the worksheet and the financial statements. Under these circumstances, the trained bookkeeper might well use reversing entries to set up the accounts for the coming period. Thus, given the instructions the clerks operated under, he could always know exactly what kinds of transactions were recorded during the period and how they were recorded. This would lessen the chances for oversights or mistakes both on the part of the clerks and in his own completion of the bookkeeping cycle at the end of the period. Then somewhere along the line reversing entries became a conventional part of the process.

Corporate
Financial
Statements

This appendix contains recent published financial statements for six large publicly-held corporations. A table of contents for these statements, indicating the page numbers for quick reference is presented below:

Indian Head, Inc.

The financial statements on pages 480–491 are reprinted from the 1971 financial statements of Indian Head, Inc. and Subsidiaries.

Financial Review

Sales

Record sales in 1971 of $446 million were 8% over sales reported in 1970. Part of this improvement is attributable to the inclusion of The Schwarzenbach Huber Company, which was acquired in February.

Operating Profit

Operating profit reached $33.9 million, up $2.2 million from results reported in 1970. Operating profit as a percentage of sales was 7.6% versus 1970's reported 7.7%.

Pretax Income

Pretax income of $26.8 million was 9% higher than 1970. This increase is due primarily to greater sales volume.

Net Income

Net income increased 9% to $13.3 million from the $12.2 million reported in 1970. Income taxes increased to $13.5 million from $12.5 million reported in 1970.

Earnings Per Common Share

Earnings per common share were $2.67 in 1971 on an average of 4,543,309 shares outstanding during the year. This represents a 5% increase from earnings of $2.55 per share in 1970 based on an average of 4,241,071 shares outstanding.

Convertible Securities and Dilution

The company has certain securities outstanding which may result in the issuance of additional common shares at some point in time. These securities are described below.

Convertible Preferred Stock, Series A— This $4.50 preference stock is convertible into common stock at: 3.64 shares until June 30, 1972; 3.08 shares to June 30, 1977; 2.67 shares to June 30, 1982; 2.35 shares to June 30, 1987 and 2.11 shares thereafter. The maximum number of common shares into which the currently outstanding preferred may be converted is 798,091. After June 30, 1987, the last date of change in conversion rates, the preferred shares currently outstanding would be convertible into 462,053 shares of common stock.

Convertible Subordinated Debentures— The $25 million of 5½% convertible subordinated debentures due April 15, 1993 are convertible at any time prior to maturity into common stock at a conversion price of $38.50 per common share. The debentures are redeemable at the option of the company at decreasing redemption prices ranging from 104.67% of principal amount currently to 100% if redeemed after April 15, 1988. Conversion of all of these debentures would result in the issuance of 649,350 common shares.

Warrants— In 1965, the company issued warrants to purchase 400,000 shares of common stock in connection with its sale of $20 million of 5½% subordinated debentures due 1990. There are presently 399,355 warrants outstanding which may be exercised to purchase common stock at $25 per share until May 15, 1975, with $5 price increases each five years thereafter until expiration in 1990.

Options— There are options outstanding for 216,309 common shares of which options for 200,100 shares are not presently exercisable. Exercise dates run through 1981. The exercise price of all outstanding options totals $5,074,000.

A pro forma calculation of earnings per share assuming the full conversion of these securities into common stock would result in earnings per share of $2.20 in 1971 compared with $2.09 in 1970. This pro forma calculation of earnings per share does not reflect the increased earnings that could result from the enlarged equity base that such conversion would provide.

Cash Flow

Cash flow (net income and depreciation) was $25.0 million compared with the $23.9 million generated in 1970. This amounts to $5.24 per common share after providing for preferred dividend requirements, compared to $5.30 per common share a year ago.

Working Capital

Working capital at year-end was $99.8 million, up from the $95.0 million at the end of last year. Principal changes in working capital in 1971 are detailed in the Consolidated Statement of Changes in Financial Position, page 30.

Capital Expenditures

Capital expenditures in 1971 were $13.9 million. This amount is down modestly from the $16.2 million expended in 1970, which included our $2.0 million equity investment in Madera Glass Company. The continued high level of capital expenditures, which we have maintained over the last few years, reflects our emphasis to modernize and make more efficient our plant and equipment and to expand operating capacity, where required, to augment our marketing programs. Depreciation in 1971 was $11.7 million.

Long-Term Debt

The company continues to have no bank or other short-term debt outstanding. The company's long-term debt has been structured to maximize the use of leverage for the benefit of common stockholders and to avoid large debt repayment requirements in any one year. The Prudential Insurance Company of America's loan of $70.0 million bears interest at 6.95% and the company's $17.8 million subordinated debentures bear interest at 5½%. The overall average interest cost for our long-term debt in 1971 was 6.5%.

A graphic illustration of our debt repayment requirements over the next 10 years appears on this page and shows that $4 million of our debt comes due in 1972, slightly less than that in each of the years 1973 through 1976 and just over $5 million in each of the years 1977 through 1981. This contrasts with our current cash flow of approximately $25 million annually.

The following table summarizes the annual requirements for debt repayment:

	Debt Repayment Schedule (In Thousands)			
Year	Prudential Loan $70,000	Other Notes $1,287	Sub-ordinated Debentures $17,822	Annual Total
1972	$ 3,500	$512	—	$ 4,012
1973	3,500	150	—	3,650
1974	3,500	71	—	3,571
1975-76	3,500	59	—	3,559
1977	5,000	48	—	5,048
1978	5,000	42	$ 72	5,114
1979-82	5,000	49	250	5,299
1983-84	5,000	34	250	5,284
1985	12,500	34	250	12,784
1986	—	27	250	277
1987-89	—	7	250	257
1990	—	—	15,000	15,000

Stockholders' Equity

Stockholders' equity at year-end was $113 million, a $13 million increase over our record equity at last year-end. Equity per common share, after making provision for the rights of preferred stock in involuntary liquidation, increased to $21.71 from $20.35 last year.

Return on Investment

Return on investment, calculated on average stockholders' equity for 1971, was 12.5%, compared to 12.6% in 1970.

Cash Dividends on Common Stock

Four quarterly dividends of 20¢ per share each, for a total of 80¢, were paid in 1971.

Report of Certified Public Accountants

The Board of Directors and Stockholders, Indian Head Inc.

We have examined the accompanying consolidated balance sheet of Indian Head Inc. and subsidiaries at November 27, 1971 and November 28, 1970 and the related consolidated statements of income, earned surplus and changes in financial position for the years then ended. Our examination was made in accordance with generally accepted auditing standards, and accordingly included such tests of the accounting records and such other auditing procedures as we considered necessary in the circumstances.

In our opinion, the statements mentioned above present fairly the consolidated financial position of Indian Head Inc. and subsidiaries at November 27, 1971 and November 28, 1970, the consolidated results of operations and the consolidated changes in financial position for the years then ended, in conformity with generally accepted accounting principles applied on a consistent basis during the period.

Arthur Young + Company

New York, N. Y.
January 7, 1972

Consolidated Statement of Income
Indian Head Inc. and Subsidiaries

Years ended November 27, 1971 and November 28, 1970

	1971	1970
Net sales	$446,065,000	$413,582,000
Operating costs and expenses		
Cost of sales, excluding depreciation	347,570,000	321,550,000
Depreciation, principally straight-line	11,695,000	11,652,000
Selling and administrative expenses	52,913,000	48,694,000
	412,178,000	381,896,000
Operating profit	33,887,000	31,686,000
Other deductions		
Interest expense—net	6,162,000	6,205,000
Loss on disposal of capital assets	285,000	864,000
Other expenses (income)	610,000	(37,000)
	7,057,000	7,032,000
Income before income taxes	26,830,000	24,654,000
Income taxes		
Federal and foreign (Note B)	12,145,000	11,220,000
State	1,340,000	1,230,000
	13,485,000	12,450,000
Net income	$ 13,345,000	$ 12,204,000
Net income per common share based on average number of shares outstanding	$2.67	$2.55
Pro forma net income per common share assuming full dilution (Note C)	$2.20	$2.09

See accompanying notes to financial statements.

Consolidated Balance Sheet
Indian Head Inc. and Subsidiaries

November 27, 1971 and November 28, 1970

Assets

	1971	1970
Current assets		
Cash	$ 8,350,000	$ 5,666,000
Short-term investments, at cost (approximating market)	26,266,000	20,527,000
Accounts receivable, less allowances of $1,812,000 in 1971 and $1,558,000 in 1970	62,059,000	57,975,000
Inventories, at lower of cost (first-in, first-out) or market:		
Raw materials and supplies	19,849,000	17,796,000
Work in process	19,933,000	18,200,000
Finished goods	21,369,000	18,553,000
	61,151,000	54,549,000
Prepaid expenses	4,073,000	4,101,000
Total current assets	161,899,000	142,818,000
Property, plant and equipment, at cost		
Land, buildings and improvements	50,434,000	46,106,000
Machinery and equipment	127,263,000	113,659,000
	177,697,000	159,765,000
Accumulated depreciation	80,063,000	66,576,000
Net plant investment	97,634,000	93,189,000
Other assets		
Equity in and advances to non-consolidated subsidiaries (Note A)	7,397,000	6,531,000
Cost in excess of net assets of companies acquired (Note A)	17,372,000	16,866,000
Other	10,011,000	9,780,000
Total other assets	34,780,000	33,177,000
	$294,313,000	$269,184,000

See accompanying notes to financial statements.

Liabilities and Stockholders' Equity	1971	1970
Current liabilities		
Current instalments of long-term debt	$ 4,012,000	$ 1,383,000
Accounts payable	29,645,000	21,262,000
Accrued expenses	25,449,000	19,734,000
Federal and foreign income taxes	2,963,000	5,474,000
Total current liabilities	62,069,000	47,853,000
Long-term liabilities (Note D)		
6.95% note payable to The Prudential Insurance Company of America,		
due in instalments 1972-1985	66,500,000	70,000,000
5½% subordinated debentures, due 1990	17,822,000	17,822,000
Other notes payable	775,000	739,000
Deferred income taxes and other liabilities	9,115,000	7,556,000
Total long-term liabilities	94,212,000	96,117,000
5½% convertible subordinated debentures, due 1993 (Note E)	25,000,000	25,000,000
Stockholders' equity (Notes D, E and F)		
Preferred stock, without par value, 1,000,000 shares authorized:		
$4.50 convertible preferred stock, Series A, at stated value		
(involuntary liquidation value—$8,779,000 in 1971)		
issued 229,477 shares in 1971 and 281,265 in 1970	834,000	1,023,000
$6 preferred stock, Series B, at stated value, issued and outstanding		
28,358 shares	2,836,000	2,836,000
Common stock, par value $1 per share, authorized 10,000,000 shares,		
issued 4,710,884 shares in 1971 and 4,289,718 in 1970	4,711,000	4,290,000
Capital surplus	13,671,000	9,490,000
Earned surplus	92,592,000	84,166,000
	114,644,000	101,805,000
Stock held in treasury, at cost	1,612,000	1,591,000
Total stockholders' equity	113,032,000	100,214,000
	$294,313,000	$269,184,000

Consolidated Statement of Changes in Financial Position
Indian Head Inc. and Subsidiaries

Years ended November 27, 1971 and November 28, 1970

	1971	1970
Source of funds:		
Net income	$13,345,000	$12,204,000
Depreciation and other items not requiring funds	12,492,000	13,242,000
Funds from operations	25,837,000	25,446,000
Increase in long-term debt	—	2,438,000
Common stock issued:		
For acquisition	4,311,000	—
Exercise of stock options, warrants and Series A preferred stock converted	311,000	157,000
Sales and retirements of capital assets	1,764,000	2,491,000
Other—net	53,000	338,000
Total	32,276,000	30,870,000
Application of funds:		
Capital expenditures	13,855,000	16,222,000
Cash dividends declared	4,919,000	4,368,000
Decrease in long-term debt	3,757,000	—
Purchase of treasury stock	—	1,523,000
Non-current assets of companies acquired—net:		
Property, plant and equipment	3,736,000	—
Other	1,144,000	—
	4,880,000	—
Total	27,411,000	22,113,000
Increase in working capital (Note G)	$ 4,865,000	$ 8,757,000

Consolidated Statement of Earned Surplus

Years ended November 27, 1971 and November 28, 1970

	1971	1970
Balance at beginning of year	$84,166,000	$76,330,000
Net income	13,345,000	12,204,000
	97,511,000	88,534,000
Cash dividends		
Preferred stocks	1,226,000	1,395,000
Common stock, 80¢ per share in 1971 and 70¢ per share in 1970	3,693,000	2,973,000
	4,919,000	4,368,000
Balance at end of year (Note D)	$92,592,000	$84,166,000

Notes to Financial Statements

Note A—Principles of Consolidation

The consolidated financial statements include the accounts of all subsidiaries except certain non-significant subsidiaries which are carried at equity.

Cost in excess of net assets of companies acquired is not being amortized, except for $1,900,000 which is being amortized over a 10 to 20 year period.

The company purchased The Schwarzenbach Huber Company in February 1971 for $3,900,000 in cash and 226,900 shares of common stock. Sales included in 1971, from date of acquisition, were $24,000,000. There was no material effect on earnings per share.

Note B—Income Taxes

Deferred income taxes relate primarily to depreciation. The provision for Federal income taxes for 1971 and 1970 includes $815,000 and $1,233,000 of deferred taxes, respectively.

Investment credit, not material in amount, has been applied as a reduction of Federal income taxes.

Note C—Pro Forma Net Income Per Common Share

Pro forma net income per common share assuming full dilution reflects conversion of Series A preferred stock and convertible debentures with adjustment of related preferred dividends and interest, exercise of warrants to purchase common stock with application of related proceeds in reduction of 5½ % debentures, and exercise of stock options with application of related proceeds to purchase common shares.

Note D—Long-Term Debt and Surplus Restriction

Annual maturities of long-term debt during the next five years are 1972—$4,012,000; 1973—$3,650,000; 1974—$3,571,000; 1975—$3,559,000 and 1976—$3,559,000.

Certain loan agreements contain restrictions on the purchase, redemption, retirement or payment of dividends (except stock dividends) on common stock of the company. Under the most restrictive provision, $18,200,000 of the company's earned surplus at November 27, 1971 was not so restricted.

Note E—Stockholders' Equity

Changes in issued shares for fiscal 1970 and 1971 are shown in the table below.

The Series A preferred stock is redeemable, at the option of the company, after September 15, 1972 at $100 per share. Each share is convertible into 3.64 shares of common stock until June 30, 1972, 3.08 shares to June 30, 1977 and at decreased amounts thereafter. The Series B preferred stock is not convertible and is redeemable, at the option of the company, at any time at $105 per share.

At November 27, 1971, a total of 2,433,976 shares of common stock were reserved for issuance comprising 834,462 shares for conversion of the Series A preferred stock, including treasury shares, 649,350 shares (at $38.50 per share) for conversion of the convertible subordinated debentures, 399,355 shares for exercise of warrants to purchase common stock at $25 per share to May 1975 and at increasing prices thereafter, 397,209 shares for options (of which options for 216,309 shares are outstanding) under the company's stock option plan and 153,600 shares for sale to the Trustee of the Employees Stock Purchase Plan and for sale to certain employees under the company's key executive equity plan.

The increase of $4,181,000 in capital surplus in 1971 includes $4,084,000 excess of fair market value over par value of common stock issued in an acquisition and $97,000 of other items. In 1970, the $547,000 increase is attributable to amounts in excess of par value of common stock sold under options, warrants and key executive equity plan.

	Convertible Preferred Stock, Series A		Preferred Stock, Series B	Common Stock	
	Issued	Held in Treasury		Issued	Held in Treasury
Balance at November 29, 1969	284,476		28,358	4,244,447	2,416
Series A preferred stock converted	(3,211)			11,671	
Stock options and warrants exercised				10,000	
Stock sold under key executive equity plan				23,600	
Purchases for treasury		10,002			37,012
Other					(2,415)
Balance at November 28, 1970	281,265	10,002	28,358	4,289,718	37,013
Stock portion of acquisition				226,900	
Series A preferred stock converted	(51,788)			188,261	
Stock options and warrants exercised				6,005	
Purchases for treasury					3,200
Other					(1,796)
Balance at November 27, 1971	229,477	10,002	28,358	4,710,884	38,417

Note F—Stock Options
During 1971, the stockholders approved the 1971 Stock Option Plan reserving 300,000 shares of common stock for options and terminated the company's previous stock option plans, under which 32,050 shares had been available for grant at the beginning of the year. Such termination does not affect options which were outstanding under these plans.

Options are granted at the quoted market price at grant dates and expire at various dates to 1981. There were 180,900 shares reserved for grant at the end of the year.

Changes during the year in the company's stock option plan are summarized below:

	Shares under Option	Prices per Share
At beginning of year	203,500	$15.75 to $46.13
Options granted	128,809	$27.25 to $30.50
Options exercised	(6,000)	$18.13 to $24.63
Options cancelled	(110,000)	$15.75 to $46.13
At end of year (of which 16,209 shares are exercisable)	216,309	$15.75 to $30.50

Note G—Changes in Working Capital
The changes in components of working capital were as follows:

	1971	1970
Increase (decrease) in current assets:		
Cash and short-term investments	$ 8,423,000	$10,471,000
Accounts receivable	4,084,000	(5,840,000)
Inventories	6,602,000	(6,374,000)
Prepaid expenses	(28,000)	976,000
	19,081,000	(767,000)
Increase (decrease) in current liabilities:		
Current instalments of long-term debt	2,629,000	(45,000)
Accounts payable and accrued expenses	14,098,000	(9,179,000)
Federal and foreign income taxes	(2,511,000)	(300,000)
	14,216,000	(9,524,000)
Increase in working capital	$ 4,865,000	$ 8,757,000

Note H—Pension and Profit-Sharing Retirement Plans
Contributions to various pension and profit-sharing retirement plans were approximately $3,400,000 in 1971 and $2,700,000 in 1970. The company's policy with respect to pension plans is to accrue and fund current cost plus interest on unfunded prior service cost.

Note I—Long-Term Leases
Annual rentals payable under long-term leases for office space and plant facilities at November 27, 1971 were approximately $2,200,000. Under certain of these leases, the company is also required to pay for insurance, taxes and repairs.

Ten-Year Summary
Indian Head Inc. and Subsidiaries

(Dollars in thousands except amounts per share)	1971	1970	1969	1968
Operating results				
Net sales	$446,065	$413,582	$435,469	$369,531
Operating profit	33,887	31,686	34,796	30,645
% to sales	7.6	7.7	8.0	8.3
Interest expense	6,162	6,205	6,787	4,000
Income before income taxes	26,830	24,654	28,617	26,122
% to sales	6.0	6.0	6.6	7.1
Per common share, net of pretax income required for preferred dividends	$ 5.39	$ 5.15	$ 6.10	$ 5.65
Income taxes	13,485	12,450	15,200	14,050
Net income	13,345	12,204	13,417	12,072
Per common share	$ 2.67	$ 2.55	$ 2.86	$ 2.61
Capital expenditures	13,855	16,222	17,691	15,899
Depreciation	11,695	11,652	10,784	8,975
Cash flow from operations	25,040	23,856	24,201	21,047
Per common share	$ 5.24	$ 5.30	$ 5.44	$ 4.86
Financial position				
Working capital	99,830	94,965	86,208	76,683
Net plant and equipment	97,634	93,189	92,808	85,851
Total assets	294,313	269,184	267,099	248,782
Long-term debt	85,097	88,561	86,123	80,609
Convertible subordinated debentures	25,000	25,000	25,000	25,000
Stockholders' equity	113,032	100,214	93,335	81,541
% return on average stockholders' equity	12.5	12.6	15.3	15.6
Dividends				
Preferred stock requirements	1,226	1,395	1,472	1,617
Common stock—declared	3,693	2,973	2,517	1,805
Per common share	$ .80	$ .70	$ .60	$ .60
Average number of common shares outstanding	4,543,309	4,241,071	4,175,348	4,000,434

Financial data are as reported in the company's annual reports without adjustment for subsequent poolings of interests.

1967	1966	1965	1964	1963	1962
$287,784	$225,455	$188,914	$158,398	$153,390	$151,627
19,607	13,679	10,762	8,286	5,642	7,144
6.8	6.1	5.7	5.2	3.7	4.7
3,689	3,300	2,552	:1,669	1,640	1,645
15,511	9,890	7,330	6,144	4,055	5,840
5.4	4.4	3.9	3.9	2.6	3.9
$ 4.81	$ 4.40	$ 3.44	$ 2.60	$ 1.64	$ 2.87
7,850	5,000	3,625	3,115	1,530	1,752
7,661	5,280	3,705	3,029	2,525	4,088
$ 2.38	$ 2.35	$ 1.74	$ 1.28	$ 1.02	$ 2.01
6,993	2,990	5,598	3,295	2,276	1,640
7,203	5,076	4,372	3,133	2,461	2,039
14,864	10,356	8,077	6,162	4,986	6,127
$ 5.23	$ 4.61	$ 3.89	$ 2.80	$ 2.22	$ 3.12
52,658	43,744	41,252	28,015	28,784	29,347
53,049	45,358	29,616	16,728	18,890	11,564
161,563	139,565	111,571	73,445	77,704	65,626
62,080	66,637	55,000	22,000	25,000	20,000
—	—	—	—	—	—
52,713	30,625	24,112	27,006	25,760	24,660
15.3	18.6	14.5	11.5	10.0	17.8
1,669	—	182	389	411	430
1,367	982	802	824	585	344
$ .55	$ .47½	$ .40	$ .40	$ .28⅓	$ .16⅔
2,521,902	2,245,815	2,028,597	2,058,460	2,065,312	1,823,113

Gould, Inc.

The financial statements on pages 493-504 are reprinted from the 1971 financial statements of Gould, Inc., and Consolidated Subsidiaries.

Financial Review

Sales set new record, earnings decline: In 1971 Gould Inc.'s sales were a record $342,166,000. 1971 was the tenth consecutive year of record sales. As compared to the prior year, sales were up 1.0%. Profits, however, were down 6.7% to $14,311,000 or $2.91 per share. Comparable earnings last year were $15,439,000 or $3.18 per share. Sales and earnings figures for 1971 include the results from operations of Ferraloy, Inc., a powder metal producer, from September, 1970, when it was purchased.

Accounting procedures require 1970 earnings to be reported on a part-purchase, part-pooling basis. As a result, 1970 net earnings are shown in our audited statement at $15,337,000, $3.16 per share. We believe the 1970 pro forma earnings of $3.18 versus 1971's $2.91 more accurately compares those two years. "Earnings per share assuming full dilution" in 1971 were $2.87 compared to $3.04 in 1970. Note "J" to our financial statement explains in detail the calculation of "earnings per share assuming full dilution."

Working Capital Declines: There were several important changes in our balance sheet during the year. Working capital declined $10.0 million during 1971. This decrease was due primarily to a reduction of $6.0 million in marketable securities which were abnormally high, $14.5 million, a year ago. Much of this decrease financed our capital expenditures. In addition, current maturities of long-term debt rose over $6.7 million. Negotiations are now in their final stages for a $45.0 million revolver-term loan with our major banks. This

loan will reduce current maturities of long-term debt and improve our working capital position.

The Company re-entered the commercial paper market in the fall of 1970 for the first time in two years. Use of this important market for short-term funds permitted us to retire all short-term U.S. bank borrowings for a 30 day period last year. Presently, approximately 50% of our short-term needs are filled by commercial paper borrowings, all of which are covered by open bank lines.

Capital Expenditures Increase: Total assets of Gould Inc. rose to $302,423,000 in 1971, an increase of $15 million over 1970's $286,944,000. Investment during the year in fixed assets was $20.4 million of which over $10.0 million was for new machinery and equipment. In the liability accounts, there was no material change in long-term debt.

However, we expect long-term debt in the year ahead to increase $5.0 to $10.0 million as we continue our growth both here and abroad. Also in the liability accounts, deferred income taxes, an important cash source, rose substantially because of our use of accelerated depreciation for tax purposes.

Leasing Operations: Gould Inc. initiated significant lease operations in fiscal year 1971. These operations are an important aid to our marketing activities. The balance sheet and income statement of our leasing companies are not included in our consolidated statements, although the net income of the operations are included in the statement of

earnings. Note "K" to our financial statements describes the financial condition of our leasing activities in detail.

Accounting policies and methods used by various companies differ. A brief description of the major policies used by Gould Inc. may, therefore, be helpful in evaluating the Company's financial statements and other data contained in the report.

Principles of Consolidation: The consolidated financial statements include the accounts of the Company and all of its subsidiaries except several minor non-manufacturing subsidiaries which are carried at the Company's approximate equity therein. All subsidiaries of the Company are wholly-owned except for an immaterial minority interest in a domestic subsidiary.

Determination of Income: The following accounting methods have been applied in the determination of income: Cost of goods sold has been determined by using inventories which are carried in our statement of Financial Position at the lower of cost (first-in, first-out method) or market.

A portion of the cost of buildings and equipment is charged against earnings as depreciation expense. This amount is computed by the straight-line method, which means that approximately equal amounts of depreciation expense are charged against operations each year during the economic life of the building or equipment. For tax purposes, however, accelerated methods of depreciation are used which charge a greater amount of expense to income in the early years than in the later years of the life of the property. Earn-

ings are charged for deferred taxes resulting from the differences between the two depreciation methods.

A portion of the cost of goodwill and similar intangible assets acquired after October 31, 1970, is charged against earnings each year on a straight-line basis over the economic life of the asset.

Expenditures for research and development are charged to earnings each year as they are incurred.

Earnings Per Share: In computing earnings per share of common stock, certain securities, such as stock options and warrants, are called "common stock equivalents", and are included in the average number of shares outstanding provided they were issued after May 30, 1969. The Company has only a minor number of such common stock equivalents outstanding and their effect is not material.

Leasing Companies: The Company has several wholly-owned leasing companies which have not been consolidated in the financial statements. The Company's investment in these companies is recorded on the financial statements at cost adjusted for the earnings of the companies. These earnings are also included in the income of the Company for the year.

Statement of Stockholders' Equity

Gould Inc. and Consolidated Subsidiaries

Financial Summary: Ten Year Comparison   Gould Inc. and Consolidated Subsidiaries

For Year Ended June 30, (a)	1971	1970	1969
Net Sales	$342,166,194	$339,979,798	$328,413,525
Increase in Sales—Percent	1.0%	3.5%	11.5%
Pre-Tax Earnings	$ 26,276,866	$ 29,358,503	$ 25,737,037
Pre-Tax Earnings as a Percent of Net Sales	7.7%	8.6%	7.8%
Income Taxes	$ 11,966,000	$ 14,297,011	$ 13,049,459
Net Earnings(b)	$ 14,310,866	$ 15,337,104	$ 13,288,640
Increase (decrease) in Earnings—Percent	(6.7%)	15.4%	16.1%
Dividends Declared Per Share of Common Stock(c) (e)	$ 1.40	$ 1.40	$ 1.40
Amount Retained for Use in the Business (c) (d)	$ 7,425,770	$ 10,234,776	$ 5,838,020
Average Number of Shares Outstanding—Net	4,916,584	4,857,958	4,837,069
Earnings Per Share(b)	$ 2.91	$ 3.16	$ 2.75
Income Taxes as a Percent of Pre-Tax Earnings	45.5%	48.7%	50.7%
Income Tax Per Share of Common Stock	$ 2.43	$ 2.94	$ 2.70
Return on Invested Capital (Net Worth Plus Long-Term Debt) — Percent	6.28%	6.95%	6.75%
Return on Net Worth—Percent	8.80%	9.95%	8.96%
Dollar Sales Per Employee	$ 26,163	$ 26,249	$ 21,723
Capital Expenditures(f)	$ 20,408,897	$ 16,093,561	$ 13,706,639
Depreciation(f)	$ 8,535,135	$ 7,327,706	$ 8,517,660
As of June 30,			
Book Value of Property—Net	$ 86,351,203	$ 71,354,182	$ 68,671,728
Working Capital	$ 80,257,104	$ 90,321,869	$ 69,322,720
Number of Employees	13,078	12,952	15,118
Number of Stockholders	14,912	15,240	15,505
Stockholders' Equity	$162,615,691	$154,199,839	$148,286,130
Shares of Common Stock Outstanding	4,935,100	4,895,643	4,842,247
Book Value Per Share of Common Stock	$ 32.95	$ 31.50	$ 30.62

(a) The amounts since 1964 have been restated for acquisitions (including those accounted for as part-pooling, part-purchase) and divestitures. The amounts for 1962 through 1964 represent the combined accounts for Gould and Clevite on an historical basis. Depreciation and Capital Expenditures, however, have been restated.

(b) Earnings and earnings per share after deduction of pre-acquisition earnings applicable to Clevite stock purchased.

(c) Due to a change in dividend declaration dates to conform to the change in fiscal year, only dividends for three quarters were declared during the year ending June 30, 1970.

1968	1967	1966	1965	1964	1963	1962
$294,624,304	$289,713,081	$282,481,341	$265,716,194	$204,518,729	$199,540,427	$194,842,473
1.7%	2.6%	6.3%	29.9%	2.5%	2.4%	9.57%
$ 21,427,641	$ 18,143,915	$ 22,521,134	$ 22,685,575	$ 16,215,703	$ 15,892,633	$ 17,402,918
7.3%	6.3%	8.0%	8.5%	7.9%	8.0%	8.9%
$ 10,452,419	$ 8,321,693	$ 10,333,378	$ 11,076,798	$ 8,080,910	$ 7,785,785	$ 8,500,759
$ 11,449,975	$ 10,417,498	$ 12,430,749	$ 11,391,421	$ 8,134,793	$ 8,106,848	$ 8,902,159
9.9%	(16.2%)	9.1%	40.0%	.3%	(8.93%)	14.66%
$ 1.40	$ 1.40	$ 1.40	$ 1.35	$ 1.30	$ 1.30	$ 1.20
$ 5,878,413	$ 5,261,016	$ 7,459,845	$ 6,958,397	$ 3,947,484	$ 3,960,718	$ 4,958,988
4,818,026	4,848,142	4,800,958	4,922,524	4,370,354	4,317,515	4,305,590
$ 2.38	$ 2.15	$ 2.59	$ 2.31	$ 1.86	$ 1.88	$ 2.07
48.8%	45.9%	45.9%	48.8%	49.8%	49.0%	48.8%
$ 2.17	$ 1.72	$ 2.15	$ 2.25	$ 1.85	$ 1.80	$ 1.97
6.38%	6.69%	8.49%	9.64%	7.09%	7.34%	8.38%
8.11%	7.64%	9.80%	9.91%	7.47%	7.81%	8.98%
$ 20,641	$ 19,453	$ 17,678	$ 18,325	$ 16,153	$ 15,435	$ 15,095
$ 11,874,588	$ 13,196,936	$ 10,290,078	$ 10,511,969	$ 9,533,625	$ 9,407,842	$ 5,879,380
$ 7,967,968	$ 6,889,071	$ 5,867,215	$ 6,341,912	$ 6,701,366	$ 6,534,745	$ 6,528,823
$ 64,276,343	$ 62,948,233	$ 56,229,735	$ 51,053,579	$ 46,980,763	$ 46,266,630	$ 44,668,265
$ 94,576,985	$ 88,604,531	$ 94,512,461	$ 75,870,699	$ 60,377,197	$ 57,956,372	$ 56,324,313
14,274	14,893	15,979	14,500	12,661	12,928	12,908
18,512	16,363	13,971	12,937	12,136	11,612	11,289
$141,097,806	$136,404,302	$126,818,823	$114,897,264	$108,936,312	$103,824,403	$ 99,025,020
4,834,649	4,842,679	4,808,858	4,791,758	4,402,396	4,324,591	4,309,291
$ 29.18	$ 28.17	$ 26.37	$ 23.98	$ 24.74	$ 24.01	$ 22.98

(d) Dividends declared on Common Stock and Amounts Retained for Use in the Business are net of the amounts attributable to the purchased portion of the Clevite, Sonotone and Servel acquisitions.

(e) Dividends Declared Per Share represents the historical amounts for Gould only.

(f) Depreciation and Capital Expenditures have been restated for all acquisitions.

Statement of Earnings   Gould Inc. and Consolidated Subsidiaries

Year Ended June 30	1971	1970
Net sales	$342,166,194	$339,979,798
Costs and expenses (including provision for depreciation: 1971 — $8,535,135; 1970 — $7,327,706)		
Cost of products sold	259,345,980	256,301,449
Selling, administrative and general expenses	54,941,155	50,968,083
Interest expense	6,764,236	6,660,359
Other (income)	(5,162,043)	(3,505,183)
	315,889,328	310,424,708
	26,276,866	29,555,090
Preacquisition earnings before taxes thereon applicable to Clevite stock purchased	—	196,587
Pretax Earnings	26,276,866	29,358,503
Federal, state, and foreign income taxes — Note C	11,966,000	14,297,011
Net Earnings of Continuing Operations	14,310,866	15,061,492
Net earnings of divested businesses	—	275,612
Net Earnings for the Year	$ 14,310,866	$ 15,337,104
Earnings per share of Common Stock — Note J	$2.91	$3.16
Earnings per share assuming full dilution — Note J	$2.87	$3.04

See notes to financial statements.

Statement of Stockholders' Equity   Gould Inc. and Consolidated Subsidiaries

For the Two Years Ended June 30, 1971	Common Stock		Additional Paid-in Capital	Earnings Retained for Use in the Business	Treasury Stock	
	Shares	Amount			Shares	Amount
Balance July 1, 1969	4,957,336	$19,829,344	$31,727,232	$ 99,677,533	115,089	$2,947,979
Net earnings for the year ended June 30, 1970				15,337,104		
Cash dividends declared on Common Stock — $1.05 a share				(5,102,328)		
Exercise of employee stock options	22,684	90,736	445,466			
Purchase of treasury stock					6,840	275,944
Repurchase of 220,000 warrants			(4,400,000)			
Dividends and other capital transactions of pooled companies	949	3,796	(1,096,314)	(32,272)	(36,603)	(943,465)
Balance June 30, 1970	4,980,969	$19,923,876	$26,676,384	$109,880,037	85,326	$2,280,458
Net earnings for the year ended June 30, 1971				14,310,866		
Cash dividends declared on Common Stock — $1.40 a share				(6,885,096)		
Exercise of employee stock options	35,984	143,936	743,033			
Issuance of restricted stock for management incentive program			(32,082)		(3,473)	(135,195)
Balance June 30, 1971	5,016,953	$20,067,812	$27,387,335	$117,305,807	81,853	$2,145,263

(   ) Indicates deductions
See notes to financial statements.

Statement of Financial Position   Gould Inc. and Consolidated Subsidiaries

Assets

June 30	1971	1970
Current Assets		
Cash	$ 15,814,248	$ 13,112,347
Marketable securities at cost, which approximates market price	7,948,354	14,482,457
Accounts receivable less allowances: 1971 — $415,591; 1970 — $778,840	51,689,218	49,327,483
Inventories — Note B	66,165,838	70,526,361
Other current assets — Note D	8,185,791	6,769,604
Total Current Assets	149,803,449	154,218,252
Investments and Other Assets		
Unconsolidated subsidiaries at underlying equity — Note A	865,170	269,437
Affiliated companies at cost	5,029,297	4,748,316
Other assets — Note D	7,989,471	4,412,311
Total Investments and Other Assets	13,883,938	9,430,064
Property, Plant and Equipment—on the basis of cost		
Land	3,852,538	3,931,954
Buildings	52,551,384	47,732,348
Machinery and equipment	96,955,789	86,941,540
Construction in progress	8,901,664	4,038,184
	162,261,375	142,644,026
Less allowances for depreciation	(75,910,172)	(71,289,844)
Total Property, Plant and Equipment	86,351,203	71,354,182
Cost of Acquired Businesses in Excess of Net Assets at Acquisition Dates — Note A	52,384,110	51,941,262
Total Assets	$302,422,700	$286,943,760

See notes to financial statements.

Liabilities and Stockholders' Equity

June 30	1971	1970
Current Liabilities		
Notes payable	$ 15,458,000	$ 18,267,748
Accounts payable and accrued expenses	42,074,715	38,928,586
Income taxes — Note C	2,886,372	3,651,622
Current maturities of long-term debt	9,089,308	2,360,176
Deferred credit — current	37,950	688,251
Total Current Liabilities	69,546,345	63,896,383
Long-Term Debt less current maturities — Note E	65,249,491	66,488,940
Deferred Credits (principally federal income taxes)	4,971,179	2,278,301
Minority Interest in Subsidiary	39,994	80,297
Stockholders' Equity — Notes E and F		
Preferred Stock—par value $1 a share: Authorized—3,000,000 shares Issued—none		
Common Stock — par value $4 a share: Authorized — 20,000,000 shares Issued — 1971 — 5,016,953 shares; 1970 — 4,980,969 shares	20,067,812	19,923,876
Additional paid-in capital	27,387,335	26,676,384
Earnings retained for use in the business	117,305,807	109,880,037
Less cost of Common Stock in treasury: 1971 — 81,853 shares; 1970 — 85,326 shares	(2,145,263)	(2,280,458)
Total Stockholders' Equity	162,615,691	154,199,839
Commitments and Contingencies — Notes G and I		
Total Liabilities and Stockholders' Equity	$302,422,700	$286,943,760

See notes to financial statements.

Notes to Financial Statements   Gould Inc. and Consolidated Subsidiaries

Note A — Principles of Consolidation and Data Regarding Acquisitions: The consolidated financial statements include the accounts of the Company and all of its subsidiaries except several minor non-manufacturing subsidiaries which are carried at the Company's approximate equity therein. (See Note K for summarized financial statements of the Company's wholly-owned unconsolidated leasing companies). All subsidiaries of the Company are wholly-owned except for an immaterial minority interest in a domestic subsidiary.

The cost of acquired businesses in excess of net assets at the dates of acquisition arose substantially in the merger with Clevite Corporation (a wholly-owned subsidiary) and amortization is not required.

In September, 1970 the Company acquired Ferraloy, Inc. for approximately $4,500,000 cash. This transaction was accounted for as a purchase. Sales and results of operations of Ferraloy, Inc. since acquisition were immaterial in relation to the consolidated financial statements.

Note B — Inventories: Inventories are priced at the lower of cost (first-in, first-out method) or market. Principal classifications of inventories at June 30 were:

	1971	Percent Increase (Decrease)	1970
Finished products	$27,907,064	(7.97%)	$30,324,412
Finished parts and work in process	19,849,157	9.19	18,178,318
Materials and supplies	18,409,617	(16.41)	22,023,631
Total	$66,165,838	(6.18%)	$70,526,361

Note C — Income Taxes and Renegotiation: Federal income tax returns of the Company and a major subsidiary have been examined and settled through April 30, 1968 and December 31, 1964, respectively. Clearance from the Renegotiation Board has been received by the Company and the subsidiary through April 30, 1969 and December 31, 1966, respectively. Management believes that final settlement of taxes and renegotiation for years not settled will not have a material adverse effect.

Note C — Income Taxes and Renegotiation (continued)
The income tax provision was:

	1971	1970
Federal — current	$ 8,494,159	$12,301,121
State and foreign — current	1,329,988	1,689,187
Deferred (arising principally from the use of accelerated depreciation for tax purposes)	2,141,853	401,290
Income taxes applicable to pre-acquisition earnings of Clevite	—	(94,587)
Total	$11,966,000	$14,297,011

The income tax provision for the current year as a percentage of earnings before taxes thereon (45.5%) is below that of the previous year (48.7%) due principally to lower federal income tax rates and an increase in foreign income which is being taxed at rates substantially lower than United States rates.

Note D — Other Assets: Other current assets include principally prepaid insurance, supplies and short-term notes receivable.

Other assets include principally non-current accounts and notes receivable, investments in common stocks, licenses and deferred federal income tax benefits.

Note E — Long-Term Debt: Long-term debt including current portions at June 30 was:

	1971	1970
Notes payable to institutional investors:		
A note of $700,000 bearing interest at 4.65% was paid November 1, 1970. The balance of the notes bearing interest at 4.85% are due $1,430,000 annually beginning November 1, 1971	$14,300,000	$15,000,000
Notes bearing interest at 5.65% are due $500,000 annually to March 31, 1977 and $1,000,000 on March 31, 1978	3,500,000	4,500,000
Notes bearing interest at 3.25% were paid on March 1, 1971	—	847,500
Bank Loans:		
Under credit agreement, 6% borrowings converted into term notes on December 1, 1970	—	23,400,000
Term notes bearing interest not to exceed 6.25% due $7,500,000 annually to November 30, 1974	30,000,000	—
Foreign notes, paid in September, 1970	—	2,000,000
Sinking fund debentures, 9.25%, due in amounts of not less than $1,100,000 per year beginning in 1976 with the balance due February 15, 1995	25,000,000	20,960,000
Convertible debentures of subsidiary	800,000	800,000
Notes of foreign subsidiaries	351,967	640,561
Other	386,832	701,055
Total	74,338,799	68,849,116
Less amounts due within one year included in current liabilities	9,089,308	2,360,176
Total Long-Term Debt	$65,249,491	$66,488,940

The agreements relating to the notes payable to institutional investors, bank loans, and the sinking fund debentures include prepayment requirements and the usual covenants and restrictions for the protection of the lenders. The agreements impose limitations upon, among other things, the creation of funded debt; the disposal of businesses or creation of funded debt of consolidated subsidiaries; cash dividends and other restricted payments ($25,205,000 of retained earnings at June 30, 1971 were free of restrictions under the most restrictive of such limitations).

Note E — Long-Term Debt (continued)
Aggregate maturities of long-term debt for each of the following five years are:

	Year ending June 30
1972	$9,089,000
1973	9,557,000
1974	9,530,000
1975	9,514,000
1976	3,108,000

Note F—Stockholders' Equity: As of June 30, 1971, 469,548 shares of Common Stock were reserved for issuance to key personnel under the Company's two Qualified Stock Option Plans, including 153,580 shares for additional options which may be granted under the plans. The options are granted at prices equal to market value on the dates granted and are exercisable over a period of up to five years. Changes during the year ended June 30, 1971 and the outstanding options are summarized as follows:

	Option Price Per Share	Number of Shares Optioned
Balance July 1, 1970	$20.29 to $54.88	296,109
Granted	$23.56 to $33.50	22,619
Exercised	$20.29 to $29.76	(35,984)
Cancelled	$20.29 to $54.88	(40,177)
Balance June 30, 1971	$20.29 to $54.88	242,567
Exercisable		163,817

On August 17, 1970 the Company granted alternate options covering an aggregate of 199,794 shares of Common Stock to holders of outstanding options. Each alternate option refers to a specific outstanding option and covers the number of shares remaining unexercised under such outstanding option, but was granted at the market price ($28.32) of Common Stock on August 17, 1970. The number of shares covered under each alternate option is automatically reduced from time to time to the extent of the shares purchased on exercise of the referenced option. Each alternate option is exercisable only when and to the extent the option referred to expires unexercised and all alternate options expire on August 17, 1975.

The Company has outstanding 1,875,345 warrants for the purchase of an equivalent number of Common Shares at $55 per share. There was no change in outstanding warrants during the year ended June 30, 1971.

Notes to Financial Statements — continued

Note G — Commitments and Contingencies: As of June 30, 1971, the Company was guarantor of approximately $895,000 of notes receivable of an affiliated company sold in 1967.

The Company leases office and research facilities at Mendota Heights, Minnesota, and a manufacturing facility at Woodruff, South Carolina under long-term leases which require annual rental payments of approximately $500,000 through 1990, plus taxes, insurance, and maintenance.

In connection with bank borrowings by unconsolidated leasing subsidiaries, the Company is required to maintain cash reserves ($725,000 at June 30, 1971) which are based upon the line of credit extended and the amount of the outstanding borrowings. If the subsidiaries fail to pay principal and interest when due, the banks may draw against the reserves and the Company will be required to reinstate the deficiencies.

Note H — Pension Plans: The Company and its consolidated subsidiaries have several pension plans which cover substantially all of their employees. The total pension expense for the years ended June 30, 1971 and June 30, 1970 was approximately $2,500,000 and $2,230,000, respectively.

It is the Company's policy to fund pension cost accrued and to amortize prior service cost over 40 years. The actuarially-computed value of vested benefits exceeded the value of the pension fund assets and balance sheet accruals of the Company for all plans as of June 30, 1971 by approximately $4,700,000.

Note I — Proposed Mergers: The Company and Allied Control Company, Inc. have entered into an agreement whereby Allied will be merged into the Company. The agreement is subject to approval by the Allied shareholders, and other conditions. If consummated the transaction will be accounted for as a purchase. The Company has purchased 140,242 shares (or approximately 28.5%) of Allied Common Stock for approximately $2,083,000. The Company has offered to acquire the remaining 71.5% interest in Allied through the issuance of 112,429 shares of Common Stock.

Subsequent to June 30, 1971, the Company announced plans to acquire Beta Instruments Corporation for approximately 54,000 shares of Common Stock.

Note J — Earnings Per Share: Earnings per share of Common Stock were computed by dividing net earnings by the weighted average number of shares of Common Stock outstanding (4,916,584 and 4,857,958 for the years ended June 30, 1971 and 1970, respectively). Stock options and warrants outstanding are not included in the computation as their inclusion is not required or would not have a material effect.

Note J — Earnings Per Share (continued)
The following condensed calculation of earnings per share, assuming full dilution, was based on the assumption that all warrants and options have been exercised and the proceeds used first to repurchase 20% of the shares outstanding at the end of the period and the balance used to reduce interest expense through the retirements of debt in decreasing order of interest rate and without regard to call and prepayment penalties.

Year ended June 30	1971	1970
Net Earnings	$14,310,866	$15,337,104
Interest expense reduction (net of taxes) attributable to proceeds from assumed exercise of options and warrants after assumed repurchase of 20% of outstanding shares	3,030,111	3,043,403
Adjusted Earnings	$17,340,977	$18,380,507
Average shares outstanding	4,916,584	4,857,958
Possible additional Common Shares issuable on exercise of warrants and options outstanding at year-end	2,117,912	2,170,180
Assumed repurchase (20%) of shares outstanding	(987,020)	(979,129)
Adjusted Shares Outstanding	6,047,476	6,049,009
Earnings per share assuming full dilution	$2.87	$3.04

Note K — Leasing Companies: The Company has several wholly-owned unconsolidated subsidiaries which are engaged in the leasing of equipment.

Combined summary financial statements of these companies (which began operations during 1970) for the year ended June 30, 1971 are:

Combined Balance Sheet

Assets

June 30	1971
Cash	$ 77,526
Accounts receivable	294,930
Contracts receivable for equipment on lease (due in one year — $1,420,000)	4,459,388
Less unearned income	(856,166)
	3,603,222
Machinery and equipment	5,923,395
Less allowance for depreciation	(2,078,204)
	3,845,191
Total Assets	**$7,820,869**

Liabilities and Stockholder's Equity

Accounts payable and accrued expenses	$ 93,414
Notes payable to banks	4,416,715
Federal income taxes	24,624
Deferred credit	16,163
Long-term debt (bank loans, 6% due $75,000 monthly to April 15, 1974) including current maturities of $900,000	2,526,814
Total Liabilities	**7,077,730**
Stockholder's Equity	
Common Stock	30,000
Paid-in capital	633,379
Retained earnings	79,760
Total Stockholder's Equity	**743,139**
Total Liabilities and Stockholder's Equity	**$7,820,869**

Note K — Leasing Companies (continued)
Combined Statement of Income

Year ended June 30	1971
Income from leases	$2,275,655
Income from services	333,834
	2,609,489
Expenses:	
General and administrative	45,168
Depreciation	2,078,204
Interest	332,732
	2,456,104
Pretax Earnings	**153,385**
Federal income taxes	73,625
Net Income	**$ 79,760**

The leasing companies have entered into leases which provide for full cost recovery of leased property and are accounted for under the financing method by recording the total amount of rentals receivable for the entire lease period. Unearned income is the amount by which total rentals and estimated residual value of the equipment (which in all cases is less than 10% of total cost) exceed the cost of the equipment. Income is recognized as earned during the terms of the leases in decreasing amounts related to the declining balance of the unrecovered investment.

The leasing companies also have a decreasing dollar value of outstanding leases which are accounted for under the operating method by recognizing income on a straight-line basis. Depreciation on this leased equipment is recognized in the income statement on a straight-line basis.

Statement of Source and Application of Funds   Gould Inc. and Consolidated Subsidiaries

Year Ended June 30	1971	1970
Cash at beginning of year	$13,112,347	$17,462,117
Source of funds:		
From operations:		
Net earnings for the year	$14,310,866	$15,337,104
Preacquisition net earnings applicable to Clevite stock purchased	—	102,000
Deferred income taxes	2,141,853	401,290
Provision for depreciation (computed principally on straight-line method)	8,535,135	7,327,706
Amortization of cost of products on rental	62,444	1,152,658
Fair value of treasury stock as compensation	103,113	
Total from Operations	$25,153,411	$24,320,758
Decrease in inventories	$ 4,360,523	$ 3,439,331
Sale of divested businesses	—	4,912,452
Increase in accounts payable and accrued expenses	3,146,129	4,511,395
Increases in long-term debt, less retirements (1971 — $28,550,317 1970 — $13,080,064)	5,489,683	18,179,936
Decrease (increase) in marketable securities	6,534,103	(10,539,363)
Proceeds from exercise of employee stock options	886,969	536,202
Total Source of Funds	$45,570,818	$45,360,711
Application of funds:		
Cash dividends	$ 6,885,096	$ 5,102,328
Decrease (increase) in deferred credits	99,276	(1,088,891)
Increase in accounts receivable	2,361,735	2,733,174
Additions to other assets	4,959,166	1,960,503
Additions to properties, less carrying amount of disposals	23,532,156	14,922,612
Decrease in notes payable	2,809,748	15,250,025
Repurchase of warrants	—	4,400,000
Cost of Common Stock acquired for treasury	—	275,944
Other changes (for 1970, includes decreases of $3,259,307 in other current assets and $1,700,540 in dividends payable)	2,221,740	6,154,786
Total Application of Funds	$42,868,917	$49,710,481
Increase (Decrease) in Cash	$ 2,701,901	$(4,349,770)
Cash at End of Year	$15,814,248	$13,112,347

See notes to financial statements.

Accountants' Report

Board of Directors
Gould Inc.

We have examined the statement of financial position of Gould Inc, and consolidated subsidiaries as of June 30, 1971 and the related statements of earnings, stockholders' equity and source and application of funds for the year then ended. Our examination was made in accordance with generally accepted auditing standards, and accordingly included such tests of the accounting records and such other auditing procedures as we considered necessary in the circumstances. We previously made a similar examination of the financial statements for the preceding year.

In our opinion, the accompanying aforementioned financial statements present fairly the financial position of Gould Inc. and consolidated subsidiaries at June 30, 1971 and the results of their operations, changes in stockholders' equity and source and application of funds for the year then ended, in conformity with generally accepted accounting principles applied on a basis consistent with that of the preceding year.

Ernst + Ernst

Chicago, Illinois
August 11, 1971

Great Northern Nekoosa Corporation

The financial statements on pages 506–511 are reprinted from the 1971 financial statements of Great Northern Nekoosa Corporation and Subsidiaries.

CONSOLIDATED STATEMENTS OF INCOME AND RETAINED EARNINGS
GREAT NORTHERN NEKOOSA CORPORATION AND SUBSIDIARIES

INCOME	For the Years Ended December 31, 1971	1970
Net Sales	$355,458,000	$355,291,000
Cost of Sales	296,467,000	288,061,000
Gross margin	$ 58,991,000	$ 67,230,000
Selling, General and Administrative Expenses	26,896,000	28,352,000
Operating income	$ 32,095,000	$ 38,878,000
Interest on Long-Term Debt	(6,442,000)	(7,593,000)
Other Income—Net	968,000	971,000
Income before provision for taxes on income	$ 26,621,000	$ 32,256,000
Provision for Taxes on Income:		
Current	$ 9,714,000	$ 12,316,000
Deferred	2,658,000	3,460,000
	$ 12,372,000	$ 15,776,000
Net Income	$ 14,249,000	$ 16,480,000
Earnings Per Share (6):		
Primary	$2.65	$3.42
Fully diluted	$2.61	$3.32

RETAINED EARNINGS		
Retained Earnings at Beginning of Year	$132,957,000	$124,568,000
ADD—Net income	14,249,000	16,480,000
	$147,206,000	$141,048,000
Deduct:		
Cash dividends declared—		
Common stock $1.60 per share	7,504,000	6,158,000
Preferred stock	1,409,000	1,220,000
Dividends paid by Nekoosa-Edwards Paper Company prior to merger March 31, 1970	—	713,000
Retained Earnings at End of Year	$138,293,000	$132,957,000

The accompanying notes are an integral part of these statements.

CONSOLIDATED BALANCE SHEETS

GREAT NORTHERN NEKOOSA CORPORATION AND SUBSIDIARIES

ASSETS	December 31, 1971	December 31, 1970
Current Assets:		
Cash	$ 7,295,000	$ 9,933,000
Short-term marketable securities, at cost (approximately quoted market).............................	6,466,000	8,832,000
Receivables, less allowances for possible losses................	52,405,000	49,312,000
Inventories, at the lower of cost (partly last-in, first-out) or market—		
Finished goods	16,417,000	15,567,000
In-process, materials and supplies	19,733,000	18,054,000
Pulpwood	6,086,000	8,852,000
Prepaid expenses	2,089,000	2,393,000
Total current assets	$110,491,000	$112,943,000
Noncurrent Assets and Deferred Charges	$ 7,224,000	$ 6,194,000
Property, Plant and Equipment, at cost:		
Plant and equipment	$515,701,000	$489,490,000
Less accumulated depreciation	214,510,000	194,411,000
	$301,191,000	$295,079,000
Timberlands—net of depletion	18,812,000	17,532,000
Total property, plant and equipment (net)	$320,003,000	$312,611,000
Cost in Excess of Assigned Value of Tangible Assets Acquired	$ 3,426,000	$ 3,426,000
	$441,144,000	$435,174,000

The accompanying notes are an integral part of these balance sheets.

LIABILITIES	December 31, **1971**	December 31, **1970**
Current Liabilities:		
Current maturities of long-term debt	$10,878,000	$ 13,097,000
Accounts payable and accrued expenses......................	29,549,000	26,539,000
Accrued Federal and state income taxes	5,128,000	4,555,000
Total current liabilities	$ 45,555,000	$ 44,191,000
Deferred Taxes on Income	$ 42,906,000	$ 38,992,000
Long-Term Debt, excluding current maturities (2):		
4.10% to 4.75% industrial revenue bonds due in		
installments to 1988	$ 32,200,000	$ 34,500,000
4¼% convertible subordinated debentures due 1991	8,376,000	8,376,000
4¾% and 5% bank notes due in installments to 1975	10,714,000	14,286,000
4.95% notes due in installments to 1982	23,250,000	25,575,000
6% notes due in installments to 1984	18,750,000	20,250,000
Revolving credit notes due banks	5,400,000	—
Mortgage debt and miscellaneous obligations	10,588,000	11,023,000
Total long-term debt	$109,278,000	$114,010,000
Stockholders' Equity (2, 3, and 4):		
Capital stock—		
Preferred stock, cumulative, issuable in series,		
without par value—		
Authorized—3,000,000 shares		
Outstanding—1,882,114 convertible shares at		
December 31, 1971 (liquidation preference		
aggregates $26,734,000)	$ 25,097,000	$ 26,167,000
Common stock, $10 par value—		
Authorized—9,000,000 shares		
Issued—4,713,056 shares at December 31, 1971..............	47,131,000	46,509,000
	$ 72,228,000	$ 72,676,000
Additional paid-in capital	33,941,000	32,348,000
Retained earnings	138,293,000	132,957,000
Common stock in treasury, 25,000 shares, at cost	(1,057,000)	—
Total stockholders' equity	$243,405,000	$237,981,000
	$441,144,000	$435,174,000

CONSOLIDATED STATEMENTS OF CHANGES IN FINANCIAL POSITION

GREAT NORTHERN NEKOOSA CORPORATION AND SUBSIDIARIES

	For the Years Ended December 31,	
	1971	1970
Source of Funds:		
Net income	$14,249,000	$16,480,000
Add charges to income which require no expenditure of funds:		
Depreciation (straight-line method)	22,270,000	21,445,000
Depletion	657,000	642,000
Increase in deferred taxes on income.	3,914,000	4,553,000
Funds provided by operations.	$41,090,000	$43,120,000
Net proceeds from sale of 500,000 shares of common stock.	—	19,146,000
New borrowings	6,461,000	—
Sale of capital stock under stock option programs.	1,147,000	77,000
Total funds provided	$48,698,000	$62,343,000
Disposition of Funds:		
Additions to property, plant and equipment, net of sales and retirements of $3,975,000 in 1971.	$30,319,000	$30,881,000
Dividends declared	8,913,000	8,091,000
Increase in noncurrent assets and deferred charges, etc.	1,032,000	(2,022,000)
Decrease in long-term debt	11,193,000	20,929,000
Purchase of common stock for treasury.	1,057,000	—
Total funds used	$52,514,000	$57,879,000
Increase (Decrease) in Working Capital.	$ (3,816,000)	$ 4,464,000
Increase (Decrease) in Elements of Working Capital:		
Cash and marketable securities.	$ (5,004,000)	$ (6,471,000)
Other current assets.	2,552,000	8,092,000
Current liabilities	(1,364,000)	2,843,000
	$ (3,816,000)	$ 4,464,000
Working Capital:		
Beginning of year	$68,752,000	$64,288,000
End of year	$64,936,000	$68,752,000

The accompanying notes are an integral part of these statements.

NOTES TO CONSOLIDATED FINANCIAL STATEMENTS December 31, 1971
GREAT NORTHERN NEKOOSA CORPORATION AND SUBSIDIARIES

(1) PRINCIPLES OF CONSOLIDATION

The consolidated financial statements include retroactively the accounts of, and the shares issued in exchange for, Nekoosa-Edwards Paper Company merged on March 31, 1970, on a pooling-of-interests basis and include other subsidiaries, after eliminations of intercompany balances, transactions, and investments.

(2) LONG-TERM DEBT

The 4.10% to 4.75% industrial revenue bonds due in installments to 1988 cover a lease on the Ashdown, Arkansas mill. The transaction is being treated as a purchase for accounting and tax purposes. The mill is mortgaged under the bond indenture.

The 4¼% convertible subordinated debentures due April 1, 1991, may be converted at any time into shares of common stock of the Company, at a price of $56.50 per share, such conversion price being subject to adjustment in certain events. At December 31, 1971, there were 148,247 shares of common stock reserved for conversion of the debentures. A sinking fund for redemption of the debentures is to be provided, beginning in 1977, in an amount sufficient to retire $500,000 of debentures annually. The Company may at its option begin to make these sinking fund payments to retire debentures at any time prior to 1977.

Under the provisions of the 4.95% notes due October 1, 1982, the 6% notes due October 1, 1984, and the 4¾% and 5% bank notes due to 1975, retained earnings not restricted against the payment of dividends (except stock dividends and regular cash dividends on the Company's preferred stock) were $71,855,000 at December 31, 1971.

Under the terms of revolving credit agreements with banks, the Company may borrow up to $40,000,000. Loans under these agreements may be converted in 1973 to four and five year term loans. Commitment fees of one-half of one percent are payable on the unused portion of the loans during the revolving credit period.

Mortgage debt of $8,145,000 is due in installments to 1992. The mortgages have interest rates ranging from 4¼% to 7¾%. Mortgage debt of $4,932,000 is secured by certain operating facilities in Wisconsin and the capital stock of Butler Paper Company, a subsidiary; and mortgage debt of $3,213,000 is secured by the Company's plywood plant and equipment.

(3) CAPITAL STOCK AND ADDITIONAL PAID-IN CAPITAL

Changes in capital stock and additional paid-in capital during the year ended December 31, 1971 were as follows:

	Capital Stock				Additional Paid-in Capital
	Preferred		Common		
	Shares	Amount	Shares	Amount	
Balance, December 31, 1970	1,998,877	$26,167,000	4,650,862	$46,509,000	$32,348,000
Preferred stock converted	(119,583)	(1,093,000)	34,730	347,000	744,000
Stock options exercised	2,820	23,000	27,464	275,000	849,000
Balance, December 31, 1971	1,882,114	$25,097,000	4,713,056	$47,131,000	$33,941,000

There are 3,000,000 authorized shares of preferred stock, cumulative and issuable in series, without par value. All series outstanding at December 31, 1971 are convertible into common stock, have voting rights and are summarized below:

Series	Annual Dividend Per Share	As Of December 31, 1971			Shares Of Common Stock Into Which Each Share Is Convertible
		Shares Outstanding	Stated Value	Redemption Price Per Share	
A	$ .40	1,090,858	$ 9,272,000	$10.00	.286
B	1.60	291,772	5,835,000	21.60	.359
C	1.00	181,955	3,639,000	20.00	.436
D	1.00	317,529	6,351,000	20.86	.369
		1,882,114	$25,097,000		

The series B is redeemable starting July 1, 1975; the other series are currently redeemable. Redemption prices for series B and series D decrease until reaching $20.00 per share; after July 1, 1983 for series B and after July 1, 1976 for series D. Conversion rates for all series are subject to change to protect against dilution in certain events. As of December 31, 1971, there were 618,694 shares of common stock reserved for the conversion of outstanding preferred stock and preferred stock options.

As approved by the stockholders on May 4, 1971, the authorized common stock of the Company has been increased from 6,000,000 shares to 9,000,000. On March 9, 1972, all outstanding shares of series A preferred stock will be redeemed at the redemption price of $10.00 per share plus accrued dividends of $.18 per share. Until March 7, 1972, such shares are convertible into common stock at the rate shown above.

(4) STOCK OPTIONS

At December 31, 1971, the Company had outstanding stock options covering 80,875 shares of common stock, 4,720 shares of series A preferred stock and units consisting of 49,308 shares of common stock and 12,327 shares of series B preferred stock. Option prices per share ranged from $43.25 to $69.94 for the common stock and were $8.046 for the series A preferred. The option price per unit of common and series B preferred was $27.75 to $36.50. Such options (including 39,275 shares of common in 1971) were granted under stock option programs for officers and key employees. In addition, the Company had 176,727 shares of common stock reserved for stock options authorized but not granted.

Options to purchase common stock under the Company's qualified stock option plans are exercisable in annual amounts but no later than five years from the dates of the respective grants. Options to purchase series A preferred stock expire in ten years from the date of the respective grants. Options to purchase units consisting of ½ share of common stock and ⅛ share of series B preferred stock (resulting from the merger with Nekoosa-Edwards Paper Company) become exercisable over four years and expire not later than April 27, 1973. Option prices under the qualified common stock option plans are equal to not less than 100% of the quoted market price of the stock at the date of the respective grants. No additional options for series A preferred stock or units consisting of common stock and series B preferred stock may be granted.

Options covering 27,464 shares of common stock and 2,820 shares of preferred stock were exercised during the year and options covering 8,658 shares of common stock and 1,123 shares of preferred stock lapsed during the year.

(5) RETIREMENT AND PENSION PLANS

Retirement and pension benefits are available to most full-time employees of the Company and its subsidiaries under provisions of several plans. It is the Company's policy to fund retirement costs in accordance with actuarial determinations and other pertinent factors. The unfunded cost for prior services is being amortized over periods up to 40 years. Under two of the plans, the value of vested benefits exceeded the total of the retirement funds and balance sheet accruals at December 31, 1971 by approximately $2,224,000.

Retirement and pension expense included in the consolidated statements of income was approximately $2,285,000 at December 31, 1971 and $2,238,000 at December 31, 1970.

(6) EARNINGS PER SHARE

Primary earnings per share were computed on the weighted average number of shares of common stock outstanding during the year plus the shares of common stock issuable upon conversion of series A preferred stock, considered to be the equivalent of common stock from the time of its issuance.

Fully diluted earnings per share were computed based on the assumed conversion of all series of preferred stock (except series B which would have been anti-dilutive), the 4¼% convertible subordinated debentures and the effect of dilutive stock options. For computation purposes, interest, less Federal income tax effect, applicable to the convertible debentures was added to net income.

(7) COMMITMENTS

The Company is lesee under a number of long-term leases which grant continuing timber cutting rights to the Company. These leases require annual payments of approximately $494,000. The total commitment for future payments was approximately $29,956,000 at December 31, 1971.

In addition to the lease for the Ashdown, Arkansas mill referred to in Note 2, the Company has various other equipment and real estate lease agreements, some of which provide for the payment of property taxes and other occupancy expenses in addition to the base rentals. The base rentals under these other leases approximated $1,221,000 for 1971 and the remaining aggregate lease obligation under these leases was approximately $13,668,000 at December 31, 1971.

The Company has previously announced a major expansion program at its Millinocket, Maine mill. At December 31, 1971, the remaining costs to complete this program are estimated at $15,000,000.

Green Giant Company

The financial statements on pages 513–519 are reprinted from the 1971 financial statements of Green Giant Company and Subsidiaries.

Green Giant Company and Subsidiaries

Statement of Earnings and Retained Earnings

Years ended March 31, 1971 and 1970 (note 1)

	1971	1970
Sales, net after returns and allowances	$241,390,949	231,408,605
Costs and expenses:		
Cost of goods sold	168,372,177	163,045,823
Marketing, distribution and general expense	57,500,405	54,045,840
Interest expense	4,860,118	5,317,288
Amortization of excess of cost over equity in subsidiary (note 1)	190,362	190,362
Income taxes, including $1,289,076 of deferred income taxes ($1,187,054 in 1970) (note 3)	5,280,020	4,054,322
Total	236,203,082	226,653,635
Net earnings	5,187,867	4,754,970
Retained earnings at beginning of year:		
As previously reported	42,523,588	41,079,734
Adjustment for retained earnings of pooled companies (note 1)	3,549,440	3,113,402
As restated	46,073,028	44,193,136
	51,260,895	48,948,106
Dividends declared:		
Convertible preference stock — $1.60 and $.157 per share on Series A and B, respectively	56,224	—
Preferred stock — $5.00 per share	121,592	121,665
Common stock — $.96 per share	2,796,502	2,713,413
By pooled company prior to acquisition	42,500	40,000
	3,016,818	2,875,078
Retained earnings at end of year	$ 48,244,077	46,073,028
Per average share of common stock outstanding (note 5):		
Net earnings	$ 1.64	1.49
Net earnings — assuming full dilution	$ 1.55	1.42

See accompanying notes to financial statements.

Green Giant Company and Subsidiaries
Statement of Financial Position

March 31, 1971 and 1970 (note 1)

	1971	1970
Current assets:		
Cash	$ 6,683,594	5,193,281
Receivables from customers and others, less allowance for doubtful accounts (note 2)	19,538,343	20,788,587
Inventories, at the lower of cost (first-in, first-out) or market (note 2):		
Finished products	39,020,618	40,823,803
Containers and supplies	25,720,648	24,700,004
Prepaid expenses	3,276,806	2,623,394
Total current assets	94,240,009	94,129,069
Current liabilities:		
Notes payable (note 2)	14,469,450	15,879,493
Current maturities of long-term debt	1,471,125	1,561,640
Accounts payable	8,730,105	8,115,353
Accrued expenses	5,750,559	5,074,722
Income taxes	1,499,632	1,573,316
Total current liabilities	31,920,871	32,204,524
Working capital	62,319,138	61,924,545
Property, plant and equipment, at cost less accumulated depreciation (note 3)	54,160,735	52,021,425
Unamortized excess of cost over equity in subsidiary (note 1)	2,791,990	2,982,352
Deferred charges and other assets	1,977,630	2,054,915
	121,249,493	118,983,237
Deferred income taxes (note 3)	3,619,185	2,330,109
Long-term debt, less current maturities (note 4)	45,130,439	46,644,506
Minority interest in subsidiary	162,441	153,914
	48,912,065	49,128,529
Excess of assets over liabilities	$ 72,337,428	69,854,708
Stockholders' equity (notes 4, 5 and 6):		
Convertible preference stock (liquidation preference $6,592,000)	$ 64,000	64,000
Preferred stock	2,429,900	2,433,300
Common stock	21,578,632	21,265,180
Additional paid-in capital	20,819	19,200
Retained earnings	48,244,077	46,073,028
Commitments (notes 7 and 9)		
	$ 72,337,428	69,854,708

See accompanying notes to financial statements.

Green Giant Company and Subsidiaries

Source and Application of Funds

Years ended March 31, 1971 and 1970 (note 1)

	1971	1970
Funds provided:		
Net earnings for the year	$ 5,187,867	4,754,970
Add charges against earnings not requiring funds:		
Depreciation (note 3)	5,770,694	5,437,866
Deferred income taxes	1,289,076	1,187,054
Amortization of excess of cost over equity in subsidiary	190,362	190,362
Sundry	6,746	7,692
Funds derived from operations	12,444,745	11,577,944
Additions to long-term debt	95,000	7,681,000
Proceeds on disposal of property and equipment	662,891	618,265
Capital stock issued to employees	313,452	247,102
Decrease (increase) in deferred charges and other assets, net	77,285	(353,438)
Total funds provided	13,593,373	19,770,873
Funds used:		
Dividends	3,016,818	2,875,078
Additions to property, plant and equipment	8,572,895	7,315,688
Reduction of long-term debt	1,609,067	1,557,554
Total funds used	13,198,780	11,748,320
Increase in working capital	$ 394,593	8,022,553

See accompanying notes to financial statements.

Accountants' Report

The Board of Directors and Stockholders
Green Giant Company:

We have examined the statement of financial position of Green Giant Company and subsidiaries as of March 31, 1971 and 1970 and the related statements of earnings and retained earnings and source and application of funds for the respective years then ended. Our examination was made in accordance with generally accepted auditing standards, and accordingly included such tests of the accounting records and such other auditing procedures as we considered necessary in the circumstances.

In our opinion, such financial statements present fairly the financial position of Green Giant Company and subsidiaries at March 31, 1971 and 1970 and the results of their operations and source and application of their funds for the respective years then ended, in conformity with generally accepted accounting principles applied on a consistent basis.

Minneapolis, Minnesota
May 7, 1971

Peat, Marwick, Mitchell & Co.

Green Giant Company and Subsidiaries
Notes to Financial Statements

March 31, 1971 and 1970

(1) Principles of Consolidation

The accompanying financial statements include the accounts of Green Giant Company and all active subsidiaries (100% owned other than for a minor 1.49% interest in the Canadian subsidiary). All material intercompany accounts and transactions have been eliminated in consolidation. The accounts of foreign subsidiaries have been converted at appropriate historical or current rates of exchange. During the year ended March 31, 1971, the Canadian government allowed the Canadian dollar to float freely in the world currency market, with the result that net earnings were favorably affected by $215,072.

On November 29, 1969, the Company acquired all of the outstanding shares of Schweigert Meat Co. in exchange for 101,603 common shares of the Company. This acquisition was accounted for as a pooling of interests and, accordingly, the accounts of Schweigert have been included for the entire two year period.

On October 29, 1970, the Company acquired all of the outstanding shares of Copeland Sausage Co., Inc. in exchange for 32,000 shares of the Company's Series A Convertible Preference Stock. On February 19, 1971, the Company acquired all of the outstanding shares of Bama Meats, Inc. in exchange for 32,000 shares of the Company's Series B Convertible Preference Stock. These acquisitions have been accounted for as poolings of interests and, accordingly, the financial statements for 1970 have been restated to include the accounts of Copeland Sausage Co., Inc. and Bama Meats, Inc. These restatements increased previously reported 1970 consolidated net earnings by $476,038 ($.06 per common share).

Unamortized excess of cost over equity in net assets as shown by the books of a subsidiary at date of acquisition, $3,807,254, is being amortized over a period of twenty years.

(2) Short-term Borrowings of Canadian Subsidiary

In accordance with the usual practice under provisions of the Canadian Banking Act, approximately $3,052,440 of receivables and $10,797,702 of inventory of the Canadian subsidiary were pledged to secure short-term indebtedness to banks of $5,902,450 at March 31, 1971.

(3) Property, Plant and Equipment

	1971	1970
Land and land improvements	$ 4,006,080	3,840,628
Buildings	29,585,627	28,799,950
Machinery, equipment and fixtures	55,768,762	54,691,534
Construction in progress	4,084,005	3,012,758
	93,444,474	90,344,870
Less accumulated depreciation	39,283,739	38,323,445
	$54,160,735	52,021,425

For financial reporting purposes, the companies compute depreciation principally by the straight-line method. For Federal income tax purposes, accelerated depreciation is being used and deferred taxes have been appropriately provided based on the resultant difference between financial and taxable income.

Investment credit recapture in the amount of $25,000 has been added in computing the 1971 provision for income taxes. An investment credit in the amount of $451,000 was deducted in computing the 1970 provision for income taxes.

(4) Long-term Debt, Less Current Maturities

	1971	1970
4¼% Convertible subordinated debentures due August 1, 1992	$12,000,000	12,000,000
5% Series B notes, due $900,000 annually December 31, 1971 to 1981 and $3,100,000 on December 31, 1982	12,100,000	13,000,000
Revolving credit loans, due May 1, 1973 with interest at ½ of 1% per annum above prime rate	9,800,000	9,800,000
8¾% Notes due $2,500,000 annually September 15, 1974 to 1976	7,500,000	7,500,000
Sundry notes and contracts with stated interest rates from 4¼% to 9% due in varying instalments to 1982	3,730,439	4,344,506
	$45,130,439	46,644,506

Aggregate annual maturities of long-term debt for each of the five fiscal years following March 31, 1971 are as follows: 1972 — $1,471,125; 1973 — $1,406,439; 1974 — $11,152,157; 1975 — $3,838,203; 1976 — $3,784,787.

In addition to requiring maintenance of working capital, a 150% current asset ratio, and other covenants, the long-term debt agreements contain provisions restricting the payment of cash dividends and the purchase or redemption by the Company of shares of its capital stock. At March 31, 1971, the amount of unrestricted retained earnings was approximately $3,300,000 and working capital exceeded the required minimum, as defined, by approximately $32,300,000.

The 4¼% convertible subordinated debentures are convertible into shares of common stock at $44.00 per share, subject to adjustment under anti-dilution provisions, and 272,727 shares of authorized and unissued common stock are reserved for issuance on such conversion. On or before each July 31, beginning in 1977, the Company is required to make sinking fund payments equal to 5% of the principal amount of debentures outstanding on July 31, 1976.

The Company's revolving credit agreement with banks provides for borrowing up to $9,800,000 through May 1, 1973 at ½ of 1% per annum above prime rates and for payment of a commitment fee of ½ of 1% per annum on average daily unused balances.

(5) Stockholders' Equity

At March 31, 1971 and 1970, 500,000 shares of voting preference stock of $1 par value per share, for which the Board of Directors has the power to fix the rights, preferences and restrictions, were authorized. During the year ended March 31, 1971, 32,000 shares of Series A and 32,000 shares of Series B Convertible Preference Stock were issued in connection with the acquisitions of Copeland Sausage Co., Inc. and Bama Meats, Inc. (see note 1). Shares of both series provide for a $4.75 per share per annum cumulative dividend. Each share is convertible into 3.5 shares of common stock and, accordingly, 224,000 shares of common stock were reserved at March 31, 1971 for issuance upon conversion. The Company may redeem the shares at any time after three years at $103 per share, which amount is also the involuntary liquidation value.

Authorized capital stock of the Company at March 31, 1971 and 1970 also consisted of 50,000 shares of 5% cumulative preferred stock of $100 par value per share (callable at $110 per share) and 4,000,000 shares of common stock without par or stated value. Changes in common and cumulative preferred stock during the two years ended March 31, 1971 were as follows:

	Shares	Amount
Common stock:		
Outstanding at March 31, 1969..........	2,895,976	$21,018,078
Equivalent shares issued in connection with restrictive stock plan of pooled company	1,603	26,920
Shares issued upon exercise of options....	2,000	39,900
Restricted shares issued in payment of liability to employees for contingent cash bonuses	5,460	180,282
Outstanding at March 31, 1970..........	2,905,039	21,265,180
Shares issued under Employees' Stock Purchase Plan	15,967	313,452
Outstanding at March 31, 1971..........	2,921,006	$21,578,632
Cumulative Preferred Stock:		
Outstanding at March 31, 1969 and 1970..	24,333	$ 2,433,300
Shares purchased by the Company	(34)	(3,400)
Outstanding at March 31, 1971	24,299	$ 2,429,900

Additional paid-in capital arose during the year ended March 31, 1971 from acquisition of a pooled company, $19,200, and from discount on purchase of cumulative preferred stock, $1,619.

Primary net earnings per share has been determined by dividing net earnings (after reduction for dividend requirements on preference and preferred stock) by the average number of common shares outstanding. The issues of Series A and B preference stock have been determined not to be common stock equivalents and dilution from dilutive options is less than 3%.

Net earnings per common share assuming full dilution is based on shares outstanding, shares issuable upon conversion of debentures and convertible preference stock to common stock, shares issuable under outstanding stock options which would be dilutive in effect and net earnings adjusted for interest expense on the debentures and dividends on the preferred and convertible preference stock less effect of retirement trust, bonus and income tax provisions.

(6) Stock Option and Stock Purchase Plans

Under terms of employee stock option plans, options to purchase 72,500 shares of common stock of the Company have been granted and are outstanding to officers and key employees at March 31, 1971 and an additional 56,800 shares are reserved for granting of future options. Options granted are at prices not less than 100% of fair market value at dates of grant, exercisable over a maximum of five years. Options outstanding at March 31, 1971 have been granted at prices ranging from $21.00 to $40.00 per share and at dates of grant had an aggregat·· fair market value of $2,083,915 or an average of $28.74 per share. Changes in outstanding options during the two years ended March 31, 1971 are summarized as follows:

	Outstanding		Currently exercisable	
	Shares	Option price	Shares	Option price
Balance at March 31, 1969	46,700	$1,423,952	25,000	$676,150
Options granted or becoming exercisable:				
1970	47,500	1,251,638	11,175	346,000
1971	6,400	136,025	16,524	486,920
Options cancelled:				
1970	(2,100)	(75,800)	(1,200)	(42,025)
1971	(24,000)	(612,000)	(24,000)	(612,000)
Options exercised — 1970..	(2,000)	(39,900)	(2,000)	(39,900)
Balance at March 31, 1971	72,500	$2,083,915	25,499	$815,145

Under terms of an Employees' Stock Purchase Plan, all regular employees of the Company and its subsidiaries are granted options to acquire the Company's common stock through a payroll deduction plan. The term of the plan is five years, to be operated in one or more phases of one year each. Options are granted at 90% of the fair market value on the date the phase begins or on the date the phase terminates, whichever is lower. Of the options for 20,100 shares granted in the year ended March 31, 1970, options for 15,967 shares were exercised on September 30, 1970 at a price of $19.63 and the remaining options were cancelled. Options to purchase an additional 28,437 shares of the Company's common stock, which were granted on December 1, 1970 at a price of $21.66 per share, were outstanding at March 31, 1971, and an additional 55,596 shares are reserved for granting of future options.

(7) Commitments

Commitments for purchase or construction of property, plant and equipment aggregated approximately $6,100,000 at March 31, 1971.

The companies use certain plants, warehouses, crop land, and plant and field equipment under arrangements which resulted in total rental expense of $8,354,140 for the year ended March 31, 1971 ($7,454,671 for fiscal year 1970), including amounts payable under noncancelable leases which require fixed annual or seasonal rentals and, in some cases, payment of taxes, maintenance and insurance, and additional payments based on crop yields or usage. Total minimum rentals under noncancelable leases in force at March 31, 1971 amounted to $21,293,734 and are payable in fiscal years as follows: 1972 — $4,755,438; 1973 — $3,590,396; 1974 — $2,467,453; 1975 — $1,879,752; 1976 — $1,505,618; 1977 and thereafter — $7,095,077.

(8) Retirement Plan

Provisions under the Company's noncontributory (profit sharing) retirement plan were charged to earnings in the amounts of $1,515,815 and $1,148,175, respectively, for fiscal years 1971 and 1970, including $368,470 and $273,206, respectively, representing elective portions paid in cash directly to employees.

(9) Pending Acquisitons

During the year ended March 31, 1971, the Company agreed in principle to acquire (subject to Board of Directors' approval) the business of John R. Thompson Co. and subsidiaries by issuance of 236,099 shares of a new series of convertible preference stock (to be convertible into 330,539 shares of Green Giant Company common stock). As disclosed by its latest annual report for the year ended December 31, 1970, Thompson had total assets of $13,940,000 and stockholders' equity of $9,006,000; sales were $31,408,000 and the net loss was $1,027,000 (earnings of $254,000 before extraordinary charges).

Also during the year ended March 31, 1971, the Company agreed in principle to acquire (subject to Board of Directors' approval) the business of Florida Quick Freeze and Cold Storage Company (the parent company of Don's Prize Foods, Inc.) by issuance of 40,000 shares of a new series of convertible preference stock (to be convertible into 160,000 shares of Green Giant Company common stock). As disclosed by its financial statements for the year ended September 26, 1970, these companies had total assets of $2,119,000 and stockholders' equity of $1,461,000; sales were $9,319,000 and net earnings were $265,000.

Green Giant Company
Ten Year Summary (A)

YEAR ENDED MARCH 31	1971	1970	1969
Income and Dividends			
Net Sales	$ 241,391	$ 231,409	$ 220,686
Net Earnings After Income Taxes	5,188	4,755	5,678
Preferred and Preference Dividends Paid	178	122	122
Common Dividends (B)	2,839	2,753	2,612
Earnings Reinvested	2,171	1,880	2,944
Per Share of Common Stock: (C)			
Net Earnings	1.64	1.49	1.81
Dividends (Current Annual Rate 96¢)	.96	.96	.92
Percent Net Earnings on Sales	2.1	2.1	2.6
Percent Return on Average Common Stock Equity	7.7	7.3	8.8
Financial Position			
Working Capital	$ 62,319	$ 61,925	$ 53,589
Property, Plant and Equipment (Net)	54,161	52,021	50,568
Other Assets	4,769	5,037	4,900
Total Capital Employed	121,249	118,983	109,057
Less Long Term Debt	45,130	46,644	40,323
Less Other Liabilities	3,782	2,484	1,289
Stockholders' Equity	72,337	69,855	67,445
Common Stock Equity per Share (C)	21.68	20.94	20.17
Other Statistics			
Ratio — Current Assets to Current Liabilities	3.0-1	2.9-1	2.2-1
Capital Expenditures	$ 8,573	$ 7,316	$ 14,251
Depreciation	5,771	5,438	4,784
Income Taxes	5,280	4,054	4,421
Common Shares Outstanding (Average) (C)	2,912,408	2,902,486	2,895,976
Price Range — Common Stock (Calendar Year) (C)	29¾-17½	37⅝-25⅝	37⅝-30½

(A) Comparative figures from 1967 have been restated to include
the accounts of Copeland Sausage Co. and Bama Meats, Inc.
on a pooling of interests basis.
(B) Includes dividends paid by pooled company prior to
acquisition.
(C) After adjustments for 2-for-1 stock split April 1965.

(Dollars in Thousands, except per share figures)

1968	1967	1966	1965	1964	1963	1962
$ 212,683	$ 207,341	$ 147,672	$ 115,713	$ 97,632	$ 78,195	$ 75,039
7,056	6,493	5,045	3,113	1,812	1,476	2,193
122	122	122	122	122	122	122
2,383	2,011	1,440	1,113	987	869	769
4,551	4,360	3,483	1,878	703	485	1,302
2.30	2.19	2.05	1.47	.84	.69	1.05
.84	.75	.65	.57½	.52½	.47½	.42½
3.3	3.1	3.4	2.7	1.9	1.9	2.9
12.5	14.3	13.9	10.6	6.4	5.3	8.5
$ 53,328	$ 40,884	$ 32,567	$ 29,537	$ 28,276	$ 27,493	$ 20,294
41,618	38,129	28,145	18,835	18,658	17,119	15,197
4,758	5,781	6,688	2,536	1,753	1,509	996
99,704	84,794	67,400	50,908	48,687	46,121	36,487
35,108	25,057	23,481	18,942	19,090	18,000	8,975
126	415	413	6	5	109	5
64,470	59,322	43,506	31,960	29,592	28,012	27,507
19.15	17.56	16.53	14.27	13.35	12.95	12.71
2.4-1	2.1-1	2.1-1	2.7-1	2.4-1	3.1-1	2.9-1
$ 11,623	$ 12,683	$ 9,735	$ 3,801	$ 4,153	$ 5,017	$ 2,980
7,092	5,623	4,176	3,409	3,279	3,088	2,673
6,020	5,761	4,794	3,202	1,791	1,134	2,425
2,885,303	2,776,310	2,405,963	2,041,521	2,002,963	1,974,322	1,971,198
48⅜-30¼	44-27	36⅛-21½	34¼-20⅞	21¾-17	22¼-14¾	23-14½

The Singer Company

The financial statements on pages 521–53C are reprinted from the 1971 financial statements of The Singer Company and Consolidated Subsidiaries.

The Singer Company and Consolidated Subsidiaries
Financial Review

Summary of Accounting Policies

Principles of Consolidation

The accompanying financial statements include the accounts of all subsidiaries other than wholly-owned finance and home building companies. These finance and home-building companies are reported in the financial statements as investments carried on the equity basis and, accordingly, their earnings are included in income.

The accounts of the home building subsidiary, acquired as of December 31, 1970 and accounted for as a pooling of interests, were included in the consolidated financial statements for 1970. However, its operations differ in many respects from those of the Company's other businesses and, in order to present more meaningful financial information, this company has been included on the equity basis for 1971 and prior years' financial statements have been restated retroactively. This change had no effect on net income for 1971 or prior years.

Beginning in 1970, the Company consolidated the accounts of its European mail order subsidiary, Schwab A.G., the ownership in which increased from 51%, the initial interest acquired in 1966, to 91% at December 31, 1970. The Financial Summary has been restated retroactively for this change.

Current assets and liabilities of branches and subsidiaries located outside of the United States are converted into U.S. dollars at the rates of exchange in effect at the balance sheet dates and non-current assets and liabilities are converted at historical rates.

All significant intercompany transactions are eliminated in consolidation.

Inventories

Inventories are stated at the lower of cost (generally on a first-in, first-out basis) or market. In the determination of cost, certain indirect manufacturing expenses are excluded.

Property, Plant and Equipment

Land, buildings, equipment and improvements which significantly extend the useful life of existing plant and equipment are carried at cost. Depreciation generally is recorded on a straight-line basis over the estimated useful lives of the assets. Maintenance and repair costs are expensed as incurred.

Income Taxes

The accompanying financial statements reflect the income from instalment sales and the elimination of unrealized intercompany profits in inventories. Income tax laws of the United States and certain other countries permit or require different treatment of these and other items, such as depreciation, for the determination of taxable income, generally resulting in the postponement of income tax payments. The net related tax effect of the above practices has been deferred in the accompanying financial statements. The effect varies widely from year to year principally due to the number of taxing jurisdictions and the variety of tax laws with which the Company must comply.

United States income taxes have not been provided on the unremitted earnings of subsidiaries incorporated outside the United States since it has been the practice and is the intention of the Company to continue to reinvest these earnings in the growth of the business outside of the United States.

The Company accounts for the investment tax credit as a reduction of tax expense in the year in which the related asset is placed in service (flow-through method).

Other Assets

Other assets consist primarily of prepaid and deferred expenses. The Company amortizes deferred expenses such as major start-up costs and plant rearrangements over the periods estimated to be benefited, generally not to exceed three years.

Research and Development Costs

Company funded research and development costs (excluding customer sponsored projects) are charged against operations as incurred.

Pension Plans

The Company has a number of pension plans which cover substantially all of its employees who meet eligibility requirements. The Company amortizes prior service costs over periods generally not exceeding 20 years. Pension costs are generally funded as accrued after giving consideration to the financial condition of each pension fund.

Long-term Contracts

Certain long-term contracts, principally in the aerospace and simulation products areas, are accounted for on the percentage of completion method. Sales under such contracts were less than three percent of total Company sales.

Marketable Securities

Marketable securities are valued at cost, which approximates market value at the respective balance sheet dates. Securities not intended for resale or not readily marketable are included in "Investments".

The Singer Company and Consolidated Subsidiaries

Earnings Per Share

Primary earnings per share is calculated by dividing net income after deducting the preferred dividend payments on the Series $3.50 preferred stock by the weighted average number of shares of common stock and common stock equivalents outstanding during the year, 16.6 million shares in 1971 and 16.2 million shares in 1970. Common stock equivalents are shares of common stock reserved for issuance upon conversion of Series $1.50 Class A and $12.50 Series A through G cumulative convertible preferred stocks and shares relating to common stock options granted if the average market price exceeded the option price during the period. The number of such equivalent shares has been reduced to reflect the assumption that proceeds of such options would be used by the Company to acquire its common shares.

Fully diluted earnings per share is calculated by dividing net income by the weighted average number of shares of common stock and common stock equivalents outstanding during the year, with the additional assumption that the Series $3.50 preferred stock had been converted.

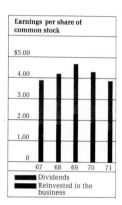

Earnings per share of common stock

Accounts Receivable

Accounts receivable-net as shown on the balance sheet is after deduction of unearned carrying charges on instalment sales and allowances for doubtful accounts. These deductions totaled $65.5 million and $64.2 million at December 31, 1971 and 1970, respectively. In accordance with trade practice, instalments not due within one year aggregating $56.9 million in 1971 and $58.5 million in 1970 are classified as current assets.

Inventories

Inventories at December 31, 1971 and 1970 are summarized as follows:

	1971	1970
	(Amounts in Millions)	
Finished goods	$333.0	$297.4
Work in process	215.8	229.0
Raw materials and supplies	57.6	57.2
	$606.4	$583.6
Contracts in process included above:		
Cost	$109.2	$122.3
Less progress payments received	22.0	37.1
	$ 87.2	$ 85.2

The Singer Company and Consolidated Subsidiaries

Investments

Investments at December 31, 1971 and 1970 consisted of the following:

	1971	1970
	(Amounts in Millions)	
Finance Companies	$ 94.8	$ 67.2
Singer Housing Company	42.0	21.2
Others	30.7	21.5
	$167.5	$109.9

Investments in and advances to wholly-owned finance and home building companies are included at equity aggregating $136.8 million, while other investments are included at a cost of $30.7 million.

The net income of the finance companies, which is included in the accompanying statements, totaled $7.9 million in 1971 and $4.9 million in 1970. The combined balance sheet of the wholly-owned finance companies at December 31, 1971 and 1970 is summarized below:

	1971	1970
	(Amounts in Millions)	
Instalment and trade accounts receivable .	$338.1	$297.1
Cash and other assets	34.4	16.8
	$372.5	$313.9
Notes payable	$253.8	$225.9
Other liabilities	16.4	7.1
Payables to affiliates	56.6	34.0
Long-term debt	7.8	14.0
Equity	37.9	32.9
	$372.5	$313.9

The net income of the Singer Housing Company included in the accompanying statements totaled $5.5 million in 1971 and $4.0 million in 1970.

The balance sheet of this company at December 31, 1971 and 1970 is summarized below:

	1971	1970
	(Amounts in Millions)	
Real estate projects	$58.6	$51.5
Cash and receivables	4.6	5.3
Investments and other assets	6.3	5.9
	$69.5	$62.7
Accounts payable and other liabilities	$12.7	$ 8.1
Notes and loans payable—secured	14.8	33.4
Payables to affiliates	15.3	—
Equity	26.7	21.2
	$69.5	$62.7

The Singer Company and Consolidated Subsidiaries

Property, Plant and Equipment

Gross additions in 1971 amounted to $83.0 million. Disposals of property, plant and equipment (net of accumulated depreciation) amounted to $27.3 million. The provision for depreciation in 1971 was $56.4 million compared with $52.5 million in 1970.
Balances at December 31, 1971 and 1970 were:

	1971	1970
	(Amounts in Millions)	
Property, plant and equipment, at cost:		
Land	$ 16.4	$ 19.9
Buildings, less accumulated depreciation of $69.6, 1971 and $70.6, 1970	91.5	99.0
Machinery and equipment, less accumulated depreciation of $323.8, 1971 and $309.6, 1970	211.1	211.4
Construction in progress	31.5	20.9
	$350.5	$351.2

Other Assets

Other assets at December 31, 1971 and 1970 were as follows:

	1971	1970
	(Amounts in Millions)	
Prepaid and deferred expenses	$55.5	$59.6
Mortgages and other	11.9	13.5
Intangibles, less amortization	17.3	17.4
Deposits	9.3	6.5
	$94.0	$97.0

Net Assets Located Outside the United States

The amount of these assets at December 31, 1971 and 1970 by major geographic area was:

	1971	1970
	(Amounts in Millions)	
Europe	$198.0	$164.7
Latin America	52.1	51.8
Far East..............................	16.8	20.5
Africa and the Near East	20.7	21.1
Canada	28.6	26.5
	$316.2	$284.6

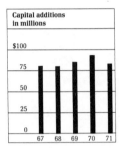

Capital additions in millions

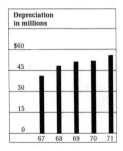

Depreciation in millions

The Singer Company and Consolidated Subsidiaries

Long-term Debt

Long-term debt, less amounts due within one year, consisted principally of unsecured promissory notes, many of which require payments each year to maturity, and debentures. The amounts due within one year, $25.5 million at December 31, 1971 and $17.8 million at December 31, 1970, are included in current liabilities.

The long-term debt is summarized by type of borrowing, as follows:

	Interest Rates	1971	1970
	(Percent)	(Amounts in Millions)	
Debentures	8¼	$100.0	$100.0
Notes payable to institutional lenders	4¼-6	66.2	72.2
Bank loans:			
Eurodollar	6⁹⁄₁₆-9¼	38.1	47.6
Revolving credit	6-8	8.0	8.0
Foreign currency	6½-9¾	13.2	20.8
Miscellaneous	various	12.5	17.1
		$238.0	$265.7

The aggregate maturities of long-term debt during the five years subsequent to December 31, 1971 are as follows:

Year	1972	1973	1974	1975	1976
Amounts in millions	$25.5	$29.4	$20.5	$16.2	$117.9

Pension Plan

Pension plan expense, including amortization of prior service costs, was $9.0 million in 1971 and $9.8 million in 1970. The unfunded prior service cost amounted to $12.4 million at December 31, 1971. The assets of the pension funds and the assets and liabilities with respect to pensions reflected in the accompanying balance sheet were sufficient to cover the actuarially computed value of vested benefits for all plans at December 31, 1971.

Commitments and Contingent Liabilities

The Company has been advised that there are no refunds of profits required relating to sales to the government under renegotiation proceedings for 1970 and prior years and it is expected that no refunds will be required for such sales during 1971.

The Company conducts a large part of its marketing operations in leased premises. Leases which expire are generally renewed or replaced by leases on other similar properties. The minimum annual rental commitment under leases and rental agreements in effect as of December 31, 1971 aggregated $41.0 million.

Executive Incentive Compensation Plan

The Company has an Executive Incentive Compensation Plan which can be cancelled at the discretion of the Board of Directors. Under the Plan, incentive awards to selected executive and key employees are administered by a Committee and may be in the form of cash and/or common stock, restricted as defined by the Plan. Net income has been charged with the estimated fair value of the anticipated awards. Awards of 28,662 and 35,550 shares of common stock, net of cancellations, were distributed in 1971 and 1970, respectively. At December 31, 1971, a total of 305,395 shares of common stock were reserved for issuance under the Plan.

Common Stock Options

Under the Company's stock option plan, options to purchase common stock of the Company may be granted to executive employees at prices not less than market value on the dates of grant. Generally, these options expire in five years. Under the 1968 Employee Stock Purchase Plan, employees are granted options to purchase common stock at 80 percent of market value.

The number of shares available under the stock option and stock purchase plans at December 31, 1971 were 394,650 and 551,393 shares, respectively.

The changes for the year in options outstanding under the stock option and stock purchase plans were as follows:

	Shares	Option Prices
Options outstanding at December 31, 1970	396,081	$24.05-93.71
Options granted	173,328	43.75-74.94
	569,409	
Less:		
Options exercised	192,464	30.12-64.06
Options terminated	32,900	26.83-85.50
	225,364	
Options outstanding at December 31, 1971	344,045	24.05-93.71

The Singer Company and Consolidated Subsidiaries

Shareholders' Equity

The capital stock of the Company at December 31, 1971 and 1970 is summarized below:

	December 31, 1971			December 31, 1970		
	Shares Issued	Stated or par value	Liquidation preference	Shares Issued	Stated or par value	Liquidation preference
		(Amounts in Thousands)			(Amounts in Thousands)	
Convertible preferred stock, without par value; Authorized 3,500,000 shares:						
Series $3.50, authorized 2,110,000 shares	1,604,385	$ 20,857	$160,439	1,686,567	$ 21,925	$168,657
Series $1.50, authorized 452,571 shares	452,571	4,073	31,680	452,571	4,073	31,680
$12.50 Series A through G, authorized 100,000 shares	71,557	7,156	35,779	95,409	9,541	47,705
	2,128,513	$ 32,086	$227,898	2,234,547	$ 35,539	$248,042
Common stock, par value $10 per share; Authorized 25,000,000 shares (1970—20,000,000 shares)	15,738,396	$157,384		15,175,835	$151,758	

Common stock issued includes treasury stock of 214,468 and 141,116 shares at December 31, 1971 and 1970, respectively, which is carried at cost.

The Series $3.50 voting preferred stock has a stated value of $13 per share and is convertible into 1.3 shares of common stock. Holders are entitled to receive cumulative cash dividends at the rate of $3.50 per share per annum prior to payment of dividends on common stock. The stock is callable for redemption on or after July 31, 1973, in whole or in part, at a redemption price of $102.50. The redemption price will decrease by 50 cents per share each year thereafter until it reaches $100.00.

The Series $1.50 Class A voting preferred stock has a stated value of $9 per share and is convertible at the option of either the holders or the Company into .9 share of common stock on or after January 1, 1972. Holders are entitled to receive cumulative cash dividends at the rate of $1.50 per share per annum prior to payment of dividends on common stock. The stock is callable for redemption after December 31, 1974, in whole or in part, at a price of $70 per share.

As of December 31, 1971, the $12.50 voting cumulative preferred stock consists of 719 shares of Series A, 24,571 shares of Series B, 9,829 shares each of Series C thru F and 6,951 shares of Series G. This preferred stock has a stated value of $100 per share and a redemption price of $500 per share after it becomes unconditionally convertible. The stock is convertible into 10 shares of common stock on April 1, 1976 for Series A thru C and April 1, 1977 thru April 1, 1980, respectively for the remaining Series. On or after April 1, 1971 and April 1, 1973 for Series A and B, respectively, and after April 1, 1976 with respect to Series D thru G, the holders will have certain rights to accelerate their conversion privileges in order to consummate a public sale of common stock. During 1971, this right was exercised as indicated in the following table. Prior to payments of dividends on common stock, holders are entitled to receive cumulative cash dividends

at the initial rate of $12.50 per share per annum, and commencing March 16, 1971 for Series A, March 16, 1973 for Series B and March 16, 1976 for the remaining Series at a rate equal to the lesser of $125 per share per annum, or a rate equivalent to the dividends payable on the underlying common stock, but subject to a minimum of $5 per preferred share.

Capital stock issued during 1971 is summarized as follows:

	Convertible Preferred			
	Series $3.50	Series $1.50	Series $12.50	Common
Shares issued at December 31, 1970 ...	1,686,567	452,571	95,409	15,175,835
Conversion of Series $3.50	(94,897)			123,348
Conversion of $12.50 Series A			(23,852)	238,520
Exercise of stock options	12,715			169,870
Issued for Executive Incentive Compensation				30,823
Shares issued at December 31, 1971 ...	1,604,385	452,571	71,557	15,738,396

At December 31, 1971, there were 3,208,583 shares of common stock reserved for the conversion of preferred stock and 1,619,915 shares reserved for the exercise of stock options, the stock purchase plan and the Executive Incentive Compensation Plan.

The Singer Company and Consolidated Subsidiaries

Statement of Income

For the Years Ended December 31, 1971 and 1970

	1971	1970
	(Amounts in Thousands)	
Revenue:		
Net sales	$2,099,454	$2,058,723
Income before tax of unconsolidated subsidiaries	24,169	16,571
Other	10,950	12,559
	2,134,573	2,087,853
Costs and expenses:		
Costs and other operating charges	1,276,170	1,246,312
Selling and administrative expenses	699,061	667,149
Interest	44,791	50,892
Provision for income taxes:		
Current	30,212	33,476
Deferred	13,527	14,901
	2,063,761	2,012,730
Net Income	$ 70,812	$ 75,123
Primary earnings per share	$ 3.92	$ 4.25
Fully diluted earnings per share	$ 3.78	$ 4.05

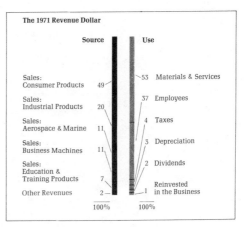

The 1971 Revenue Dollar

Source			Use
Sales: Consumer Products	49	53	Materials & Services
Sales: Industrial Products	20	37	Employees
Sales: Aerospace & Marine	11	4	Taxes
Sales: Business Machines	11	3	Depreciation
Sales: Education & Training Products	7	2	Dividends
Other Revenues	2	1	Reinvested in the Business
	100%	100%	

The Singer Company and Consolidated Subsidiaries

Balance Sheet

December 31, 1971 and 1970

	1971	1970
	(Amounts in Thousands)	
Assets		
Current assets:		
Cash and marketable securities	$ 58,619	$ 53,512
Accounts receivable—net	392,691	381,559
Inventories	606,414	583,609
Total current assets	1,057,724	1,018,680
Investments	167,499	109,949
Property, plant and equipment—net	350,476	351,189
Other assets	94,017	97,004
	$1,669,716	$1,576,822
Liabilities and Shareholders' Equity		
Current liabilities:		
Notes and loans payable	$ 266,118	$ 212,197
Accounts payable and accrued expenses .	245,728	239,642
Income taxes payable	44,578	40,960
Income taxes deferred	68,392	55,705
Total current liabilities	624,816	548,504
Long-term debt	237,958	265,742
Other non-current liabilities	32,462	18,087
	895,236	832,333
Shareholders' equity:		
Convertible preferred stock	32,086	35,539
Common stock	157,384	151,758
Additional paid-in capital	26,738	18,510
Retained earnings	572,176	547,306
	788,384	753,113
Less treasury stock	13,904	8,624
Total shareholders' equity	774,480	744,489
	$1,669,716	$1,576,822

The Singer Company and Consolidated Subsidiaries

Statement of Retained Earnings

For the Years Ended December 31, 1971 and 1970

	1971	1970
	(Amounts in Thousands)	
Amount at beginning of year	$ 547,306	$ 517,751
Net income	70,812	75,123
	618,118	592,874
Less:		
Dividends paid:		
Preferred	7,192	6,816
Common (per share—$2.40)	36,891	35,400
Prior to merger by pooled companies	—	206
Cost of treasury stock in excess of net assets of pooled companies	1,859	3,146
	45,942	45,568
Amount at end of year	$ 572,176	$ 547,306

Statement of Additional Paid-in Capital

For the Years Ended December 31, 1971 and 1970

	1971	1970
	(Amounts in Thousands)	
Amount at beginning of year	$ 18,510	$ 10,777
Excess of proceeds over par value of common stock sold to employees	8,228	7,733
Amount at end of year	$ 26,738	$ 18,510

The Singer Company and Consolidated Subsidiaries

Statement of Changes in Financial Position

For the Years Ended December 31, 1971 and 1970

	1971	1970
	(Amounts in Thousands)	
Source of Funds		
Net income	$ 70,812	$ 75,123
Depreciation and amortization	62,151	54,528
Less net income of unconsolidated subsidiaries	13,362	8,908
Funds provided from operations	119,601	120,743
Long-term debt issued	45,357	146,495
Increase in:		
Notes and loans payable	53,921	—
Income tax liabilities	16,305	21,086
Other current liabilities	6,086	39,687
Changes in other non-current items	11,601	—
Sales and other dispositions of capital stock	8,542	12,512
Dispositions of property, plant and equipment	27,328	15,384
Decrease in accounts receivable	—	36,128
Decrease in cash and marketable securities	—	2,789
Total	$ 288,741	$ 394,824
Use of Funds		
Reduction of long-term debt	$ 73,141	$ 133,350
Additions to property, plant and equipment	83,005	94,468
Dividends	44,083	42,422
Increase in:		
Investments	44,188	10,312
Inventories	22,805	56,526
Accounts receivable	11,132	—
Cash and marketable securities	5,107	—
Purchases of treasury stock	5,280	—
Decrease in notes and loans payable	—	48,281
Changes in other non-current items	—	9,465
Total	$ 288,741	$ 394,824

PEAT, MARWICK, MITCHELL & CO.
CERTIFIED PUBLIC ACCOUNTANTS
345 PARK AVENUE
NEW YORK, NEW YORK 10022

To the Shareholders and
Board of Directors
of The Singer Company

We have examined the balance sheets of The Singer Company and consolidated subsidiaries as of December 31, 1971 and December 31, 1970 and the related statements of income, retained earnings, additional paid-in capital and changes in financial position for the two years ended December 31, 1971. Our examinations were made in accordance with generally accepted auditing standards, and accordingly included such tests of the accounting records and such other auditing procedures as we considered necessary in the circumstances.

In our opinion, the accompanying financial statements present fairly the financial position of The Singer Company and consolidated subsidiaries at December 31, 1971 and December 31, 1970 and the results of their operations and the changes in their financial position for the two years ended December 31, 1971, in conformity with generally accepted accounting principles applied on a consistent basis.

Peat, Marwick, Mitchell & Co.

March 9, 1972

A. O. Smith Corporation

The financial statements on pages 532–543 are reprinted from the 1971 financial statements of A. O. Smith Corporation.

Sales   Earnings

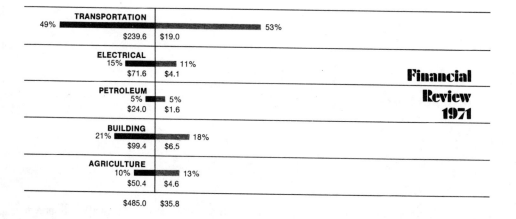

TRANSPORTATION
49% 53%
$239.6 $19.0

ELECTRICAL
15% 11%
$71.6 $4.1

PETROLEUM
5% 5%
$24.0 $1.6

BUILDING
21% 18%
$99.4 $6.5

AGRICULTURE
10% 13%
$50.4 $4.6

$485.0 $35.8

Financial Review 1971

SALES

Sales of A. O. Smith Corporation and its consolidated subsidiaries reached a record $456,846,000 in 1971, an increase of 10.6% over 1970 sales of $413,098,000, the previous record year. Automotive division sales increased about 35% over 1970, when the United Auto Workers' union strike against General Motors Corporation materially affected volume. Important volume gains were also achieved by the company's elevator and Harvestore subsidiaries and by the Consumer Products division.

Volume declines occurred in the Electric Motor, Meter Systems and Clark Control divisions. The distribution of the company's sales by major divisions and subsidiaries for 1971, 1970 and 1969 is shown below:

	$ IN MILLIONS		
	1971	1970	1969
Automotive (including Railroad Products)	220	163	182
Armor Elevator Company, Inc. and Armor Elevator Canada Limited	59	43	-0-
Electric Motors (including Bull Motors Limited)	52	59	45
A. O. Smith Harvestore Products, Inc.	37	34	29
Consumer Products	40	34	31
Meter Systems	20	27	19
Electrical Controls (including Canadian Controllers Ltd.)	20	24	25

International sales in 1971 were $41 million, or 9% of the company's consolidated sales. The company's operations located outside the United States produced $33 million of these sales. The balance represented exports from U.S. plants. These sales do not include sales of affiliates located in foreign countries.

EARNINGS

Earnings for 1971, excluding an extraordinary loss, were $12,808,000, or $5.23 per share. Earnings for 1970, excluding a net extraordinary gain, were $7,287,000 or $2.95 per share. Measured by earnings per share before consideration of either extraordinary gains or losses, 1971 was the third best year in the company's history. The reinstated investment tax credit added $0.19 per share to the company's 1971 results. Other consequences of the freeze and Phase II controls reduced company earnings. Some of the adverse effects of the government's programs were the inability of the water heating and Harvestore portions to increase prices. The Automotive division's results were adversely affected by the costs of the retroactivity feature of the Milwaukee, Wis., union settlement, as these costs cannot be recovered by price increases. On the other hand, material costs were favorably affected because undoubtedly many of A. O. Smith's suppliers' prices would have increased without the freeze. Also, A. O. Smith Corporation Of Texas, an affiliate, received a large line pipe order late in 1971 which, without the import tax and without the return of the investment tax credit, probably would not have been obtained. The net result was a reduction in earnings, the precise amount of which cannot be measured .

The provision for taxes was $11,400,000, in 1971 and $8,900,000 in 1970. The effective tax rates in 1971 and 1970 were 48% and 50% respectively.

An extraordinary loss of $1,760,000 or $0.72 per share resulted in 1971, from both the sale of Layne & Bowler Pump Company, a subsidiary, to the General Signal Corporation, and the sale earlier in the year of the irrigation system segment of Layne & Bowler's business. While the growth potential of the irrigation systems market, which originally led to A. O. Smith's acquisition of Layne & Bowler, is substantial, it appears that this potential can be more profitably realized by regional manufacturers. In 1970, a net extraordinary gain increased 1970 earnings by $2,146,000 or $0.87 per share.

The earnings improvement in 1971 was primarily caused by:

- A substantial improvement by the Automotive division, which in 1970 suffered the impact of the United Auto Workers' union strike against General Motors Corporation.
- Improved profit performance by the elevator subsidiaries and A. O. Smith-Inland Inc., an affiliate company.
- A substantial reduction in the operating loss of A. O. Smith Corporation Of Texas, another affiliate company.
- Continuing strong profit performance by the Consumer Products division and A. O. Smith Harvestore Products, Inc., a subsidiary.

For the fourth quarter of 1971, before extraordinary items, the company earned $3,952,000, or $1.61 per share. For the same period of 1970, also before extraordinary items, a loss of $800,000, or $0.32 per share, was incurred.

DIVIDENDS

Dividends paid on common stock amounted to $3,431,000 in 1971 and $3,457,000 in 1970. The dividend payment was $1.40 per share in both years. Dividends have been paid every year since 1940.

WORKING CAPITAL

At December 31, 1971, working capital totaled $99,132,000. At year end, 1970, working capital amounted to $96,512,000. Current assets were 2.7 times current liabilities at December 31, 1971, compared with 2.6 times last year. A statement setting forth the changes in financial position for the years 1971 and 1970 is shown on page 13.

CAPITAL EXPENDITURES

During 1971, $17,335,000 was invested in improvements and expansion of facilities. Capital expenditures amounted to $23,267,000 in 1970. Significant expenditures were made in the Automotive division to develop increased truck frame capacity, to provide for model change requirements for passenger frames and for a major consolidation and modernization of the intermediate-size passenger frame production facilities. The Electric Motor, Armor Elevator, Clark Control and water heater segments of the company also required additional facilities to support anticipated growth, and, particularly in the case of Clark Control, new product introductions.

CASH FLOW

Cash flow, defined as the sum of net earnings and depreciation, amounted to $21,840,000 or $8.92 per share in 1971.

During the prior year, cash flow totaled $19,284,000 or $7.81 per share. The improvement in 1971 is primarily attributable to increased earnings. Depreciation in 1971 and 1970 was $10,792,000 and $9,851,000 respectively.

LONG-TERM DEBT

Total debt, due after one year, including lease purchase obligations, totaled $61,480,000 at 12/31/71 compared to $62,224,000 at 12/31/70. Long-term debt equaled 41% of stockholders' equity at 12/31/71 versus 44% at 12/31/70. A schedule of the company's long-term debt appears in note 3 to the financial statements on pages 16 and 17.

STOCKHOLDERS' EQUITY

Stockholders' equity in the company increased to $150,143,000 at 12/31/71 from $142,936,000 at 12/31/70. Earnings, excluding extraordinary items, equaled a return on average stockholders' equity of 8.5% in 1971, compared to 5.1% in 1970. As of 12/31/71 there were 2,519,479 shares of common stock outstanding, including 63,839 shares held as treasury shares. The company completed the program initiated in 1969 to acquire 100,000 shares of its common stock in the open market. These shares are available for use in connection with the company's employee stock option program, for acquisitions or other proper corporate uses which may arise, without diluting the proportionate interest of present shareholders. A total of 22,198 shares were purchased in 1971 at a cost of $1,099,000. Treasury stock transactions (in shares) during the year were as follows:

Balance 12/31/70	66,019
Acquired	22,198
Issued for Stock Option Purposes	24,378
Balance 12/31/71	63,839

STOCK OPTIONS

At year end, 155,013 shares of common stock (including 22,614 shares of treasury stock) were reserved for stock options under the company's 1962 Restricted Stock Option Plan, 1964 Qualified Stock Option Plan and 1970 Employees' Stock Option Plan.

Option transactions (in shares) during the year were as follows:

Options outstanding 12/31/70	80,672
Granted	-0-
Exercised	24,378
Options outstanding 12/31/71	56,294

In addition to the 56,294 options outstanding at December 31, 1971, there were non-qualified stock options totaling 47,050 shares outstanding at the end of the year. The non-qualified stock options were granted under the 1970 plan to employees holding an equivalent number of qualified stock options granted under the 1964 and 1970 plans. The optionee may exercise either the qualified or non-qualified stock option and the option not so exercised is then cancelled. The shares released by such cancelled options then become available for new option grants.

As of December 31, 1971, there were 54,569 shares available for additional grants, including 51,950 shares under the aforementioned 1970 plan. Further information regarding stock options is contained in note 4 to the financial statements on page 17.

A. O. SMITH CORPORATION

CONSOLIDATED STATEMENTS OF EARNINGS AND RETAINED EARNINGS

Years ended December 31, 1970 and 1971

1970	1971	
		EARNINGS
$413,097,543	**$456,845,662**	NET SALES
		OPERATING COSTS AND EXPENSES:
358,911,167	**392,657,178**	Cost of goods sold
34,375,607	**36,767,912**	Selling, general and administrative
393,286,774	**429,425,090**	
19,810,769	**27,420,572**	PROFIT FROM OPERATIONS
		OTHER INCOME (deductions):
(4,224,122)	**(5,672,414)**	Interest expense
2,337,701	**1,867,182**	Miscellaneous—net
(1,886,421)	**(3,805,232)**	
17,924,348	**23,615,340**	EARNINGS BEFORE INCOME TAXES
8,900,000	**11,400,000**	PROVISION FOR INCOME TAXES (1971 after investment tax credits, flow through method, of $475,000)
9,024,348	**12,215,340**	EARNINGS BEFORE EQUITY IN EARNINGS (LOSSES) OF UNCONSOLIDATED AFFILIATES AND EXTRAORDINARY ITEMS
(1,737,344)	**592,886**	EQUITY IN EARNINGS (LOSSES) OF UNCONSOLIDATED AFFILIATES—NET
7,287,004	**12,808,226**	EARNINGS BEFORE EXTRAORDINARY ITEMS
2,146,000	**(1,760,000)**	EXTRAORDINARY ITEMS, net of applicable income taxes (Note 5)
$ 9,433,004	**$ 11,048,226**	NET EARNINGS
		PER SHARE OF COMMON STOCK:
$2.95	**$5.23**	Earnings before extraordinary items
.87	**(.72)**	Extraordinary items
$3.82	**$4.51**	Net earnings
		RETAINED EARNINGS
$101,197,733	**$107,174,231**	BALANCE AT BEGINNING OF YEAR
9,433,004	**11,048,226**	NET EARNINGS
110,630,737	**118,222,457**	
3,456,506	**3,430,865**	CASH DIVIDENDS, $1.40 per share
$107,174,231	**$114,791,592**	BALANCE AT END OF YEAR (Note 3)

See accompanying notes.

A. O. SMITH CORPORATION

CONSOLIDATED
STATEMENT
OF CHANGES
IN FINANCIAL
POSITION

Years Ended December 31, 1970 and 1971

1970	1971	WORKING CAPITAL
		SOURCE:
$ 7,287,004	$12,808,226	Earnings before extraordinary items
9,850,821	10,792,192	Depreciation
627,275	2,700,000	Deferred income taxes
1,737,344	(592,886)	Equity in (earnings) losses of unconsolidated affiliates
677,674	1,414,952	Other items not involving working capital
20,180,118	27,122,484	Total from operations exclusive of extraordinary items
2,146,000	(1,760,000)	Extraordinary items
1,419,672	3,969,870	Amounts applicable thereto not involving working capital
3,565,672	2,209,870	Total from extraordinary items
34,291,224	—	Proceeds from sale of debentures, less related costs of $708,776
—	1,340,293	Long-term borrowings—banks
451,797	688,253	Proceeds from exercise of stock options
58,488,811	31,360,900	
		USE:
3,456,506	3,430,865	Cash dividends paid
1,641,438	2,033,528	Payments on long-term debt
23,267,000	17,335,205	Plant and equipment expenditures
5,450,815	412,665	Investment in subsidiaries and affiliates
—	2,100,000	Prepaid pension costs
1,494,850	1,098,612	Purchase of treasury stock
1,936,001	917,231	Deferred model change-over expenditures
266,034	1,413,159	Other
37,512,644	28,741,265	
$20,976,167	$ 2,619,635	INCREASE
		INCREASE (DECREASE) IN COMPONENTS OF WORKING CAPITAL:
$ 2,123,520	$(1,387,518)	Cash and marketable securities
5,707,364	1,858,073	Receivables
8,809,957	(329,300)	Inventories
3,031,647	3,943,682	Accounts payable
2,512,633	3,389,956	Income taxes
(1,205,045)	(3,676,229)	Accrued payroll
(3,909)	(1,179,029)	Other
$20,976,167	$ 2,619,635	

See accompanying notes.

A. O. SMITH CORPORATION	1970	1971	
CONSOLIDATED BALANCE SHEET December 31, 1970 and 1971			**ASSETS** CURRENT ASSETS:
	$ 7,914,301	$ 3,829,190	Cash
	4,900,000	7,597,593	Marketable securities, at cost (approximates market)
	55,724,364	57,582,437	Receivables
			Inventories, at lower of cost (first-in, first-out) or market:
	20,668,040	24,110,588	Finished goods
	39,601,718	35,711,093	Work in process
	25,463,768	25,582,545	Raw materials and supplies
	85,733,526	85,404,226	
	3,764,205	3,118,551	Prepaid expenses
	158,036,396	157,531,997	Total current assets
			OTHER ASSETS:
			Investments in and advances to:
	10,292,039	11,227,010	50% owned companies (Note 1)
	5,040,386	5,110,966	Unconsolidated finance subsidiary (Note 1)
	3,600,000	5,700,000	Prepaid pension costs (Note 2)
	5,892,790	6,391,942	Other, at cost
	24,825,215	28,429,918	Total other assets
			PLANT AND EQUIPMENT, AT COST:
	4,753,794	3,434,903	Land
	23,504,282	23,938,886	Buildings (less accumulated depreciation, 1971—$25,927,690; 1970—$24,885,565)
	58,639,501	62,080,550	Equipment (less accumulated depreciation, 1971—$75,827,180; 1970—$73,824,675)
	86,897,577	89,454,339	Net plant and equipment
	2,281,569	2,384,304	DEFERRED MODEL CHANGEOVER COSTS, LESS AMORTIZATION
	5,554,195	5,234,503	EXCESS COST OF INVESTMENT IN SUBSIDIARIES over net assets at date of acquisition less amortization (40 year basis)
	$277,594,952	$283,035,061	

See accompanying notes.

1970	1971	
		LIABILITIES AND STOCKHOLDERS' EQUITY
		CURRENT LIABILITIES:
$ 4,098,828	$ 3,355,075	Notes payable—banks and others
18,773,944	14,830,262	Accounts payable
6,182,426	2,792,470	Income taxes
4,598,203	4,666,993	Taxes, other than income taxes
9,595,498	13,271,727	Accrued payrolls
16,030,235	17,284,303	Other liabilities
2,245,000	2,199,270	Long-term debt due within one year
61,524,134	58,400,100	Total current liabilities
62,224,488	61,480,203	LONG-TERM DEBT DUE AFTER ONE YEAR (Note 3)
6,665,000	9,365,000	DEFERRED INCOME TAXES
4,245,355	3,646,781	DEFERRED CREDITS, LESS AMORTIZATION
		STOCKHOLDERS' EQUITY:
		Preferred stock, $1 par value:
—	—	Authorized—1,000,000 shares
		Issued—none
12,598,745	12,598,745	Common stock $5 par value (Note 4):
		Authorized—6,000,000 shares
		Issued—2,519,749 shares
25,820,774	25,459,401	Capital in excess of par value
107,174,231	114,791,592	Retained earnings (Note 3)
(2,657,775)	(2,706,761)	Treasury stock, at cost, 1971—63,839
		shares; 1970—66,019 shares
142,935,975	150,142,977	Total stockholders' equity
$277,594,952	$283,035,061	

See accompanying notes.

A. O. SMITH CORPORATION

NOTES TO CONSOLIDATED FINANCIAL STATEMENTS

1. PRINCIPLES OF CONSOLIDATION

The consolidated financial statements include the accounts of the Company and all subsidiaries except for its wholly owned finance subsidiary, AgriStor Credit Corporation. The investments in and advances to the finance subsidiary and affiliates (50%-owned) are carried at cost plus equity in undistributed net earnings since acquisition.

Accounts maintained in foreign currencies are converted to U.S. dollars based on year-end exchange rates for net current assets and certain long-term liabilities. Fixed and other non-current assets, long-term liabilities and capital accounts are converted at exchange rates prevailing at date acquired or incurred. Income accounts are converted at the average exchange rate for the year except for amounts related to items converted at historical rates. Unrealized gains and losses on conversion to U.S. dollars, which have not been material, are credited or charged to earnings.

2. RETIREMENT PLANS

The Company and its consolidated subsidiaries have non-contributory pension plans covering substantially all employees. Total pension expense for 1971 and 1970 was $5,555,000 and $3,830,000, respectively, which amounts include current cost plus interest on unfunded prior service cost for

all plans. In addition, the 1971 expense includes amortization of prior service cost for substantially all plans on a 30-year basis; whereas the 1970 expense includes, for two plans, amortization of the prior service cost on a 40-year basis. The increased pension expense in 1971 is principally attributable to increased benefits. The change to the amortization of prior service cost for substantially all plans and the change in amortization period did not materially affect 1971 earnings. The actuarially computed

values of vested benefits under certain of the plans exceed the assets of the related trusts by $34,900,000 at December 31, 1971. The present policy is to fund, at a minimum, pension cost accrued. The Board of Directors has authorized contributions to the pension trust of $5,700,000 in excess of amounts charged to earnings; this amount is shown as prepaid pension costs in the balance sheet and the applicable deferred income taxes have been provided.

3. LONG-TERM DEBT AND RESTRICTION ON DIVIDEND PAYMENTS

Long-term debt at December 31, 1971 and 1970 is as follows:

	1971	1970
10¼% sinking fund debentures	$35,000,000	$35,000,000
4¾% notes payable, due $1,600,000 annually—final maturity July 1, 1983	19,200,000	20,800,000
Lease purchase obligations expiring 1984 and 1986, interest rates 4% to 6% per annum	3,780,000	3,960,000
Notes payable—banks (Eurodollar and Sterling), due in 1974, current interest rates 6½% to 11% per annum	2,080,000	2,080,000
9½% notes payable in quarterly installments of $37,500 through November 1, 1979 (secured by the plant and equipment of Armor Elevator Canada Limited, a consolidated subsidiary)	1,200,000	1,350,000
9% note payable—bank (Deutsche Mark), payable October 1, 1977	621,118	—
8½% note payable—bank (Sterling), payable May 17, 1976	600,000	—
Miscellaneous mortgage notes, due 1972 through 1975, interest rates 4½% to 8½%	1,198,355	1,279,488
	63,679,473	64,469,488
Less amount due within one year	2,199,270	2,245,000
	$61,480,203	$62,224,488

The indenture relating to the 10¼% sinking fund debentures requires sinking fund payments of not less than $1,750,000 and not more than $3,500,000 on July 1 in each year beginning with the year 1976 to and including the year 1994. The right to make any sinking fund payments in excess of $1,750,000 in any one year is not cumulative, and no such excess payment will relieve the Company of its obligation to make minimum sinking fund payments. The debentures are redeemable through operation of the sinking fund annually beginning July 1, 1976, at the principal amount thereof or at any time at the Company's option, as a whole or in part, at a redemption price of 109.326% to July 1, 1972, and at prices declining .424% thereafter on each July 1. The agreements relating to the 4¾% notes payable and the indenture relating to the 10¼% sinking fund debentures contain provisions restricting the payment of cash dividends and the retirement or acquisition of the Company's common stock. Under the more restrictive of these provisions, retained earnings of $21,300,000 was not so restricted at December 31, 1971.

4. STOCK OPTIONS

At December 31, 1971, 22,614 shares of treasury stock and 132,399 shares of authorized but unissued common stock were reserved for options outstanding and for options which may be granted in the future. Options for 56,294 shares were outstanding at December 31, 1971 at per share prices ranging from $25.04 to $39.50 or a total of $1,748,308. The options expire either five or ten years from date of grant and are exercisable at various dates (14,262 exercisable at December 31,

1971). No options were granted in 1971. Options for 51,050 shares were granted in 1970 at per share prices ranging from $31.25 to $39.50 or a total of $1,627,487. Of the options granted, 26,050 replaced options granted in prior years which were cancelled. Non-qualified options for 44,150 shares at a per share price of $30.30 and for 2,900 shares at $33.58 per share were outstanding at December 31, 1971. These options were granted in 1970 to employees holding an equivalent number of shares under qualified plans. The grantee has the option of exercising either the qualified or the non-qualified option and the option not so exercised is then cancelled.

Treasury stock was issued for options exercised in 1971 (24,378 shares at prices ranging from $27.51 to $33.58 per share or a total of $688,253) and in 1970 (16,423 shares at a price of $27.51 per share or a total of $451,797). The excess of the cost of the treasury stock ($361,373 and $234,135 in 1971 and 1970, respectively) over the proceeds of options exercised was charged to capital in excess of par value.

5. EXTRAORDINARY ITEMS

The Company sold, effective January 1, 1972, Layne & Bowler Pump Company (wholly owned subsidiary) for cash. The loss on this sale, after income tax credit of $570,000, has been included in the 1971 statement of earnings as an extraordinary item. The operations of this subsidiary for the two years ended December 31, 1971 are not significant.

The extraordinary items in 1970 include the gain ($3,076,000) resulting from the sale of the oil well casing business, less costs associated with the discontinuance of a product line of the Railroad Products division and the Company's equity in the estimated loss in connection with the disposition of the Specialty Products division of A. O. Smith-Inland Inc., a 50%-owned company. The 1970 extraordinary items of $2,146,000 are stated after income tax effect of $810,000.

6. DEPRECIATION

For financial statement purposes, depreciation on plant and equipment additions prior to January 1, 1954, and subsequent to December 31, 1966, is computed using the straight-line method; depreciation on additions between the above two dates is principally computed using accelerated methods. For income tax purposes, the Company uses accelerated methods and guideline depreciation. Deferred income taxes are provided for the excess of depreciation claimed for income tax purposes over depreciation provided for financial statement purposes.

7. LONG-TERM CONSTRUCTION CONTRACTS

Armor Elevator Company, a consolidated subsidiary, adopted the percentage of completion method of accounting for long-term construction contracts in 1971 whereas previously it had used the completed contract method. The new method of accounting for long-term contracts was adopted to provide a more meaningful measurement of the operations of this subsidiary. The effect of this accounting change in 1971 and 1970 income and expenses was nominal and accordingly the 1970 statements of earnings, retained earnings and changes in financial position have not been restated. This subsidiary was acquired on December 30, 1969 in a transaction accounted for as a purchase, consequently the change has no effect on consolidated operations prior to that time or on the consolidated retained earnings at December 31, 1969. This change does affect the valuation of the net assets acquired in December, 1969 and the consolidated balance sheet at December 31, 1970 has been restated as follows:

Decrease in excess cost of investment in subsidiaries over net assets at date of acquisition	$ 542,000
Decrease in current liabilities	$1,112,000
Increase in deferred income taxes (since the completed contract method will continue to be used for income tax purposes)	$ 570,000

REPORT OF CERTIFIED PUBLIC ACCOUNTANTS

The Board of Directors and Stockholders
A. O. Smith Corporation

We have examined the accompanying consolidated balance sheet of A. O. Smith Corporation at December 31, 1971 and the related consolidated statements of earnings, retained earnings and changes in financial position for the year then ended. Our examination was made in accordance with generally accepted auditing standards, and accordingly included such tests of the accounting records and such other auditing procedures as we considered necessary in the circumstances. We have previously made a similar examination of the consolidated financial statements for the prior year.

In our opinion, the statements mentioned above present fairly the consolidated financial position of A. O. Smith Corporation at December 31, 1971 and December 31, 1970 and the consolidated results of operations and changes in consolidated financial position for the years then ended, in conformity with generally accepted accounting principles applied on a consistent basis during the period after restatement of the 1970 consolidated balance sheet as explained in Note 7.

ARTHUR YOUNG & COMPANY

MILWAUKEE, WISCONSIN
January 17, 1972

A. O. SMITH CORPORATION

TEN-YEAR
FINANCIAL SUMMARY
($000 Omitted Except for Per Share Values)

(1) In 1963 the Company changed its fiscal year from July 31 to December 31. Data shown are for the short period August 1, 1963 to December 31, 1963.

(2) Net Earnings, Cash Flow and Cash Dividends Per Share are based on average shares outstanding in each year adjusted for subsequent stock dividends.

(3) Book Value Per Share is based on year-end stockholders' equity and shares outstanding at year-end adjusted for subsequent stock dividends.

(4) Restatements of 1969 and 1970 amounts have been made to give effect for the 1971 change in accounting for long-term elevator construction contracts from the completed contract method to the percentage of completion method.

	1971	1970
NET SALES	456,846	413,098
EARNINGS BEFORE EXTRAORDINARY ITEMS	12,808	7,287
Per Share (2)	5.23	2.95
As % of Sales	2.8%	1.8%
As % of Average Stockholders' Equity	8.5%	5.1%
NET EARNINGS (After Extraordinary Items)	11,048	9,433
Per Share (2)	4.51	3.82
CASH FLOW (Net Earnings and Depreciation Only)	21,840	19,284
Per Share (2)	8.92	7.81
CASH DIVIDENDS	3,431	3,457
Per Share (As Declared)	1.40	1.40
Per Share (2)	1.40	1.40
As % of Net Earnings	31.1%	36.6%
STOCK DIVIDENDS	—	—
WORKING CAPITAL		
Cash and Marketable Securities	11,427	12,814
Receivables	57,582	55,724
Inventories and Other Assets	88,523	89,498
Total Current Assets	157,532	158,036
Current Liabilities (4)	58,400	61,524
Net Working Capital (4)	99,132	96,512
Current Ratio (4)	2.7	2.6
CAPITALIZATION		
Stockholders' Equity	150,143	142,936
Book Value Per Share (3)	61.14	58.25
Long-Term Debt:		
Notes Payable	57,885	58,444
Lease Purchase Obligations	3,595	3.780
Total Long-Term Debt	61,480	62,224
Total Capital	211,623	205,160
Long-Term Debt As % of Total Capital	29.1%	30.3%
PLANT AND EQUIPMENT		
Gross	191,209	185,608
Accumulated Depreciation	101,755	98,710
Net	89,454	86,898
CAPITAL EXPENDITURES	17,335	23,267
ANNUAL DEPRECIATION	10,792	9,851
AVERAGE NUMBER OF EMPLOYEES	16,030	16,008

1969	1968	1967	1966	1965	1964	1963(1)	1963	1962
354,518	372,798	329,976	318,433	,358,441	299,852	112,585	281,819	249,053
14,560	11,643	9,627	8,738	7,918	1,512	1,819	5,513	5,922
5.84	4.68	3.87	3.51	3.18	.61	.73	2.22	2.38
4.1%	3.1%	2.9%	2.7%	2.2%	.5%	1.6%	2.0%	2.4%
10.9%	9.4%	8.4%	8.0%	7.6%	1.5%	1.8%	5.6%	6.0%
14,560	11,643	9,627	8,738	7,918	1,512	1,819	5,513	5,922
5.84	4.68	3.87	3.51	3.18	.61	.73	2.22	2.38
23,088	21,518	19,799	17,580	17,493	10,387	5,361	13,664	14,501
9.26	8.65	7.96	7.07	7.03	4.18	2.16	5.49	5.83
3,494	3,198	2,808	2,567	2,148	2,147	536	2,145	2,145
1.40	1.30	1.20	1.15	1.00	1.00	.25	1.00	1.00
1.40	1.29	1.13	1.03	.86	.86	.22	.86	.86
24.0%	27.5%	29.2%	29.4%	27.1%	142.0%	29.5%	38.9%	36.2%
—	5%	5%	5%	—	—	—	—	—
10,691	28,706	8,299	9,558	14,155	7,434	12,313	10,198	9,175
50,017	42,766	41,598	39,415	35,520	38,947	36,322	36,262	32,555
79,229	63,172	67,379	67,866	59,178	62,811	49,919	54,168	44,657
139,937	134,644	117,276	116,839	108,853	109,192	98,554	100,628	86,387
64,401	49,905	37,551	38,509	31,507	42,874	22,508	23,726	19,536
75,536	84,739	79,725	78,330	77,346	66,318	76,046	76,902	66,851
2.2	2.7	3.1	3.0	3.5	2.5	4.4	4.2	4.4
138,003	127,956	119,440	112,621	106,445	100,675	102,498	101,216	101,740
55.73	51.38	48.07	45.33	42.85	40.52	41.30	40.79	41.00
24,906	22,400	24,000	27,000	31,000	32,440	32,570	32,570	25,000
3,960	6,081	6,348	6,601	—	—	—	—	—
28,866	28,481	30,348	33,601	31,000	32,440	32,570	32,570	25,000
166,869	156,437	149,788	146,222	137,445	133,115	135,068	133,786	126,740
17.3%	18.2%	20.3%	23.0%	22.6%	24.4%	24.1%	24.3%	19.7%
170,757	160,457	157,040	151,165	128,610	137,012	127,975	126,958	116,200
96,310	96,442	91,385	85,919	77,933	78,138	74,083	72,258	64,237
74,447	64,015	65,655	65,246	50,677	58,874	53,892	54,700	51,963
16,275	9,258	10,979	16,318	6,596	16,657	3,491	8,581	8,422
8,528	9,875	10,172	8,842	9,575	8,875	3,542	8,151	8,579
12,844	13,754	13,728	13,356	14,752	14,146	13,091	12,609	11,228

index